HEGEL

One of the founders of modern philosophical thought, Georg Wilhelm Friedrich Hegel (1770–1831) has gained the reputation of being one of the most abstruse and impenetrable of thinkers. This first major biography of Hegel in English offers not only a complete, up-to-date account of the life, but also a perspicuous overview of the key philosophical concepts in Hegel's work in a style that will be accessible to professionals and nonprofessionals alike.

Terry Pinkard situates Hegel firmly in the context of his times. The story of that life is one of an ambitious, powerful thinker living in a period of great tumult dominated by the figure of Napoleon. Hegel's friendships and encounters with some of the great minds of this period feature prominently in the narrative: Hölderlin, Goethe, Humboldt, Fichte, Schelling, Novalis, the Schlegels, Mendelssohn, and others. The treatment of the philosophy avoids Hegel's own famously technical jargon in order to display the full sweep and power of Hegel's thought.

The Hegel who emerges from this account is a complex, fascinating figure of European modernity who offers a still-compelling examination of that new world born out of the political, industrial, social, and scientific revolutions of his period.

Terry Pinkard is professor of philosophy at Georgetown University and the author or editor of five previous books, including most recently *Hegel's Phenomenology* (Cambridge, 1996).

Hegel
A Biography

Terry Pinkard
Georgetown University

CAMBRIDGE
UNIVERSITY PRESS

PUBLISHED BY THE PRESS SYNDICATE OF THE UNIVERSITY OF CAMBRIDGE
The Pitt Building, Trumpington Street, Cambridge, United Kingdom

CAMBRIDGE UNIVERSITY PRESS
The Edinburgh Building, Cambridge CB2 2RU, UK   http://www.cup.cam.ac.uk
40 West 20th Street, New York, NY 10011–4211, USA   http://www.cup.org
10 Stamford Road, Oakleigh, Melbourne 3166, Australia
Ruiz de Alarcón 13, 28014 Madrid, Spain

First published 2000

Printed in the United States of America

Typeface Ehrhardt 10.5/13 pt.   *System* DeskTopPro$_{/\text{UX}}$[BV]

A catalog record for this book is available from the British Library.

Library of Congress Cataloging in Publication data
Pinkard, Terry P.
Hegel : a biography / Terry Pinkard.
p.   cm.
Includes bibliographical references and index.
ISBN 0–521-49679–9
1. Hegel, Georg Wilhelm Friedrich, 1770–1831.   2. Philosophers –
Germany – Biography.   I. Title.
B2947.P56   2000
193 – dc21
[B]   99–34812

ISBN 0521 49679 9 hardback

To Susan

"Wem sonst
als
Dir"

You can define a net in one of two ways, depending on your point of view. Normally, you would say that it is a meshed instrument designed to catch fish. But you could, with no great injury to logic, reverse the image and define a net as a jocular lexicographer once did: he called it a collection of holes tied together with string.

You can do the same with a biography. The trawling net fills, then the biographer hauls it in, sorts, throws back, stores, fillets and sells. Yet consider what he doesn't catch: there is always far more of that. The biography stands, fat and worthy-burgherish on the shelf, boastful and sedate: a shilling life will give you all the facts, a ten-pound one all the hypotheses as well. But think of everything that got away, that fled with the last deathbed exhalation of the biographee. What chance would the craftiest biographer stand against the subject who saw him coming and decided to amuse himself?

Julian Barnes, *Flaubert's Parrot*

The events and actions of this history [of philosophy] therefore have the characteristic that in their content and worth it is not so much personality and individual character which enters, whereas in political history the subject of deeds and events is the individual in his particular natural make-up, genius, passions, energy, or weakness of character—in a word, what makes him *this* individual. Here [in the history of philosophy] on the other hand the productions are all the more excellent the less is their merit attributed to a particular individual, the more, on the other hand, do they belong to freedom of thinking, to the general character of man as man, the more is thinking itself, devoid of personality, the productive subject.

Hegel, *Introduction to the Lectures on the History of Philosophy*

Contents

Preface

HEGEL IS ONE of those thinkers just about all educated people think they know something about. His philosophy was the forerunner to Karl Marx's theory of history, but unlike Marx, who was a materialist, Hegel was an idealist in the sense that he thought that reality was ultimately spiritual, and that it developed according to the process of thesis/antithesis/synthesis. Hegel also glorified the Prussian state, claiming that it was God's work, was perfect, and was the culmination of all human history. All citizens of Prussia owed unconditional allegiance to that state, and it could do with them as it pleased. Hegel played a large role in the growth of German nationalism, authoritarianism, and militarism with his quasi-mystical celebrations of what he pretentiously called the Absolute.

Just about everything in the first paragraph is false except for the first sentence.

What is even more striking is that it is all clearly and demonstrably wrong, has been known to be wrong in scholarly circles for a long time now, *and* it still appears in almost all short histories of thought or brief encyclopedia entries about Hegel.

But if that isn't Hegel, who then was Hegel? And how did he come to be so badly misunderstood?

Hegel was born on the cusp of our modern era, and his life spanned the two great revolutions of the modern age. Born in 1770, Hegel grew up at a time when kings were secure on their thrones, and to the casual observer, society was in the shape it had assumed many years before. In his teenage years, the French and the American revolutions exploded that world forever, and by the time he died in 1831 the industrial revolution was gearing up; train travel and photography were on the scene, steam engines were driving industry, and the world was witnessing the stirrings of the move toward economic globalization that we now find such a normal part of our world.

Although we in our own day like to think of massive technological change as rapidly altering our lives, probably no generation lived through such a wrenching transformation of ways of life as did Hegel's. The impact that industrialization and the upheavals of the political revolutions of the time had on people's lives was exceptional; the world was suddenly drawing closer, the prospect of revolution hung permanently in the charged atmosphere of the times, wars of revolution spread both hope and destruction across the continent, and by the 1830s former backwaters were suddenly being linked by steamships and locomotives to each other and to the great metropolises of the world. Whole new professions were suddenly springing up to service the rapidly emerging economies of the modern world. Young men and women of the time, not without justification, felt quite strongly that they were leading unprecedented lives, that the past and even the world of their parents were no longer adequate guides to life in the new world emerging before them. Some reacted against that giddy feeling of being cut free and longed for a restoration of the world that had been; others entertained revolutionary hopes of a transformed humanity in the future.

Hegel himself was not indifferent to those revolutionary events and to those deeply felt experiences of his own generation. He was drawn to them, he embraced them, and he made it his life's vocation to try to comprehend those circumstances and that experience, to make sense of the vast changes he and others personally encountered as young Germans and Europeans growing up at the end of the eighteenth century and living through the disruptions of that period and the dawn of the nineteenth century. Much of his philosophy was an attempt to come to terms with what those events might and must mean to us, "we moderns," who are still trying to grapple with the meaning for our own lives of market societies and the celebration of freedom. Hegel has been called, not without reason, the first great philosopher to make modernity itself the object of his thought.

Despite his influence on so much subsequent thought, Hegel remains a figure of great mystery within a great deal of contemporary philosophy, and the mystery deepens and varies depending on whether one looks at the reception of his thought in the context of Anglophone philosophy or of continental European philosophy. In continental European thought, almost everybody has reacted to him, and he remains a force in that tradition of philosophy, a thinker whose influence can be picked up almost everywhere. Behind so many worries about, for example, the status of modern culture, the relation of science to the humanities, the role of the state, how we are to understand history itself, what are the possibilities for modern art – there stands Hegel, looming as one of the central figures in the debate.

Curiously enough, though, his thought has also repeatedly been declared to be definitively, once and for all, dead and gone, something that has long since been overcome – yet, equally curiously, the alleged corpse keeps reviving and reappearing. A contemporary French philosopher once remarked that the great anxiety for all modern philosophers is that no matter how many new paths they take, they will find all of them to be dead ends, with Hegel waiting at the end of each of them, smiling.

For many, of course, Hegel's own reputation has been inextricably entwined with the reputation of the most famous person to claim to adapt his thought to new circumstances, Karl Marx. Marx and his followers claimed to have transformed Hegel's supposedly "idealist" dialectic into a "materialist" theory of history, society, and revolution. Not unsurprisingly, the reaction to Hegel after Marx became intermingled with the reaction to Marxism itself, and depending on what one thought about that, one took a different stance toward Hegel. For much of the twentieth century, "Hegel" seemed only to be the nonindependent part of a phrase, "from Hegel to Marx."

Likewise, because of a bowdlerized presentation of his philosophy by the deservedly obscure Heinrich Moritz Chalybäus, which was immensely popular in Germany in the middle of the nineteenth century (and read by Marx), Hegel's thought quickly became synonymous with the rather arid formula of thesis/antithesis/synthesis, a formula that Hegel himself never used and which in any event misrepresents the structure of his thought. But the characterization stuck, and to many, Hegel remained simply the idealist progenitor of the materialist Marx, which (depending on one's attitude toward Marxism) made him a hero or a villain, but in both cases, somebody whose own thought was not important and whose only real importance lay in the people he influenced.

Hegel's reception in Anglo-American philosophy has always been much different from his reception on the European continent. Although Hegel has always had his devoted readers in Anglophone intellectual circles, he has also been firmly, sometimes even vociferously, rejected by a large and important segment of Anglophone philosophy as having nothing of any importance to say.

In many places in Anglophone philosophy, it is probably safe to say that he has not been so much rejected as simply ignored. It is not out of the ordinary to find major departments of philosophy where he is not taught at all, especially at the graduate level. It is hardly a secret that there are large numbers of Anglo-American philosophers who refuse to read Hegel, who seem to have completely absorbed Bertrand Russell's criticisms of Hegel without ever having paused at Hegel himself. Among them, the suspicion remains, first fostered by Russell and the other great analytic critics of German Idealism at the beginning of the century, that the clarity and argumentative rigor that count as one of the great achievements of modern analytic philosophy can only be attained and sustained by a thorough refusal and avoidance of the dark prose and dense continental thought of Hegel. For these people in contemporary philosophy, Hegel stands not as one of the great thinkers of the modern era, someone with whom one simply must come to terms, but as somebody to be avoided virtually at all cost, who has nothing of importance to say, and whose thought is at best only a wicked temptation from which pliable young minds especially must be protected.

Almost as if he were an unwanted guest, though, Hegel has refused to go away even in analytic philosophy itself; instead, he keeps popping up on many of the byways of contemporary intellectual life. Why, though, was he shunted off to the side? What happened to Hegel to make him such a pariah?

Part of the explanation is straightforwardly historical. Hegel was blamed in Anglophone countries for the German authoritarianism that led to the First World War and for the kind of nationalist worship of the state embodied by the Nazis that led to the Second World War. Not only was he suspected of teutonic obfuscationism and of being an imposter within the halls of the academy, his name became associated with the moral disasters of the twentieth century. When after the Second World War Karl Popper published his immensely influential book *The Open Society and Its Enemies*, laying blame for much of the German catastrophe on the baleful influence of Hegel's thought, the final nail in the coffin for Hegelianism seemed to have been put in place. That Popper's treatment of Hegel was a scandal in itself did nothing to assuage the fears of many that the study of Hegel's works as if they might have something to say was itself a dangerous enterprise.

Hegel survived the attacks and still remains around, although not entirely so. It is still not unusual at any number of major universities to find famous professors in one department celebrating Hegel as one of the intellectual giants of the modern world while equally famous professors in another department at the same university deride him as humbug, poppycock, maybe even a fraud. Hegel, the mystery figure, still remains as controversial as if he had been lecturing on the campuses only yesterday.

Why, though, if he is long since dead and gone, if his thought has clearly long since been superseded and shown to be false and maybe even dangerous – why has he remained around? The passions he provokes within the academy seem oddly out of place for a figure in the history of philosophy whose influence has supposedly already come and gone.

Who then was Hegel?

Acknowledgments

ROBERT PIPPIN read some early drafts of this work; if I footnoted all the instances where a formulation was made better because of his criticism, the book would probably be twice as long as it is now.

Footnoting all the points at which Rolf-Peter Horstmann gave me invaluable advice about various things would constitute a manuscript in itself.

H. S. Harris also generously read the whole manuscript in draft and offered a wealth of tips and criticisms, bringing his own vast erudition regarding this subject to my assistance. I have profited from Professor Harris's insights into the subject, and I am very grateful to him for sharing his busy schedule with my manuscript.

Sally Sedgwick and Robert Stern also read some of the earlier portions of the manuscript and offered a variety of helpful suggestions. Conversations with Peter Gay at the very outset of this project helped me get my bearings; his tips and encouragement are much appreciated. Terence Moore at Cambridge University Press offered invaluable suggestions about the manuscript and encouragement along the way.

Axel Markert of Tübingen University helped me out with all kinds of details, both logistical and otherwise, during my periodic trips to Germany, which were financed by summer research grants from the Graduate School at Georgetown University and by a stint as a visiting professor teaching a class at Tübingen.

Susan Pinkard is the real inspiration behind this work. Her historian's eye led her to suggest various lines of thought and ideas for improving the manuscript. Without her input and suggestions, it simply would not have been written.

Notes on the Text

IN ORDER TO accommodate the variety of readers who might want to read something about Hegel, I have broken the book up into sections that might appeal to those different readers, where feasible. Some will be more interested in the story of Hegel's life, some will be more interested in the particular works under discussion, and some will be more interested in different parts at different times. I have tried therefore as far as possible to make room for these selective readers. Sometimes, especially when I was dealing with the earlier periods in Hegel's life, the goal of keeping the purely biographical material separate from discussion of the works was impossible; but I have tried to demarcate those sections in the relevant chapters. Some chapters (such as that on Hegel's *Science of Logic*, I would think) will be of primary interest mostly to Hegel scholars. But for those, for example, who want to know what Hegel's life was like in Nuremberg but do not particularly want to read about the *Science of Logic* (and vice versa), I have separated those chapters off from the more biographical story of his life. Likewise, I have treated Hegel's intellectual development in the extant texts from his Jena period in a completely separate chapter (Chapter 4) from the one devoted to his life during that period. Chapters 4, 5, 8, 11, and 14 are thus purely "philosophical" chapters.

≈

Besides the quantity and well-known obscurity of Hegel's own works, despite the controversy that surrounds them, there is also the fact that his life intersected with his thought in a variety of deep ways, such that one sometimes cannot firmly pry apart the biographical from the philosophical in his development. But despite that being the case, Hegel himself firmly resisted the idea that the philosophical author's life sheds any light on his works. He was never particularly forthcoming about his own life, and it sometimes seems as if he wanted simply to vanish into his works altogether. Although a voluminous amount of material has been found and published by the diligent and careful scholars associated with the Hegel Archives in Germany, there thus still remains much about Hegel that is not and perhaps never can be known.

A *fully* comprehensive study of Hegel's life and work would therefore necessarily be a multivolume affair, and this was to be a one-volume work intended for a wider audience than that of Hegel scholars and professors of philosophy. To create such a work, I have had to make some compromises along the way. For example, I have had to cut short what for specialists would have been many interesting discussions, and I have sometimes been forced to take a stand on some issue or another without being able to go into all the details explaining why I took that stand or why I disagree with some other readings. To give only one example: There is by now an immense amount of literature on the authorship of one extremely short Hegelian text (a couple of pages in its transcription) that has gone by the name "The Oldest System Program in German Idealism." Although the manuscript is in Hegel's own handwriting, Hegel's authorship of the text is hotly disputed. I devote only a few sentences to who the author may be, even though an entire book could be devoted exclusively to that issue.

Nonetheless, I have tried to make my case for telling this particular story about Hegel's life, how his works are to be interpreted, and how his life and his works intersect within the body of the book, taking into account the exigencies of keeping it shorter than it obviously could have been. Such a goal demands that one take a variety of shortcuts. I have not given, for example, much emphasis to Hegel's relationship to his onetime friend Issak von Sinclair, although there are those who think that his influence on Hegel's life and thought is much more profound than I do; I disagree, but making the full case for my disagreement would have taken more pages than would be feasible here. In all instances, though, I have tried to indicate at least what I take the points to be, even if sometimes those assertions might strike those Hegel scholars whose concern is with a very particular and limited period in his development as a bit dogmatic. I have also not given much consideration at all to the differences between the various editions of Hegel's *Encyclopedia of the Philosophical Sciences* (1817, 1827, 1830), although that is surely an interesting and important story in itself. Unfortunately, taking into account all the small nuances of Hegel's relationships and concerns would produce something like a virtually unreadable eight-volume biography, and that was not my aim. I have also tried to situate Hegel's life within the revolutionary events that transpired around him, since one simply cannot understand Hegel's own experience without also having some grasp of the circumstances surrounding his life and the connections among them.

ᵴ

Translation of Hegel's key terms has not always been easy, and there does not exist even an unvarying set of agreements among translators about how to render certain key terms. I have therefore taken the liberty of altering almost all of the English translations where I cite them in order to preserve a certain uniformity of language and style throughout the text.

This of course required me to make some decisions about how to render key terms. Sometimes in a translation I give the German word in parentheses, but I have tried to avoid this practice as much as possible. With some words such as *Willkür*, which I render as "freedom of choice" and sometimes as "choice," I often enclose the German word in parentheses, since that particular rendering is not without controversy among philosophical scholars, and it is good for those who care about those controversies to be able to see where those terms occur. In most cases where I thought that an issue of translation might be at hand, I have put the German terms in the footnote. Unlike some other translators of Hegel, I have always rendered *Begriff* as "concept."

Many of Hegel's earlier translators – dubiously, to my mind – decided that Hegel's technical terminology was so special that it deserved capitalization, but I have resorted to capitalizing only one word in Hegel's lexicon: "Idea" for "*Idee*." That term has a technical meaning that departs sharply from the English word "idea," so that calling attention to it via capitals and quotation marks seemed the prudent choice.

As any reader moderately familiar with Hegel knows, there simply is no good term by which to directly translate his use of *Aufhebung* and its cognates. On the whole, I have used the term of art earlier translators coined expressly for the purpose of translating the term, namely, "sublation." "Sublation" means raising, canceling, and preserving simply because that is what the coiners stipulated; Hegel used the ordinary German term because it actually does carry those different meanings in different contexts.

For those readers who might skip a couple of chapters and find themselves encountering what seem to be unexplained technicalities or German words, a quick look at the index should point one to the pages on which an explanation of the term is given. There are several places where I use the German terms "*Bildung*" and "*Wissenschaft*" in their original forms, having explained them earlier. The index is also a guide to getting at the meanings of those terms.

ᨳᩛ

Those who find footnotes distasteful can, on the whole, safely ignore the tiny superscripted numbers in the text. The notes to the text are mostly there to give sources for quotations and references and for the most part will only be of interest to other Hegel scholars (particularly for all chapters after the first two). I should also point out that in those notes, I have self-consciously violated one or two common conventions of footnoting where following them would, I thought, make life more difficult for the reader; thus, I have avoided entirely the use of "op. cit.," since, when one is trying to track down the source of a note, finding an "op. cit." is usually more irritating than enlightening; instead I give a shortened citation for the source in question. Full citations can always be found in the list of Works Cited.

I have also had to resist the always-present temptation to enter into various lengthy debates with other scholars in the footnotes; the grounds for doing so were simply to restrict the size of the present volume. This will be regretted, I am sure, by those who will think that I really should have bothered to argue against so-and-so's alternative interpretation on such-and-such point or who think that so-and-so's views on some controversial point really should have been aired. On the whole, I have to admit that I agree with them. I too regret it, but in a book such as this, there would simply be too many such points to argue, and the notes would have ended up being as long as the text itself. This is a decision that obviously involves a lot of trade-offs, not all of them entirely happy; but at least it keeps an already weighty volume down in size.

I can only hope that all those who think that this or that point should have been stated differently will take that as an invitation to state that disagreement itself. Disagreement is the nature of contemporary philosophy in a fragmented world, and if the book serves as a catalyst to such disagreements and objections, so much the better. Hegel, who loved the power of oppositions, might himself have been ironically amused, and, who knows, maybe even deeply pleased by that prospect.

Hegel's Formation in Old Württemberg

"Wilhelm"

I N 1770, A LONG-STANDING CRISIS in the small south German
duchy of Württemberg seemed to have found its resolution. The
prince of Württemberg, Duke Karl Eugen, and the representative assembly of the estates, the *Landtag*, reached a constitutional settlement
on the rights of Württemberg subjects and the appropriate powers of
various bodies in the Württemberg government. The results of this
settlement were to lead a British politician some years later to proclaim
that there were only two constitutions worth noting, the British and the
Württemberg.[1] The constitutional settlement itself and the circumstances surrounding it were both odd and yet also strangely typical for
the time. The mere statement of the issues is enough to give a sense of
the complexities of the old regime in Württemberg: The Protestant
estates of Württemberg, a more or less untypical feudal institution that
had survived into the modern world, had brought a suit before an
imperial court of the increasingly irrelevant Holy Roman Empire, of
which Württemberg was a member, to force their Catholic prince, Duke
Karl Eugen, to legally acknowledge what they took to be their traditional
rights; and Duke Karl Eugen, himself always inclined to absolutism and
Catholic pageantry, and who had always rigidly resisted any such pressures from the Protestant estates, had come under immense pressure
from the emperor of the Holy Roman Empire – the archduke of Austria,
himself an absolutizing Catholic monarch – to settle in favor of the
Protestants. To add to the complications, much of the pressure on the
Catholic emperor of the Holy Roman Empire had come from Karl
Eugen's wife's uncle, Frederick the Great, the Protestant monarch of
Prussia, against whom Karl Eugen had allied Württemberg in a recent

war, and who was the enemy of the Catholic Austrian archduke. The settlement nonetheless reaffirmed the traditional rights and privileges of the Württemberg estates, and the Protestant victors took this as the triumph of a righteous Protestant people defending their traditional rights against the absolutizing despotism of a Catholic duke.

In the same year that the duke and the estates reached their constitutional settlement, a minor Protestant functionary at the court of Duke Karl Eugen, Georg Ludwig Hegel, and his wife, Maria Magdalena Louisa Hegel, announced on August 27 the birth of their first child, Georg Wilhelm Friedrich Hegel.

G. W. F. Hegel (addressed as "Wilhelm" by his parents, very close friends, and family) was thus born into and grew up in a world comprised of an odd and not terribly coherent mixture of the old and the new. In fact, Hegel did not grow up in anything that could really be called "Germany" at all; he was born instead into the duchy of Württemberg, which itself was part of the Holy Roman Empire – the butt of the joke that it was neither Holy nor Roman nor an Empire. That world was in fact to vanish early in Hegel's life: By 1806, the Holy Roman Empire in which Hegel had spent his youth suddenly ceased to exist; the small provincial duchy of Württemberg had become the much-expanded kingdom of Württemberg by virtue of a later duke's having allied himself with Napoleon Bonaparte; and the epochal "constitutional settlement" of 1770, the year of Hegel's birth, had been ignored, dismantled, and, given its rapid slide into irrelevance, completely forgotten. The vivid contrasts between Hegel's cultural background, complexities and oddities of old Württemberg, and his youthful introduction to the world of the Enlightenment both at home and through his education were to color his understanding of both himself and the world around him for the rest of his life. These odd pieces of an incoherent patchwork of practices and traditions set the stage for much of Hegel's later thought, as the mature Hegel of the nineteenth century tried to come to terms with his eighteenth-century youth.

Hegel's Family and His Early Education

Hegel came from a moderately well-to-do family of solid Württembergers.[2] His father, Georg Ludwig Hegel, had studied law at Tübingen University and was at the time of Hegel's birth a secretary to the

revenue office at the court. Hegel's father's family had several generations before been émigrés to Württemberg from Austria in the sixteenth
century; when Austrian Protestants were required to convert to Catholicism in the 1500s, the ancestor of the Hegel family of Württemberg,
Johannes Hegel, a pewterer, had moved from Catholic Austria to Protestant Württemberg rather than give up his Lutheran faith (or at least
that was the story the Hegel family told themselves).[3] Generations of
Hegels had been pastors in Württemberg, a position of no little esteem
and importance in the duchy. (The poet Friedrich Schiller was, for
example, baptized by a pastor named Hegel in Marbach.) Hegel's grandfather (Georg Ludwig Christoph) had been the *Oberamtmann* (ducal
commissioner, a kind of high bailiff) for the town of Altensteig, and his
great-grandfather (also Georg Ludwig Christoph) had been the *Stadt-
vogt* (also a type of ducal commissioner) for the town of Rosenfeld.
Hegel's mother, Maria Magdalena Louisa Hegel (whose maiden name
was Fromm), had a father who had been a lawyer at the High Court of
Justice at the Württemberg court; her family had been in Stuttgart itself
for more than a century, and she traced her lineage on her mother's
side back to Johannes Brenz, a noted Württemberg Protestant reformer
of the sixteenth century.

Hegel was one of six children born to his parents; only he and two of
his siblings survived into adulthood: a sister, Christiane Luise, and a
brother, Georg Ludwig. This is not surprising, since high rates of child
mortality were a fact of life in those days; smallpox alone killed one out
of every thirteen children in Württemberg in the 1770s, and Hegel
himself had to survive several serious life-threatening illnesses as a
youth. Indeed, his health was for the rest of his life to be plagued off
and on by various illnesses. When Hegel was eleven, his mother died
(September 20, 1781) of a "bilious fever" that was raging in Stuttgart,
which also came close to claiming Hegel and his father. That Hegel
survived and his mother did not no doubt affected him more than we
can ever discover; Hegel developed a kind of speech impediment, and
the underlying reason may well have had to do with his mother's death,
his own survival, and some antagonism between himself and his father,
although these are virtually impossible to ferret out. (Hegel almost never
speaks of his father in his letters; there was apparently some tension
between them; for example, when he was at university, he and his father
apparently engaged in some rather impassioned disputes about the vir-

tues of the French Revolution.) Hegel's brother, Georg Ludwig, had a
brief but apparently glorious career as a military officer, rising to the
rank of captain; he was ennobled and thereby became Georg Ludwig
von Hegel; he marched off with Napoleon on the Russian campaign in
1812, never to return. His sister, Christiane, was to outlive him only by
a few months; a very cultured, independent woman, she never married,
electing to stay home and care for her father.

Education and "culture" were clearly stressed in the Hegel household. Hegel's parents put him in what was called the German School at
the age of three, and at five he was put in what was called the Latin
School. His mother taught him Latin at home so that when he went to
the Latin School, he already knew the first declension of Latin and the
nouns that went with it. Indeed, Hegel's life-long infatuation with
learning and his unconditional respect for it almost certainly began with
those early experiences of learning Latin from his mother and his
attachment to her. That Hegel's mother was capable of doing this
already says something about the remarkable state of learning in the
Hegel household, since it was, to put it mildly, uncommon for women
in this period to receive the kind of education that would have enabled
them to teach their four- and five-year-old sons Latin at home (a fact
noted explicitly by Christiane Hegel in her recollections of their youth).[4]
Hegel's father in fact paid for his son's private lessons in geometry by a
noted local mathematician, K. A. F. Duttenhofer, when Hegel was only
ten years old; as Hegel grew older, his father continued to pay for
private lessons in other subjects. (For example, Hegel most likely
learned French in this way).[5]

Although Hegel almost never spoke of his father in any letters, there
is a striking difference with regard to his mother. In 1825, at the age of
fifty-five, he sent off a short note to his sister, Christiane, that said only,
"Today is the anniversary of our mother's death, which I will hold
forever in my memory."[6] It seems clear *whose* memory dominated his
adult life. He and sister were united by an identification with their
mother; their brother, Georg Ludwig, seems to have taken after their
father, which seems to have been part of the painful estrangement that
Hegel had with his father. Both Hegel and his sister took after their
mother in their bookishness, and their mother's death left them without
their "protector" in the family, elevating Georg Ludwig most likely
into the position of favorite. Hegel dealt with this by rebelling, devel-

oping a stutter, and pursuing a career of which his father did not exactly approve; Christiane dealt with it by remaining at home to care for her father until his death and turning down a number of different suitors for marriage during that period.

Hegel's family life after the death of his mother was probably quite strained, and all the evidence points to a sharp sense of alienation on his own part toward his family. In keeping with his mother's ideals for him, Hegel was from the standpoint of his teachers (if not of his father) a model student who read voraciously, was always the first in his class from the age of ten until he left for university at eighteen, and, like many young men of his day and age, kept a diary during his teenage years. In his diary, he recorded long excerpts from his many readings, a practice also not uncommon in an age where owning books was still a luxury. One indication of the sense of alienation he felt was that as a teenager, he tended to spend Wednesdays and Saturdays entirely at the ducal library, which was open to the public and which was also quite close to his home. Since his home was not without its cultural resources – the family subscribed to the *Allgemeine deutsche Bibliothek*, an influential journal of ideas (in which, incidentally, some of the early debates about Kant's philosophy appeared) – the decision to spend so much time away from home all the more sharply reflected his sense of not being "at home" in his home in Stuttgart. Hegel did, however, enjoy the company of his teachers, and, as the model student he was, would go for walks with them, during which the conversations would turn to academic subjects in which the young man showed such a keen interest. One of his teachers, a Mr. Löffler, gave him at the age of eight a present of Shakespeare's works translated by Eschenburg, with the advice that although he would not understand them at that point, he would soon learn to understand them. (Hegel recorded years later in his teenage diary a laudatory remembrance of Löffler when he died.)

Hegel's family was certainly well connected but was not included among what in Württemberg were known as the *Ehrbarkeit*, the "non-noble notables," who staffed the Württemberg assembly of estates (its parliament) and who had a near-monopoly on the better, more prestigious positions in Württemberg. The *Ehrbarkeit* had achieved their status largely because of the sheer oddness and complexity of Württemberg's history; the Württemberg nobility took no part in the governance of the duchy, instead understanding their noble status as having to do entirely with a direct, "immediate" relation to the Holy Roman Emperor, and thereby de facto leaving everything to the *Ehrbarkeit*, which more or less consisted of some important clergy, certain urban elites, and important rural magistrates. The *Ehrbarkeit* continually contested with the duke for power. To add to the complexity of Württemberg's (and Stuttgart's) social milieu, the duke's own privy council (*Geheime Rat*) had over the years gradually ceased to be simply an extension of the duke's authority and had come instead to regard itself as a semi-independent body, which itself then contested with not only the duke but also with the estates (and thereby with various parts of the *Ehrbarkeit*) for power and influence.[7] The privy council itself had come to be composed of what had more or less gradually evolved into a professional class of bureaucrats, almost always trained in law at the university in Tübingen (located in Württemberg just a few miles south of Stuttgart).

In addition to Württemberg's idiosyncratic political arrangements, the form of social life that prevailed within the Württemberg of Hegel's youth can be described (following Mack Walker) as that of the German "hometowns," a form of life that took root in other German *Länder* within the Holy Roman Empire, but not so much in places like Prussia.[8] The structure of the hometowns could in a broad sense be called "communitarian." There was clearly a sense of who belonged (and equally as clearly and forcefully, who did *not*) in the hometowns, and each hometown had a clear social sense of what groups had what rights and privileges without there being any need for a written statement of them. The guild system in Württemberg played a central role in the structure of its hometowns in the sense that the guild functioned as a kind of "second family" (a description that Hegel was later to use in his mature political philosophy in his attempt to revivify the old corporate structures within the modern Prussian state): It served to protect its members' particular privileges and rights, to buffer individuals against life's contingencies; it convened elaborate ceremonies at various stages of a member's life, it provided the circle in which one socialized, it offered assistance when bad luck befell one or one's family, it oversaw moral and professional standards – in short, it regulated a person's life from apprenticeship to death.[9] In the year that Hegel was born, the hometown structure of Württemberg seemed finally to have triumphed against the contrivances of its absolutizing Catholic duke; however, only a few years later, the structure of hometown life all over Germany was to be threatened by the modernizing influences emanating from the French Revolution.

We cannot know with certainty what Hegel's mother and father actually thought about the political events in Württemberg and the developments in Württemberg culture at the time of Hegel's birth, but the evidence strongly suggests that they were a family who were at once quite comfortable with the old Württemberg traditions and at the same time clearly oriented toward the ideas of the German Enlightenment and its modernizing tendencies. They most likely saw no contradiction between the Enlightenment's goals and the traditions and patterns of existing Württemberg life. Although not members themselves of the *Ehrbarkeit*, Hegel's family clearly moved in the social circles close to them; and they also moved in the circles of the people who staffed the privy council. Hegel's parents were thus the kind of people who were tied into the traditional order of Württemberg and, no doubt, as Protestants also disdainful of the impertinence of their Catholic ruler and proud of Württemberg's constitutional tradition, but who were attempting, however unconsciously, to go beyond the confining borders of their limited Württemberg world. As already mentioned, they subscribed to the *Allgemeine deutsche Bibliothek*, one of the major publications of the German Enlightenment, and Hegel's mother was uncharacteristically well educated for a woman of her day. Shortly after Hegel was born, the family moved to a very fashionable address in Stuttgart, which indicates that they both were and thought of themselves as a family on the way up. If anything, it seems to be the case that Hegel grew up in a family that communicated to him a strong sense of being "somebody" while at the same time also being an outsider to the official circle of the *Ehrbarkeit*; moreover, on his mother's side, Hegel was descended from a long line of prominent Protestant reformers. The up-and-coming Hegel family staked their claim to social status on the basis of a certain attitude toward learning and achievement rather than on family connections.

This strong sense of his own proper standing in the world, along with his touchiness about possible affronts to it, characterized Hegel for his whole life. Firmly etched on the young Hegel's view of the world was that his family, which was just as middle-class and probably more educated than most of the members of the *Ehrbarkeit*, were nonetheless effectively excluded from the very best positions in the Württemberg government simply and solely because they were not part of the "non-noble notables." Hegel's sense of social inclusion and exclusion was thus not that of the middle-class *Bürger*'s exclusion from the world of the aristocracy; it was the sense ingrained at an early age of the simple injustice of exclusion from status by virtue of something completely contingent, of being the same and yet excluded. It also gave him a certain anger that often came to full expression in his more polemical writings.

Most telling was his father's decision to send Hegel in 1784 to the Stuttgarter *Gymnasium Illustre*. The school was in some respects a complete mess, as most schools in Württemberg were at the time; however, it was a place in which Enlightenment thought had taken some foothold alongside the more traditional Protestant humanistic learning of the Renaissance (although the school could hardly be said to have been a bastion of Enlightenment thought). Since it seems that quite early in his life he or his parents (very likely his mother) decided that he was to study theology, the more natural choice would have been to send Hegel to one of the "lower seminaries," the "cloister schools," which were the traditional path in Württemberg for students destined for theological study at the university at Tübingen and a subsequent career in the omnipresent Protestant church of Württemberg. (Hegel's friend at Tübingen, the poet Hölderlin, for example, went to such a "cloister school.") The importance of theological studies is shown by the fact that even in Hegel's *Gymnasium* more than fifty percent of the graduates went on to pursue some kind of career that involved theological studies.[10] Although Tübingen University reserved the great majority of its places in theological studies for the students graduating from the lower seminaries, it also reserved a few places reserved for students of the *Gymnasium Illustre*, and this seems to have been one of the likely reasons for sending Hegel there. At the *Gymnasium Illustre*, Hegel could get an Enlightenment education and still be prepared and qualified for theological training at Tübingen.

Of course, Hegel might have been sent instead to the *Karlsschule* in Stuttgart – a military academy founded by Duke Karl Eugen to train officials and military officers in the new sciences – which was regarded not only as the better institution but also as the more "Enlightenment oriented" of the two schools. Since Hegel's father seems to have cared deeply for his son's education, there must have been a special reason to send him to the *Gymnasium Illustre* rather than to the *Karlsschule*. The decision could not have been based on any special dislike that Hegel's father had for the *Karlsschule*, since he later sent Hegel's younger brother, Georg Ludwig, there. Indeed, it seems likely that it was Hegel's mother's desire that he become a theologian and not his father's; after all, she taught him Latin at an early age, clearly preparing him for a career in the church or as a learned man. Hegel's father, on the other hand, was a civil servant, a prudent, rational man trained in law, who displayed (at least in the records) no particular ecclesiastical piety and did not seem in any way inclined to send Hegel's brother to seminary training. His mother's desire that the young Hegel become a theologian and his father's desire that he nonetheless attend some "modern" (that is, Enlightenment, vocationally directed) institution must therefore have been the motivating factors in the decision. According to Hegel's own memories, it was at least one year after his mother's death that his father decided that he was to study theology at the Protestant Seminary in Tübingen.[11] The decision in favor of the *Gymnasium Illustre* was very likely a compromise between Hegel's father and his dead mother's wishes, a wish to keep a foot in both camps.

Whatever the grounds for sending Hegel to the *Gymnasium Illustre*, however, the decision turned out to have fortunate consequences for him. The bookishly inclined young Hegel, attached to his mother and missing her after her death, was thus not packed off to a "cloister school" but instead continued living with his father and siblings in a family environment that clearly indulged his bookish interests; and he was able to spend four years at a school in which he came into contact with teachers who were to recognize and encourage his love of learning and in which he was given a humanistically oriented education that steeped him in the classics, in ancient and modern languages, and in modern science and mathematics.[12]

The main importance of Hegel's stay at the Stuttgart *Gymnasium* was that its environs and its mixture of Enlightenment and Renaissance humanistic approaches introduced the young Hegel to the world of modern, up-to-the-minute ideas and promoted a sense of distance from the traditional world of the Württemberg "non-noble notables." His sister, Christiane, remembered her brother especially loving the study of physics at the *Gymnasium*, and we know that he was also fascinated with mathematics during this period.[13] He himself remembered learning by the age of twelve the Wolffian doctrines of "clear ideas" in school, and by the age of fourteen having learned all the classical rules of the syllogism taught to him in school.

Quite commonly, in his diary, he would also make long excerpts from various books. In his diary he did not, however, tend to record his feelings, nor did he record, with one exception, any adolescent musings on girls, something one might expect from a teenage boy. Hegel's diary entries clearly show him to be a voracious reader of all kinds of material even if, as one can expect from a diary kept by a fourteen- to sixteen-year old boy, they do not contain much that is of overwhelming philosophical interest. The entries nonetheless display a keen and observant adolescent trying out different ideas, doing his best to appear earnest even to himself, and recording various things he was reading and took to be noteworthy.

Hegel's diary entries might thus seem to make him out to be some kind of reclusive bookworm, a kind of premature old fogy – his nickname, after all, among his friends while he was a student at Tübingen University was "the old man" – unless one keeps in mind that diary entries, like all forms of autobiography, tend to be highly selective. They present not so much the unvarnished truth about someone as they do the diarist's own attempt to appear to himself (or to his "best friend," as the addressee of diary entries of the time were often called) in a certain light. Hegel's diaries thus give us a slightly one-sided picture of Hegel's personality as a youth, but nonetheless one that he was intent on creating for himself in his own imagination. His sister, for example, remembered him as having many friends (although she also remembered him as lacking any "bodily agility" and, while loving gymnastics, being very "clumsy" at dancing, one of Hegel's enduring deficiencies that is also attested to by other young women who danced with him at the time).[14] Hegel, on the other hand, in his diary entries keeps trying to portray himself as living up to his mother's dreams for him as a future man of learning and Württemberg theologian. But even Hegel, the youth who tried so hard to appear to himself as the ever-serious and oh-so-earnest young man of learning, notes in his diary on the first of January, 1787, that he went to a concert apparently given every year, that he could not hear the music for all the toasts being given, but that since he got to see some old friends, time passed quickly and pleasantly, and "looking at pretty girls added no little amount to our entertainment."[15] Hegel's gregarious nature and sociability were features of his personality for his entire life, and there is no reason to doubt that they were present in him as a youth. Hegel's youthful diary nonetheless reveals his intellectual bent; even in his adolescence, he does not talk much about himself or his feelings, a trait he was to keep his entire life.

He also records on that same day in 1787 that he could not tear himself away from reading *Sophies Reise von Memel nach Sachsen* (*Sophie's Journey from Memel to Saxony*), a sentimental, picaresque novel famous both for its lack of any real literary merit and for its extreme popularity in its day. (When Hegel's first biographer, Karl Rosenkranz, publicized this fact in the 1840s, it prompted Arthur Schopenhauer, who harbored a lifelong passionate dislike for Hegel, to write to a friend, "My favorite book is Homer; Hegel's is *Sophies Reise*.")[16] What interested Hegel in the novel were no doubt what were for him the vivid descriptions of the landscape, both natural and human, in Sophie's travels, and the descriptions and accounts of the various characters she met along the way; to the young sixteen-year-old Hegel, who tried to think of himself as quite the serious fellow, who came from an ambitious, rising family and whose own ambitions were growing, but who had spent all of his life in relatively provincial Stuttgart, these descriptions of far-away parts of the empire must have seemed particularly enticing and romantic, the kind of thing, no doubt, it would have seemed that a serious young fellow like himself should explore. But this was hardly appropriate reading for a pure "man of learning," much less for a premature old fogy. Hegel had plenty of adolescent enthusiasm for matters that did not fit his own picture of what he liked to think he was about.

More interesting than whatever Hegel's boyish lapses in literary taste might have been are the diary excerpts Hegel made from various books that he read, for they reveal not only the books he was reading but also the kinds of things he was thinking about at the time (or at least that he liked to appear to himself to be thinking about). He excerpted extensively from a book on world history, for example, and he shows himself to be reading modern authors such as Klopstock. He also excerpted passages from various figures of the German Enlightenment. In many of those excerpts, he copied out various passages from those authors on what "Enlightenment" consists in, and he himself recorded his own reflections on the matter, namely, that he took Enlightenment to come from the study of the sciences and the arts and to have various levels of learning within itself (a received view of the time).[17] This self-conscious fascination with the Enlightenment is consistent with entries that display no deep skepticism about religion (a trait not merely to be ascribed to a Protestant Württemberg teenager recording thoughts in a diary, but a feature of the mainstream of the German Enlightenment that distinguished it, for example, from the French version). He displayed a knowledge of Rousseauian themes (although it is very unclear whether he actually read Rousseau at this stage in his life or whether he only read *Neuer Emil*, the work of the German Rousseauian J. G. Feder).[18] His entries also show that he read and liked Christian Garve, one of the leading "popular philosophers" – the German equivalent of the Scottish Enlightenment "educators" – and even the Scottish philosopher Adam Ferguson (whom Garve translated). He seems to have been particularly attracted by Garve's distinction between personal knowledge and the knowledge one gets from books, which itself would have fit well into Hegel's interest in Rousseauian ideas and with the kind of pietistically influenced, emotionalist Protestantism prevalent in Stuttgart in those days. His entries also show him to be in the process of acquiring a sense of the alleged superiority of Greek culture to modern life, an idea that Johann Joachim Winckelmann had established in German culture and which Garve had helped to refine for a larger public.

The young Hegel was also very aware of the Württemberg hero J. J. Moser; he made a note in Latin in his diary on the date of Moser's death about the status of the great man.[19] (Moser only lived a few houses down from the Hegels in Stuttgart.) More importantly, Hegel's own Württemberg background, and the articulations of it by people like Moser, endowed him in his youth with a keen appreciation for the rhetoric of constitutionalism and rights and, more importantly, implicitly gave him a conception of the basis of such rights as lying somehow in social practice; as a young and aware Württembergian, he would have naturally had the idea that these rights can be derived not from abstract precepts but only from the way the traditions and practices of a form of life are interpreted. The young Hegel cut his intellectual teeth hearing stories about how Württemberg had defended itself against tyranny, not by appealing to the rights of man but appealing to what it had established as valid within its own history, to its own socially bounded sense of the way things are to be done, which was itself deeply rooted in the hearts and characters of Württembergers themselves by virtue of their religious, social, and political institutions.[20]

Interestingly enough, Hegel also seems to have been at least vaguely aware of Kant's philosophy in his Stuttgart days, although given Kant's difficulty and Hegel's age at the time, he can be excused for not saying much about it and can be completely exempted from questions about whether he understood it. He excerpted essays from authors who wrote about Kant; for example, one of his favorite authors, Garve, wrote the first review of Kant's *Critique of Pure Reason*, only to have the editor of the journal in which it appeared, J. G. Feder (the German Rousseauian whom Hegel also excerpted), chop it up and insert certain accusations into it – namely, that Kant's idealism was only a replay of Berkeley's idealism – which were not in the original. (The intact original was printed in 1783 in the *Allgemeine deutsche Bibliothek*, so Hegel may have seen it.)[21]

Perhaps most significant, though, was his friendship with Jacob Friedrich von Abel, who was on the faculty of the *Karlsschule* and who was one of the older teachers who played an important role in Hegel's life. Hegel's sister said in an account of Hegel's life that von Abel "fostered" Hegel (or made Hegel his "protégé," depending on how one translates her letter).[22] Abel, who had earlier taught and befriended Schiller, later became a professor of philosophy at Tübingen in 1790 (although this was after Hegel had formally finished his prescribed course of "philosophical" studies there and had already begun his theological training). Abel had joined the debate on Kant's philosophy and had in fact published in 1787 (while Hegel was still in the *Gymnasium*) a book on Kant – *Versuch über die Natur der speculativen Vernunft zur Prüfung des Kantischen Systems* (roughly, *An Assay into the Nature of Speculative Reason for a Test of the Kantian System*) – which concerned itself with Kant's *Critique of Pure Reason* and *Prolegomena to Any Future Metaphysics*.[23] In that work, Abel defended the findings of traditional rationalist metaphysics against Kant's critique, asserting against Kant the idea that the world simply must have a creator and that this divine creator establishes the relation of our experience to the world. Whereas Kant had argued that the ways in which we must experience the world and conceive of it could not be extended to apply to things-in-themselves beyond our experience, Abel rebutted that claim with the simple assertion that Kant's major points, as he put it, were "unconvincing" and did not follow from Kant's own premises.

Abel's book was short in length and even shorter in argument, but it was probably known to Hegel as one of the first things he learned about Kantianism. It is likely that the teenage Hegel thereby inherited some slightly anti-Kantian ideas from Professor Abel, particularly the ideas, first, that Kant's "pure reason" was simply too general and too formal to do the work that Kant said it could do (something that his Württembergian background would have predisposed him to believe); and second, that the traditional proofs of God's existence and of the necessity of a final cause of the world had been left untouched by Kant's system, which itself would have meshed nicely with everything else Hegel was learning about Kant from his excerpts. In addition, it may have filled the young Hegel's mind with the idea that Kant, for all his brilliance, had not offered a serious challenge to the traditional metaphysics of religion, so that he could remain convinced that the truly serious issues had to do only with what an enlightened heart could discover for itself (all opinions he was later, of course, to revise entirely, although his suspicion of what he took to be Kant's formalism was never to go away).[24]

Whatever knowledge the young Hegel had about Kant, though, he was clearly influenced by and quite taken with Gotthold Ephraim Lessing. Hegel even recorded in his diary that he had read Lessing's play *Nathan the Wise* (published in 1779). The play, although rather didactic, made a big impression on Hegel (as it did on countless other young men at the time). In the play, Nathan, a Jew, exemplifies what Lessing took to be the ideals of Enlightenment religion: that all religions are inherently one, that the true teaching of enlightened religion is that we should acknowledge our fundamental common humanity, but that nonetheless the differences between people are neither to be eradicated nor disavowed but instead tolerated. Nathan's "message" – that the same basic moral and spiritual characteristics that make one man a Jew make another man a Christian, and that therefore many different forms of religion can peacefully and fruitfully coexist in an enlightened, cosmopolitan polity – both expressed and affirmed that the young Hegel's religious convictions and his Württemberg heritage were not at odds with his Enlightenment and humanistic education, that he could be a good Württemberger *and* a man of the Enlightenment (although his diary entries show him nonetheless manifesting a typical Württemberg Protestant disdain for Catholic practices). More generally, Nathan's "message" expressed for Hegel the idea that adherence to one's traditions and practices was both important and did not necessarily exclude one from recognizing the common humanity of others. If one followed Nathan's example, one could be both religious and rational, emotional and enlightened, proud of one's own traditions without impugning those of others – all the kinds of things that were quite radical for their own day, however clichéd they may seem to us now. They were the kinds of things to fill the mind of a young man like Hegel with heady dreams of Enlightenment progress. In the very youthful essays on religious and political topics that he was to write immediately after leaving the university, he was to return time and again to the figure of Nathan as a paradigm of enlightened, humane religiosity.

The figure of Lessing himself made, it would seem, an equally big impression on Hegel. When Lessing began his career, there was little to no German literature, no German theater, no German literary criticism to speak of, and virtually no public for such things had they existed. Lessing carved out for himself a German equivalent of the career of a "man of letters" (an idea imported from France), and to do this he had first to educate and virtually create his public. Lessing admirably succeeded in almost all of his tasks; his accomplishments and his character (particularly, his uncompromising honesty about himself) made him the uncontested hero of German literary culture. In this sense, he was the absolute paradigm of an "educator of the people," a *Volkserzieher* – Lessing even titled one of his better-known books *The Education of the Human Race* – and Hegel cluttered his diaries with observations on what it would mean to be such an "educator of the people," clearly imagining such a role for himself. For Hegel, the example of Lessing helped to flesh out in imagination the idea of being a "man of letters," one who would live off his writings (and perhaps also preach at a parish to help pay the bills, since "men of letters" rarely earned a living simply from their letters), who would educate a public towards its enlightenment, and who would embody in his own life the unities of Enlightenment rationality, Rousseauian emotionalism, religious piety, and open-minded, wide-ranging thought.

In short, Hegel's diary entries, his excerpts, and the essays of his school days in Stuttgart display a keen young mind that is throwing around a lot of thoughts without coming down to anything like a settled position on things. He reveals himself as "for" the Enlightenment in the sense of an unbiased, critical approach to things; he is "for" religion, especially a religion that actually claims the hearts of people and can make equal claim to being "enlightened"; he is "against" dry abstract reason and "mere" book learning (although, ironically, he is clearly a person steeped beyond his years in such "book learning"); he is "for" progress; and, like any good young Rousseauian, he is "for" learning from "experience," from "life," from "activity." He seems to have fully absorbed the emerging German ideal of *Bildung* – a multipurpose term that included the ideals of education, art, culture, and the formation of cultivated taste – which people such as the revered Moses Mendelssohn had identified with Enlightenment itself. A person of *Bildung* was thus "fit" to be the kind of person who was morally entitled to be an "educator of the people," since he himself could make good claims to being supremely "cultivated and educated" himself. In Württemberg, the ideal of *Bildung* was also fused with a religious dimension – a person of *Bildung* would also have a properly formed religious conscience, and Hegel was no exception. The young Hegel thus applied himself to his studies to become such a man of *Bildung*, and he did so with a striking confidence in his own intellectual powers, a trait that was to be with him for his entire life; the teenage Hegel never seemed to be especially worried that he might be in over his head, or that he might be misrepresenting to himself the content of what he had been reading. He was instead fully confident that he could master any subject, and his experience at the Stuttgart *Gymnasium* (and, we assume, at home) had only helped to support that self-conception and self-confidence.

Hegel was one of a few students selected to give graduation speeches at the *Gymnasium*. Like the others who were selected, he was required to speak on the topic of Turkey. Hegel chose to speak on "The abortive state of art and scholarship in Turkey." The conventions of the talk were to give the schoolboy the opportunity to display his erudition, praise his teachers, and, of course, to praise the wise administration of Karl Eugen for providing them with a much superior educational environment than was supposedly available in poor, benighted Turkey. Hegel accomplished both tasks dutifully, even if somewhat long-windedly. With that, he brought his life as a *Gymnasium* student to a close.

His head full of mixed ideas, Hegel set off – full of confidence in his powers but also, no doubt, with a little anxiety about his future – to study theology at the university at Tübingen, a seat of learning where almost all the notables of Württemberg had studied since the fifteenth century. In his own mind, he most likely foresaw himself following a career path partly modeled on that of Lessing: He was to become a minister or at least a theologian; he was to help to "educate" and "enlighten" the public with his learning – in science, philosophy, theology, languages, and literature – and he was to become a "man of letters." Since almost one quarter of the books being published at the time in Germany were theology books, his career path as a theologian seemed no doubt to him a wise, although – given the already small and rapidly diminishing number of positions for ministers available at the time – also a somewhat risky choice. But, after all, had not Lessing started out his career as a student of theology? At this point in his life, Hegel had firmly allied himself with the Enlightenment, at least as he understood it, and the future he ambitiously imagined for himself as a young man had him playing a role in continuing that progress promised by more Enlightenment. The issue of what was genuinely modern and of how to bring the past up to date, make things more enlightened, formed the hazy edges of the future he was beginning to envision for himself. To that end, so he thought at the time, he would pursue a career in theology, he would preach a new, "enlightened" religion to his parish, and he would write essays (or novels or plays or poetry – at this stage the teenage Hegel could not really have said which) that would assist in the project of increasing enlightenment.

Once at Tübingen, however, he was to strike up a friendship with two other students that would change his life forever; he was to find that the ideas he so self-confidently brought with him were not as clear as he had thought, nor was their fit with each other as seamless as he had imagined it to be; and he was fully to abandon the idea of becoming a pastor, deciding instead at first to embark on the more dangerous path of leading something like an independent life as a "man of letters." Although Hegel could not have known it at the time, as he left for Tübingen, his Württemberg upbringing had equipped him with an ambition, a somewhat overweening self-confidence, and a set of ideas that were to generate many of the problems that would eventually lead him fairly late in his career to decide to become a professor of philosophy in a university setting. Indeed, as Hegel's world began to widen for him at the university and immediately thereafter, he came to find that reconciling the particularistic appeal to social mores he had acquired through his Württemberg upbringing with the demands of the more universalistically inclined Enlightenment rationality that he had acquired at home and at the Stuttgart *Gymnasium* was neither personally easy nor immediately achievable. His doubts and frustrations about these ideas would begin at Tübingen but would not be resolved, as he was to find out, until much later.

2

The Protestant Seminary in Tübingen

Disappointments and Charms of University Life

HEGEL COULD NOT HELP but have been disappointed with his circumstances at Tübingen University when he arrived there. The university, which had enjoyed a fairly glorious past, had gone into steep decline and was in danger of ceasing to exist altogether. In 1769 Karl Eugen had decided to rename the university after himself; instead of being called the Eberhard University (named after Duke Eberhard, who had founded the university in 1477), it was to be known henceforth as the Eberhard-Karls University. However, despite its renaming, Tübingen University remained at the time a bastion of outmoded thought and courses of instruction, differing very little in this regard from most other German universities at the time. Nepotism was also rampant in Tübingen, another unfortunate feature it shared with the other German universities; the professors there tended to come from a small number of families who intermarried, with the fully predictable result of a drastic lowering of the overall quality of the professoriate.[1] Thus, by the time Hegel was ready to go to the university, universities in Germany had become the object of widespread contempt; they were seen as mere relics of an outmoded medieval scholasticism, where new knowledge was not produced, and as places where youth became corrupted by the anti-intellectual student culture of duels and drunkenness prevalent at most all of them. Universities remained semifeudal "corporations," institutions governed by the professoriate, who were far more interested in exercising their inherited medieval privileges than in anything else, and who thus tended to resist strenuously all efforts to reform the universities. Moreover, like many other German universities, Tübingen maintained an idea of its educational mission as that of

19

passing on orthodox, correct belief to its students, a pedagogical idea reinforced by the predominance of the theological faculty of the university.

For theses reasons, there were many people in Germany calling for the total abolition of universities and their replacement by more specialized academies of science and useful knowledge. Karl Eugen had tried to get Tübingen to modernize its teaching and its research, but finally gave it up as a lost cause and began to focus his energies on his own creation, the *Karlsschule*, also named for himself. The *Karlsschule* was typical of the new "academies" being formed at the time in opposition to the staid, theologically bound universities with their medieval charters and privileges and outmoded curricula. In 1782, Karl Eugen decided to promote the *Karlsschule* in Stuttgart to the rank of a university, and the *Karlsschule* began to drain off resources and energy from the university in Tübingen.

By the time Hegel arrived, there was little more to the university in Tübingen than the Protestant Seminary – the *Stift* – where he was to live and study. What was left of the law and medical faculties could not even be described as a skeleton crew. The fact that by 1788 the university itself had become more or less a mere appendage of the Protestant Seminary supposedly attached to it was, moreover, not something that further endeared it to its devout Catholic duke, Karl Eugen. Thus, Hegel arrived at a university that had the feel of someplace frozen in time, where somehow (and in great contrast to his *Gymnasium* in Stuttgart) the Enlightenment had not yet quite arrived. (The university was only to be saved by Karl Eugen's death in 1793, his successor's decision to rebuild the Tübingen university, and the subsequent transfer of the best minds of the *Karlsschule* to Tübingen.)[2]

Hegel reacted to this situation by rebelling. Although he entered the Seminary as the top-ranked student of his class, he quickly became both uninterested in his official studies and a bit headstrong in his attitudes and did not manage to keep his first-place ranking after the first test. Hegel the model student was quickly transformed into a somewhat surly young scholar who neglected good bits of his studies. He did not abandon his idea of himself as following his chosen career as a "man of letters," nor did he abandon his passion for reading and reflection, but he did change his attitude toward his teachers and his schooling, even if he kept many of the behaviors he had acquired as a schoolboy.

In addition to the low quality of the university, the circumstances of the Protestant Seminary were themselves not of the kind that would have appealed to Hegel's temperament. The Protestant Seminary was built on the foundations of an older Augustinian seminary, and, for the duration of their studies, the students became in effect Protestant monks. They were required to wear long black coats (which vaguely resembled cassocks) with white cuffs and collars. The seminarians' hours were strictly regulated, and they were regularly scrutinized and watched. Failure to abide by the rules meant punishment, usually in the form of being deprived of one's ration of table wine for the day or being incarcerated in the student jail (the *Karzer*). The chancellor of the university was fond of saying, "It is good and salutary for one whose future occupation will be the care of souls that his will should be broken whilst he is young."[3] Hegel was in no mood to have his will broken, and the strict regulations and the low level of the instruction only served to further alienate him from his official studies.

The "Three Friends"

During Hegel's first year, however, he made the acquaintance and became good friends with another student who, like him, was both highly ranked in the class and equally alienated from the life at the Seminary: Friedrich Hölderlin, who was to become one of the greatest of all German poets. In the fall of 1790, he and Hölderlin also became good friends with another much younger student who had just arrived, Friedrich Wilhelm Joseph Schelling.[4] Schelling was five years younger than Hegel and Hölderlin, but his precociousness had so impressed the authorities at the cloister school he had attended that he had been given an early admission to the Seminary. Both Hegel and Hölderlin quickly discovered that Schelling shared their antipathy to the Seminary, and the three became fast friends and shared a room together there. They jointly resolved not to become pastors, and Schelling and Hölderlin came to be among the chief catalysts for Hegel's eventual turn towards a career in philosophy.

A deep sense of shared experience and expectation combined to bring the three friends together and to drive them more to philosophical and less to theological studies. As they entered the university, things were slowing down in Germany. Having only recently recovered from the devastation of the Thirty Years War, Germany had been growing economically and demographically. The economic situation, however, was starting to stagnate, and the number of suitable positions for young men with expectations of holding a "learned" position in society was shrinking. Yet all the while that the prospects for their futures seemed to be receding, there was a continuous introduction into Germany of new French and English "Enlightenment" ideas that reinforced a growing view among the young that the "old ways" were restricting Germans from improving their lot both socially and educationally. Life really could be improved, it increasingly seemed evident, by the application of reason to human affairs, and to the young seminarians what especially seemed to be blocking such renewal in their own environment were precisely the hometown structures of the Württemberg life in which they had been raised. Their shared experience – the felt tension between social promise and the antiquated structures of hometown life – put these three rather studious young fellows in the position of being especially open to prospects of change and to new ideas that would give them a comprehensive view of things that would outline how it would be possible to "reform" the present situation. They were thus experientially already open to something like Kant's philosophy, with its emphasis on "freedom" and "spontaneity." That Hegel initially had some doubts about this is also instructive.

The Revolution

Hegel's and Hölderlin's first year at the Seminary was thus spent in alienation from their surroundings. Hölderlin, who had been engaged to a pastor's daughter (typically, a young seminarian married a pastor's daughter in order to inherit the pastor's position) painfully broke off his engagement to the young woman in 1789. That, however, was to prove insignificant in light of what happened next: The French Revolution in 1789 quite simply changed everything for Hegel and Hölderlin. The Revolution led Hegel, Hölderlin, and, after his arrival, Schelling, to become increasingly exasperated by the provinciality and corruption of the Württemberg world in which they lived, which their experience of the Seminary had only brought home all the more vividly to them. They were, moreover, not alone at the Seminary in their embrace of Revolution, and their initial enthusiasm for the Revolution only deepened over the next few years with French victories over counterrevolutionary German armies. They cheered the Revolution in 1789, and they followed the events closely in France and hoped for something similar in Germany. For Hegel, his initial disappointment with the Seminary gave way to heady feelings of hope for the future and identification with the revolutionary cause.

However, after the Declaration of Pillnitz in 1791, in which Austria and Prussia pledged themselves to defend the principles of monarchy against the threats of revolution, there was much concern in France (and outside France, particularly among the pro-French faction at the Seminary) that France was to be invaded by hostile forces intent on reversing the Revolution. For a while, things seemed to have calmed down when the French king accepted the new constitution in 1791. However, the western part of the old empire, of which Württemberg was part, had seen a huge influx of émigré nobility from France, who formed a pressure group calling for a counterrevolutionary coalition to invade France. The situation between the two sides deteriorated with the various angry charges being traded, and on April 20, 1792, the French declared war. The duke of Braunschweig, recognized as one of the foremost military leaders of his day, took command of a force that at first successfully marched into France. But on September 20, he engaged the forces led by the French General Dumouriez at Valmy near Paris. The French won the battle, the duke of Braunschweig took his forces with him into retreat, and the French pursued them deep into Germany. The day after the victory at Valmy, the newly elected National Convention in France abolished the monarchy. (Goethe, who was present at the battle of Valmy, remarked on that night that a new epoch in world history had begun.)

The pro-French element of the German population, of which the young students Hegel, Hölderlin, and Schelling were most decidedly members, rejoiced at this turn of events, since it seemed to promise fulfillment of their hopes that the retrograde forces of the old empire were not long for the world. For the partisans of the Revolution at the Seminary, the defeat of what they could only regard as the forces of moral and spiritual enfeeblement could not help but be encouraging. Excitement about the events in France was also stirred by the presence of French students at the Seminary, who brought the news from France directly into the Seminary. Some of the seminarians came from areas in

France that belonged to the duke of Württemberg, who because of
various vagaries of Württemberg history possessed lands in France in
Alsace and in the area around Montbéliard (known then by its Württemberg name of Mömpelgard). In addition to those students, there
were also some French seminarians from other Protestant areas in
France. One of the entries in Hegel's university album, for example,
was by Jean Jérôme Kolb from Strasbourg. (Kolb's entry read, "Vive la
liberté!!").[5]

Some fellow students later recounted an anecdote about this period
according to which the trio of Hölderlin, Schelling, and Hegel erected
a "freedom tree" – a kind of revolutionary Maypole – on the fourteenth
of July, 1793 (a year into the Terror, during which the guillotines were
working full time) on a field near the town of Tübingen and danced the
revolutionary French dance, the Carmognole, around it, all the while
singing the words to the *Marseillaise* (which Schelling had translated
into German). The story has been repeated so many times that it has
become part of the Hegel-Schelling-Hölderlin legend, but unfortunately, except for the part about Schelling's translation, the story is
almost surely false. However, its believability for those who later told it
lay in its adequately capturing the spirit that was undoubtedly animating the three friends.[6] A political club had formed in the 1790s at
Tübingen to discuss the Revolution, to read various revolutionary tracts,
and in general to raise the spirits of the seminarians who were inspired
by the events of the Revolution; Hegel was a member of the club. The
club had itself been founded by another friend of Hegel's at the Seminary, Christian Ludwig Wetzel, who had apparently brought the text
to the *Marseillaise* with him from a sojourn in Strasbourg, where he
had been in 1792 in order to fight on the French side in their battles
with the Austrians. The trio of Hegel, Hölderlin, and Schelling, moreover, were also enthusiastic readers of a German journal, *Minerva*,
edited by Johann Wilhelm von Archenholz, which avidly supported the
Revolution.

If the Revolution and its celebration sat well with the three friends,
it certainly did not particularly please the duke of Württemberg. He
had lost many of his lands in France when the revolutionaries of 1789
abolished feudal privileges, and so from his point of view, since it was
bad enough that the Seminary in Tübingen was Protestant, it would be
intolerable if it turned out to be training antiroyalist revolutionaries.

The political club at Tübingen especially had not gone unnoticed by the authorities, and the duke himself made a personal visit to the Seminary to see just how subversive the institution bearing his name had become. After fighting with the French forces in 1792, Hegel's friend Wetzel had returned to Tübingen in order to take his master's exam, but when the duke visited in 1793, Wetzel decided that discretion called for him to absent himself from the area, since he was almost certainly to be arrested and incarcerated. (He later became a commissioner in the conquering French army of the Rhine and the Mosel and finally moved to Paris, where he founded a piano factory.) Schelling himself was interrogated by the ducal visitors, at which point he apparently confessed to having made some youthful errors; he was not arrested, and Hegel was never interrogated. But after Wetzel's flight to France, the political club gradually ceased to exist.

Hegel and his friends thus began to imagine different futures not only for themselves but for Württemberg and even for the Holy Roman Empire as a whole. This conception of being a "partisan of the Revolution" fit well with and revitalized Hegel's view of himself as having a career as a "teacher of the people" on the model of Lessing. Some of his friends, such as Wetzel, had already presented themselves as partisans of the Revolution, willing to go off to join its battles. An older seminarian, Karl Friedrich Reinhardt, who had published articles highly critical of life in the Seminary, had taken enthusiasm for the French one huge step further: After becoming the vicar in Balingen (a Württemberg town near Tübingen), he had gone to France in 1787, participated in the Revolution, and become a figure of some importance there – indeed, he rose to such influence within the ruling circles in France that he later even replaced the great Tallyrand, becoming, even if only briefly, the French foreign minister under the Girondins.[7]

Such things no doubt filled Hegel's head with dreams of what his nonpastoral career might turn out to be. More importantly, though, the Revolution and his imaginative involvement in it with his friends had altered his view of his own ambitions, even if he himself was slow to realize it. He had come to Tübingen imagining a future for himself as an enlightened pastor and theologian assisting in the project of bringing Württemberg, and maybe even the "German nation" as a whole, into modern life (much as Lessing had created a public for literature and theater). He had quickly abandoned the idea of becoming a pastor, after the Revolution had suggested to him and others that more was at stake in becoming "modern" than merely becoming "enlightened." Hegel, like many German intellectuals of the time, tended to see the emerging French Revolution as a newer version of the older Protestant Reformation, destined to lead society to a better ethical condition. The more general ideas of moral reform and spiritual renewal had, of course, been with him since he had imbibed the related ideals of Enlightenment and *Bildung* ("cultural formation," "taste," "cultivation") in Stuttgart, but the political nature of the Revolution and the involvement of his fellow seminarians had gradually led him to think more concretely about the social embodiment of the rather hazy ideas of "moral reform" and "spiritual renewal" that he had brought with him to Tübingen. His Württembergian background had endowed him with a sense of constitutionalism and with the idea that indistinct notions such as rights had to be anchored in some kind of social practice; his Enlightenment education had prepared him for the idea that it was both possible and desirable to make a career of assisting the process of spiritual renewal, and that the application of human reason was to play a large role in this; and the Revolution and his association with his seminary friends (both German and French) had thrown into question just how his Württembergian ideals and his Enlightenment sympathies were actually going to play out. The major role that Pietism played in Württemberg also played a large role in this conception – despite the fact that he was not a Pietist himself and was not personally in any way attracted to Pietist ideas, Hegel was nonetheless greatly influenced by the central Pietist idea that reform of the *church* had not been enough and that a thoroughgoing reform of the *world* was equally required, and that the Revolution was to lead to this reform of the world.

The "Old Man" and the "Summer of Love"

Nonetheless, however rebellious against the ways of the Seminary Hegel became, he remained the industrious, serious fellow he always was; his friends at the Seminary referred to him by the nickname "the old man," and one of them drew in his university album a picture of an old man on crutches with a long beard, under which was the inscription, "God help the old man." Hegel may have visited the taverns, cut classes, and ridden off on afternoon adventures with his other friends, but the nickname shows that (probably unlike many of them) he was not content with simply pub crawling, carousing, and making merry; he was still reading quite a bit and still remained extremely serious about learning, however much contempt he might have had for the low quality of the professoriate at Tübingen.

Although Hegel continued to do just enough in his studies to remain respectable, his heart was not in them. Instead of focusing on his required studies, he threw himself into his reading and, in particular, into the works of Jean-Jacques Rousseau. Many of his student friends when thinking about him in later life remembered him as being an ardent partisan of Rousseau at the time. (He and his classmates would, for example, write "Vive Jean-Jacques" in each other's albums.) Notwithstanding that, Rousseau was not his sole reading matter; he was also avidly reading Friedrich Schiller, Friedrich Heinrich Jacobi, Montesquieu, Plato, and much else.

But his mind was not completely absorbed in such abstruse matters. Hegel remained a gregarious soul, and, like many students before and since, he and his fellow students reacted to the strictness of their academic environment by forming bonds of camaraderie with each other. Hegel loved to play cards (something he appreciated as a schoolboy in Stuttgart and throughout the rest of his life), discuss issues with friends, and engage in friendly drinking bouts at the many pubs around Tübingen. These escapades (along with Hegel's cutting of lectures and his continual oversleeping) did not go unnoticed by the proctors, and the records show Hegel being cited several times for such breaches of the rules. The records also show him being thrown into the student jail for a couple of hours in 1791; Hegel's infraction had to do with his having ridden on horseback without permission with a couple of friends to a neighboring village and then having arrived back at the Seminary too late – the reason being that the horse belonging to one of Hegel's friends, a Frenchman studying at the Seminary, became sick, and Hegel and another friend, J. C. F. Fink, refused to ride back without him; the result of Hegel's disobedience to the rules was some mandatory time spent in the student jail, the *Karzer*.[8] As is often the case with students, Hegel also become fond of frequenting the taverns with his friends. His condition on returning to the Seminary late one night prompted one of the older porters at the Seminary gates to exclaim, "Oh Hegel, you're for sure going to drink away what little intellect you have."[9] On yet another occasion, when the porter admonished him with, "Hegel, you're going to drink yourself to death," Hegel replied (surely in a slurred and bleary tone) that he had "just had a little refreshment."[10] His sister remembered Hegel in his students days as a jovial sort who loved both to dance and to visit the ladies.[11]

However much it might be tempting to romanticize Hegel's time at Tübingen – as a time of good friends, wine, ideas, revolution (and unfortunately fleeting attempts at romance) – such romanticizing would obscure the fundamental anxieties that plagued Hegel and his friends Schelling and Hölderlin for their entire stay there. Although the lack of open positions for pastors was so great that they did not reasonably have to worry much about being forced into the profession against their wishes, like all the students at the Seminary they attended the institution on a stipend, and in order to secure entry to the Seminary each had been required to sign an oath of obligation that he would devote himself to theology and to becoming a minister. Each was therefore under legal obligation to the authorities in Württemberg to take a pastoral post if assigned to one. Hegel must have found some relief in the fact that a person such as himself, who regularly got very low marks for his sermons, would not be among the few who would be chosen for such scarce positions.

To thwart even the remote possibility of such a fate, Hegel attempted (as did Hölderlin) to shift over to the study of law after his master's exam (that is, after he had completed his two-year program of general and philosophical studies and before he was to begin his three-year program of theological studies). His father, however, refused to let him make the switch. This quite obviously irritated Hegel no small amount. Unlike so many other generations of Hegels, his father had not become a pastor but had instead studied law at Tübingen; it is probably fair to assume therefore that the relations between father and son were a bit strained on this issue, as they also apparently were on the issue of the Revolution. Hegel had no qualms about debating his father on the contentious issue of the Revolution, an issue about which his father took an emphatically different position from Hegel's own, siding with the aristocrats.[12]

There is no record of why Hegel's father actually refused to let him make the switch, but one obvious ground was that young Hegel had been required to sign a paper obligating him to the study of theology, and his father had been required to pledge his property to sustain his son's studies if he were to be accepted for a stipend at the Seminary. No doubt his father's upright old Württemberg sense that "a man's word was his word" played a role in this; no doubt his worries about possible legal claims on his property also played no small part. Perhaps some dismay and irritation over his son's revolutionary leanings also inclined him to want to keep him out of a political career (fearing the worst for him were he to pursue it). In any event, the young Hegel was compelled to complete his theological training, always under the constant worry that the authorities of Württemberg might force him after all to assume some pastor's post in some village somewhere in the duchy. What had seemed a few years before like a good career choice had come to seem like a possible life sentence; the threat was, moreover, to hang over him for many years to come. If anything, that disappointment only caused him to dive into his extracurricular reading with even more dedication and intensity than he had before.

In his great year of youthful rebellion, 1791, he also became quite taken with the daughter of a deceased professor of theology in Tübingen, Auguste Hegelmaier. Auguste lived with her mother in a baker's house in town. The baker also ran a wineshop where students congregated, so Hegel naturally found himself at home there. He was continually to be found at the baker's shop, drinking the wine and wooing Auguste, who worked at the wine bar. Hegel inscribed in his friend J. C. F. Fink's album in 1791, "Last summer was beautiful; this one more beautiful! The motto of the former was: Wine; of this one, Love!" and he wrote after it, "V.A.!!!" (for Vive Auguste).[13] His friend Fallot also wrote "Vive A!!!" in Hegel's album, and his French friend from Montbéliard, Bernard, wrote, "V. La belle Augustine" – but then added (in French) "for you! And C . . . for me alone!", indicating that he was not a competitor for Auguste's affections.[14] Hegel was even led to help organize a summer ball of which Auguste was named the queen.[15] (Hegel maintained a life-long love of balls and dancing.) Unfortunately for him, Hegel's affections were not requited; it seems that Auguste's affections, even if only for a while, went instead to Hegel's good friend J. C. F. Fink. (Unfortunately, we cannot tell just how good a friend Fink remained after this affair.) Hegel was surely disappointed by his failure in love, although, typically, he made no comments in his diary about this emotional issue; his sister later remarked, though, that at this time he seemed to hold out few hopes in the area of romance. His "summer of love" ended only with a broken heart.

Philosophical Controversies at the Seminary

The Pantheism Controversy

By the 1790s, the three friends had also devoted themselves to reading F. H. Jacobi's works and were particularly enthralled by what came to be called the "pantheism controversy" surrounding Jacobi's 1785 book, *Über die Lehre des Spinoza in Briefen an Herrn Moses Mendelssohn* (*On Spinoza's Doctrines in Letters to Herr Moses Mendelssohn*). The controversy surrounding Jacobi's book on its own would have been enough to lead the three friends to it, but in addition the professor in charge of teaching philosophy at the Seminary, Johann Friedrich Flatt, although a "supernaturalist," was himself an admirer of Jacobi's work, wrote laudatory reviews of Jacobi's books, and was even mentioned approvingly in the second (1789) edition of Jacobi's book (the edition that the three friends no doubt read).[16] For Hegel, Schelling, and Hölderlin, the widely followed controversy surrounding Jacobi's supposed "disclosure" of Lessing's alleged pantheism struck an experiential key.[17]

Jacobi, a figure in German intellectual circles at the time, claimed to have befriended Lessing and to have had a series of conversations with him shortly before his death in which Lessing confided to him that he was a "Spinozist." The charge of "Spinozism" was no light charge to throw around in Germany at the time; for many, Spinoza, a secular Jew, stood for all that was wrong in the modern world. A reliance on reason and science had led Spinoza to a denial of a personal god, and to many Germans this was tantamount to attempting to undermine (Christian) religion and moving to atheism. Since the authority of so many German princes rested on their also being the heads of the churches in their respective *Länder*, anything that could be construed as an attack on religion was ipso facto also to be construed as an attack on the princes' position and authority and therefore on the political authority of the *Land* itself. Accusing Lessing of having admitted to being a Spinozist was therefore bound to be explosive, for Lessing was a widely venerated figure, not only for his writings but for his exemplary, self-critical character. To attack Lessing was to attack the Enlightenment itself.

Jacobi's "revelation" of Lessing's alleged Spinozism was in the form of some letters written to Mendelssohn, who at the time was embarking on writing a biography of his good friend Lessing; Jacobi's alleged motivation for the letters was to inform and warn Mendelssohn before he wrote his account of what Jacobi would have understood as the scandalous revelation that Lessing had secretly been a Spinozist. Jacobi's strategy in all this seems to have been that if he could show that as fine a mind and character as Lessing had been led to "Spinozism" by virtue of following out the ideas of the Enlightenment, then he would have conclusively shown just how dangerous those ideas could be. By asserting that Lessing himself had "confessed" to being a Spinozist, Jacobi got the public debate with Mendelssohn that he had sought. Worrying that Mendelssohn was going into print with his own version of their correspondence, Jacobi published the letters and some other material in 1785 under the title *Über die Lehre von Spinoza in Briefen an Herrn Moses Mendelssohn* (*On Spinoza's Doctrines in Letters to Herr Moses Mendelssohn*). Unfortunately, from Jacobi's point of view, instead of undermining Lessing's authority the whole affair and the publication of the book seemed to have had the opposite effect: With the authority of Lessing behind it, Spinozistic thought was legitimated and the Spinozists came out of the closet. The "pantheism controversy," as it came to be called, was one of the most widely followed events in German intellectual life at the time, eventually pulling in even Kant himself. Schelling in particular was impressed by this debate and was to confide in Hegel in a letter written two years after Hegel had left the university that he too had become a Spinozist (referring to Hegel in the letter as an "intimate of Lessing's," thereby indicating that he thought Hegel too was a secret Spinozist).[18]

The "pantheism controversy" made an indelible mark on the three friends. In Hegel's student album, there is an inscription from Hölderlin, which quotes a line from Goethe (roughly translated: "Pleasure and love are / that which fits great deeds"), and below the date (1791) is added in a different pen and ink the Greek letters "S. Hen kai Pan" ("S. εν και παν"). The "S" stands for "Symbolum," and the "Hen kai Pan" is the expression that Lessing allegedly used when he spoke with Jacobi; it is a "pantheistic formula" and means "one and all," that

is, "God is one and is in everything," a notion that rules out a conception of a personal God as an individual being.[19] This shows that Hegel
and his friends were clearly beginning to entertain in addition to their
politically heretical thoughts certain religious ideas that were equally far
away from what was being officially taught to them at the Seminary. It
is probably not going too far to make out of the added script, "Hen kai
Pan," something like a shared position at the time between the three
friends, namely, that of some kind of "Spinozism": a rejection of the
dualism of soul and body in favor of the view that soul and body are
only aspects of the same underlying substance; and a view that true
wisdom is to be attained by trying to achieve a fully objective and
detached point of view (by achieving, as it were, the point of view of
the universe, rather than remaining in one's own perspectivally limited
point of view).

The use of the symbol "Hen kai Pan" also fit into another part of
Hegel's development during this period. Hegel, Hölderlin, and Schelling began to share an admiration of ancient Greece in the period of the
Athenian empire (something not uncommon at that time for German
intellectuals) around the same time that they developed their enthusiasm
for the Revolution, and in their minds, the two ideas fused. They
continued to understand the Revolution as new kind of Reformation,
and the three friends came to picture that renewal in terms of an
idealized image of ancient Athenian Greece. The Greece that Hegel and
Hölderlin idealized was also shaped in part by their understanding of
Rousseau's idealized utopias. The idealized classical Greek polis – taken
by them as a form of social life in which the individual was not alienated
from the surrounding social order, and in which politics, religion, and
the social conventions of everyday life served to affirm the individual's
sense of his own place in the world instead of undermining it – came to
stand for what they hoped the Revolution would bring to Europe and
in particular to the decrepit structure of the Holy Roman Empire. They
saw in Greek art a kind of perfection that had not been attained in later
Western art, and under the influence of the enormously influential
writings of Johann Joachim Winckelmann, they understood this to be
due in primary part to the Greek devotion to freedom. Winckelmann's
view of Greek art thus meshed well with the views of the Enlightenment
authors who attracted them, and the whole form of classical Greece life
came for them to be associated with the Revolution's invocation of

liberty, equality, and fraternity. In particular, it stood for them as a positive religious and social alternative to what they saw as the debased condition of contemporary Christian and German civilization. The Greeks had united divine beauty with human life, and they had done it under the banner of freedom. The "Hen kai Pan" thus symbolized their devotion to non-Christian (or deviantly Christian) ideals of thought and to the Revolution, and the way in which in their own minds they linked their ardor and hopes for the Revolution with their growing admiration for classical Greece – the Revolution had come to stand for the promise of a new dispensation, a future social order in which divine beauty and human freedom would become part of the everyday life of ordinary people (in contrast to what they saw as the authoritarian ugliness of contemporary life).

Diez, Storr, and the "Kant Club"

The ties between Hölderlin, Schelling, and Hegel seem to have been very close, and thus it is striking that when a group was formed in the Seminary to study Kant, Hegel did not elect to join the group, although Schelling and Hölderlin were avid members. Although Hegel was certainly reading Kant during this period, Kant apparently failed to capture his imagination sufficiently for him to join the other enthusiasts at the Seminary. Hegel had most likely brought with him to the Seminary both his skepticism about Kant's overall theory and some ideas about the implausibility of Kant's reliance on reason as the sole motivating force behind moral action; his growing passion for Rousseau during this period perhaps only served to underscore those doubts about the final viability of Kantian theory, even though Rousseau had been one of the major influences on Kant's own thought. But perhaps most importantly, Hegel's own vision of his future at this point did not include becoming a philosopher in the strict sense; he was still focused on becoming a "man of letters," a person who would apply "enlightened reason" to the study of human affairs for the purposes of moral and religious reform. For Hegel at this point, Kant was just one more Enlightenment figure, one who, to his mind, severely neglected the more experiential, "subjective" aspects of human life. He certainly found it to be important to know what Kant was saying in order to be able to incorporate some of his ideas into the rational criticism of existing social and religious customs; but he did not find it especially important to study Kant as closely as Hölderlin and Schelling did.

This was to lead a few years later to tensions between him and Schelling. It can only be a surmise, but one suspects that in Schelling's mind, Hegel had been the slow one to catch on to the importance of Kant's ideas – he was too stubborn to see any of this for himself and without Schelling's encouragement, would have never come to see the value of any of it – which in turn led Schelling continually to undervalue any possible creative contributions to philosophical debate that Hegel might make. There was also quite likely a tension in the friendship itself between Schelling and Hegel; Hölderlin and Hegel were the same age and had originally become friends; Schelling joined the circle later, and he and Hölderlin together became much more enamored of Kant than Hegel was at first. Schelling's closer intellectual friendship with Hölderlin at this time, together with a certain sense of haughtiness on Schelling's part, probably irked Hegel just a bit; after they left the Seminary, Hegel continued to stay in touch with both of them, but after a few years he let the correspondence with Schelling lapse. Schelling's rather meteoric rise a few years later to prominence in philosophical circles while Hegel was still languishing as an unpublished, unknown house tutor no doubt only further underwrote Schelling's initial view of Hegel.

Nonetheless, although Hegel was not particularly interested in joining the Kant group, he was surrounded by enthusiastic discussions of Kant, and Kantian ideas clearly made an impression on him. In particular, there was – at least among the students and certainly among Hegel's friends – an impassioned debate between the followers of Gottlob Storr (a professor of theology and one of the handful of esteemed professors at the place) and Carl Immanuel Diez, an older student at the Seminary who was responsible for assisting in the instruction of the younger students. Diez was a theologian who had turned against the kind of theology being taught at Tübingen, in part because of Kant's writings, and had become a radical, antireligious Kantian.[20] (Diez was the son of one of the professors of medicine, which partly explains how, within the nepotism-laden structure of the university, he was able to hold such radical views within the theology faculty.)

Diez had reacted strongly to the teachings of the theologian Gottlob Storr. Storr was Hegel's, Hölderlin's, and Schelling's teacher and a figure against whom all of them reacted. Storr embodied both a supremely imposing intellect with a manner of congeniality that led even those who disagreed with him to value and respect him; he also embodied an uncompromising attitude toward biblical interpretation; he took it as his vocation to refute the idea that the Bible represents only a historical accommodation of human beings to the times in which they lived (and thus to refute the idea that the job of the theologian is to extract the "rational truth" from the merely "symbolic" and "historical" elements of the Bible); his self-proclaimed pedagogical mission was to communicate to his students a sense of their obligation to defend orthodoxy against what he called heterodoxy. Storr's theology was based on what he termed "supernaturalism," by which he meant the idea that the Bible was a sacred text and was to be taken therefore as having been divinely inspired; its authority could therefore only come from revelation. Storr the "supernaturalist" classified all his opponents as "naturalists," by which he meant all those who believed that the acceptable truths of Christianity could only be those that were also consistent with or demonstrable by the powers of "natural" human reason. Interestingly, Storr employed Kantian means to show this: Since Kant had shown, Storr argued, that we could have no knowledge of things-in-themselves, of the "ultimate metaphysical structure" of the world, he had also shown that the so-called application of reason to the critique of the dogmatic truths of Christianity by a whole generation of Enlightenment thinkers was completely beside the point. Nothing can be known by unaided reason about the ultimate nature of things; to know about the ultimate nature of things, Storr concluded (contra Kant), we therefore need a revelation from God, and Jesus' life (along with the Bible) was exactly that sort of revelation. Storr thus tried to marry orthodoxy to the developing Enlightenment conception of reason. (Storr's arguments and his standing among German intellectuals were high enough to induce Kant to mention him respectfully as exercising his "accustomed sagacity" in the 1794 preface to the second edition of *Religion within the Limits of Reason Alone*.)[21]

Storr thereby brought Kant into the defense of orthodoxy, a move which found no sympathy at all among Hegel, Hölderlin, and Schelling, whose reactions to Storr were themselves partly shaped by Diez. Since Kant had at this point not yet published anything specifically on religion – his book *Religion within the Limits of Reason Alone* was not to be published until 1793, Hegel's last year at the university – there was little specifically in Kant's writings to draw on except for the discussions of the practical postulates of the existence of God and the immortality of the soul in the *Critique of Practical Reason*, and Kant's own claim in the *Critique of Pure Reason* that he was only clearing the way for reasonable faith. Diez therefore based his critique of Storr in particular and of religion in general on Kant's *Critique of Pure Reason*, taking it much further than the orthodox Kantians had ever dared. He argued that since Kant had shown that we could have experience only of those things that conformed to the conditions under which experience was possible, and since Kant had shown that among these conditions is that all our experience must be of spatio-temporal substances interacting within a causal order, the kind of revelation of which Storr spoke was in principle impossible and the kind of knowledge that Storr imputed to Jesus' disciples was equally impossible.

Diez's use of Kant against Storr's defense of orthodoxy greatly impressed the three friends. Known among the students at the Seminary as a Kantian *enragé* – a term that was also used in the Seminary to characterize those with Jacobin sympathies – Diez outfitted Hegel, Schelling, and Hölderlin with Kantian tools that could be turned against Storr's attempt to preserve the idea of the Bible as a sacred text and therefore as something that simply had to be accepted as authoritative. Moreover, although Diez apparently did little to move Hegel to a Kantian position at this point, he certainly inspired Schelling and Hölderlin to study the great transcendental idealist, and both of them eventually took Hegel down that path. Diez himself quickly came to realize the absurdity of his continuing to study theology while holding such views and left for Jena to study medicine. He exercised some influence on the development of idealism in Jena with regard to Karl Leonhard Reinhold, the first famous "post-Kantian" philosopher in Germany; he also maintained a friendship and philosophical correspondence with another older student at the Seminary, Friedrich Immanuel Niethammer (b. 1766), who was later to have a decisive influence on both Hölderlin and Hegel. Diez himself died of typhus while working at a hospital in Vienna in 1796.[22]

Thus, although Hegel did not at first become a partisan Kantian at Tübingen, he was nonetheless clearly influenced by the discussions of Kant going on in Tübingen, and by the end of his stay in Tübingen, after Kant had actually published something on the topic of religion, Hegel himself switched over to using the Kantian language of the "religion of reason," and he, Hölderlin, and Schelling took to using key Kantian phrases as code words in their conversations with each other. Kant had reconstructed Christian thought in terms of his theory of morality and autonomy in a way that the three friends came to identify with their own adoration of Greek life, support for the French Revolution (which Kant also supported), and distaste for the Christianity that was being doled out to them in the Seminary. Kant's Christianity was exclusively a religion of morality, and for the radical Kantians, Jesus was only the foremost teacher of morality, not some supernatural God-man walking the earth: In Kant's words, "there exists absolutely no salvation for man apart from the sincere adoption of genuinely moral principles into his disposition."[23] The members of such a moral community, he said, form an "invisible church" as distinct from the public, institutional embodiment in a "visible church."[24] The "kingdom of God" (one of the three friends' code words, which was used by Hegel in his last required sermon at the Seminary) is, in Kant's words, "the principle of the gradual transition of ecclesiastical faith to the universal religion of reason, and so to a (divine) ethical state on earth" which "is self-developing . . . which one day is to illumine and to rule the world."[25] Hegel, Hölderlin, and Schelling began to identify their youthful revolutionary aspirations with this Kantian idea of the "kingdom of God" and to speak of themselves as members of that "invisible church."

Hegel nonetheless still remained at this early point in his life somewhat suspicious of Kantian thought, ever lagging behind his two friends in his enthusiasm for the fine points of Kantian doctrine. For him, it still seemed a bit too arid, too reliant on an intellectualized reason, neglecting, so he thought, the moral force of the passions and therefore failing to give a complete account of the living embodied human agent. Like the good son of a pragmatic civil servant in Württemberg that he was, he continued, despite his equally deeply felt Enlightenment sympathies, to be deeply suspicious of claims about "universal reason," holding instead that what motivates people is what their surrounding social practice instills in them and what they can feel for themselves. His Württembergian upbringing, however much he was now distancing himself from it, made such Kantian ideals difficult for him fully to accept, however much they were capturing the fancy of his equally

Württembergian comrades. It was also clear that this tension within his own view troubled him to no small extent.

Hegel's Return to Stuttgart

In the summer of 1793, Hegel's continuing bouts of bad health gave him an unexpected opportunity to try to work out some of his anti-Kantian ideals. Hegel was continually having to go home during his student days in Tübingen because of bad health (although the nature of his maladies remains unknown); but his grounds for doing so likely had to do equally well with his desire to escape from what he regarded as the restricting environment of Tübingen. Tübingen was a small, provincial town that had become even smaller and more provincial as the university had gradually declined in status; while not a metropolis or a cosmopolitan city of any note, Stuttgart was nonetheless a "residence city," that is, a city in which the duke made his home and which therefore attracted the kind of artisans and intellectuals who typically gather around such places. Moreover, Stuttgart had an active, Enlightenment-oriented intellectual life, whereas Tübingen seemed intent on keeping the Enlightenment firmly outside the city walls. Hegel's preferences as a child growing up in Stuttgart stayed with him; he clearly preferred Stuttgart with its wide, open streets and its more open intellectual atmosphere to the narrow, dark, medieval and early Renaissance streets of Tübingen that seemed to accommodate themselves fully to its atmosphere of old-fashioned Pietist repression. A particularly bad bout of ill health allowed Hegel to get permission to spend his last semester at home recuperating; but while there, he indulged in much reading, the study of botany, and a thorough reading of Greek tragedy with special emphasis on Sophocles – which leads one to question just how ill he really was.

While recuperating at home, Hegel received an offer to be a house tutor for the children of a patrician family in Berne. Having managed to get away from Tübingen for health reasons, Hegel jumped at the chance not to have to return, and so petitioned the authoritative church body in Stuttgart (the *Konsistorium*) to allow him to take the theological exam early, and they concurred. Hegel easily passed his exam and thereby managed to finish his theological studies earlier than expected (and certainly earlier than his friends). This seems to have perked up

Hegel's spirits, for it meant that he could begin his career as an author and critic, and, even better from his point of view, that he would not have to return again to Tübingen to study theology. He managed to take a brief vacation before his trip, and he passed the time in Stuttgart with the poet Gotthold Friedrich Stäudlin, a friend of Hölderlin's who also helped to promote Hölderlin's career as a poet. Stäudlin and Hegel struck up an instant friendship; Stäudlin's enthusiasm for the French Revolution (which was to get him ejected from Württemberg at the end of 1793, forcing him to flee to Strasbourg) meshed with Hegel's own sympathies. The two made frequent trips to Cannstatt, a suburb of Stuttgart, where they would drink wine and discuss ideas, and, one can only assume, share their enthusiasm for the Revolution. Stäudlin later wrote to Hegel, when Hegel was in Berne, "These serene hours were so sweet, that I know to give you, dear Hegel, my very warmest thanks for them. You are one of those upright, sincere people, who are good for me and whom I consequently would always want on my side."[26]

While at home in Stuttgart, Hegel also worked on a manuscript that was almost surely begun in Tübingen but completed in the summer of 1793 during his stay in Stuttgart. The essay (nowadays called simply the "Tübingen Fragment" or the "Tübingen Essay") was Hegel's first constructive attempt at doing the kind of thing he had set his heart on doing when he originally left for Tübingen: It was his attempt at writing a critical essay in the style of Lessing or of the French *philosophes* on the current situation facing European life. The essay is distinctly not academically philosophical in tone or argument, although it touches on many philosophical questions, broadly construed. It is Hegel's attempt to come to terms with a set of conflicting ideas in his own mind, some of which he had brought with him to Tübingen, but most of which he had acquired while he was there. Hegel was never to publish the essay, but he was to rework various themes in it for later, also unpublished, essays. The problems he posed for himself in these essays eventually drove him out of the framework in which he had posed them and led him to become the philosopher he was later to be.

The essay is in one sense an attempt to reply to the Kantian enthusiasms of his two Seminary friends, Hölderlin and Schelling. The key element in the essay is a discussion of the role of religion in individual and public life. Hegel sounds themes here that reverberate throughout his later works, but the tone and emphasis are all quite different in the

early essay. The main distinction he draws in the paper is that between
what he at that time called "subjective" and "objective" religion. Objective religion is equated with theology, with established, promulgated
doctrines of belief and with institutional embodiment in a church.
Subjective religion, on the other hand, is something that informs a
person's whole life; it is a matter of the heart, not of doctrine, and it
provides the individual who participates in it with motivations to act in
a way that the dry doctrines of objective religion could never do. In the
metaphors that Hegel uses in the essay, objective religion is "dead,"
whereas subjective religion is "alive." When one inquires therefore into
the role of religion in the life of an individual or in the life of a
community, one must investigate the people's subjective religion – what
the people really believe and feel – and not the established doctrines
that the theologians promulgate or the official words professed by the
pastors in the pulpits. The task of moral and spiritual reform falls to
subjective religion – which Hegel, using the term of art of his day, calls
the religion of the *heart* – and not to objective religion. Moral and
spiritual reform therefore cannot come merely from the theologians; it
must also come from the practices of a "religion of the people" (a
Volksreligion), an idea that he may very well have taken over from
Rousseau.

Interestingly enough, Hegel argues here against a purely Enlightenment understanding of religion and against Kant in particular (although
the arguments are very attenuated at best). In his *Religion within the
Limits of Reason Alone*, Kant had argued in favor of a pure religion of
morality, an "invisible church," to which he opposed the "visible
church"; Kant contrasted the "pure faith" of reason with the "ecclesiastical faith" of the established churches. (This was particularly easy for
Kant, since he himself was never comfortable with any ceremonial
religious service.) Kant's problem in the book was to show how a
religion was possible that did not rely on any form of revelation or
nonrational basis; one might say that Kant posed the problem of what a
"modern," that is, a "rational" religion would look like, a problem that
was to provoke Hegel for his entire career. At first blush, Hegel's
distinction between subjective and objective religion looks like a reworked version of the Kantian distinction. However, Hegel draws a
sharp contrast between his ideas and the Kantian conception, claiming
that a pure religion of reason could never serve as a "subjective"

religion; pure reason alone cannot motivate us, cannot claim our hearts. The idea of a "pure faith" that consists entirely of the motivation to act virtuously in light of the demands of practical reason is therefore an empty ideal; as Hegel puts it, "man needs motives other than pure respect for the moral law, motives more closely bound up with his sensuality . . . hence what this objection really comes down to is that it is altogether unlikely that humankind, or even a single individual, will ever in this world be able to dispense entirely with nonmoral promptings."[27]

For the young Hegel, still under the influence of Rousseau (and probably, even if only indirectly, of the earl of Shaftesbury), the idea of Enlightenment reason *alone* motivating us was simply unbelievable. In the essay, he offers no real arguments against Kant's idea that reason provides us with its own incentives for action; instead, he simply voices his conviction that Kant's view is incredible. What he sees as needed instead is a union of Enlightenment reason and the human heart; the Kantian ideals of reason and human dignity require a "people's religion" to be put into practice.

Hegel's criticisms of the idea of a purely detached, Enlightenment criticism of religion are, no doubt, also a bit autobiographical in tone. Hegel claims that such Enlightenment criticism and putative reform necessarily fails. Partially echoing Aristotle, Hegel claims that Enlightenment reason can only produce a *Wissenschaft*, a "science" or "learned discipline," whereas what is needed is *wisdom*, which can never come out of such theories, out of *Wissenschaft* alone.[28] (This disparagement of *Wissenschaft* is, of course, another issue on which Hegel later was to decisively reverse himself.) Enlightenment criticism of the practices of religion necessarily confuses the richness of heartfelt, "subjective" religion with that of superstition and fetishism; it prides itself on its detachment from such superstition, and it is the "arrogance typical of adolescents . . . having got a couple of insights out of books they begin scoffing at beliefs they had up to now, like everyone else, unquestioningly accepted. In this process, vanity plays a major role."[29] (One suspects that Hegel is thinking of himself and perhaps also of Diez.) The work of Enlightenment is at best to assist in the production of a genuine religion of the people, a genuine sense of moral and spiritual renewal; on its own, it cannot do this. As Hegel puts it, "Part of the business of enlightening understanding is to refine objective religion. But when it comes to the improvement of mankind (the cultivation of strong and great dispositions, of noble feelings, and of a decisive sense of independence), the powers of the understanding are of little moment; and the product, objective religion, does not carry much weight either. . . . It is nonetheless of the utmost importance for us to discourage any fetishistic mode of belief, to make it more and more like a rational religion. Yet a universal church of the spirit remains a mere ideal of reason."[30]

One can see several of Hegel's youthful influences at work in the essay. For someone of Hegel's upbringing, the distinction between subjective and objective religion would have been a natural way to cast Kant's distinction between the "invisible church" and the "visible church." Kant's distinction echoes Pietist thought, and, as we noted, although Hegel was no Pietist, he could not help but have been influenced by the importance of Pietist ideas in the Württemberg climate. (His close friend at Tübingen, Hölderlin, was, for example, raised as a Pietist.) For the Pietists, what was important was religious experience and its transformative effect on one's life; they were deeply suspicious not simply of some of the particular theological statements of Christian faith at that time but in general of any intellectual articulation of religious faith. Moreover, in Württemberg, the Pietists had come to understand their reliance on the transformative power of faith as being connected to the successful political movements of Württemberg history, of a godly people who had successfully resisted the encroachments of their absolutizing Catholic monarchs. Hegel's distinction between subjective and objective religion nicely fit into the Pietist division between real, emotional religious experience and the dry, falsifying intellectual articulation of that experience.

Hegel himself, however, could not and would not have understood his distinction between objective and subjective religion as a Pietist recasting of Kantian thought, since he did not think of himself as a Pietist of any sort. In the essay, the problem Hegel sets for himself has to do with his understanding of the consequences of the French Revolution, namely, the issue of what conditions would be necessary to bring about a spiritual and moral renewal of "the people." The only possible answer, so he thinks, must come from a genuine religion of the people (from a genuine *Volksreligion*). To show how this could take place, he constructed an idea of how such a genuine religion of the people would develop, drawing on the things he knew to do so: his Württemberg past (with its implicit Pietist distinction between the true religion of subjective emotion and the dead hand of orthodoxy), the Kantian ideas he has acquired at the Seminary, his devotion to the Revolution and its cause of freedom, and, very importantly, his emerging love of ancient Greece, into which he has stirred various Rousseauian themes.

To this end, he identified a genuine *Volksreligion* with the religion of ancient Greece, which he in turn identified with the ideal of freedom: "The folk festivals of the Greeks were all religious festivals, and were held either in honor of a god or of a man deified because of his exemplary service to his country. . . . A religion of the people (*Volksreligion*) – engendering and nurturing, as it does, great and noble sentiments – goes hand in hand with freedom. But our religion [i.e., orthodox Christianity] would train people to be citizens of heaven, gazing ever upward, making our most human feelings seem alien."[31]

The unstated problem in the essay is that of what form the revolution in Germany – understood always as a social program of moral and spiritual renewal – ought to take. In this first stab at an answer to that question, Hegel develops the general form of what a solution would look like: It would be possible to have moral and spiritual renewal only if a genuine "religion of the people" could be developed, that is, only in a religion that would touch both people's hearts and minds, unite the public and private sides of life, and do this for *all* the people, not merely for a small few of them. From his schoolboy Stuttgart readings of Christian Garve and Johann Gottfried Herder, Hegel had picked up the idea that the modern fragmentation of society into different estates and classes made modern life incapable of forming any conception of a common interest; in his essay, Hegel comes to see subjective religion, the "religion of the people," as the means by which such fragmentation is to be overcome.

However, Hegel could not explain in the essay exactly how such a subjective religion uniting all people in both their reason and their hearts could actually come about in such fragmented circumstances, nor could he point to any clear direction in which a solution could lie. Hegel had set himself a problem, he had failed to solve it, and he knew it. But he was to take up these problems again during his sojourn in Berne and Frankfurt and would raise the question of whether Christianity could

be reformed so that it could serve as the vehicle for the kind of revolution Hegel had in mind. He gradually came to see that the questions he
had been asking himself about were not exactly the ones he needed to
raise if he was to fulfill the very general task he had set for himself, and
that realization gradually took him away from his original goals.

3

From Berne to Frankfurt to Jena: Failed Projects and Fresh Starts

Berne: Second Thoughts

IN SEPTEMBER OF 1793, Hegel took his examination from the church authorities in Württemberg (the *Konsistorialexamen*) and passed. In October of 1793, he began the first of his two stints as a *Hofmeister*, a private tutor to well-off families, having acquired his position as tutor in the usual way that young men in those days acquired such positions: totally by accident. A Berne patrician, Captain Carl Friedrich von Steiger, had set out to find a private tutor for his two children. A young graduate of the Tübingen Seminary, a certain Herr Schwindrazheim, had been recommended to Captain von Steiger, and he decided to do some secret checking up on Mr. Schwindrazheim's qualifications and character. He had a confidante investigate him in Stuttgart, and the results were not exactly favorable for Herr Schwindrazheim. However, another young man, a certain young Hegel, was instead recommended by the relevant people in Tübingen, including the proprietor (Johannes Brodhag) of an inn called the Golden Ox. (The innkeeper was later to become famous in biographies of Schiller, who had earlier frequented the place.) Captain von Steiger managed to get in touch with Hegel, there was some dickering on Hegel's part about the money involved (Switzerland was even then recognized as an expensive place to live), and the deal was finally struck.

Hegel's stint as a private tutor was typical of the career of young educated men of those days. In the prevailing system of education, many aristocratic and even fairly well-off bourgeois families hired private tutors for their children. (Hegel, for example, had some private tutors while attending school in Stuttgart.) To this end, young men were contracted to provide education for the children at home or often

45

simply to accompany a young aristocrat on something like his grand
tour, a fashion that the German aristocracy had taken over from the
English. On the grand tour, the young aristocrat would journey to
various important cities, visit the local luminaries, and come back not
only having seen the world but also presumably having acquired some
education along the way. This last was not always the case: The aristocracy hired private tutors not generally because they valued education
highly; just as frequently, the young tutor was hired simply to watch
over his young lord's bad habits, help him to avoid some of their nastier
consequences, and explain to the otherwise clueless young aristocrat
why this particular intellectual luminary he was about to visit or that
particular church he was seeing was important. Indeed, manuals for
tutors at the time advised the tutor to keep his aristocratic charge away
from the three bad W's: "Wein, Weiber, Würfel" (wine, women, and
dice).[1] The young men hired were frequently those who had achieved a
diploma in theology, since there was an enormous surplus of them (thus
driving their price down), and because it was felt that such novice
divines would be the proper moral accompaniment for a young, impressionable, wealthy aristocrat out for the first time on his own (and who,
after all, was destined to become a patriarchal figure to his peasantry
after his father departed the scene). As far as such things went, such
tours were the kinds of things that young theologians often desired since
they gave them a chance to be introduced to society and to see the
world for themselves. Schelling, for example, himself was hired to
accompany a young noble on a tour of England and France, and although he was originally quite enthusiastic about this opportunity, his
enthusiasm dampened after the revolutionary upheavals of the time
caused his employer to switch the itinerary to a tour of major German
cities. Schelling ended up not with Paris and London but instead with
Leipzig and Jena.

   Hegel was not so lucky: He was engaged not for a grand tour of the
world or, for that matter, even for a venture to Leipzig, but instead
simply to tutor two young children (ages six and nine) at home. Captain
von Steiger was particularly interested in having the young tutor teach
his children reformed religion, languages, history, geography, arith-
metic, and music.[2] Dismal as such a prospect might have seemed, it
appealed to Hegel because it offered him both the excuse to conclude
his studies in Tübingen early and the possibility of beginning his career

as a *Popularphilosoph*, a "popular philosopher," the German equivalent of both the free spirited *philosophes* of the French Enlightenment and of the Scottish philosophers. Like the *philosophes* and their Scottish counterparts, the German "popular philosophers" set themselves the task of doing philosophy in a manner accessible to the educated public and of explaining to the general public the more demanding ideas of modern, enlightened philosophy (such as Kant's). The idea behind the movement of the "popular philosophers" was that the widespread discussion and dissemination of such philosophical ideas would assist the overall Enlightenment goal of promoting the application of reason to human affairs. The expanding number of popular journals of culture also made it possible for such "popular philosophers" to earn money from writing articles. Although the honoraria for pieces published in such journals were certainly not on the grand scale, neither were they trivial.

The alternative to becoming a "popular philosopher" was getting a position at a university, but this was fraught with its own special difficulties. First, there was no clear way (besides being a member of a professor's family) to gain a position in a German university, and second, the state of German universities at the time was, with few exceptions, so dismal that nobody with Hegel's ambitions would have even desired such a position. Since the position of private tutor – *Hofmeister* – was often taken as a good way for a young man to make contacts with the wider world, to be introduced into society, and to have time for his own scholarly work, a person like Hegel would naturally have been attracted to such a position. If nothing else, the position of *Hofmeister* held out the possibility of making a name for oneself with the people that counted, so that later one could lay claim to being the kind of learned gentleman who would be appropriate for a university post, if such a thing became desirable.

Like so many other young intellectuals of that period (and even like Kant a generation before), Hegel thus began his career as a *Hofmeister*, and the experience did not exactly endear the aristocracy to him. The position was almost certain to disappoint him; in fact, the whole encounter led Hegel into a serious depression. Again, Hegel shared that experience with many young intellectuals of his generation. The position of *Hofmeister* was by the end of the eighteenth century racked with social stresses and contradictions: On the one hand, the *Hofmeister* was a servant, a domestic; on the other hand, he was not only more educated

than the other domestics, he was almost certainly better educated than
his employers. The husband and wife of the house therefore generally
treated him only *slightly* better than the other, more lowly domestics,
which is to say that they did not treat him well at all. (For example, one
of the burning issues of the time for such families concerned whether
the *Hofmeister* should eat with the family or with the servants.) For a
young man like Hegel, who came from a family of good social status,
such a position of social inferiority was especially grating.

This position of being both socially below the husband and wife but
slightly higher than the rest of the domestic staff also did not exactly
endear the typical poor young *Hofmeister* to the other domestics, so he
was generally alienated not only from the husband and wife but from
the other domestics as well, and indeed quite often was treated by them
with rudeness bordering on contempt. Even in those situations where
he was treated much better than the other domestics and was even
allowed to eat with the family instead of with the other domestics, he
was still clearly a social inferior and was always treated as such. The
literature of the time abounds with anecdotes of incidents in which a
Hofmeister unwittingly oversteps the social boundaries and assumes a
familiarity with the family to which he is not entitled and for which he
is immediately and publicly humiliated and rebuffed. Moreover, the
children whom he was teaching quite often also held him in disconcert-
ingly low regard, since they had often internalized not only a sense of
their own social superiority but also an understanding that they would
one day be running things whether they were educated or not, hence
making his admonitions to behave and do their lessons seem quite
irrelevant. Quite often he became against his own wishes the unhappy
mediator between not only the children and their parents but between
the parents themselves. Along with all that, the position came with low
pay and absolutely no job security.

The results of such a set of tensions and contradictions were predictable. The isolation, the petty humiliations, and the insecurity common
to the position of *Hofmeister* led regularly to bouts of resignation, depression, and crushing loss of self-confidence among such young men –
and Hegel was no exception. By the end of the eighteenth century, not
only was this becoming increasingly noted in the literature surrounding
the institution of the *Hofmeister*, the *Hofmeisters* themselves were be-

coming both very self-conscious regarding their bad treatment and very critical of the institution itself.[3]

More importantly, Hegel had been imbued from his early Stuttgart days with the ideals of *Bildung*, that is, of education and self-cultivation, of becoming a man of knowledge and good taste, and he had fused his commitment to *Bildung* with his ideals of the Revolution as a moral and spiritual renewal of the German people. Hegel was the young man who had excerpted Moses Mendelssohn's essay "What Is Enlightenment?" in his teenage journal and had noted how Mendelssohn had virtually equated Enlightenment itself with *Bildung*, the idea of education as the cultivation of taste and good judgment. During his stay at the university, which had coincided with his passionate endorsement of the French Revolution, he had, like many other young men of his generation, come to think of the revolutionary moral and spiritual renewal of Germany in terms of establishing a new elite of educated leaders (men of *Bildung*) to rule the country. In Hegel's mind, the new revolutionary order would bring about a state of affairs in which men of learning, taste, and cultivation would be running things instead of the undereducated, pompous, corrupt aristocracy represented by families such as the von Steigers.

The idea itself of *Bildung* was one of those things that was in the air at the time and came with considerable controversy attached to it. By Hegel's time, the idea had been distinguished from that of *Erziehung*, education. *Bildung* incorporated within itself the notion of true education and cultivation as in turn demanding self-formation. As it were, one could *become* educated (in the passive tense, represented by the term *Erziehung*), but one had to *make oneself* into a cultivated-educated person (in the active tense, represented by the term *Bildung*).[4] *Bildung* required self-activity, self-development, and self-direction.

In Hegel's day, one of the major issues about the nature of *Bildung* was its relation to Enlightenment. Was a cultivated-educated person also an enlightened person? Although some thought that the two were distinct, many suspected that in fact they were so essentially linked that the call for young men to acquire *Bildung* was ipso facto a call for them to become "enlightened," which in turn for the more retrograde elements of German life, was itself tantamount to a demand to make them into French revolutionaries, perhaps even into Jacobins intent on murdering the aristocracy and the leaders of the church. Mendelssohn, after all, had identified *Bildung* with Enlightenment, and Kant had claimed that to be enlightened was equivalent to thinking for oneself, and to many of the retrogrades, that in itself was equivalent to Jacobinism. Needless to say, this debate was also joined by those who wished to distinguish "true" *Bildung* from "false" or "corrupted" *Bildung*, that is, true self-cultivation from that kind that led one to become a revolutionary or a democrat. There were cries against the idea of *Bildung*; there were even suggestions that, with all the new "reading societies" springing up across what still counted as the Holy Roman Empire, a new disease, that of "reading addiction" (*Lesesucht*), was arising, an ailment which was believed likely to strike impressionable young students, loose women, servants not properly respectful of their masters, and other questionable sorts of people.[5]

One of the most striking characteristics about the idea of *Bildung*, of course, was that it transcended the idea of the old society of orders, of "estates" to which one belonged by birth, much as the earlier French idea of a "man of letters" had done.[6] To be a person of *Bildung* had nothing to do with one's birth but with how one directed and formed oneself; men (and women) of *Bildung* thus had a claim to status that directly contradicted the traditional claims of birth and estate. A man like Hegel could claim, for example, to be the kind of person who had the "right" to be at the center of things by virtue of how he had made himself into a cultivated-educated man, independent of whether his family was or was not a member of the *Ehrbarkeit* of Württemberg, and certainly independent of whether he had been born into any kind of aristocratic patriciate (such as was the case with the ruling class in Berne, including the von Steiger family). Nor was the idea of *Bildung* as something that legitimated claims to leadership or to ruling status confined to the bourgeoisie in their conflict over status with the nobility; the men who claimed *Bildung* for themselves were usually laying claim to an elite status that separated them both from nobility and from what they often took to be the philistine bourgeoisie. The man of *Bildung* often took himself to be "above" both the nobility and bourgeoisie.

In Tübingen, Hegel had come to identify the French Revolution with moral and spiritual renewal and, under the influence of his admiration for ancient Greece, to equate it with the coming reign of beauty and freedom. For Hegel as for many others, the idea of *Bildung* fused into this revolutionary-Greek ideal; it was thought that a revolution in Germany would lead to the displacement from leadership of people like the von Steigers and to their replacement with people like Hegel, men of *Bildung*. For Hegel, the son of a ducal functionary, whose family were people of note (if not "notables") in Württemberg, who was an educated-cultivated man, who had *Bildung*, to be treated as a lowly servant by a family that in his eyes represented a dying and corrupt social order with no right to be at the center of things – all this was destined not to sit particularly well with him.

Berne at the time was a self-styled "aristocracy" that in fact was an oligarchy ruled by a small set of families, the von Steigers among them. It had gradually taken control of the area surrounding it (the Vaud) and then suppressed all attempts by the inhabitants to break free of Bernese rule. The city indulged in the charade of "choosing" its town council by vote of a set of aristocratic families; in fact, the so-called election of which it claimed to be so proud was more a set of power plays by a familiar group of well-entrenched families who regarded their offices as matters of inheritance rather than as dependent on any kind of plebiscite. Not only was the family for which Hegel worked a member of this patrician oligarchy; worse, from his point of view, they were allied with the elements of the Berne patriciate who opposed the French Revolution and advocated an alliance with the Prussians and Austrians against the French. (Relatives of Captain von Steiger belonged to the Bernese "war party" advocating war with revolutionary France.) In one of those odd twists of fate, the young partisan of the Revolution thus found himself working for a family that stood for just about everything he opposed.

The whole arrangement was bound to break down, and, sure enough, it eventually did. Apparently at first Hegel made a good impression on the family, and they got along quite well. (In the early stages of his stay in Berne, Hegel is mentioned approvingly in the family's letters.)[7] Captain von Steiger even entrusted some oversight duties to him, and in one of Hegel's letters at the time to Captain von Steiger, Hegel dutifully reports to him on household matters, on the return of a servant and von Steiger's wife from a spa, on the progress of some workers at a gravel dig, and on a few other household matters.[8] Hegel therefore probably appeared to Captain von Steiger to be a man of good character, reliability, and standing, and certainly Hegel seems at first to have been trusted.[9] But in contrast to the glowing mentions by Captain von Steiger about him, Hegel complained in a letter to Schelling that "I am not completely idle but my occupation, heterogeneous and often interrupted as it is, does not allow me to really come into my own," thus echoing the typical *Hofmeister's* complaint that he is forever at the arbitrary beck and call of his master and that his time is rarely his own.[10] In any event, whatever amicable relations there had been between Hegel and Captain von Steiger at the outset of the arrangement seem to have withered away by the end of Hegel's stay. Captain von Steiger's brother remarked in a letter to him in November 1796 that he is "extremely displeased at the disagreement that the said Hegel has caused you," that whatever it was that Hegel did was typical of Württembergers, and that as a condition of not being so stupid "it's necessary not to be [a Württemberger]."[11] It thus seems that Hegel and the von Steigers were equally displeased with each other, and one can understand why.

The combination of generally depressing conditions involved in being a *Hofmeister* would probably by themselves have been enough to undermine the amicability of any such arrangement. That Hegel with his rather self-assertive personality might have been particularly unsuited for the position of *Hofmeister* had already been noted by the head of the Seminary at Tübingen. When von Steiger employed Hegel, the relevant authorities at the Seminary were not consulted about his appropriateness for the post, and in what seems to be an expression of pique about this, the *Ephorus* (head) of the Seminary, Ch. F. von Schnurrer, on learning of Hegel's appointment, wrote to a friend in Holland that "I very much doubt whether [Hegel] has in the meantime learned to let himself patiently bear those sacrifices that always, at least at the beginning, are normally connected with the position of private tutor. He has been absent for almost the whole summer from the Seminary under the pretext of taking a cure, and his long residence at home, where he perhaps himself counts for more than his father, may surely be no real preparation for the not exactly unconstrained life of a *Hofmeister*."[12] Hegel's rather headstrong nature (at least at this point in his life), to which Schnurrer's letter attests, only added fuel to what was already a combustible mixture.

However, despite the irritations, there were some compensations for Hegel at the von Steiger household. The massive collections of the Berne library were just down the street from the von Steigers' city house, and Hegel almost certainly took advantage of that fact. Perhaps more importantly, the von Steiger family had a private library second to none in Europe. The library had been built by Captain von Steiger's father, and it concentrated on the literature of the French and English Enlightenment. Hegel's own master, Captain von Steiger, had made no substantial additions to it himself, despite the fact that having failed in politics – he was unsuccessful in an attempt to become the equivalent of mayor – he had retreated into a life supposedly devoted to *Bildung* and art (at least that is what he told himself).[13] Thus the library had had no substantial additions made to it since the time of the elder von Steiger, with the result that, although the library contained quite a bit of pre-Kantian literature, it contained no Kant per se, and, needless to say, not a trace of Fichte.[14] Hegel almost certainly used the Steiger library as a resource for his studies (when he had free time). During his period in Berne, he read, for example, Gibbon's *Decline and Fall of the Roman Empire*, and he may well have read it in Captain von Steiger's library. He also began an intensive study of the British economists, particularly Sir James Steuart and, probably at the same time, Adam Smith, whose ideas almost immediately began to have an enormous impact on his thought.[15] Indeed, he no doubt became acquainted with British culture and literature during this period in a way that was to influence him all his life. Captain von Steiger's father, Christoph Steiger, was an unabashed Anglophile, making trips to London, Oxford, and Cambridge, and he had amassed an enviable collection of English-language books in his library (190 books in all, ranging from the well-known figures of English literature to political, historical, and economic writings).[16] Hegel, who still wanted to be a popular philosopher, began exploring the works of English modernity in the von Steiger library, and he was later able to incorporate many of the ideas he encountered there into his more mature writings.

There were also other compensations and gratifications to Bernese life. Hegel made friends with a fellow Stuttgarter, a painter named Johann Valentin Sonnenschein. They spent happy evenings together with acquaintances at Sonnenschein's place, often singing together around the piano one of the pre-Beethoven settings of Schiller's poem "Ode to Joy." Hegel also reported to Schelling in a letter that he had made the acquaintance of a Silesian, Konrad Engelbert Oelsner, who had been reporting from Paris in the German journal *Minerva* on the events of the Revolution, and who himself had already begun to despair about the course that the Revolution had been taking in the years since the uprising of 1789.[17] (Oelsner himself was later to remark in reference to a translation of the Abbé Sieyès' work by another later acquaintance of Hegel's, Johann Gottfried Ebel, that "the burgher of Frejus and the teacher of Königsberg form an immense chain of thought, from the coasts of the Mediterranean to the Baltic Sea. Calvin and Luther, Sieyès and Kant, a Frenchman and a German, reform the world."[18] Such ideas were to become part of Hegel's own repertoire.) In May of 1795, Hegel visited Geneva; in July of 1796 he took a long hike in the Bernese Alps with some fellow Germans. (Hegel's recorded impressions of the hike are revealing: The young follower of Rousseau found that although Nature as an idea excited him, nature as a reality did not; for the rest of his life, he was almost always to prefer urban life to the life of the great outdoors, however much in his youth he continued at least to profess a kind of Rousseauian appreciation for Nature.)

The Revolution and its implications, however, dominated much of his thought. In Germany, all the various discontents that had been welling up for years were beginning to take on a new significance for the Germans themselves in the light of the French Revolution, and, naturally enough, there were many articles and discussions about whether an event such as the Revolution could happen in Germany itself. There were those who argued that the Germans were too religious and that the so-called Third Estate that had existed and led the revolution in France (at least in the way that Abbé Sieyès described it) did not have the same status in Germany; there were also German Jacobins who hoped for a full-dress upheaval in the German principalities. Like other Germans (and like Oelsner himself), Hegel was beginning to experience some consternation about what was going on in France. Hegel's own Girondist sympathies were strengthened when he learned of the guillotining of Carrier; in a letter to Schelling, he concluded that it "has revealed the complete baseness of Robespierre's party."[19] However, Hegel's basic stance towards the events and issues surrounding the Revolution continued to be the one that he had developed in Tübingen: The Revolution held out the possibility of moral and spiritual renewal of what he understood to be the corruption of German social and cultural life. His earlier interest in what would be required generally for there to be the kind of moral and spiritual renewal he longed for became increasingly connected to considerations of the ways in which social institutions and practices had to be changed if such renewal were even to be possible. In particular, the ecclesiastical orthodoxy ruling Württemberg in general and Tübingen in particular began to seem more and more onerous. In a letter to Schelling, he concluded that "orthodoxy is not to be shaken as long as the profession of it is bound up with worldly advantage and interwoven with the totality of a state."[20] Using the watchwords that he and his Tübingen friends had used at the university, he declaimed to Schelling, "May the kingdom of God come, and our hands not be idle. . . . Reason and freedom remain our password, and the invisible church our rallying point."[21]

Nonetheless, during this period Hegel continued to see the Revolution and his own attempt at playing a role in it in Germany in terms of a new Reformation. In light of his new dedication to Kantianism, he remarked to Schelling: "From the Kantian philosophy and its highest completion I expect a revolution in Germany. It will proceed from principles that are present and that only need to be elaborated generally and applied to all hitherto existing knowledge."[22] Of course, Hegel was not really imagining the masses, armed with Kant's *Critiques*, storming some German Bastille as much as he was looking for a system of thought that would unite politics and religion and lead to the establishment of something like the idealized Greek *polis* that he and friends had first begun to imagine in Tübingen. Still, he found that whatever his ambitions, he was getting nowhere; to Schelling, he raised his usual lament: "My remoteness from various and sundry books and the limitation on my time do not allow me to work out many of the ideas that I carry around with me."[23]

Disappointed with his own lack of progress and feeling isolated, Hegel had also acquired a clear and distinct disdain for the corruption of the aristocratic Bernese system he was seeing at close hand, noting to Schelling that "to get to know an aristocratic constitution one must have gone through a winter such as is encountered here before" the Bernese go through their charade of elections.[24] His absolute scorn for the inequities and half-witted ways of the Bernese oligarchy and its political system – which, as a member of the von Steiger household, he got to observe firsthand – led him to translate and publish (with an attached, anonymous commentary) a pamphlet written by a French-speaking Swiss, Jean-Jacques Cart, in which the Bernese aristocracy was castigated as being the oppressor of the inhabitants of the Vaud in full violation of all their traditional rights. What interested Hegel was Cart's story about the decline of freedom in the Vaud: The people of the Vaud were initially a free people but gradually lost their freedom, not because of any lack of virtue on their own part but simply and solely because of German-speaking Bernese oppression. In his commentary, Hegel noted that although the people of the Vaud had been given tax relief to compensate them for their loss of freedom, such compensation is necessarily completely unsatisfactory for all those who genuinely value freedom. Those who assert that tax relief adequately compensates the loss of freedom only show, Hegel said with no small distaste, "how it is still very generally believed that enjoying no civil rights at all counts for much less than having a few less Thalers yearly in one's wallet."[25] In the commentary, Hegel also heaped praise on the American revolutionaries: "The taxes that the English parliament put on tea imported into America were extremely small; however, what made the American revolution was the Americans' feeling that the wholly insignificant sum that the taxes would have cost them would at the same time have been the loss of their most important rights."[26] Hegel also commented (no doubt on the basis of personal experience) on the complete lack of any real legality in Berne, something only barely obscured by the pretense of what passed for legal process in the city. Hegel published the pamphlet anonymously in 1798 (after he had left Berne and was living in Frankfurt); it was his first published work. (Curiously enough, Hegel told very few people about this episode; when Hegel's own copy of the pamphlet was discovered among his personal papers after his death, even his own family did not know that it had been written by him, and it was auctioned off as an anonymous work.)

Probably generational conflicts too were being mirrored in Hegel's distaste for the Bernese. He and his father had hotly disputed the Revolution, with his father – a non-noble minor functionary in a ducal court – taking the side of the aristocrats. In the Bernese system, Hegel would have thought he was seeing the full working out of what his father advocated. All the worse, he must have thought to himself.

The picture of Hegel's situation that emerges is, of course, fairly comical: Hegel the young revolutionary, devoted to *Bildung*, imagining himself a man of letters, finding himself living with an arch-reactionary family opposed to the Revolution and which pretentiously thinks of itself as devoted to *Bildung*, all the while failing to keep its great private library current with the latest in philosophy; and, having no real free time to write anything very original, the young *Hofmeister* secretly translating in his free time an anti-Bernese pamphlet attacking the quasi-feudal system from which that very family profits (all the while singing "Freude, schöne Götterfunken" at Sonnenschein's residence).

Hegel, however, was in no position to see any comedy in the situation. In his letter to Schelling, he laments his "remoteness from the showplaces of literary activity" and describes how he "longs very much for a situation – not in Tübingen – where I could bring to fruition what I formerly let slip by, and could even on occasion set my hand to work."[27] In stark contrast with his own isolated, unproductive existence in Berne, his old friend Schelling had in the meantime left Tübingen and staged a meteoric rise in German intellectual life after having landed at Jena, where the philosopher Johann Gottlieb Fichte was electrifying packed audiences with his thoughts on the development of post-Kantian philosophy. Hölderlin had already written Hegel about his having attended Fichte's overwhelmingly popular lectures at Jena, and Schelling continued to write him enthusiastic letters about all the things he had read, was reading, and was thinking about (Kant, Fichte, the nature of self – all of the things Hegel was wishing he could read and write about himself). Hegel could only dejectedly reply to Schelling that he was just getting around to looking at these things, and, despondent about his own lack of progress, note to Schelling that in contrast with Schelling's astounding productivity and early fame, "my works are not worth speaking of."[28]

Hegel's depressed mood was evident, and both Hölderlin and Schelling picked it up in his letters. Seeking to help his old friend, Hölderlin began looking for a position for Hegel in Frankfurt; discovering that a prosperous wine merchant, Gogel, was seeking a *Hofmeister* for his children, Hölderlin managed to maneuver an offer of the job to Hegel. He announced this triumphantly to Hegel: the working conditions, he told Hegel, are really quite good, and "you will drink very good Rhine wine or French wine at the table. You will live at one of the most beautiful houses in Frankfurt, on one of the most beautiful squares in the city, Rossmarktplatz." His employers, the Gogel family, are, Hölderlin assured him, quite sociable, "free of pretension and prejudice," who "prefer not to associate with *Frankfurt society folk*, with their stiff

ways and poverty of heart and spirit."[29] And, of course, best of all, the
position is in *Frankfurt*, a bustling commercial center. Indeed, Hölderlin
assured Hegel, "by next spring you will once again become the old
man" (his nickname at Tübingen).[30] The deep emotion Hölderlin felt
about being able to reunite with his old friend was only too evident: I
am, he told Hegel, "a man who has remained faithful to you in heart,
memory, and spirit despite rather variegated transformations in his
situation and character, who will be your friend more deeply and
warmly than ever, who will freely and willingly share every moment of
life with you, whose situation lacks nothing but you to complete its
happiness . . . I truly need you, dear friend, and I believe you will be
capable of needing me as well."

Hölderlin warmly concluded: "I would still have much to tell you,
but your coming here must be the preface to a long, long, interesting,
unscholarly book by you and me."[31] Hölderlin, already undergoing much
personal difficulty in his own life, clearly was looking forward to Hegel,
his truest friend, joining him in Frankfurt.

Hegel gladly accepted the position and left Berne as soon as he could.

Christianity, Modernity, and Hegel's Bernese Kantianism

Although Hegel himself was crushingly disappointed with his activities
in Berne, his time there was not completely wasted. Notwithstanding
that he was failing in terms of his own aspirations, in terms of where he
was eventually headed he had been laying some crucial groundwork. He
had begun an intense study of Kant, Fichte, and Schelling – although
with some chagrin he admitted to Schelling that "you cannot expect
observations from me on your writing. In this matter I am but an
apprentice"[32] – which was to pay off a few years later. In his few
writings in Berne, he at first continued the line of thought that he had
begun in his "Tübingen Essay," continuing to employ the distinction
between objective and subjective religion, all the while spicing it up
with some of his new readings and new reflections. The fragments of
his work from this period show that his Enlightenment background (as
tempered by his admiration for Rousseau) continued to play a role in
this thought. For example, on the one hand, he claimed that any division of society into "estates" (*Stände*) is a danger to freedom, since it
fragments the whole – a theme that had also been voiced in an essay

written during his period at the Stuttgart *Gymnasium*, in which he drew on his youthful readings of Johann Herder and the "popular philosopher" Christian Garve to explicate the difference between ancient and modern literature.[33] He also began to echo Edward Gibbon in his discussions of how the introduction of Christianity had undermined the Roman empire; Gibbon's irony coupled with his passionate attachment to his subject obviously made a big impression on Hegel – indeed, he was to adopt some of Gibbon's manner in his own masterpiece, the *Phenomenology of Spirit*. On the other hand, he praised the individuality of Socrates and compared Jesus unfavorably to Socrates; Socrates, he says, "left behind no Masonic signs, no mandate to proclaim his name. . . . He did not, in order to bring people to perfect goodness, outline some detour by way of *him* . . . dispensing with mediators, he led the individual only into himself."[34] He revived the idea found in the "Tübingen Essay" of transforming an "objective" religion into a "subjective" religion, except that now he ascribed this task to the state, noting that somehow the state must do this while preserving freedom for the individual conscience.[35] (Exactly how the state was to do this, he did not say.)

In making these kinds of claims, however, he once again found himself in a bind of his own making: On the one hand, he wanted to call for some way of overcoming the fragmentation of modern life and establishing some form of community without at the same time violating individual liberty of conscience; on the other, he wanted to praise the reliance on individual insight and understanding taught by Socrates without letting such self-reliant individuals go on to fragment themselves from the social whole and from each other. In his Berne fragments, just as in his "Tübingen Essay," he still had found no concrete way to bring these kinds of conflicting claims together, to unite his ideas of a unified, unfragmented "beautiful" social whole with the idea of the preservation of the rights and practices of the individual conscience. He seemed to realize that his prescriptions ended up being only moralistic calls for "something better" without any real possibility of their being realized. And as a Württemberger, he of course certainly knew the pitfalls of having a "state" simply mandate a particular religion; Duke Carl Eugen would have gladly mandated Catholicism for his subjects, if only he could have gotten away with it.

Most significant for Hegel's development during his Bernese period was his growing concern with what it would mean, as he had put it to Schelling, to "complete" the Kantian philosophy. Indeed, his fragments and his more developed pieces from that time bear witness to his early forays into Fichte's writings and, more importantly, to the growing influence of Kant on his thought. In Berne, his more explicitly Rousseauian commitments began to fade as the more overtly Kantian elements came more and more to the fore, and Aristotle's notion that the good man finds happiness in what virtue requires started to become linked with Hegel's increasingly Kantian stance in ethics. By the very end of his stay in Berne, Hegel was beginning to redescribe everything in terms of the basic notions of Kantian ethical theory. Although there were strains of Fichte in some of the fragments from that period – his friend Schelling was clearly going in the direction of Fichtean thought at this time, and Hegel was not immune to it – it was Kantian language that began to overtake Hegel's earlier ways of formulating things. For example, in one of the fragments from the Berne period, we find Hegel claiming, like a good Kantian, that "the effect of religion is to strengthen, by means of the idea of God as moral lawgiver, ethical life's motives and to enhance the satisfaction we derive from performing what our practical reason demands, specifically with regard to the ultimate end that reason posits: The highest good."[36]

Hegel also began to enlist Kant in his battle against Tübingen orthodoxy. In a letter, he dismissively asked Schelling, "How are things otherwise in Tübingen? . . . In truth, nowhere is the old system so faithfully propagated as there."[37] Taking the Tübingen theologians as his target, he even went so far in his Berne period as to write an entire "Life of Jesus" (unpublished in his lifetime) in which Jesus' life and teachings were redescribed so as to fit more or less the ideas articulated by Kant in his *Religion within the Limits of Pure Reason Alone*. In the "Life of Jesus," Jesus emerged not as the natural/supernatural deliverer of a divine revelation (as Hegel's theology professor at Tübingen, Gottlob Storr, had tried to demonstrate) but instead as one of the foremost exponents of Kant's "religion of morality."

Hegel did not, however, make himself over into a fully orthodox Kantian. For him the question continued to be: If Christianity is to be made into a "people's religion" (a "subjective" religion), and if that is to be identified with a quasi-Kantian understanding of the "kingdom of God" and the "invisible church" – that is, if it is to be fully reinterpreted in light of the code words used by Schelling, Hegel, and Hölderlin at the Seminary in Tübingen – then it must be given a purely *moral* interpretation that is also compatible with Hegel's, Hölderlin's, and Schelling's admiration for the idealized ancient Greeks as models for what a renewed social order would look like. Thus, Hegel attempted to fuse Kant's idea of a "religion of morality" with his own critique of the fragmentation of modern life inspired by his youthful readings of Garve, Herder, and Rousseau, and out of this he hoped to produce a "popular philosophy" that would bring about, as he had put it to Schelling, the "revolution in Germany" that would follow from the "application" of Kant's philosophy.[38]

Indeed, at this point, Hegel was still quite explicit about his desire to be such a "popular" philosopher, noting to Schelling that the special features of Kantian and Fichtean ideas were not things he thought needed to be worked out in such a "popular presentation"; it was important for intellectuals to understand the fine points of the post-Kantian movement, but it was not important to make them part of the "popular philosophy": "An esoteric philosophy will, to be sure, always remain, and the idea of God as the absolute 'I' will be part of it. . . . The philosophers are proving the dignity of man. The people will learn to feel it."[39] In seeing his future in this way, Hegel was also quite obviously planning to carve out new ground for himself: The "popular philosophers" had until then mostly contented themselves with reproducing, reworking, and applying British (and particularly Scottish) ideas; Hegel, on the other hand, was looking to make himself into a "popular philosopher" who was going to apply *Kantian* ideas in light of the British ideas he had picked up along the way.[40]

Indeed, the "completion" of Kantian philosophy at this point meant for Hegel only the *application* of Kantian philosophy in a "popular" way, the construction of a more or less Kantian conception of what would be a genuinely practical stimulus to action. In commenting on his study of the philosophical movement from Kant to Schelling (and on his relative ignorance of the ways in which post-Kantians like Karl Leonhard Reinhold were developing the critical philosophy), he remarked that the more recent attempts to get to the bottom of Kant's theory (Reinhold's and Fichte's) were, for him, only "speculations, rather than being of great applicability to universally usable concepts, [which] seem of more direct significance mainly to theoretical reason alone."[41] Hegel's ideas on "subjective" religion and a "people's religion" were all constructed in light of what he thought at the time was necessary to transform Kantianism into something more practical, more applicable, something that could be expressed in the kind of essay written by a *Popularphilosoph*. However, despite Hegel's quantitative productivity during this period (judging from the amount of manuscript material he produced), he never thought any of it worth publishing, and he never wrote to anyone (not to Schelling, not to Hölderlin) to ask for help or advice about getting his works into print. (The exception is the pamphlet by J.-J. Cart.) Hegel was clearly dissatisfied with what he had produced. Despite the task he had set for himself of becoming a "popular philosopher," a man of letters, despite the fact that he had produced quite a bit of work along those lines during this time, and despite the likelihood that publication would have advanced his self-chosen career as a man of letters, he simply put those manuscripts in the drawer.

While at Berne, Hegel also wrote an ambitious book-length manuscript, which he clearly expanded and altered after having arrived in Frankfurt, and even worked on somewhat after arriving in Jena at the turn of the century; he never found it satisfactory, however, and it was only published long after his death, under the title "The Positivity of the Christian Religion." In it, Hegel tried to synthesize the basic influences on his thought at the time. For example, he brought Gibbon's account of the decline of the Roman empire and the role Christianity played in it to bear on Kant's reconstruction of Christian religion as the "religion of morality," as religion "within the limits of reason alone," and tried to show how these two accounts could be reconciled in an examination of the nature of the "positivity" of the Christian religion. Hegel used the term "positivity" in a sense derived from jurisprudence: "Positive" law is that law which is in force in a particular legal and political community. In Hegel's own time, "positive" law had come to be contrasted with what was then called "natural law." "Natural law" had a much wider meaning than it does nowadays; it was the doctrine of the normative foundations of law in general, not just the normative foundations of law as lying in the "natural" order. For Hegel, positive religion – which is analogous to what he had been calling in his earlier efforts "objective religion" – is any religion and its associated doctrines whose normative force depends on their being the established religion of a people. Christianity was a positive religion in this sense, since both Catholics and Protestants had clear ideas about what counted as doctrine, who could take the Eucharist, who could not, and so on. *Positivity*, thus, in law and in religion, is that which relies only on the dictates of authority instead of on those dictates that come from "thinking for oneself" (which, according to Kant, is the very definition of Enlightenment itself). *Any* positive religion, so it seems, must therefore be at odds with the demands of reason, of "thinking for oneself." Reviving some arguments from his manuscript "The Life of Jesus," Hegel argued that Jesus never intended to institute a positive religion, at least in the sense of a religion that was to claim humanity's allegiance by reference only to Jesus' own authority. Instead, Jesus set out to create a religion of morality that would restore freedom to a world that had lost it, in which people would embrace virtue because they would impose it on themselves.

The themes of freedom and the self-imposition of the law – both of them involving striking bits of Kantian language – reoccur throughout the essay.[42] In his ethical theory, Kant had argued that the only thing that was unconditionally good in itself was a good will, which, in Kant's well-known characterization, would if even "by its utmost effort it still accomplishes nothing ... still shine like a jewel for its own sake as something which has full value in itself."[43] Whereas the other great influence on Hegel, Aristotle, had argued that the only thing that was unconditionally good, that was a final end of an agent's deliberations – that is, that which rational human agents ultimately cared about it for its own sake – was *Eudaimonia*, happiness in terms of flourishing, prospering, and getting along well in a virtuous life, Kant argued that this unconditional good and final end had to be the free will itself. Since no agent could be indifferent to freedom as a final end, as a requirement of practical reason no agent could therefore be indifferent to what was a priori required for the agent's freedom. Kant argued that the a priori requirements of full freedom demanded that the agent determine his will according to principles that he had fully and freely adopted for himself, that is, that he act only on those principles that he has autonomously imposed on himself; and to make such self-impositions, the agent is required to determine his will only according to principles that abstract away from all contingencies that might determine his will (such as any contingent desires or needs he might just happen to have) and determine his will instead according to principles that answer to that element within him that is authoritative for him.

Since Kant holds that that which is authoritative for us is "self-determining reason" – reason that accepts no standards other than those which it can vindicate for itself, that survive the kind of self-critique that reason continually practices on itself – the only principles that can count as self-imposed are those that would hold for any rational being.[44] The principle of principles, therefore, for practical reason is the categorical (unconditional) imperative, that the agent determine his will according to principles that he could at the same time and always determine as "universal law," as the kinds of principles which any other rational agent would also elect to determine his will.[45] Of course, what is striking about Kant's doctrine – and would have been particularly striking to Hegel at this stage in his life – is that Kant might have seemed, at least at first glance, to have resolved the problems Hegel had bumped up against in the "Tübingen Essay," namely, how to reconcile a demand for full unconditional freedom and individual liberty of conscience with the demands of a community having a unified moral voice. At this point in his development, Hegel took Kant to have shown how each individual, relying only on his own reason, would in his own conscience reach the same conclusions as all other rational individuals, and how thus a Kantian moral community would not morally be at odds with itself. A fully Kantian moral community would thus be an "invisible church," constituting itself as a "philosophical sect" in which each individual member, in Hegel's words, "adopts no duties except the ones imposed on himself."[46]

In the "Positivity" essay as in the "Life of Jesus," Hegel took Jesus to have been preaching a doctrine that fit those Kantian prescriptions. However, he also took the corruption of the Jewish people (a theme that he seems to have taken from Chapter 15 of Gibbon's *Decline and Fall of the Roman Empire*) to have made it impossible for them to have received such a message.[47] The Jews, on Hegel's understanding at this time, had transformed their religion into one of base servility to law and made it thereby into a religion from which all elements of personal freedom had been extirpated. Because Jesus' own disciples were corrupted by the Jewish adherence to the divine law, even they found it impossible to accept Jesus' teachings for what they were – teachings that called on them to attain "truth and freedom by their own exertions" and thereby to lead a life of virtue[48] – and they therefore ended up proclaiming that they accepted Jesus' teachings not by virtue of their insight into their truth but by virtue of Jesus' own personal authority, by virtue of *his* having said them. The contrast with the followers of Socrates, who had been taught to think for themselves, could not be greater: as Hegel put it, the "followers of Jesus . . . had no political interest like that which a citizen of a free republic takes in his native land; their whole interest was confined to the person of Jesus," whereas the followers of Socrates "loved Socrates because of his virtue and philosophy, not virtue and philosophy because of him."[49]

The contrast Hegel draws is thus between Jesus, who is portrayed as a ethical–religious Kantian hero, who only wanted people to be free and to develop their own powers to impose the moral law on themselves (and thereby to become virtuous in a Kantian sense), and the founders of Christianity (the disciples, the early church fathers), who are portrayed as corrupting Jesus' teachings and setting up Christianity as a positive religion, one whose teachings are based on authority rather than on free reason. Jesus' own teachings are not "positive," they are not meant to substitute a new authoritarian system for the old authoritarian system. Nonetheless, to get his teachings heard, Jesus had to confer some authority upon his own person, for, given the corrupted conditions of the time, "to propose to appeal to reason alone would have meant the same thing as preaching to fish."[50] And thus the movement was set in motion toward "positivity."

Hegel, interestingly, does not speak of the early Christians as *betraying* Jesus' teachings; instead he attributes the corruption to the context in which those teachings appeared. The Greek and Roman republics were free in the sense that "Greeks and Romans obeyed laws laid down by themselves"; each citizen found the free republic itself to be "the final end of *his* world," and their religions supported this freedom.[51] With the collapse of Greek and Roman freedom, Greek and Roman religion also disintegrated, and what had previously been a motivating force for the better in citizens' lives vanished. The loss of such a good left people with nothing to inspire them except the cold ideals of protecting property and the fear of death. In this context, Christianity, which promised eternal life to those who slavishly followed its dictates, stepped into the void left by the disappearance of the Greek and Roman divinities.

The followers of Jesus and the early Christians thus were almost unwittingly led to establish Christianity as a positive religion, although in its early stages even they could not even have been aware of the commitments they were undertaking. They were a small sect, whose members joined voluntarily (and thus "imposed" the rules of the sect on themselves), and they were able thus to be a society of friends in the Aristotelian sense.[52] But as they grew in size and influence, the "positivity" of their views became all the more apparent. As they took over the state and the realm of positive law, their religion itself became all the more "positive" in character. They eventually eliminated freedom of thought, and their positive commands to their members to *feel* certain ways resulted in an unspiritual society of hypocrites and self-deceived people who had lost all sense of freedom and beauty.

Unlike Gibbon, however, Hegel was not content to attribute the rise of Christianity simply to a series of contingent, heterogeneous social factors. Hegel's interest in the Kantian ideas of freedom and therefore of the self-imposition of the moral law lead him to offer a hypothesis that went far beyond the bounds of Gibbon's Enlightenment historiography. Hegel noted in relation to Christianity's having supplanted the great pagan religions of antiquity that "great revolutions which strike the eye at a glance must have been preceded by a still and secret revolution in the spirit of the age, a revolution not visible to every eye, especially imperceptible to contemporaries, and as hard to discern as to describe in words. . . . The supplanting of a native and immemorial religion by a foreign one is a revolution which occurs in the spiritual realm itself, and it is thus of a kind whose causes must be found all the more directly in the spirit of the times."[53] The "secret revolution" of which Hegel spoke made reference to his Tübingen concerns: the collapse of ancient freedom and the possibility of a revolution-reformation in modern life that would restore the spirit of Greek freedom and lead to moral and spiritual renewal. Christianity became a positive religion *in spite of* Jesus' teaching because the "spirit of the times" in Jesus' day and immediately thereafter had lost the ideal of freedom; what actually separated the followers of Jesus from the followers of Socrates was Greek social and religious life, which had prevented the Greeks (in Hegel's eyes) from having any positive religion. Accusations of heresy in Greek life were, after all, virtually nonexistent; the Greeks did not seem so intent in their religious practices on propounding doctrine against which one could measure one's "true" religiosity.

Despite Hegel's own description of himself as wanting to "apply" Kant's thought, in the "Positivity" essay he was also clearly trying to develop it in light of his own interests. In "What Is Enlightenment?", Kant had called for an end to mankind's "self-incurred tutelage."[54] In the "Positivity" essay, Hegel took this a step further, explaining this self-imposed tutelage as having come about because of the loss of Greek and Roman freedom, and attributing the transformation of Christianity into a positive religion to that loss; Hegel "applied" Kant's notion of freedom as self-legislation to history to explain how Christianity became a "positive religion." Echoing Kant's essay, Hegel noted that "every day anyone can see examples of how far men can renounce their own native powers and freedom, how they can submit to a perpetual tutelage with such willingness that their attachment to the fetters they place on reason is all the greater the heavier these fetters are. In addition to recommending a virtue religion, Jesus was also bound continually to bring himself, the teacher of this religion, into play; he had to demand faith in his person, a faith which his virtue religion required only for its opposition to the positive doctrines."[55]

The unspoken but clear implication of the essay is that the question of whether Christianity could therefore *cease* to be a positive religion and become again a "religion of freedom" was necessarily connected with the issue of whether the French Revolution would succeed in restoring freedom and spirituality to modern life. But, oddly enough, the question of whether Christianity actually could be this new "religion of freedom" was left unanswered in the essay, and the reason seems to be that Hegel simply had not made up his mind on the issue. He suspected that Christianity might simply be inadequate to the role of a "religion of freedom." At one point he noted that its imagery does not lend itself to the kind of "poetic adaptation" that is capable of "refining our people," because the images of "positive" Christianity have been so inculcated in people's minds in such a "positive" manner that they "carry a sense of uneasiness running counter to that enjoyment of beauty which arises from the free play of our mental powers."[56] (The notion of beauty as arising from the "free play of our mental powers" is, of course, an indirect reference to Kant's notion in his *Critique of*

Judgment that beauty results from the sensuous embodiment of our spontaneity, that in enjoying beauty, we are really enjoying the spontaneous free play of our mental powers.) If because of its cultural and historical baggage, "positive" Christianity is incapable of being beautiful, then it is incapable of motivating people to be free, and, if that is true, "positive" Christianity simply cannot satisfy the demands of modern European life.

At that point in his development, though, Hegel could not bring himself to conclude authoritatively that Christianity *could not* satisfy such demands. However, the lack of a definitive answer to that crucial question was, as Hegel surely came to see, fatal for the "Positivity" essay, and without an answer to that question, the "application" of Kant had not really succeeded, for the basic practical question remained unanswered.

Even worse for Hegel's point of view, the answer that was coming from France, as it were, was not encouraging: In 1793, the revolutionaries had officially "abolished" Christianity and replaced it with Robespierre's "cult of reason," something that was as silly as it was uninspiring. Indeed, Christianity of any sort did not seem to be playing a critical role in the development of revolutionary events. The "Positivity" essay thus ended without really coming to grips with the very problems that had inspired it.

Hegel was almost without doubt discouraged by his attempts at "popular philosophy." He had written much, but none of it he deemed suitable to see the light of day. His position seemed, furthermore, to be more syncretic than synthetic: He was pasting together bits and pieces of Kantian practical philosophy, his theological training at Tübingen, and his interest in what he took to be the problems and promises of the Revolution, and the result was a whole that not only looked cobbled together but also failed to provide crucial answers for the basic problems it was written to address. Hegel's attempt to "complete" the Kantian philosophy by applying it to the problems of a "people's religion" thus seemed to be coming to a dead end.

It was, in part, the failure of his efforts to "apply" Kant to practical life that eventually would lead him to question even more fundamentally just what the completion of Kantian philosophy would imply. At first, however, the failure of his efforts simply left him depressed and at odds with himself; but he had reason to be hopeful: He was escaping Berne for the more cosmopolitan community of Frankfurt, apparently to work for a more congenial family and for a reunion with his close friend Hölderlin.

Stopover in Stuttgart: Flirtation and Politics

At the end of the year of 1796, Hegel set off from Berne to Frankfurt. He had to get permission from the *Konsistorium* (the church authorities) in Württemberg to take his position as *Hofmeister* with the Gogel family, since he still technically owed them service as a pastor. However, because there were many other young men who actually wanted the few church positions that were available, and who were obviously better suited for them than Hegel (who was in any event hardly the darling of the theological faculty at Tübingen), his permission to go to Frankfurt seemed a sure bet. Playing the odds, Hegel began his service with the Gogel family at the beginning of January, although his official permission from the *Konsistorium* to do so was not granted until January 10, 1797.

On the way home, Hegel stopped off to visit his family in Stuttgart for a few weeks. Even with the brighter prospects of Frankfurt ahead of him, his sister remembered him as sad and withdrawn. After all, although he was moving to a better city, and would be in the company of Hölderlin once more, he was simply trading one *Hofmeister* position for another. He was not, for example, going on to edit a journal or even to write for one, nor was he going to a university to assume a position as a salaried intellectual. However, as things turned out, two things during his stay in Stuttgart helped him to recover himself and get his feet planted again: He become involved with the growing revolutionary movements in his home state of Württemberg, and he became involved in a flirtation with a young woman by the name of Nanette Endel, who was living at the time with his sister and father.

Nanette Endel was apparently a friend of Hegel's sister, Christiane. She later became a milliner, and she was probably engaged in training to become a milliner while she was living and working at the Hegel household to earn her keep and to pay for her training. Nanette Endel was five years younger than Hegel and a devout Catholic. Although Hegel arrived at Stuttgart feeling quite low, it seems clear that he and Nanette became good friends rather quickly. The two teased each other

quite a lot and carried on an extended flirtation (much to the consternation of Hegel's sister, whom Hegel jokingly characterized in a letter
to Nanette Endel as the "privy councilor" who had accused Nanette of
being a bit "roguish" in her relations with him).[57] Hegel, whose own
distaste for Catholicism was to last for the greater portion of his life, no
doubt at first reacted strongly to Nanette Endel's devout adherence to
it. However, Nanette Endel was good-spirited enough to joust with
Hegel on these matters. She teased him about his dour nature and his
Protestant high-mindedness, gently poking fun at his self-important,
self-appointed task of becoming an "educator of the people" and establishing a "people's religion." She teased him by calling him Saint
Alexis, a Christian saint from the year 400, who fled on the day of his
wedding and renounced all his worldly possessions in order to live the
life of a monk. He teased her by calling her Sister Jacqueline, a reference
to Jacqueline Arnauld, the abbess of the Jansenist cloister of Port Royal.
It seems that she at least tried, however good-naturedly and maybe even
half-heartedly, to get Hegel to consider becoming a Catholic or at least
going to Mass or undertaking some Catholic practices; he in turn tried
to get her to convert to Protestantism.

They no doubt disputed with each other about the relative merits of
Catholicism and Protestantism, although there is no reason to think that
these conversations ever went very deep. Hegel apparently could never
take women seriously as intellectual equals; the idea of the modern
emancipated woman was not one with which – to put the most charita-
ble reading on his behavior – he felt comfortable. No doubt he could
not take seriously the disputations of a young Catholic woman of so
much less education than he. However, Nanette Endel could give as
well as take; she teased him about his vaunted intellectual superiority,
addressing him as *Magister* (Master, his degree title from the university), and Hegel quite obviously was willing to accept such teasing from
someone who was willing to engage with him on a less than fully serious
level. (Even later in Berlin, Hegel had a preference for passing a good
part of his time with less educated people who liked to joke and play
cards rather than those who insisted on discussing more heady intellectual matters; in fact, Hegel's circle of friends always included a diverse
throng of people.)

The flirtation and joking with Nanette Endel obviously helped to
revive Hegel's spirits and put his all-too-serious reflections on modern

religion into perspective. Each morning she would help him tie his cravat, and in the evening he would read to the gathered family and Ms. Endel portions of a popular novel that had been serialized in Schiller's magazine, *Die Horen*. (The fact that Hegel's family subscribed to Schiller's magazine is further evidence of the importance attached to *Bildung* in his family.) In a letter to her from Frankfurt – her letters to him were all, alas, probably destroyed by Hegel's sons after his death – Hegel mentions her going to "confession" for some unmentioned wrongdoing, and the context indicates that it was probably on account of a pass that Hegel made at her and her subsequent worrying that she had somehow "initiated" his behavior. He remarks jokingly on how much more strict the Catholics seem to be in Frankfurt and how she would not get off as easily there, and about how she had absolved him without "inflicting a penance."[58] Hegel remarks on how they danced a lot on the night of his departure from Stuttgart. In a very revealing letter to Nanette Endel from Frankfurt in 1797, Hegel interrupts himself after going on about serious moral themes, and notes simply, "I do not know why I always fall into general reflections. But you will forgive a man who was once a *Magister*, and who drags himself around with this title and its accessories as with a thorn in the flesh from an angel of Satan . . . I have every reason to assume that longer association with you would have liberated me more and granted me a greater capacity for merrymaking."[59] He clearly missed her while in Frankfurt. In the little piece of verse she wrote almost thirty years later for her friend Christiane Hegel, about Hegel himself, she remarks on how, on Hegel's departure from Stuttgart, she (ever the proper Catholic girl) had to assume a "penance" for herself, holding out both hands in order to avoid the kiss Hegel obviously wanted to give her.[60]

No doubt Hegel tossed around in his mind the idea of a more lasting relationship with Nanette Endel, and it is more than likely that Nanette Endel thought about much the same thing. How far these ruminations went, we cannot say, nor can we know if Hegel ever expressed his thoughts about this to Nanette Endel or if she expressed hers to him. Hegel's relationship with Nanette Endel was surely colored by a romantic interest, but its extent and seriousness cannot be determined. Perhaps the religious difference, and maybe the class difference, were simply too great for either of them to overcome. In any event, they seemed to have had a jolly time together, and Hegel even mentioned the possibility, almost a year later, of their "visiting" each other, something that never came to pass.

There were, however, other nonerotic matters afoot in Württemberg at the time that also attracted Hegel's attention and held it even for quite a while after he had relocated to Frankfurt. For the first time since 1770, the Württemberg Parliament (the *Landtag*) had been summoned to meet on September 22, 1796, for the purpose of discussing the issue of war payments to France. (The "constitutional settlement" of 1770 had made the issue of such payments a matter for the assembly of estates to decide, so the duke had no choice but to summon the *Landtag*.) There was quite a bit of talk in the air that perhaps it would lead to a revolution in Württemberg, just as the calling of the Estates General in France had led to the French Revolution. Moreover, after the troops of the revolutionary Republic of France had in 1796 and 1797 invaded Baden and Württemberg from Strasbourg under the leadership of General Moreau, what were called the Swabian patriots – "patriot" at this time meaning "those who showed the love of their country by wishing to renew it by reform or revolution"[61] – cheered on the incursion, expecting the revolutionary French troops to support the revolutionary cause in Württemberg.

The incentives for unrest in Württemberg had been building for some time. After his death in 1793, Karl Eugen was at first succeeded by his two brothers. His first successor was Ludwig Eugen, who ruled from 1793 to 1795. Under pressure from the other powers in Württemberg and in light of Prussia's treaty with France in 1795, Ludwig Eugen – who abolished the *Karlsschule*, Tübingen University's great competitor – tried to enter into peace negotiations with France to keep Württemberg away from the growing atmosphere of war in Europe. After his death, Friedrich Eugen (the other brother) succeeded him and ruled from 1795 until his death in 1797. Friedrich Eugen had been a Prussian general and Karl Eugen's governor in the (French) territories of Mömpelgard (Montbéliard). It was on his watch that General Moreau had crossed into Württemberg in 1796 and effectively brought it into the French sphere of power; in 1796, the French had driven a hard bargain in the peace negotiations with Friedrich Eugen. Among other things, they had demanded both four million francs in war reparations and the right to freely march through Württemberg. Because of losses suffered in skirmishes with Austrian troops, however, the French had to with-draw in the autumn of 1796 from all of southwest Germany. As a consequences of this withdrawal, Württemberg was freed from plunder-ing by French troops but was left open to plundering by Austrian troops. The situation, however, was again also made unstable by Napo-leon's coming in 1797 to within striking distance of Vienna after having routed Austrian troops in Italy. On July 9, 1797, a Cisalpine republic composed of Milan, Modena, Ferrara, Bologna, and Romagna was pro-claimed by the victorious French troops. The Swabian patriots obvi-ously hoped that something similar would fall to them once the French set foot in Württemberg.

However, their hopes for support were to soon to be dampened. By the time of their incursions into Württemberg, the French had assumed a much more self-interested policy. The Revolution had been continu-ally under attack, and the French had thereby become less interested in spreading revolution in general than with preserving the successes of the Revolution at home. After the defeat of the Prussian–Austrian forces at Valmy in 1792, the counterrevolutionary German powers had contin-ually tried to regroup, but French troops had continued to win scores of decisive battles in Germany. In April, 1795, the Prussians, badly battered, finally broke ranks with the Austrians and signed a treaty with the French, and in 1796 Napoleon Bonaparte, having just become a general, shifted the war to Italy and defeated the Austrians there. None-theless, despite these victories, the French had reason to fear (and history was to prove them right) that the counterrevolutionary coalition would spring up again. Moreover, they had to deal with counterrevolu-tionary activity within France itself: The revolt of the Vendée in west-ern France – where pro-Catholic, antirevolutionary forces had asserted themselves – was putting great stress on the revolutionary regime in Paris. The last thing the regime believed it needed was to have a revolution break out in Germany in places where they were establishing beachheads for their protection against the Austrians and Prussians. Consequently, the revolutionary armies under Moreau tended to restrict themselves to pillaging the huts and houses of ordinary people in Würt-temberg, leaving the castles of the nobility largely untouched. In Octo-ber 1797, the French signed a treaty with the Austrian Habsburg regime at Campio Formio, which required the Austrians to cede the left bank

of the Rhine and which in principle guaranteed compensation to Württemberg for the lands west of the Rhine that the French had seized
from it.

In these circumstances, Württemberg under Friedrich Eugen's reign
simply became more and more ungovernable. The *Ehrbarkeit* began
asserting themselves as never before and on their own initiative sent
representatives to the Congress at Rastatt (a congress first convened in
1797, at which the Germans ceded the city of Mainz to the French and
which Hegel's friends, Isaak von Sinclair and Hölderlin, also attended).
Thus Friedrich Eugen found himself in the embarrassing position of
having his own governmental representatives at the conference competing with the representatives appointed by the estates, with no clear line
of authority to decide who had responsibility for what. The battle of
the estates with the monarch, however, took a much different turn when
on December 23, 1797, Friedrich Eugen died, and his oldest son,
Friedrich II, assumed power. Friedrich II almost immediately launched
into a protracted battle with the estates – a battle that he was eventually
to win by using French power to consolidate his position against the old
estates of Württemberg and thereby bring to an end the entrenched
gutes alte Recht (good old law). Not only was Friedrich II able to destroy
the power of the estates; he was with French help to have himself
elevated from duke to king in 1806. However, in 1797, none of this was,
of course, foreseeable.

Although the Swabian patriots were certainly rankled by the refusal
of the French to support their cause, this did not stop them from trying
to foment some sort of revolution in Württemberg. If anything, the
incursions of the French only made their claims against the duke all the
more pressing. The patriots ranged from those who merely wished to
reassert against the duke the traditional claims of the estates in Württemberg (which he was fighting tooth and nail) to those who wanted to
do away with the duke and establish, à la France, a Württemberg
Republic. Moreover, the French incursion led to the postponing of the
meeting of the *Landtag*, something that in itself did nothing to stop the
political agitation going on in Württemberg. It might indeed have actually fanned further discontent. As a consequence, Stuttgart itself became
deluged with political pamphlets. It is virtually certain that Hegel read
a great many of these; he even saved them, and several such pamphlets
were found in his collection after his death in 1831.

Although he became aware of these developments while staying at home in Stuttgart, after arriving in Frankfurt Hegel attempted to enter the debates in Württemberg with a pamphlet of his own about the need for reform there (which also remained unpublished in his lifetime). In that pamphlet (or what survives of it), he struck out against the conservatives in the debate and argued that the institutions of the "constitutional settlement" in Württemberg no longer corresponded to the shape that life in Württemberg had come to assume. For the "new" Württemberg, he proposed a system of representation in which the *Landtag* would have regular, periodic meetings, instead of the irregular ones that the duke would call only when pressured to do so.[62] Echoing his Bernese Kantianism, he made a moral appeal to the Württembergers for the "courage to practice justice." The title of the manuscript in Hegel's own handwriting is, "That the Magistrates Must be Elected by the Citizens (*Bürgern*); To the Württemberg People," but that was at some point crossed out and (in somebody else's handwriting) is written instead, "On the Most Recent Internal Relations of Württemberg, in particular on the Violation of the Magistrate's Constitution; To Württemberg's Patriots.") He sent the manuscript to three unnamed friends in Stuttgart, who, to his disappointment, talked him out of publishing it, claiming that the actions of the French in Württemberg had discredited all apologies for and defenses of the Revolution in Württemberg, and that Hegel's manuscript would therefore serve only to set back the cause of reform rather than to help it.[63] Hegel, no doubt reluctantly and somewhat dejectedly, put it aside, but he did not put aside his continuing reflections on the political state of affairs in Germany. (It was during this period that his translation and commentary on J .J. Cart's pamphlet was anonymously published in 1798.)

Frankfurt: Hölderlin and New Horizons

Hölderlin's Friendship, Hölderlin's Influence

In Berne, Hegel had felt isolated, but in Frankfurt, Hegel now found himself in the middle of things. Frankfurt was a bustling commercial town with a more cosmopolitan air than Berne at that time, and life with the Gogel family was a world away from the smug, reactionary family of the von Steigers. While in Frankfurt, Hegel wrote several

letters to Nanette Endel, jokingly telling her about how little space there
was for a Saint Alexis in Frankfurt. The prosperous, materialist Frank-
furters, he said, certainly would be loathe to give up sex, but they would
be even less inclined to give up their property. Hegel remarked that
"upon mature reflection I have decided not to try to improve anything
in these people, but on the contrary to howl with the wolves" (citing a
German proverb that means, roughly, something between "when in
Rome, do as the Romans do" and "if you can't beat them, join them"),
a far cry from the slightly depressive, moralizing tone he had brought
with him from Berne to Stuttgart.[64] In keeping with that new outlook
of "if you can't beat them, join them," he also related to Nanette Endel
how he was going to balls and to the opera in Frankfurt and how he
had become more "equal to the world," more *like* the world than the
alienated, moralistic "educator of the people" in Berne could ever have
been.[65] He even indulged in Rousseauian exaggeration, noting that the
experience of big city life would from time to time drive him out of
Frankfurt to the country, where, as he told her, "I reconcile myself
there in the arms of nature with myself and with men" and how the
"stillness of nature" allowed him to "collect himself."[66] (All this from
the man who only a year before had found a walk through nature in the
Alps to be almost a complete waste of time.) In a remark intended to
raise Ms. Endel's eyebrows, he even remarked on how little he went to
church: "As soon as you stopped holding me to piety, it was all over. I
never more than pass by churches."[67]

Most importantly for Hegel, he was reunited with his friend Hölderlin. At the Seminary, Hölderlin had been Hegel's closest friend, and
the attachment that the two felt for each other had clearly survived the
few years since both had left Tübingen. During that period, Hölderlin
had attended Fichte's lectures at Jena and was brimming with ideas
about post-Kantian philosophy. Although moving swiftly into his short
but brilliant career as a poet (he was to suffer a permanent mental
breakdown in the early 1800s), Hölderlin was at that point also passionately occupied with philosophy. He and Hegel lived only a short distance from each other, and they apparently engaged in a constant,
intense discussion of politics, poetry, and philosophy, and camaraderie.
The first volume of Hölderlin's poetic "novel," *Hyperion*, was published
shortly after Hegel's arrival in Frankfurt, and he was at work on his
poem *Empedocles* during Hegel's stay there. (That the two discussed

this work, and that the two friends influenced each other's ideas during this period, is abundantly clear.)[68]

While he was at Berne, Hegel had even written a long, Hölderlin-like poem to his friend entitled "Eleusis," a reference to the Eleusinian mysteries of ancient Greece. The poem is basically a long, Rousseau-inspired tribute to their friendship and common ideals, among them the shared Spinozism of their youth. Indeed, it is a rather strikingly "early Romantic" piece by someone who was later to become one of Romanticism's strongest critics. Along with some of his other writings during this period, "Eleusis" suggests that under Hölderlin's influence Hegel had half-heartedly tried to become a Romantic of sorts, both before and during the first part of his move to Frankfurt. However, it was an attempt that was bound to fall short. Hegel's personality and interests were simply at odds with Romanticism, just as they were at odds with his theoretically Rousseauian attitude toward nature, and as his stay at Frankfurt lengthened, he shed his little bits and pieces of Romanticism as quickly as he had acquired them. By the time he moved from Frankfurt to Jena, he had permanently abandoned whatever remained of his brief self-conscious dalliance with that kind of Romanticism.

Hölderlin himself had begun his career after the Seminary in the same way that Hegel had. He too had become a *Hofmeister*, and the experience had, like Hegel's, been none too pleasant. The poet Schiller had convinced Charlotte von Kalb that Hölderlin would be ideal for what she was seeking in a *Hofmeister*, and at first everything seemed to be going well. But Hölderlin soon began to feel that he was simply being used by the family (something that obviously came with the position but which offended his sense of himself), and he had an affair with a divorced governess in the house, who became pregnant by him. (The child died at eighteen months of age.) Moreover, Hölderlin's relation to his young pupil deteriorated from an initially affectionate affair into one characterized by, to put it euphemistically, the infliction of discipline. In a lapse of judgment, Charlotte von Kalb had sent Hölderlin to Jena with her ten-year-old son, and the results were disastrous: Hölderlin, naturally enough, wanted to be around Schiller, Goethe, and Fichte; he resented having to attend to the boy; and he ended up by inflicting beatings on the boy. (Hölderlin became obsessed with the boy's masturbating and wished to "cure" him of the desire.)[69] Luckily for Hölderlin, Charlotte von Kalb dismissed him without censure, even giving him three months' salary so that he could set himself up in Jena.

Hölderlin took the offer and moved to Jena, where he made the acquaintance of the leading literary lights there and renewed his friendship with Isaak von Sinclair, a friend who had been at Tübingen with Hegel and himself. (Von Sinclair had studied law.) For reasons that remain obscure (but probably having to do with his running out of money), he rather abruptly left Jena in 1795 to return home. At the same time, his friend, von Sinclair, was in effect dismissed from the university for some unspecified political disturbance. (Von Sinclair, being noble, was not actually dismissed, since nobles could not be dismissed; he was instead "advised to leave.")[70] In January of 1796, however, Hölderlin managed to land a position with the household of Jakob Friedrich Gontard and his wife Susette as *Hofmeister* for their children. Jakob Gontard, only six years older than Hölderlin, was the heir of a banking family in Frankfurt and had become a very successful banker and textile producer himself. His wife, Susette, a beautiful and cultured woman, was only one year older than Hölderlin. Jakob Gontard was a bit of a philistine, who neglected his poetry-loving wife, and the result was predictable. By July of 1796, Hölderlin was writing his friend C. L. Neuffer of his love for Susette, and it is clear that the feelings were requited on her part. Hölderlin quickly idealized Susette Gontard as a new embodiment of the Greek ideal to which he, Hegel, and Schelling had earlier dedicated themselves. (He was not alone in this; the sculptor, Landolin Ohmacht, did a bust of Susette Gontard in the classical style.) Susette became "Diotima" in his poems, the character from Plato's *Symposium* who speaks so eloquently of love as the ascent from the beautiful body to the form of beauty itself. In September of 1798, Hölderlin left the Gontards' employ; his sudden departure almost certainly had something to do with the ongoing affair with Susette Gontard, although the exact nature of what occasioned his leaving remains a bit murky. But it is quite clear that it upset both himself and Susette Gontard quite a bit, and they continued to see each covertly for a good while thereafter – indeed, until Hölderlin finally left the Frankfurt area altogether. Hegel was often used as an intermediary to deliver messages between the two lovers and to arrange rendezvous between them.

After leaving the Gontard family, Hölderlin moved over to the little

Landgravate of Homburg vor der Höhe, a postage stamp principality situated next to Frankfurt, where Isaak von Sinclair had become the minister to the prince of Hessen-Homburg. Homburg vor der Höhe had been carved out of a larger family domain as a particular principality in 1622, and there had been disputes ever since about to whom it really belonged, where its revenues were to come from, and so on. Because of this, the family of Hessen-Darmstadt was forever claiming rights against Hessen-Homburg. (Curiously enough, for a brief period in the late 1740s, J. J. Moser, the hero of Hegel's parents' generation and architect of the "constitutional compromise" in Württemberg, had been the privy councilor and chief of chancellery there, but had been dismissed on account of his too-vigorous attempts to rein in the *Landgrave*'s spending.)[71]

Hölderlin's passionate belief in the emancipatory potential of the French Revolution, a belief he shared with Hegel and Sinclair, had not been diminished either by the turn of events in France or by the growing French incursions into German territory. Hölderlin got a chance to see the war close up when, on Jacob Gontard's orders, he took Susette Gontard and the children away from Frankfurt when the French were shelling the city – a command from Jacob Gontard that, given his wife's and Hölderlin's feelings for each other, amounted to sending the rabbits off to guard the lettuce. Nonetheless, despite the suffering Hölderlin witnessed, he did not budge from his rather idealized belief that the French were the new bearers of the promise of the renewal of Athenian freedom and beauty. He compared the French foes of the Revolution – there was, after all, an immense emigré community of French nobility living in Germany – with the despotic Persians against whom the Athenians defended their freedom.[72] His idealization of the Revolution and its promise began to be reflected in the poems of that period, which more and more reverted to images of an upheaval (*gähren*) that would restore humanity to its original free and lovely state.[73]

Hölderlin had obviously looked forward eagerly to Hegel's arrival. Hölderlin even remarked to his friend Neuffer that his old friend was a more "calm, matter-of-fact" type of person and therefore someone around whom he could "orient" himself.[74] He told Hegel in a letter that Hegel had always been "his mentor," and pointed out to Hegel that he could be "of use" to him, since "the infernal spirits that I took with me from Franconia and the ethereal spirits with metaphysical wings that have accompanied me since Jena have abandoned me since I have been in Frankfurt."[75] It is also likely that Hölderlin's feelings about his relations with Hegel put a lot of stress on the friendship, especially given the situation in which Hölderlin had landed himself with Susette Gontard and the way in which Hegel sometimes had to serve as a liaison between them.

Nonetheless, the years at Homburg vor der Höhe were a period of deeply passionate conversations among Hegel, Hölderlin, Issak von Sinclair, and another friend, Jakob Zwilling, about Fichte, art and poetry, idealist philosophy in general, and radical politics.[76] Hölderlin's half-brother even remembered, years later, how during a visit to Frankfurt, Hölderlin immediately took him to meet Hegel, and how, after Hegel warmly greeted Hölderlin's half-brother, both Hegel and Hölderlin promptly forgot he was even present as they launched into a vigorous philosophical debate.[77] Hegel obviously felt that he had much to learn from his two old friends, Hölderlin and von Sinclair, and from Zwilling. He, after all, had been marking time in Berne in the company of such intellectual luminaries as the von Steiger family, while they had been at Jena hearing Fichte's lectures on the completion of the Kantian project and talking to the leading literary figures of the day, such as Schiller and Goethe. Never again in his life was he to be so caught up in the kind of intense intellectual friendship that he sustained during this period in Frankfurt.

Hölderlin's influence on Hegel's thought during this period was immense; indeed, he completely re-oriented Hegel's intellectual direction. While at Jena, Hölderlin had given much thought to what he thought was wrong in Fichte's system, and his reflections on Fichte (and post-Kantian idealism in general) came as a complete revelation to Hegel. They served to make it clear to Hegel that his own efforts at "realizing" the Kantian philosophy by "applying" it had severely underestimated the extent of the problems that still remained Kant's and Fichte's own attempts at rendering it into a final form. Hegel thus became convinced that what he had only a few years before dismissed as merely "esoteric" matters were in fact the heart of the matter, and that for him to do what he had set out to do – to construct a line of thought that would guide modern life to its realization – he had to alter completely his plans for his future.

The philosophical discussions were given added urgency by the increasing tempo of events in France. Neither Hegel nor Hölderlin had ever given up on the French Revolution – both of them seeing it as an emancipatory movement and both of them hoping that something like it, without its accompanying violence, would also come to pass in Germany. During Hegel's stay in Frankfurt, this looked as if it might come even sooner than either had anticipated. After the Austrians had signed a treaty with the French at Campo Formio in 1797 to end hostilities, direct negotiations between representatives of the Holy Roman Empire and the French commenced at the town of Rastatt in November 1797 and continued until April 1799. The German city of Mainz, which had been continually occupied since 1797 by the French, was during this period taken over by a set of "German Jacobins" led by Georg Forster, which in turn made the threat of the Revolution coming to Germany ever more palpable. After 1798, in fact, Mainz came to belong entirely to France and remained a French possession for a number of years. As the ranking minister of Homburg vor der Höhe, Isaak von Sinclair attended the congress at Rastatt as the prince's representative and brought Hölderlin along with him to the meetings. (Also attending the conference at various times were Napoleon, Goethe, and Metternich.) Even if Hegel and Hölderlin had run out of topics in philosophy and literature (which they had not), Rastatt alone would have been enough to occupy their discussions.

In Prussia, Friedrich Wilhelm II died in November 16, 1797, leaving Prussia, one of the members of the coalition to defeat the Revolution, disordered, in debt, and tottering on the edge of vanishing as a power altogether. Napoleon had with the Abbé Sieyès staged a coup d'etat and on November 9–10, 1799 (18–19 Brumaire on the revolutionary French calendar), had made himself first consul of France; shortly thereafter the Directory, which had been the ruling body of France for most of the Revolution, was abolished. Modern life's tempo was suddenly picking up.

Hegel's Choice: Renewed Contact with Schelling

Although Hegel and Hölderlin shared a lot in those days, there were nonetheless always fundamental differences between the two in personality and general outlook. Hölderlin was correct to see Hegel as a more "matter-of-fact" person than he was. While clearly quite philosophically gifted, Hölderlin nonetheless remained first and foremost a poet, capable of producing unmatched lines of haunting beauty and perfect, complex meter. He had been influenced in Jena by the early Romantic talk of the unity of philosophy and poetry, and he wanted, at least at this stage of his life, to do both philosophy *and* poetry. He was, though, a sensitive personality, not the more prosaic, "matter-of-fact" fellow that Hegel was. He also came to depend on Hegel more than Hegel depended on him, and that put additional, even perhaps eventually unbearable, strains on their relationship. Nonetheless, in the intensity of their conversations on common interests, Hölderlin and Hegel managed to stake out a common position, with most of the influence at this time coming from Hölderlin. They did this despite the fact that Hölderlin was moving into his mature poetic period while Hegel was intensely studying Kant's *Metaphysics of Ethics* and the Scottish economists. (Hegel even wrote a commentary during this period on Kant's book, although that manuscript has since been lost).[78]

The interests binding the two young men, though, were deep. Hölderlin has been called, rightfully, the first great "modern" European poet, and Hegel's strong interest in modern life were echoed by his friend's interest in creating a "new sensibility" that would help to usher in the modern age. Hölderlin's conviction that it was the poet's responsibility to fashion a new language appropriate to the new age – and to create a responsibility on the part of his readers to participate in fashioning this "new sensibility" – had a profound effect on Hegel; it was to lead him to make a decisive shift near the end of his stay in Frankfurt to abandon in his philosophical writings the more easygoing prose style of his earlier years and to adopt instead his own analogue of Hölderlin's notion of demanding that his readers actively participate in fashioning this new way of assuming responsibilities to the world and to each other. It was certainly Hölderlin's most ambiguous legacy to his old friend that he convinced him to cast his philosophy in a form that demanded of his readers that they take him on *his* terms. The sudden and profound shift in the style of writing and the growth of a recognizable "Hegelian" style of prose around the end of his Frankfurt stay and during his sojourn in Jena were indications of the depth of influence that Hölderlin exercised on him – an influence that extended up until Hegel's death.[79]

The results of Hegel's own philosophical labors during this period were, however, to his mind disappointing, and although he certainly intended those pieces for publication, they did not appear until long after his death. Hegel's impasse in the development of his thought during his Frankfurt period was, however, soon to receive a jolt from outside. On January 15, 1799, his sister Christiane wrote to Hegel to inform him that that their father had suddenly died. In March, Hegel set off for Stuttgart, where he stayed for three weeks to help straighten out his family's affairs and work out the inheritance. He and his brother took roughly equal shares (Hegel received 3,154 florins [i.e., Guilders], 24 Creuzers, and 4 Pfennigs; his brother received 3,354 Guilders, 24 Creuzers, and 4 Pfennigs), and they gave Christiane a bit more since she had not had the opportunity for any higher education (4,000 Guilders, 24 Creuzers, and 4 Pfennigs).[80] After having settled the terms of the inheritance, Hegel returned to Frankfurt, probably entertaining seriously the idea that he would bring his activities as a *Hofmeister* to a close and try once again to stake out a career as a writer. He worked on his manuscript "The Spirit of Christianity and Its Fate" along with several other texts on the same themes; and he did intensive studies of Kant and of Scottish theories of the economy, trying to bring all of his ideas about the emerging modern capitalist economy together with his ideas about the reforming powers of a true religion. It was also becoming quite clear to him that he was going to have to pursue a more rigorously philosophical course than he had previously thought, and, although he had some very general ideas about the direction in which he was moving thanks to his conversations with Hölderlin, it was still not clear to him what precise form his thought should take.

By 1800, yet another factor had entered the scene in Frankfurt. The stress had become too great for Hölderlin and Susette Gontard; they loved each other but had become worn down by the impossibility of their respective situations. On May 8, 1800, Hölderlin and Susette Gontard had their last meeting, and Hölderlin returned home to Nürtingen after the death of his brother-in-law. While in Nürtingen, he wrote one of his most beautiful pieces, "Der Abschied" ("The Farewell"), in which he spoke to Susette (as Diotima) about the contradictions in the practical world that had driven them apart and how one day he hoped they would encounter each other again after their original desires had faded away, at which time they could calmly walk in the garden taking in their lovely memories (making it nonetheless clear in the poem how their desire for each other could never really cease).

By the autumn of 1801, Hölderlin had managed to land another position as *Hofmeister* with a German official in Bordeaux, France, and set out on December 10 for Bordeaux, finally arriving there on January 28. In 1802, Susette Gontard, already suffering from tuberculosis, died of measles contracted from her children; Hölderlin, unaware of this, ran into some unexplained difficulties in Bordeaux and returned home. Once there, he learned of Susette Gontard's death, and his precarious mental health only worsened. Very soon thereafter he began his rapid slide into the severe schizophrenia that was to render him more or less helpless for the rest of his life.

By 1800, it was thus more than clear that Hegel's partner in philosophical conversation and closest friend was leaving, and there is some reason to suppose that the two friends were in fact already growing apart. Hölderlin was more and more undergoing a crisis in his life, whereas Hegel was finally coming to terms with the world and getting his own thoughts in order. The combination of Hölderlin's increasing personal crises and the death of Hegel's father almost certainly played the leading role in Hegel's reassessment of just where his life had been heading and his taking stock of himself and his future. Although it seems quite evident that Hegel had not been especially close to his father, there is, on the other hand, also no evidence of anything like a complete rupture between the two. There are no letters or accounts of Hegel at the time being laid low by his father's death or bemoaning the event to anyone; but it is significant that Hegel waited until the March following his father's death in January to return to Stuttgart, where he was needed to help consolidate and divide what was not exactly a large estate. Hegel was not overwhelmed, and he did not feel he had to leave immediately for Stuttgart. Hegel could not have helped being affected by his father's death, and being led into the kind of self-evaluation that often accompanies such events. His decision to change the course of his life occurred during that period; he finally decided that he had moved around enough; the period of his life where he could put off decisions, remain a *Hofmeister*, and continuously toy with ideas about making a life for himself as some kind of ill-defined "popular philosopher" was now over; he needed to become more serious; he needed a *career*.

After a trip in September of 1800 to Mainz to see at first hand the results of the Revolution as it been put into practice in Germany, Hegel, now possessed of a small inheritance, decided to see if he could make it as an *academic* philosopher. To do this, he summoned up his courage and got in touch with his old friend Schelling, with whom he had not corresponded since his Berne days. Schelling had since become quite a figure; having been introduced into literary circles by Immanuel Niethammer, a former seminarian at Tübingen and an organizing figure among the intellectuals at Jena, at the age of only twenty-three he had become in 1798 an "extraordinary" professor at the same university as Fichte, and, after Fichte's dismissal from the university in 1799 on spurious charges of atheism, had come to be seen by virtually everyone there as Fichte's legitimate successor at Jena. In his letter to Schelling (dated November 2, 1800), Hegel informed him about his plans to move to another location, citing Bamberg as a possible place, and asked him for some advice about where he should stay in Bamberg, saying that he was "determined to spend a period of time in independent circumstances, devoting it to works and studies already begun" and noting that he was not yet ready for the intensity and the "literary revels" of Jena, that he was looking instead for a town where there are "inexpensive provisions, a good beer for the sake of my physical condition, a few acquaintances." (Hegel even mentioned that he "would prefer a Catholic city to a Protestant one: I want to see that religion for once up close" – was he thinking of Nanette Endel?) After begging Schelling's pardon for bothering him about such trivialities, he noted that he "hoped that we will once again find ourselves as friends." Having said that, Hegel rather portentously informed Schelling that "in my scientific development, which started from more subordinate needs of man, I was inevitably driven toward science, and the ideal of youth had to take the form of reflection and thus at once of a system" – the death of his father perhaps prompting that phrase about transforming the "ideal of youth" and also signaling to Schelling, perhaps a bit ruefully, that he, Schelling, had been right all along about the importance of systematic philosophy. Hegel had originally set out to involve himself in practical affairs as an "educator of the people" who would accomplish his mission through writings that would lead the people to a moral and spiritual renewal by assisting them in the construction of a "people's religion." In light of his failure to fulfill that project, Hegel remarked in his letter to Schelling, "I now ask myself, while I am still occupied with it, what return to intervention in the life of men can be found."[81] This was no doubt a set of terribly emotional admissions for Hegel to make to Schelling. He had stubbornly for several years held onto his conception of himself as a man of letters despite what his close friends at the Seminary had no doubt urged him to do. He had disparaged the intricacies and subtleties of the post-Kantian movement as perhaps necessary parts of an "esoteric" philosophy that were nonetheless unnecessary for the more practical "application" of Kant's philosophy; he had thus more or less insinuated that Schelling was indulging in mere speculation, in the "esoteric," while he, Hegel, was working on more practical and immediate "intervention" in the form of "popular philosophy." Now he had to admit to himself and to Schelling that his earlier ambitions had failed, that he had got it wrong, that Schelling had been right all along. He signed the letter in the familiar, "Wilhelm Hegel."

The imploring tone of Hegel's letter to Schelling is not hard to miss, and Schelling replied in exactly the way Hegel had no doubt deeply hoped he would: Instead of sending him some addresses in Bamberg, he urged him instead to come to Jena and stay with him, and in January 1801, in a move that was to prove decisive for him, Hegel arrived in Jena. He must have been both delighted and fearful of the prospect. For Hegel, his stay in Frankfurt had been a mixture of the best of times and the worst of times. On the one hand, there were reasons for a certain despondency on his part: His attempt at entering the debate in Württemberg had been quashed; his own career was still going nowhere – he was, after all, still just an unpublished *Hofmeister*, whereas Hölderlin was beginning to achieve some renown for his published poetry, and Schelling's career had been simply dazzling. Moreover, not only was the Revolution not progressing well in France, sympathy for it in the Holy Roman Empire was decidedly on the wane. His father's death at the end of this period had jarred him, prompting him to realize that he had to provide himself with a career and not just live on youthful daydreams of being a man of letters. He was now thirty years old with not much to show for himself; his grand ambitions about being a "teacher of the people" had produced no great publications, no public recognition, and little money. The death of his father only brought home to him how he had been living in a bit of a daydream, that he was no longer the slightly pampered young intellectual at the head of his class but only a barely employed man approaching what counted then as middle age.

His decision to go to Jena, though, gave him some reason for optimism: He had been in lively company in Frankfurt, his new ideas were beginning to take form, and he was still fairly confident about the kind of social, moral, and religious renewal for which he longed and in which he wanted to play an important role. Now he had a chance to go to, of all places, Jena itself to pursue a career in letters and philosophy, a chance to be an academic and not a *Hofmeister*. Nonetheless, as if it were a reminder of just how beholden to others he still was, he once again had to apply to the Württemberg church authorities for permission to visit a "foreign" university.

The young man who always found it virtually impossible to talk about himself, who always found it easier to speak in generalities than in personal terms, who had mused to Nanette Endel that "I do not know why I always fall into general reflections," was of course quite naturally emotionally attracted to the ideal of university life taking shape in Jena. He had obviously decided, no doubt at first with some reluctance, that such "intervention" in the life of men could come only by his producing some writing "in the form of a system." He had decided that in order for *him* to become an "educator of the people," it was first necessary to become a philosopher following Fichte's model and to join the newly conceived Fichtean university within modern life. That decision was not only to affect Hegel's career, it also decisively changed the very style in which he wrote. After having made that decision, Hegel's prose became much more "Fichtean" and *wissenschaftlich*; he abandoned the free-flowing prose style he had chosen in his earlier writings in favor of what he regarded as the more rigorous, "scientific" mode of presentation – like Hölderlin, framing his thoughts in a kind of unrelenting style that refused to allow the reader to fall back on his own familiar use of language. The paradigmatically obscure Hegelian use of self-created technical terms remained the most ambiguous of the modernist ambitions he inherited from his old friend.

Still, although his ambitions remained high, he had been chastened by his experiences in Frankfurt and by having to come to terms with the death of his father; he belatedly came to the realization that he had to throw himself wholeheartedly into becoming what Schelling already was: a systematic philosopher. No other decision Hegel was ever to take was so decisive for him as that resolution to move to Jena and try his luck at something at which, thus far, he had experienced no real success.

Jena: Hegel's Transformation

In making the decision to go to Jena, Hegel thus also resolved to effect a decisive transformation of his old project and his plan for his life. His early identification with *Bildung* easily fit into the Fichtean model of the university: If the university was the central institution of modern life, and was to be staffed and run by "philosophical minds," men of *Bildung*, then people like himself rightfully belonged in the university and in the field that was at the summit of university life: systematic philosophy. His failure at practical "intervention" in the process of moral and spiritual renewal could now be redeemed by following in the footsteps of his friend Schelling.

Indeed, this decision was to give a definitive shape to the rest of Hegel's life. Although he was not to get a regular (what was called an "ordinary") appointment at a university until 1817, when he was forty-seven years old, he never abandoned the goal of securing such an appointment after having committed himself to that ideal. After 1800, he firmly believed that the university was the sole institution in which he could achieve the objectives he had set for himself while at Tübingen, and he was never again to waver in his conviction that not only was systematic *philosophy* the unifying point of all the disparate faculties of the modern university, but systematic *philosophizing* was *a* central if not in fact *the* central activity of modern life.

Jena: The Modern University Takes Shape

The town and the university had become famous at the end of the eighteenth century for their dazzling intellectual and cultural life, a development significant not just for Jena itself but for all of Germany. All universities in Germany were in a state of crisis by this time. They were widely seen an antiquated, medieval institutions, corrupt to the core, run by a professoriate that was increasingly seen as teaching completely outmoded, useless knowledge, and fit only to be abolished (as the French had in fact done immediately after the Revolution). Even worse, the universities were turning out young men with no prospects for employment; there were simply not enough government and pastoral positions for all the men emerging with degrees of *Magister* from the German university system. Not surprisingly, student attendance at the universities was also dropping off precipitously, and many universities had become only expensive shells supported by increasingly uninterested princes. They were objects of increasing scorn; Goethe, for example, savagely mocked them in his play *Faust*. Because of this, many old German universities in fact simply ceased to exist during this period, and others were soon to pass away. Among others, Cologne (founded in 1388) ended its life in 1798; Helmstedt (founded in 1576) ceased to be after 1809; and Frankfurt on the Oder (born in 1506) expired in 1811.[82] In fact, twenty-two German universities (more than half of the previously existing number) ceased to exist during the Napoleonic period.[83]

Moreover, given the ways in which universities seemed to promote a disorderly life among students and the nepotism and corruption that plagued all of them, it increasingly seemed that not only were universities outmoded institutions, they were actually morally harmful institutions for their youthful students. Universities thus seemed like the last place from which an important cultural movement of any kind would emanate, much less a movement as vibrant as had come out of the small, unimportant backwater town of Jena, whose university had traditionally been well known only for the exceptional rowdiness of its students. Jena's students were famous for their crudity, their habit of dueling, their secret societies, their drunkenness, and their bullying of townsfolk lower in station than themselves. The students at Jena – as contemptuous of learning as any students had ever been anywhere at any time – practiced the ritual of conferring on each other the title of *Doctor cerevisiae et vini* (doctor of wine and beer), the ceremony for which consisted in a candidate's drinking as much beer as three other selected opponents.[84] Jena was, to put it mildly, not known as a place where the life of the mind flourished.

There were of course some exceptions in Germany to this model of university life, but they were few and far between. The most significant of these was Göttingen University, founded by the Hannoverian princes in 1737 and dedicated to modern principles.[85] The founders of Göttingen gave theology – traditionally the dominant subject in the university, and at many universities for all practical purposes the only subject – a very subordinate position. Having seen the damage that religious disputes had caused at Halle – an uncharacteristically prosperous university that had declined sharply when the Pietists there managed to get Christian Wolff (at that time the leading philosopher in Germany) dismissed from his position on doctrinal grounds – the founders of Göttingen were anxious to avoid the sectarianism that had often plagued German universities. The corresponding academic freedom that resulted from playing down the role of theology curiously enough even made Göttingen the leader in Enlightenment biblical criticism. The founders also consciously deemphasized philosophy, the other characteristically central faculty of a traditional German university; unlike the case of theology, however, that did not lead to its becoming a center of philosophical thought.

Göttingen offered its professors both high salaries relative to other universities and freedom of thought, and it sought to attract only famous professors. It quickly excelled in what we would now call the social sciences. Most importantly, Göttingen made a conscious effort to attract a clientele not traditionally oriented to university life: the nobility. The nobility had typically ignored university life, preferring instead to go to a "knightly academy" (a *Ritterakademie*) where the emphasis was not so much on knowledge as it was on becoming the German version of a Renaissance gentleman.[86] Göttingen made a conscious attempt to attract these types (who typically paid higher fees) and thus offered instruction not only in law and social science (knowledge useful for running a *Land*) but also in "dancing, drawing, fencing, riding, music, and conversation in modern languages."[87] Göttingen succeeded; even though the nobility made up only two percent of the population, they composed more than thirteen percent of the students at Göttingen.

Jena's intellectual supplanting of Göttingen was due to some contingent factors that put it in the position to answer some deeply felt needs of the time. Jena had none of Göttingen's natural advantages. It was a small, insignificant town whose population almost never rose above 4,500. The wealthy Hannoverians, linked to the English royal family, lavishly supported their university at Göttingen, but the Thüringen princes in charge of Jena were more or less indifferent to their own, both in enthusiasm and in financial support. The salaries at Jena were notoriously low, amounting to between 460 to 260 Thalers per year, whereas a student was assumed to need 200 Thalers a year just to subsist.[88] However, for completely accidental reasons having to do with the history of Saxony (the *Land* in which Jena was located), the university, unlike all the other German universities, was not answerable to one individual noble for its patronage but instead to the four different Thüringen nobles of Weimar, Coburg, Gotha, and Meiningen. This was fortunate for Jena; beholden to four different princes, it ended up for all practical purposes answering to none; the respective nobles could never meet or agree on anything, and they could not have cared less about the university. Although this meant that none of the Thüringen princes was willing to give the university much support (or to increase professors' salaries), it also meant that the Jena professoriate could achieve for themselves an unprecedented arena for freedom of thought and teaching, all of which they began exploiting around 1785.

Jena was also fortunate because it lay in those territories protected by the 1795 Treaty of Basel, which exempted it from the Napoleonic decrees that had disrupted the activities of other German universities. Largely because of this and the freedom of thought it offered to intellectuals, in the period following 1785 Jena quickly attracted a series of literary and scientific leaders who came to enjoy the liberty offered them by the university, and it quickly developed an outstanding faculty in medicine, theology, law, and of course philosophy. In 1784 (or maybe as late as 1785), Christian Gottfried Schütz began lecturing on the philosophy of Immanuel Kant, and Jena (not Königsberg, where Kant lived) almost instantly became the center for the propagation of Kantian philosophy. Schütz founded a journal, the *Allgemeine Literatur Zeitung*, which also quickly acquired a wide circulation across Germany and became the chief organ for the discussion and dissemination of Kantian ideas. The Jena professors were able to augment their meager incomes by writing for the *Allgemeine Literatur Zeitung*, which also paid uncharacteristically high honoraria for published articles.

One of the most important elements in the development of Jena's university was the acquisition in 1775 of a far-sighted minister of culture in Weimar who oversaw the university: Johann Wolfgang Goethe. When he came to Weimar, Goethe was already a figure of immensely high esteem in German life and letters and had also become quite a celebrity – indeed, perhaps the first real literary celebrity, in the sense of being an author whom people wanted to meet, and to hear him connect his personal experiences with his literary creations. Goethe took a keen interest in the development of the university and appointed a capable official, Christian Gottlob Voigt, to oversee the development of the institution. He was able to convince the poet and dramatist Friedrich Schiller to come to the university in 1789 as an "extraordinary" professor (so called because his position was not one of the officially funded "ordinary" chairs). Although Schiller was to leave Jena to move to Weimar in 1793, the joint prospect of being in the vicinity of two such famous men (Goethe and Schiller) was enough to draw intellectuals to Jena and, following in their wake, more serious students.

The coming of Schiller and then shortly thereafter of Fichte changed the course of the university at Jena and helped to establish a more or less "Jena view" of the world. In his inaugural lecture in 1789 on "What Does It Mean and To What End Do We Study Universal History?" Schiller sharply distinguished between what he called the *Brotgelehrte* (literally, bread-scholars) and the *philosophischer Kopf* (the philosophical mind), the difference being that between the student who comes to the university to learn some skills in order to enter a profession (the *Brotgelehrte*) and the student who comes solely from the love of learning (the *philosophischer Kopf*). Only the latter pursues a noble purpose and really belongs in a university, and Schiller called on the students to assume, each on his own, this responsibility for themselves. In 1794, Fichte came to the university (also as an "extraordinary" professor) and intensified the line that Schiller had already taken vis-à-vis the relationship between the university and intellectual life. Fichte's lectures quickly became a sensation, and students began flocking to Jena to hear him speak; soon his lecture halls were so packed that students stood on ladders to peer in the windows when Fichte was lecturing.[89] Declaring himself a "priest of truth," Fichte argued that the scholar is both the teacher and the educator of mankind, since only the scholar is able to come to grips and articulate the truth that is the necessary condition for all people to achieve their proper humanity.[90] Moreover, the apex of the scholarly world is occupied by the philosopher, since only he can possibly grasp the unity that is implicit in all the other scholarly activities of the university and hold the university together in its scholarly and moral mission. Even more strongly than Schiller, Fichte called on the students to assume such responsibilities for themselves.

In Fichte's formulations, the university and, by implication, really *only* the university at Jena, was therefore to be the central institution of modern life, the place where knowledge was to be unified and the freedom of humanity was to be underwritten. In one fell swoop, Fichte had transformed the idea of the university from that of the antimodern institution *per excellence*, an outmoded, morally and intellectually bankrupt corporate holdover from medieval times, into the central institution of modernity's wishes and demands. In some ways, just as Fichte's philosophy was a radicalization of Kantianism, his ideas on the university were a radicalization of the Enlightenment conception of the Republic of Letters, according to which the central institutions of modern life were comprised of the network of writers, publishers, booksellers, and those who ran the Enlightenment salons.

Kant himself was a proudly self-proclaimed member of the Republic of Letters, which, as the phrase at the time had it, claimed to know no national boundaries, and in his piece *The Conflict of the Faculties*, Kant had paved the way for Fichte by arguing that not only had the philosophical faculty matured enough to break away from dependence on other faculties (particularly the theological faculty), it could in fact now assume preeminence among them since it and it alone was a fully autonomous study, not beholden to any other body for its core doctrines (making it different, for example, from law, which was beholden to what the legislators had enacted).

As always, Fichte radicalized Kant's doctrine and laid the foundation for the typically modern claims about the centrality of the university as the gatekeeper for admission to the elite. Certainly before Fichte, few people would have thought that the *university* was destined for anything more than a subordinate status in the emerging new world of political, economic, and personal freedom. Fichte's calls for freedom and responsibility and his charge to the university to become *the* institution of modern life had no less than a revolutionary effect on the students. Many freely offered to disband their secret societies and devote themselves to the ideals of learning, offering also in the process to hand themselves over to Fichte's leadership. (Fichte's rigidly moralistic personality led him to bungle things badly, leaving the students feeling betrayed by him, which led them in turn to disrupt his lectures, throw stones through his windows, and run him out of town; but after military troops were dispatched to Jena from Weimar and the student insurrection was decisively quashed, Fichte was able to reestablish himself, and

his student supporters formed a short-lived *Gesellschaft freier Männer* –
Society of Free Men – to combat the old fraternities.)[91]

What is more striking is how the students rapidly accepted Fichte's
claims and even demanded them. The generation of students attending
Fichte's early lectures was, of course, more or less Hegel's own generation. During the late and post-Enlightenment period in which they had
grown up, traditional religion had lost much of its hold on them. Many
felt that the established churches had become far more interested in
simply persecuting the unorthodox and protecting their privileges than
in being the leaders of any kind of spiritual or moral movement. Fichte's
calls for the students to liberate themselves by assuming moral responsibility offered them an alternative to the orthodox religion they had
rejected. They were now joined in a cause that went beyond their own
private interests; they were called to be participants in a common social
project that was to liberate them all collectively and individually.

Perhaps just as important, Fichte's new conception of the university
gave intellectuals a new place in the world. Before the Revolution,
young men in France had flocked to Paris with dreams of becoming
"men of letters" only to discover that, contrary to what they had hoped
and expected, the Republic of Letters simply had no salaried positions
in it, and it was not therefore possible actually to make a living as an
"author." Many of these disappointed young men began increasingly to
sympathize with the growing calls for a revolutionary transformation of
society. Fichte's reconceiving of the role of the university, however,
effectively gave young German intellectuals (such as Hegel) an alternative to a free-standing career as a man of letters. They could instead
pursue their intellectual careers as salaried professors *within* the institution of the university rather than being locked out of an intellectual
career altogether. In effect, young men with modernizing ambitions
could within a modern, Fichtean university assume a salaried position
in the social order while remaining intellectuals.

Fichte's reconception of the university turned out to be one of the
fundamentally modern stratagems for handling intellectuals, not just in
Germany but elsewhere as well. By making them into salaried professionals in charge of what was supposed to be *the* crucial institution for
the modern order, the danger that they would instead turn into smol-
dering, resentful men and women working outside the accepted social
framework was put aside. After Fichte's revolutionary reconceiving of

the role of the university in modern life, the intellectual acquired the ability – and maybe even an odd sort of duty – to imagine his or her life henceforth as a Professor, not as a man or woman living outside society in some idealized state of the Republic of Letters. In some ways, the Professor became the salaried position within that idealized Republic.

Fichte thus managed to recast the image of the university from that of a backward, outmoded institution inimical to all that was modern to the focal point of modern life itself, the agent of social and moral renewal; and philosophy was to be the pinnacle of that movement, the point in the university where all those elements came together. Fichte also succeeded in transforming the image of the professor from that of a pedantic, narrowly focused, antiquated fellow fit only to be an object of ridicule into that of a heroic, modern individual, the moral exemplar of modern life – into, in Fichte's phrase, the "priest of truth."

Jena's "Literary Revels" and the Birth of Romanticism

The intellectual efflorescence at Jena that had drawn in Schelling and now Hegel himself had attracted not only academics. The Jena environment – and particularly Fichte himself – drew in others who were only tangentially associated with the university. Fichte had put a great set of personal and moral demands on his hearers, summoning them to accept fully and individually the responsibility for their own actions and beliefs, but those demands had, almost paradoxically, been enthusiastically received. The dogmatists, Fichte claimed, were incapable of understanding the deep truths of the post-Kantian idealist turn in thought because they had yet to understand just how free they were; they simply failed to see that the buttresses holding them up were only self-erected props. Thus, no refutation of dogmatism (such as that offered by Kant's and then Fichte's philosophies) could gain any foothold in their minds because, as Fichte put it, they were incapable of understanding their own radical freedom.[92] Fichte called out to the audience at his lectures to assume their own freedom, to realize it within their own lives and reflections, and, implicitly, told them that those who continued to abide by the old order were personally incapable of perceiving this truth unless and until they somehow "converted" and came to grasp their own freedom.

Obviously, a troubling set of questions would have arisen for those who took this message to heart. One was: How does one bring the "dogmatists" around to understanding their own freedom? How does one effect such a change of soul? In the context of Germany at the time, this question had a real, deeply felt practical force to it. How was the moral and spiritual renewal of Germany – the very idea of the revolution – to be brought about if it was to be accomplished by those who continued to think of themselves as "unfree" (and to rely on the accepted canons of tradition and church)? The answer that quickly emerged came from a creative and brilliant misreading of what Kant and Fichte were demanding: The power of the *imagination*, especially as employed by self-possessed artists (those willing to break with the accepted, given "classical" standards of art), would be the vehicle by which people would be brought around to this spiritual change. The Romantic artist (and not the classical artist slavishly following the so-called classical forms) would be the vehicle for the dispensation of the new order. By exhibiting freedom at work, art would become emancipatory and thereby also become political.

That Fichte's rather abstract philosophical reflections would have served as this kind of flashpoint for poets is not surprising. The idea of the "imagination" as the unifying point between art and philosophy – indeed, as the most important part or function of the human mind itself – had been hovering over European thought for some time before the upheaval of Kantian and Fichtean philosophy brought it to the forefront of discussion. Because the moderns had taken themselves to be attempting to understand the nuances of the human mind (in opposition to what they thought were their medieval predecessors' preoccupation with investigating the nuances involved in God's creation of the world), the idea of the human "imagination" had come to play a larger and larger role for them. Thus, even Thomas Hobbes, the great proselytizer for jettisoning the shackles of the Aristotelian/Scholastic past in favor of the "new science," elevated imagination to a high rank, claiming in a late piece, "All that is beautiful or defensible in building . . . and whatsoever distinguisheth the civility of Europe from the barbarity of the American savages, is the workmanship of fancy," which Hobbes had in earlier works identified with "imagination."[93] The idea of "fancy" or the "imagination" had gradually been welded into neo-Platonic themes by the early eighteenth-century figure Anthony Ashley Cooper (the third earl of Shaftesbury), who in turn had attributed to the "imagination" the ability to forge a unity of sensibility and reason, of emotion and thought, which enabled us ultimately to be able to discern the "mutual dependency of things."[94]

Indeed, so much attention had been paid to the role of the "imagination" in human affairs that it is not surprising that it suddenly became a central object in philosophical and literary discussions during this period. Kant himself in his *Critique of Pure Reason* had claimed that it was the faculty of the "transcendental imagination" that united the contributions of sensible intuition and spontaneous conceptual activity into the unity of consciousness; Schiller had taken Kant's claim even further; and Fichte (typically) had completely radicalized it, claiming that "the whole enterprise of the human spirit issues from the imagination, and the latter cannot be grasped save through the imagination itself."[95] For Fichte, the imagination suddenly became *the* faculty of the mind, the basis for all other activities. What had been an emerging theme in European intellectual life was suddenly promoted by Fichte to the status of the first rank. Freedom, the idea supposedly animating the Revolution, was to be shown to be more deeply rooted in human life than had previously been thought, and freedom was now linked firmly with the exercise of the imagination.

This only charged the atmosphere all the more at Jena, spurring the development of early Romanticism there. Two of the key figures in the development of Romanticism, August and Friedrich Schlegel, both lived in Jena for a period. August Schlegel moved to Jena in 1795 shortly after his marriage to Caroline Michaelis Böhmer, the daughter of a famous theologian in Göttingen, whose previous husband, a small-town physician named Böhmer to whom she had been married at an early age, had died in 1788. Caroline Michaelis Böhmer Schlegel, an accomplished intellectual figure in her own right, had led an emancipated life that was to old-fashioned types quite simply scandalous; she had been part of the German Jacobins in Mainz, had been imprisoned by German authorities when they temporarily retook Mainz, and had suffered social banishment from her hometown when it was discovered that she had become pregnant following a short liaison with a younger French officer named Jean-Baptiste Dubois-Crancé. August Schlegel, who had become infatuated with her at an early age (she did not reciprocate) offered to marry her, and despite her initial disinclination (she wrote to a friend that she still found the prospect of marriage to August Schlegel "laughable"), she finally decided after her imprisonment that marriage to him would, after all, be the safe and prudent thing to do.

Friedrich Schlegel also moved to Jena in 1799 with his new wife, Dorothea, herself also an intellectual in her own right; and she and Friedrich Schlegel were linked together in their own well-known scandal. The daughter of the famous philosopher, Moses Mendelssohn, she had at eighteen entered into an arranged marriage with Simon Veit, a wealthy banker in Berlin with no serious interest in intellectual matters. When Friedrich Schlegel was in Berlin, he and Dorothea began an affair, which led to her leaving her husband and divorcing him in 1798. Friedrich Schlegel then published his famous novel *Lucinde*, a thinly veiled autobiographical rendering of himself and Dorothea and the union of physical and spiritual passion they found with each other. The book itself caused a scandal – its portrayal of the union of sexuality and love was a bit risqué for many temperaments at the time, including Hegel's own – and made its author famous and notorious. Both Schlegels thereby cultivated a sense of having unconventional marriages in an age that was busy undermining all the old conventions.

The Schlegels quickly attracted a circle of like-minded people to join them in Jena. August Schlegel had been invited to Jena in the first place by Schiller to work on Schiller's magazine, *Die Horen*, and on the *Allgemeine Literatur Zeitung*. He became an "extraordinary" professor at the university. Friedrich Leopold Freiherr von Hardenberg (known better by his pen name, Novalis), who had been Friedrich Schlegel's friend, also came to join the circle at Jena, as did the early Romantic Ludwig Tieck. (Hölderlin had met Novalis during his earlier stay in Jena.) Schelling naturally fit into this circle, becoming the acknowledged philosopher of the group. Friedrich Schlegel himself became an "extraordinary" professor of philosophy (although his lectures on philosophy were by everyone's admission a bit of a disaster). A whole host of other minor figures complemented the scene, and the intellectual energy created by the group spurred the development of Romanticism. (Indeed, the term "Romanticism" itself was coined and popularized by Friedrich Schlegel.)

Friedrich Schlegel joyously referred to the university at Jena as a "symphony of professors."[96] August and Caroline Schlegel's house was the center of activity: Dorothea Schlegel wrote to friends in Berlin, "Such an eternal concert of wit, poetry, art, and science as surrounds me here can easily make one forget the rest of the world."[97] Others such as the Romantic theologian Friedrich D. E. Schleiermacher were more or less honorary members of the group even though they did not live in Jena. Together, Friedrich and August Schlegel edited a journal, *Athenäum*, which had a short life but which became one of the founding works of the early Romantic movement.

If anything, the early Romantics took Fichte's lectures on the freedom of the "I" in positing the "Not-I" as providing a springboard for the new movement, although the early Romantics hovering around the Schlegel circle gave it a twist that Fichte himself would not have condoned. Friedrich Schlegel proclaimed in one of his "fragments" for *Athenäum*: "The French Revolution, Fichte's philosophy, and Goethe's *Meister* are the greatest tendencies of the age. Whoever is offended by this juxtaposition, whoever cannot take any revolution seriously that isn't noisy and materialistic, hasn't yet achieved a lofty, broad perspective on the history of mankind."[98] Schlegel was to use Fichte's idea about the freedom of the "I" to develop his own theory of "irony," which in turn was used to undermine the familiar distinction between ancient and modern art (a distinction that had already come under attack from Lessing). Fichte (by following and radicalizing Kant) had shown that all people are radically free, that nothing can count for the "I" unless he actively lets it count; Schlegel argued that a true artist would not let any inherited forms count for him except insofar as he, the artist, "let them" count.

Schlegel thereby proposed replacing the older distinction between classical and modern art with what he argued was the more fundamental distinction between classical and *Romantic* art: Romantic art was to be characterized by the artist's ironic distance from his own works, by his refusal to let himself and his works be completely absorbed into some external ("classical") ordering. That this new distinction was not just the older distinction in different words was evinced by Schlegel's including Shakespeare as one of the paradigmatic "Romantic" artists, an artist who was never completely "absorbed" in his plays. The Romantic artist could not let his creative imagination be ordered by rules (such as those of classical tragedy) that he himself did not posit. Indeed, as guided by the *imagination*, the artist was subject to no rules he did not impose on himself, and ironic distance from even those rules meant that the artist could never be completely absorbed or wholly revealed in his works.[99]

The Romantics took Fichte's idea of the self-authorization of the "I" seriously but gave it an existential twist that went far beyond anything that Fichte himself would have envisioned. Fichte had argued that the intrinsic revisability of all our judgments was linked to our complete freedom to make such revisions, that only the "absolute I" could determine for itself what was to count epistemically, morally, and aesthetically. Thus, the full and "boundless" spontaneity of the subject of thought and action could only be *self*-bounded. Romantics such as Friedrich Schlegel took this "self" to be not Fichte's "absolute I" but the real, existing self of the poet and critic, the self which can ironically both detach itself from its immediate environment, look on everything as something it could either accept or reject, and still situate itself in terms of a striving for the "absolute" that remains only an infinite "ideal," not something ever achieved.[100]

This in turn seemed to them to call for a more personal approach to art. For the Romantics, the exploration of the self, of the personal world of emotions and sensuality within the context of a rather abstract, holistic conception of "Being," was more important than the abstract determinations of the categories of knowledge that Fichte had sought. Those people for whom the older ties of religion had weakened but who were still looking for something that could redeem their lives found in Fichte's call to actualize their own freedom a summons to explore themselves and in doing so to usher in a new world of freedom and reconciliation.

The Romantic movement that was born in Jena (partly out of Fichte's lectures) was the product of a number of different personalities and, despite its professed ideals of unifying philosophy and poetry, was not particularly inclined to the kind of systematic philosophical thought that Fichte championed. Friedrich Schlegel, for example, found the paradoxical aphorism and the "fragment" to be the ideal manner of expressing his ideas on irony and on the essential incompleteness of all experience, of the constant forward movement of self-consciousness in the very activity of its more backward-looking recollections. As a movement, Romanticism tended to oppose itself to all previous schools of thought, and hence it is notoriously difficult to ascribe any unity to the Romantic movement since it self-consciously resisted any systematization or fixed and final categorization of itself.

Nonetheless, the Jena Romantics tended to have four related ideals. First, they tended to believe in the unity of knowledge, not as the Enlightenment had – as a structured tree with various branches – but as a set of fragments developing itself from an inchoate whole, which could therefore not be a matter of "logic" but only of experience and imagination. Second, they fervently upheld the ideal of "subjective inwardness," *Innerlichkeit*, the notion of the irreducibility and usually the primacy of subjective experience, all the while holding to a "realist" view of the world, refusing to hold that "Being" itself could be exhaustively comprehended in such subjective experience. They thus rejected Fichte's idealist notion of the I's fully comprehending the Not-I, holding instead that the background for any comprehension of experience necessarily includes a large element of uncomprehended (and maybe even incomprehensible) experience and that the function of art and theory is to call our attention to the relative open-endedness of the horizons of conscious life. Third, most of them reacted against the Enlightenment disenchantment of nature by calling for a kind of re-enchantment of nature; but they also wished to do this without returning to anything like traditional or orthodox religion. (That the breakdown of the Romantic program would lead some – such as Friedrich Schlegel himself – to convert to Catholicism is not in this respect surprising; certainly Hegel did not find it surprising.) Fourth, and implied by their other views, they championed what they took to be the Fichtean notion of the primacy of the imagination over the "mere" intellect.

In all these respects, the Romantic movement in Jena responded to exactly that to which all the rest of Fichte's admiring students responded: the breakdown of what had been traditionally authoritative, the sense that modern life was up for grabs, the search for something to replace the now-exhausted reconciling force of the older religion. The world of freedom first formulated by Kant and radicalized by Fichte, which the French Revolution had promised but which to many now seemed to be betrayed, was a world in which everything that had counted was in the process of being newly established or reestablished.

Thus, Friedrich Schlegel could write to his friend Novalis that he intended "to write a new Bible and follow in the footsteps of Mohammed and Luther."[101]

Some Romantics thus began to speak in poetic terms about death, denying its opposition to life and seeing it instead as the culmination of life. The Romantic interest in death was, however, not some kind of life-denying fascination with mortality but an attempt to affirm life itself. The Romantics seemed to think that what makes life worth living is what redeems death, but since the older ways of redeeming human mortality had lost their authoritative grip on people, it was necessary to create a new understanding of the relation of life and death that was itself reconciliatory. Thus, Novalis and Schlegel began offering the idea that death was part of life, was its completion, and that it gave the living a reconciling reason for their life. This quickly got out of hand, however, as the Romantic concern with seeing what might redeem life took on more and more the character of a fascination with death per se. Novalis's seductive *Hymns to the Night*, written after his young fiancée, Sophie von Kühn, died at thirteen, speak of death as the fulfillment of life: "What once sunk us into deep sorrowfulness / now draws us onward with sweet longing"[102] Even Friedrich Schlegel in *Lucinde* spoke of the two lovers longing for death in the section of the novel called "Yearning and Rest," since death would detach their union from the contingencies of the world and render it eternal.

The incendiary personalities that made up the Jena Romantic movement, however, soon found multiple reasons to squabble with each other. The Schlegel brothers, typically quarreling with all the others connected with the editorial board of the *Allgemeine Literatur Zeitung*, had resigned from the board in the autumn of 1799; this in turn had led Christian Gottfried Schütz – the influential editor of the journal, an important philologist who was a key figure in Jena's promotion of the ideals of Greek art and life – to publish an article in the journal that more or less accused the Schlegel brothers of mental instability.[103] All of this internal squabbling finally led to the Romantic circle's full dissolution by 1803. The ideas that they set into motion, though, were to be significant for Hegel's development; he took over some of them himself, all the while attempting to distance himself from what he saw as their extravagances and having very strained personal relations with many members of the movement.

Jena's Decline, Hegel's Entry

Hegel was certainly drawn by Jena's fame and was personally attracted to the Fichtean ideal of the university. Although he was always much better disposed to the Classicism coming out of Goethe's Weimar than to the specific kind of Romanticism that found its birth in Jena, his sojourn in Jena was to involve a personal struggle about how to combine these intellectual movements within his own thought. Nonetheless, the young man from an up-and-coming family in Württemberg, always touchy about his status in the world, would have found the more or less bourgeois environment of Jena more to his taste than the aristocratic pretensions of Göttingen. In Göttingen, the riding stables were among the largest and most conspicuous buildings; in Jena, the professors lived like paupers but engaged in constant conversation and had a sense of themselves as engaged in the common project of creating modern life from the ground up. Unlike Göttingen's semiaristocratic mission to produce "well-rounded" people, Jena's intellectuals were self-consciously edgy, more interested in *Bildung*. Moreover, Goethe's own increasing interest in the content of classical models and in the emerging natural science of the day helped the Jena university to become a center of new learning and not merely a place for the transmission of outdated knowledge.

Unfortunately for Hegel, the university that had spawned this intellectual explosion had already begun to fall apart even before he arrived. Although the university had become a magnet for intellectuals, not all people in the university were particularly thrilled by the new colleagues surrounding them. The older "ordinary" professors felt especially threatened by the newcomers. The incomes of the "extraordinary" professors was not dependent on that of the guildlike structure of the medieval universities (as were those of the "ordinary" professors) but came directly from the government itself. The sudden upsurge in the number of more distinguished "extraordinary" professors thus was not only a threat to the status of the older, established "ordinary" professors, it was also a threat to their continued governance of the university.

The appointment of Schiller is a case in point about the emerging tensions in the structure of the university at Jena. Because of his book, the *History of the Secession of the United Netherlands from the Spanish Government*, Schiller had been called to Jena to serve as a professor of history. However, the "ordinary" historians scoffed at the fact that Schiller had no formal historical training, and they scoffed even more at the fact that he was not capable of delivering his lectures in Latin (surely a prerequisite for a historian). One "ordinary" professor of history at the university, Christian Gottlob Heinrich, led an uncompromising campaign against Schiller's appointment, and Schiller finally had to have his title changed to "extraordinary" professor of philosophy instead of history. (Denying Schiller an appointment to the history faculty was, unfortunately for Professor Heinrich, the only thing of note he ever did.) The two "ordinary" professors of philosophy, however, Justus Christian Hennings and Johann August Heinrich Ulrich, were no more happy than the historians about the new appointments and tended to resist the intrusions of the new Kantian and post-Kantian philosophy with as much vehemence as the historians had rejected Schiller.

Thus, Fichte's success at the lectern, which had caused student enrollments at the university to shoot up, served only to anger the old guard at Jena. Moreover, since students paid fees to individual professors to attend their lectures, the old guard saw the students' attendance at Fichte's lectures as cutting into their incomes.

Fichte soon gave them a wider target at which to aim. In a well-intentioned but presumptuous act, Fichte scheduled some lectures on Sunday morning at the same time as church services in town. (Fichte firmly believed that the moral content of his lectures absolved him of any charge of interfering with piety.) This provided the springboard for those resentful of the newcomers to undermine Fichte, who was already rumored to be a dangerous Jacobin because of his 1793 published defense of the French Revolution. Fichte also helped to edit a journal (the *Philosophisches Journal einer Gesellschaft Teutscher Gelehrten*, i.e., the *Philosophical Journal of a Society of German Scholars*) together with Immanuel Niethammer, a transplanted Swabian who had also been a student at the Tübingen Seminary and who after first being on the philosophical faculty at Jena had shifted to the theological faculty. (Niethammer had been good friends with Hölderlin at the Seminary and had tried to further Hölderlin's career as a philosopher when Hölderlin was at Jena; he was later to play a crucial role in furthering Hegel's career.) When Fichte published a piece in the journal on the ethical basis of religion, insisting all the while that such religion required practical postulates about the existence of God, he was accused of atheism by the old guard. A series of articles began to circulate that accused Fichte of this and, by implication, imputed Jacobin sympathies to him. Karl August, the duke of Weimar, was particularly upset with his minister, Goethe, for not keeping a more watchful eye on what he regarded as the subversive tendencies surrounding "his" university. Goethe himself, who could not have cared less about Fichte's alleged atheism even if it were true, was incensed at what he saw as Fichte's obdurate imprudence and did nothing to help him. After Fichte bungled the whole affair by assuming a strikingly haughty and moralistic stance towards the obviously and patently unfair charges against him, Christian Gottlob Voigt, Goethe's aide in charge of the university, refused to defend him further. By March 27, 1799, the decision was made to remove Fichte from his professorship, and at meetings on April 14 and 25, the decision was finalized.

The old guard was overjoyed with Fichte's dismissal, particularly Professor Ulrich in philosophy (who dismissed the students' calls for Fichte's reappointment as the moral equivalent of calls for the construction of a bordello).[104] When other professors threatened to leave if Fichte were dismissed, the university authorities wrote it all off as empty threats. However, as the number of students attending Jena suddenly began to sink after Fichte's dismissal, the "extraordinary" professors who had made Jena's fame suddenly began to become more aware of Jena's provinciality and its abysmally low pay. They had felt themselves compensated by Jena's unprecedented freedom, but Fichte's dismissal showed how precarious that freedom actually was, and, to add to their unease, as "extraordinary" professors, the newcomers did not have secure positions or incomes but were wholly dependent on the benevolence of the officials of the government in Weimar. At the same time, the university at Halle was rebuilding itself, and after 1803, the university at Würzburg (which had just come under Bavarian control) had been declared free from clerical control, thus offering the newcomers a way out of the Jena malaise. In the midst of all this turmoil and new competition from other places, Karl August, the duke of Weimar, only made things worse by deciding to build himself a new palace, and money that might have been spent on competing with Halle and Würzburg was instead directed to the construction of the palace (the work on which, according to Voigt, employed 400 people). Karl August was spending 4,000 Thalers per week on the construction of the palace, almost none on the university, and the result was that the most prominent among the professors began looking for better offers elsewhere.

Hegel would have known about the decline of Jena as he arrived in 1801 to join Schelling, and he thus arrived with some anxiety but with confidence that he was finally at a place that was proper for a person of his station and his ambitions. On January 21, 1801, Hegel arrived and took up residence at Schelling's place at "Klipsteinishchen Garten." The only likely picture of him at this time (a silhouette) shows him sporting the very fashionable "Titus" haircut (probably best known as Napoleon's haircut), a style identified with "modernity" (and sometimes with the Revolution), which he was to keep all his life.[105] (A silhouette of him during his university period shows that he probably never sported the more traditional, long-haired, braided look of the generation immediately preceding his own; indeed, he seemed to have had an unkempt, rather spiky, "revolutionary" haircut during his university years.)

Having got his bearings, Hegel moved shortly after his arrival to a garden apartment directly beside Schelling's place and set himself to working to have himself named an "extraordinary" professor at Jena.[106] For the time being, though, he had to make do with being a *Privatdozent* – a private, unpaid lecturer – at the university, and, indeed, his hopes of becoming an "extraordinary professor" were to be disappointed until 1805. The position of *Privatdozent* was not altogether a happy one; not paid any salary by the university, the *Privatdozent* charged fees for lectures and thus was dependent for all of his income on how many paying students he could coax to hear him profess; had Hegel not had his small inheritance to live on during this period, being a *Privatdozent* would not even have been an option for him, since no *Privatdozent* could live on the meager fees gained from lectures. However, even to obtain this hardly elevated status, he had to convince the philosophical faculty (which, it must be remembered, comprised more than what would be included in a twentieth century "philosophy department") that his degree from Tübingen was a sufficient license for him to be a teacher, and he had to submit a "habilitation" thesis (part of the traditional German university system in which a kind of second dissertation is required in order to obtain the right to give lectures) and defend it.

He therefore immediately set about preparing a short Latin thesis, the materials for which he had apparently brought with him from Frankfurt.[107] There was a bit of a mix-up between Hegel and some members of the faculty about how and whether he was entitled to defend a thesis, but the matter was finally decided in his favor, and on his birthday, August 27, 1801, Hegel defended a short habilitation called, "On the Orbit of the Planets."[108] Hegel's defense took the form of his defending some theses, with some official "supporters" of his view and some official "opponents" to his view present. Hegel's "opponents" were Schelling himself – not much of an "opponent," since Hegel was defending some more or less Schellingian theses – and another Swabian, Immanuel Niethammer. On his own side as a "supporter" he had Schelling's brother, Karl. Needless to say, Hegel passed his defense. With that, Hegel's life in Jena more or less officially began.

The thesis gave rise to one of the oldest Hegel legends, that in his habilitation thesis he had a priori deduced the impossibility of there being anything between the planets Jupiter and Mars, only for it to turn out that an Italian astronomer at virtually the same time had empirically discovered the existence of some asteroids in exactly the area where Hegel had supposedly declared that it was a priori impossible for them to be. As with many legends about Hegel, this one is untrue. The basis of the legend lies in Hegel's discussion at the end of the thesis about various disputes concerning the mathematical descriptions of the distances of the planets from each other. He began the discussion by making the quasi-Schellingian remark, "There remains a bit to be added about the ratios of the distances of the planets, which to be sure appears only to belong to experience. But the ratios cannot form a measure and a number of nature which are alien to reason: Experience and the knowledge of natural laws bases itself on nothing other than that we believe that nature is formed out of reason, and that we are convinced of the identity of all natural laws." He then added that different researchers approach that "identity" differently: After giving mathematical expression to a natural law and then finding that not all observations fit the equation, some come to doubt the veracity of the preceding experiments and try to smooth things out, whereas some are convinced that if the equation says something is there, then it simply must be there, and since "the distances of the planets from each other suggests a ratio of a mathematical series, according to which for the fifth member of the series there exists no planet in nature, it comes to be suspected

that between Mars and Jupiter a certain planet must really exist, which
– indeed, unknown to us – makes its way in space, and is zealously
sought in research. Because this series is arithmetical and does not even
follow a numerical series that the numbers produce out of themselves,
i.e., out of potencies, they have no significance whatsoever for philosophy." He then discussed various Pythagorean speculations about the
force of such numerical series, about how they were taken up by Plato
in his *Timeaus* as the arithmetical series in terms of which the demiurge
had constructed the universe, and he noted, "if in case this series yields
the true order of nature, then it is clear that between the fourth and the
fifth place there is a large space and no planet will be missing there."
He never endorsed the idea that Plato's numerological series offered
anything like the true description; but he did not explicitly say it was
wrong, and thus the legend began. The context makes it clear, though,
that in the circumstances surrounding a hastily written thesis, he was
only throwing this out as one possibility and not one he seriously
entertained.[109]

He began immediately offering lectures during the winter semester of
1801–02; the public announcements of the lectures show him offering a
course on "Logic and Metaphysics" and two courses with Schelling, an
"Introduction to the Idea and Limits of True Philosophy" and a "Philosophical Disputorium" in which students were obliged to defend certain theses every week. One student – a Mr. Bernhard Rudolf Abeken,
later to be the rector of a *Gymnasium* in Osnabrück and to remain on
friendly terms with Hegel – reported in his memoirs how little talent he
had in philosophy and how against his better judgment he joined the
class, only to find himself being forced to defend theses such as "History
repeats itself ideally in art; the project of a history of art would be
therefore to show how the unity in art corresponds to the multiplicity in
history" and "Epic and tragedy stand to each other as identity and totality; lyrical poetry stands in the middle and exhibits doubledness (*Du-
plizität*)" – all very clearly Schellingian themes of the time.[110]

Hegel decided to write his own textbook for such a class, and the
Cotta publishing company – a prominent firm (in fact, Goethe's publisher) located at that time in Tübingen – announced in a small notice
on June 24, 1802 that they would have such a book on "Logic and
Metaphysics" from Dr. Hegel. In the meantime, Hegel's *Magister* de-

gree had somehow blossomed into a *Doktor*, apparently with the approval of the Jena examiners.

Unfortunately, the announced book never appeared, although Hegel was working feverishly on such matters during his initial stay in Jena. During that first year, he wrote and published his first short book: *The Difference between Fichte's and Schelling's Systems of Philosophy*, which appeared in September 1801, shortly after his habilitation defense, and which was taken by everyone to be a polemical defense of Schelling's philosophy against Fichte's philosophy– a striking thesis, since Schelling had until then been widely taken to be an orthodox defender of Fichte's ideas.[111] The publication of the book was timely. Although Schelling certainly wanted to establish himself as the obvious successor to Fichte, he had to contend with the great following that Fichte still had at the university. Not only had Niethammer's journal shifted from one emphasizing discussions of the Kantian philosophy into basically a journal disseminating the Fichtean philosophy, the university still had a devoted and popular Fichtean lecturing on Fichte's philosophy: Johann Baptist Schad, who like Fichte had been born into exceedingly modest circumstances – he was the son of Catholic farmers and had originally studied to be a priest – and who had taken his doctorate in philosophy at Jena and lectured on Fichte's thought from 1799 until 1804 to large and sympathetic audiences.[112] Schad made no attempt at developing any original thoughts, contenting himself with simply developing in more popular form Fichte's philosophy. Despite the unoriginal light Schad cast on things, he was nonetheless a representative of the remaining Fichtean influence at the university that made it difficult for Schelling to establish himself as the next logical step in the progression of post-Kantian thought that was beginning to take shape at Jena. Hegel's essay was therefore clearly a boost for Schelling's career.

It is also clear that although Hegel had finally committed himself to publication, he was again not fully satisfied with the results of his efforts. Nonetheless, he managed to turn out an astonishing amount of work during this period. Shortly after the *Difference* book had appeared, he and Schelling embarked on editing a critical journal together. The success of journals coming out of Jena, such as the Schlegels' *Athenäum*, Niethammer's and Fichte's *Philosophisches Journal einer Gesellschaft Teutscher Gelehrten*, and above all Schütz's *Allgemeine Literatur Zeitung*, had convinced J. F. Cotta to inaugurate another critical journal. The *Allgemeine Literatur Zeitung* had been the main organ for the dissemination of Kantian philosophy, the *Philosophisches Journal einer Gesellschaft Teutscher Gelehrten* had become the journal disseminating the idealist/Fichtean philosophy, and the *Athenäum* had disseminated the new ideas of Romanticism. Schelling began negotiating with Cotta to bring out a new journal, which (although he did not say this) would clearly be oriented towards disseminating the Schellingian point of view. At first, he had planned to do this together with Fichte, but as the philosophical differences between them began to sharpen and as Hegel suddenly arrived on the scene, Schelling changed his mind and suggested to Hegel that he and Hegel coedit the journal, to be called the *Kritische Journal der Philosophie* (*Critical Journal of Philosophy*). Hegel published a variety of lengthy essays in the journal, all of them having a Schellingian cast. Indeed, this association with the Schellingian point of view was to hover over Hegel's reputation to some extent for the rest of his life. Although the essays were unsigned, most people could detect from Hegel's notorious writing style and sharp polemical asides which ones had been written by Hegel.

As work on the journal progressed, trouble began brewing between Hegel and Schelling. In letters to others, Schelling showed himself to be distancing himself at a fairly early stage from Hegel, even going so far as to attribute gaffes and infelicities in his own essays to failures on Hegel's part to polish them up adequately before publication.[113] In Schelling's mind, no doubt, Hegel was an old friend whom he was helping out but who had no claims of his own to raise, whose role was simply to be a good soldier in the newly launched Schellingian movement in philosophy. That Hegel might have had his own views to work out that might not themselves be simple elaborations of the Schellingian point of view seems not to have occurred to Schelling. As far as Schelling was concerned, *his* own point of view was their *shared* point of view. Hegel was thus put in an uncomfortable position: To continue to serve as a loyal servant in the Schellingian cause was perhaps to abandon his own ambitions; yet to abandon the Schellingian cause was to subject himself to the risk of having no livelihood whatsoever and to disappoint an old friend who had come to his aid. He was, moreover, quite sensitive to any insinuation that he was merely a factotum or apologist for Schelling's views. For example, when it was announced in a newspaper in Stuttgart that "Schelling has now fetched a stout warrior to Jena from his fatherland Württemberg, through whom he gives notice to the astonished public that even Fichte stands far below his own viewpoint," Hegel felt compelled to denounce this in an issue of the *Critical Journal of Philosophy*.[114] However, Schelling continued to see himself and Hegel as working on a "common project," which for him amounted only to Hegel working on *his* (Schelling's) project. The tensions continued to mount between the two friends.

In addition to the growing tensions between himself and Schelling, the bright lights of Jena that had beckoned Hegel were growing dimmer and dimmer. The decline of the university and of the town of Jena as an intellectual center was each year accelerating and making itself felt. When Hegel came in 1801, this decline, although under way, was not yet in clear sight. To be sure, Fichte had been driven out of Jena, but Schelling had taken his place, and he and Schelling were editing a potentially important journal together. However, rather suddenly, just as there had been a mass movement of intellectuals to Jena in the last part of the eighteenth century, there occurred a rapid mass exodus of talent from Jena at the beginning of the nineteenth century. By 1803, none of the key members of the Romantic movement were any longer living in Jena. In 1802, the noted Kantian-inspired jurist Paul Johann Anselm von Feuerbach moved to Kiel. When in 1803 the university at Halle offered the outstanding sum of 1,400 Thalers to Professor Justus Christian Loder – an anatomist and surgeon on the medical faculty, who commanded immense moral authority and was thus known as the "true chancellor of the university" – he of course accepted the offer despite Goethe's entreaties to him to stay and, adding insult to injury, took his invaluable collection of anatomical "specimens" with him.[115] After Loder announced his departure in 1803, Christian Schütz announced a few weeks later that he too was moving to Halle, and, adding to Jena's woes, that he was taking the *Allgemeine Literatur Zeitung* with him.

Worse, Hegel's friend Schelling was the subject of one of the great scandals of the period in Jena and, because of the scandal, felt he had to abandon Jena and take a position elsewhere. In 1798, Schelling made the acquaintance of Caroline Schlegel, August Schlegel's wife. He was twenty-three, she was thirty-five and had a history of falling for men who were younger than she. It is more than apparent that Caroline

Schlegel possessed an independence of mind and spirit that attracted many of the men around her but simply frightened most of the others; for example, although Goethe liked her, Schiller referred to her as "Dame Lucifer." Schelling was a frequent guest at the Schlegel's house; as things happen in these situations, it was not long after that Caroline Schlegel and Schelling began a genuine affair of the heart. With this state of affairs obvious to absolutely everyone, Caroline, August Schlegel, and Schelling all met in Berlin in 1802 and amiably worked out an agreement about what was an obviously touchy situation; with Goethe's intervention, Caroline managed to get a divorce (with August Schlegel's full cooperation), and she and Schelling were married in 1803.

That in itself would have been enough to cause a minor scandal. However, before their affair had begun, Caroline had sought to have her daughter from her first marriage, Auguste Böhmer, engaged to Schelling. In 1800, the daughter became ill, and, according to the rumors that circulated all around Jena, Schelling's and Caroline's attempts to cure her using the techniques of the "philosophy of nature" that Schelling was propounding had directly caused the fifteen-year-old Auguste's death. Another rumor, circulated mostly by the wife of the theologian Heinrich Eberhard Gottlob Paulus, and Friedrich Schlegel himself, was that Caroline had deliberately killed her daughter in order to have Schelling for herself. (Caroline and Dorothea Schlegel seemed to have felt a particular animosity toward each other.) The insinuations against Schelling and Caroline even made the pages of the *Allgemeine Literatur Zeitung*, prompting Schelling to file a lawsuit against the editor, Christian Schütz. August Schlegel took Schelling's side in this matter, supporting his lawsuit against Schütz and defending him and Caroline against the rumors of murder.

Hegel, who never had an easy time with independent women, also had a particular dislike for Caroline, and this put a great strain on Hegel's relations with his old friend. Hegel valiantly tried to keep up the relationship with Schelling; after learning from Schelling that he and Caroline had been officially married (in a ceremony in Württemberg presided over by Schelling's father), Hegel wrote to congratulate him, joking that "I should at least send a sonnet marking the occasion, but you are in any case already used to making do with my prose, which does not permit one to be any more expansive in such matters other than a handshake and an embrace are."[116] But the tensions were not to be papered over so easily; Hegel quite simply disapproved of Schelling's wife. Although relations between Hegel and Caroline were officially polite and cordial, Caroline sensed Hegel's dislike and reciprocated in kind. She derisively remarked in one of her letters to a friend on February 18, 1803 about how in Jena society Hegel "plays the Gallant and the general Cicisbeo" (the latter term coming from the Italian, originally meaning a cavalier who accompanies married women but by 1800 a term of derision and mockery).[117]

After Schelling's departure from Jena and the cooling down of their friendship, Hegel's feelings about Caroline became more open. In a letter to Immanuel Niethammer's wife in 1807, Hegel remarked that the wife of a new friend of his was also a friend of Caroline Schelling, and he added a bit scornfully, "her friendship with Mrs. Schelling might perhaps – depending on *one's* judgment of the latter – add some timidity to one's curiosity to get to know her."[118] Hegel's negative attitude toward Caroline Schelling also surfaced in some remarks he made after her death in a letter to Immanuel Niethammer. He said that many "have enunciated the hypothesis that the Devil had fetched her" (hinting that he shared their low opinion of her) and made his own views about her fairly explicit, saying of Niethammer's wife that God should "preserve her as befits her merit ten times longer than" Caroline Schelling.[119] Hegel was hardly playing the "gallant" in that case.

In 1803, another option opened up for Schelling himself. Yet another coalition against the French had met the same fate as the earlier coalitions, and in the aftermath of its defeat, the map of the Holy Roman Empire had been redrawn in 1803 more or less according to French design; the result was that Würzburg had come under Bavarian control – the Bavarians were allied with the French – and the enlightened, modernizing Bavarian administration had founded a new "nonclerical, modern" university in Würzburg, which immediately began to draw the Jena luminaries to itself. The scandal and the rumors of murder left Schelling in 1803 with no real choice after his marriage to Caroline except to accept the offer from the newly organized university at Würzburg and forsake Jena. Nor was Schelling the only one who felt the need to get out. In addition to Schelling, the prominent theologian Paulus, the philosopher-theologian Immanuel Niethammer, and the well respected (Kantian) jurist Gottlieb Hufeland all left for Würzburg. In 1806, the jurist Thibaut left for Heidelberg. Hegel, no luminary at the time, was not invited. Schelling's departure ended Hegel's employment at the *Critical Journal of Philosophy*, since without Schelling to coedit the journal, it immediately folded. Hegel was left with no paying job, and both the city and the university at Jena were, so it seemed, in a state of rapid collapse.

Worse personal news followed. Schelling, writing to Hegel in July 1803 about a meeting with Hölderlin, remarked on how shocked he was at the complete breakdown of Hölderlin's mental capacities since he had last seen him, commenting that "the sight of him quite shook me: he neglects his appearance to the point of disgust; and though his speech does not greatly indicate a state of insanity, yet he has completely adopted the outer manner of those in such a state." He then suggested that Hölderlin return to Jena (apparently something Hölderlin had expressed a wish to do) and that Hegel agree to take care of him, even though Schelling warned Hegel that to take care of Hölderlin at that point he would have to "rebuild him from the ground up."[120] Hegel was shaken by the news; but at that point, Hegel was barely capable of supporting himself, and he was thus reluctant to act on Schelling's suggestion, although he clearly wanted to do so. No doubt recognizing Schelling's description of Hölderlin from the last time he had seen him in Frankfurt, Hegel told Schelling that Hölderlin "is beyond the point where Jena can have a positive effect on a person," adding "I hope that he still places a certain confidence in me as he used to do, and perhaps this will be capable of having some effect on him if he comes here."[121] Hegel was obviously more than a little anxious himself about Hölderlin's illness and wished to avoid the whole issue. Hölderlin had been his close friend at the university and in Frankfurt; now it seemed he was slipping away, beyond his help.

Hegel managed nonetheless to hang on in Jena, and he even acquired more students after Schelling's departure. In 1804 he was named an "assessor" of the Mineralogical Society of Jena, and he even made some forays into the surrounding Harz mountains to gather specimens. He was also made a member of the Westphalian Society for Natural Research. But this was small consolation for an aspiring scholar who was facing both the collapse of the university around him and his own ever-shrinking prospects for finding some salaried position elsewhere. After hearing rumors that there might be some new salaried appointments in philosophy at the university, and that J. F. Fries (whom Hegel detested and who detested Hegel) might get one of them, Hegel plaintively wrote to Goethe in 1804 practically begging for one of them: "I am thus reminded that I am the oldest *Privatdozent* in philosophy of those currently here," and "I fear being held back from working at the university according to my abilities should the high authorities grant such a distinction to others" (that is, to Fries).[122] He did not, however, receive the appointment he wanted. He also wrote letters to just about anybody who might, just might, be able to put him forward for a salaried position. All these too were to no avail.

Among those who met him at Jena, Hegel seemed to inspire two kinds of reaction: he was either highly admired and even idolized, or he was disparaged. Reports from Hegel's admirers describe him in only the fondest terms, but others did not have such high opinions of him. Whereas K. F. E. Frommann (the bookseller and one of Hegel's good friends in Jena) remarked that Hegel was "praised and beloved" by those who heard his lectures in the winter of 1804–1805, Friedrich Schlegel in an 1804 letter from Paris to his brother August Schlegel remarked that "still more nauseating to me are the Hegelites (*Hegeleien*); only with great difficulty will I read something again from these people."[123] Hegel in this period displayed the characteristics that for his whole life caused people to line up with him or dismiss him for his arrogance. He had a self-assurance that many found attractive and many others found off-putting; but he also manifested a genuine concern for his students, going out of his way to help them and taking great interest in helping one particularly sickly student. In another case, a young Catholic student from the Netherlands, Pieter Gabriël van Ghert, became interested in Hegel's philosophy but could not speak German well enough to understand the lectures; Hegel not only helped him with his German but also had him over to his apartment for slower conversations about the points being made. The result was that van Ghert became a life-long friend and devotee of Hegel's philosophy, maintaining his allegiance to Hegel long after he had become an important person in the government of the Netherlands. Curiously, Hegel thought until 1817 that van Ghert was Protestant and was surprised to learn that his friend was in fact Catholic. Despite attracting followers, even disciples who took every utterance and every grimace as the sign of something profound (a practice that immensely rankled some of Hegel's contemporaries), Hegel himself always seemed to take a slightly ironic, dis-

tanced, sometimes even bemused attitude toward such disciple-like behavior, which the student-disciples, however, simply interpreted as
more evidence of his "deep interiority."[124]

Hegel had come to Jena full of enthusiasm and touched by a bit of
anxiety. Always the sociable sort, he had quite rapidly made friends in
Jena and had participated in the heady intellectual discussions that were
the milieu of Jena at the time. He became especially good friends with
Karl Ludwig Knebel (a retired Prussian officer and kind of free-floating
dabbler in intellectual matters), Thomas Johann Seebeck (a scientist
with a particular interest in *Naturphilosophie* and Goethe's theory of
colors), the bookseller Frommann and his family, at whose house he
indulged his life-long passion for playing cards, and with Immanuel
Niethammer and his wife. After Niethammer moved to Würzburg,
Hegel began a long correspondence with him, inquiring in almost every
letter about possible jobs; by 1805, as Hegel's situation was worsening,
he was even borrowing money from Niethammer.

At first during his stay in Jena, Hegel ordered quite a bit of wine; his
orders reveal tastes that clearly went beyond his limited income (tastes
presumably acquired during his stay in Frankfurt as *Hofmeister* to the
wealthy wine merchant Gogel). There are records of several orders for
Medoc and, quite striking for a poor academic, for Pontac. Pontac was
the wine of the de Pontac family in Bordeaux, who were the first to
make a wine recognized by the name of the ancestral chateau of the de
Pontac family, Haut-Brion, then as now recognized as one of the pre-
mier wines of the world. The odds are, however, that Hegel's orders
for Pontac were for the more generic Pontac wines, which are now
called St. Estèphe, then as now still not a bad choice. Hegel was not,
moreover, the first philosopher to be enchanted by the wines of Haut-
Brion; John Locke had made a special trip there on May 14, 1677, to
marvel at how such a wine was made.[125] Hegel had more than a passing
interest in wine, and his students often picked up that interest in
imitation of the "master." His tastes in wine also tended to exceed his
budget.

But as time went on, Hegel's circle of friends shrank as everybody
picked up and left for other universities. Hegel came to be more and
more isolated, and his wine orders shrank in both volume and quality.
Faced with the collapse of everything around him, with inflation rapidly
eating away at what little was left of his inheritance, and with the fact

that he did not have a salaried position or any real prospect of one, Hegel seems to have gradually and quite understandably begun to sink into a kind of slow, mounting depression. He was coming to the end of his ambitions to be a philosopher or literary figure of any sort, and it was not clear what else was open to him. His father had almost certainly wanted him to pursue some other career (such as his brother had); but Hegel had followed his mother's wishes and decided to be a man of learning; now it was beginning to look as if his father had been right and his own act of self-assertion had failed. The conflict in his own emotions was no doubt almost too much to bear.

However, although Schelling's departure in 1803 had meant the end of his work on the journal, it had also freed Hegel to develop his own thoughts. Thus, although he was rapidly running out of money, he was nonetheless no longer beholden to Schelling, no longer forced into the public role of the loyal Schellingian churning out essays for the journal intended to propagate Schellingian philosophy, however much his own published views had begun to diverge from Schelling's. On his own, with his whole future, so it seemed, on the line, he had to establish himself by writing his own book and establishing his own presence in the philosophical and literary community. It would have been terribly easy for him to have given up at this point or to have simply gathered up the extensive manuscripts that he was producing during the period 1801–05 and quickly published them, in hopes that such a book would land him a salaried position at Jena or elsewhere. That he did not, that he held out until he had prepared what he thought was good enough to send out to the world as the Hegelian system, displays the ability for focused, hard work that had always characterized him and that continued to characterize him for the rest of his life. Hegel brought his family's very old-fashioned but proud sense of personal integrity with him; he was simply not going to present to the public a work in which he himself could not believe. It also shows his supreme self-confidence that he was capable of such a project, a trait that people less friendly to Hegel were always to characterize instead (and not entirely wrongly) as his arrogance and obstinacy.

That he did this during a period of intense personal difficulty and deep depression was all the more remarkable.

4

Texts and Drafts: Hegel's Path to the *Phenomenology* from Frankfurt to Jena

Part One
Philosophy in Frankfurt:
Hegel's and Hölderlin's New Position

The Background: Kant's Transcendental Idealism

IN THE *Critique of Pure Reason*, Kant had taken up Hume's challenge to the very authority of reason itself. Hume, a key figure in the Scottish Enlightenment, had quite ironically thrown much of Enlightenment thought into doubt: The idea that there was an order to the world that "reason" could discover – unaided, on its own – was undercut by Hume's powerful arguments for the claim that there was in fact no necessary order to our ideas other than the ways in which they were combined in our minds according to habit and the laws of association. In light of Hume's criticisms, Kant had tried to redeem reason's claims for itself, arguing that there were indeed rationally necessary rules for the combination of ideas, and that these rules could be derived from the conditions for an agent's coming to be conscious of himself. In one of the most important and darker passages of the *Critique of Pure Reason*, Kant claimed that for any "idea" or "representation" (*Vorstellung*, in Kant's German vocabulary) to be a representation of mine, I had to be able to ascribe it to myself, to be able to say of it (roughly put) that it was a representation *of mine*, something that I actively *took* as mine by virtue of ascribing it to myself.[1] An "idea" or "representation" that I could *not* ascribe to myself would, of course, be unthinkable; it would be, for all practical purposes, a "representation" that would not even exist for me. It therefore followed that all "ideas," "representations," had to fit the conditions under which they could be ascribed to myself as a self-conscious agent (that is, as an agent who is not only aware of "representations" but who is also capable of becoming aware that such "representations" are his "own," belong to "his" experience of things).

Kant's notoriously difficult argument was meant to buttress something like the following claims. First, there are ways in which our "representations" *must* be combined; it cannot all be *just* a matter of habit and association; we make judgments on the basis of those representations, and judgments can be right or wrong, unlike associations of ideas, which merely happen or do not. Second, those modes of combination depend on what is necessary for beings like ourselves to become *self-conscious*; it follows that the necessary ways in which we combine our "representations" fully constitute the structures in which the world can experientially appear to us, and Kant calls these structures the necessary "categories" of experience. Kant called these categories "transcendental" in something like the following sense: Although Hume was correct to assert that we do not experience any kind of "power" of causality but rather regularities of events, categories such as "causation according to necessary law" are nonetheless the *conditions* without which we could not have experience of objects at all. Such categories "transcend" experience in the sense that they are not capable of being empirically validated, but as the necessary conditions of experience, they are "transcendental," part of the necessary "structure" of our experience.

The complex act of identifying oneself as the *same* subject of experience of an *objective* world of objects in space and time *distinct* from those experiences of it – that act, Kant argued, was neither a "given" nor a matter of "habit" or "association." Just as much as this self-consciousness was *necessary*, it was, as Kant put it, therefore also "original," *underived* from anything else: It could not be a matter of applying "criteria" to discover that we are the same "I," the *same point of view* in all our experiences. Kant drew the conclusion that the *activity* of combining these representations can therefore only be that of full *spontaneity*, an activity that does not rest on anything else but itself – it is, as Kant put it, a "self-activity," a *Selbsttätigkeit*.[2] The unity of self-consciousness could not be produced by the objects of experience, since our various "representations" had already to be combined for there to be objects *for us* at all. As spontaneous, this activity of combination was "self-bootstrapping"; there was no further agent behind the agent, no man behind the curtain, who could be doing the combining for us. Each agent had to combine his own experience himself according to the rules of combination universally valid for all rational agents.

Kant in effect took himself to have shown how we were capable of combining two different and apparently exclusive views of ourselves into one overall conception of ourselves. Although we necessarily viewed ourselves as material beings *in* the world, we also necessarily viewed ourselves as subjective points of view *on* that world. The necessity for seeing ourselves as a unified, subjective point of view *on* the world had to do with the transcendental conditions of experience in general; for there to be any conscious experience, we had to unify all our representations into one consciousness, and that was possible only if we both unified those representations into an overall representation of an *objective world* populated by material substances interacting according to deterministic causal laws, and we unified those representations as being the representations of one unified consciousness, one *subjective point of view.* The unity of consciousness itself, however, as the transcendental "I," never *appeared* in that objective world but was instead a *transcendental* condition of the experiential appearance of that world itself. That we necessarily think of ourselves as subjective points of view that do not appear in the objective world – as embodied beings we make our appearance in that world alongside other material objects, but as subjective points of view we do not – was, Kant contended, to be made intelligible not only by reflection on what was necessary for experience in general but also by the distinction between what he called phenomena (roughly, the world as appearing to us in experience) and noumena (the world as consisting of unknowable things-in-themselves, things that cannot be experienced).

In a footnote to his argument, Kant drew a revolutionary conclusion that seemed to some readers to contradict other things that he said in the book. He said that the necessary unity of self-consciousness "is therefore that highest point, to which we must ascribe all employment of the understanding, even the whole of logic, and conformably therewith, transcendental philosophy. Indeed this faculty of apperception is the understanding itself."[3] (Hegel was much later in his *Science of Logic* to call these statements the "profoundest and truest insights" to be found in Kant's first *Critique*.)[4] That is, Kant *seemed* to be saying that all the principles of knowledge should be derivable from the conditions necessary for a rational agent to become self-conscious. Kant, however, had explicitly denied that, claiming instead two striking things: first, that the rules of combination had to be *applied* to what he called "intuitions" (such as sensory "givens"), the necessary structures of which were themselves simply given and not derivable from the conditions of self-consciousness itself; and second, that these principles, although necessary for any *experience* of objects at all, could not be said to give us knowledge of "things-in-themselves," of what things were "really like" independent of all our experience of them.

Invoking a realm of unknowable things-in-themselves, Kant meant something like the following. Metaphysicians had disputed for centuries about what the ultimate structure of reality was; some said it was all one thing – for example, one substance – of which thought and extension were only different "modes"; whereas others said that it was composed of eternal Forms, which were more real than their phenomenal instantiation, whereas still others claimed that reality was a set of noninteracting, self-contained monadic entities divinely arranged so that their internal movements just happened to correspond to the internal movements of the others.

In Kant's terms, these were all differing conceptions of what reality was like in-itself. In denying that we could ever have knowledge of things in-themselves, Kant was in effect claiming that we were required to take a fully agnostic position toward such metaphysical conceptions. We could with full justification claim that the world necessarily had to appear to us as a world of physical, mutually independent substances interacting with each other in space and time according to necessary causal laws (since Kant thought he had shown in the rest of his *Critique* that such categories were the necessary conditions of self-consciousness). But as to whether this appearing world of physical objects in causal interaction with each other was "really" in-itself a manifestation of eternal, supersensible forms or was a set of self-enclosed monadic entities was unknowable; all such claims about the metaphysical structure of reality in-itself were completely, fully, totally ungrounded and, moreover, could never be grounded, since human knowledge was necessarily limited to the way the world had to appear to us and to the "transcendental" conditions of that appearance. Human knowledge could not extend itself with any legitimacy whatsoever to what metaphysically existed in-itself. When it tried to do so, it merely ended up authorizing a series of mutually contradictory propositions, which Kant labeled "antinomies."

Many in Germany quickly understood that Kant's denial of knowledge of things as they were in-themselves had potentially explosive consequences. First of all, it implied that there could be no theoretical knowledge of God, since God was precisely the kind of metaphysical entity about which Kant said we could in the literal sense *know* nothing. But in Germany, since the authority of the myriad German princes was almost always bound up with their being the heads of the churches in their respective *Länder*, Kant's demonstration that we could not know about these supernatural things was taken to suggest that we also could not know whether the authority of the princes was in fact legitimate. Many of the great "rationalists" of the German Enlightenment had relied on their proofs of the existence of God to shore up claims for the authority of enlightened absolutist princes. Although Kant's work seemed to answer the charges raised by Hume's attack on the authority of reason as claimed by the "rationalists," it simultaneously undermined the "rationalists' " own claims by demonstrating that reason could never pretend to have knowledge of things-in-themselves.

Kant's protests that his work had shored up the new science in a way that only cleared the way for faith did nothing to assuage the fears about its undermining of princely authority. Most of the princes did not want their authority merely taken on "subjective" faith; they wanted their authority in its full, robust form as based on something demonstrably true. Kant's austere theoretical philosophy therefore quickly became an object of intense public discussion, for it quickly came to appear to many as belonging to the same "revolutionary air" that was all-too-threateningly hovering over the princely domains of the Holy Roman Empire.

Reinhold, Jacobi, and the Battle over Kant's Legacy in Jena

By the late 1780s, the word was out that going to Königsberg to study with Kant was wasted effort; Kant was busy, he was old, and he was obsessed with finishing his project before he died. That provided the opening for the small university town of Jena to establish itself as the real home of Kantianism. Indeed, the first person ever to give public lectures on the Kantian philosophy (besides Kant himself) was Christian

Gottfried Schütz, the founder and editor of the *Allgemeine Literatur Zeitung*, who had been lecturing on the subject at Jena since 1784, three years after the appearance of the *Critique of Pure Reason*. Soon Kant's works were being studied at Jena, and soon the jurist Gottlieb Hufeland was giving a Kantian twist to the study of jurisprudence at Jena, and the theologian Karl Christian Erhard Schmid was lecturing on the *Critique of Pure Reason* in the winter semester of 1785. Moreover, the *Allgemeine Literatur Zeitung* itself quickly became one of the chief organs for the propagation of the new Kantian revolution in philosophy, and Jena thus became the center of the debate over that revolution.

Jena's prominence as the center of the new Kantian line of thought was reinforced by the publication in 1786 of Karl Leonhard Reinhold's *Letters on the Kantian Philosophy* (*Briefe über die kantische Philosophie*). Born in Vienna on October 26, 1758, Reinhold had been a Jesuit novitiate until the order was dissolved in 1773, after which he attended a college from which he acquired the right to teach philosophy.[5] Reinhold himself came of age during the reign of Josef II of Austria, one of the paradigmatic enlightened despots of the age, who, in attempting to set the Austrian state on a firm, rational, bureaucratic footing, among other things abolished many traditional privileges for the Catholic Church, issued edicts of toleration for non-Catholics and for Jews, and expelled the Jesuits from all parts of the Holy Roman Empire, all the while setting up a political police that arrested dissenters from his policies.

Reinhold himself moved to Leipzig in 1783, where he converted to Protestantism, then to Weimar in 1784, where a year later he made a very judicious marriage to the daughter of Cristoph Martin Wieland, the great German writer and man of letters. His marital connections led him to become coeditor with Wieland of the *Teutsche Merkur*, a prominent journal. Reinhold quickly became well known as one of the "popular philosophers" writing about Enlightenment themes, and in 1785, spurred on by Schütz's article on Kant, he began a thorough reading of the Kantian philosophy. The result was his *Letters on the Kantian Philosophy*, in which he tried to show in a clear, "popular" fashion how Kant had resolved the great debate between reason and faith.

The conflict between faith and reason, brought to the forefront by Jacobi and experienced intensely by Reinhold in his own upbringing, provided the background for Reinhold's encounter with Kant. Very roughly, Reinhold argued that Kant's significance lay in his having demonstrated once and for all that faith and reason were not opposed to each other. Since Kant had shown that the proofs of God's existence actually rested on practical and not theoretical reason, there was nothing to fear from modern science or speculation. Moreover, since Kant had also shown that reason cannot venture to make pronouncements about "things-in-themselves," he had thereby demonstrated that the rationalists would also have to admit the reality of "faith."[6] As Reinhold explained matters, one could be both modern *and* religious, provided only that one was a Kantian. Jacobi's worries about the deleterious consequences of the extension of "reason" to all areas of life seemed to have been decisively answered.

Reinhold's book catapulted the discussion of Kantian philosophy to the forefront of German life and brought with it the meteoric rise of Reinhold himself as the recognized leading exponent of the Kantian philosophy. This led to his procuring the position of "extraordinary professor" at Jena in 1787 and later to his becoming an "ordinary supernumerary professor" (*ordentlicher überzähliger Professor*) in 1792. His lectures, famous for their lucidity and rhetorical flourish, became a magnet for students. By 1788, more than 400 students (an unheard-of number for that time, particularly at a backwater such as Jena) showed up for his summer semester lectures on Wieland's *Oberon*. Reinhold had overnight become the new star of German intellectual life.

However, during this same period, Jacobi had gone further in his criticism of Kant's philosophy.[7] Jacobi argued that the vaunted Kantian distinction between "appearances" and "things-in-themselves" only led to an even deeper and more corrosive skepticism, to the idea that we could not know what things were really like, and that the reassurances of so-called practical reason could not be enough to convince us otherwise. Coining a new term, Jacobi threw down the challenge: The consistent application of reason to human affairs could only lead to "nihilism," to the notion that *nothing* really mattered.

Further, Jacobi accused Kant's philosophy of being inconsistent and self-defeating. Kant held that things-in-themselves cause certain representations (intuitions) passively to arise in us, to which our spontaneous synthesizing activities then apply a categorial form; but Kant also held, as Jacobi pointed out, that causality was one of the categories that we arrived at in the application of this form to those intuitions, and that no "category of the understanding" could apply to things-in-themselves; Kant thus necessarily applied a category of appearances to things-in-themselves in direct contravention of his own theoretical strictures. All this showed, Jacobi argued, that no philosophical theory can do without some "given," something that simply has to be taken as accepted, and this was as true in epistemology as in religion.

Jacobi's arguments clearly struck at the heart of Kant's project, and how seriously one took them depended on how one interpreted the Kantian project. What made Jacobi's attacks all the more distressing for Enlightenment figures was that Jacobi himself was considered to be a progressive figure of the times. Jacobi was a physiocrat (that is, he held that agriculture was the basis of a country's wealth, and he was in favor of free trade), a passionate defender of free speech, and a proponent of a form of constitutional government for the Holy Roman Empire that would be resemble that of England.[8] Nonetheless, he also thought that the unqualified application of standards of "reason" to all human conduct only led to a mechanized view of the world in which there was no room for human freedom, which inevitably led in turn to the excesses of Josef II in Austria and to the French Revolution.[9]

Jacobi's wholesale attack on the Kantian system itself compelled Reinhold to the conclusion that what needed rehabilitating in Kant's philosophy were not its conclusions but its very foundations, its first premises. Taking his newfound fame to heart and no longer content with merely being a mouthpiece for Kant, Reinhold began working out his own thoughts on how to complete the Kantian philosophy by providing, as he put it, the missing premises for the true foundation of Kant's thought. The result of this project, and Reinhold's failure at it, was epochal for the development of German idealism.

If the Kantian philosophy were to be put on a sure footing, so Reinhold argued, then its basic principles had to be derived from some principle that was itself absolutely *certain*, a principle that one could not throw into doubt once one had come to understand it, and that would in its wake thus secure the claims of the Enlightenment. What was at stake, Reinhold argued, was not the "letter" of the Kantian philosophy but its "spirit," not its "results" but its very "premises."

To that end, Reinhold argued that since Kant's philosophy was primarily a philosophy of consciousness, we needed a fundamental account of how this consciousness is constituted. Such a basic account would itself constitute an *Elementarphilosophie* (a philosophy of the "basic elements" of consciousness), and the most fundamental "element" or proposition of the *Elementarphilosophie* would be what Reinhold called the "principle of consciousness" (*Satz des Bewußtseins*): "In consciousness the subject distinguishes the representation from the subject and object and relates it to both."[10] This was taken by Reinhold to be an indubitable "fact" of consciousness, something that can serve as the foundation for all further philosophy. The Reinholdian picture of consciousness thus came to be that of a "subject" standing in relation to an "object," with a "representation" standing between the subject and the object; for Reinhold, this subject actively relates the representation to the object (that is, takes it as a representation and not just a piece of "mental stuff") and at the same time ascribes the representation to itself and distinguishes itself from that representation. On the basis of that conception, Reinhold went on to "deduce" the nature of the distinction between the form and content of representations and the rest of what he took to be necessary to the Kantian critical apparatus. With that deft move, Reinhold's fame only increased; students flocked in greater numbers to Jena to hear Reinhold, the "purified Kant," expound the *Elementarphilosophie* from his lectern.

Fichte's Radicalization of the Kantian Project

Reinhold's so-called discovery of the true basis – the premises, as it were – of the Kantian philosophy quickly ran into a devastating objection from G. E. Schulze in a widely read book at the time, *Aenesidemus* (published in 1792). Schulze pointed out that Reinhold's characterization was clearly involved in an infinite regress: The subject doing the relating must be conscious of itself, and since all consciousness, on Reinhold's definition, involves a representation, the subject doing the relating must have a representation of itself, which in turn requires another subject to relate it to itself and the first subject, ad infinitum. Given the widespread view that Reinhold's accounts were only Kant's views made more precise and readable, Schulze's review might also have proved devastating to the Kantian project as a whole – except for the intervention of another young philosopher, Fichte, who in a review of *Aenesidemus* came to the conclusion not that the critical philosophy was to be abandoned but that it needed a better foundation than Reinhold had given it, namely, an account of self-consciousness that was not representationalist in character and therefore did not rely on the Reinholdian idea of the notion of "representation" being the fundamental concept in philosophy.[11]

The results of Schulze's book and Fichte's response were catastrophic for Reinhold's career; his star sank as rapidly as it had risen, and Reinhold was never again to regain the prominence he briefly enjoyed. Paid the absurdly low salary typical of the professoriate at Jena, Reinhold accepted a better offer from Kiel in 1794 and left Jena for good just as his reputation was beginning a rapid slide downhill. Away from Jena, he came to abandon the Kantian critical philosophy entirely and to adopt a theory of philosophy as equivalent to logic, all of which pushed him even further toward the philosophical periphery at the time.

Fichte arrived in Jena as Reinhold departed, and he quickly supplanted Reinhold as the great star in the German intellectual firmament. Although at first Fichte seemed to accept certain basic Reinholdian claims – in particular, the claims about the need to arrive at an indubitable starting point for philosophy, the related distinctions between the "premises and the conclusions," and between the "spirit and the letter" of Kant's thought, and the need only to "complete" Kant's philosophy – in fact he was to effect a wholesale shift in the nature of the debate, moving it away from Reinhold's worries and in the direction of asking how it was possible in the first place for there to be the kind of self-determining subjectivity that Kant claimed was necessary.[12] Fichte stopped asking how we "constitute" a web of experience and started asking instead about the *authority* for the norms by which we make judgments about that experience.

Fichte's principles are notoriously obscure, and Fichte spent many years trying to work them out before finally abandoning altogether his project of completing Kantian idealist philosophy. Fichte's principles are, in their barest outline, something like the following. The first principle was the Kantian principle of the necessity of self-consciousness, which Fichte characterized as the principle of "I = I" (and which he sometimes characterized as the I's "self-positing"). The second principle was Fichte's version of the Kantian notion that the unity of self-consciousness required some material to synthesize; Fichte characterized this necessity as the principle of the "Not-I": The "I" (the principle of the necessary unity of self-consciousness) is said to "posit" the not-I (that is, the necessary unity of self-consciousness requires some material that is not itself part of self-consciousness for its synthesizing activities to combine, and it must posit this material as something "other" than itself, something "given" to it).[13]

The third principle (which even Fichte himself had trouble stating and which went through numerous revisions) went something like this: Since the necessary unity of self-consciousness (Fichte's "I = I") itself necessarily requires something other than itself, but since it is necessary that *it* posit something as not-posited by itself, as "given," it finds itself in a "contradiction" between holding that everything is a "posit" by the "I" and that among the things that the "I" must posit is that not everything with normative force is a "posit." Because, Fichte argued, an agent cannot abide such a contradiction at the heart of his self-conception, he must eternally strive to overcome this contradiction by showing how any apparent "not-I" (a brute "given" serving as a norm of judgment) is actually not just a "given" but can in fact be shown to be constructible out of what counts as the necessary conditions of self-consciousness itself.[14]

To put Fichte's conclusion in another way: None of the "givens" of experience possess any certainty, any unrevisability; their status as objects of knowledge is a status bestowed on them by our own self-grounding activity.[15] Even the status of a relatively simple experience, such as "something looks red," which just seems to be "given" to us, is a status that we bestow on that experience: It "looks" red to us because we construe it in terms of color concepts, in terms of something like, "the way things that *really are* red *look* in certain lighting conditions," and so on.

Indeed, articulating the third principle gave Fichte so much trouble that during his development of it over the course of several years, he came to hold that the "I" could never *theoretically* demonstrate the full constructibility of the "Not-I" out of itself but must instead take it as a *practical* and infinite task to be achieved, thus leading himself to assert that the demands of practical reason were prior to the claims of theoretical reason – that "dogmatism" (the acceptance of the "Not-I" as a brute "given") could not be overcome theoretically but only practically.[16]

Fichte radicalized the Kantian idea of the "spontaneity" of the subject in synthesizing his experiences – the idea of a spontaneity that lay at the heart of all experience and theoretical knowledge – in a way such that even the notion of our own experiential passivity is something that "we" spontaneously "posit" for ourselves, and he took to describing the awareness of this radical, self-positing spontaneity as "intellectual intuition," a kind of nonrepresentational awareness of our own activity of representing.[17] In Fichte's hands, the joint ideas of the revisability of all our experience and our freedom in doing so – our "boundless" spontaneity which can only be *self*-bounded – became the hallmarks of what it would actually take to complete the Kantian project. The opposite view, that of taking the world as externally acting upon us and generating beliefs and actions in us, was characterized by Fichte as "dogmatism."[18] Fichte's obscure but nonetheless powerful and highly original development of Kantian philosophy away from all reliance on "givens" quickly transformed what had been an Enlightenment ideal into something else: a Romantic exploration and celebration of freedom itself.

Schelling and the Romantic Turn in Idealism

If Fichte set the tone, Schelling helped to raise the stakes (and the embellishment of the language in which it was described) of philosophical idealism. Schelling was the quintessential Romantic. Experimental in temperament, always focused on the large view rather than the fine details, throwing off brilliant insights along the way, Schelling quickly became "the" philosopher for the Romantic circle that had formed at Jena, especially after Fichte's spectacular dismissal from the university surrounding the charges of his alleged "atheism." During that early period in Jena, Schelling's thought developed rapidly, his publications were coming out as fast as he could write them, and each one, so it seemed, took a stance slightly different from the earlier ones. After his own rise to fame later in Berlin, Hegel was to offer a withering observation on much his old friend's output during this period: "Schelling conducted his philosophical education in public."[19]

In the period from roughly 1794 to 1800, Schelling went through his rapid development. Beginning as a Spinozist, he quickly became a Fichtean; in 1795, he published *Of the I as the Principle of Philosophy or On the Unconditional in Human Knowledge*, in which, although still appearing Fichtean in his overall argumentation (he still spoke of the "I's" positing a "Not-I," and so on), in fact he began to depart from

Fichte's thought in important ways. He then began to see the problems in Fichte's own system, and by 1800 had published his *System of Transcendental Idealism* in which he articulated his own distinctive Romantic post-Fichtean form of idealism. Schelling drew out what he took to be the central principle of Fichte's development of idealism and phrased it in a way that was to appeal to his Romantic admirers: "The beginning and end of all philosophy is – *freedom*!"[20]

Just as Fichte had radicalized Kant, Schelling radicalized Fichte. Fichte had spoken of how the "I" necessarily posits for itself a "Not-I" to account for its own activity; but Fichte's "I," Schelling argued, remained conditioned by something else. What was at stake, even on Fichte's own terms, was the status of the "unconditioned" in our activities of self-positing, and Schelling took to calling this unconditioned totality at first the "absolute I" and later simply "Being."[21] Likewise, Schelling radicalized Fichte's notion of "intellectual intuition," claiming that apprehension of the full, unconditioned freedom of the "absolute I" was such a nondiscursive "intellectual intuition" and drawing the conclusion that since the "ultimate goal of the finite I is therefore an expansion toward identity with the nonfinite," the "ultimate goal of all striving can also be represented as an expansion of personality to infinity, that is, as its own destruction."[22] Fichte's "infinite task" of overcoming all reliance on any "given" had suddenly been given a much more religious, even existential and Romantic twist.

However, Schelling himself became worried within a very short time about some of his own conclusions, and began working out what became known as the "philosophy of nature" (*Naturphilosophie*). Schelling thus embarked on his ambitious and greatly influential project of showing how the nature studied by the physicists was itself possible only if there was a "Nature" to be uncovered a priori by the philosophers that made it possible.[23]

One of the key notions in Schelling's philosophy of nature (which was crucial for the development of Hegel's thought in his early writings in Jena) was his idea that nature divides itself into various "potencies" (*Potenzen*). (The term *Potenz* was taken from the mathematical use of "power," as when one speaks of 4 being 2 to the "second power.")[24] Schelling's general idea was roughly the following: An investigation of nature finds that nature necessarily divides itself up into various opposed "potencies" out of a primordial unity that contains a primordial opposition (*Ur-Gegensatz*) within itself. One of the guiding images at work in Schelling's reflections, as in so many other writings of the period, was that of the magnet: The magnet has positive and negative poles, but the poles are not self-subsistent; they exist only in terms of being united within the whole magnet. If one cuts a magnet in half, one does not have two magnet parts, one with a positive pole and one with a negative pole; one has two magnets, each with positive and negative poles. Each pole therefore can exist only when united with its opposite. Schelling called this union the "indifference point" (for example, the point at which the magnet is neither positive nor negative). Each "potency" involves opposites that attract each other (like the positive and negative poles of a magnet), and nature progresses from simple to complex forms by multiplying its "potencies"; when the opposites come together, they multiply each other's "potencies," and the result is a new, higher, more "potent" natural form. Nature is inherently productive and develops of itself all these stages by virtue of its productivity, being spurred on by self-produced "checks" in nature that oppose such expansive, productive forces. (Schelling in fact tried to work out a kind of algebra for this conception of oppositions and potencies in nature, a formalism taken up by his less inspired imitators but which he himself soon discarded.)

The various alleged "indifference points" to be found in nature are, however, all unstable; they are not *genuine* "indifference points," since a genuine "indifference point" would mean the cessation of all development in nature. The only true "indifference point" would be the "absolute" itself out of which all the other various oppositions (and therefore "potencies") of nature develop, but, as he put it, the "absolute indifference point exists nowhere, but is, as it were, distributed among several individual points," which in turn ensures the boundlessness of the universe.[25]

In asserting all this, Schelling denied the validity neither of experimental empirical science nor of empirical investigation – his focus was always on what he saw as the false picture of nature presented by atomism and by the purely mechanical understanding of matter – nor did he advocate any kind of spiritualist conception of nature. He would have nothing to do with those who postulated a "vital force" to explain the way life emerges out of "dead" matter.[26] His point was always that the study of the "potencies" revealed the a priori presuppositions about nature involved in the empirical scientific study of nature.

Thus, so Schelling argued, post-Kantian idealism must pursue a double-edged strategy to avoid the skeptical charge. On the one hand, it must pursue the construction of the "Not-I" out of what the "I" finds necessary for its own self-identity, which culminates in a system of Kantian-Fichtean transcendental idealism. On the other hand, we must also develop a *Naturphilosophie* that shows how nature's own dynamics require that it develop some "point" at which it can reflect on its own productive processes. At the end of both developments – transcendental idealism and *Naturphilosophie* – there is an "intellectual intuition" of the absolute, of a natural human creature nondiscursively intuiting the activity of nature's freely determining itself to produce exactly those "points" at which nature comes within human self-consciousness to a full consciousness of itself.

The absolute itself is therefore that unity that unites the subjective "I" and nature itself, and, as the condition of everything else, it can *only* be the object of an "intellectual intuition." Schelling took himself to have shown that the division between "subject" and "object" can only be the self-display of the absolute itself, which is itself neither subject nor object, and as neither subject nor object, cannot be the "object" of discursive thought or sensible intuition. Schelling almost immediately thereafter began calling this "absolute" the "absolute Identity," and his philosophy became known as "Identity philosophy."

But if the absolute is the object of neither thought nor sensibility, then of what faculty is it the object? Schelling concluded in his *System of Transcendental Idealism* that it could only be the "object" of *imagination*, and in particular, of artistic imagination. The artistic genius, as it were, "shows" us what cannot be "said." In art we achieve the genuine "intellectual intuition" that shows us the unity of self-conscious life and nature, that shows us that we really are the way we must be if we are to be the free agents that we must think of ourselves as being. The hidden conclusion in all of this was of course the idea that those who did not "see" this, who did not have this kind of "intellectual intuition," were those who were incapable of understanding and appreciating art in the first place. "Intellectual intuition" thus turned out to be available to the philosopher and the artist – who in these terms are conceived not so much as the "priests of truth," as Fichte had described the philosopher, but more as a small circle of apostles of the absolute – and unavailable to those who are so mired in the finite that they cannot "see" what are the so-called necessary presuppositions are of their own self-consciousness.

Schelling's aesthetic turn in his understanding of the intuition of the "absolute" was combined, not unsurprisingly, with a very anticommercial understanding of the relations between modern society and such philosophical truths. As Henry Crabb Robinson, an English student at Jena (and one of the first to bring the "new philosophy" to English attention), put it in a letter to his brother in 1802, Schelling simply dismissed all empiricist English philosophy, indeed even England itself, with the assertion, "it is absurd to expect the science of beauty in a country that values the Mathematics only as it helps to make Spinning Jennies and & Stocking-weaving machines. And beauty only as it recommends their Manufactories abroad."[27]

Hölderlin's Philosophical Revolution and His Influence on Hegel

Although Schelling's views obviously had quite an influence on the development of Hegel's own philosophy, the genuine impetus for Hegel's development of his own views was his encounter in Frankfurt with Hölderlin's thoughts on Fichtean idealism. It is quite clear that in 1795, Hölderlin belonged to an animated circle in Jena involved in serious conversation about Fichte's idealism and its relation to Kant. The best surviving evidence of Hölderlin's own entry into that debate consists of a short fragment of two pages titled (not him but by his editors) "Judgment and Being" ("*Urteil und Sein*").[28] Although Hölderlin never published it – the very existence of the piece itself was not even known until 1961 – Hölderlin almost certainly discussed the ideas in it with Hegel, and it was those ideas that decisively turned Hegel away from the direction he had been taking at Berne. As Hölderlin reconstructed things, Fichte's three principles could be understood as falling into a schema of unity, sundering of the unity, and restoration of the unity (of the "I," the "Not-I," and the infinite progress). Hölderlin argued, however, that the initial principle itself (the principle of self-positing self-consciousness, which Fichte characterized as "I = I") could not in fact be the "absolute beginning" because self-consciousness already involves a "division" of itself from itself: The self (the "subject" of awareness) becomes aware of itself as an "object" of awareness. The first principle, therefore, cannot be "absolute," since it already contains an "opposition" within itself.

Hölderlin was proposing, as it turned out, something vaguely similar to what Schelling was about to propose at the same time (although it is unclear if Hölderlin was aware at that point of Schelling's own attempt).[29] Hölderlin argued that the way in which Fichte had separated the "subject" from the "object" – that is, the way in which he had radicalized the Kantian project – made it impossible to see how such a separated "subject" and "object" could ever get back together again. Fichte's solution – that it was the subject's own activity that did this, that the "subject" was the "absolute" ground of this – seemed wrong because the "subject" itself did not appear even to itself to be absolute but rather to refer to something else which was deeper and more fundamental than itself. The separation of "subject" and "object," Hölderlin concluded, was only the expression of a much deeper unity, which Hölderlin called (following Spinoza and Jacobi) "Being."[30] "Consciousness," in Hölderlin's treatment, as a relation of "subject" to "object" could not itself be basic; it had to derive from a yet more basic unity, a more basic apprehension on our part of something that, prior to all our particular orientations, served to orient us in general. Before we can deliberate on anything, we must already be oriented toward some terms that guide that deliberation and which are not themselves established by deliberation; that fundamental standpoint within our own consciousness out of which we orient ourselves was the "one," "Being," that of which we are experientially aware but of which we cannot be explicitly, fully conscious, since consciousness already presupposes a split between "subject" and "object," between our being able to discriminate between our subjective experience of something and the object of that experience (between, for example, our experience of a tree and the tree itself). This "one" forms a kind of "horizon" of our consciousness without itself being an object of that consciousness, and the key to all of this lay in our own *judgmental* activities, in our own attempts at articulating judgments that "get it right" about ourselves and the world.[31]

This implied that Reinhold's and Fichte's search for a "first principle" in philosophy was itself already doomed, since there could be no such first principle; instead, there could only be a prior, holistic predeliberative orientation within some "whole" that included our consciousness and its objects within itself. Fichte's notion that the "I" must posit the "Not-I" was thus also doomed: It assumed that one side of the relation had to do all the work, as it were, when in fact we begin with a unity of thought and being that precedes all reflection on it. Neither the "subject" nor the "object" has any "original" determinateness on its own that would serve to ground or establish the determinateness of the other; if "realists" make the mistake of thinking that the "world" bestows determinateness on thought, "subjective idealists" such as Fichte make the mistake of thinking that thought imposes all the determinateness on the world. Neither "subject" nor "object" is primary or originary, and we must accept that we are always in touch with the world in all its general outlines. This acceptance necessarily precedes all our reflection, including even our various skeptical doubts about it. That we have a sense of the "whole" that includes us, even if we cannot at first articulate it (except perhaps poetically), was the implication of Hölderlin's reflections.[32]

Hölderlin's reflections on Fichte and on the development of idealism in general had no less than an explosive impact on Hegel. In Berne, as Hegel had set himself to completing the Kantian program by applying it, he had dismissed Fichte's and Reinhold's works as being merely of interest to theoretical reason alone. Hegel's own concern up until that point had been rather straightforwardly with the idea of the self-imposition of the moral law, with how that might be "applied" to history to show how Christianity had become a positive religion, and how mankind had, in Kant's words, thereby imposed a form of tutelage on itself. In all these cases, though, Hegel's diagnosis of the problem had landed him at a theoretical dead end. Now, under the influence of Hölderlin, he saw how his project of *applying* the Kantian idea of self-imposition to specific social problems (particularly those connected with the Revolution) had in fact begged the question of what constituted self-imposition in the first place, indeed, had begged the question about all our judgmental activities. Fichte had shown that the theme of self-determination, if taken seriously, had to be developed on its own, and by virtue of his own difficulties in working out his system, had shown that it was not a self-evident idea that could simply be "applied."

Hölderlin had now indicated to him not only that Fichte's own philosophy had deeper problems within itself, but also that something like even a history of Christianity could not be understood outside of some deeper understanding of the kind of prereflective situating that goes on in conscious life before more determinate plans and projects are laid out. Hegel also came to see under Hölderlin's guidance that idealism as it had been developing could not be written off as ignoring the more experiential aspects of human life; at the heart of conscious life itself was an element of spontaneous activity that was not simply the application of underived conceptual form to given sensuous content. "Subjective religion," as a way of orienting people's "hearts," required some account of how we orient our conscious lives in the first place, and Hölderlin had shown that a full account of that was still outstanding.

As Hegel absorbed Hölderlin's radical ideas, it became clear to him that his whole project of staging a career as a Lessing-like "educator of the people" was coming to a crashing end, since he had been trying to "apply" a set of ideas that were themselves already deeply in conflict with each other. If he really wanted to do what he set out to do, he simply was going to have to do things differently, and that realization shifted Hegel's course onto the path he was finally to take.

"The Oldest System Program of German Idealism"

Around this time Hegel wrote out a short manuscript which has come to be known as "The Oldest System Program of German Idealism." (It is usually dated 1797.) The essay is very short and contains little argument; instead, it contents itself with simply announcing various lines of thought and with indicating in a sketchy way how they might possibly fit together in some future development. Although the manuscript is in Hegel's own handwriting, it is by no means clear that it his own creation, and the question of its actual authorship has always remained a matter of controversy. In fact, it was originally attributed to Schelling, although for a while much scholarly opinion shifted to the view that attributes authorship of the piece to Hegel himself; the author, however, is most likely Hölderlin.[33]

There are several things that make the manuscript problematic as a Hegelian text, which we unfortunately cannot go into here. Nonetheless, whoever its author may be, "The Oldest System Program" was either written or copied out during a crucial transition in Hegel's own development and in the development of German idealism in general, and even if Hegel was not the author, the piece still reflects many ideas and concerns he had during that period and is a reliable piece of evidence as to the direction of his own intellectual development. Having taken Hölderlin's criticisms of Fichte to heart, Hegel would have seen in this piece how his Bernese program would have to be modified in light of his newfound interest in the most basic conceptions of idealist philosophy. The author of the manuscript speaks, for example, of how he wishes to "set down the principles of a *history of humanity* and expose the whole miserable human work of state, constitution, government, legislation, etc."[34] Hegel's interests in Berne in combining, as it were, Gibbon with Kant had expanded in Frankfurt into combining Gibbon and idealist philosophy in general into a more ambitious history than even Gibbon himself would have envisaged. The author of the manuscript announces some theses dear to Hölderlin (which Hegel, Schelling, and Hölderlin all no doubt themselves took from Schiller, perhaps even from Shaftesbury), namely, that "the Idea that unites all is the Idea of *beauty*," that the "philosopher must possess just as much aesthetic power as the poet," that in forging a unity of poetry and philosophy, "poetry (*Poesie*) acquires a higher dignity, it becomes again what it was in the beginning – the *teacher of humanity*."[35]

The author also speaks, in terms that at least Hegel himself never again repeated, of a "new mythology . . . [which] must stand in the service of Ideas, it must become a mythology of *reason*."[36] The notion that modernity had to break with the past and that it would be the destiny of philosophers and poets to create a correspondingly new sensibility, a "new mythology" – an idea already powerfully at work in Hölderlin's poetry – to match the new times thus linked up with some of the ideas earlier found in Hegel's "Tübingen Essay," namely, the project of creating a "people's religion" that would actually move people's hearts in the direction of moral and spiritual renewal. What had earlier been a call for "subjective religion" had transmuted itself into a call for a "new mythology," a new sensibility to be created by philosophers and poets. Hegel's own version of radical modernism, ignited by Hölderlin's influence, was thus expressed forcefully, and in its earliest form, in the manuscript (again, whoever its true author may be). Just as Hölderlin was led to create new mythological landscapes and a new form of language to help create that modern sensibility, and to refuse to employ the jargon common to his time in order to adopt the kind of modernist stance on life that he considered necessary to the expression of that sensibility, Hegel concluded that for his philosophy to be the kind of modernist, rigorous *Wissenschaft* he intended for it to be, he had to create a new vocabulary that would force the reader to think for himself, that would avoid convention so as not to lull the reader into simply accepting past conceptions of things. (Indeed, it was shortly after Hegel wrote out this piece – again, leaving it open who the actual author may be – that his prose style began its decisive shift; that choice of obscure vocabulary, it turned out, was to be one of Hegel's most enduring and most dubious legacies.)

The most important aspect of "The Oldest System Program," however, is that it is a step on the way toward what its editors named it: a *system* program. In Frankfurt, Hegel's line of thought was rapidly shifting away from attempts at completing the Kantian philosophy by "applying" it to pressing social issues and toward issues of what it would take to work out the internal dynamic of the complex of ideas associated with the notions of self-consciousness and freedom. He was increasingly concerned with the issue of what was entailed, as the author of "The Oldest System Program" puts it, in our thinking of "the first Idea [being] naturally that *of myself* as an absolutely free being" and with how we were to think about nature, society, history, and philosophy itself if such an "Idea" were to have any effective basis in our lives.[37] The "system program" notes that there can be no corresponding "Idea of the *state*," since "what is called the *Idea* can only be an object of *freedom*," and that is clearly inapplicable to anything mechanical; the state thus cannot serve as the realization of freedom because, as the manuscript states, "the state is something *mechanical*" – a clear reference to the conception, widespread in philosophical and cameralist thought in Germany in the eighteenth century, of the state as a "machine" and a clear indication that the kind of "modernist" sensibility at work in the piece looked to poetry and philosophy, not conventional political reform, to create the "new sensibility" for modernity.[38]

Hölderlin had apparently convinced Hegel at this point that freedom was possible only when human action was structured in terms of principles whose outcome was a "beautiful" state of affairs, and that the realization of the ideal of "beauty" would somehow provide the answer to the problems provoked by Kant's and Fichte's works.[39] The manuscripts Hegel produced in Frankfurt while under Hölderlin's influence are, by and large, unsuccessful attempts to blend those various interests together into a coherent whole.[40] It was not until he got to Jena that he was able to develop those ideas originally inspired by Hölderlin into his own distinctive vision.

Christianity, Modern Life, and the Ideal of Beauty: "The Spirit of Christianity"

Under Hölderlin's influence, Hegel was motivated to work up a completely new manuscript on the subject that had provoked him in Berne: whether Christianity could be a "modern" religion – that is, whether it could become a genuine "people's religion" and thereby serve as a vehicle for social and moral renewal. The essay is known under the title "The Spirit of Christianity and Its Fate."[41] The ideas at work in "The Spirit of Christianity and Its Fate" were in some ways continuous with those of "The Positivity of the Christian Religion," but new themes and concepts were introduced, old ideas underwent a transformation, and a new conclusion appeared.[42]

The "Spirit of Christianity" is animated by the central notion that the "fate" of a people cannot be understood as the result of contingent factors in their historical development nor in terms of forces imposed from outside a people's collective self-understanding. It is rather the logical outcome of the "principles" inherent in their common life, the logical development of the commitments undertaken by a people about what ultimately matters to them.

The theme allowed Hegel to reflect again on which kinds of commitments to what ultimately matters are compatible with a modern understanding of freedom and which are incompatible with that understanding. In that light, Hegel returned to the differences between Judaism and Christianity to make his point. The "spirit" of Judaism, he argued, must be characterized as that of servility and alienation, since it understands the "law" as being imposed on it by an alien, divine being (an "infinite Object," as Hegel put it). Hegel explained this in a Fichtean idiom colored by Hölderlin's notion of the unity of "subject" and "object": Because the Jewish nation conceived of itself in terms of the "antitheses" of itself and nature and of itself and the rest of humanity, the only "synthesis" available to them was the abstraction of a God who was beyond nature and humanity and who was simply their "master."[43] The result was a "spirit" that *wedded itself* to bondage, that embodied a self-incurred subservience: As Hegel puts it, the claim that "there is one God" becomes equivalent to "there is one master, for whom we are the bondsmen."[44] Judaism could therefore never be a religion of freedom, for its "spirit" could never allow it to achieve the "synthesis" that would be necessary for understanding freedom as self-legislation, as involving more than the imposition of laws by an alien being. (At this period in his life, not surprisingly, Hegel shared the widely prevalent view in Germany that the Jews would continue to be maltreated until they abandoned Judaism; as he put it, the Jews "will be continually maltreated until they appease it by the spirit of beauty and so sublate it by reconciliation.")[45]

However, in the "Spirit of Christianity," Hegel also took issue with his earlier, by and large Kantian identification of the essence of Christianity with a pure "religion of morality." Departing from his Bernese conception, Hegel instead argued that Kant's own conception of the self-imposition of the categorical imperative was only a form of "self-coercion," only another expression of the alienation of people from nature and from each other. Although the Kantian conception of morality as autonomous self-legislation by rational agents makes up for the deficiencies in the notion of being dominated by an alien "other" (by the Jewish God, for example) and thus marks an advance over Judaism, it still does not overcome the idea of domination in general, for, as Hegel puts it, "in the Kantian conception of virtue this opposition [that between universal and particular, objective and subjective] remains, and the universal becomes the master and the particular the mastered."[46] The great Kantian split therefore between "inclinations" (coming from the natural self) and the "rational will" merely raises domination to another level rather than overcoming it.[47]

The "spirit" of Christianity, on the other hand, was understood in terms of *love*, which supposedly transcends both the allegedly slavish obedience of the Jews and Kant's rigid moralism.[48] Jesus preached an ethic of love and therefore of true freedom; in the ethic of love, we do that which answers to our particular, embodied lives while at the same time performing our universal duties. In love, there is no domination: "Its essence is not a domination of something alien to it . . . it is rather love's triumph over these that it lords it over nothing, is without any hostile power over another."[49] Kant had held that love cannot serve as the basis of morality because it could not be commanded; Hegel turned this around, arguing that this was precisely its superiority to the rigid Kantian notion of "self" domination.

This conception of the "spirit" of Christianity, of course, required Hegel to offer some explanation as to how love is supposed to actually to overcome these hostilities, some account of that in which love's alleged superiority consists. The answer came from Hegel's newly acquired, Hölderlin-inspired conception of the way in which a subject can said to be free. The imposition of any duty cannot come from the individual agent's imposing a "law" on himself; it must come instead from the individual's integrating himself into a loving relationship with some ground deeper than his own finite subjectivity, with something which is both himself and yet more than his own individual life, what Hegel called the "infinite," meaning that which is self-bounding and not bounded by something "other" than itself. Love does not need the opposition of duty and inclination; the lover is inclined to do things for the sake of the beloved all the while finding it right that he do so. Love, not self-coercive Kantian autonomy, is thus the true basis for the ethical virtues.

However, love as a subjective phenomenon cannot be satisfactory or self-sufficient; as Hegel put it, although "morality sublates domination within the sphere of consciousness; love sublates the barriers in the sphere of morality; but love itself is still incomplete in nature."[50] In another fragmentary manuscript dating from roughly the same period as the composition of "The Spirit of Christianity and Its Fate," Hegel spoke of something that he called "infinite life," which he identified with God, and he there claimed that religion is the elevation of "finite life to infinite life."[51] In yet another manuscript of the same period, he said that "this love, when made by the imagination into essence is divinity."[52]

Hölderlin's influence in Hegel's thought at this time was thus quite evident. Love consists in a deeply experiential going beyond one's own restricted, personal point of view, in transcending one's own finite "I" in the direction of an other, and it brings out the deeper unity among the various points of view, a unity that precedes all consciousness of division; this process of self-transcendence, however, has its logical stopping point in the idea of one's uniting with "infinite life" (an activity that Hegel identified with worship itself), and it results in a vision of "beauty," which is identified with "truth."[53] Such infinite, divine life is Hegel's surrogate for Hölderlin's idea of "Being": It is more basic than any of the seemingly basic oppositions of self and other, lord and master, or mind and nature that we experience as finite beings, and it underlies them. Therefore, Hegel concludes, "subjective" love cannot be self-sufficient; it requires completion in religion, which is itself the synthesis of "reflection" and love: When love as something subjective and personal manages to become something objective yet still remain fully personal, one then has religion. This objective love is, in turn, described as "infinite life," something in which the individual living agent participates, understanding it as the basis of his own finite life.

In "The Spirit of Christianity and Its Fate," Hegel concluded that we are each individually free when we act according to principles that follow from the *free* spirit of the *people* to whom we belong, for only the "spirit" of the people as a whole, not the isolated individual, can be fully self-determining in the relevant sense. In the daily world of everyday life, ethical duties and particular virtues will inevitably come into collision with each other; but the "spirit" of a people in which love is the principle overcomes those contingent collisions. Or, as Hegel phrased the matter, "only when it is simply the one living spirit which acts and restricts *itself* in accordance with the whole of the given situation, in complete absence of external restriction, then and only then does the many-sidedness of the situation remain, though the mass of absolute and incompatible virtues vanishes."[54]

Of course, the question this raised was: What then is the "fate" of Christianity? Is it the religion that Hegel had been seeking, that would be capable of providing a spirit of freedom for its adherents and thus be capable in a reformed state of leading a people to social and moral reform? Hegel's answer turned out to be negative. Although, as he put it, there can be "no Idea more beautiful than that of a nation (*Volk*) of people related to one another by love," nonetheless the *world* in which Jesus lived made it impossible for him to realize that goal. The Roman-Jewish world of Jesus' time was corrupt, and thus "Jesus could only carry the Kingdom of God in his heart . . . in his everyday world, he had to flee all living relationships because they all lay under the law of death, because men were imprisoned by Judaism."[55] Jesus (characterized in the essay as a "beautiful soul") found himself in an impossible dilemma: He could either abandon what was most deeply true about himself (his dedication to a religion of love), or he could flee the world and live a life without worldly pleasure, which itself was only a "one-sided," unsatisfying resolution of the issue. Likewise, Jesus' followers had to cut themselves off from the world, and thus the love they professed became only an ideal; as they became more numerous, it also became impossible to maintain the affiliations of love that had been the intended basis of Christianity. Instead of "infinite life," the idea of the individual uniting himself with something both continuous with himself and yet deeper than his own individual life, the image of the risen Jesus, distant and transcendent, necessarily became the dominant image of Christianity, an image of longing for a redeeming love that Christians in principle could not experience in this life. What had been the ideal of "elevation to the infinite" in love increasingly became a "positive" religion based on the authority of a teacher and on belief in a God who became increasingly and necessarily conceived not as an object of love but merely as a master who commands.[56]

Christianity was thus necessarily led to create an insurmountable opposition between God and the world, and the "fate" of Christianity was that what was originally intended to overcome the relationship of dominator and dominated, of lord and bondsman, necessarily reintroduced such dominance into itself. In the form it had come to assume, Christianity, as the religion of Jesus, simply *could not* become the modern religion that Hegel had earlier hoped that it would be. The "fate" of Christianity is that it never could have really been or become a religion of freedom since it was never able successfully to unite "finite life" with "infinite life," despite its initial promise to do so. What had been the story in Berne of the unfortunate loss of freedom, of Christianity's becoming a positive religion despite the intentions of its founder, now in Frankfurt became a story of "tragic destiny," of its being inevitable that Christianity could never become a religion of freedom, however exalted and (for its times) otherwise justified its founder may have been in assuming the stance he did.

If Christianity cannot be the modern religion that will lead to moral and spiritual renewal and thus to social reform, and if religion is necessary for this end (a view Hegel continued to hold), it followed that some other form of religion had to be the vehicle for this reform. But could this new religion be based on what the "Oldest System Program" calls a new "mythology of reason"? Or – and this must have been clear to Hegel – would that be only another version of the ill-fated, almost laughable "cult of reason" attempted in France by Robespierre and his followers?

Driven to that conclusion but not happy with it, Hegel at least briefly toyed with the idea of investigating what would be entailed in the idea of founding a new religion – what would it take, what would it look like, would it even be possible? – and he even wrote an extremely short piece provocatively labeled, "Religion, founding a religion."[57] Hegel's essay clearly illustrated the unresolved state of his own thoughts at the time. On the one hand, little can done *within* the spirit of a people if it is not already free. If one is brought up in an unfree "spirit," then in order to be free, one must break out of it and integrate oneself within another "spirit," something that itself is not possible on the purely individual level. On the other hand, he also wanted to integrate these ruminations about freedom and the "fate" of a form of "spirit" into the scheme of thought recently inspired in him by Hölderlin: We can transcend the inevitable oppositions of life only by elevating ourselves to the infinite, by coming to identify ourselves with the "infinite life" that lies at the basis of our own finite lives, and we can only do that if the "spirit" to which we belong enables us to have a self-understanding that makes such identification possible. Hegel was thus at this stage of his thought somewhat at odds with himself. He still held a belief in an essence of humanity (Kantian in Berne, Hölderlin-inspired in Frankfurt) that is variously expressed in different periods in history or in different "spirits" but which remains constant over time, yet at the same time he also wanted to hold that our humanity takes its determinate shape in light of the "spirit" and its associated "fate" in which we form our self-understandings, which itself seems to imply that our "humanity" can historically also take very different shapes. In Frankfurt, Hegel was still not sure just *what* he thought. His essay on "The Spirit of Christianity and its Fate" thus became one more (in his eyes) failed attempt to come to terms with the complex set of issues about modern life that was troubling him.

Part Two
Jena: Texts and Drafts

Hegel's arrival in Jena signified his entry into the very center of the movement of post-Kantian philosophy, of all the exuberant attempts to go "beyond Kant" in philosophical discussion. However, even before his arrival, quite a number of young intellectuals, under the prodding of Immanuel Niethammer, had begun a quiet move "back to Kant."[58] This "re-Kantianization" of philosophical discussion, however, still regarded as unacceptable Kant's various "dualisms," his conception of experience as the application of conceptual "form" to neutral sensuous "content," and his conclusions about unknowable things-in-themselves. Hegel's friend Hölderlin had participated in those early discussions, and Hegel himself arrived in Jena with a position that had already been decisively shaped by his friend's own arguments and conclusions about those issues. He was, however, immediately drawn into Schelling's orbit and found the appeal of Schelling's own understanding of these issues attractive; but he was also quite definitely influenced by the atmosphere, still alive in Jena, that encouraged returning to Kant to see if within Kant's own works there was a way out of Kant, using Kant himself. If anything, Hegel's attempt to find his own voice by combining Hölderlin's influence with the ideas coming out of Schelling's formidable talent for speculative philosophy was one of the prime motivations for his development in his early years in Jena.

1797–1800: Rethinking the Problem of "Germany"

Hegel brought with him to Jena a manuscript that he had started in Frankfurt, which dealt with the problem of the status of the Holy Roman Empire in the age of the French Revolution. He drafted a good part of the essay near the end of his stay in Frankfurt and began work on it again in his first year at Jena, but then, as he had done with "The Positivity of the Christian Religion" in Berne and with the "Spirit of Christianity" in Frankfurt, he put it aside without ever attempting to publish it. Although quite philosophical, the essay – known as "The German Constitution" – was also very topical, and Hegel most likely decided not to publish it because his intensive work on establishing his credentials in systematic philosophy left him no time to make any further revisions to a piece that political events in Europe were quickly rendering obsolete.

The Rastatt conference, begun in 1797, began to bring home both to otherwise hopeful and to skeptical Germans how ineffectual and practically useless the old Holy Roman Empire had become. In the past, the smaller political units of Germany (such as the *Landgravate* of Homburg vor der Höhe and the many relatively small imperial cities) had always rested their claims to independence on the laws of the Holy Roman Empire and had counted on its support to prevent them from being swallowed by their larger, more aggressive neighbors. However, in the wake of the growing evidence of the empire's ineffectiveness against the French, they had acquired good reasons to fear for their existence, even though few could imagine that in a few short years almost none of them would continue to exist as independent political entities. These smaller political entities were surrounded by the French (who seemed unstoppable), the Prussians (who had demonstrated that they respected no territorial rights when they saw conquest to be in their interests and thought they could get away with it), and by the Austrians (who also had good reasons to extend their political domain). Indeed, to the various independent principalities, it was not at all clear just which of them – Prussia, Austria, or the French – was the greatest danger.

When the Rastatt congress was still in session, war broke out again. The Habsburgs in Austria had formed a new coalition with England, Bavaria, Franconia, and Württemberg; once again feeling threatened, Russia and France declared war. However, on December 3, 1800, the Austrian forces were completely routed by the French in a forest not far from Munich. In February 1801, the Austrian emperor, Franz II, in the name of Austria and the Holy Roman Empire had no other real choice than to accept the treaty proposed to him. The Treaty of Lunéville – signed on February 9, 1801, only a few weeks after Hegel's arrival in Jena – forcefully brought home the complete political impotence of the Holy Roman Empire. Because of some difficulties, however, the *Reichstag* (the official representative body, as it were, of the Holy Roman Empire) was forced to conclude the details of the treaty, and this delayed a final settlement on the issues for a few years. Finally, the Report of the Imperial Deputation (*Reichsdeputationshauptschluß*) of 1803 – about a year after Hegel had ceased work on "The German Constitution" – proclaimed exactly what many of the smaller political units had come to fear: The map of the Holy Roman Empire was totally redrawn, and the smaller political units by and large disappeared, swallowed up by their more powerful neighbors. Moreover, it was evident to all clear-eyed observers that these results came from France's simply dictating the terms of the treaty to the representatives of the Holy Roman Empire, with the old *Reich* having little room to maneuver.

Hegel began work on the essay "The German Constitution" while the Congress of Rastatt was in session, and he continued to work on it during the outbreak of war between France and the new coalition against it. Although it was abundantly clear to him that the creaky old machinery of the Holy Roman Empire was breaking down, even he was no doubt a bit taken aback at just how rapidly the whole empire managed to fall apart between 1801 and 1803.

He began the essay (in a forward composed some time after the major body of the essay) with the striking thesis, "Germany is no longer a state."[59] He went on to explain that his reason for this assertion was that for anything to *count* as a state, it must be able to mount a common defense, and Germany had shown that it could not perform that task.[60]

But Hegel meant much more by a "state" than merely some body possessing a monopoly on force within a territorial unity. From his days at Tübingen through Berne and Frankfurt, Hegel had been attracted to what he took to be a Greek ideal of a way of life that would unite religious, social, and political life within itself. A way of life (or "spirit," as he had come to call it in Frankfurt) had to be something that could give its participants some orientation, a point to living. In arguing for the overarching importance of a "common defense," Hegel was not therefore arguing that the state should somehow *assert* itself. (Hegel was not a "statist" in that essay.) He argued instead that only when a state has united its citizens in a *common project* with which they can freely identify can it lay claim to their full and uncoerced allegiance.[61] Germany was "no longer a state" because it no longer constituted such a common point of view for "the Germans"; it was not any kind of body in whose collective ends they could see their own ends reflected, and it was for that reason incapable of rousing them to a common defense.

In developing that analysis of contemporary German political life, Hegel was still operating within the ambit of the issues that had motivated his unsatisfying attempts at outlining the conditions for a modern religion, asking what could provide the basis for moral, spiritual, and social reform in modern times. Originally, Hegel had asked this question of Christianity, only to find it wanting. Now Hegel asked the same question of the Holy Roman Empire – could it be the basis of moral, spiritual, and social reform or must something new replace it?

The background to the issue that Hegel was raising in the essay had to do with the failures of the Holy Roman Empire in the face of the challenges put to it by the French Revolution. On the one hand, the behavior of the members of the Holy Roman Empire clearly illustrated that the individual German principalities did not have any particular allegiance to the Holy Roman Empire. The smaller states were largely unenthusiastic about joining the imperial war effort, and the great powers (Austria and Prussia) showed no solidarity at all with each other, each dropping out of the war from time to time to conclude their separate short-lived peaces with France.[62] The French had proved to be militarily overwhelming in part because of their ability to raise large, spirited, devoted conscript armies, whereas the princelings of the various German states neither could nor wanted to do any such thing. (Karl August of Weimar – on whose watch Goethe had built up the university at Jena – succinctly summed up the matter: "I would rather pay my last *ecu* to the elector of Saxony to have a couple of his good regiments march than to arm five hundred of my peasants.")[63] The distrust that the princelings of the Holy Roman Empire felt toward the common folk, such distrust that they were unwilling to arm them, was reciprocated; the common folk had no desire whatsoever to go off and fight for their princes; to most of them, one oppressor was as good as the other, and they felt no particular loyalty to any one of them.

The French, on the other hand, had rallied the people by means of the Revolution to the cause of the *nation* of France. The conscripts of the French army had come to believe that they were fighting for the Revolution and for France, which for them was not the abstraction that the distant duke or king was for the professional German solider. This identification with the "cause" (and the way in which the French combined this large army with superior tactics and with new ways of handling the problems of logistics) made the French unbeatable against the old-fashioned armies of the *Reich*, whose discipline came from long training and from the fear of failure instilled in them by their commanding officers (usually through harsh measures). To Hegel's way of thinking, the mass conscription and the spirited fighting of the French soldier were closer to the Greek ideal of citizenship than was the out-moded, dull professional soldiering typical of the armies of the Holy Roman Empire. Revolutionary France offered its members something that elicited their full allegiance, gave them an orienting point and something to redeem their lives. The Holy Roman Empire only offered its men modest pay for service and the threat of severe punishment if they failed at their duties.

In that situation, the question that had to be raised was fully analo-gous to the key issue that Hegel had raised in his earlier essay "The Positivity of the Christian Religion." In that essay, the question was not "*Is* Christianity a positive religion?" but rather "Could Christianity *become* a people's religion?" Likewise, the central question for the essay on the "German Constitution" was not: *Is* the Holy Roman Empire a state in the sense that it elicits allegiance to itself on the part of its members, that it offers them something worth living and dying for? It was instead: Could the Holy Roman Empire *become* such a state? To understand the possibilities open to the Holy Roman Empire, Hegel argued, one had to understand its spirit – the defining norms that articulated what ultimately mattered to the German people – in order to determine "Germany's" possible *fate*.

On Hegel's account, the defining norm for the German "spirit" had to do with "freedom." Original Germanic freedom involved the individ-ual's refusal "to be restricted by the whole; his limitations he imposed on himself without doubt or fear."[64] However, as the Germanic peoples and the Roman peoples mixed at the end of the Roman Empire, this freedom was transformed as the various states in what was eventually to become Europe became ever larger.[65] The combination of Germanic "freedom" and the ever-increasing size of the political units of Europe resulted in the development of feudalism, in which groupings of indi-viduals as estates came to be represented in the state. The system of original Germanic freedom thus developed into the system of represen-tation, which in turn became "the system of all modern European states."[66] Weaving his understanding of Gibbon into his analysis of Germanic freedom and the principle of representation, Hegel claimed that this marked an "epoch in world history. The nexus of the cultiva-tion and formation of the world has led the human race beyond oriental despotisms, through a republic's world-dominion, and then out of the fall of Rome into a middle term between these two extremes. And the

Germans are the people from whom this third universal formation of the world-spirit was born."[67]

Unfortunately, Germany, which gave the idea of modern representative government to the rest of the world, was incapable itself of fully realizing that ideal. Because its "principle" was that of "abstract freedom," the Germanic nation continued its cleavage to the way of life embodied in the hometowns of the Holy Roman Empire with their set of accumulated and fiercely defended arcane rights and privileges. This attachment to the individual and the hometown made it impossible for Germany to be really free, since the continued existence of these self-contained, very traditional, supposedly "free" communities "does not rest on their own power and force; it is dependent on the politics of the great powers."[68] Thus, the *fate* of German "freedom" was that it necessarily turned into a loss of freedom, into merely apparent and not actual, efficacious freedom. German freedom, as evidenced in the freedom of the individual and the hometown to adhere to their traditional ways of doing things, necessarily became entwined with a freedom-undermining dependence on the goodwill of the great powers.

In rejecting the claims of the hometowns to be adequate embodiments of "Germanic freedom," Hegel rejected large portions of his father's world and his own Stuttgart youth. Indeed, he reserved his most scathing comments for his own youthful hero and the hero of his father's generation, J. J. Moser, the great Württemberg lawyer who had argued that the validity of the laws of the Holy Roman Empire rested on the foundation of what tradition had established, who had done the most to write out those laws, and who was the champion of the "constitutional settlement" in Württemberg in 1770. (Although Moser is not explicitly mentioned, the object of Hegel's scorn has always been clear to commentators.) Against all those lawyers and followers of Moser who were continuing to argue that the Holy Roman Empire was still a state because of the existence of imperial law and of the so-called traditions of imperial law, Hegel argued that the Holy Roman Empire was a state only in "thought" and not in "actuality."[69] Since the Holy Roman Empire could neither enforce its laws, nor defend itself according to its laws, it could not be said to be an *actual*, effective state, however much it may have looked like one in Moser's law books.

Hegel thus firmly rejected the Moser-inspired celebration of tradition in the "good old law" of Württemberg. His attraction instead to the

Revolution in France has to do with the way its very modernity had cast aside such appeals to tradition and substituted instead the ideal of actualizing freedom within the institutional structures of a modern political order. The vaunted "freedom" of the hometowns, so dear to so many German political thinkers at the time, had, Hegel suggested, simply rotted away because of the incoherence at the heart of German hometown life.

The issue then clearly was: Given that this is the *fate* of Germany, is there anything to be done about it? Must Germany transform itself into something else? Or, analogous to the question of whether Christianity could become a modern religion, could "Germany" remain "Germanic" in the conditions of the modern world? Or does "Germany" necessarily have the same fate that Hegel at the time ascribed to ancient Greece or to the Jews – that, having played its role on the world stage, it now is fated to sink gradually into oblivion?[70]

For Germany to be a true state, it would have to unite its people in such a way that they could come to identify with it. To do that, it would first have to have as its objective "the immutable maintenance of rights." Second, for such Germanic freedom to be possible in the modern world, a people must "be bound to a state by law."[71] Third, this legal formation of a people would clearly require representation: "people must share in the making of laws and the management of the most important affairs of state . . . without such a representative body, freedom is no longer thinkable."[72] The problem was that all these conditions had been made virtually unrealizable because of the fact that the modern German principalities were composed of essentially contradictory sets of rights rooted in the restricted and self-undermining world of the hometowns. Where there are such contradictions, there can be no solution, for there is nothing higher to which one can appeal than the spirit of the state itself, which, if riddled with such contradictions itself, cannot resolve the contradictions of its parts.[73] (War itself, Hegel notes, cannot decide which rights in the contradictory pairs are legitimate; it can only decide "which of the two rights is to give way.")[74] Is such freedom possible when the form of life is so clearly shaped by the structure of the hometowns?

Two factors shaped Hegel's response to this question and made his own results unsatisfactory even for himself. First, Hegel's sympathies had always been with the more moderate Girondist wing of the Revolution, but the experience of the Terror had led him to have second thoughts about the Revolution's direction, even if he still believed in its necessity and its ultimate justification. He thus clearly denounced what he called the French Jacobin "freedom frenzy," which in the name of freedom tears down all the structures that actually make freedom possible.[75] It was therefore out of the question simply to try to copy the Revolution in Germany. Second, when he came to describe the social conditions in Germany that he thought might make the realization of modern freedom possible there, he was left with nothing except to draw on some of the basic structures of the Württemberg society of his youth. In his original Tübingen and Berne writings, he had argued that any division of society into "estates" was a threat to freedom, since it necessarily fragmented what was really an organic whole; older now, he argued instead for their necessity for an adequate realization of freedom and "organic wholes."[76]

His conclusion was that the Rousseauian "general will" could thus only be made effective within a state having a form of representative government, in which representation is effected by various mediating structures and not within the "freedom frenzy" of Revolutionary direct democracy (which itself can only lead to factionalization and confusion).[77] The freedoms of the hometowns with which Hegel was familiar (and in which he grew up) had given Germans, so he thought, the correct idea of representative government and a core set of mediating institutions to actualize that idea, but those hometowns had undermined their own freedoms by making it impossible for the Holy Roman Empire to be a genuine state. They themselves were doomed, since they could only continue to exist within the protecting structure of the Holy Roman Empire, which was itself doomed. For what was still alive in hometown life to survive, it had therefore to meld with the ideals of the French Revolution, even if not with the specific development of that revolution.

The question for Hegel was therefore: How can such representation be accomplished in Germany, given the corrupted condition in which Germany finds itself and given the way in which "Germanic freedom" had institutionalized itself in the structures of hometowns and not in a true state? Once again, just as he had in his earlier essays on Christianity, Hegel found himself at an impasse. He described what he took to be the conditions under which freedom could be achieved, but he had no clear idea about how any of that could be actualized. He rejected

Prussian leadership for the maintenance (or restoration) of the Holy Roman Empire – Prussia was in such a state of both decay and increasing centralization that it could not in any way serve as the natural center for preserving the independence of the estates – and he toyed with the idea that Austria, where he thought that the estates had managed to hang on to their independence, was the only real hope for a rejuvenated Holy Roman Empire. Hegel was clearly trying to find a middle way between the ongoing struggles among the forces leading to centralization in Germany (which Prussia adequately symbolized) and the old, decentralized, overlapping ruling authorities, that is, the structure of *Herrschaft* in the Holy Roman Empire, the complex orderings by which groups and individuals exercised authority over others.[78] But how, he wondered, was this to be accomplished?

Just as he had no answer to his earlier question about how a "people's religion" could be established, in 1801 he also had no real answer to how a proper German state could be brought about. Indeed, the only possible, thinkable solution necessarily involved the imposition of statehood by force. Since the Germans were all too corrupted by their stubborn adherence to the debased consequences of "Germanic freedom" – to the structure and assumptions of the life of the hometowns – all that remained as a possibility was that some wise leader, a "Theseus" of Germany, would somehow compel the Germans to unite and "treat themselves as belonging to Germany."[79] (Hegel praised Machiavelli for having this kind of insight about how modern states can be formed.)[80]

But even Hegel himself could see that this solution was essentially no solution at all; it was at best merely a hope that things would turn out right, that the proper "Theseus" would come along and would institute a modern representative republic of sorts and not some worse tyranny. Even worse, the "fate" of Germanic freedom, of the structure of hometown life, seemed destined to vanish unless this sort of "Theseus" were miraculously to appear.

1801–1802: Hegel Comes to Terms with Schelling

The Difference *Essay: Kant, Schelling, and "Authentic Idealism"*

Hegel's first published foray in the debate about post-Kantian philosophy was a short book, *The Difference between Fichte's and Schelling's Systems of Philosophy*, which appeared in September 1801, less than a year after his arrival at Jena. This small monograph defined Hegel for the next several years in the public eye: To the philosophical public, he had emerged on the scene rather suddenly as a follower of Schelling who had drawn a line between Fichte and Schelling in support of Schelling's understanding of what was required for the post-Kantian project. Despite that general reception, however, the work was not a purely Schellingian effort. In his efforts to mold himself into a systematic philosopher, he began by defending Schelling's own ideas and terminology in a different way than Schelling himself had done, bringing to bear on this task his own, very similar ideas that he had worked out in his conversations with Hölderlin in Frankfurt. The result was a highly original, "Hegelian" text that nonetheless offered itself to the public as a piece of "Schellingian" philosophy. It also showed that Hegel was hard at work during this period on the most fundamental issues in the development of post-Kantian idealism and was always more than merely a political or religious thinker.

Schelling was widely viewed by the philosophical public at the time as simply carrying forward Fichte's philosophy. Hegel surprised his readers by arguing that Schelling and Fichte disagreed at the most basic level on exactly what it would take to carry forward Kant's project without falling into what were perceived as Kant's own dogmatisms. Reinhold had proposed that what Kantianism needed was a clear statement of its highest and first principle, which he claimed to have provided with his "principle of consciousness," and Fichte had to a certain extent (in Hegel's reconstruction of the line of post-Kantian thought) only taken that approach one step further. In Hegel's construction of the progress made in post-Kantian thought, Reinhold and Fichte had not fully liberated themselves from certain Kantian "dogmatisms," whereas Schelling had fully done so.

In particular, both Reinhold and Fichte assumed that the Kantian distinction between "conceptual form" and "intuited content" was valid. However, in Schelling's and Hegel's eyes, Kant had already intimated in his later *Critique of Judgment* a way out of the various impasses created by his notions of unknowable things-in-themselves and contradictory conceptions of "unconditioned totalities" by developing a notion of an "intuitive intellect," a form of understanding that did not apply concepts to pre-given material from the senses but understood the sensory particulars in light of a prior grasp of the "whole" that was constructed by "reason." Kant seemed to be suggesting, that is, that prior to the application of conceptual form to sensuous givens, there had to be an orientation to a whole that preceded and made intelligible the later, more derivative application of such conceptual form to sensuous content. Reinhold (and by implication, Fichte), in effect, had stayed mired in Kant's original formulations and had therefore been led to their conclusions that Kantianism only required a clearer statement of its "first principle" as the ultimate condition for the possibility of there being experience of objects, which meant that they still dogmatically accepted Kant's dualism of conceptual form / nonconceptual content that would make such a search for "first principles" appropriate at all.[81]

In Hegel's presentation, therefore, the difference between Fichte and Schelling was a fundamental difference in what they understood the post-Kantian project to be about. Fichte, by seeking a first principle, was inevitably led to seeing the "I" as that principle, and he thus could only understand the "Not-I" as something posited by the "I"; he was thus a "subjective" idealist. Realism is simply the flip side of subjective idealism, understanding the "first principle" to lie on the side of the object, not the subject. As Hegel explained it, "dogmatic idealism posits the subjective as the real ground of the objective, dogmatic realism the objective as the real ground of the subjective."[82] The endless oscillation within modern philosophy between realism and idealism, however, is only indicative of something deeper, of a set of shared presuppositions that neither the realists nor the idealists articulate, and for which Kant's notion of the conflicted nature of consciousness was the clue. Within our ordinary consciousness of ourselves and the world, there are necessarily two opposing points of view. When we regard ourselves "theoretically," objectively, we see ourselves as bodies in space and time subject to the same causal laws as other bodies; when we regard ourselves "practically," subjectively, we see ourselves in terms of what we *ought* to believe, that as, as freely subject to norms. The subject of consciousness can thus take both a purely personal, subjective point of view on himself, seeing things from "within" his own experience; and he can take a detached, purely objective point of view on himself, seeing himself, as it were, from the outside. We see ourselves from the "inside" when we think of ourselves only in first-person terms as having a point of view *on* the world around us. We see ourselves from the "outside" when we think of ourselves as objects *in* a world of other objects (for example, locating ourselves on a map, seeing ourselves as others see us, or thinking of ourselves in third-person terms). That is, we see ourselves as a subjective point of view on the world and experience ourselves as spontaneous and free from that subjective point of view; we also see ourselves objectively, not as a point of view *on* the world but as another object *in* the world. As Hegel noted, "The opposition [between realism and idealism] is in consciousness, and the reality of the objective, just as much as that of the subjective is founded in consciousness."[83]

Hegel diagnosed the futility of such a search for "first principles" that would resolve the modern debate between "realism" and "idealism" as having to do with what he called "reflection." In the technical sense that Hegel used it, "reflection" designated an approach to philosophical thought that takes one of the basic oppositions in consciousness (the subjective or objective point of view) and then holds it fixed and uses it as a basis for constructing or criticizing the other point of view. The purpose of true philosophy is to show that the kind of "reflection" that takes itself to be necessarily driven to the antinomial oppositions of Kantian philosophy is actually implicated in something that precedes such opposition and without which such opposition would not be possible. Both Hegel and Schelling called that the "absolute," which Hegel identified with reason itself. Moreover, just as Kant in the *Critique of Pure Reason* had said that "reason has insight only into that which it produces after a plan of its own," Hegel says in the *Difference* book that "reason comes to know itself and deals only with itself so that its whole work and activity are grounded in itself."[84]

Hegel contrasts reason with "the understanding." "The understanding" is a faculty *conditioned* by the world, but reason is a faculty that takes the conditioned findings of "the understanding" and weaves them into an *unconditioned* account of subjectivity and objectivity, of the personal and the objective points of view. "The understanding" must work on things given to it, whereas reason works only on materials it has given itself, "after a plan of its own"; reason is self-bounding and therefore "infinite," whereas "the understanding" is bounded by things outside of itself and therefore "finite." Reason aims at a grasp of the "unconditioned totality" that must include and resolve the oppositions of "the understanding" within itself.

When "the understanding" tries to grasp something fundamental about a way of life, it inevitably ends up positing the kinds of oppositions that also appear in the unending debates between "realism" and "idealism." When this happens, the form of life has become, to use a term that is increasingly crucial for Hegel, *entzweit*, "disjointed," "severed," "ruptured," within itself. Hegel's conception of this kind of rupturing, disjointing, *Entzweiung*, was already at work in his unpublished essay on the need for Württemberg reform written while he was in Frankfurt – "That the Magistrates Must be Elected by the Citizens." In that essay, he had spoken of the way in which the "yearning . . . for a more pure, more free condition had moved all hearts and severed (*entzweit*) them from actuality."[85] This kind of disjointing – *Entzweiung*, splitting in two – creates the need for philosophy. As Hegel puts it, "When the might of union vanishes from the life of people, and the oppositions lose their living connection and reciprocity and gain independence, the need of philosophy arises."[86] The failure of philosophy (and its alliance with reason) to perform this task is indicative of a form of life whose fate is gradually to deteriorate and pass away, as happened with the Greeks and Romans.[87] For Hegel the implication in all this is clear, even if he does not state it: The issue of whether modern life can succeed in Germany and in general depends on the possibility of *philosophy's* showing *whether* that way of life is indeed a possibility for us.

The need for philosophy thus arises out of a need for social life to overcome or heal its internal ruptures. It most certainly is not the need for some new, alternative authority that would replace the older authorities that have lost their hold on people. Philosophy, that is, does not replace the older system of religion with its "system." In an 1802 reproach to the notorious defender of modern skepticism, G. E. Schulze – who had argued that philosophy had historically failed to produce a proper "system" to guide people – Hegel responded by ridiculing Schulze as having "presented the relation between philosophy and the public as that between a [state] administration and a people; the philosopher would hold the office of Pastoral Duty for the People's Reason and would have taken the duty upon itself to construct for the people a constitutional philosophy and to administer the People's Reason."[88] The implication was obvious: philosophy can and should aspire to no such thing.

The kinds of "disjointing" that philosophy treats thus depend on the way of life itself and what "counts" for it. As examples of dualisms that were important in the past, Hegel lists "spirit and matter, soul and body, faith and intellect, freedom and necessity," which, as he notes, "used to be important" but which have been supplanted in our time by the opposition between subjectivity and objectivity.[89]

In trying to heal those ruptures, philosophy does not propose new and alternative explanations of the phenomena so much as it tries to shift the nature of the questions being asked about what ultimately counts, what is normative for us – as Hegel put it in the journal he kept during his years in Jena, "The questions which philosophy does not answer are answered in that they should not be so posed."[90] In the case of the rupture between the "subjective" and the "objective" points of view, philosophy therefore had to ask if there was necessarily a viewpoint that included both of them and in terms of which they both are derivative.

Both the subjective and the objective points of view are, however, *our* points of view, and the opposition between them is an opposition within "us." Consciousness, as a subjective awareness of an objective world, can in fact only be possible if the same agent can assume both points of view within himself. The point of view of consciousness presupposes therefore that the conscious agent have a grasp on something that is itself neither subjective nor objective, a unity of thought and the world, or conceptual form and sensuous content, that is prior to any such division between them. The "absolute" is thus the unity of subject and object, the unity of thought and being that underlies all our disrupted consciousness of ourselves and our world.

The dispute between realism and idealism thus had to be over the deeper ground and unity of what Hegel in the *Difference* essay called the "subjective subject-object" and the "objective subject-object." The unity of those points of view – what Hegel calls a "subject-object" – must include within itself a conception of how our subjective experience relates to a world of objects. However, there are two ways of misconstruing this "absolute," paralleling the oppositions of "realism" and "idealism." A "subjective subject-object," as he calls it, would be a conception of objects as constructed out of subjectivity; an "objective subject-object" would have to be a conception of how the character of our experience is determined by the way in which objects interact with our minds. Any conception of the world as being somehow a construct or a "posit" out of our experiences thus has to be a "subjective subject-object"; any conception of what is normative for our experience as deriving merely from the causal product of our interactions with nature or a grasp of some extra-mental item that determines in turn how we are to judge it would have to be an "objective subject-object."

Since we find ourselves in our own conscious lives always embodying both the objective and the subjective points of view, the temptation is always to try to eliminate the incompatibility by constructing one point of view in terms of the other. Fichtean idealism, for example, attempts to construct the world out of the subjective positings of the "I," and thus embodies the strategy of constructing everything out of a "subjective subject-object." All materialists do exactly the opposite. (In the *Difference* essay, Hegel actually defends materialism against Reinhold's objections, arguing that Reinhold has failed to take seriously the intellectual motivations that would make someone into a materialist.) Schelling, on the other hand, has seen that both points of view are necessary to account for conscious life, "so that the absolute presents itself in each of the two subject-objects, and finds itself perfected only in both together as the highest synthesis in the nullification of both insofar as they are opposed."[91] In Schelling's terminology, the "absolute" must be therefore the "indifference point" of the subjective and objective points of view.

Hegel thus supplied a kind of argument for the absolute that was only adumbrated in Schelling's formulations but which, so Hegel thought, was nonetheless implicit in such formulations. He also supplied what he no doubt took to be the missing argument for the necessity of "intellectual intuition." That we can entertain the opposition of the subjective and objective points of view in *one* consciousness could not be explained by either the subjective or objective point of view itself; therefore, the explanation had to be in terms of something that included each as factors within itself, and this could only be the *intuitive awareness* of the *activity* of which both points of view are themselves constituted. It is an *intuition* in that it has an "object" (our *experience* of the unity of the two points of view) of which it is aware, namely, the activity that constitutes the two different points of view; and it is *intellectual* in that it is not sensuous while still being an awareness within conscious life of the constitution of these two points of view. Schelling's division of philosophy into transcendental philosophy (which explores things from the subjective point of view) and *Naturphilosophie*, which explores things from the objective point of view, is explained as being rooted in the

unity of the intuition of the absolute, of the self-limiting activity that
makes up the two points of view.

In putting it in this way, Hegel was subtly trying to pull Schelling
back toward Kant via the ideas he had worked out with Hölderlin in
Frankfurt. At the outset of the *Difference* essay, Hegel claimed that
Kant's "Transcendental Deduction of the Categories" is indeed the
authentic (*echter*) idealism in its spirit, not its letter.[92] That spirit had to
do with what the post-Kantians had taken to calling "pure speculation,"
whereas the letter had to do with the oppositions set by "the understanding" from within the Kantian system itself. Even there, however,
Hegel characterized "speculation" in very Kantian terms, as the "activity of the one universal reason [directed] on itself" which thereby
"grasps its own grounding within itself" – thereby echoing Kant's own
claim that "reason must in all its undertakings subject itself to criticism
. . . [and] reason depends on this freedom for its very existence."[93]

"Faith and Knowledge": Kant's Way out of Kant

It was one thing to analyze the fundamental oppositions in philosophy
as stemming from a misunderstanding by the "reflective understanding"
about the unity of the absolute. Hegel, however, had larger targets in
mind. One year following the publication of his *Difference* essay, Hegel
again took up the related themes of how fundamental oppositions surface within a way of life and their relation to philosophical thought in
an extended essay in the *Critical Journal of Philosophy* published in 1802
called "Faith and Knowledge or the *Reflective Philosophy of Subjectivity*
in the Complete Range of Its Forms as Kantian, Jacobian, and Fichtean
Philosophy."[94] In that piece, he argued that there was more at stake
than just a set of merely theoretical philosophical errors, that in fact the
culture (*Kultur*) of his own time had come to be based on *reflection*, and
that Kant's, Jacobi's, and Fichte's "philosophies have to be recognized
as nothing more but the culture of reflection raised to a system. This is
the culture of the ordinary human understanding."[95] The errors of
philosophy were only expressions of a deeper malaise in the culture
itself.[96]

In putting matters this way, Hegel was also throwing into question
something he had long held dear, the value of *Bildung*. If to become
"cultivated" and "formed" were features of the "culture" of the time,

and the culture of the time was itself fraught with ruptures within itself, then acquiring *Bildung* – doing the kind of thing his parents had done and which he had been raised to do – would by itself not be enough. *Bildung* required something beyond what it had traditionally included, namely, the kind of systematic philosophy Hegel was now advocating.

The modern "culture of reflection" is in fact the "culture" whose basic characteristics have been expressed by the philosophies of Locke and Hume, according to which the task of philosophy can be only to have "the world assessed and from now on explained from the stand point of the subject."[97] At its best, "reflection" can produce only a more or less coherent ordering of the assertions emerging from taking one of those points of views as fixed, not a resolution of the fundamental division between them.[98] The result is a proliferation of "systems" of philosophy, each with its own degree of plausibility, and no apparent way of settling the disputes among them.

In positing one of the sides of the subject-object dualism as more basic than the other, as explaining somehow how the other acquires its determinateness, both such Lockean and Kantian "reflective" philosophies invariably degenerate into some form of psychologism. That is, they inevitably lead to some kind of theory about how the "operations of the mind" are structured by certain laws such that the mind performs these operations on some discrete bit of experiential data so as to produce the experienced world. If, after all, one operates with the picture of the world (of the set of things-in-themselves) as *interacting* with a subject (either by causing intuitions, as Kant says, or by causing some even more generally conceived *Anstoß*, some "check" or "impingement," as Fichte says), and one goes along with the picture of "mind" (or the "I") "processing" the "data" according to its own set of laws to produce the world of appearance (which can never be said to be the same as the world-in-itself), then of course it makes sense to ask for the laws governing this kind of operation. Philosophies of reflection are thus led to some picture of one set of principles being *applied* to some given data to produce a product that is somehow the unity of both; the paradigm becomes that of *application* of a scheme to some given *content* rather than *development* of both from something else.

Hegel argued that Jacobi's thought formed an especially interesting case because Jacobi wished to deny the Kantian and Fichtean picture of the mind's "processing data" or "applying" forms to some given content while holding onto the basic picture of subject and object that drove Kant and Fichte to their own conclusions. Rejecting both Kant and Fichte as transcendental skeptics, Jacobi is simply left with a great divide between subject and object which he bridges by the deus ex machina of positing that we *just immediately know* that there is a world external to our experiences and a God that answers to our need for Him. (In both cases, Jacobi calls this immediate knowledge "faith.") Jacobi, however, could only come to this conclusion if in the first place he took "the [transcendental] imagination and self-originating reason as something arbitrary and subjective, and . . . sensuous experience as eternal truth."[99] That is, Jacobi is led into his doctrine that we *just know* that there is a world out there *because* he psychologizes Kant's and Fichte's points.

Hegel's point was that one could not simply write off Jacobi's strategy as only a psychologistic misunderstanding of Kant and Fichte, since their philosophies inevitably require such a reading. Since we cannot say what things-in-themselves are, we are inevitably led back to the idea that it is "we" (or the "transcendental I") that put the relations of causality onto "givens," and once we begin to reflectively focus on what we mean by saying that we put these constructions on things, "transcendental idealism has passed over into this formal or more properly, psychological idealism."[100] That is, the idea that *we transcendentally* apply the categories to the givens of experience quickly passes over into the idea that the categories are simply something that we *humans* just "project" onto experience.[101] Thus, "Kantian, and more particularly Fichtean philosophy are forever sliding into this psychological idealism."[102] This is the consequence of "explaining the world from the standpoint of the subject." Kantian and Fichtean idealisms are thus essentially "dualisms" and are "nothing more than an extension of Lockeanism."[103]

In saying all that, though, Hegel proposed what he saw as Kant's own way out of Kant's troubles. Despite his dualism of "concept" and "intuition," Kant had come to the conclusion that there could be no "unsynthesized intuitions" of which we could be conscious, that is, that there is nothing in experience that is simply "immediately given," of which we can be aware without having to be in possession of any conceptual faculties or that we can know without having to know anything else: As Hegel puts it, indirectly quoting Kant himself, "The

Kantian philosophy has the merit of being idealism because it does show that neither the concept in isolation nor intuition in isolation is anything at all; that intuition by itself is blind and the concept by itself is empty."[104] Both concepts and intuitions are "moments" within the whole that is consciousness. They are not independent elements that must be somehow brought together and combined in order for consciousness to come to be. Furthermore, Kant himself seemed to acknowledge as much when he argued that the synthetic unity of consciousness was original, that is, underived, and formed the basis of everything found within consciousness. Hegel makes the point thus: "The original synthetic unity must be conceived, not as produced out of opposites, but as a truly necessary, absolute, original identity of opposites."[105] The "opposites" here are concepts and intuitions, which are "identical" because they are only constituents of a whole, which Hegel identifies with "the absolute and original identity of self-consciousness."[106]

On Hegel's view, Kant argued otherwise only because he was in the grip of a "reflective," dualistic picture of the mind as consisting of separate elements that had to be psychologically combined instead of a picture of the mind as having various "moments" within its overall organic unity. Thus, Kant was led to argue that transcendental philosophy must supply the *rule of application* for its concepts, that is, its categories, and it must do this a priori.[107] In making that move, Kant thus shifted the focus of transcendental philosophy away from the *unity* of experience as oriented to a "whole" and toward the *application* of categories to the "given." The application of the categories to the givens of sensuous intuition, however, requires some kind of *interplay* between the two faculties, that is, some kind of mediation between the pure categorial concepts (the "scheme") and the empirical intuitions (the "content") to which they are "applied." Kant, of course, concluded that time had to be that intermediary, since it is both pure (a priori) and empirical (it is a form of intuition, that is, a form in which objects can be "given" to us); and since all representations appear in what Kant calls "inner sense," everything appears in time. Kant calls this intermediary the *schematism*, with the schema being a system of rules that applies the category to an object of sense and which thereby gives the otherwise empty category its determinateness, or its "meaning" (*Bedeutung*). The schema is set up by the faculty Kant calls the productive imagination, and Kant himself notes that how it does this – apply the rules – is a mystery.[108]

Hegel scoffed at the very idea that Kant needed to have any such doctrine of schematism, arguing that the only reason for introducing it had to do with his "reflective" conception of the mind as "processing" discrete data in the first place. Indeed, if one pursued Kant's line of thought vis-à-vis the notion of an original, underived unity of self-consciousness instead of his idea of consciousness as divided into distinct faculties of concept and intuition, then the productive imagination itself would be seen *not* as an intermediary but as the original unity *itself*: "This power of imagination is the original two-sided identity. The identity becomes subject in general on one side and object on the other; but originally it is both. And the imagination is nothing but reason itself . . . as it appears in the sphere of empirical consciousness."[109]

What in Kantian idealism had therefore looked like a division into two distinct faculties of spontaneity and receptivity (of "the understanding" and "intuition") really involved an original unity in which spontaneity was already at work in what only seemed to be the sheer givenness of experience. It is not so much that we *receive* contents in our experience of the world as we *take up* our experience in a kind of spontaneous activity. Thus, the model of "reflection" – that we apply a formal "scheme" to a sensible "content" – does not actually fit what Kant says about productive imagination. In *taking up* a content, we are not *applying* anything to a "given" so much as we are actively *orienting* ourselves in experience by *attending* to various manifestations of the world to us or by actively taking up certain incentives to action by determining our will in accordance with them. Hegel identifies this "taking up" as the *appropriating* of the manifold of sense as spontaneity.[110] However, this spontaneity is not simply free, unattached activity, as if one had an inert world on one side and a free-spinning spontaneity on the other side. Rather, it must be conceived as an active taking up of something, of a way in which the world manifests itself to us by virtue of our taking up its manifestations to us.

In the *Difference* essay, this was called "intellectual intuition," but, significantly, Hegel does not put that term to such use in "Faith and Knowledge," although a similar idea is at work there. In "Faith and Knowledge," Hegel is more concerned to show how Kant in particular is driven by the logic of his own thoughts to something like a doctrine of "intellectual intuition," and to show how the logic of Kant's philosophy also indicates a way out of dependence on "intellectual intuition."

In this light, Hegel focuses particularly on Kant's 1790 *Critique of Judgment*, especially §§76–77 of that work.[111] Kant argues there that we necessarily require a conception of a purposive whole for two kinds of judgments even if we can never infer that any such purposive whole actually exists.[112] Those judgments are those concerning, for example, organisms whose parts can only be understood in terms of their serving some function in the whole that is the organism; and those judgments about the beauty of certain natural objects and human artifacts.

What especially caught Hegel's eye was Kant's claim that since, first of all, we cannot do without the concept of purposiveness, and, second of all, we cannot say the world is actually purposive, we are led to the *regulative* idea of an intuitive intellect, in his terms, to "a complete spontaneity of intuition . . . a cognitive power different from and wholly independent of sensibility,"[113] which requires us to "conceive of an understanding that, unlike ours, is not discursive but intuitive, and hence proceeds from the *synthetically universal* (the intuition of a whole as a whole) to the particular, i.e., from the whole to the parts."[114] That is, we are led to the regulative idea of an intellect that actively takes up a teleological whole and elicits out of that whole what the parts *must* be, even if we cannot say that such an intuitive intellect actually exists. Kant added to this the extraordinary claim that we could regard thereby the "substrate" of the material world as a thing-in-itself and "regard this thing-in-itself as based on a corresponding intellectual intuition (even though not our own). In that way there would be for nature, which includes us as well, a supersensible basis of its reality, although this basis would necessarily remain beyond our cognitive grasp."[115] In the second introduction to the *Critique of Judgment*, Kant added that "judgment . . . provides nature's supersensible substrate (within as well as outside us) with *determinability* by the intellectual power . . . This judgment makes possible the transition from the domain of the concept of nature to that of the concept of freedom."[116]

Hegel seized on Kant's idea that he had provided a link between nature and freedom in the reflective judgment, saying that Kant had found the "middle term" between the two, indeed, their "identity."[117] However, he charged Kant with *failing* to show that this idea of an intuitive intellect could *only* be regulative, a conception that although necessary for us to have, could not be said to actually exist. This was, Hegel argued, most clear in Kant's own explanation of judgments about the beautiful. The experience of the beautiful, on Kant's analysis of it, is intrinsically *normative*: As Kant puts it, "When we make a judgment declaring something to be beautiful . . . we cannot base it on experience; for it seeks to justify us in making judgments that contain an ought: It does not say that everyone *will* agree with my judgment, but that he *ought* to."[118] (Kant makes the same kinds of claims about teleological judgments.)[119]

The difference between teleological and aesthetic judgments, Kant says, is that the former are objective while the latter are subjective. By this Kant means that in making teleological judgments, I judge that an *object* is as it *ought* to be in fulfilling its purpose. (Kant's cited the eye as an example of such an object.)[120] If I judge it merely in terms of mechanical laws, I make no such normative judgment: A defective eye violates no rules of physics; its defectiveness lies in its failure to achieve the *purpose* of seeing. On the other hand, when I make an aesthetic judgment that something is beautiful, I make a judgment that *others should judge it as I do*, that is, that the object *ought* to be judged as *I* judge it.

In teleological judgments, therefore, I judge that the object ought to *be* a certain way; in aesthetic judgment, I judge that the object ought to *be judged* in a certain way.[121] Furthermore, I do not claim that the *object* that is being judged is defective if somebody fails to judge it as it ought to be judged; I am judging that *my judging* the object to be beautiful is as *it* ought to be, and that my *judging* (or the other's judging) is defective if it is not as it ought to be. I cannot state a *rule* for this, except to say that others ought to judge as *I* judge (a normativity that Kant calls "exemplary" necessity).[122] Kant (infamously) called this "purposiveness without a purpose," by which he apparently meant that although my judgment is normative (purposive), it has no specific rule to guide it (it is without a purpose).[123]

Yet in making the self-referential (exemplary) normative judgment that others *ought* to judge as I do (and hence come to feel the same aesthetic pleasure that I do), I am also making the normative judgment that I ought to be judging as others (who have taste) do. That is, I seem to be presupposing that my own subjective *tastes* (that is, judgments) are also universal, or at least universally communicable. (My own subjective *pleasures* may not and need not be so universally communicable.) In making normative aesthetic judgments, therefore, we seem to be engaged in a non–rule bound way of *adjusting* our own judgments of tastes to what others ideally *would* do and of making normative demands on others as to what kinds of judgments they therefore *should* make. We presuppose, that is, that a community of rational beings would have to *mutually* adjust their own judgments of taste so as to maintain the normative force of their own judgments.[124]

This only shows, Hegel argues, that the experience of beauty on Kant's own terms demonstrates that "the opposition between intuition and concept falls away."[125] I cannot perceive the beautiful by just receptively taking in some experience and then applying a formal norm to that experience. Rather, in order to have the aesthetic perception, I must already have a sense of myself as situated in a larger whole, namely, the community of rational agents in terms of which I adjust my reflective judgments as to what I am experiencing and who, I must presuppose, are also adjusting their reflective judgments to the normative demands I place on them. However, this implies that this *reflective* judgment cannot therefore be a matter of *reflection* (in the sense that Hegel uses it), since it does not involve the *application* of any norm to some given content. The pleasure that comes from the aesthetic judgment about an object is not a sensation, not any kind of elemental "vibration" in experience, but a pleasure that is the feeling that my cognitive powers are working *as they ought to*; it is a pleasure that results from my grasp of their harmonious "free play," from the self-legislating *spontaneity* of the mind. Most importantly, Kant seems to be saying that I impose a norm on myself by adjusting my judgments in light of a prior *orientation* toward what I take other rational agents to be doing.[126] This self-orienting must be presupposed in order for me to make any reflective aesthetic judgment at all. The problem, of course, is, as Kant admits, that this orientation is itself rather indeterminate and general; the important point, however, is that it cannot be a matter of rules, since it is the community of rational agents themselves that are legislating the rules for themselves in a kind of idealized form of mutual imposition as mutual adjustment of judgments.

Kant's conception of aesthetic judgment as involving mutual adjustment of judgments thus gave Hegel a new way of thinking about something that had long bothered him. The author of the "The Oldest

System Program in German Idealism" had stated that the *state* could not be a realization of freedom, since the state was only a Hobbesian or Wolffian social "machine." But in exploring the *Critique of Judgment*, Hegel must have taken notice – although he does not mention it in "Faith and Knowledge" – of the crucial footnote in which Kant had explicitly compared his idea of the way in which we judge organisms to be purposive to the way in which "a" society had been similarly "read-justed" by recent political events (almost certainly an allusion on Kant's part to the American Revolution). In that note, Kant asserted, "For each member in such a whole should indeed be not merely a means but also an end; and while each member contributes to making the whole possible, the Idea of that whole should in turn determine the member's position and function."[127] Hegel would have seen Kant's enticing analogy between the intrinsic purposiveness of organisms and rational social life to be further support for his notion of the way the Kantian conception of aesthetic judgment should be developed beyond the realm of aesthetic judgments per se.

In "Faith and Knowledge," Hegel still retained much of Schelling's explanatory apparatus for expressing all these claims even as he was starting to depart from Schelling's own specific employment of the apparatus. Thus, he accounted for this mutual adjustment of judgment by invoking Schelling's notion of there being a "potency" (*Potenz*) in each level of things that is raised to a higher "potency" by virtue of the tensions within it. The higher "potency" of the original identity of intuition and understanding is "the understanding" itself. The original unity of self-consciousness has its lower "potency" in the multiplicity of sensuous intuitions, and when this original identity "simultaneously sets itself against the manifold, and constitutes itself within itself as universality, which is what makes it a higher potency," then it constitutes within one and the same consciousness "the understanding," which itself must be taken only as a more developed function within the whole (or the "identity") that is conscious life.[128] (And, like Schelling, Hegel is drawn to the image of the magnet as the proper metaphor for this activity.)[129] Since this reflective judgment requires some orientation, Hegel concluded, rather strikingly and without much argument, that the idea of the intuitive intellect was not a *regulative* ideal at all but the "Idea of the transcendental imagination that we considered above."[130]

What gives "reflective" philosophy its appeal over and against such philosophies of the absolute, so Hegel argued, is its partial, one-sided assumption of the revolution in philosophy that was brought about in Kant's works. It embodied what he called the "coloration of inwardness" and the tendencies of the most recent "fashionable culture," namely, the notion that the "subject" must assume his own freedom, learn to think for himself, and choose his own ends. The "philosophies of reflection" therefore are not written off by Hegel as mistakes so much as they are seen as the penultimate stage of (or as evidence for) the completion of the historical process that has seen its political expression in the Revolution. This final stage can only come about through the offices of systematic philosophy, which by introducing us to the absolute reestablishes "the Idea of absolute freedom and along with it the absolute passion, the speculative Good Friday that was otherwise only the historical Good Friday."[131] Hegel was probing once again his notion of radically reinterpreting religion in terms of idealist philosophy, of finding in Christianity the practice by which this "mutual adjustment" of judgments could be carried out in a modern, reconciliatory way.

1802–1804: The Embryonic Hegelian System

Recognition and Social Life: The Break with Hölderlin's Conception

Hegel's viewpoint was rapidly evolving, and more hints of its direction can be gleaned from several works written between 1802 and 1804. One was a long essay published in parts in the *Critical Journal of Philosophy* in 1802 and 1803: "On the Scientific Ways of Treating Natural Law, Its Place in Practical Philosophy, and Its Relation to the Positive Sciences of Law."[132] Around the same time, Hegel worked on two manuscripts, neither of which were published in his lifetime: a set of lecture notes (including what is now known as the "First Philosophy of Spirit") and a lengthy sketch of part of his whole system, which has become known under the title the editors gave it, the *System of Ethical Life* (*System der Sittlichkeit*), a topic on which Hegel was lecturing at the time.[133] In those works, Hegel was still attempting to bring his Frankfurt position into line with his newly adopted Schellingian views, combining those two influences in developing his own views vis-à-vis his long-standing interest in the developing political situations in France and

Germany, Hegel ended up extending Schelling's ideas in ways that find
little parallel in Schelling's own thought.[134] Most importantly, he was
led to take one of the most crucial and decisive steps toward formulating
his own distinctive view.

In the essay on "Natural Right," Hegel took on what he saw as the
two modern false starts in understanding natural rights: the empiricist,
psychologistic theories of natural right typified by Hobbes and Locke,
and the transcendental theories of natural right, typified by Kant and
Fichte. The essay developed at some length what he took to be their
myriad failures to acknowledge their hidden presuppositions, and he
diagnosed the basic reason for such failure to be the way in which both
types of theories attempted to develop a conception of a social "whole"
out of the idea of a social contract among individuals already vested
with normative authority outside of that social whole. Both of them
failed, in Hegel's eyes, because they could not understand how individuals are only "potencies" of a larger social whole and ultimately of the
"absolute," that is, ultimately "potencies" of "spirit."[135]

To explain this, Hegel also brought into play a Fichtean idea of
mutual "recognition" that gave him the key for which he had been
looking in his attempts to work out his own views vis-à-vis Schelling's
and Hölderlin's.[136] Hölderlin had convinced Hegel in Frankfurt that
Fichte's own procedure was too "subjective"; one simply could not
begin with the "subject's" certainty of itself and then ask how the
"subject" manages to posit a world of "objects"; instead, one must
begin with a commitment to an unarticulated unity of subject and
object, which Hölderlin considered to be implicitly, nondiscursively in
play in all the activities of our conscious lives. Hegel's great insight in
1802 had been to develop Hölderlin's point that one cannot begin with
an isolated, individual subject experiencing the world and then ask how
a world of objective experience gets built up out of the "inner" world
of purely subjective experience; one must begin with an already *shared*
world of subjects *in* a world making judgments in light of the "possible
judgments" of others (the theme developed out of Kant's third *Critique*
in "Faith and Knowledge"). In 1803, Hegel developed that idea further:
The "original unity" was not to be articulated in terms of Hölderlin's
conception of a nondiscursive grasp of "Being"; it was to be understood
as an *intersubjective* unity, a unity of *mutually recognizing agents* in the

natural world. In the *System of Ethical Life*, his term for this unity was "absolute ethical life."

This concept of "recognition" gave Hegel a nondualistic, yet also nonreductionist account of the relation between spirit and nature. Hegel argued that the "ethical life" (*Sittlichkeit*) of any particular "people" must be construed entirely in terms of the patterns of entitlements and commitments that those individuals confer and sustain by acts of mutual recognition; it must not be construed as any kind of separate realm requiring its own special causal powers, nor as simply the result of a natural process. The difference between spirit and nature is thus not that between two different types of substance; it lies in the way in which humans are led to self-consciously *regard* themselves, to establish points of view *on* the world in addition to being natural entities *in* that world. "Spirit," as Hegel put it, "is the absolute intuition of itself as itself (or absolute knowing)."[137]

Moreover, we articulate this intersubjective unity in different ways depending on the purposive contexts in which we find ourselves. At any given moment, either "concepts" or "intuitions" can be playing the preponderant role in our conscious life. When our consciousness of things is preponderantly intuitive – when we are primarily aware of particular items and things – the conceptual element in experience is muted and blurred (but not absent); Hegel calls this the "subsumption of the concept under intuition." It is that aspect of conscious life in which the appearance of things as simply being "given" to us is strongest. For example, our "practical feelings" (called the "practical potency") of the need for something as elemental as food appears to us as an "intuitive" awareness of a singular and seemingly just "given" need for a particular object, and the element of conceptual (normative) activity at work in such needs is submerged within our consciousness. Nonetheless, even in those cases of the "concept's being subsumed under intuition," we still see things *as* such and such, for example, our seeing an apple *as* the *kind* of thing that would satisfy hunger, so that our "taking up" of the manifold of sense incorporates the elemental conceptual mediating activity at work in it.

On the other hand, when the element of conceptual mediation is more obviously in view, as when we perceive something *as* a tool, we have a case of "intuition's being subsumed under the concept." Seeing something *as* a tool is seeing it more self-consciously in terms of certain "concepts" it instantiates, in terms of the ways in which it fits into our practical projects. The intuition of apples thus *seems* like a "given," but the intuition of tools *seems* much less "given." Both ways of "seeming" are the result of the interplay of "concept" and "intuition" and of the relative weight each plays in their different purposive contexts.

We progress from being natural creatures with relatively straightforward organic needs to being complex laboring creatures who work in order to satisfy those needs; labor and its concomitant use of tools in turn raises us to being social creatures, mutually shaping each other through an even more complex process of "formative culture," *Bildung*, and this progression is articulated in the language of the "potencies."[138] The law-governed regularities of nature (the first "potency") are thus necessary for the normativity of social life (the second "potency"), but these normative features of human agency are not thereby reducible to these natural regularities. The great difference between the two kinds of life – organic and social – is that just as "the single individual was dominant in the first potency, the universal is dominant" at the potency of the social level.[139] Thus, in Hegel's preferred Schellingian way of putting the matter: "Man is potency, is universality for the other, but the other is just as much the same for him; and so he makes his reality, his unique being, his effecting this into himself into an incorporation into indifference, and he is now the universal in contrast to the first potency."[140]

Hegel returned to these themes a year later in 1803 and developed them even further. With Schelling's departure for Würzburg in the summer of 1803 the personal and professional demands of fitting his rapidly developing thought into Schellingian form began to ease, and in his lectures during this period Hegel took the opportunity to sharpen his own thoughts with the aim of producing his own system in the form of a book (which he desperately needed to secure a salaried position). What remains of the lecture notes written between 1803 and 1806 has become known to us as the *Jena System Drafts* (*Jenaer Systementwürfe*).[141]

In the 1803–04 manuscripts, there is much more emphasis on the notion of "consciousness" than there is in, for example, the *System of Ethical Life*, but the lines of thought are fairly continuous. Hegel uses the perception of color to illustrate how the "potencies" work in explaining sensuous "consciousness." There is first of all the sheer givenness of the sensation of color, but "spirit as sensing is itself animal, submerged in nature."[142] This first "potency" does not give us the consciousness of color but merely the animal-like discrimination of color. To have *consciousness* of a color, one must be able to *report* on the experience, and one's report on the experience (as a sensing of blue, for example) is a *correct* report only if it is sanctioned as reasonable according to the norms of one's linguistic community. For the agent to be able to make such a normatively correct report, a particular sensation of color must be taken up by him and inferentially linked to other color concepts, and he must, moreover, be able to understand a "particular" sensing of blue as an instance of the "general" color blue. Thus, there are three such "potencies": in Hegel's own words, "[1] in sensation as determinateness of blue, for example, and [2] then as concept, formally and ideally related to others as names, as opposed to them and at the same time as identical with them in that they are colors, and [3] in this, simply, universally as color."[143] (These three "potencies" for Hegel correspond to the functions in consciousness of sensation, imagination, and memory.)

"Consciousness" mediates between the individual agent and "spirit." The individual organic agent comes to be conscious of the natural world insofar as he manages to respond judgmentally, normatively, and not merely habitually to nature: not merely to have sensations of blue or to be able to discriminate blue things from non-blue things but to be able to report that he is experiencing blue and to *evaluate* that report in terms of whether it meets the standards of correctness held by his linguistic community. (That is, to be able to say both things like, "That looks blue to me," *and*, "Oh, it's not really blue, it only *looked* blue.") The norms for being able to respond appropriately to episodes of sensing blue by saying things like, "That's blue" or "That's funny; it looked blue in that light," are relative to the relevant linguistic community; or, as Hegel puts it, "the preceding potencies, in general, are ideal, they exist for the first time in a people: *Language only is as the language of a people*, and *understanding* and *reason* likewise."[144]

In the 1803–04 manuscripts, the notion of "recognition" received some substantial reworking. The Kantian idea of "mutual adjustment of judgments" in "Faith and Knowledge" became transmuted into an original *struggle* for recognition that possessed its own logic. Agents, as

occupying a particular physical part of the world and having a subjective, personal point of view on that world necessarily *appear to each
other* as *particular* points of view, as "excluding" each other: As Hegel
puts it, "each appears in the consciousness of the other as that which
excludes him from the whole extension of his individuality," and this
leads to a struggle to determine whose point of view is to be normatively
dominant.[145] Since there is no given objective point of view to which
the agents can turn to resolve such epistemic disputes between themselves, they must struggle to the death. The reasoning in the rather
condensed lecture notes of 1803–04 seems to be that each agent must
orient and situate himself with some conception of a "whole" of such
judgments, and thus each at first claims to be that "whole," an "absolute
consciousness," not as a matter of fulfilling some Hobbesian desire for
power or security, but in order to be recognized simply "as rational, as
totality in truth."[146] He who capitulates, who would rather live than risk
his life to preserve his claims to being an "absolute consciousness,"
becomes "for the other immediately a non-totality, he is not absolutely
for himself, he becomes the slave of the other."[147]

This lopsidedness of recognition – its going one way and not the
other – is, he says, an "absolute contradiction," something that cannot
be sustained.[148] He who becomes the slave is posited in the relationship
as someone whose claims to knowledge and truth can only be interpreted as being subordinate to somebody else's point of view, and the
slave thus becomes the type of being who is incapable of bestowing the
recognition that is necessary upon those for whom he is the slave. In
his lecture notes, Hegel concluded that the mutual failure at securing
such recognition compels both agents to acknowledge and develop that
"absolutely universal consciousness" within themselves that makes it
possible to conciliate their respective positions.[149] (In the surviving lecture fragments, this is as far as the argument goes; the rest of the
surviving notes after the section on recognition are short, but they
indicate that Hegel intended to carry out his argument in a similar vein
to that found in the *System of Ethical Life*; the problems of economic
dependence treated in the earlier manuscript are also articulated through
examples taken directly from Adam Smith – at one point Hegel invokes
Smith's notion of the division of labor in a "pin factory" only to argue
that it is only "machinelike" and therefore ultimately degrading to
people.)

In the unpublished *System of Ethical Life* Hegel showed that he was struggling to put this new conception of "spirit" and "freedom" into play as a conception of how freedom is both a necessary feature of agency and something that is to be socially achieved. For us to understand the ways in which we deny or affirm that we or others are entitled to certain claims to knowledge or rights to action, we must understand the more fundamental unity in which such recognitional activities and statuses operate as an "Idea" of reason: As he put it, since the "Idea" is the "identity of concept and intuition," we must always be operating with a notion, however obscure, of what it would mean to "get it right" in our judgmental activities.[150]

But it was also clear that we did not always "get it right" and that we have not always been in a position of freedom. That has to do, so Hegel argued, with the *stance* we *assume* toward nature. Nature does not determine our stance toward it; *we* spontaneously determine that, and it is our "distance" from natural determination that determines how adequate our realization of freedom is. Thus, he noted that natural "life" always has an element of "inequality" to it, that some have more "power" than others, and that when encounters between agents occur without the right kind of social mediation, the result cannot be complete mutuality of recognition but instead must be relations of domination, of "lordship and bondage."[151]

Hegel took the transition point between nature and sociality to be the family as a social unit founded on natural relations (those between the sexes) but incorporating within itself normative commitments and ethical ideals. The family is the "supreme totality" – that is, the most complex normative unity – "of which nature is capable."[152] Other modes of sociality would then be founded on increasing departures from nature toward the ideal of "absolute ethical life," which would be completely "indwelling within individuals and is their essence,"[153] in which "the ethical life of the individual is one pulse beat of the whole system and is itself the whole system," and in which the stances individuals jointly assume toward each other are free from natural determination.[154] These increasing departures from nature toward sociality correspondingly mark increasingly adequate realizations of freedom (that is, of conditions under which the self-determination of norms rather than behavior according to natural regularities is possible). Following the family is therefore the economy, which arises out of the system of

natural needs, of work with tools, of the organization of labor and the
like; the economy eventually produces and gives way to what Hegel
calls an "absolute ethical totality," a people, a *Volk*, which is defined
not along ethnic or racial lines (that is, not in terms of nature) but in
terms of what ultimately collectively matters for it.[155] The "universality"
of a people "in which they are one is absolute indifference . . . in which
all natural difference is nullified,"[156] which implies (in the Schellingian
framework Hegel is using) that a "people" is not an unstable unity that
pushes itself on toward any higher set of "potencies."

   Nonetheless, a particular "people" is not the "absolute indifference,"
the point at which the tensions and oppositions in lower-order "potencies" no longer exist to drive the system on toward higher and higher
unities.[157] Behind all the different peoples is an unchanging spirit of
"humanity." Hegel noted that "the world-spirit, in every one of its
shapes, has enjoyed its self-awareness, weaker or more developed but
always absolute; it has enjoyed itself and its own essence in every nation
under every system of laws and customs" – an indication, if nothing
else, of just how strong was the hold that Hölderlin's ideas still exercised
on Hegel.[158] Rather than bring into play Schelling's notion of history as
the progressive revelation of God, Hegel stayed with the notion of *fate*
that he had worked out in the "Spirit of Christianity" and that had
been inspired by Hölderlin: Each people is destined to a "tragic fate,"
and the rise and fall of peoples is "the performance within the realm of
the ethical of the tragedy which the absolute eternally plays on itself.
. . . *Tragedy* consists in this, that ethical nature segregates its inorganic
nature (in order not to become embroiled in it) as a fate (*Schicksal*), and
places it outside itself; but by the recognition of this fate in its struggle
against it, ethical nature is reconciled with the divine essence as the
unity of both."[159] This conception of the way in which "spirit" appears
in different historical forms, the particular conception of fate and divinity, is virtually the same as that found in Hölderlin's own notes on
history and tragedy, an idea that informed much of Hölderlin's poetry
in his short, brilliantly creative period after 1800.[160] Thus, like Hölderlin, Hegel asserted that such "divinity" appears in forms relative to the
"people" for whom it is a divinity – "In this way the ideality as such
must be given a pure absolute shape, and so must be regarded and
worshipped as the nation's God."[161] In the *System of Ethical Life*, Hegel

makes it clear that he thinks that there is an "absolute" conception of divinity but that it appears in particular forms for different peoples – "This universality which has directly united the particular with itself is the divinity of the people, and this universal, intuited in the ideal form of particularity, is the God of the people."[162] Nonetheless, Hegel seems to think that history must have an overall unity, noting rather darkly that "over the single stages [of each shape of spirit] there floats the idea of totality which, however, is mirrored back by its whole scattered image, and sees and recognizes itself therein" – another, rather oblique reference to the views of his former Frankfurt companion.[163]

Cameralism, the Estates, and Modernity in Germany

These kinds of fundamental considerations permitted Hegel to return to the theme of Germanic freedom he had earlier discussed in the "German Constitution." The crucial issue was, again, that of the "fate" of "Germanic freedom" and its correlated notion of "representation." As he had done in "The German Constitution," Hegel argued that a legal organization of society into *estates* was necessary for a free people, and he knew that in arguing in this way he was going against the trend. The estates were already an outmoded institution in Hegel's own day, and, by 1802, they seemed clearly to be destined to vanish. An estate was a social grouping according to legally recognized social rank (which tended to correlate with economic status but was not equivalent to it) in which members had certain rights and privileges peculiar to that estate. The classical medieval distinction of the estates had sorted them into nobility, ecclesiastics, and commoners according to the formula of one estate doing the work, one estate being in charge of spiritual activities, and one estate doing the fighting necessary for the common defense (at least according to Philip de Vitry's virtually canonical 1335 description).[164] But as many had already recognized for quite some time, the category of those who did the "work" inadequately grouped together two very different economic groups: prosperous merchants and all the others who worked, including peasants. Even in the medieval world in which the tripartite division of the estates was most at home, the "townspeople" and the rural populations were still very different in wealth and power. By 1800, it seemed not only that the continued existence of the traditional estates was incompatible with the emerging sense of personal freedom in European life, but also that it was also putting a stranglehold on economic progress.

Hegel's argument for their continued existence rested on his radical reinterpretation of them as *ethical* unities instead of natural or primarily economic social formations. Each estate, he argued, was constituted by the type of shared *stance* that its members took toward themselves, each other, and members of other estates. Thus, even though between 1802 and 1803 Hegel divided the three estates in a way that more or less mirrored the conventional distinctions at work in German law at the time – nobility, *Bürger* (townsman), and peasant – he quite distinctively reinterpreted each of them: The estate of *Bürger* (townsmen) was about the principle of "uprightness" (*Rechtsschaffenheit*); the aristocracy was about courage; and the peasantry about the virtue of "simple trust" in the nobility.[165]

Hegel's ideas on the necessity of the estates were clearly colored by his reactions to German cameralism, a doctrine developed during the seventeenth and eighteenth centuries by and for German civil servants in the employment of various monarchs; the doctrine concerned itself with the proper methods for rationally administering a state with the goal of increasing its wealth. Cameralism assumed that society (specifically, German society) was in essence a harmonious whole and that the state should rationally administer the whole only so as to increase wealth for the state and should intervene in the workings of the social whole only in order to remedy distortions in it (for example, when individuals or groups were demanding more than their naturally just share or were engaged in activities that did not follow from their historical privileges).[166] Cameralism was a theory of *fiscal* administration, holding that fiscal tasks should be both administratively centralized and made more uniform; it was thus very much tied into the leading ideas of the German Enlightenment and its related concepts of "enlightened absolutism" and the state as a "machine." It did not hold that *society* itself should become more uniform, only that the rational, enlightened *administration* of society should become more uniform. According to cameralist theory, the fiscal administration of the "state" helped to *coordinate* the various corporate bodies of society; it did not *reform* them.[167]

Cameralism's highly flawed foundations came into clear view around 1803–06 as the Holy Roman Empire was starting to exhale its last breaths. Its most basic problem was that, given the complex, particularistic existence of the hometowns, the intrinsic harmony that it postulated in German society simply did not exist. After the first wave of reaction to revolutionary French incursions into Germany, cameralist theory necessarily, although only gradually, began to shift toward notions of centralized social reform. At that point, it seemed that the state could only pursue the goal of increasing its aggregate wealth by claiming sovereignty over all elements of society, that is, by claiming that all the local, particularized corporate bodies with their unwritten, centuries-old sets of norms and practices had to submit to the rationalizing dictates of the centralized administration.

This latter course, in effect, was the Prussian way, but Hegel had come to the conclusion in "The German Constitution" that Prussia was unsuitable for the restoration of the Holy Roman Empire because of its own decline and because its centralizing policies threatened the existence of the estates.[168] In his 1802–03 writings, Hegel was trying to thread the needle, to support something like the Prussian idea of locating the authority of the estates in a larger social whole while at the same time avoiding the risks of eliminating the estates altogether, as he feared was actually happening in Prussia.

Hegel thus found himself in the dilemma that was to occupy him for a good part of his life when he turned to thinking about political matters. On the one hand, he rejected J. J. Moser's methods; to Hegel, Moser seemed to have contented himself with the useless task of simply compiling the various traditional claims of rights and privilege without making any attempt to impose any kind of rational unity on them. On the other hand, Hegel did not want to take the Prussian route of potentially eliminating the estates altogether. In 1802 and 1803, Schellingian theory combined with a concept of "recognition" seemed to give him the way out he needed, since it seemed to be able to offer an account of the estates as "potencies" of the whole society, as corporate bodies that on their own created a dynamic that led to the creation of a "state" that was their unity but still presupposed their existence; and it did this by virtue of a non-naturalistic but not reductionistic theory of "spirit" and agency.

In reinterpreting the estates as embodying fundamental ethical *stances* toward social life, Hegel also thereby radically reinterpreted who could be included in membership in them. What he called at the time the "absolute estate" included the nobility as members; since the members of this estate live "general lives wholly belonging to the public," only that estate was fit for life in politics.[169] Hegel thus included in that estate not only the nobility but also philosophers – a conclusion that made sense only in light of Fichte's redefinition of the university and of philosophy's place in it.[170] (Hegel also drew on Plato's authority for combining the tasks of the political nobility and the philosophers.)[171] From a biographical point of view, it is striking that Hegel thereby included himself but would have excluded his father from membership in the "absolute estate."[172]

A major point of Hegel's argument was obviously to demonstrate that old-fashioned cameralist jurisprudence should be replaced by speculative Hegelian/Schellingian philosophy. A speculative theory of what would count as an adequate realization of freedom would, Hegel concluded, make "a good part and perhaps all of the sciences called positive jurisprudence . . . fall within a completely developed and elaborated philosophy," and, by implication, not within the domains of the cameralistic faculties.[173] "Philosophy," Hegel said, "stands in the Idea of the whole above the parts; thereby it keeps each part in its limits and also, by the majesty of the Idea itself, prevents the part from burgeoning by subdivision into endless minutiae."[174]

Philosophy speaks from the standpoint of the "absolute" – but from what point of view was the philosopher speaking when he said that? At this point, Hegel did not find even his own answers to that question very convincing; and he had to worry that his own doctrine of the "mores" of a "people" only threatened to be replace cameralism's dogmatics with some more communitarian and equally dogmatic conception of law. The *System of Ethical Life* remained unpublished and unfinished.

1804–1805: Logic and Metaphysics

Hegel's First "Logic"

Hegel's only reputation at this time was that of being Schelling's disciple, and since their journal had closed he had been publicly silent, publishing nothing. Moreover, the small inheritance on which he had been living was dwindling fast, and the small supplements from the nominal students' fees and honoraria for his work in journals were nowhere near enough to compensate.

Clearly, Hegel needed a salaried position, and, just as clearly, he needed a book to get one; but none seemed to be forthcoming. In 1802 he announced that "his" system would be forthcoming; this was repeated in 1803 when he told his students that his own "compendium" for the lectures would soon be forthcoming; when he wrote to Goethe on September 29, 1804, requesting an appointment as a professor in philosophy, he added that "the purpose of a work I hope to complete this winter for my lectures – a purely scientific elaboration of philosophy – will permit me to present it to Your Excellency, should I be kindly permitted to do so."[175] In 1805, he wrote a letter to Johann Heinrich Voss, seeking to enlist his help in attaining a position at Heidelberg, saying, "By fall, I will give an exposition of my work as a system of philosophy."[176] In 1804–05, Hegel wrote out a clean copy of a long manuscript on "Logic, Metaphysics, and Philosophy of Nature," which was almost certainly intended to be the basis for the book he had been promising since 1802. Yet again, despite his earnest promises of a book to all concerned and despite his desperate need for one, Hegel became completely dissatisfied with his efforts and as he had before, simply and abruptly stopped work on it and began work on another manuscript.

The 1804–05 manuscript – The *Jenaer Systementwürfe II: Logik, Metaphysik, Naturphilosophie* (*Jena System Draft II: Logic, Metaphysics, Philosophy of Nature*) – presents a curious development in Hegel's thought.[177] It is almost certainly written during the period 1804–05, but it contains none of the social and political reflections of the earlier attempts at a system. It surely was a reworking of some older lecture notes (or an older manuscript for a book) that Hegel had developed for his courses on logic and metaphysics in 1802; most likely, his abandoning this manuscript had to do with how he came to see its incompatibility with the state of his thought as it was developing during the period 1805–06. Indeed, it seems that he quite suddenly stopped working on it altogether. The manuscript thus marked yet another stage in the growing crisis in Hegel's career. The very obscurity of the surviving manuscript is evidence of just how distraught Hegel was becoming at this point in his life.

Early on in his career at Jena, Hegel had come to the idea that his

"system" would be divided among what he had taken to calling logic
and metaphysics, philosophy of nature, and philosophy of spirit, but it
was not clear to him just how the three (or maybe four) parts of his
system were to be related to each other. Uniting all these different
sections would be a truly speculative philosophy conceived, as Hegel
now put it, as the *articulation* of the absolute, that is, the articulation of
the basic structure, the unity, underlying both the objective and the
subjective points of view.

Hegel's unpublished manuscript of 1804–05 was an attempt to accomplish this via a "logic" of relations. Hegel's decision to call this a
"logic" followed the trend of the times. If nothing else, other people at
Jena (including Fichte) had been doing much the same thing, and
Hegel's own course in philosophy as a student at Tübingen in the winter
semester of 1788–1789 had been called "Logic and Metaphysics"
(taught by J. F. Flatt).

The key idea of Hegel's 1804 "Logic" seems to have been that the
system begins with something like Hölderlin's conception of the unity
of thought and being, some notion of a fundamental identity, and one
then shows that the *articulation* of this identity itself presupposes an
articulation of "difference," following which one shows how the articulation of this relation of identity and difference must develop itself into
a yet richer, more determinate relational system. Although the crucial
introductory sections of the manuscript are missing, it seems most likely
that Hegel began the manuscript with the concept of what he called
"simple relation" – Hölderlin's notion of the deep unity of thought and
being – from which the surviving portions show that he then proceeded
to develop the relations of "reality" and "negation," out of which the
conceptions of qualitative difference and quantitative difference were
then themselves developed. The articulation of the conception of
"quantitative difference" was used to argue the point that traditional
syllogistic logic was incapable of handling conceptions of the "infinite,"
which had been otherwise quite capably handled in the mathematics of
the differential and integral calculus.[178] The way in which the infinite is
expressed as a "ratio" in the calculus shows that there is indeed a purely
conceptual basis for articulating the infinite, and that mathematics has
thereby shown that a new type of "logic" is required in order that the
"infinite" not be conceived as some kind of "thing" – as an infinitesi-

mally large or small quantity – but as having an "ideal" existence in its expressions in the formulas of the calculus.[179]

Indeed, the mathematical example shows, Hegel argued in the manuscript, that thinking in terms of simple "relations" (*Beziehungen*) requires us to articulate them in terms of a more basic conception of "ratios," or "relationships" (*Verhältnisse*), "totalities" grasped in thought that are the conditions of our conceptual grasp of the "relations" between things (such as the individual elements in an infinite series). In the manuscript, two such "relationships" are singled out: the relationship of being and the relationship of thought. Under the heading "relationship of being," Hegel includes what he calls the relationships of substantiality, of causality, and of reciprocal interaction, which together commit us to understanding the various individual substances of the world as only moments in the process of the world's coming to be and passing away as a whole, "moments" at which that "infinite" process coalesces into individual "points."

If the "relationship of being" is the conceptual articulation of the way in which the particular items of the world are both absorbed into and produced by the universal process of nature itself, then the "relationship of thought" is the pure "logic" of the unity of and relations between the "universal" and the "particular" aspects of that process, the logic according to which the primordial divisions in the "judgment," and later in the "syllogism," are produced.[180]

In the manuscripts, Hegel argues for the conclusion that any rigorous, "logical" typology of judgments must itself be derived from what is necessary to articulate the larger totality within which such judgments are made, in particular, to articulate the implicit relations between universals and particulars. The guiding thread in that discussion has to do with the notion that if there are only so many ways that universals and particulars can be related to each other, then there can be only that many types of correctly formed judgments. However, all attempts to establish this in any kind of rigorous fashion only demonstrate, so Hegel concluded, that a putatively purely *formal* classification of judgments itself already depends on a more substantial, *material* treatment of what it is correct to assert, and that the doctrine of judgment thus naturally gives way to a doctrine of what it is correct to assert, which itself comprises the classical theory of the syllogism, the theory of inference.

In the 1804 "Logic," Hegel argued that the classical theory of the syllogism, however, required as a condition of its own possibility another nonsyllogistic totality. This was not, however, an entirely new conclusion; already in his 1802 essay on the "Relationship of Skepticism to Philosophy" for the *Critical Journal of Philosophy*, he had shown that he was quite familiar with the criticisms of formal syllogistic structure made by the third-century skeptic, Sextus Empiricus. On Sextus' account, a familiar syllogism such as "Every man is an animal, Socrates is a man, therefore Socrates is an animal" is inadequate; it itself rests on syllogisms that are *either* incomplete – how do we know that every man is an animal until we have investigated all men? – *or* are complete and therefore make the syllogism circular – since if we have investigated every man, then we have also investigated Socrates, so we already know Socrates is an animal, and we have already presupposed the conclusion, "Socrates is an animal," in even stating the syllogism. Other similar criticisms had been voiced in Hegel's own day about the sufficiency of syllogistic structure. To put it in the contemporary terms coined by Gilbert Ryle: What was at stake were the *inference licenses* at work in the syllogism; the argument was that we cannot understand the validity of syllogisms until we have shown the validity of the inference licenses themselves (since they cannot be included in the premises of the system). Hegel concluded not only that it was simply dogmatic to presuppose that all such inference licenses must be formal, but also that an investigation of both the way in which judgments must be classified and the proof the validity of syllogisms themselves shows that the whole of syllogistic logic cannot be explained in terms of a purely formal enterprise.

Hegel's treatment of syllogisms themselves in his 1804–05 "Logic" is very abbreviated. His general argument, though, is something like the following. The traditional explanation of the validity of syllogisms had to do with the way in which the subjects or predicates were said to be "distributed" as the middle terms of the inference. The syllogism, "All men are mortal, Socrates is a man, therefore Socrates is mortal," involves a major term ("mortal"), a minor term ("Socrates"), and a middle term ("man") that "binds" the major and minor terms together in the conclusion. The invalidity of syllogisms such as "Socrates is white, white is a color, therefore Socrates is a color" was to be explained by the notion that the subject and predicate terms were not "distributed" correctly in the premises (or were not "distributed" at all). The idea of "distribution" was traditionally explained in terms of what "fell under" the term and what did not.

Since, however, the understandings of the terms and their "distribution" were not themselves formal in nature, the determination of what counts as a valid syllogism cannot depend solely on resources internal to the formal structure of syllogisms themselves but must also depend on the material content of certain concepts; what counts as purely logical vocabulary (for example, connectives such as "and" and "or") and what counts as "distributing" the terms depends on what counts as a substantive understanding of conceptual content in the first place. The very understanding of the validity of syllogisms themselves, he concluded, had to do with our implicit grasp of the larger "whole" of thought and being that gave sense to such judgments and their syllogistic connections in the first place.

Metaphysics as the Completion of Logic

Since the validity of the syllogism depends on the "distribution" of terms, any rigorous definition of the basic terms already presupposes some kind of "definition by essence," the paradigm of which is that of geometrical procedure. The formal validity of syllogisms therefore depended, so Hegel reasoned in the 1804–1805 manuscript, on a more complex unity that would mediate between the "relationships of being" and the "relationships of thought." This would be "metaphysics," and the "totality" of such metaphysical definition and division would be a form of cognition (*Erkennen*).[181]

"Metaphysics" conceived in this fashion would be articulation of the unity of "thought" and "being," the "absolute," the "logic," that is, of what Hölderlin had called "Being." Metaphysics thus is the doctrine of the way in which what appear to be basic oppositions are conceptually articulated in terms of their deeper unity and connection with each other.[182] The basic principles of such unities are those of identity and contradiction, the "principle of the exclusion of a third" (bivalence), and the "principle of sufficient reason." These principles cannot be proved within syllogistic logic itself, since syllogistic logic presupposes them.

Staying true to the inspiration of Hölderlin, Hegel divides "meta-

physics" into three main subdivisions: cognition as a system of principles, the "metaphysics of objectivity," and the "metaphysics of subjectivity," each of which have a deeper unity in the "absolute" that is
prior to their division from each other. In the metaphysics of objectivity,
we think of "cognition" (which Hegel identifies in the manuscript with
the "absolute I") as making objective claims about ourselves and the
world. This necessarily leads to something like the classical pre-Kantian
metaphysical conceptions of the soul, the world, and the "highest essence" (God), which themselves generate the paradoxes that motivated
classical metaphysics and which eventually necessitated the Kantian
revolution in philosophy, which is then itself grasped in an intuition of
the "absolute" as the unity of this kind of "subjectivity" and "objectivity."

The Articulation of the "Absolute" and the Early Philosophy of Nature

In 1802 and 1803, Hegel began to assemble clippings concerning natural
science from various journals and newspapers, and he returned intensively to one of his earlier interests as a schoolboy in Stuttgart, the
study of physics and mathematics, in an effort to gather material for a
philosophy of nature that would mesh with his reflections on the possibility of human freedom. The philosophies of nature that he produced
during these years display a detailed knowledge on his part of a good
bit of what was going on in the natural science of the time. (Certainly
Jena, with its collection of budding natural scientists, was a good place
to learn about these things.) They vary quite a bit in detail – the two
earlier drafts begin with the system of the sun, the movement of the
planets, the earth, and then move to mechanics, whereas the final draft
in 1805–06 begins with pure mechanics and derives things from that –
but they all retain (as Rolf-Peter Horstmann has shown) the idea that
the two basic factors in nature are what Hegel calls the "aether" and
"matter."[183] The "aether" is the way the absolute appears most basically
in nature as "unity," and it develops into "difference" in various ways
(or as the "universal" that is differentiated into "particulars"); the
aether develops itself into "matter," and this "matter" then develops
itself into the various appearances of nature.

The details of Hegel's philosophy of nature in this period are not important here. Hegel himself abandoned and modified many of the ideas he sketched out, and he certainly never saw fit to publish those notes, copious as they were. Their importance lies in the way in which they show the manner by which Hegel tried to flesh out his conviction that he needed a nonreductionist and still non-naturalist account of the genesis of spirit out of nature.[184]

Nonetheless, during this period Hegel was trying to fit such ideas into his newly developing "logic and metaphysics" of "unity and multiplicity," and "universality and particularity," and he was also still trying to squeeze all of this into a Schellingian theory of the "potencies." His idea was that nature's processes, which lead to the dispersal of all things into a "multiplicity" of entities, also lead to nature's capturing this "multiplicity" in a "unity." Out of this "logic" of unity and multiplicity, universality and particularity, Hegel then tried to show that the heavenly bodies maintain their unity as individuals within a "universal," the solar system; that the earth is a single thing only insofar as it unites all the differences (physical, chemical, and biological) within itself; and that ultimately these relative identities can only be comprehended by *spirit*, by something that comes to mirror all this motion in itself through the medium of language and consciousness. The result of all this was a set of notes that constitute some of the densest prose Hegel ever wrote.[185]

In the draft of his "Logic" in 1804, Hegel returned again to the philosophy of nature, taking up the same themes, such as the appeal to a dynamic of an "aether" or "absolute matter." There is, however, a new ordering of the parts (motion as studied by the science of mechanics comes to play a more important role) and a new treatment of details, none of which, however, are important enough to recount here. If "logic" is about the standards for correct thought, and "metaphysics" is about the primordial unity of thought and being, then "philosophy of nature" would be about the way in which the natural world must be constituted for the kinds of agents that are explained in metaphysics really to be possible. That is, the essence of nature itself must be shown not to exclude the possibility of what has been claimed in "logic" and "metaphysics." Nature must be shown in its own dynamic (as studied by the sciences) to lead to spirit, even to require it.

Why then is "philosophy of nature" not simply a part of "metaphysics"? Hegel's answer seems to be that "metaphysics" studies the structure of the unity of "subjectivity" and "objectivity" (the subjective and objective points of view), whereas "philosophy of nature" studies the way in which nature must metaphysically develop within itself such "minded" creatures in the first place. As Hegel puts it, nature's "existence as much as its ideality, or its coming to be absolute spirit is the metaphysical coming to be or the coming to be of cognition as self-cognition."[186] Nature itself is unaware of this aspect of itself; only human agents as "minded" natural beings have this awareness of nature's dynamic: "The spirit of nature is a hidden spirit, it does not step forth in spirit's shape; it is only spirit for the cognizing spirit; or, it is spirit in itself but not for itself."[187] The "philosophy of nature" thus regards the "whole," the "absolute," as the primordial unity of mind and nature.

What remains of the 1804–05 manuscript, however, abruptly ends with introduction of the concept of "the organic." Hegel, it would seem, simply and suddenly ceased working on the manuscript and put it aside. His earlier work and other fragments from that period suggest he had intended to follow the "philosophy of nature" with something like a philosophy of "existing spirit" in the manner of the *System of Ethical Life*. It was, however, apparently clear to Hegel that the whole enterprise simply did not hold together. On his own terms, the final division of the "system" would have to be self-contained, it would be the logical stopping point that articulated all the conditions under which each of the prior divisions were themselves necessary; but, as Hegel puts it in his notes to himself, the idea that there would be such a final section – which in the notes he calls an "absolute proposition" – would amount to saying that the relation between it and the other divisions would have "just as well either the form of an infinitely extending straight line or that of a circular line returning back into itself."[188] If that were the case, though, then either the third division, "philosophy of nature," would have to be self-contained (and there is no reason to think that Hegel thought it could be), or there would have to be a fourth division, which could only be that of something like the doctrine of "ethical life," which would then entail that metaphysics, even the whole of logic, would be relative to a particular "people's" intuition of the "absolute." If so, then he needed an argument as to why any particular "people's" point of view could take priority over any other "people's" points of view. Running out of time and money, in desperate personal circumstances and suffering from depression, Hegel started over again to see if he could actually produce what he had long been promising. That led him to a new conception of the history of such formations of "spirit" and to the final establishment of his own, authentic voice in philosophy.

1805–1806: Hegelian Idealism: The Penultimate Shape

Sometime around the fall or summer of 1805, Hegel began work on yet another manuscript for use in his lectures. Preserved in relatively good condition, it presents a kind of snapshot of Hegel's thought about what would be necessary for the proposed "system" that he had been promising to publish for some time. The manuscript is known to us as the *Third Jena System Draft: Philosophy of Nature and Philosophy of Spirit* (*Jenaer Systementwürfe III: Naturphilosophie und Philosophie des Geistes*), and like the preceding ones, it was never published in Hegel's lifetime.[189] But in it, Hegel suddenly appears as Hegel, almost in his full voice, much as he was to appear for the rest of his life.

Nature and Spirit

Quite significantly, in the 1805–06 draft of the "system," the Schellingian language of the "potencies" dropped out completely. In the preserved draft, Hegel opened the section on nature with the statement that his conceptions of "absolute matter or the aether . . . [are] equivalent in meaning to pure spirit, for this absolute matter is nothing sensuous but is rather the concept as pure concept within itself, spirit existing as such."[190] "Absolute matter," that is, is not something that we empirically encounter in the observation of nature; it is a "posit," an "ideality," the "totality" presupposed by the more determinate explanations offered by the physicists. The promise made in the "Oldest System Program of German Idealism" to give "some wings again" to physics, to understand the scientific account of nature in terms of the deeper experience of nature as a "whole," seems to be driving the account. What is at stake are the ways in which we must conceive of nature as a whole – not just in terms of what the scientists say about it but in terms of our various experiences of it and how it matters to us.

After having written a new *Naturphilosophie*, Hegel went on to sketch out a new section about *Geist* for his lectures.[191] The manuscript on spirit is much less polished than the one on nature. Much of it is completely telegraphic, consisting of short phrases, often with little explanation as to how they are supposed to connect with each other. Indeed, the whole set of notes on spirit have the obvious shape of cribs for Hegel to use in his lectures. Hence, one must often read between the lines to reconstruct what Hegel's arguments must have been.

His introductory sections on *Geist* develop in a more extended fashion the point made in the *System of Ethical Life*, that our basic "stance" toward nature is spontaneously determined by ourselves but that this does not occur in one fell swoop, that our "mindedness" emerges out of natural determination and progressively distances itself from such natural determination as it gradually determines itself from within its own resources. Hegel's own chosen examples are colorful: While asleep, we are at our least self-determining; we passively combine images in our mind following both the so-called laws of association and the associations of phantasmorgoric images that appear in sleep and which defy being put into the form of any so-called laws: "A bloody head shoots up, there another white shape, only to suddenly disappear."[192] Our "waking up" and bringing our judgmental capacities into play depends, as he also earlier argued, on our acquisition and use of language.[193] Likewise, the employment of our judgmental capacities takes place in the practical context we share with others of trying to accomplish something, out of which emerges the practices of human labor and the creation of tools to accomplish those ends.

Recognition and Sexual Union

The creation and use of tools gives one an implicit grasp of oneself as a rational goal-setting agent, but the mere use of tools is not enough to make that implicit self-awareness into a fully explicit self-awareness. To be reflectively aware of oneself as having a point of view, one must be able to contrast it with some other point of view. To make such a contrast presupposes, however, that one is already aware of another agent as being reflectively self-aware, and thus in the manuscript, Hegel introduces his notion that when two agents who are only implicitly reflectively self-aware come to encounter each other, the unity between them, the rational will, splits itself into two types. The will, as he puts it, disrupts (*entzweit*) itself into "two powers, two characters."[194]

Hegel returned to his notions of "recognition" to articulate this generation of self-consciousness, and, quite strikingly, in the 1805–06 manuscript he employed a theorized sexual encounter between man and woman to make that point. In the use of tools, agents encounter nature as a means to satisfy their impulses, but in the encounter of the sexes, "impulse comes to an intuition of itself . . . becomes knowledge (*Wissen*) of what it is," and in being naturally aroused by the other, each agent thereby acquires a new "impulse" for the union with the other, which also results in a "tension" in each agent. Hegel quaintly describes this by saying that at first, each approaches the other "with uncertainty and timidity, yet with trust, for each knows itself immediately in the other."[195] In the union with the other, each cancels and preserves his and her individuality, each comes "to have his essence in the other," and each comes to self-knowledge in being "external to self."[196] Each, that is, comes to know him- or herself as an agent in the union of the sexes; mindedness emerges out of nature through a natural attraction. The primordial unity of self-consciousness thus divides itself into (for Hegel, the always sharp) divisions between men and women.

In such sexual union, both agents participate in the basics of creating a *common* point of view, which in "love" has its first and most immediate shape as a type of cognition. Sexual union makes explicit the very perspectival nature of the consciousness of such embodied agents. Self-conscious sexual union is thus more than the "natural," biological attraction of the sexes; each understands that both their own radically perspectival, subjective point of view and the *recognition* of each by the other together fashions the beginning of a point of view that is not so perspectival yet not divorced from human individuality and embodiment. As Hegel puts it, in such self-conscious sexual union, his or her "uncultured (*ungebildetes*) natural self is recognized."[197]

Much of Hegel's characterization of the sexes in this manuscript is also consistent with the views he had held since his youth about men and women, and which he continued to hold with only slight modifications until his death. The differences are almost always put in terms of a duality of activity and passivity, knowing and not knowing, animal and plant, and so on. In the margins of the manuscript, for example, Hegel revealingly wrote: "The man has desires, impulse; the feminine impulse is rather to be only the object of impulse; to *entice*, to awaken impulse and to allow it to satisfy itself in it."[198] Why he had such trouble with Caroline Schlegel Schelling should be no great mystery; on the whole, Hegel simply could not entertain the idea of independent, active women, even if he did come later in life to endorse a very weak version of women's equality and even if he does speak in this manuscript of the "positing oneself as the same" as the other, and of the opposition of the sexes being converted into an "equality."[199] One can hardly help speculating about whether it is only coincidental that around the time that Hegel was composing these notes, he was also engaging in a sexual liaison with Christiana Charlotte Johanna Burkhardt, his landlady and housekeeper, which resulted in the birth on February 5, 1807, of his illegitimate son, Ludwig Fischer.

Life-and-Death Struggles for Recognition: Families, Property, and Social Life

Hegel lectured on how the establishment of sexual union creates the notion of a family, a social unity whose normative status is more than that of a contract between individuals, and then went on to discuss the *struggle* for recognition, a notion that had played such an important role in earlier manuscripts and which continued to play a crucial role in later works. Speculating in a very Rousseauian mode, he argued that the confrontation of independent *families* in the state of nature, with men as the heads of families, would eventuate in the "struggle" for recognition, which begins as a struggle over claims to family possessions. Each male head of a family seeks to *exclude* other male heads of families from his own domain; each therefore demands from the others a recognition of his own status as having the right to lay claim to such and such as possessions; each seeks, that is, "to count (*gelten*) for the other."[200] In demanding to be recognized by the other as having *rightful* claims on the other's possessions, each *insults*, so Hegel says, the other, challenges not the other's impulses or desires but the other's "self-knowledge."[201] But in coming to see that they have thereby committed themselves to a struggle over life and death, each agent comes to see that more is at stake than he had thought, that he is putting himself, in Hegel's words, in danger of committing suicide.[202] These life-and-death struggles for recognition thereby lead the agents to grasp that what is at stake in such struggles is not the same as what is at stake in the satisfaction of various impulses: What is at stake now is "that taking cognizance becomes recognition," "willing without impulse," as Hegel puts it, acting on the basis of a *conception* of what ultimately matters in life and not just on the basis of *impulses* that each happens to have. In the manuscript, Hegel surprisingly assumes that the confrontation with their possible deaths would simply lead each immediately to offer recognition to the other.[203]

Becoming such explicitly recognized social beings, they also become *property* holders, bearers of property *rights* and not merely heads of families in *possession* of certain family goods. This in turn leads them to establish lawful relations of exchange, to set up a system of punishment and enforcement of rights, and so on.

Commercial Society, the Revolution, and the Task of Philosophy

In his lectures, Hegel applied his systematic idealism to his longstanding interests in the shape of a revolutionized Germany. The text shows that he was presenting to his students a series of arguments about the benefits and dangers of the emerging commercial society championed by the Scots and the forms of political freedom championed by the French. Freedom, he argued, is realizable only in a modern, law-governed commercial society and is also fundamentally threatened by the institutions and practices of that very same commercial society. For example, even though tastes become refined and wealth increases in modern industrial society, there are the dangers of machines taking over much of production, of a growing disparity of wealth and poverty. Like the mixture of hometowner and reformer that he was, Hegel claimed that the state has a duty to make sure that the suffering classes – he uses the term "*Klassen*" and not "*Stände*" in this connection – find alternative employment and to exercise a "universal oversight" in these matters. On the other hand, as a good reader of Scottish political economy, he also argued that state intervention in markets should be restrained and unobtrusive and that using taxes to prevent consumption is counterproductive. (His example is that of taxes on wine; presumably, that struck home for him.) He even made some passing remarks on the rationality of the idea of fashion: the emergence of the practice of changing fashions in clothing and decoration (itself part of the multiplication of needs in modern commercial society) is a social condition for the realization of freedom, for it gives individuals the opportunity to participate in a "free use of forms," a way to relate to each other that "excites impulse and desire," in which the very fluidity of modern life is made evident to their consciousness.[204]

Hegel's great worry at this time was clearly about what could and could not be preserved in the transition to a reformed, modernized Germany. He noted that "freedom of commerce" must be maintained and that the state cannot "wish to save that which cannot be saved" – it cannot artificially prop up local artisanal means of production that are doomed to extinction in the competition with more efficient modes of production in the emerging capitalist economy.[205] But he also noted in a short fragment that this most likely meant for Germany the "sacrifice of this generation," the "increase in poverty," and hinted that therefore "poor taxes and institutions" for the support of those who suffer in this transition must also therefore multiply.[206]

The third division of the manuscript, following "Spirit According to Its Concept" and "Actual Spirit," is simply labeled "Constitution"; there Hegel discussed his systematic conceptions of how the "universal will" is to be *rationally* embodied in a particular "people," a *Volk*. He used it, moreover, to update himself and his students on what he saw as the deeper significance of the French Revolution now that Napoleon was emperor and France was an empire. Certainly the Revolution had taken a different course during his stay in Jena. Napoleon, having already abolished the Directory and made himself first consul, managed on August 2, 1802 (16 Thermidor on the revolutionary French calendar), to have himself proclaimed consul for life; and then on May 18, 1804, after a decisive plebiscite, Napoleon was made hereditary emperor of the French and on December 2 staged his coronation. (The vote in the plebiscite was 3.6 million for, 2,569 against.)

By 1805–06, Hegel thus was of two minds about the Revolution, and his manuscripts of that period clearly show it. He had still not given up his hopes for a "revolutionizing" of Germany, but his conclusion that the structure of the old Holy Roman Empire was simply incapable of accommodating itself to those changes had only become better founded. Although France itself had at first presented the odd spectacle of a country gradually drifting into anarchy while at the same time seemingly growing stronger in foreign affairs, it had apparently stabilized itself by Bonaparte's seizure of rule; indeed, the so-called Code Napoleon went into effect on March 21, 1804, not only in France but also in

Luxembourg, the German Palatinate, parts of Rhenish Prussia and Hesse-Damstadt on the left bank of the Rhine (which France had won from Germany in the treaty of Lunéville), and in Geneva, Savoy, Piedmont, and the duchies of Parma and Piacenza. The new code embodied many of the goals of the Revolution, indeed, of modern life in general: It favored freedom of contract, underwrote modern ideas of property and inheritance, and, in a move that expressed Napoleon's own feelings on the matter, put an end to revolutionary ideas about women's equality by making wives subordinate to their husbands as a matter of the civil law. France thus seemed to be stabilizing itself in a way of which Hegel could partially approve and with which he could partially identify. Like many people in France, who had become tired of the anarchy, Hegel too continued at this time to be seduced by the idea of a strong leader, a "Theseus," a Napoleon of the Germans who would do the equivalent of founding a new Athens in Germany, and he said as much in his lectures.

Hegel was not, however, completely taken in by the French example. Despite his ongoing high regard for the Revolution, Hegel's Württemberg past made him uneasy about many parts of it. Although Napoleon had effectively put into practice the new civil code, he had done so at the price of effectively dismantling representative government. Hegel was struggling to bring together what he saw as the affirmative aspects of the French upheaval with his other studies in Scottish political economy and his belief that something like the system of "estates" had to be preserved in Germany if freedom were to be adequately realized there. For example, whereas the Abbé Sieyès had sharply distinguished the "nation" from what the Scottish philosophers had called "commercial society," Hegel took a different line; he distinguished between the "constitution" of a *Volk* (which made up their *Geist*, formed them as a "people") and "actual spirit," which corresponded very roughly to "commercial society" (and included marriage and the family).

Sieyès had insisted that (in his words) "the nation is prior to everything. It is the source of everything. Its will is always legal; indeed it is the law itself."[207] Hegel at first seemed to speak similarly when he said that the state "is the simple absolute spirit that is certain of itself and for which nothing counts but itself."[208] However, from Hegel's point of view, Sieyès's conception simply failed to comprehend the way in which modern individualism takes root within the normative structures of a "people." Hegel calls this a "Nordic essence," the "principle of absolute individuality," "absolute being-within-self"[209]; and he claimed that individuality emerges as the "higher principle of modern times" in the way in which individuals "return back fully into themselves," which, as he noted, contrasts modern life with ancient Greek life.[210]

In phrasing it that way, Hegel set up the problem as one of combining "Germanic" freedom (with representative government), Scottish commercial society, and French revolutionary politics. (In the lectures, he scathingly remarks on what he took to be the utter boneheadedness of the Germans with regard to the momentous changes that were being required of them, returning to his claim that the "great man" must come along who is "to know the absolute will, to express it, to gather everyone under his banner.")[211] The *estates*, he argued, were crucial for such a combination to have any validity. Hegel simply rejected Sieyès's solution for modern life – that the third estate was "everything" – but, more importantly, by 1805–06 Hegel had divided the estates in a revealingly different way than he had in 1803–04. In the 1805–06 ordering, the aristocracy dropped out altogether as an essential estate, and instead Hegel ordered things into an estate of peasants, of trade and law (*Stand des Gewerbes und des Rechts*), and of merchants (the *Kaufmann*) – and then, in addition to all these, he introduced what he called the "universal estate," his new characterization of what he had earlier called the "absolute estate." This included three very different types of groups: the soldier, who puts his life on the line in the name of the "people"; the businessman (*Geschäftsmann*), who deals in goods and monetary transactions from all over; and "those who work for the state."[212]

The introduction of this conception of "universal estate" into the scheme shows how much Hegel was continuing to grapple with his hometown background in light of developments since the Revolution. The distinguishing characteristic of the universal estate is precisely that its members are *not* tied to particularistic hometown life. The merchant, the peasant, and the local tradesmen (the people who are not *Geschäftmänner* but do engage in local trade, *Gewerbe*) are deeply tied to local custom and local privilege and can only form their opinions on the basis of that local custom and privilege. The members of the universal estate, however, are those whose talents and occupations do not bind them to any particular community but to the "people" as a whole and who are therefore most suited to reworking the implicit universal principles of the "people" into explicit form. The other estates are too particularistic to be able to generalize; and, of course, philosophers working for universities (state-sponsored institutions) are members of the "universal estate."

The universal estate is thus identified with the people whose "stance" in life is that of "universality," that is, whose knowledge and interests are not tied to particular communities. In Hegel's own lifetime, he had witnessed a new and highly visible group come into being – that of the mobile government advisors, government ministers, and the new style of professors – which had brought along with it great tensions into German life. The reformers, of which Hegel was one, wanted to bring rationality and legal uniformity to German life and, naturally enough, they were often met with the entrenched hostility of local custom and privilege. As Hegel himself had witnessed, the result up to that point had been that reform was carried out at either the most general level, leaving local privilege untouched (in other words, no real reform at all); or efforts at reform came into direct conflict with local custom and privilege, and reform generally had to yield. Indeed, the sheer diversity and eccentricity of local custom and privilege and the absolute determination of the locals not to yield had made the issue of "reform" one of the flashpoints in Germany during the period that Hegel was lecturing.

The alternatives thus seemed to be either yielding to localism and forgoing reform; or adopting liberal, individualistic principles and riding roughshod over the locals, which was met with only the greatest hostility by the locals themselves. Hegel obviously wanted neither of these: he wanted to preserve some of the mediated nature of the hometowns while at the same time pushing centralizing reform onto them. He thought that "liberalism," as a doctrine of sheer individualism, was completely inadequate to this task, since it was incapable of capturing the necessary background predeliberative norms of a "people" without which any deliberation about the future of "Germany" would only result in sterile speculation, not in anything actual.

In this respect, Hegel was responding to his own time and in some sense even mirroring it. Only since the Revolution – indeed, really only since 1800 – had there opened up for a wider class of young men (roughly of his generation) a way of life that was not tied to the hometowns. In Hegel's case, this new, more modern form of life, on which he had set his sights as a teenager in Stuttgart, had its legitimating ideal in the concept of *Bildung*, that is, of "education, culture, and self-cultivation." The young men of *Bildung* saw themselves as free from the strictures of hometown life, as having a right to be "somebody" by virtue of their cultivated characters, not by virtue of their birth. As the "movers and doers" of German society, cosmopolitans who were not tied to any particular hometown, they were in direct conflict with the structures of the hometowns and usually understood themselves to be in conflict with them.

In speaking of the "universal estate" as "those who work for the state," Hegel also seemed to be coming to terms with his father's generation; Hegel's father had been a cameralist bureaucrat in Duke Karl Eugen's administration and had thus been a member of what Hegel had *now* taken to calling the "universal estate," namely, those trying to bring rationality and order to hometown life. Thus the experience of his own family in old Württemberg had left deeply ingrained in his own experience the model of a class of educated, cultivated individuals whose function was to bring order and rationality to society and whose claim to legitimacy rested on their educational credentials and not on being any part of the aristocracy – the Württemberg aristocracy, after all, played no role in the Württemberg parliament, the *Landtag*.[213]

In developing his ideas about the "universal estate," Hegel was clearly trying to come to terms with and combine two very different features of his own personal experience: the *universalism* of his upbringing – of his father as a member of the universal estate, entitled to his position because of his diploma in law from Tübingen – and the *particularism* of hometown life, something whose value and emotional pull he obviously also deeply felt. This refusal to give up either his Enlightenment-inspired universalism or his deeply felt particularism sharply distinguished Hegel from a number of other thinkers working within the old Holy Roman Empire at that time. It obviously distinguished him from all those who continued to argue for Enlightenment universalism and for the simple abolition of traditional hometown privileges. However, it also distinguished him from the German "counter-Enlightenment," which by and large tended to argue in the opposite way – against universalistic, Enlightenment "reason" in favor of particularistic feeling and communal tradition.

The particularistic pull of the hometowns colored the thought of many such people, and found its most forceful expressions in the writings of the irrationalist Johann Georg Hamann and the always eloquent F. H. Jacobi; both attacked the Enlightenment's ideal of a universalistic reason as standing for all that was "dead" and "mechanical" in opposition to what was "living" and "organic." In making such arguments, both Hamann and Jacobi were in effect intellectually playing out on a larger scale the encounter of the hometowners of the Holy Roman Empire with the forces of reform and rationalization of which Hegel's family had been partially representative. Thus, when Hamann and Jacobi tended to make claims to the effect that only the particular was real, they were also in effect endorsing the immediate experience of German hometownness against the claims made by the "universal estate," which itself was only gradually making its appearance.

Indeed, hometown life was for many essentially bound up with the very idea of leading an ethical life at all; the corporate structure of hometown life made it necessary for members of each corporation to provide for each other's needs, and thus for such people the policing of other people's ethics – how responsible they were, whether they generated illegitimate children for which the corporation would then have an obligation to provide sustenance, and so on – was intimately connected with the economics of hometown life. This was complicated by the fact not only that the reformers wished to limit or abolish the traditional privileges of the hometowns in the name of "reason," but also that many in the French and British Enlightenment had attacked religion itself in the name of "reason." The conflation of "reason" with both "reform" and an attack on religion only made the confrontation between "hometown" life and rational reform all the more combustible. In combining particularism with the defense of religion, Hamann and Jacobi in effect identified the continuance of hometown life with the continued survival of religion and morality itself. They helped make the idea plausible that the so-called reformers were calling not merely for a more efficient administration of the state but in effect for a wholesale abolition of all that was true and beautiful.[214] For Hegel, the "either-or" of both "reform or hometown life" and "universalistic reason or particularistic feeling" had to be overcome, and he set out to bring the two together in his thought. He still, however, saw no means to bring about this transition except through the intervention of some "Theseus" who would, somehow, insure that it all happened.

In response to the obvious danger of such a "Theseus" transforming himself into a tyrant, in his lectures Hegel offered the French Revolution as an example of "tyranny" transforming itself into a "rule of law."[215] Although "tyrants" often appear in the early stages of revolutions, once the revolution's goals have been securely anchored in institutional practice, the need for such tyranny vanishes and so does the hold that the "great man" has on the "people." Thus, in Hegel's 1806 analysis, as the Revolution was under attack by the coalition of counter-revolutionary (German) forces, the Jacobins were able to hold onto power and institute the Terror in order to secure the Revolution; but once it was clear that the Revolution had been secured – once French troops had proved themselves to be the masters of Europe in virtually all their campaigns – there was no longer any need for the Terror, and in 1794 Robespierre and the Jacobins were therefore overthrown. As Hegel put it in his lecture notes, "[Robespierre's] power left him because necessity had left him, and thus he was overthrown by force."[216] The implication is that by 1805–1806 Hegel had come to agree with the assessment of the French Council of State in 1800 that "we have finished the novel of the Revolution: now we must begin its history."[217] From his standpoint in Jena, it seemed as if the excesses of the Revolution were over, that the Revolution itself was secure – who, after all, was capable of taking on the seemingly invincible French army? – and that the only outstanding issue had to do with what would become of "Germany." (Hegel's own account of the French Revolution as "absolute freedom and terror" in the *Phenomenology* – an account often taken as a negative assessment of the Revolution but which appeared in the book he was writing as he gave those lectures – has to be considered in light of what he was saying in public at the time.)

Political reorganization in the style of the French, however, would not be enough. There must be an articulation by the "universal estate" of what ultimately matters to the community if such political action in Germany were not to descend into the kind of anarchy and terror practiced in France. For that, something other than a purely political practice is needed, and Hegel identified those practices in the manuscript as "art, religion, and science (*Wissenschaft*) ," whose goal must be "to self-knowingly create this content as such."[218]

Art does this by creating the "illusion" of a self-enclosed world of beauty; in this way, art appeals to a "people's" highest interests, in what is "infinite," through its creation of a beautiful "veil, that covers the truth."[219] Art can thus present only a beautiful, dreamlike illusion about its self-contained nature.

A better likeness of the true nature of "spirit" is found in religion. In what Hegel calls "absolute religion" (by which he meant Protestant Christianity reinterpreted in the terms of modern, speculative philosophy), what ultimately matters in human life is brought to full self-consciousness: In his words, "The absolute religion, however, is the depth brought to daylight," and, as he puts it, "This depth is the I, it is the concept, the absolute pure power."[220] Thus, in "absolute religion" one has the representation in rite and symbol of the idea that "the divine nature is none other than human nature,"[221] that "God, the absolute essence in the beyond, has become man,"[222] that "God is the self, God is man."[223] Still, although "absolute religion" can *assure* a people of this, it cannot *demonstrate* it; it can only *reveal* this to us without "insight."

For such "insight," one requires philosophy, the "absolute science (*Wissenschaft*)."[224] Philosophy does fully what art and religion can do only partially; it thus completes the task of self-knowing that art and religion begin: bringing to self-consciousness not merely what matters to a particular "people" but what ultimately matters to mankind in general – that is, what "spirit" really is. As such, it divides itself into two parts: speculative philosophy and philosophy of nature. It begins in immediate consciousness of the world, and it culminates in spirit's knowing itself as free.

Despite their rather telegraphic, fragmented form, these lecture notes end in such a way as to make it clear that Hegel had in his own mind come to some resolution regarding the shape his system was to assume. There would be an introduction, a way of guiding the reader into philosophy, which would, of course, begin with "immediate sensuous consciousness."[225] It would then proceed to the way in which we must make judgments about nature – to the "expression of the Idea in the shapes of immediate being"[226] – and would be followed by a treatment of spirit as shaping itself into a "people." It would then culminate with a section on philosophy's reflection on its role in the whole process, on how it makes fully explicit what had been only implicit in all the divisions that had preceded it. Philosophy's task would thereby be to articulate the "whole" in terms of which we must situate ourselves and in terms of which we must orient ourselves in order to make the judgments that we must make.

Hegel at first seemed to think that this only required some minor adjustments to the "system" that he had worked out in 1805–06, and that it would serve as a good introduction to that "system." Having done the introduction, he could then proceed to finish his "logic" – of which in 1805–06 he already very likely had a good draft (which has since been lost) – and follow it with the "philosophy of the real" (the philosophy of nature and the philosophy of "spirit" that he had worked out in his lectures of 1805–06). He did not know as he started out on this project that once again, just as it had before, his conception of a quick introduction to the "system" would fall apart, and he would be forced to begin again.

This time, however, his failures were to lead to his masterpiece, the *Phenomenology of Spirit*, a book whose very conception Hegel ended up revising even as he was writing it. There were, however, many personal troubles yet to befall Hegel before he reached that goal.

5

Hegel Finds His Voice: The *Phenomenology of Spirit*

The Project of the *Phenomenology*

HOWEVER DESPERATE Hegel's situation may have been while composing the *Phenomenology of Spirit*, in completing it he finally came to terms with the influences of Hölderlin and Schelling in his own original way. As one of his students from his later Berlin years, Karl Ludwig Michelet, observed, Hegel "was in the habit of calling this piece, which appeared in 1807, his voyage of discovery, since here the speculative method, which for him uniquely befitted the history of philosophy, in fact encompassed and traversed the whole sphere of human knowledge."[1] Indeed, Hegel's use of the cliché "voyage of discovery" seems particularly apt for the *Phenomenology*, since in it he managed to bring together many of his youthful concerns into a comprehensive philosophical conception that was to stay with him for the rest of his life.[2]

The experimental character of the book was evidenced in his ambivalence about what to title it; he in fact ended up giving it several different titles, thereby confusing the printer and the binders so much that many of the earliest copies ended up with several of the different titles bound together. (The original title finally came out as "System of Science: First Part: The Phenomenology of Spirit," with another title stuck between the "Preface" and the "Introduction," which in some editions came out as "Science of the Experience of Consciousness" and in other editions as "Science of the Phenomenology of Spirit.")[3]

Quite likely, the change in title had to do with Hegel's assumption of a Kantian idea for use in a new context. In *The Metaphysical Foundations of Natural Science*, Kant – in the context of arguing against Newton's way of distinguishing "true motion" from merely "apparent motion" –

had said that his own transcendental investigation into the a priori presuppositions of physics was to be called a "phenomenology"; the aim of such a "phenomenology," Kant went on to say, was "not of the transformation of mere appearance (*Schein*) into truth, but of appearance (*Erscheinung*) into experience (*Erfahrung*)."[4] As Hegel began to grasp that his original idea for a "science of the experience of consciousness" was itself necessarily turning out to be a history of the shapes and formations of consciousness itself, he saw his construal of the historical "movement" of spirit to be analogous to Kant's "phenomenology" of the "true" movement in nature, and he thus titled his book somewhat metaphorically the "phenomenology" of spirit, a study of spirit's "true" movement in history, to be distinguished from its only "apparent" movement.[5]

In his *Phenomenology*, Hegel attempted to lay out the basis for his whole system of philosophy and to convince his audience – "we moderns" – that they in fact *needed* something like his system.[6] He and Hölderlin together in Frankfurt had concluded that the modern world was something qualitatively new and demanded therefore a "new sensibility" appropriate to it. That meant that the older appeals to tradition, nature, and other forms of authority were necessarily going to be unsatisfactory in modern times, and the issue before "we moderns" thus seemed rather stark: Either we found some way in which to establish a new philosophy appropriate for modernity; or we had to face Jacobi's indictment that the Enlightenment appeal to reason itself was mistaken, an act of human hubris, whose outcome could only be, to use the term Jacobi coined, "nihilism."

The *Phenomenology* was in some respects a direct confrontation with Jacobi's indictment of modernity. Kant's proposal for an investigation by reason of its own powers had foundered on the defects in Kant's own development of his system; the post-Kantian project thus was required, if it was to answer Jacobi's charge, to develop a thoroughgoing skepticism even about reason itself and its own pretensions; simple blind faith in reason could not supplant a trusting faith in anything else. A procedure modeled on such a thoroughgoing skepticism, though, could only appear "as the path of doubt, or, more authentically, as the path of despair," as an effort to destroy any and all attempts at establishing any kind of truth.[7] Such despair, of course, could only be assuaged by reason's demonstration of its own self-sufficiency. The *Phenomenology* was therefore to be a form of "self-consummating skepticism," a way in which a thoroughgoing skepticism undid itself, and reason's commitments were thereby established and secured.[8]

In keeping with that idea, Hegel crafted a book with a highly unorthodox structure, evident in even a quick overview of the work's range of concerns. Beginning with "consciousness," Hegel tried to show that there are no "given" objects of direct awareness that determine the judgments we make about them; that "consciousness" already involves "self-consciousness," and that self-consciousness itself is highly mediated and dependent on structures of mutual recognition among self-conscious agents; that attempts to establish "successful" patterns of mutual recognition have foundered because of their inability to sustain allegiance to themselves when set under the microscope of reflective self-criticism; that what we therefore must take as authoritative for ourselves has to do with what has come to be required of us by virtue of the failures of past attempts at sustaining a set of normative structures of mutual recognition and that to understand what is required of us at the present, we must understand how the past came to demand that of us; and that the attempt to understand such reflective, social activity in modern life requires us to rethink a Christian view of the nature of religion as the collective reflection of the modern community on what ultimately counts for it; and that only such a historically, socially construed philosophical account of that whole process can adequately introduce us to such a fully "modern" standpoint and provide us with an elucidation of both itself and its own genesis.

Consciousness and Self-consciousness

Hegel confronted Jacobi's indictment at the very beginning of his book. Jacobi had argued that not only must we accept religious faith as a groundless act of belief, a *"salto mortale,"* we must accept the existence of a world external to our own consciousness as a matter of such "faith," which Jacobi called "sense-certainty." However, Hegel argued, even the simplest act of awareness in such "sense-certainty" already involves us in much more than an awareness that individual things just "are"; in making judgments about "sense-certainty," we articulate those experiences as complexes of individual things-possessing-general-properties, which in turn requires us to articulate a background set of laws and forces that are not "given" in direct awareness but construed by our faculty of "understanding." However, even that act of understanding the world as a totality of individual things possessing general properties interacting according to laws itself produces a set of contradictory, antinomial results. The result is that Jacobi's original claim – that "consciousness" is a simple awareness of things as they immediately are (either through sense-certainty or, more complexly, through perception or, even more complexly, in their supersensible background supplied by the "understanding") – turns out to involve much more than simple consciousness itself. We are in fact always aware of things *as* such and such, *taking* things to be this way or that, and are supplying a meaning to our experience that it does not automatically have. Jacobi's "faith" thus turned out to involve more complexity than he had thought it would.

The only way to deal with the antinomial consequences of the norms that govern our "consciousness" of the world is to understand them in terms of our "self-consciousness" about what we are doing, what goals we are trying to achieve in making such judgments. Those goals would at first seem to be given by the demands of "life" itself, by what is necessary to sustain ourselves and reproduce ourselves, and what counts as "the norm" for such self-consciousness would depend therefore on what is necessary for "life."

However, a self-conscious agent never simply "is" what he is in terms of life itself. He always has what Hegel calls a "negative" relation to his own natural states of desire and sensation, since (as the opening of the *Phenomenology* had shown) those natural states never fully determine the norms by which they are judged. This only becomes fully clear, however, when one self-conscious agent encounters another. In seeking reassurance that his norms are correct, are what all agents would affirm, each agent demands that the other agent *recognize* his normative grasp of himself and the world as the truth, as the norms that all agents would rationally follow. In making those demands, though, each finds that it is not "life" itself that is setting the terms of judgment but his own self-conceived *project* for his life that determines which of his desires have a normative ranking above the others and which of his desires have a rightful demand to fulfillment. Each becomes aware, that is, of his own "negativity," of the way in which his project is never fully determined by the strength or the intensity of any particular desire.

To the extent that one of the parties decides that his own self-conception is indeed more important than life itself, the demand for recognition becomes a struggle to the death. When out of fear for his life, one agent thereby submits to the authority of the other, both enter into a relationship of mastery and servitude. The "master" imposes the norms, the principles of correct judgment, on the vassal, who, in order to fulfill his natural desires, lets those principles be imposed on him. The master's project for his own life determines which of the vassal's desires are worthy of satisfaction; the vassal's own project for his life, his conception of what ultimately ought to matter to him, is subordinate to and even determined by the master's project.

However, through the discipline of his work for the master, the "vassal" comes to distinguish more clearly between his own subjective point of view and a more impersonal, normative point of view represented by the master. Although the master's point of view comes to represent the "totality" in terms of which the vassal must orient himself, it nonetheless remains only a *particular* point of view whose claim to authority really is only that it has been compelled by the master; and once it becomes explicit just how one-sided the relationship is, that what has counted as the true norms is only the result of some contingency of power, neither the master nor the vassal can any longer sustain a normative allegiance to that set of norms. Just as the vassal reflects on his status and comes to understand the sheer contingency of the master's hold on him, likewise the master comes to understand that the recognition he requires from the vassal, because it is only compelled, cannot serve as the free recognition he himself requires, cannot serve to vouchsafe his original claim that these were the norms that *any* agent *would* adopt.

Reason and History

Having reached that point in the *Phenomenology*, Hegel then shifted his narrative – in a fashion without much precedence in his earlier manuscripts – to overtly historical considerations, taking the normative failure of relations of mastery and servitude to explain the depth of the cultural crisis that followed the demise of the slave-owning societies of antiquity. Various other attempts to sustain a kind of self-mastery and independence in light of that failure (Stoicism and Skepticism) themselves failed to make good on their own promises, and the ancient world's despair at attaining anything like an adequate normative framework was finally answered by Christianity, with its claim that "we" must willingly put ourselves in servitude to this higher truth, which itself can only be "revealed" to us. The discipline of Christian worship throughout the medieval period (a period of universal servitude), however, prepared the way for an assertion of self-activity through the application of norms of impersonal reason to the world.

Following up on that idea, Hegel wrote an even longer, historically shaped chapter entitled simply "Reason" to show how the development of the idea of applying impersonal reason to nature and then to human affairs had culminated in a modern recognition that the unconditionality of the claims of reason have to do with their being necessary constituents of an admirable or worthy way of life, and that this modern realization itself had provoked a crisis in reason and therefore in modern culture itself. In that chapter, Hegel argued that European "spirit," by applying the standards of impersonal reason to both nature and human affairs, had only further developed and articulated the kind of "negativity," the self-undermining skepticism that was in fact essential to the European conception of what ultimately mattered to it. Such "negativity" had first become explicit in ancient Greek society, and it had shaped European "spirit" into a way of life that embodied within itself a kind of intrinsic demand for reflective self-doubt that in turn continuously undermined the various alternative claims to authority that appeared within that way of life. Having developed itself in this fashion, European "spirit" thus embarked on the "path of despair" that Hegel characterized the *Phenomenology* as portraying.

In the chapter on "Reason," Hegel attempted to illustrate, in a dazzling although obscure series of portraits of the development of early modern European life, just how the various attempts of European life to shore up its normative commitments in the early modern period by a reliance either on reason itself or on something else beyond reason that would somehow "ground" and reassure reason about itself had, each *on its own terms*, undermined themselves and come to generate out of the specific ways in which they failed new attempts at such reassurance. In Hegel's sweeping account, neither Faustian faith in knowledge as the power to compel the world and other agents to give us what we want, European sentimentalist faith in a unity of hearts, neo-Stoic appeals to "virtue" as disinterested altruism, nor even more modern ideals of communities of "expressive freedom" were able to survive the magnifying glass of such skeptical, corrosive rational reflection on themselves. In Hegel's broad picture of the development of European life's failure to rationally underwrite the authoritativeness about what mattered to it, Kant emerged as the great hero of modernity; Kant heroically rescued modern reason's claims to authority by showing that reason could indeed establish a "substantial" form of *Geist* in the shape of the "kingdom of ends" mutually legislating for itself, taking no authority for itself except that which it could generate out of its own "spontaneous" activities. However, while that turned out to be fully *necessary* as a modern self-conception, it also turned out, Hegel argued, to be *empty* as an actual guide to action. Thus, the stage was set for the spiritual crisis over whether the modern authority of reason was itself sustainable or was itself simply too empty and arid to produce anything worthy of full allegiance.

Geist and History

Having written such a long – and almost certainly originally unanticipated – chapter on "Reason" that culminated in the notion that the unconditional force of reason's basic claims had to do with the worthiness of the way of life of which it was an essential constituent, Hegel found himself committed to writing an even longer chapter entitled "Spirit" ("*Geist*") in order to make good on that assertion. In the "*Geist*" chapter, Hegel attempted to show how past ways of life – various "shapes" of *Geist* – had undermined their own claims to worthiness and to allegiance wholly within their own terms just as the early modern attempts at shoring up reason's claims themselves had foundered; and that by virtue of their own specific modes of failure, the historical succession of such failed forms of *Geist* had come to require modernity's appeal to reason as basic and essential to itself.

Just as the historical section in the beginning of the book had begun with a reflection on the failures of the ancient ways of life to sustain a kind of Stoic or Skeptical form of independence and self-sufficiency for self-conscious agents, the section on "*Geist*" opens with a consideration of the Greek introduction of "negativity," of the corrosive, undermining power of reflective thought into Western history. Ancient Greek life presented the picture of an "ethical harmony" unified within an ideal of beauty. Within ancient Greek life, individuals acting only on the particular demands of their own social roles were thus confident that the combined results of their actions would be ethically harmonious, and that the "whole" that was produced out of these various actions was itself beautiful and self-sustaining. However, ancient Greek life had no place within its conception of itself for the notion of an individual stepping *outside* of his role to appeal to some kind of ethical standard that was not itself completely embodied in a particular social role. Although this contained a set of contradictions that were always implicit within Greek life, those contradictions were only fully articulated in the heyday of its flowering, achieving one their most eloquent articulations in the Sophoclean tragedy *Antigone*.

The narrative of the tragedy *Antigone* tracks the downfall of Oedipus' family. Oedipus' son Eteocles sits on the throne of Thebes, but the other son, Polyneices, who believes the throne should be his, attacks the city, and both he and Eteocles are killed in the attack. Their maternal uncle, Creon, assumes the royal power and orders that although Eteocles' body is to be given the proper burial rites, these are to be prohibited for Polyneices because of what Creon claims are his traitorous acts. In defiance of this edict, Antigone (the daughter of Oedipus and therefore the sister of both Polyneices and Eteocles) performs the burial rites for her dead brother, Polyneices. She is caught at doing this, and Creon sentences Antigone to be entombed alive. As a result, Antigone commits suicide, Creon's son (who had been betrothed to Antigone) also commits suicide, Creon's wife dies, and Creon is thus faced with his own ruin as a result of his actions.

In explicating *Antigone*, Hegel developed his own original theory of tragic drama. Tragic drama consists in the portrayal of individual agents being required to do something that is *right* that is also at the same time unequivocally *wrong* and that leads to the agent's destruction. In Greek tragedy, it is the clash within the way of life itself that requires its participants to perform wrong actions that are also necessarily right in terms of what is required of them by the way of life itself. Greek tragedy thus typically presents a conflict between characters who each embody some particular "ethical principle" of Greek life, and since both sides to the conflict are in the right and yet commit wrong, there can be no happy or "moral" answer to the dilemma posed by the play.

As Hegel construed it, Antigone does what she has to do as defender of the divine law of the household and Creon does what he has to do as defender of the civic state. The result is mutual destruction, and the result of such tragic reflection for the Greeks was the gradual undoing of their faith in their ethical harmony and "beauty" and their becoming more reflective and "philosophical," which resulted in turn in the gradual and necessary undermining of the beliefs necessary to sustain their way of life.

The attempts by the successors to the doomed Greek ethical harmony to fashion a worthy way of life for themselves could only result in a long period of European self-alienation in the absence of such harmony. As he had in the "Reason" chapter, Hegel sketched out a brilliant, obscure, and provocative account of the logic of the line of development from Roman to contemporary times. The alienated, "formal" unity of the Roman Empire, bound by no common substantial ends, was maintained only by the force of its legions, the formal character of its laws, and the power and authority of the emperor, who was represented as an "absolute person," a "titanic self-consciousness that thinks of itself as an actual living god," who is only "really conscious of what he is . . . in the destructive power he exercises against the self of his subjects."[9] The "legal person" in Roman life, deprived of any "social substance," thus had to find his "substance" within himself, in the stoical contemplation of his life and the alienated give-and-take of the legal relations of the empire. The result was the creation of a new type of "interiority" among its citizens, a new type of concern with inwardness and subjectivity.

The dissolution of the Roman Empire and its crystallization into "Christendom" and then even later into "Europe" provided only a further fragmented and alienated set of ideals. The warriors dominating the scene in early medieval Europe came to understand themselves to be the spiritual descendants of the Roman patricians, to be *aristocrats*, and since the Roman way of life had bequeathed a conception of the self as fundamentally lacking any substance on its own, all that could count for these "aristocrats" was obtaining honor and glory in the eyes of appropriate others. The logic of such aristocratic recognition eventually required there to be a single point of authority that bestowed such recognition, and this achieved its historical apogee in the figure of the absolute monarch, Louis XIV, the Sun King, who effectively turned what might have been a sullen and rebellious aristocracy into a fawning set of courtiers eager for favors and valuable opportunities for investment. With that, the ideals of the aristocracy effectively merged with those of the merchants, the bourgeoisie; and since the aristocrats had defined themselves in terms of being devoted to king and country and not to the "common" and vulgar pursuit of money and comfort, the linchpins of belief in the right of the aristocracy to govern collapsed when that form of negative self-definition dissolved.

The collapse of the aristocratic ideal left only a fragmented world that presented its participants with conflicting and contradictory demands for belief and action. (Hegel appealed to and cited Denis Diderot's short dialogue "Rameau's Nephew" – translated only in 1805 by Goethe – to illustrate the emptiness and lack of orientation experienced by such agents trying to make their way in such a fragmented world.) Something like a "pure consciousness" that was "above" the fragmented forms of social life seemed to be required, and by the eighteenth century that demand itself had become the scene of another form of modern fragmentation. The oddly sectarian skirmishes between the coexisting movements of skeptical modern Enlightenment and emotionalist modern religion – Pietism in Germany, Jansenism and Quietism in France, Wesleyanism in Great Britain – embodied this fragmented outlook. One side, the Enlightenment, believed that the exercise of "pure insight" by individuals, abstracted away from all tradition and social relations, could generate a set of ideals that would command allegiance; the other side, "Faith," believed that an emotional encounter with God and a corresponding orientation in life would follow if one personally opened one's heart in the right way, and that one required no treatises from learned theologians to accomplish this.

The failure of either "Enlightenment" or "Faith" to decisively resolve that dispute (and the premature triumph of Enlightenment against "faith" in European intellectual life) resulted in the completely fragmented social "whole" of modernity, itself seemingly incapable of providing any real guidance for people since it embodied completely contradictory ideals within itself. Out of this fragmented social life, however, the modern, despairing experience of "groundlessness" gradually reshaped itself into a project of "self-grounding," of working out one's rational commitments from within a conception of free, self-determining "subjectivity." This was given political expression in what for Hegel was *the* decisive modern event, the French Revolution. How-ever, without any "grounded" social institutions to mediate the claim to "absolute freedom" embodied in the revolutionary upheaval – with all the old social roles discredited and with no guidance except the general injunction to "be free" – no group in the Revolution could establish itself as anything more than just another particular point of view, just another "faction." With nothing more to guide it than the abstract utilitarian thought bequeathed to it by the Enlightenment, that "absolute freedom" violently obliterated the distinction between indi-viduals, and the Revolution became the Terror, with the sanitized exe-cutions of the guillotine serving to protect the "whole" from those who supposedly threatened it. The routinized mass executions in the name of revolutionary justice resulted in nothing more, as Hegel put it, than "the coldest and stalest of deaths, with no more significance than cutting off a head of cabbage or swallowing a mouthful of water."[10]

As he had suggested in his lectures of 1805–06, Hegel argued some-what obliquely in the *Phenomenology* that the revolutionary terror had to end when it was no longer felt by the citizens of revolutionary France to be necessary to protect the country from attack from without. With the fall of Robespierre, the Revolution began to institutionalize itself, a process that was completed only with the arrival of Napoleon, whom Hegel saw as the key figure in finishing the "novel" of the Revolution and a central personage in the story of the way the abstract ideals of modern freedom began to take form in social practice.

Modern Life, Modern Morality, and "Beautiful Souls"

A major point of Hegel's discussion of the development of the spirit of modern Europe in the chapter on "*Geist*" was to show how the political revolution in France had effectively broken with the old ideals, thus setting the stage socially and intellectually for a fundamental rethinking of what a worthy way of life based purely on the norms and commit-ments that would precipitate out of our own activities of fully *mutual* recognition would look like. Hegel argued that although the French had begun the political phase of the modern revolution, the torch had nonetheless passed to German philosophy to complete in theory what the Revolution had only begun in practice.[11]

The first phase of this activity lay in Kant's own theoretically revo-

lutionary claim that freedom should be an end in itself. The Enlightenment had culminated in a view of the "whole" that orients us in life as
consisting only in the abstract claims of "utility," of the greatest happiness for all. The Revolution, under Rousseau's influence, had culminated in a vision of "absolute freedom" as determined by a "general
will," which in the development of the Revolution became identified
with the "nation." Kant saw that what was required had to be a self-
determined whole that made room for the individual agent and neither
swallowed him in abstractions such as "utility" nor reduced him to
moral insignificance as merely a cog in the machine of the "nation."
Instead, in Kant's hands, the emphasis on spontaneity and freedom
committed us to a "moral worldview," an ideal of a way of life that
recognizes the dignity of all and in which each autonomously wills as a
member of the "kingdom of ends."

To conceive of oneself as a "moral" agent and to will as a member of
the "kingdom of ends" requires one to do one's duty, that is, both to
do what is right and to be motivated to perform the action solely on
account of its rightness, its justifiability, and not on account of some
other attractive, empirical feature of the action (such as its utility or its
promoting one's own happiness). Thus, the "moral worldview," so
Hegel argued, always sets into opposition "morality" and the "actuality" of the individual willing agent (his relationships, his inclinations,
his own project for his life, and so on). The proponents of the "moral
worldview" put the *individual* at center stage; but they claimed that he
was required to act from *universal* duty alone.

The "moral worldview," so eloquently elaborated by Kant and developed to its one-sided conclusion by Fichte, thus had to feign and
dissemble about acting only for duty's sake, since, by putting the self-
determining individual at the center of their account, they made such a
thing impossible. The philosophers of the "moral worldview" displayed
their implicit acknowledgment of this dilemma in the ways in which
they were forever smuggling in additional motivation to make up for
their overly rigorous conception of moral duty. Kant himself even
argued for commitments to various "postulates" concerning rewards for
virtue in the next life. Such "postulates," however, only demonstrated
that the proponents of the "moral worldview" had implicitly although
not explicitly acknowledged that self-determining individuals neither do
nor can act from duty alone and for that reason, such postulates could

only be "feigning" maneuvers to avoid coming to terms with the implicit contradictions at work in the "moral worldview."

It is thus no surprise, Hegel concluded, that the early Romantics in the late eighteenth century – and in Jena in particular – picked up on this deficiency of the "moral worldview" and took the Kantian and Fichtean emphasis on "spontaneity" and "autonomy" in a different direction. The "moral worldview" had shown that as self-determining moral agents, we had to be true to our own *consciences* as to whether we were acting out of respect for the moral law or out of more mundane considerations; the early Romantics attempted to effect a shift of moral consciousness away from the idea of obedience to a self-imposed *law* and toward the idea of being "true to oneself," of finding one's way around in the world in a manner that "fits" one's own nature. Kant had tried to make room for individuals but had dissolved all significant notion of individuality into the rigorism of his theory; the early Romantics reacted by bringing the individual fully back into the picture. Whereas Kant, in his notion of the universal "moral law," stressed the *impersonality* of reason's demands, the early Romantics stressed the *uniqueness* of each individual and the need to appeal to a sense of being both true to oneself and of being capable of attaining an ironic distance from oneself and one's surroundings, all the while being open to the claims of the emotions in finding one's way around in the world.

That emphasis on conscience and uniqueness, however, necessarily collapsed into a self-defeating doctrine of "beauty of soul," of maintaining the purity of one's own convictions independent of the social consequences of one's actions and the judgments of others.[12] Hegel characterizes the "beautiful soul" as an agent of such purity of motive that he never acts from "mere" "inclination" but always and solely on the basis of what is most essential about himself. The alleged "beauty" of the "beautiful soul" supposedly consists in the way in which the fragmentation characteristic of modern social reality is thereby absent from his unsullied unity, purity, and innocence. However, exactly because the "beautiful soul" is unified and undivided within himself – he is "beautiful" in opposition to the degraded and fragmented "ugly" characteristics of the modern world in which he lives – he essentially cannot *act* in that fragmented world without thereby also sullying that undivided "beauty" of his soul. Seen in that way, the "beautiful soul" is the "moral worldview's" agent completely withdrawn into himself, who can no longer dare to act because action in a fragmented world would inevitably stain the purity of the moral motive. To act is to take a stance in the actual world, to do something that in fragmented circumstances will necessarily be seen by others, perhaps even by oneself, as wicked or misguided. Facing up to that, the "beautiful soul" also assumes the shape of the Romantic ironist (perhaps embodied in the form of Friedrich Schlegel, Hegel's nemesis at Jena), who realizes the necessity for acting but eschews all justification in terms of general principles, so only his "beautiful" conscience can discern what the particularities of each situation require.

The result of the stress on the primacy of maintaining beauty of soul is that the community of "beautiful souls" itself fragments into two camps. One camp consists in those "beautiful souls" who suffer from the kind of paralysis that comes from fear of doing anything at all and who thereby become judgmental moralists, holding fast to the rigorist purity of their moral vision; the other camp consists of those who realize the necessity of action but who eschew having to offer justification for it, since they claim they are only being true to themselves in particular situations. The result is the very modern frenzy for accusations and counteraccusations of hypocrisy, charges of only pretending to have a "beautiful soul," countered by charges of "radical evil," of substituting one's own particular interests for those of morality itself. Such accusations and counteraccusations, though, set the stage for a fully modern Christian *reconciliation*, for the acknowledgement and confession by each agent that each of them is, after all, only a particular point of view and that out of the whirl of competing unique points of view, we are nonetheless obligated to act on reasons that can be shared by all. Such reasons must be negotiated and struggled over; they can never be just "given," and the struggle can be reconciliatory only to the extent that it is guided by a Christian religious viewpoint that we are all "sinners," all in need of mutual forgiveness.

Religion and Absolute Knowing

If modern life is reconciliatory only by virtue of a certain type of mutual forgiveness carried out in a religious practice, then it had to be established just what would count as such a religious practice for "we moderns." Hegel's book had already turned out to be much longer than he had originally planned, and he now added yet another long chapter in an already very large book, a penultimate chapter offering an account of how and why Christianity could lay claim to be *the* modern religion. There were both systematic and personal reasons for doing so: Hegel's reflections on *Geist* as the "I that is We and the We that is I" – that we are each "minded" only to the extent that others are so "like-minded" – put him in a position to return to his earliest concerns about what would count as a "modern" religion and to give them full voice in his newfound philosophical view.[13]

From Hegel's 1806 standpoint, religious practice is essentially a collective reflection on what ultimately matters to us, on what humanity's highest interests are – in short, on what it means to be the kind of *geistig*, "minded" creatures we are. In religious reflection, as in artistic and philosophical reflection, we encounter "the spirit that knows itself as spirit."[14] Quite strikingly, though, Hegel argued that religious reflection is fundamentally different from theoretical reflection, offering something that theoretical, philosophical reflection simply cannot offer, *even though*, as his argument turns out, in modern times it must also be subordinate to philosophical reflection.[15]

Religion is the collective reflection on the "divine" through rite, ritual, and symbol. It "represents" the divine instead of "conceptually" articulating it. As such a form of reflection, it too progresses historically as part of a way of life; the various shapes of religious practice and reflection emerge from the very specific ways in which earlier forms of such reflection fail on their own terms, and what counts as sacred and divine can only be understood by grasping the way in which it has come to be sacred and divine for a people.

The earliest forms of such reflection on divinity take the form of "nature religions," in which the divine is interpreted as an abstract natural "whole" that does not necessarily concern itself especially with humanity; such "natural" religious reflection culminates in the "nature religions" of Egyptian life. Egyptian religion, though, was unsatisfactory because it only abstractly combined human and natural concerns in its highly symbolic works of art; its divinities remained fundamentally opaque even to the Egyptians, and the creators of its statuary and relics were thereby never able to rise to the level of art, remaining instead only "artisans," capable of great craftsmanship but incapable of using their talents to direct communal reflection on the divine.

It took the Greek breakthrough, in which the gods took on the forms of idealized human beauty, to depart from "nature religions." In "nature religions," the divinity's concerns are simply different from humanity's concerns, and thus man and the divine can never be reconciled in such religions. Moreover, as idealized forms of human beauty, the Greek divinities call on the creators of statuary to do more than produce well-crafted results; they call on them to adequately capture the sheer beauty of divinity in their works. The Greek artisans thus gradually became instead artists, men (and women) involved in leading the communal thought on what was at stake in mortal life. Likewise, the people themselves ceased to be mere supplicants begging for the gods' favors; the community itself became a necessary participant in the ways of the gods and in the way the gods appeared.

This introduced, however, a kind of "negativity" already implicit in all religious reflection into Greek life. As they crafted their works, the internal tensions in the ideals to which they were collectively committed began to be made explicit. In their epic of self-creation, of how they came to be the "people" they were – Homer's *Iliad* and *Odyssey* – the role of fate came to the fore and the general issue of whether Troy's destruction was in fact in accordance with *justice* emerged. The creation of tragedy (already discussed by Hegel in the book in the section on *Antigone*) only accentuated this "negativity," and in comedy, that "negativity," that practice of reflective criticism and "criticism of criticism," emerged in full force. In comedy, the pretensions and self-deceptions of everyday life are put in the foreground and made the object of laughter in order to point out the deeper substantial truths at work in a way of life. In Greek comedy, that only served to bring out the role of the detached, reflective individual, the ironic character who sees the folly of what is going on around him. By no accident, tragedy, comedy, and Socratic philosophy emerged at the same time, and the "beautiful whole" of Greek life could not survive being put under the scrutiny of that kind of ultimately philosophical, reflective, individualized attention to itself. The Greeks own triumphs in art (epic, tragedy, and comedy) ultimately undid the allegiance they had formerly held to the way of life that brought those triumphs about.

Greek religion thus created the necessity for the kind of Stoic religion of the Romans, and out of the practices of individualized and alienated self-reflection of the Roman period following the denouement of Greek beauty and harmony, Christianity emerged as the "revelation" in the teachings of Jesus of Nazareth that God was *Geist*, that His nature was fully manifest to us, that the concerns of divinity and humanity were not at odds with each other, and that the divine had in fact become human. Christianity taught that God was "love," and that the divine's claims on us were therefore to be found in human "hearts" after they had opened themselves to the potential transformation in their own "hearts" that was necessary for them to appreciate this "love." Moreover, the Christian rites and practices of introspection, of forgiving one's enemy, doing penance for one's sins, and asking for forgiveness oneself – only fostered the kind of self-transformation that enabled people to absorb the Christian teachings.

Jesus' death was the death of God, the way in which God became human. The divine, Hegel argued, had thereby been made manifest as rational self-conscious *Geist* itself. This did not imply that man was God; in Christian religion, Hegel argued, we acknowledge that we worship not ourselves, which would be absurd, but the "divine principle" within ourselves, a claim he was later to try to make good in his "philosophy of nature." The divine in Christianity is the rational structure of the whole in which we live and work, are born and die, not some transcendent entity beyond human life and concerns. The divine is in one sense only the way in which the world embodies within itself the potential for *Geist*, for our "mindedness" and "like-mindedness," which comes to its penultimately full realization in the human religious community.

Even modern Christian religion itself, however, is not capable of formulating that truth about itself. For that, we require "philosophy," the kind of "absolute knowing" that consists in our own historicized self-understanding that expresses itself in the *Phenomenology*'s account of modernity as the necessary result of humanity's own history – not as a result of blind causal forces but as a way of life that can justify its own claims to allegiance and continually reinvent itself along rational lines. The modern faith in reason is capable of redeeming itself and continually renewing itself, guiding itself only by the lights of the kind of self-bootstrapping, communally understood project of rationally comprehending what ultimately matters to us. That project completed itself in the philosophical self-knowing that was "our" self-knowledge in the *Phenomenology of Spirit*, the final chapter of Hegel's book, his own self-described "voyage of discovery." In that book, Hegel, the Seminary student and failed "popular philosopher," became, irrevocably and finally in a form satisfactory to himself, *Hegel*, the systematic philosopher of *Geist* and modern life.

6

Life in Transition: From Jena to Bamberg

Hegel's Life Unravels

AS HEGEL WAS WORKING on the *Phenomenology*, his situation at Jena was becoming more and more tenuous. His inheritance was rapidly running out, and his position at Jena did not pay him a salary. When another *Privatdozent* at Jena, J. F. Fries, was promoted to "extraordinary professor," Hegel found himself particularly incensed. There was certainly no love lost between Hegel and Fries; both Fries's comments about Hegel in his letters to friends and Hegel's comments on Fries are equally nasty. Fries represented what to Hegel was a shallow and wrongheaded way to continue the Kantian revolution, namely, through a kind of psychologistic study of the ways in which the mind synthesized ideas (a strategy Hegel thought he had laid to rest in "Faith and Knowledge"). Fries, who had been raised in a famous Pietist community and continued to have warm contacts with it, also professed a "religion of the heart" that Hegel held in even lower regard. Moreover, and perhaps most importantly, Fries was an outspoken public and private critic of the whole line of thought that ran from Fichte to Schelling, did little to conceal his opinion that the whole movement – especially that represented by Schelling – was not just mistaken but was outright patent nonsense, and was professionally at first more successful than Hegel. As a *Privatdozent* at Jena, Fries was also a direct competitor with Hegel for students – Fries also lectured on "natural right" and on "logic and metaphysics," and he was just as ambitious as Hegel. The two men, moreover, belonged to very different circles of friends in Jena; indeed, the lists of those whom the two regarded as friends overlap in only a few places. Fries, for example, had never met Goethe, whom

Hegel had come to know and whose friendship he cultivated, and he had never met Schiller.

Fries's animosity to the line of post-Kantian idealism of which Hegel was part became all the more evident in 1803 with the publication of his book *Reinhold, Fichte und Schelling*. The book was a highly polemical tract against what Fries saw as the rubbish put forth by Jena's post-Kantian idealists, against which Fries propounded his own anthropologized and psychologized Kantian view: "Our reason," Fries said, "is an excitability, which only through particular stimulations or affections can be determined to be expressions of life (*Lebensäußerungen*); its expressions are knowledge."[1] In 1803, Fries even went so far as to publish an anonymous satirical piece – although everybody knew who the author was – called, in a play on a title by Fichte, *Sonnenklarer Beweis, daß in Prof. Schelling's Naturphilosophie nur die von Hofrath Voigt in Jena schon längst vorgetragenen Grundsätze der Physik wiederholt werde, ein Neujahrsgeschenk für Freunde der Naturkunde* ("A Crystal Clear Demonstration that in Prof. Schelling's Philosophy of Nature Only the Principles of Physics that Have Already Been Long Since Presented by Privy Councilor Voigt in Jena Are Repeated, a New Year's Gift for Friends of Natural History") – in which he accused Schelling of more or less plagiarizing some lectures given by Voigt in 1793.[2]

In addition to being a competitor with Hegel for students at Jena, Fries also rapidly became a competitor for the scarce positions at other universities for which Hegel longed. Both Fries and Hegel had their eyes on a position at the newly reformed university of Würzburg, and Hegel was to be particularly stung by Fries's connections there. The rationalist Enlightenment Protestant theologian, H. E. G. Paulus, who had been one of Hegel's friends and who had moved from Jena to Würzburg at the same time as Schelling, had never particularly liked Schelling and in Würzburg had come to regard Schelling with undisguised contempt. Paulus was the one friend that Fries and Hegel shared, but, unfortunately for Hegel, Paulus' loathing for Schelling and Schelling's philosophy led him to write to Fries to tell him that he was trying to attain a position for Fries at Würzburg in order to have a "Kantian" counterweight to what Paulus could only view as the Schellingian silliness taking root there. Hegel's friendship with Schelling, whose star was starting to set, and Paulus's friendship with Fries, whose star was on the rise, thus virtually insured that Hegel would not get a position at Würzburg. It was painful to Hegel that the one place where he had friends and might hope for some help in securing a position thus turned out to be a place where one of his own acquaintances was promoting someone whose ideas Hegel could only look on with derision and who was publicly outspoken in his denunciations and ridicule of the line of thought into which Hegel had thrown his lot.[3] Fries, moreover, was outpublishing Hegel, having published not only *Reinhold, Fichte und Schelling* but also a volume in 1803 on the philosophy of law (*Philosophical Doctrine of Right and Critique of All Positive Legislation*).[4] Because of all these complications, Hegel and Fries established a deep antipathy for each other that lasted their whole lives.

In Hegel's eyes, the fact that Fries and not he was to be promoted could only have been experienced as the deepest affront. Acutely aggrieved, Hegel politely protested in a letter to Goethe that if Fries were going to be promoted, then he too certainly deserved promotion, and he laid out his case for his deserving promotion (including his usual promise to bring out his "system" in book form very soon); his ploy was successful, and in 1805 he managed to have himself promoted along with Fries to "extraordinary professor." Unfortunately, the position carried the same salary as his former position: nothing. Moreover, to accept the position also meant that he had both to gain permission from the Württemberg Consistorial Church authorities and, since accepting the position at Jena was accepting employment by a foreign prince, to forsake the minor stipend he had been receiving from the consistory in Württemberg. This was difficult: His Württemberg stipend had never amounted to much, but at least it was *something*. In 1806, Goethe finally managed to get Hegel a salary of 100 Thalers, but this amounted to little more than an honorarium; the lowliest student was expected to have 200 Thalers simply to be able to support himself at the barest subsistence level.

The untenability and precariousness of Hegel's overall situation in Jena comes out clearly in his letters to his friend Immanuel Niethammer. The letters written to Niethammer during this period make continual references not only to various jobs that Hegel hopes Niethammer might assist him in procuring but also to the money he has borrowed from Niethammer, and finally resort to outright pleading for money. For lack of funds, Hegel was forced to leave his old apartment and move to a smaller, cheaper place on Löbdergraben (at or very near the place that his friend Hölderlin had occupied some years earlier and next-door to where Fichte had earlier lived). By 1806, Caroline Schelling was writing to Friedrich Schelling about how bad things were getting in Jena and how people were reduced to having very little, noting, "One cannot say how Hegel managed to bring himself through it all."[5]

Hegel was desperate for a position, and to get a position, he needed a book. During this period, he wrote a letter (drafted at least three times, the final draft probably being written in May, 1805) to Johann Heinrich Voss, the translator of Homer and a major figure in his time, hoping to enlist Voss's help in securing a position at the newly reconstituted university at Heidelberg. (After the rearrangement of the German map following the *Reichsdeputationshauptschluß* of 1803, Heidelberg fell under the rule of the principality of Baden, and the grand duke of Baden took it upon himself to rebuild the virtually ruined university there very much along the lines of the then rapidly disintegrating university at Jena; Voss was one of the luminaries he lured to Heidelberg to achieve his aim.) In his letter to Voss, Hegel lays out what he hopes to be his career path; he remarks on philosophy as the "queen of the sciences" (indicating his full acceptance of the Fichtean understanding of the role of philosophy in the university), and he even flatters Voss by comparing his translation of Homer to Luther's translation of the Bible, noting that he (Hegel) hopes himself to "teach philosophy to speak German," and hints not so subtly about how his having some position at Heidelberg would enable him to pursue the "common aims" that he suggests he and Voss share. He even suggests, no doubt sincerely, that he "would wish to cover a particular field of philosophy not represented at Heidelberg, i.e., to lecture on aesthetics in the sense of a *cours de littérature*," and he notes that "by fall I will give an exposition of my work as a system of philosophy" (referring, almost certainly, to his work on what was to become the *Phenomenology of Spirit* – as always, though, Hegel failed to make good on the claim, this time fortunately being off by only about a year).[6] Nothing came of Hegel's entreaties to Voss, although he received a very courteous and seemingly heartfelt reply wishing him good luck. Niethammer was also unable to find anything for him. Finally, to pile insult on top of desperation, his adversary J. F. Fries was able in 1805 to land the position in Heidelberg for which Hegel had entertained hopes; Fries had done so

with the help of his friend Henry Crabb Robinson, the English student
at Jena, who by various accidents had come to be taken seriously enough
by a number of important people to exercise some influence in German
academic circles; Fries thus acquired – to Hegel's chagrin, with Voss's
assistance – the salaried position of an "ordinary professor" at Heidelberg.

Writing to a friend (the Catholic physician and mystic Karl Joseph
Windischmann) several years later (1810), Hegel spoke of a dark period
in his life, a "mood of the soul, or rather of reason" during which he
had no clear idea of where he was heading, which he characterized both
as a "hypochondria" – a depression – from which he suffered "to the
point of exhaustion," and as nonetheless a "turning point in his life"
during which his self-confidence grew.[7] Hegel was no doubt referring
to his overall stay in Berne, partially to some events late in his stay in
Frankfurt, but most of all he was referring to his time spent in Jena and
to the "turning point" he experienced there in 1805–06. Certainly, if
there was ever a period during which, as Hegel puts it in the letter, his
soul, confronted with a "chaos of phenomena," was in a state in which
"though inwardly certain of the goal, [it had] not worked its way
through them to clarity and to a detailed account of the whole," it was
during that stretch in Jena when he was constantly revising his various
"system drafts" and hanging on as best he could to his unsettled
existence. Hegel's account shows that he dealt with his slump into deep
depression by working even harder.[8]

He offered some advice to Windischmann, which is significant for
what it says about himself: "It is science (*Wissenschaft*) which has led
you into the labyrinth of the soul, and science alone is capable of leading
you out again and healing you." What is especially striking about this
piece of advice – other than its being one of the few instances in which
Hegel talks about himself in any emotional terms at all – is that Hegel
does not mention *religion* as his salvation, nor does he recommend it to
Windischmann. In the dark night of the soul, for Hegel (at least in
1810), not religion, not even God, but devotion to scholarly work is
alone capable of providing salvation for people like himself. The priority
of "science" over religion was thus not merely something that Hegel
proposed in theory; at that point in his life, his own experience had
obviously shown him that religion was not, *for him*, the full answer to
his own problems.

Depressed as he was becoming about the turn of events in his life, Hegel nonetheless was not paralyzed by it, even though his situation was depressing enough. A Danish romantic poet, Adam Oehlenschläger, who visited Jena in the summer of 1806, remembered finding Hegel a particularly lively and good-hearted fellow. He and Hegel became friends after sharing a comical evening at a piano recital, where someone was trying to play some sentimental piece on the piano while singing along with it; apparently, his playing was awful, his singing worse. Both Hegel and Oehlenschläger were standing behind the chair of the person singing and playing, and as the piece wore on and got worse, the absurdity of the situation crept up on them; they kept exchanging glances and while straining to be polite, found that the more they tried to stifle their laughter, the harder it became to do so, and that every time they glanced at each other, it only increased the impulse to laugh. The two became good friends and took walks and talked every day. On one walk with some other friends, one of them, Professor Franz Joseph Schelver, a renowned botanist, gathered some cherries and berries from someone's garden, which Hegel jokingly explained away as not being the theft of fruit so much as it was serious botanical research on Schelver's part.

G. A. Gabler remembered Hegel's being honored by the festive singing of students outside his house, a homage customary for a new *Prorector* to receive but which was only done for particularly popular professors. Hegel, as always a bit clumsy in such a public setting, was clearly surprised by this show of affection and, as Gabler put it, uttered "some obscure words about the meaning of science" to the students, remarking, typically, that he accepted the honor in the name of "respect and recognition" for such science.[9]

Hegel was trying his best to hold up his spirits, but it was nonetheless clear to everyone that his professional options were drying up. Even his old friend and protector Schelling was continuing to experience troubles since his move to Würzburg, troubles that went beyond Paulus's enmity for him. The Catholic clergy there, having decided that he was an enemy of their religion, had furiously turned against him, and the Catholic bishops even forbade Catholic students from attending Schelling's lectures, threatening them with excommunication if they did. In 1805, however, after the Treaty of Pressburg (following yet another defeat of the Austrians by the French), Bavaria, which had been given

Würzburg only a few years before, had to give it over to Austrian interests in exchange for a significant enlargement of its own territory and its becoming a kingdom (its reward for having sided with France). Schelling refused to take an oath of loyalty to the new regime, and in compensation the Bavarian government made him a member of the Bavarian Academy of the Sciences in Munich. On April 17, 1806, Schelling left Würzburg for Munich. Schelling could thus be of no help, and even Goethe, the magisterial figure whose friendship Hegel had carefully cultivated since coming to Jena and who actually looked quite favorably on Hegel's work, was incapable (to his own regret) of doing much for Hegel.

Realizing that he was now under extreme pressure to publish his long-promised book, Hegel arranged to have his "system" brought out by a publisher in Bamberg named Goebhardt, who agreed to pay him eighteen florins per page, with the first payment coming only after the first half of the book had been delivered to him. Of course, that raised the question of when a book is half-finished, and Hegel, it turned out, could not provide an answer, since he found his manuscript to be growing almost out of control as he wrote it. The publisher began to lose patience with his recalcitrant client and reneged on his promise of guaranteeing 1,000 copies of the *Introduction to the System of Science*, and not only reduced his part of the bargain to a promise of 750 copies but also refused all payment to Hegel until the whole manuscript, not just half of it, was delivered to him. After several mournful entreaties from Hegel, Immanuel Niethammer intervened and promised the publisher that he himself would buy up the entire run if Hegel did not get the manuscript in by the deadline (which was fixed at October 18, 1806).

Whether Niethammer knew the risk he was running – this was the same Hegel who had been promising a book since 1802 – is not clear. (Perhaps Niethammer had seen enough of the manuscript to believe that, for once, Hegel had an excellent chance of actually finishing it on time.) Hegel thanked Niethammer profusely, and set to work trying to bring the manuscript to an end. But as he was doing this, Hegel was also writing to just about everybody he knew asking them about possible leads for employment (as an academic, as editor of a journal, as doing *anything* in intellectual life that paid a salary).

Just as he was finishing the book, something else happened that he could not have predicted: Napoleon, the man who wished to "finish the novel" of the Revolution, appeared with French troops outside of Jena. Prussia had not engaged French troops since the calamitous Battle of Valmy in 1792. In the meantime, Prussia had occupied British Hannover, thereby upsetting the British; in the summer of 1806, in talks with the British about peace, France suggested that Hannover be returned to Britain, all of which caused Prussia to align itself with Russia against France. On September 13, Prussia sent its troops into Saxony. On October 14, as Hegel was finishing up what was to become the *Phenomenology of Spirit*, Napoleon engaged the Prussian troops on a plateau outside of Jena. The battle lasted only for the afternoon and ended with the Prussians in a full, anarchic, chaotic retreat, their once-dominant army having been decimated by the French troops. (Friedrich Gabriel von Clausewitz, the great theorist of modern warfare and a later acquaintance of Hegel's in Berlin, was with the Prussian troops that day; his reflections on the causes of the Prussians' humiliating defeat at the Battle of Jena motivated him to begin his famous reconceptualization of the nature of modern warfare.)

During the battle, the city of Jena was shelled and many houses on one of the main streets of the town (the Johannisgasse) were set aflame. Before the battle, Hegel had packed up his things and gone to stay at first with the well-placed parents of one of his students – Georg Andreas Gabler, who ironically enough was later to become the first successor to Hegel's chair at Berlin – and then later with his friends the Frommanns, who had a large house on the other side of the small town; on returning to his own place, Hegel found it ransacked by the French, remarking in a letter to Niethammer that the "knaves have, to be sure, messed up my papers like lottery tickets."[10] On October 13, one day before the climactic battle, Napoleon entered the town of Jena, and Hegel, ever the admirer of the Revolution, noted famously in a letter to Niethammer that "I saw the Emperor – this world-soul – riding out of the city on reconnaissance. It is indeed a wonderful sensation to see such an individual, who, concentrated here at a single point, astride a horse, reaches out over the world and masters it . . . this extraordinary man, whom it is impossible not to admire."[11] That Hegel said this to Niethammer at that time is all the more striking since at that point he had already composed the crucial section of the *Phenomenology* in which he remarked that the Revolution had now officially passed to another land

(Germany) that would complete "in thought" what the Revolution had only partially accomplished in practice – as it were, that the "novel of the Revolution" was to be completed by German philosophy, not by French politics.[12] The fact that Hegel had mostly completed the book at this point gave rise to the legend, most famously put in words by his student Eduard Gans, that "under the thunder of the battle of Jena he completed the Phenomenology of Spirit."[13] (Hegel himself helped to supply material for that legend, even describing the *Phenomenology* in a later letter to Niethammer as "my book, which I completed the night before the battle of Jena," a statement which, of course, was only partially true.)[14]

The *Phenomenology* was, though, completed under heady and, for Hegel, also depressing circumstances. On July 12, 1806, Napoleon had used his influence to officially establish the Confederation of the Rhine, an alliance of sixteen German states (soon to become twenty-three) that included almost all the old member states of the Holy Roman Empire (excluding, notably, Prussian and Austria). One of the conditions for membership (which was forced on the participants by the French) was that the members of the confederation had to renounce membership in the Holy Roman Empire. That condition effectively ended the existence of the empire. On August 6, 1806, the official herald of the Holy Roman Empire, the old *Reich*, read a proclamation in Vienna (with all the usual flourishes and after the appropriate trumpet fanfare) that announced that the emperor had abdicated his position as emperor of the Holy Roman Empire; in doing so, the emperor had thereby illegally but nonetheless effectively dissolved the empire itself. Thus, the empire under whose terms and laws Hegel had always lived vanished right before his eyes; moreover, in later smashing what was once the vaunted Prussian military at the battle of Jena, Napoleon had snuffed out any possible hope for its reconstitution. The seemingly invincible French now had a sturdy buffer between themselves and Austria and Prussia: The new member states of the Confederation of the Rhine were large enough to defend themselves (unlike the *Länder* of the old Holy Roman Empire) but not large enough to pose any real threat to France, to whom, in any event, they were allied.

Hegel himself apparently regretted neither the empire's dissolution nor Napoleon's coup de grace, but he was certainly unnerved by the whole set of events. On the eve of the battle of Jena itself, Hegel sent most of the last pages of his book by special courier to the publisher; on October 18, he claimed to be carrying the last sheets with him in his pocket, fearful that they might get lost. Shortly after the battle and its aftermath, Hegel, who only a few days before had admired Napoleon from his window, remarked in one of his letters to Immanuel Nietham-mer, "nobody has imagined war as we have seen it."[15]

But as the publication of the book drew near, what Hegel had hoped would be the high point of his life – the publication of *his* system, *his* chance to take what he saw as his rightful place in the post-Kantian disputes – started turning out to be something completely different. On February 5, 1807, two weeks after Hegel, now virtually penniless, had finished a new Preface for the book, the housekeeper and landlady of the house where Hegel was living, Christiana Charlotte Johanna Burk-hardt, gave birth to his illegitimate son, Ludwig. With no money, no real paying job, and a child by a woman who was married to someone who had recently abandoned her, Hegel's situation now became com-pletely and totally desperate.

Farewell to Jena

The Demise of the University

The Battle of Jena and its aftermath left the university and the city devastated. By 1805 the war situation and the continual movement of troops in and out of the city had brought hard economic times to Jena; during that time, food became more expensive and other prices steadily rose. The departure of the university's leading lights had also meant that many fewer students were now coming to the university to study, thereby further worsening the already declining economic situation of the town. With the city already in bad shape, matters became even worse as French troops went on a spree of plundering in the city both before and after the battle. Whole libraries belonging to professors disappeared along with many of their other possessions and just about any money they had with them. As French troops first entered the city, two emissaries from the university even went to speak with one of the French marshals to plead with him to spare the university; their reward for this effort was that their money and their watches were stolen from them on the spot.[16] One professor, Christian Gruner, suffered the most:

he had 18,000 Thalers taken from him. (Hegel himself noted in a letter to Niethammer how indeed "Gruner suffered very greatly.")[17] Only the few houses that had quartered French troops were spared from such looting, among them that belonging to the Frommann family (to which Hegel had retreated from his apartment on Löbdergraben). In fleeing his own residence, Hegel was certainly not alone; anyone who knew anybody who owned one of those houses and whom the owners permitted to move in prudently and quickly abandoned where they had been living. Johanna Frommann noted that at the time when Hegel was there that she had between 70 and 80 French people staying at her house, and the number of Germans raised the total number of people living in her house in those few days to about 130.[18] Moreover, for some time after the battle, the city was effectively turned into a military hospital for recovering French soldiers; many private homes, including those of many professors, were packed with convalescing French servicemen.

Things looked particularly bad for the university, since Napoleon, with his eye on administrative efficiency in newly conquered lands, had closed many German universities, saying that there were simply "many too many academies in Germany; one could arrange for instruction with many fewer."[19] (Halle, for example, temporarily suffered such a fate at Napoleon's hands.) However, Napoleon decided to spare the university at Jena. Meeting with a delegation of three people from the university (which included *Prorector* Gabler, at whose house Hegel had first taken refuge), Napoleon noted how the university had distinguished itself through the fame of its professors and in effect promised not to haul all of its goods away; by November 24, a letter to that effect was given to the university.[20] Napoleon partially made good on his promises, and by 1808, Jena had been compensated for the burning of its buildings with a payment of 30,000 Francs.[21]

(Napoleon did not meet with Goethe himself at this point, but almost two years later, in October 1808, he commanded an audience with the great man, from which a famous Napoleonic saying emerged. When asked by Goethe about whether tragedy could be still written around the idea of fate, Napoleon is said to have replied, "What do we want with fate now? Politics is our fate."[22] Hegel in fact liked that particular line so much, he later cited it as a classic Napoleonic line in his lectures in Berlin on the philosophy of world history. The actual conversation between Goethe and Napoleon, however, turned less on such grand themes; it was mostly concerned with Goethe's youthful novel *Sorrows of Young Werther*, which Napoleon claimed to have read seven times![23] Goethe was a public celebrity, someone whom people wanted personally to *meet*, and Napoleon was no exception.[24] Being as starstruck with Goethe's celebrity as any of the other passionate devotees of *Werther* at the time, Napoleon used his own renown to stage a conversation with the author so that he could ask him which parts of the novel were "real" and which were not. Napoleon's infatuation in meeting personally with such a celebrity probably contributed to Jena's receiving compensation for the damage.)

The damage to the university, however, had been done. When the winter semester began on November 3, 1806, only 130 students returned, and the university reached its lowest point for new students (only 31). Needless to say, these returning students had even less money to spend around town than before. Even those professors who had elected to stay in Jena while all others were abandoning the university now found themselves forced for economic reasons to look for employment elsewhere. Hegel was no different: He had no money, an illegitimate son, and he desperately needed some form of employment. He even had some reason to worry that he might be denied the money due him for turning in the whole manuscript of the *Phenomenology*, because he had missed the deadline for submitting it. His lawyer, however, assured him that acts of war created exculpatory reasons in such cases and that he had nothing to worry about.

During this period, Hegel was in constant correspondence with his old friend Immanuel Niethammer, who was by this time living in Bamberg. Like Paulus and Schelling, Niethammer had left Jena for the university at Würzburg, but when the city (and hence the university) was given over to the Austrians, Niethammer, a Protestant, had been dismissed and as compensation given a job in the Bavarian civil service. (The rich ecclesiastical city of Bamberg had been given to Bavaria in the reorganization of 1803.) The printer and publisher of the *Phenomenology* was situated in Bamberg, so Hegel suggested in a letter to Niethammer that it would be best if he (Hegel) came to stay for a while in Bamberg to look over the proofs, since he would just be able to make it through the winter on the money that the publisher, Goebhardt, owed him for completion of the manuscript (and, no doubt, because he owed Niethammer money and hoped to be able to continue to rely on the good will of the Niethammer family for support). Hegel's personal situation was desperate; he was mortifyingly compelled to ask Niethammer to "send me money without fail. I need it most urgently."[25]

Hegel traveled to Bamberg for a brief trip to oversee the proofs, and then he returned to Jena. But the event of February 5, 1807 – the birth of Hegel's illegitimate son, Ludwig – changed things for him. He not only needed money, he now had a child that he felt at least some moral obligation to support. (His legal obligations in this matter, to the extent that he had any under the laws of the time, were not at all clear.) When, out of the blue, Niethammer offered him a position as editor of a newspaper in Bamberg, Hegel jumped at the chance, although it is clear that he did it with some regret. He wanted to stay on at the university in Jena or move to some other university; his whole plan for his life that had taken root in his heart already in Berne if not even earlier at Tübingen had required him to be in a *university*. Instead, he was having to leave the university at which he had developed his thoughts and take another, completely unrelated job.

Although Fries had landed the professorship at Heidelberg for which Hegel had himself longed, Hegel had still held out hopes that he might go to Heidelberg, since so many of his former colleagues and friends from Jena had gone there. Jena itself had lost its luster for him; as he remarked in a letter written around this time, Jena "seemed like a cloister." The glory days of Jena had come and gone, and what had been only a few years before a vibrant center of German intellectual life had become a self-deceived small town in which, as Hegel put it, insignificant books "of which hardly a hundred copies had come before the public" were regarded as having worldwide importance.[26] Everyone else was moving on; but Hegel was stuck with no money and no real prospects for income.

Hopes for Other Appointments

Hegel jumped at every opportunity to hang onto his university career. One of his former Jena students, Karl Wilhelm Gottlob Kastner, had gone on to become a professor of chemistry at Heidelberg; Kastner raised Hegel's hopes by informing him of the possibility of a new literary journal being founded at Heidelberg, and hinted that Hegel might be able to assume the editorship of it. Another former Jena colleague and friend, Franz Joseph Schelver, who had also assumed a professorship at Heidelberg, wrote encouragingly to Hegel, holding out hope that Hegel would eventually gain some kind of post at Heidelberg (and noting that the rumors he had heard that Hegel was an unintelligible lecturer were only being circulated by students, not professors, and that he was trying to put them to rest). In that letter, Schelver asked Hegel about his thoughts on the kind of journal about which Kastner had earlier spoken, and Hegel quickly responded with a piece called "Maxims for the Journal of German Literature."

Hegel's reply exhibited some typical themes for him. The purpose of such a journal, he said, would be the "furthering of scientific and aesthetic cultivation (*Bildung*)."[27] (It would be, that is, the kind of journal to which his mother and father in Stuttgart would have subscribed.) This was to be accomplished by publishing "critiques" of existing works in which the general reader would be introduced to what were the basic *issues* in the various developing "sciences" in German life. It was definitely not to contain merely *reviews* of works in which the contents of various books were to be presented, nor was it to go into the special details of particular "sciences" (theology, law, medicine, whatever). Instead, it was to have the overall aim of achieving "universal spiritual cultivation (*Bildung*), and science and taste," which it was to do not by having authors insert their own "personal meanings" into the reviews, even when they were posing as "representatives of the public" by doing so.[28] (Hegel might well have been arguing for a German version of the *Edinburgh Review*, which followed much the same principles and had a wide readership in Britain and around the world at large – counting, for example, Napoleon, Madame de Stael, and Stendhal among its readers. It is clear that Hegel was reading the *Edinburgh Review* in his Heidelberg and Berlin periods, and he might well have been reading it earlier, since it was first published in 1802.)[29]

Moreover, it would above all avoid what Hegel saw as the kind of weak-minded philosophy that substituted feeling and mere opinion for reason. Hegel had particular reason to be envious of what he saw as the weak-minded philosophy that had emerged in Germany in those years, since it seemed to be becoming clear that it, and not the post-Kantian line of thought that he represented, was becoming the dominant trend in German philosophy. However, the vogue for such philosophy of "feeling" was only to heighten, and Hegel was not effectively able to stake out his own counterclaim until his years in Berlin after 1818.[30] Asked by Schelver to comment on particular authors, including Schelling, Hegel took the opportunity to take a swipe at his old friend Schelling, who, he ruefully noted, was now "solemnly beginning to renounce" the basic principles of true science that he had once championed.[31]

This did not, however, stop him from writing to Schelling himself in February 1807 to inform him of his move to Bamberg to assume the editorship of the newspaper – which he characterizes in the letter as "not even completely respectable" but "at least not dishonest" – and to inform him that he would nonetheless be more than happy to edit a critical journal of German literature if the Bavarian Academy of the Sciences (which Schelling was joining) were to support such an endeavor, commenting on how well suited he would be for such an endeavor and how such a journal under his supervision would support the attempts under way at that time to reform education in Bavaria (in which Niethammer was playing a key role).[32]

But nothing was to come of those attempts. No journal and no offer of editorship came from Heidelberg. Schelling more or less advised him to lay low for a while and take things slowly, throwing cold water on Hegel's hope that Schelling might be able to arrange something for Hegel with regard to any such journal in Munich; Schelling tried to soften the blow by speaking of the governing authorities in Munich as "anxious, small-minded" men who would only have a certain "anxiety" in the face of men such as Hegel.[33]

Finally, Hegel's last hope at Jena was dashed. He had hoped that after Schelver's (the botanist's) departure for Heidelberg, the authorities could be persuaded to replace a botanist with a speculative philosopher and that Schelver's salary might somehow thus be diverted to him. Hegel had even tried to convince Goethe that he might be suitable for giving lectures on botany in addition to his lectures on philosophy and for serving as the caretaker of the botanical gardens, even noting that he had "collected a herbarium in Switzerland, part of which I still preserve as a keepsake," and that being able to "move into the currently unoccupied apartment of the Ducal Botanical Garden" would be very helpful to him.[34] But, despite Hegel's efforts, the authorities finally decided that indeed they preferred to replace a botanist with another botanist and not, as Hegel had hoped, with someone like himself. (Hegel also tried to court a bit of favor with Goethe by mentioning a report that had come to him from Schelling: Schelling had written enthusiastically to Hegel about a discovery of a diviner – a person who locates underground water by feeling its "pull" on a stick he holds – on the "Tyrolian border." Schelling took this as empirical confirmation of some of the theses in his philosophy of nature, noting that the diviner's actions permit "unknowable polarities" to be displayed.[35] Unfortunately, and much to Schelling's embarrassment, the man was quickly exposed as a charlatan and conjurer. In a later letter to Schelling himself about the matter – before the exposure of the diviner as a fraud – Hegel rather gingerly responded to the whole issue by noting that he had perhaps too much "unsteadiness of hand" to do the experiment correctly himself.)[36]

With the position in Botany closed off to him, Hegel finally ran out of options. Bamberg was now his only choice.

Move to Bamberg

One of the striking features of Hegel's personality at this point was that he refused to blame the French for his troubles. His whole life was being disrupted by the French invasions of the German states and the way they had turned things topsy-turvy for the Germans. It would have been extremely easy for a person in his situation to have become embittered and to have explained his misfortunes away by making excuses of the form, "if only the French had not . . . ," but he never once succumbed to the temptation to blame them for his difficulties. Instead, Hegel came somewhat regretfully to the conclusion that he had no real alternative except to accept the offer of the editorship in Bamberg, something to which he was not completely averse but which was clearly second-best for him.

He was, however, still not willing to burn all his bridges in Jena. In his letter to Goethe about his move to Bamberg, he fudged the whole issue, saying that he had received a "temporary private business offer on the occasion" of his earlier trip to Bamberg and that "seeing that by accepting the offer I can for the time being provide my subsistence," he felt he should request "a leave of absence this summer from my professorship," noting that he hoped the day would come when his teaching at the university in Jena actually would "enable me to earn my subsistence as well as engage in higher occupations."[37] Obviously worried that his little ruse might be exposed, he even mentioned to Niethammer in his letter of acceptance of the Bamberg editorship that he was in fact going to dissemble to Goethe in just such a way, asking Niethammer not to contradict him should anyone ask.

In moving to Bamberg, though, Hegel had some reason to be more hopeful. Since Niethammer had just been appointed to a high position in Munich in the educational establishment of the kingdom of Bavaria, Hegel could hold out hope that Niethammer's influence would lead to some university appointment in one of the soon-to-be-organized or reorganized Bavarian universities. It clearly occurred to Hegel that it would be helpful to be in Bavaria if something like that were to become possible.

That he was also fleeing his awkward personal situation in Jena – the birth of his illegitimate son – no doubt also played a role in Hegel's thoughts on moving. The child was christened Georg Ludwig Friedrich Fischer (since his mother's maiden name was Fischer). Two godfathers were listed on his baptismal certificate (along with a statement that Ludwig Fischer was Johanna Burkhardt's third illegitimate child and that she was an abandoned wife): Hegel's close friend, the bookseller Friedrich Frommann, and Hegel's brother Georg Ludwig Hegel, who is identified in the documents as "Lieutenant in the Royal Württemberg Regiment, Crown Prince."[38] The child was named after both Friedrich Frommann and Hegel's brother, and this is one of the very few instances in which Hegel's brother makes any appearance in Hegel's post-Stuttgart life; for all practical purposes, Hegel never refers to him. Hegel also began shortly thereafter to refer to the child by the French name Louis instead of as Ludwig, as if he were trying to distance himself psychologically from the reality of his illegitimate child; he only became Ludwig to Hegel when in 1816, five years after his marriage, Hegel decided to accept him into his household.

It is also clear that this matter hung heavily on his conscience; in a letter to Frommann in July, 1808, he stated about Ms. Burkhardt that "I continue to regret painfully that so far I have not been fully able to extricate from her present situation the woman who is the mother of my child, and who thus has a right to call upon me to perform obligations of all sorts. I am very obliged to you for facilitating for me what relief I am able to provide in the matter."[39] From this it may be gathered that he borrowed money from Frommann (other parts of the letters speak of loans from Frommann) to provide something for Ludwig Fischer's support. (Later in 1811, Ms. Burkhardt for unknown reasons gave Ludwig Fischer to Friedrich Frommann's sisters-in-law, who had started a home for boys without parents.) Hegel also ambiguously noted that he regretted that he had "not been fully able to extricate [Ms. Burkhardt] from her present situation." There is some evidence, not completely reliable, that Hegel made an offer of marriage to Ms. Burkhardt or at least insinuated that marriage was a possibility. In fact, Ms. Burkhardt's husband, who had abandoned her, died shortly after the boy's birth, and one rumor had it that Hegel promised marriage to her shortly after her husband's death, but then conveniently forgot about the matter after moving to Bamberg. That may be true – it is unsubstantiated – but one of Hegel's motives for moving to Bamberg may have been simply that it would put some distance between himself and an awkward situation. In any event, irrespective of what Hegel's conscience may have told him, Ms. Burkhardt and Ludwig Fischer remained behind in Jena.

Bamberg's Professorial Journalist

The Napoleonic Reorganization of Germany and University Life

The reorganization of Germany under French hegemony in 1803 had been followed by another tumultuous reorganization of Germany under Napoleonic French hegemony in 1806, including the formation of the Confederation of the Rhine, itself a completely Napoleonic invention. (It is estimated that about sixty percent of Germans came under new rulers during the revolutionary period.)[40] The charter that founded the Confederation of the Rhine (of which Bavaria was a member) stipulated a series of obligations for France's "allies" having to do with the kind of support they were required to give France during time of war; these obligations in turn fostered various reform movements within the German states as their governments tried to come to terms with new rulers and new boundaries and with the ever-increasing need to become "modern" in order to support the large armies and governmental trappings that came along with the new world the French had unleashed upon them.

Universities themselves were completely swept up in the modernizing reforms, and Hegel fervently hoped that he would be called to one of the newly founded or newly reorganized universities. The old professorial guild that had run the universities had been under sustained attack since, at the end of the eighteenth century, it had found itself effectively challenged by Göttingen and then by Jena; during the Napoleonic era, it found itself completely on the run. Careers in universities were now open (in theory) "to talent," and powerful officials, such as Niethammer and Jacobi in Bavaria, were to have far more influence in placing their favorites than the old professorial guild could ever hope for. Thus, during this period, Hegel's letters show him to be continually on the lookout for possible openings and appointments at one of these reformed universities, always vigilant for rumors of new universities opening or old ones being reorganized; indeed, until his appointment as professor at Heidelberg in 1817, his letters are filled with constant comments on who was getting which appointments at which institutions and quite often with unconcealed contempt for the injustice involved in appointments of those whom he saw as weak-minded and not nearly as deserving as he. It also shows how continually disappointed he was that the appointments were going not to people who were pursuing the post-Kantian path but instead to those more interested in developing various romantic philosophies of "feeling" and "intuition." Unfortunately, it was they, not he, who were capturing the imagination of German intellectuals and the German public during this period.[41]

All of Germany had been turned upside down in a rather short period of time. The old Holy Roman Empire no longer existed, and, shortly after the Battle of Jena, it seemed that even once-mighty Prussia might simply cease to count for anything in the new world of the reorganized European powers. The once-vaunted Prussian army had in essence collapsed after the battle of Jena, and Napoleon had been able to advance virtually unhindered into Berlin, causing the royal court there to flee for safety to the eastern sections of the Prussian domains. After Napoleon handily defeated the Russians at Friedland in June of 1807, the Prussians were forced in July to sign what for them was the humiliating Treaty of Tilsit, which dispossessed them of all of their lands west of the Elbe and large chunks of their Polish lands. (Napoleon had actually forced the Prussians to wait on the shore while he and Czar Alexander of Russia signed a peace treaty on a raft in the middle of the

Nieman River.) The Frederickian "machine state" against which Hegel
had earlier inveighed had thus been thoroughly defeated. Bavaria, on
the other hand, had allied itself with the victorious French and seemed
to be in the process of reforming and modernizing itself.

The Bamberger Zeitung

Hegel moved to Bamberg to assume editorship of the newspaper, the
Bamberger Zeitung, sometime between the first and the middle of March
1807 (about a month after the birth of his illegitimate son); his move
was thus prior to but still near the end of the complete Prussian defeat
following the collapse of their army after the battle of Jena. A short
time after he assumed the editorship, his book the *Phenomenology of
Spirit* was finally published (in April 1807), and Hegel even went so far
as to publish a "notice" in the paper about his new book that extolled
its virtues. (Hegel also placed the same "notice" in the *Allgemeine
Literatur Zeitung*, which had since moved from Jena to Halle, and in
that journal's weak replacement in Jena, the *Jenaer Allgemeine Literatur-
Zeitung*.)

Hegel was stepping into an engaging and somewhat complicated
situation. Bamberg had been a center of publishing for some time, and
Hegel's publisher there, Anton Goebhardt, was a very established firm
with a rather prestigious list of authors and with close ties to the
university at Würzburg. Bamberg itself was much larger than Jena,
having 17,169 inhabitants in 1807.[42] The newspaper itself had an interesting history. Before Hegel assumed the editorship, the *Bamberger
Zeitung* had been successfully edited by a Frenchman, a former abbé,
Gerard Gley, who, because he was a priest, had been forced to flee
France in 1791 and, landing in Catholic Bamberg, had become the
editor of the newspaper there. Gley added a straightforwardly political
supplement to the newspaper, which he called "Charon," which debated very au courant political topics in the format of a dialogue between two "characters," Charon and Mercury. "Charon" lasted from
1797 until 1801. Gley himself was a mercurial character; he took over
the paper, then sold it in 1801, then became editor again in 1804. In
1806, caught up in the spirit of the times, he suddenly and without
warning gave up the editorship to accompany Marshall Davoust of the
French army on its way to Poland, where he was later made general

commissar of the principality of Lowkowitz. (He ended his days as professor of philosophy at the university at Tours.)[43] Whatever else he was, though, Gley was a successful newspaper entrepreneur; during his tenure as editor, Gley managed to boost the number of subscriptions to the newspaper to 2,000. When Gley decided to sell his paper in 1801, the archbishop – in 1801 Bamberg was still an ecclesiastical possession – required him both to lower his price and to sell it to a particular person, a Mr. Schneiderbanger (who apparently had good connections with the ecclesiastical authorities). Schneiderbanger, however, knew little or nothing about running a newspaper, so he had to procure some professional help in managing the enterprise, and in 1804 Schneiderbanger felt compelled to ask Gley to return as chief editor. After Gley departed with the French troops in 1806, he hired another philosopher, a Professor Deuber, who apparently managed in a short time to turn the newspaper into a forum of pedantic unreadability. As Niethammer put it in his letter inviting Hegel to become the editor, Deuber "directed the newspaper so brilliantly that he has nearly kindled its death-torch."[44] Luckily for Schneiderbanger, he had only hired Deuber as a stand-in until Gley's return, which, of course, never happened; the declining fortunes of the paper then forced Schneiderbanger to dismiss Deuber. At that point, Schneiderbanger seriously needed a new editor and asked Niethammer to take the job; Niethammer refused but recommended Hegel. Desperate for somebody – and apparently being convinced despite his experience with Deuber that philosophers make good editors – Schneiderbanger immediately agreed to offer the position to Hegel.

It was not the university position he had wanted, but Hegel put the best face on it. First, it would provide him the income and the opportunity to continue work on his "system," now that the introduction to it (the *Phenomenology*) had been finished. Indeed, he seems to have set to work on his *Logic* almost immediately, having no doubt brought with him some substantial notes on the subject that he had completed in Jena. Second, it gave him what he called a "public life": As he put it at the time in a letter to Niethammer, "as seductive as independent isolation is, everybody must maintain a connection with the state, and must work on its behalf . . . I will not really be leading a private life, for no one is more of a public man than a journalist."[45] Hegel had other good reasons to be happy with his newspaper job. As he remarked to Niethammer, editing a political newspaper would be especially interesting for him since, as he put it, "I pursue world events with curiosity," adding that "[f]or the most part our newspapers can all be considered inferior to the French. It would be interesting for a paper to approximate the style of a French one – without, of course, giving up a sort of pedantry and impartiality in news reports that above all the Germans demand."[46] And Hegel was, after all, a devotee of political newspapers and journals: While in Jena, he had even commented in his daily journal, "Reading the morning paper is the realist's morning prayer. One orients one's attitude toward *the* world either by God, or what the world is. The former gives as much security as the latter, in that one knows how one stands."[47] So if not his interest in religion, at least his interest in political realism could find expression in his new job.

The paper appeared daily including Sunday. Its news consisted mostly of reports gathered from other newspapers (particularly from those in capital cities) and from "correspondents" (that is, anybody with some interesting account of events occurring wherever he was). Moreover, Bamberg had become a nodal point for commerce and traffic from various Bavarian towns to Würzburg and to the Prussian and non-Prussian areas of Germany, thus giving the paper a strong regional importance. (The various advertisements placed in the newspaper inquiring about things such as travel connections to such places attest to Bamberg's growing regional importance in that regard.)[48] Hegel also stumbled into some good luck: Just as he had assumed the editorship, one of the newspaper's major competitors, the *Erlanger Zeitung*, was temporarily shut down for offending the censors, and the *Bamberger Zeitung* thus acquired a whole set of new customers who could no longer receive their beloved *Erlanger Zeitung*. Hegel's newspaper thus found itself on even sounder financial footing than before. Because of Schneiderbanger's pressing need for a new editor and the need to capitalize on the recent shutdown of the *Erlanger Zeitung*, Hegel was able to negotiate a very nice arrangement regarding his pay: He and Schneiderbanger were to split the profits in half. Originally Hegel had been promised only 540 florins in salary, which he had found to be barely acceptable. The new arrangement would give Hegel, by his own reckoning, a salary of at least 1,348 florins, which he found quite ample. Moreover, he noted in a letter to Niethammer that he had persuaded Schneiderbanger to agree to make the appointment "temporary" and subject to immediate annulment if Hegel were to receive an offer from an "important post" (in other words, a university).[49]

Hegel's Pro-Napoleonic Editorship

The newspaper was pro-Napoleonic in its outlook, in large part because Bavaria was an ally of the French. This suited Hegel perfectly, who was quite open in his sympathies for the French cause. Moreover, since he had argued in his *Phenomenology* that German philosophy was the necessary requirement for completing the Revolution, he must have found it perfectly appropriate for a German philosopher to be interpreting the ongoing Napoleonic reorganization of the German *Länder* for a German public. In a letter to a former student (dated January 23, 1807, roughly one month before Niethammer's February 16 offer of the editorship to him), Hegel noted that the French had now shed the "fear of death" (a theme already voiced in his essay in 1800 on the "German Constitution"), which in turn had enabled France to possess the "great power which she displays against others." Hegel noted that other nations (in other words, the Germans) are now being forced to "give up their indolence vis-à-vis actuality and to step out into it," and in doing so, they will "perhaps surpass their teachers." The reference is to post-Kantian idealist philosophy, which as Hegel put it, although having "something solitary about it" can nonetheless not "be held aloof from the activity of men, from that in which they place their interest," and only such idealist philosophy could provide people the tools they needed to understand the meaning of the historical events transpiring around them. "Science," Hegel adds, "alone is theodicy, and she will just as much keep us from marveling speechless at events like brutes – or, with a greater show of cleverness, from attributing them to the accidents of the moment or talents of an individual, thus making the fate of empires depend on the occupation or non-occupation of a hill."

In Hegel's view, the post-Jena age was one in which what had bound people together in the past was now "without spirit," no longer a constitutive element of the European collective identity; hence, the old institutions and practices that supported that earlier way of life had "no longer any stability within themselves" and had to give way to new, modern institutions, since those old practices were only the "arrange-

ments" that modern life had "outgrown like the shoes of a child."[50]
The Revolution was right and unstoppable, so Hegel thought, because
it embodied what was now required of modern people.

Since his Tübingen days, Hegel had been convinced that he was
living in a period in which a new beginning was being fashioned. As he
took over the editorship of the newspaper, this conviction that he was
in the middle of a complete revolution in forms of life only grew in
strength. Hegel had come to see the Battle of Jena itself as marking that
set of events: In a letter of August 30, 1807 (almost a year after the
battle), he referred to it as "that all-too great event that was the Battle
of Jena, the sort of event which happens only once every hundred or
thousand years."[51]

With those beliefs in mind, Hegel therefore could not have been
personally indifferent to editing a political, pro-French newspaper for a
German public, even if it was not his first choice for a salaried position.
On the whole, Hegel kept to the idea he had expressed to Niethammer,
that he would attempt to edit the paper with the "impartiality" that he
thought was "demanded by the Germans," and thus he largely kept his
own personal statements out of the newspaper – something he was
actually quite comfortable with and which he had recommended to the
authors of the literary review he had proposed for Heidelberg. However,
his principles of selection and his attempts to supply a larger political
context for his readers clearly exhibit his pro-Napoleonic ideas at work.
For example, he would encourage support for the French by including
reports on how well the French army was behaving as it marched
through various areas of Germany. In an article of May 10, 1807, one
month before the final defeat of the Russians by the French at Friedland, there is, for example, a report on how well the French troops were
behaving; it notes that everywhere "the extraordinarily good conduct of
the French had become well known."[52] (The presence of French troops
on German soil was, of course, already a sore point among many
Germans. Within a short time it was to become a flashpoint for the
growing resistance to the French occupation, as it became increasingly
clear to various Germans that the French were only in small part
"liberators" and were in large part simply an occupying force intent on
using Germany to feed its growing demand for troops and to provide
financial support for its continental ambitions. But this was not as clear
at the time that Hegel was selecting those reports for inclusion in the

news.) To draw the contrast between the good behavior of the French and the bad behavior of the Russians (Prussia's allies), Hegel included references (in the papers of March 20 and 21, 1807) to the Russian army as exhibiting "the behavior of Cossacks," burning down whole villages and murdering the villagers to make political points.[53] In a "notice" he selected for printing in the March 21, 1807, edition of the newspaper, it was said that the "rebirth" of Germany could not depend on "imitating the ethos, laws, politics, and humanity of a superstitious people" such as the Russians.[54] (The French victory at Friedland was later described in the *Bamberger Zeitung* as a "glorious victory.")[55]

He also was quite obviously interested in the way in which the French seemed to be modernizing Germany. In particular, he was fascinated with the introduction of the liberal monarchical constitution in the newly created kingdom of Westphalia and devoted many pages of the newspaper to covering developments in that newly created kingdom. The kingdom of Westphalia was created by Napoleon to provide a moral model for other German states and to give his younger brother, Jerome, a throne (though Napoleon's priorities were not necessarily in that order). It was given a liberal constitution, proclaimed in November, 1807, "which embodied the emancipatory promises of the revolutionary age: civil equality and religious liberty, the abolition of guilds, serfdom, and aristocratic privilege, and the introduction of the French legal code, open courts, and trial by jury."[56] It was, in fact, the first constitution ever given to a German state.

That Hegel would have been intensely interested in such a political body – the kingdom of Westphalia was almost the size of Prussia after the latter lost so much of its lands after the Treaty of Tilsit – goes without saying. Indeed, in 1807, when Napoleon's fortunes were riding high, the kingdom of Westphalia no doubt appeared to Hegel as the pure harbinger of the future, and thus almost every issue of the newspaper from the end of 1807 (the date of the promulgation of the constitution of the kingdom) through 1808 contained some report on the constitutional developments in the kingdom of Westphalia.[57] (Hegel's interest in Westphalia was also evidenced in his letters to Niethammer, in which he always spoke approvingly of what was going on there.)[58] The kingdom of Westphalia, as it turned out, was not what was promised: Instead of the moral spearhead of French-inspired emancipation, it quickly became a sink of corruption, the promised representative government never appeared in any real form, and the whole state was treated by the French almost exclusively as a source of revenues and men for the French war machine – in the kingdom of Westphalia, more men per capita were taken as soldiers for the French than anywhere else in Europe.[59] With Napoleon's defeat in 1813, the short-lived kingdom immediately vanished. But in 1807, Napoleon was probably in Hegel's eyes beginning to look like the "Theseus" he had wished for Germany in "The German Constitution." In a piece of August 2, 1807, reporting on the fact that astronomers at Leipzig university had named a star for Napoleon, Hegel inserted the observation that Napoleon "has not opened to our eyes new views into inaccessible worlds, but rather, what is more, he has disclosed and completed a view into a new world here at hand for our gaze."[60]

He was also fond of reporting about events in Paris, particularly matters having to do with the way Napoleon seemed (at least to Hegel) to be encouraging the development of the sciences. In one of the pieces (August 12, 1807), for example, Napoleon is cited as showing great "respect for the sciences," and as expressing "disapproval of the enemies of philosophy, of the sophists of the various parties, which seek to obstruct the progress of reason."[61] The implicit comparison with the failures of the German princes to do the same is obvious. (For example, his old friend in Jena, Thomas Seebeck, wrote to him on January 29, 1808, about exciting new experiments in physics being performed in England, noting sadly, "Unfortunately, it is only going to get more difficult for we poor German physicists to keep in step with our rich neighbors," ruefully adding that one of the English researchers had won, of all things, a scientific prize in Paris the year before.)[62] In another piece, Napoleon was described as endorsing confessional freedom and as being against the "bigoted parties" that wished to reintroduce confessional unity; as opposed to earlier French kings, who, as Hegel put it, were not so much kings of the nation as they were "kings of a caste or sect," Napoleon's status as emperor was "to be purely national" and thus above such confessional divides.[63] The moral of that story vis-à-vis the status of Protestants in the newly acquired lands of otherwise purely Catholic Bavaria was surely not missed by Hegel's reading public – Protestants had only acquired rights of citizenship (*Bürgerrechte*) in Bavaria in 1801, and the acquisition of large Protestant areas in 1803 and 1806 had made the issue of Protestants in the Catholic kingdom of Bavaria all the more pressing.[64]

Thus, although Hegel's official policy was to keep his own views out of the newspaper (as he was also supposedly required to do by the laws regulating newspapers), he simply could not suppress his admiration of the French and thus was incapable of completely removing himself from the newspaper accounts. He would even insert editorial comments into the body of reprints of the official Prussian accounts of various battles to underline what he was certain was the false nature of those accounts. For example, on May 27, 1807, Hegel inserted into the official Prussian account the statement that it was full of "the most frightful lies that it is only possible to fabricate."[65] He would also reprint Prussian accounts of Napoleon's maneuvers and then juxtapose them to more flattering (and reliable) accounts from other newspapers, inserting comments to the effect that the publication of such lies by the Prussians was clear evidence of the distress in which the Prussian government had found itself. It is also abundantly clear that this pro-Napoleonic slant to the newspaper was fully in line with Hegel's own opinions; he was in no way catering to the reigning authorities and censors in Bavaria against his own wishes or his own ideas.[66]

Life in Bamberg

Hegel quickly settled into life in Bamberg, and his natural gregariousness found a niche for itself. As the editor of the local newspaper, Hegel became an important social figure on the Bamberg scene, something that plainly flattered his sense of who he was. He became good friends with another newly arrived pair of persons in Bamberg, Johann Heinrich Liebeskind (a high official, *Oberjustizrat*, or high royal counsel) and his wife; both were noted for their cultivation (*Bildung*), Mr. Liebeskind being a virtuoso on the flute and Mrs. Liebeskind being an accomplished writer and translator, as well as knowledgeable about music. (Mrs. Liebeskind had been a close friend of Caroline Schelling and along with her had also been an enthusiastic member of the Mainz Republican Club and supporter of the Revolution; she was divorced from a prominent Göttingen historian of music.) In a letter to Niethammer, Hegel remarks that he "visits almost no other house," and the letters are full of references to playing cards – a lifelong source of satisfaction for Hegel – at the Liebeskind's house with various other Bamberg notables.[67] Hegel also notes with some satisfaction that gossip has it in Bamberg that he is courting an aristocratic "Mrs. von Jolli," something that he good-naturedly assured Niethammer had no basis in fact. (She and her husband – an officer in the Bavarian army – were apparently good friends of the Niethammers.) Hegel's satisfaction with his acceptance in Bamberg was also apparent to his old friends, particularly the Frommanns, even though his friends made it clear that they still would prefer for him to return to the university environment of Jena.[68] Hegel even mentioned attending a New Year's Day costume ball in, of all things, a *valet's* outfit, which he claimed to have procured on the spot from the "Court doorman, along with his wig."[69] (In his *Phenomenology*, Hegel had augmented the old French saying that no man is a hero to his valet by adding: "not, however, because the man is not a hero, but because the valet – is a valet, whose dealings are with the man not as a hero, but as one who eats, drinks, and wears clothes, in general, with the individuality of his needs and ideas."[70] His point there was that the "universal," moral, or heroic aspects of an action are easy to overlook; the valet is a pure "particularist" who can only see the particular, contingent aspects of the character in question, not the ways in which his actions can have a wider significance.)

As Hegel's spirits improved in Bamberg, he pursued his passion for good eating and drinking; in his letters, he spoke of how good the Bamberg beer was and even grumbled a bit about how he feared that the newly introduced Bavarian regulations might come to hurt the quality of that excellent local beer. (He also made references to drinking excellent wine, a taste that had been with him at least since his Frankfurt days.) He asked Niethammer to procure a special "Rumford Coffee Maker" from Munich for him – Hegel was an avid coffee drinker – and a few months later was joking to Niethammer (in a manner still recognizable among contemporary academics) about "how much my scientific activity is already indebted to this coffee."[71]

Hegel's Aversion to Bavaria

But despite his acceptance into the Bamberg social scene and his having a forum for nudging public opinion in a pro-French direction, Hegel was never satisfied with his job or with being in Bavaria. Bavaria had handsomely prospered by virtue of allying with the French, for although at the end of the eighteenth century its status had been was so low that it seemed for a while that the principality might be swallowed up by Austria, by 1806 Bavaria had instead become the largest and most important member of the Confederation of the Rhine, having itself swallowed up Bamberg, Augsburg, Nuremberg, the formerly Prussian counties of Ansbach and Bayreuth, and a host of other ecclesiastical states and free imperial cities. By 1806, Bavaria had even become a kingdom. Under the leadership of Count Maximilian Montgelas, an aristocratic Frenchman from the Savoy (who learned to speak German only in the 1780s) whose father had been a successful solider for the Wittelsbachs (the ruling family of Bavaria), the newly organized kingdom set about reforming itself.

The need for reform was clear, and Montgelas wasted no time. Bavaria had incorporated into itself many lands that had nothing to do with anything like Bavarian history and tradition; for example, Bavaria, formerly entirely Catholic, now possessed large Protestant holdings. In the tumultuous years of the Napoleonic era, moreover, it was clear that the state needed to develop its resources not in order to support dreams of princely glory (as Duke Karl Eugen had done earlier in Württemberg, with Hegel's father as one of the officials in charge of raising such wealth) but simply in order to survive and to support its obligations to its ally, France. In Bavaria, the Catholic Church had owned vast amounts of land and had extensive control over valuable resources; Montgelas, seeing the use to which those resources could be put, wasted no time in claiming them for the state in the name of secularization and civic equality, which, perhaps needless to say, did not exactly endear him to Catholic officials in that country.[72]

This new need for reform changed the way Germans began to think of administration in general. Administration had previously been based on cameralist assumptions, the falsity of which in pre-Napoleonic days had not been as apparent. However, as the need to codify and rationalize in the wake of the Napoleonic reorganization of Germany became more pressing, the difficulties within cameralist doctrine became more obvious. The hometown structure of German life had resisted such homogenizing moves. The problems inherent in the clash between hometown structures and modern life had been apparent to Hegel for quite some time, and, and, if anything, his awareness of them had only been sharpened in the intervening years. The consolidation of territory in places like Bavaria, however, had the practical effect of making it all too evident that the old way of simply muddling through the problems inherent in this clash between hometown life and the demands of consolidating administration was no longer possible.

Moreover, administrative activity in Bavaria not only had to bring its own previous hometown structures into line with new, "enlightened" state policies, it also had to bring into line with Bavarian policies areas that had not previously been Bavarian at all in culture or outlook. Bavarian officials with no knowledge of hometown traditions suddenly appeared in these communities as governing officers. They governed by following such authorities as cameralist doctrine and the new Napoleonic civil code, not according to norms that had been established by any tradition recognizable to those hometowns. That is, they governed in the name of what was supposedly right and rational, not in terms of what had been established by folkways and collective memory, and their putative reforms therefore naturally encountered all sorts of resistance. The hometowns found them to be anathema, and the older, Catholic portions of Bavaria were particularly threatened by them. That Hegel's best friend in Bamberg – J. H. Liebeskind – was such an official is surely no accident; Hegel's idea that such officials acquired the *right* to be the governors of such areas because of their *Bildung* would have been confirmed in Liebeskind's instance.

All the problems about which Hegel had written in Jena were now problems that he was seeing close up in Bamberg, and the Bavarian response exasperated him to no end. In particular, he was irritated by the attempt by Bavaria's official historians to shore up the legitimacy of the new kingdom by concocting a history of Bavaria that would show how the newly formed kingdom actually had a long and rich unified cultural past that made it a "people." (Among its so-called findings included asserted links between the Wittelsbachs and Charlemagne himself, thus encouraging the idea that somehow the expanded kingdom of Bavaria was of a piece with the old empire.) Hegel could not heap enough scorn on the idea of such a manufactured history.[73] Besides, as he sarcastically notes in a letter of April 21, 1808, Bavaria does not need any "justification for the antiquity of its literature and art" now that it has "Augsburg, Nuremberg, Ansbach, Ulm, Memmingen" (all previously non-Bavarian places).[74] Hegel's contempt for "old Bavaria" is apparent in the letters in which he plays on the Latin term for Bavaria (*Bayern* in German, *Bavariae* in Latin) by continually referring to Bavaria as "Barbaria."[75] Moreover, he was very much put off by the way in which the Catholics in those parts of Bavaria that had preceded its post-Napoleonic expansion – who began calling themselves "old Bavarians" to distinguish themselves from the newcomers to the kingdom, whom they called "foreigners" – indulged in what he regarded as retrograde, idiotic praise for the putative beauty and glory of medieval Catholic Germany. In speaking of one such Bavarian in particular (a Mr. Rottmanner) who was pushing this line of thought and singing the praises of the superior virtues of old-time Catholic Bavaria as compared to Protestant northern Germany, Hegel noted how "this twaddle was invented and developed in north Germany, and the solid original south German character is – now as before – merely picking it up from the disdained north Germans, parroting it now as ever."[76] (Friedrich Schlegel, who in the meantime had converted to Catholicism and become a propagandist for Austria, was a north German; Hegel's reference is obvious.) Indeed, Hegel almost never missed a chance to take a dig at what he regarded as the intolerably backward attitudes of the "old" Bavarians.

Niethammer, Hegel, and Hometown Bavaria

There was a lot at stake for Hegel in all of this. His friend Niethammer had in 1808 become a high official in Munich. (Niethammer became the *Zentralschul und Oberkirchenrat*, central commissioner of education and consistory.) Clearly Niethammer was going to be in charge of securing positions for people in what were going to be the newly reorganized universities of Bavaria, and it was more than evident to Hegel that if he was going to land a position in one of those places for himself, he would need to rely on his friend more than ever. Niethammer himself, however, was constantly having to do battle with the "old Bavarians," since he was both Protestant and in their eyes a "foreigner." The attacks by the "old Bavarians" thus represented attacks on Hegel's future, and Hegel took every opportunity to let Niethammer know he was on Niethammer's side in the controversies. F. H. Jacobi, whose writings Hegel had read in Tübingen and attacked in Jena, had, moreover, become the head of the Academy of Sciences in Munich and as a Protestant and a "foreigner" had also come under attack from the "old Bavarians." When Jacobi defended the freedom of "science" against the "old Bavarians" (and when Hegel learned that Niethammer and Jacobi had become friends), Hegel's attitude toward Jacobi suddenly changed; he ceased to attack Jacobi and instead by December of 1807 was describing himself as one of "Jacobi's party."

But it ran deep within Hegel's personality and his worldview to refuse to take sides with one group – the reformers or the hometowners – at the complete expense of the other. The great tension running throughout Hegel's life was that between his particularist, hometown experiences and his universalist, Enlightenment education; he was always attempting to mediate these two features of his own experience and bring them together into a coherent worldview. Thus, for him, the rationalistic, cameralist-inspired attempts to simply impose administrative reform from above could not work unless they were also anchored in the way of life of a people. His low opinion of the Bavarian resistance to such reforms put great strain on those beliefs, since he regarded the Napoleonic reforms as necessary and progressive, and he had little patience with the forces of reaction he witnessed daily among the Bavarians. Unadulterated hometown life was clearly a thing of the past, something the Revolution followed by Napoleon had simply swept away, but it could not be simply abolished, since the simple, "unmediated" abolition of hometown life would undermine the authority of the reform movement altogether.

Hegel's time in Bamberg was, although brief, very important for the formation of his political ideas. The general points that Hegel had been arguing in the *Phenomenology*, and in the lectures on his "new idealism" of 1805–06 in Jena, were now being fleshed out before his eyes; as the editor of one of the most important newspapers in the region, he had to observe and comment on the pace of Napoleonic reforms in what seemed to be the most important of the newly restructured kingdoms. Hegel saw his own views being confirmed: Without an anchoring in social practice, in the self-identities of the people in the reformed communities, the reforms could have no authority; they would only appear, indeed would only *be*, the imposition of one group's (the reformers) preferences and ideals on another. Without the transformation of local *Sittlichkeit*, of collective self-identity, the reformers could only be the "masters" and the populace could only be the "vassals."

In a letter to Niethammer in January 1808, Hegel speaks of the importance of a well-run press in all this and of the kind of role the press can reasonably be expected to play. It is not enough to have freedom of the "press and pen," as he puts it, unless one also has "publicity (*Publizität*)," which consists in a "dialogue of the government with its own people, about its and their interests," which, Hegel notes, "is one of the most important sources of the power of the French and English peoples." Without a proper *formation* of interests and public opinion, which can only come about through this "dialogue," freedom of the press only amounts to a frenzy of various factions devouring each other – a "*Freß-Freiheit*" instead of a "*Preßfreiheit*" (a "freedom to gobble it up" instead of a "freedom of press").[77] Echoing his earlier call in his Frankfurt essay, "That the Magistrates Must be Elected by the Citizens," Hegel remarked to Niethammer that "much is required for such dialogue; but, above all, courage."[78] His implicit critique of the way in which Montgelas's reforms (and those of all the other reformers in Germany) were proceeding is evident: In their re forms, there was no "dialogue," there was instead only administrative fiat in which, even in those cases where the "right" thing was being decreed, the self-undermining nature of decrees that seem to come only from "on high" was evident. The *press* plays its proper role when it serves a mediator for the formation of such public opinion; when the press serves to mediate things in the right way, it thereby serves to underwrite the processes of reform. In that light, Hegel thought it might be beneficial to have an official state-run press organ – like the *Moniteur* in France – to aid and assist in the process of reform. (The *Moniteur* had been founded in the Revolution of 1789 as the "Gazette Nationale, ou le Moniteur universel" and in 1800 Napoleon had made it an official organ of the government; other German *Länder*, but not Bavaria, had founded similar types of newspapers.)[79]

In November of 1807, Hegel had already been complaining of the "slow nature of the Germans" in carrying out reforms in the proper way. The rationalizing motivations of the Napoleonic aftermath to the Revolution had been taken up without the corresponding changes in institutions and social practice. Hegel disapprovingly noted that for the

German reformers "in all imitations of the French only half the example is ever taken up. The other half, the noblest part, is left aside: liberty of the people; popular participation in elections; governmental decisions taken in the full view of the people; or at least public exposition, for the insight of the people, of all the reasons behind such measures."[80] The arrogance of the high officials vis-à-vis the hometowners was only too apparent to Hegel: "Nor is anything known of the state having sufficient trust in itself not to interfere with its parts – which is the essence of liberty."[81]

Hegel continued, however, to be somewhat optimistic about the course of reform, since he thought it was inevitable and that its necessity would be clear enough to all the major figures (except for the hopelessly archaic "old Bavarians"). The various debates still raging among the antediluvian German law professors about which states were sovereign, which old rights were still in force, and about whether the Confederation of the Rhine was the successor to the Holy Roman Empire were all, to Hegel, simply and absurdly beside the point: "The great professor of constitutional law sits in Paris," he remarked in reference to Napoleon, noting also in passing that since the "German princes have neither grasped the concept of a free monarchy yet nor sought to make it real . . . Napoleon will have to organize all this."[82] What was really efficacious in the modern world, what ultimately had a purchase on people's minds and hearts, he thought, was the emerging inevitable structure of modern life itself.

Life at the newspaper, despite its nice salary and its social status, was nonetheless not what Hegel wanted for himself. He still saw the university as his natural home, and the various day-to-day practical problems editing a newspaper were gradually getting to him. As much as he enjoyed his newfound status in Bamberg, and as much as he admitted to being able to indulge his "penchant for politics," as he had told his friend Karl von Knebel, he also had to admit that the problem with editing a political newspaper such as the *Bamberger Zeitung* was that it ultimately did not allow him to focus on what was significant, since, as he put it, "the important thing for the reader is content. For me a news item has interest as an article filling a page."[83]

As Niethammer's power and influence over educational matters grew, Hegel began more and more to complain (always politely, although sometimes a bit obsequiously) to Niethammer of looking forward to his "deliverance from the yoke of journalism"[84] and to being able to "break away from my journalistic galley."[85] He came close to the breaking point when he was investigated by the state for violating some security measures by virtue of an article he published containing information on various French troop movements. In Hegel's eyes, this was just plain insanity, since the information in the article had already been published in other Bavarian newspapers. He complained that he would actually prefer *prior* censorship of the newspapers to this kind of interference, since at least with censors one would know in advance where one stood, whereas in the situation in which he found himself, the authorities could simply step in after the fact and threaten to suspend the whole operation of the newspaper if they found it offensive. Adding to Hegel's worries about his own continued livelihood was the fact that his sense of responsibility to others was also deeply offended: In his complaint, he noted that "the newspaper provides a considerable part of the income of one family; my subsistence depends entirely on it as also that of two married workers and a few other people. All that is put in jeopardy by a single article which is found offensive."[86]

In July of 1808, Hegel told his friend Friedrich Frommann that "God willing, in Bavaria a new world will arise. This has long been the hope. And I shall find a niche for myself in Bavaria even should the old world remain."[87] But it was becoming more and more clear to him that his niche was, or at least so he hoped, *not* to be in the newspaper business, especially in Bavaria. The investigation for breach of security had taken place in September 1808, and by October 1808 he was again pleading with Niethammer: "If you believe yourself unable to do something immediately for me regarding a university, do not let the reorganization of the gymnasiums or lyceums pass by in the uncertain hope of achieving something better for me later" and making clear his own specific anxiety: "The future is uncertain, and will be even more so should you leave the educational system to go over to the church."[88] Niethammer had come to seem to be Hegel's guardian angel, and Hegel feared that if Niethammer left the educational field or was forced out, he would be without protection or contacts, adrift in a world in which the kind of philosophy he did was not in fashion among the people who were making the decisions.

The Reception of the *Phenomenology*

Schelling's Response

While Hegel was living in Bamberg, his long-awaited volume, the *Phenomenology of Spirit*, appeared. Since he had finally broken with Schelling in that book, he had some reason to be anxious about Schelling's response. He thus wrote to Schelling on May 1, 1807, to complain, typically, about what he saw as the lack of culture in Bavaria, to apologize about the confusions involved in the distribution of copies of the book (which was supposed to explain why Schelling had still not received a copy), and to make the usual expressions of regret authors typically make about the various infelicities in their work and how it all could have been better phrased. (He also helped to start the legend of the book's creation by telling Schelling, "I actually completed the draft in its entirety in the middle of the night before the battle of Jena.")[89] Hegel tried to soothe what he correctly thought would be Schelling's adverse reaction to Hegel's criticism of him by explaining away those criticisms – including the (in)famous description of Schelling's "identity philosophy" as the "night in which all cows are black" – as aimed not at Schelling himself but at unnamed others who supposedly misused Schelling's ideas, at "the shallowness that makes so much mischief with your forms in particular and degrades your science into a bare formalism," as he put it to him.[90] He also told Schelling, of course, how much he would like his approval of the *Phenomenology*, a sentiment he no doubt personally and deeply felt, even if it was also true that a famous personage like Schelling could have helped to bolster Hegel's career if he had seen fit to publicly extol the book's virtues.

Schelling's reply came in August, 1807, and the tone was perhaps what Hegel had feared: "Insofar as you yourself mention the polemical part of the Preface," Schelling told Hegel, "given my own justly measured opinion of myself I would have to think too little of myself to apply this polemic to my own person. It may therefore, as you have expressed in your letter, apply only to further misuse of my ideas and to those who parrot them without understanding" – and here one can virtually hear the icy tone in Schelling's voice – "although in this text itself the distinction is not made."[91] Schelling goes on to express some exasperation at Hegel's abandonment of their joint (that is, Schelling's own) position vis-à-vis "intellectual intuition," since, as far as Schelling was concerned, concept and intuition were both just aspects of "what you and I have called the Idea – which by its very nature is concept in one of its aspects and intuition in another."[92] Schelling concluded the letter, however, on a conciliatory note: "All the best; write me again soon and keep me in your mind as your true friend, Schelling."[93]

Hegel did not reply. Schelling was clearly not happy, he obviously felt somewhat betrayed and a bit insulted by the old friend whom he had given a job, and it was clear that if Hegel had been hoping that Schelling would help to promote his book and further Hegel's cause, he was going to be disappointed. Indeed, Schelling's tendency at this point was in the opposite direction: By July of 1808, he wrote to Karl J. H. Windischmann, who was preparing a review of the *Phenomenology*, to say that "I am very curious to see what you have been getting along with Hegel. I'm dying to find out how you have disentangled the rat's tails; hopefully you . . . will not just wink at the way in which he wants to erect as a universal standard what is only suitable to, and been granted for, his individual nature" – hardly the words of a man who had any intention of promoting his old friend's career.[94] The friendship between the two men at that point began, understandably, to change its form, and the two were to be rivals for the attention of the German public for the rest of Hegel's life. The two did not by any means become enemies, but the friendship of their youth was clearly over. They were two very different personalities, and their original friendship had been based on what they had taken to be a common project. That common project had been defined at first mostly by Schelling, but as Hegel began to make his own way in the world and to separate his own project from Schelling's, the relationship between the two men also changed. Hegel continued to inquire about Schelling in letters to mutual friends and to send his regards via intermediaries, and Schelling would say kind things to others about Hegel. Schelling even visited Hegel in Nuremberg in 1812, which Hegel described as a "friendly visit" although, not surprisingly, as Hegel put it, "philosophical matters were not touched."[95] Schelling did apparently become slightly more irritated as his star began to sink and Hegel's began to rise, and he often grumbled to associates that Hegel was simply making good on ideas he had pilfered from him. Finally, in a grand historical irony, Schelling later finally became Hegel's successor at Berlin, with the terms for his appointment calling for him to "stamp out the dragon seed of Hegelian pantheism in Berlin."[96]

Anonymous Reviews: Hegel as Schellingian

Schelling was clearly going to be no help, so Hegel was of course quite eager to see how the book would be received by others. The initial reviews that appeared while he was still in Bamberg were not, however, encouraging. On August 6, 1807, a hostile anonymous review appeared in the Munich *Oberdeutsche Allgemeine Litteraturzeitung* (*South German General Literary Newspaper*).[97] The reviewer more or less refused to see that Hegel had changed his position since his *Difference* book and since his and Schelling's collaborative work on the *Critical Journal of Philosophy*. Instead, the *Phenomenology* was taken to task as being a thoroughly Schellingian piece. The reviewer, assuming on his own part what he took to be a more or less Fichtean position, laid out a charge that has followed Hegel and Hegelianism ever since, namely, that Hegel had tried to swallow up everything in "the absolute" and that he had put too much emphasis on the all-consuming power of theory. Hegel was rebuked for not having recognized that there is much "that is *not known*, which thus cannot be ordered into a system . . . a suspicion said also to have been expressed by Shakespeare." The reviewer even accused Hegel of succumbing to the kind of "French revolutionary rage" that had recently been in evidence, and lumped Hegel together with, of all people, Jacobi.[98] Since Hegel was, if anything, well known at the time only as a fierce critic of Jacobi, and Jacobi was, if anything, well known as not exactly being one of the French Revolution's greatest admirers, that polemic was all the more odd and striking, since the only halfway plausible reason for the reviewer's putting Jacobi and Hegel into one pot had to do with Jacobi's impassioned defense of the sciences in his inaugural address as the president of the Munich Academy of the Sciences in 1807. (Small wonder then that Hegel soon started describing himself as being in "Jacobi's party.")

An anonymous reply to the review was published shortly thereafter (August 1807), which defended Jacobi but still attacked Hegel for being too "intellectualistic" in his dismissal (in the Preface to the *Phenomenology*) of those who strove to make philosophy "edifying" instead of "scientific," and accused Hegel, oddly enough, of falling back into the outmoded formalism of Christian Wolff.[99] The controversy stimulated yet another anonymous reply (also in August 1807) to the first anonymous reply, which criticized the original review and the reply for not making it clear that Hegel had in fact broken from Schelling's point of view and, while not exactly praising Hegel, somewhat ironically noted that in Hegel's criticisms of Schelling, we had an example of someone versed in the misguided Schellingian system, a "master [commenting] on his art," showing us just how wayward the Schellingian system really was.[100] (If Schelling himself read this review, it would certainly have heightened his already negative feelings about the *Phenomenology*.)

Salat's, Köppen's, Windischmann's, and Bachmann's Reviews

Other reviews began to appear that only heightened the controversy surrounding Hegel's book. Some of the negative reactions were explainable as reactions to Hegel's own sharply polemical attacks on other philosophers in his and Schelling's *Critical Journal of Philosophy*. However gregarious Hegel's personality was in social settings, it also had a very aggressive side that clearly emerged from time to time in his writings. Indeed, when it came to such polemics, Hegel cut no corners and made no attempt to soften the blows he inflicted. In 1802, he had reviewed a piece by Jacob Salat (a Catholic Bavarian theologian and moralist, and an intimate of Jacobi's) in the *Critical Journal of Philosophy*, calling Salat, variously, "Bavaria's apostle," the self-appointed "Knight against the darkness," and accusing him of completely misrepresenting the Berlin Enlightenment (that is, Kant) and uttering only mistaken banalities about the Enlightenment itself. Salat had insisted against post-Kantian idealism that instead of its barren "formulas" (by which he surely meant Schelling's *Naturphilosophie*), we need instead the "spirit and not the letter." Of that, Hegel sarcastically remarked, "Spirit, only not the letter, is Salat's cry, spirit, spirit, not the formulas, not a determinate concept," which, he said, just boils down to the idea that "for him, just hand-waving is what is most spiritual (*das Geistigste*), since in hand-waving there is the least such letter." With Salat, Hegel said, we have only a shallow moralism that amounts to a scorning of morality itself, "which covers its scornfulness with a moral cloak of the better and the more perfect and which under this cover ordains by decree its unrecalcitrant vanity to be virtue . . . one cannot do otherwise than hold this camouflage of morality to be the very worst in which vain ignorance has hidden itself."[101]

Hegel therefore had reason to fear Salat's getting a turn to review him. Salat had already coauthored a book in 1803 with another conservative Bavarian Catholic entitled *Der Geist der allerneusten Philosophie der Herren Schelling, Hegel und Companie. Eine Übersetzung aus der Schulsprache in die Sprache der Welt* (*The Spirit of the Very Latest Philosophy of Mr. Schelling, Hegel and Company: A Translation from the Language of the School into the Language of the World*), which could not exactly be described as friendly toward Schelling and Hegel. In 1804, Salat on his own had sharply responded to Hegel's rather contentious attack on him in 1802. In 1808, he then took on Hegel's *Phenomenology* in his book *Vernunft und Verstand* (*Reason and Understanding*) and, surprisingly, softened his tone a bit. Understanding better than most others that Hegel had indeed decisively broken with Schelling, he nonetheless managed to misread the *Phenomenology* as criticizing Schelling exclusively and not himself as well. (Since the articles in the *Critical Journal of Philosophy* were unsigned, he had perhaps come to think that Schelling was the principal or sole author of the piece attacking him.) But he certainly wasn't ready to endorse what Hegel had to say in the *Phenomenology*. Although Hegel, Salat proclaimed, "has now powerfully declared himself against the *pious talk*" of the idealist school (meaning Schelling), one nonetheless still encountered in his system "the old or well-known spirit of the idealists," and in his thought the "old idealist game" of "transferring absoluteness, perfection to humanity" was only being played out again in a different form.[102] In any event, Salat noted, Hegel's writing had at least improved since Hegel's entries in what Salat pithily characterized as that "unforgettable journal." (Luckily for Hegel, an equally sharp review by him of another book by Salat had originally been scheduled by Niethammer to appear in the *Allgemeine Literatur-Zeitung*, but it was for some reason never published; it would almost certainly, had it ever appeared, have been aggressively negative, and Salat might not have been so generous to Hegel.)

Those were all the reviews to appear while Hegel was still in Bamberg. However, in 1809, shortly after his departure for Nuremberg, an anonymous review (but almost certainly authored by another follower of Jacobi, Friedrich Köppen) appeared in the *Allgemeine Literatur-Zeitung*. That one of Jacobi's insiders was doing the review made it all the more important for Hegel – indeed, in ways Hegel himself could not have known – since Jacobi, by assuming the presidency of the Munich Academy of Sciences, had become a powerful man in Bavarian intellectual circles, and one who, without Hegel's knowing it, was getting contradictory messages from various people about Hegel's qualifications. In August of 1809, the author, Jean Paul (Johann Paul Friedrich Richter), had written to Jacobi praising the *Phenomenology*, saying that, given all the nasty things Hegel had said in earlier writings about Jacobi, he found himself "surprised" at Hegel's "new philosophical system" with its "clarity, style, freedom, and force," noting also that Hegel had finally freed himself from "father-polyp Schelling."[103] On the other hand, Jacobi had written to Hegel's old nemesis, J. F. Fries, in November of 1807, asking him about the *Phenomenology* ("about which Niethammer had spoken with interest," he added), noting in passing that his student Köppen was in the process of writing a review of it.[104] Fries wasted no time in responding to Jacobi's inquiry, informing him that there was not much to Hegel's book, just a "universal history of the human spirit," nothing more than "Schelling's *Naturphilosophie* carried out on the side of spirit," and that the whole thing was in any event completely self-contradictory since it declared all knowledge to be in flux and relative, while at the same time declaring itself to speak from the absolute standpoint.[105]

In his review, Köppen showed that he too understood that Hegel's break with Schelling was indeed real, and that "Hegel was doing battle with his old philosophical self."[106] But he claimed that although Hegel had thus exposed the false formalism of the Schellingian *Naturphilosophie*, he had fallen into the opposite error of trying to make "all speculative philosophy into logic" and in doing so, had failed to understand what Kant had demonstrated, that logic on its own is empty and that we require the experience of particular things in order to develop any particular content for our ideas. The error into which Hegel had fallen, he said, was typical of all philosophical thought: This "blunder of the philosophers is not new, to hold the logical *abstractum* of the universal for the truth of things," as Köppen put it.[107] Of the new Hegelian speculative system, moreover, Köppen blithely said, "we wish [it] well but cannot, in light of former logic, come to declare such a thinking of contradictions to be a supersession (*Aufhebung*) of logical thought in general."[108]

That theme was picked up by another anonymous reviewer for the *Neue Leipziger Literaturzeitung* (*New Leipzig Literary Newspaper*) in 1809. Hegel had failed to "refute Kant," he said, and without such a refutation, the conversion of speculative philosophy into "logic" could only be a false start.[109] That reviewer, however, curiously failed to see how Hegel had genuinely broken with his old Schellingian position, saying at one point that "next to these strange logical games we find the author's old idea of the emergence of a being out of itself."[110] Indeed, the author finds the seemingly paradoxical passages of the book to be unintelligible, offering up as an example a quote from Hegel that "the truth of independent consciousness is the vassal's consciousness," something that obviously struck the reviewer as so odd that it did not require any explication for its oddness to be apparent.

K. I. Windischmann finally published his review of the book in 1809 in the *Jenaische Allgemeine Literatur-Zeitung*. Contrary to what Schelling had hoped, Windischmann's review emerged as an enthusiastic endorsement of everything Windischmann took Hegel to stand for. Unfortunately, Windischmann also misunderstood just about everything about Hegel's book. Windischmann, a Catholic physician and enthusiast of mesmerist cures, saw the entire book as more or less a mystical religious treatise. Windischmann seemed to understand, for example, the dialectic of mastery and servitude as a proof that we must learn to trust and fear the Lord God. Hegel had made a pun in that section of the book about wisdom beginning with the fear of the lord – the *Herr*, the master – and Windischmann had taken the pun literally, thinking that Hegel had thereby shown that out of the "fear of the Lord" in the earthly sense comes the impulse to "give our whole essence an everlasting form (*Gestalt*) from its own resources."[111] Windischmann interpreted the passages on the "moral worldview" in the *Phenomenology* as concerning not the completion of the Revolution in the philosophies of Kant, Fichte, and the Romantics but instead a demonstration that everything, including moral consciousness itself, constitutes only the various forms of appearance that religion takes. Indeed, his only criticism of the book was that voiced by everyone except Jean Paul, namely, that the book was obtusely written. (Jean Paul claimed to find it delightfully clear.) On the basis of his reading of the *Phenomenology*, Windischmann became, if only for a while, an enthusiastic Hegelian, even telling Hegel in 1810 that his book was destined to become "the book of elements for

the emancipation of man, the key to the new gospel that Lessing proph-
esied."[112] Hegel, wisely, did not point out or press the differences
between himself and Windischmann in his letter replying to him and
thanking him for the review.

Hegel was not exactly pleased with Köppen's and Salat's reviews,
since he regarded them as second-rate thinkers at best and was indignant about what he took to be the continuing injustice of their securing
the university positions that he himself so desperately wanted (and that
he thought he also more richly deserved). In 1807, two years prior to
the review, he had exclaimed about Salat's appointment at the newly
formed university of Landshut, "How is one to keep from breaking out
in howls over such a situation? It is just too much!"[113] Of Köppen's
appointment to the same university, he could only remark at the same
time – with unconcealed antipathy – that it "is, of course, quite characteristic; and what seems to me his complete incapacity for any solid
thought is all the more shocking because it shows how great is the
power [Jacobi] has courted."[114]

Some general and important themes nonetheless began to crystallize
out of the early reviews of Hegel's book. Almost everyone complained
about the turgid, dense style of the book, something Hegel himself
acknowledged but nonetheless continued all his life to defend as necessary for the presentation of such a "rigorous" (*wissenschaftlich*, "scientific") undertaking; for Hegel, the dense, compact presentation of a
complete thought – the style developed by Kant – was the only suitable
form for rigorous speculative philosophy. In a letter to his friend Karl
Knebel about the *Phenomenology*, Hegel contrasted the kind of clarity
he could achieve in the reporting of news – "that Prince so and so
passed through today, that His Majesty went boar hunting" – with, as
he put it, the kind of "abstract subject matter [that] does not permit
that clarity of exposition which discloses the object in a finished state
and clear light at first approach, and which is possible in the case of a
concrete subject matter."[115] In an 1812 letter to Peter van Ghert, he
said with reference to what van Ghert had characterized as the "pon-
derousness" of the presentation in the *Phenomenology* that "it is . . . the
nature of such abstract subjects that treatments of them cannot assume
the ease of a common book for reading. Truly speculative philosophy
cannot take on the garb and style of Locke or the usual French philosophy . . . I must be satisfied for the time being with having broken new

ground," adding that he was aware that much of his philosophy had to strike the ordinary reader therefore as "the topsy-turvy world."[116]

More important, though, was the issue of the continuing status and development of post-Kantian idealism in the *Phenomenology*, a theme on which almost all the reviewers picked up, even though as a rule they either continued to see Hegel as a Schellingian or simply confessed to being puzzled by how one was to relate Hegel's apparently new, apparently non-Schellingian views to his older, presumably Schellingian standpoint and, more broadly, to post-Kantian idealism in general. Salat in particular had insightfully seen that Hegel was breaking with Schelling but was also continuing to play the "idealist game" in a different form; more than others, he saw the continuities and discontinuities in Hegel's version of post-Kantian idealism.

The initial controversies about the book served it well. The issue of what to do "after Kant" was still very much alive in German circles, even if the idea of developing the Kantian *idealist* point of view had fallen out of favor. The controversy surrounding Hegel's book thus established him as a central figure in the *idealist* line of thought, even for those who held that particular line of thought to be mistaken. Since many philosophers and thinkers at the time, including Schelling himself, were moving away from any further development of idealist philosophy, Hegel found himself almost by default coming to be regarded as the representative exponent of what had only a few years before been the vogue but which had in the intervening years come to seem to many German intellectuals an unsustainable intellectual project.

Perhaps most importantly, though, what had *not* emerged was any generally agreed upon interpretation of the book, a matter that paradoxically was to prove quite fortunate for Hegel. Köppen and Salat had made it clear to the public that Hegel had broken with Schelling's views and taken idealism in a different direction, although neither of them approved of that new direction nor could they even agree about how it was to be characterized. In a later, famous review of the *Phenomenology* published in 1810, a former student of Hegel's at Jena, K. F. Bachmann, drove that point home, saying that it had always been a mistake to equate Hegel's and Schelling's views, that a "more precise look" at the essays published by Hegel in the *Critical Journal of Philosophy* showed that the two had always had differing points of view. Now, he said, they were almost "complete opposites." Hegel's work, instead, pointed the way to "a new epic in the history of philosophy," which would invite attacks on itself from both the Kantian and Schellingian camps, and, in a famous comparison, Bachmann said that if Schelling was the Plato of modern philosophy – a characterization that had already been widely applied to Schelling while he was at Jena – then Hegel was modern philosophy's "German Aristotle."[117] In a turn of phrase that was to prove prophetic, Bachmann said that Hegel's students, "suffused with the truth of the system," have set it as the "goal of their lives" to work together to bring about the "realization of the truths contained in his system," adding that that common effort must take "another, more practical path" than that taken by Hegel.[118]

Within three to four years after the *Phenomenology*'s appearance, the general view had thus begun to emerge that Hegel had broken with Schelling, that he had now assumed the mantle of being the foremost proponent of developing post-Kantian idealism in Germany, and that nobody was quite sure in what direction he was proposing to take it. Once the initial waves of enthusiasm for Romanticism and its aftermath had begun to die down after the downfall of Napoleon in 1813, that lack of an agreed-upon interpretation of his work allowed Hegel to begin to be seen as someone around whom *both* anti-Romantics and Romantics could rally, since without there being a definitive interpretation of Hegel (and with Hegel slyly refusing to play all his cards and publicly rule out definitively any interpretation), all the sides in the debates found that they could read *into* "Hegel-the-post-Kantian-idealist" a good bit of what they already wanted to see, which, naturally enough, was usually themselves. Even Schelling himself, in a moment of good-spiritedness, said in 1809 that Hegel as a "pure exemplar of inward and external prose must be held sacred in our overly poetical times," and that against the times' constant tendency to "sentimentality . . . such a negating spirit is an excellent corrective."[119] Fortunately for Hegel, it turned out, the times were soon to favor a sober "German Aristotle," a person of "inward prose" more than they were an over-poetic "Plato." But that time was not to come for several more years.

7

Nuremberg Respectability

The Politics of Neo-Humanism

WITH FRENCH HEGEMONY IN EUROPE seemingly secure, the burdens of editing and running the newspaper were beginning to feel more like a millstone to Hegel. He did not want to be a *commentator* on events; he wanted to *shape* them, and that could not be done, at least in the way he wanted to do it, as a newspaper editor. He was relying on his friend Immanuel Niethammer to help him out, and Niethammer was clearly doing his best to get his friend something more suited to his ambitions. In March, 1807, Niethammer had already commented to Schelling: "I am happy that I have been able to rescue Hegel from devastated Jena. Once we get him here on Bavarian soil, he will soon come to further help himself."[1]

As Niethammer had hoped, Hegel had indeed done well for himself in Bavaria, but Niethammer certainly knew that the position at the newspaper could only be temporary, that Hegel would never be satisfied editing a newspaper in a provincial town, and he set to work to obtain something more fitting for Hegel. He tried to get Hegel interested in some other projects, but Hegel balked. Niethammer, for example, offered to commission him to write a general textbook on logic for the Bavarian pre-university lyceums, surely knowing at the time that Hegel was at work on the second part of his proposed "system" (specifically, on what was to become his *Science of Logic*). Hegel replied to Niethammer's offer – and probably to Niethammer's surprise – by simply dragging his feet about the proposal, noting that although he was indeed hard at work on his logic, he needed more time to complete it, and would need even more time to put into anything like an "elementary" form suitable for the schools. Besides, he also noted, since his logic was going to be new, it might prove to be too difficult for the teachers to master well enough to teach it to their pupils.[2] Niethammer also proposed that Hegel teach theology in the schools, to which Hegel reacted even more strongly, saying that he would "have gladly taught theology in the *university*" – underlining an old point – but that teaching theology under the direction of the Protestant church in Bavaria "makes me shudder in every nerve."[3]

On May 8, 1808, Niethammer wrote to him about a variety of things, among them asking for a progress report on work on his logic and on whether he thought that commissioning him to do such a logic for the schools would really be doing him a service. At the end of the letter, Niethammer then coyly asked Hegel how he would feel in his heart if he were to propose him for the rectorship of a *Gymnasium*, preferably in Munich itself – a proposal which, as Niethammer diplomatically pointed out, would be "beset with difficulties" – or, if not in Munich, at least in one of the major provincial cities.[4] Hegel responded immediately but only with muted enthusiasm; it was not what he wanted, but it was much better than what he presently had. He made it clear to Niethammer that he would *much* prefer to be in a capital city (in other words, Munich); both Hegel's conception of how he might influence things, which required him to be located near the center of events, and his own clearly urban tastes made that clear: "Sojourn in a provincial city may always be considered a banishment, even if one has banished oneself," he remarked in his letter.[5] He made one last plea to Niethammer about a university appointment: There was much talk about the university of Erlangen being reorganized and coming under Bavarian governance – it was at that time under French military rule – and Hegel told Niethammer that "I know of no situation which I would desire more and for which I would at once more wish to be in your debt."[6] (The desire to go to the university was to become an idée fixe in Hegel's mind, appearing regularly in his letters to all concerned, until he finally received such an offer in 1816, only to turn it down in favor of Heidelberg; ironically, Hegel's son, Karl, many years later got a position there.) He also noted that his logic, on which he was hard at work, would be better suited for use in a university and might well be used to secure him some kind of appointment there. But with characteristic pragmatism, he also laid out the conditions for accepting such a rectorship, such as wanting to work under an appropriate commissioner who would allow him to do the right things, and so on.

Thus, when Niethammer responded on October 26, 1808, with an offer of a rectorship in Nuremberg, Hegel gladly accepted (remarking, as always, that he hoped that the way was still open for a university appointment) and mused that his appointment to a rectorship would be "directly linked to his literary activities, and at least do not differ in type even if they do differ in shape."[7] He would after all be a professor at a *Gymnasium*, which would be a better stepping stone to a university appointment than being an editor at a newspaper. He had to wrap things up in Bamberg – he made it clear that he understood himself to have a moral obligation to the newspaper to make sure everything was in good shape and in good hands before he left – but that took less time than he had thought. Since he was still officially a professor at Jena who was only on temporary leave, he also had to ask for permission from the duke of Weimar to be relieved of his obligations there, which was of course only a pro forma matter. He even had also to obtain permission from the Württemberg Consistory to be released from his obligations to them. (The ministerial letter to the king of Württemberg approving Hegel's request noted that Hegel's studies since leaving the Seminary in Tübingen put him in the position of having "neither the proper industry nor the necessary inclination" to occupy an "ecclesiastical office" and that no other position suitable for him was available in Württemberg.)[8] By November, 1808, Hegel assumed his new post in Nuremberg.

Niethammer's Views on Education

Niethammer had at least two related motives for bringing to Hegel to Nuremberg. It was, to be sure, an act of friendship and expression of loyalty to Hegel. But since Niethammer was in the middle of an intense political struggle for which he needed loyal allies in key places to put through the reforms he was seeking, it was clearly also in his own interests to have someone like Hegel in that particular position, a fellow he could trust and who was himself personally committed to the same project. In the great shake-up of the Napoleonic redrawing of the German map, Niethammer, a Protestant Swabian, had become a high official in the reformist administration of Count Montgelas in otherwise Catholic Bavaria. By 1808, he had risen to become the commissioner in charge of educational reform. In Bavaria, as in the other German states pursuing reform, educational matters had previously not been something in which the state had meddled and instead had been largely an area over which the church had exercised authority.[9] Now, just as reforming states were seizing church lands for their revenue – as Montgelas had done with particular vigor in Bavaria – they were also coming to see education as essentially a matter of state and not merely of clerical interest.

In this context, a movement known as neo-humanism had come to take root in German educational circles, and Niethammer, along with Wilhelm von Humboldt in Berlin, came to be known as one of its prime exponents. The leading ideas of the neo-humanist movement in education had to do with its opposition both to past German models of education and to the emerging models of education inspired by the German Enlightenment, which they identified as "utilitarian." (The "utilitarian doctrines" of which they spoke had only passing similarities to eighteenth-century British utilitarianism.) For the neo-humanists, education was to be fundamentally aimed at *Bildung*, at putting students in a position where they could realize a certain ideal of humanity, namely, that of becoming a self-directed, self-formed man of cultivation and taste. The proponents of neo-humanism, therefore, aimed at a kind of universalizing mode of education that identified it with *Bildung*. This also meant that such education had to go beyond whatever the hometown had to offer; because it was aimed at the development of a general model for humanity, it was not much interested in the particularities of hometown life. In this way, the neo-humanists saw themselves as developing a national German *culture*, which for them did not in any way necessarily imply a single, national German *state*.

Needless to say, the neo-humanist ideal met with stiff resistance from the hometowners and all from all those (such as those in the church) who had seen their wealth, power, and authority swept away from them during the revolutionary Napoleonic period. These conservative forces wished to base the ideals of education on the idea not of developing self-forming, self-directed individuals of taste and cultivation (which in their minds had come to be equivalent to the disease of the French Revolution, of modern life in general) but rather of producing people suited for a more traditional, more hierarchically organized society of ranks and orders. Using many au courant ideas, they were led to formulate an alternative program for education based on the emerging conservatism of political romanticism by invoking the Romantics' metaphorical conception of an *organic* community to justify a stratified, hierarchical social order in which people would know their proper places. They thus joined forces with the other "utilitarian" opponents in opposing neo-humanist ideals.

What the neo-humanists called "utilitarian" models of education were united by the idea that education should be focused exclusively on training people for the professions, particularly for the professions that they were by virtue of their class and estate supposedly destined to join.[10] The competing claims for political authority thus played over into the politics of education and educational reform: For people like Niethammer and Hegel, modern life was about *Bildung* and about men with *Bildung* having the right to constitute the new elite of modern social life. For the conservatives, that was both foolishly irrelevant and dangerously revolutionary; those who formed the elite should be those who belonged there by virtue of family and social status, not by virtue of some kind of "education" they had received or to which they had laid claim. Moreover, Hegel certainly understood this when he joined forces with Niethammer, and it was absolutely clear which side he was on. In January, 1807, Hegel had remarked to a friend, "But you also direct your attention to current history. And there can be indeed nothing more convincing than this history to show that *Bildung* triumphs over raw coarseness, and spirit over spiritless understanding and mere cleverness."[11] In accepting the post of rector, Hegel told Niethammer that "I am daily ever more convinced that theoretical work accomplishes more in the world than practical work. Once the realm of ideas is revolutionized, actuality will not hold out."[12] Hegel wanted to shape the new world, and to his mind, nothing shaped it better than the power of thought and *Bildung*.

Niethammer needed all the help and all the allies he could muster. In 1804, there had been a general plan for the reform of the Bavarian educational system underwritten by Josef Wismayr and heavily influenced by Kajetan von Weiller, a leading Catholic thinker among the "old Bavarians." (In 1803, Weiller had published a book written jointly with Jacob Salat attacking Schelling and Hegel.) The so-called reform plan Weiller and Wismayr developed in 1804 was heavily imbued with what the neo-humanists called "utilitarian" thought, that is, with the idea of training people for their proper places and professions. That directive also would have required that anything even resembling philosophy as Hegel understood it be strictly excluded from the curriculum; it specifically recommended that "faith in the omnipotence of the intellect should be weakened," that certain types of "feelings" instead be encouraged, and, "in that way, the teachers will overcome the prejudice that philosophy is only an affair of knowledge."[13] (The never-published review that Hegel composed of Salat's work in 1805 was in fact almost certainly intended as a shot in the battle between Niethammer and his opponents; Niethammer wanted to use it as a way of undermining Salat's and Weiller's claims.)

To make matters worse, Schelling, who was on Niethammer's side, had already committed a faux pas in criticizing the plan and had thereby endangered the whole project. Incensed by Weiller's and Salat's attacks on him and seeing clearly that the section on philosophy in the 1804 plan was intended to keep *his* philosophy out of the schools, Schelling had fired off a letter to Count von Thürheim, an important minister for Bavaria in Bamberg, about how insulted he was by the plan and how the Wismayr-Kajetan plan amounted to only "Jesuitism in reverse." The reply Schelling received from Count von Thürheim was not exactly encouraging; instead of endorsing his views, Count von Thürheim instead rebuked Schelling for his "demonstrated arrogance, which offers a convincing proof for how little speculative philosophy makes people more rational and ethical."[14] Since the forces allied against Niethammer in his battle were already formidable enough, and since Schelling's exchange with Count von Thürheim had not exactly helped Niethammer's cause, it was abundantly clear that if Niethammer was to rescue speculative philosophy for the Bavarian schools, he would need someone less rash than Schelling to help him.

The "Greek" Model

When Niethammer finally managed to outflank his foes and become the commissioner of education for Bavaria, he set to work immediately to put his ideas into place. He did this using a two-pronged strategy. First, he published a book on the subject in 1808 to make his points more widely known among the general German public and among Bavarian intellectuals in particular: *Der Streit des Philanthropinismus und Humanismus in der Theorie des Erziehungsunterrichts unsere Zeit* (*The Dispute between Philanthropism and Humanism in the Theory of Educational Instruction of Our Time*). The book took up some themes in post-Kantian philosophy and applied them in a highly polemical way to the practical disputes at hand. In effect, Niethammer traded on the Kantian distinction between treating people merely as means and treating them as ends in themselves in order to justify his labels. The conservatives were labeled "philanthropic" in the sense that they wished to do good for others by providing them with what would make them happy; they essentially embodied a paternalistic outlook that did not take into account people's capacity for self-direction and autonomy but instead tried to settle and determine important matters for them, justifying this blatant paternalism by claiming that it would make those under its direction "happy." For the conservatives, it was not important that those under their tutelage be directing themselves or exercising their own powers of free thought; because what was important was that they come to be satisfied with their proper place in life, very narrow, practical, "utilitarian" training for specific professions was all that should be expected from state-run educational institutions. "Humanism," on the other hand, aimed at making people self-directing, at bringing the students to embody within themselves the universal human ideal of self-formation which was built into the idea of *Bildung*. Using that framework, Niethammer sharpened the polemics: The "philanthropists," he claimed, were only developing the "animal" side of human nature; they thought (some) people were (like animals) only capable of happiness, not autonomy; humanists, on the other hand, recognized that what was distinctively human about people was their capacity to develop rationality and thereby to become self-directing individuals, not merely satisfied organisms. "Philanthropists" aimed only at training people for their occupations because they did not wish to train people for self-directed thought; "humanists," on the other hand, aimed at educating people to become fully flourishing autonomous agents.

Second, in his post as commissioner of education, Niethammer issued a proclamation in 1808 called the "General Normative for Organizing the Public Institutions of Learning." Although Niethammer probably intended for his book to be the theory and the "General Normative" to be the practice, in fact, his "General Normative" was in many respects necessarily a compromise document. It proposed two different types of schools, a "humanistic" *Gymnasium* and a "*Realinstitut*," the latter resembling the kind of school for professional training for which the so-called "utilitarians" had called. Both, however, were to be centered around the overall concept of humanistically oriented *Bildung*; in that way, Niethammer remained true to his program even while having to compromise with his opposition.

Niethammer's neo-humanistic approach to education was in part based on the Württemberg, Swabian experience that he and Hegel shared. As it was in many other ways, the Württemberg of Niethammer's and Hegel's youth had been an exception within the overall mosaic of German educational institutions. In Württemberg, the school system had been based on the Württemberg liturgical regulation (*Kirchenordnung*) of 1559. The "cloister schools" (which Hölderlin but not Hegel had attended) that had been established by that regulation had in effect served as a kind of higher *Gymnasium* in Württemberg from which the non-noble elite of Württemberg (and particularly the *Ehrbarkeit*, the non-noble notables) had emerged. Moreover, the existence of the *Landesexam* (the *Land*-wide examination) in Württemberg that entitled people to attend one of the cloister schools gave Württembergian education a unity that was otherwise completely lacking in other areas of the Holy Roman Empire, and the fiercely Protestant identities of Württemberg's *Ehrbarkeit* insured that the older, Renaissance "school humanism" of the sixteenth century continued as a living tradition in Württemberg education.[15] Both Niethammer's and Hegel's approaches (along with Schelling's) to educational issues thus had to do with the way in which they were reinterpreting their own Swabian, Württemberg experience in light of their later post-Kantian idealism. The "school humanism" of their youth and experience became transformed into the "neo-humanism" of Niethammer's "General Normative." Indeed, a large part of Hegel's, Schelling's and Niethammer's common commitment to idealism itself rested on their common search for a synthesis of Kant's modern insistence on human rationality, spontaneity, and autonomy and the Württemberg "school humanism" from which they had emerged.

In particular, the idea of *Bildung* for Niethammer's neo-humanistic orientation was linked to a heavy stress on philosophy, classical lan-

guages, and Greek as the primary classical language. The older Refor-
mation-inspired education models in Protestant lands had, in different
forms, taken Latin and religious instruction as the central orienting
points of the curriculum.[16] In the great educational debates of the early
nineteenth century, the conservatives continued to opt for Latin as the
basis of education, while the neo-humanists – particularly Niethammer
and Hegel – laid greater stress on the study of the Greek language,
classical Greek texts, and modern philosophy (with a heavy dose of
Greek philosophy thrown in). The neo-humanists justified this by arguing for the superiority of Greek poetry and philosophy to Latin
models and on the advantages of learning the Greek language as opposed to learning only Latin. To them, Greek works seemed closer to
the original roots of European culture (and, after all, the Romans had
taken the Greeks as teachers).

Moreover, the Greek model appealed to those Germans who thought
they could see their own situation mirrored in it. Whereas, since the
Renaissance, the Roman model had been adopted as the model for
centralizing, efficient monarchical states such as France (who could see
themselves as continuing the "Roman" tradition of empire and good
roads), the Greek model of different, independent political units (such
as the ancient Greek city-states) subsisting within a clearly discernible
national Greek culture seemed much closer to what was actually available and desirable for Germany. For these neo-humanists, Germany, like
ancient Greece itself, displayed an emerging national culture subsisting
within small, independent principalities; that is, it had a unity of *culture*
that flourished within the context of political *fragmentation*.

The stress on Greek as opposed to Latin on the part of the neo-
humanists thus also had clear social overtones. The older nobility had
taken their cue from French models, and thus they tended to insist on
Latin as primary; people such as Niethammer and Hegel, who were
claiming entitlement to an elite status on their basis of their *Bildung*,
tended to stress the superiority of Greek models to Latin models as the
basis of a truly just and good society, and in that way to differentiate
themselves from the claims made by those who wished to continue a
hierarchical social order based on (supposedly Roman ideas of) aristocracy. In elevating Greek over Latin, they were in effect saying that the
old elite (the aristocratic "Romans") were going to have to learn from
them (the democratic "Greeks").

In this debate, it was not without importance that both Niethammer and Hegel had come from the university at Jena, the great "bourgeois" alternative to Göttingen's more aristocratic mold and a hotbed of "Greek" studies; and it was also not without importance that both Niethammer and Hegel had emerged from Württemberg, where the elite consisted of non-noble notables (not aristocrats), who had almost all been educated in the classical "school humanism" of Württemberg. Finally, and perhaps equally important, they had both come from the Tübingen Seminary, where, as part of their studies, they had actually learned Greek in order to give exegeses of the New Testament. At a time when only a tiny handful of German universities offered any training at all in Greek, their theological training at Tübingen gave them a decided leg up in the emerging reliance on "Greek" models to supplant the older, "Latin" systems of authority. Thus, neither Niethammer nor Hegel found it terribly difficult to translate their Württemberg experience into a form of post-Kantian humanism with a stress on *Bildung* and the study of Greek.

Modernizing Education in Nuremberg

The Problems of "Bavarian" Nuremberg

Niethammer, sensing the intense opposition to his plan by the Catholic "old Bavarians," decided to make his play for educational reform first of all in one of the newly acquired Protestant territories. There, he figured, he would stand the best chance of succeeding and of thereby providing himself with a basis for implementing his reforms throughout the rest of Bavaria. He had to have great trust in Hegel's abilities and loyalties to put him in charge of that experiment, since he had to be aware that failure in that area would severely undermine his chances of succeeding elsewhere. Niethammer in effect made Hegel into his agent in Nuremberg; Hegel's job was to make sure that the reforms succeeded, but he was also to be given quite a bit of latitude to determine what needed to be done. Hegel was thus made both rector ("headmaster") of the *Gymnasium* and professor of the philosophical preparatory sciences. He was also made the "head teacher" for the section on philosophy according to Niethammer's ordinance declaring the necessity for such "head teachers." As professor of "philosophical preparatory sciences,"

Hegel was entrusted to implement Niethammer's "General Normative" of 1808, which required students at the *Gymnasium* to study philosophy in a certain sequence of areas, the purpose of which was, according to Niethammer's directive, "to introduce the student to speculative thought and thereby to lead them through a series of levels of practice to the point at which they would be ready for the systematic study of philosophy with which university instruction begins."[17]

The *Gymnasium* to which Hegel was called was a reorganized version of a much older, once-famous Nuremberg institution. The school had been founded in 1526 as one of the first Protestant schools in Germany, the very first humanistic *Gymnasium* in Germany, and the first to make Greek and mathematics a required part of the curriculum. One of the great figures of the Reformation, Melanchthon, had even participated in its founding. By the time Hegel arrived, however, its days of glory were long since behind it. Like many other German institutions, it had failed to modernize and had gradually sunk into mediocrity. But because it was in a firmly Protestant territory, and because the institution had such a glorious past with great affinity to the neo-humanism Niethammer was representing, it seemed the ideal place at which to begin the plan.

Hegel was also stepping into a situation with many potential difficulties. Although the assumption of Nuremberg by Bavaria had not been met with any particularly emotional resistance by Nuremberg's inhabitants, it was also the case that not everyone was happy about the fact. Nuremberg had been a free, self-governing imperial city within the old Holy Roman Empire (although surrounded by Prussia), but in the Napoleonic period, Nuremberg had suffered repeated occupation by French troops, had watched many of its art treasures shipped off to Paris, and, as imperial protection of its independence ceased, had been forced to watch itself become an object of negotiation between France, Bavaria, and Prussia without having any right to participate in the negotiations that would shape its destiny. Although Nuremberg had managed to remain one of the six free imperial cities after the *Reichsdeputationshauptschluß* of 1803, in 1806 the terms of the act that established the Confederation of the Rhine had simply given Nuremberg over to the Bavarians, and the formal dissolution of the Holy Roman Empire in 1806 only sealed Nuremberg's fate. On September 15, 1806, with great fanfare, the occupying French forces gave over Nuremberg to the relevant Bavarian official, Count von Thürheim himself (whom

Schelling had offended and who was to become the general commissioner of Nuremberg), and, overnight, all of Nuremberg's ancient governing institutions had to be reworked into Bavarian institutions, with some ancient ways of doing things vanishing altogether. For example, Nuremberg had for centuries been ruled by a few patrician families; in 1808, the Bavarian authorities simply dissolved the old patrician council, having allowed it to remain nominally in force from 1806 to 1808 only because they had regarded it, in Count von Thürheim's cynical words, as "a useless but also harmless assembly."[18] Some old, important Nuremberg patrician families – such as the von Tucher's, into which Hegel was to marry – suddenly found themselves no longer entitled by birthright to power in the city. Nonetheless, many members of the Nuremberg elite had sadly come to the conclusion that not only had their former independence become too costly, it had become in any event no longer viable once the protection of the old empire had vanished. An example was Paul Merkel, a prominent Nuremberg merchant and a later friend of Hegel, who was one of the Nuremberg elite who had come to see no other alternative than annexation by Bavaria; his wife, though, felt otherwise, telling her children with tears in her eyes on the day of annexation, "You poor children, you are now vassals of a prince."[19]

Although Nuremberg was not a large German city by the standards of its day, it was by no means a small town. In 1809, a census taken by Bavarian officials put the population of the city at 25,176.[20] Only three cities at the time in German-speaking lands – Vienna, Hamburg, and Berlin – had more than 100,000 inhabitants; Königsberg, Dresden, Cologne, and Frankfurt had between 50,000 and 60,000 inhabitants.[21] Although rich in homegrown traditions, Nuremberg had unfortunately also acquired an enormous debt during the period before and during the Napoleonic reorganization of central Europe. In annexing Nuremberg, Bavaria had to assume those debts. In 1810, Bavarian officials decided that they would continue to pay the reigning two percent interest on the debts to the Nuremberg creditors (mostly the patriciate and wealthy merchants), but, in an effort to limit expenditures, also decided to value the debts at only forty per cent of their paper value, thus effectively slashing by more than half the fortunes of many creditors, a move that did not exactly help to enamor those creditors to their new Bavarian rulers. In order to meet those debts, the Bavarian authorities began selling off property belonging to the city without regard to its place in the city's history or its artistic importance; many church properties and buildings (which had also been seized by the state) were also sold or put to other uses (such as becoming post offices). This only further served to disenchant some of the Nuremberg locals with the reforming Bavarians. As an appointee of the central commission in Bavaria and a Swabian, Hegel thus could not expect a free ride in Nuremberg; indeed, he could expect to be greeted with suspicion as an outsider arriving on the scene to reestablish a once-grand local institution of learning.

In addition to these social difficulties, Hegel had to deal with the problem of the decrepit Nuremberg school system itself. An official Bavarian report in 1807 on the state of the Nuremberg schools had essentially declared them to be worthless as preparatory schools for any higher study (such as the university) and argued that the four existing schools would have to be completely rebuilt from the ground up, administratively and pedagogically. They were described as being utterly backward, run by antiquated guilds, and taught according to outmoded models of pedagogy. (The report noted quite caustically, for example, that "outside of the Bible and the songbook, no new useful manual of religion has been introduced. The teachers are mostly old and wholly useless.")[22] But there were also some encouraging signs which offered Hegel hope in his new job. The local school commissioner to whom he had to answer was Heinrich Paulus, the rationalist theologian, who was not only an old friend from Jena but was also yet another fellow Swabian graduate of the Seminary in Tübingen; Paulus even wrote Hegel a nice congratulatory letter telling him how happy he was to learn that Hegel was to be in Nuremberg.[23] Unfortunately, and unknown to Hegel at the time, the reformers in Munich really had no idea what things cost and were embarking on too many plans and issuing too many directives for which they simply did not have the money. Indeed, Hegel could not have known that because the reformers themselves did not know it; the result was that by 1811, the Bavarian kingdom was running a debt of 120 million Guilder.[24] Paulus jested to Hegel that as an idealist, Hegel would keep all of them free of contamination by "the material, dirty essence of Mammon," joking (in English!) to Hegel, "God damn all the Idealism."[25] But little did both of them know just how bad things really were. It had taken the whole set of Napoleonic reforms for France finally to get a realistic hold on its own budget, on what things really cost, and on what kinds of revenues could be rationally predicted and assumed; the reformers in Bavaria were just beginners, and they were essentially groping in the dark, employing a mixture of small parts of more modern economics and lots of old fashioned cameralist assumptions, stirred together with large amounts of practical ignorance.

Difficulties with Teaching Duties

In addition to these difficulties, Hegel also had to assume his duties with very little information about what they were or even what he was supposed to be teaching. Everything was put off until the last minute, so that Hegel in effect had to begin his term as rector and professor by improvising on an almost daily basis. Only at the very end of November did he learn in a letter from Paulus what the "General Normative" was to require him to implement, and on December 5, 1808, Paulus opened the *Gymnasium* with a celebratory speech, with Hegel shortly thereafter – December 12, 1808 – officially beginning instruction in the *Gymnasium*. The chaos of the financial arrangements concerning the *Gymnasium* became apparent to Hegel immediately on assuming office. Directly after having been sworn in, Hegel began to note that the promised money and resources necessary to run the new institution of the *Ägidien-Gymnaisium* (so named for the church next to it, the Ägidien Church on the Ägidienberg) were wholly lacking. The walls were stained, lots of details had been neglected, and money to take care of those things was simply unavailable. Unfortunately, things did not improve in this regard very rapidly. During his tenure as rector, Hegel accumulated a long list of legitimate complaints that he had regularly to lodge with the relevant authorities: His salary would often go unpaid for months; because his salary was not paid, he had to take out loans simply to live; he had to meet school expenses out of his own pocket; the bookseller for the students charged them more for the books than did other booksellers; there was no copyist (or secretarial assistant, as we might say today), so Hegel had to copy out all the mounds of official paperwork himself ("the most annoying aspect of my office . . . a dreadful and repugnant waste of time," he called it);[26] and the list just grew and grew.

Moreover, there had been a confusion at the outset regarding the size

of Hegel's salary. Hegel had actually taken a cut in salary to move from
Bamberg to Nuremberg, and Nuremberg's cost of living was higher.
His remuneration was supposed to include 900 Guilders as professor,
100 Guilders as rector, and free lodging – he had been making over
1,300 Guilders as a newspaper editor in Bamberg – but the local administrator had interpreted this as 900 Guilders and free lodging *or* no
lodging and an extra 100 Guilders; lodging, as Hegel noted, would itself
come out to at least 100 Guilders. A bit piqued by all this, Hegel told
Niethammer, "If this is the case I must confess that I would gladly cede
the rectorship to anybody" and that if the administrator's interpretation
would allowed to stand, "I have to request you to take the rectorship
away from me."[27] An extra 100 Guilders for being rector did not seem
nearly enough to make it worth the trouble.

Of all these things, the one that seemed to Hegel to sum up the
shortcomings of the new Bavarian order was the fact that no toilets at
all were installed in any of the buildings housing any of the schools; and
the idea that there were no toilets in a building in which schoolchildren
were supposed to spend the entire day was, well, just ludicrous: Reporting back to Niethammer, Hegel sarcastically said of the toiletless
state of affairs obtaining in the Nuremberg schools that "this is a new
dimension of public education, the importance of which I have just now
discovered – so to speak, its hind side."[28] With equal sarcasm, Hegel
added that it would be nice to manage to have the requisite toilets
installed, "provided, of course, they are actually installed and not just
decreed," and, adding to his reflections on the difficulties awaiting him,
"you will be able to imagine for yourself how little such shabby external
conditions . . . are geared to instilling the confidence of the public, seeing that provision has been made for nothing, and that money is lacking
everywhere."[29] For Hegel, it had not been an auspicious beginning; and
the toilet problem itself was to endure for years.

Hegel's Success as Administrator and Teacher

But despite the practical obstacles – which, as his letters make clear,
irritated him to no end – he managed to put the *Gymnasium* on a
successful footing and to instill confidence in it. As one of his first acts
he managed to shift around some of the less productive faculty members
without antagonizing them at the same time. For example, he notes that

he had "to remove Professor Büchner, who understands nothing of algebra, from teaching mathematics to the upperclassmen and to put him in charge of religious studies and the doctrine of obligations for the lower classmen."[30] Hegel quickly gained the respect of the children, addressing the older students as "Mister" (*Herr*), a way of treating them with respect so that they would come to think of themselves as self-directing young adults and no longer as children in tutelary care. (In that way, he was being consistent with the post-Kantian pedagogical goals he and Niethammer shared, that education should be aimed at treating people as ends in themselves and fostering a sense of self-respect.) He maintained a sense of discipline and order in his classes and put great stress on being able to take good dictation and render things into good, clear German. (His own speech, as the students and his colleagues remembered, was itself thick with his Swabian accent and laden with Swabian expressions.[31] Hegel's own attitude toward his Swabian accent and mannerisms was typical of his self-distancing nature; he even once good-naturedly told the Frommanns that their nephew, who was going to visit Stuttgart, "at first will doubt whether [its Swabian inhabitants] actually speak German.")[32]

His students remembered him as an inspiring teacher; after dictating things to them, he encouraged the students to discuss what had been dictated, to learn to think for themselves and to ask questions: One student remembered that "each could demand to speak and seek to assert his opinion vis-à-vis the others; the rector himself only instructively stepped in now and then in order to guide the discussion."[33] Just as he had done at Jena, he paid much attention to his students and their needs, even though these students were much younger and obviously not nearly as advanced as the university students at Jena. Once a year, all the students in the *Gymnasium* – which in 1811, for example, amounted to 126 children – had to bring all their work, including their homework, to the rector, who would read all of it and make personal recommendations for improvement, would discuss with them the books they were reading outside of class, offer them tips for better study, and praise them for the progress they were making (when they were making any, which was frequent).[34] (All this was carried out in addition to his other administrative duties as rector, his sixteen hours a week teaching philosophy, and his own private work on the *Logic*!) He was also particularly remembered for his concern and care for students who came from backgrounds of slender means, a concern that stayed with him all his life.[35]

Schelling's friend Gottlob Schubert, who also knew Hegel in Nuremberg, reminisced later that those who knew Hegel only "from his writings or in his lecture hall" simply could not know "how amiable this man was in his personal relations" and, like many others, remembered especially well Hegel's sense of humor and, interestingly, his very characteristic smile.[36] Indeed, the reminiscences of the students in those days attest to an ongoing feature of Hegel's personality that was often at odds with other descriptions of him. He had always been a bad public speaker and lecturer; even at the Seminary in Tübingen, his sermons had been given low marks. The writer Clemens Brentano described him in 1810 as the "honest, wooden Hegel" in Nuremberg, a not untypical description.[37] But others in descriptions and recollections continually remarked on Hegel's amiability and sociability along with his honesty, sincerity, and uprightness. Hegel almost certainly had a very common type of speech impediment; when he had to speak formally before groups, he was led either to stutter or to lecture in slow, groping monotones; his (apparently well deserved) reputation for being a bad lecturer seemed to stem mainly from that. However, in personal situations, he seemed to be quite at ease and not troubled by such matters, again typical for such a speech impediment. And, like the nineteenth-century man he was, he had a very keen sense of privacy, becoming uncomfortable when people became very personal with him in what he regarded as public situations. In the small-class situations of the Nuremberg *Gymnasium* his difficulties in public speaking, however, seem not to have played a role, probably because of the age of the students and the necessarily more relaxed way in which he presented his ideas; in the *Gymnasium* classroom, he seems to have been both fluid and friendly in his demeanor.

Hegel's Public Addresses

Very quickly he succeeded in convincing both students and parents that the *Ägidien-Gymnasium* had been restored to its former glory. Just as he had done in Bamberg, Hegel managed to secure a place for himself in the social structure of the city rather quickly, which in a tradition-bound former imperial city such as Nuremberg was itself no small feat.

Hegel, moreover, made his goals and pedagogy publicly available and clear from the outset. In his address at the farewell festivities for the retiring rector (a Mr. Schenk) whose place Hegel was taking, Hegel returned to the ideas of self-direction and self-cultivation (of *Bildung*) that animated both his and Niethammer's conception of education: Stating the matter a bit floridly, as was the custom for such occasions, he said, "The value of cultivation, self-formation (*Bildung*) is so great that one of the ancients wished to say that the difference between a cultivated (*gebildeten*) person and an uncultivated one is as great as that between people in general and rocks," and added, "The riches of *Bildung* are given over to the teaching estate . . . to sustain and transmit to posterity. The teacher must look at himself as the guardian and priest of this holy light so that it does not go out and that humanity not sink back into the night of ancient barbarism."[38]

At the beginning of his tenure, Hegel had to make a yearly public address at the ceremony marking the end of the school year at which the academic prizes for that year were awarded (a kind of annual graduation address). In those addresses, he spoke to a gathering of the students, their parents, and the various Nuremberg notables who would assemble for such occasions; the addresses give a clear idea both of what Hegel wanted to communicate to the public about his goals for the *Gymnasium* and of his own pedagogical methods. Given the way in which Hegel came to be accepted in Nuremberg society, we must presume not only that he did succeed in actually communicating his views, but also that he succeeded in both convincing and reassuring the parents that the rector who had been brought in from the outside was in fact right for the job.

In his first such address, delivered in September, 1809, Hegel faced the formidable task of convincing a somewhat skeptical public and set of parents of the value of what he was doing. He began by noting the obvious, that people care more about their children than anything else and that the *Gymnasium*'s task was to help their children develop into young adults suited for higher learning. He then sounded the clarion call for the Niethammer-Hegelian modernizing line of thought. The new *Gymnasium* was to build on the foundations of classical humanist learning, which, he assured the parents and public, amounted to sustaining and continuing the illustrious humanistic foundations and traditions of the older *Gymnasium*. But the goal of the new foundation of the older

Gymnasium was to "fulfill the truest need of the time . . . putting the ancients into a new relationship with the whole and in that way sustaining what is essential in them as well as altering and renewing them."[39]

Hegel proposed two ways to accomplish this. First, instruction would be carried out in German, not in Latin, as the old so-called "Latin" schools in Germany had done: Hegel repeated in similar words what he had told Heinrich Voss in 1805 when he was inquiring about the possibility of an appointment at Heidelberg: "No people can be regarded as cultivated (*gebildet*)," as Hegel put it in 1809, "that cannot express all the riches of science in their own language" for when instruction is in a foreign language, we necessarily lack the "innerness (*Innigkeit*)" that allows us to be at home with the knowledge we seek.[40]

Second, the superiority of classical training, particularly in Greek, was to be emphasized in the new school. Hegel's public justification for this was striking, if for no other reason than for its continued application of clearly secularized versions of religious references. First, classical works, he says, are the "profane baptism that gives the soul the first and unforgettable tone and tincture for taste and science."[41] The study of the ancients thus inspires us and in a good way alienates us from our ordinary way of looking at things, making us ready to become self-forming, cultivated people – people, that is, of *Bildung*.[42] Second, and more importantly, classical works present us with an ideal of beauty, indeed, they are the "most beautiful that have been."

In characterizing the Greeks in this way, Hegel brought into play a phrase which had functioned as common rhetoric in Germany in general and Württemberg in particular, namely, "the beautiful soul." The usage of the phrase "the beautiful soul" had originally been wholly religious, but the phrase had undergone a gradual secularization during the early modern period (particularly by the earl of Shaftesbury) and had then been used in the eighteenth century to describe the Greeks in particular. Picking up on this, Hegel claimed, "If the original paradise was that of *human nature*, then this is the second, the higher paradise of the human spirit, which in its more beautiful naturalness, freedom, depth, and serenity steps forth like the bride from her chamber"[43] – that metaphor of the beautiful virginal "bride" having been the characteristic symbol of the beautiful soul for centuries.[44] This shows that Hegel, who had criticized the idea of the "beautiful soul" so trenchantly in his *Phenomenology of Spirit*, was still at least partially in its grip (unless, of course, he was just playing to his audience, which, given everything else we know about Hegel, seems unlikely).

Learning the classical languages has another advantage, Hegel argued. It brings youth to a greater awareness of the nature of the kind of logical categories they use, since "grammar has the [logical] categories, the unique creations and determinations of the intellect, for its content." Everyone can "distinguish red from blue without knowing how to give a definition of them according to Newtonian hypotheses" but we have *Bildung* vis-à vis them only when "we *have* them, i.e., have made them an object of consciousness."[45] The study of the ancients thus also contributes to our "logical formation (*Bildung*)."[46]

In closing, Hegel sounded a fully modernist note. One of the catch phrases to emerge from the Revolution was the idea of "careers open to talent." Hegel closed his remarks by addressing the students directly, saying that the purpose of the *Gymnasium* was to bring that ideal to Germany, to make it practicable in Germany, so "that in our fatherland every career stands open to your talents and diligence, but it is only practicable for those who deserve it."[47]

Nuremberg Rebellions

Although Hegel had come to Nuremberg secure in his belief that Napoleon had crushed the conservative resistance to the Revolution's demands, events quickly reminded him that the story was far from over. Napoleon's imperial ambitions grew, and he overextended himself, going into Spain on the pretext of needing to defend the Spanish coast against the British. (He also wanted to put his brother on the throne of Spain, a motive not unimportant to his decision.) At first, the Spanish adventure seemed to be working itself out as the typical Napoleonic success, but then to his surprise, the Spanish revolted and engaged him in guerrilla warfare, something to which he was not accustomed, and in July, 1808, a French army of 18,000 men was forced to capitulate to Spanish forces at the town of Bailen, an astonishing event noted throughout Europe. Napoleon was able to reinstate his brother as king in December, 1808, but the costs were excessive. In Italy in the same year, Napoleon annexed Rome, and when Pope Pius VII excommunicated him, Napoleon had him seized and put him under the equivalent of house arrest in a highly guarded residence in Savona. These events did not neutralize the Pope, as Napoleon had wished to do, but instead made him into a Catholic martyr. The Austrians, sensing a weakness in Napoleon's ranks, thus declared war in 1809, with the declaration of war being authored by Friedrich Schlegel, Hegel's old nemesis from Jena, who had since (along with his wife) moved to Austria, converted to Catholicism, and become more or less a propagandist for the Habsburgs. The authorities in Austria tried to cast their cause in the name of "Germany" and to foment a kind of popular guerrilla war in Germany like that which had come to pass in Spain. In Schlegel's "Proclamation to the Bavarians," a piece of Austrian war propaganda, he asserted that "We [Austrians] are Germans every bit as much as you are. . . . All those who are imbued with a true German patriotism will be powerfully supported, and, if they so deserve, richly rewarded by their former emperor, who did not resign his German heart along with his German crown."[48] Napoleon, however, once more proved master of the situation and, even after being wounded in one battle and then suffering his first defeat at Aspern, managed to capitalize on Austrian mistakes and defeat the Austrians at Wagram in July 1809. His army smoothly rolled into Vienna (after having been driven out only a short while before), and Napoleon was able to impose a punishing treaty on Austria.

Hegel, who had never liked Schlegel, now thoroughly and utterly detested him, and he could barely contain himself at the defeat suffered by the Austrians. Playing on Schlegel's stated desire to "liberate" Bavaria, Hegel said, with a certain amount of what the Germans call *Schadenfreude*, "the opposite liberation of Friedrich Schlegel with his Catholicization of all of us has gone down the drain, and he may consider himself lucky if only the gallows remain liberated from him."[49] He was, however, a bit rattled by the events in Nuremberg that were related to the war with Austria. An Austrian division reached Nuremberg in June 1809, and the French forces in the town had to retreat. On June 26, 1809, as Hegel was writing a letter to Niethammer to complain as usual about the lack of a copyist and the idiotic bureaucratic decrees that Bavarian officials were issuing for running the schools, the Austrians took control of the city. Matters were made worse when Countess von Thürheim imprudently referred to the Austrians in a public gathering as "a bunch of hirelings (*Gesindel*) made up of cobblers, tailors, and linen weavers (*Schustern, Schneidern und Leinwebern*)," and thereby managed to insult, enrage, and alienate the assembled Nuremberg artisans, many of whom still had greater feelings for the former emperor of the Holy Roman Empire than they did for their new king in Munich.[50] Outraged, the offended artisans rushed out to open one of the gates to the city and allow the Austrian troops to enter, at which point things began to get a bit out of hand. The Austrian troops and some townspeople went on something of a rampage, focusing their destructive energies in particular on a building housing Bavarian officials. The Bavarian insignias were torn down, and the whole place was sacked. Count von Thürheim, the Bavarian governor of the district, was seized by what some called the "rabble" and was then taken prisoner by the Austrians, who took him and a few other prominent Nuremberg officials as hostages when they had to retreat to Bayreuth. (They also took quite a bit of Nuremberg money and goods with them.) Even though the hostages were freed after the later and rather sudden Austrian retreat from Bayreuth, von Thürheim's career in Nuremberg was finished as a result of the fiasco, and he had to move on. Nuremberg's sympathy for the Austrians, however, did not go unnoticed in Munich, and in the reorganization of Bavaria in 1810, Nuremberg was no longer allowed to remain the governmental seat of a Bavarian department, with Ansbach instead gaining that title.

Hegel reported on the incident of the brief Austrian seizure of Nuremberg to Niethammer, expressing utter and thorough outrage at the behavior of the Nuremberg citizenry.[51] But at least for the time being, things had turned out well. On the one hand, Napoleonic Germany, to which Hegel was so firmly attached, had remained intact, and for the next couple of years would again seem perfectly secure. On the other hand, Hegel, with his clearly pro-Napoleonic sympathies, would have understandably been a bit nervous about his standing in a town that had witnessed such an outbreak of pro-Austrian sentiment and also a bit nervous about the stability of what he saw as the clearly more rational social order that Napoleon had brought to Germany.

As a result of all this Hegel became even a bit more troubled than before about his position in Nuremberg and about whether he would ever be able to get out of his rectorship and acquire the university position he really wanted. Hegel's anxieties were certainly not lessened by observing the ongoing battles that Niethammer constantly had to fight with those who opposed the reforms and the several close calls

Niethammer had, in which it looked as if Niethammer either would be forced out or would be impelled to resign in indignation over the whole state of affairs. Hegel's hopes were raised when, out of the blue in 1809, he received a letter from a former student of his in Jena, Peter van Ghert, informing him that van Ghert now had a fairly high position in the government in Holland and had read in a Heidelberg newspaper of Hegel's bad fortune after the devastation of Jena following the battle there. Proclaiming himself to be outraged at the very idea that Hegel "had been wholly ruined . . . that the best man in Germany" was no longer employed as a professor of philosophy, van Ghert offered to intervene for Hegel and procure for him a position at one of the soon-to-be reorganized universities in Holland.[52] (The lectures were given in Latin, van Ghert assured Hegel, so there would be no linguistic barriers for him.) Hegel was quite pleasantly surprised by all of this and reported back to van Ghert in December 1809 that he was not in fact ruined, that his position in Nuremberg was, moreover, "tolerable," although he hoped only "temporary," so that the offer of a position in Holland was not needed at that time. (Interestingly, Hegel noted that if he did indeed accept a position in Holland, he would intend to deliver lectures in Dutch soon thereafter, making the same point about the necessity of doing philosophy in one's own language to van Ghert that he had made in his address at the closing of the school year in 1809.) Hegel's rejection of van Ghert's offer to help him secure a position in Holland did not stop him, however, from using it as a tool to put pressure on Niethammer to secure a position for him at a Bavarian university, all to no avail.[53] Van Ghert's efforts to attract Hegel to Holland, however, did not end there but persisted over the next several years; indeed, van Ghert's patronage and his spirited defenses of Hegelianism made Holland one of the early places where a Hegelian school of thought sprang up.

Education, Modern Life, and Modern Religion

Bildung, *Discipline, and Education*

Hegel's initial address at the closing of the school year in 1809 must have been a success, but for whatever reason he felt compelled to alter his tone a bit in 1810. In 1810, he stressed the importance of religious education, for which he gave a somewhat secular rationale, namely, that "participation in a public worship" links students to a "tradition and to old customs."[54] Military practices, which had been introduced by governmental decree into the schools that year, were justified by Hegel as important for producing a well-rounded character. After all, he argued, a "cultivated (*gebildeter*) person has in fact not limited his nature to something in particular but rather has made himself capable of everything," and moreover, such practices remind the student that he must be ready to "defend his fatherland or prince."[55] (This was, of course, a theme that went back in Hegel's thought at least to his essay "The German Constitution," although the claim made in the 1810 address seems at best only half-hearted.)

However, in his second address, Hegel spoke more specifically about the themes of sociality that were bound up with his philosophical views and his commitment to the ideal of *Bildung*. People do not enter the world with natural inclinations toward virtue or education, he reminded the assembled parents and students; they need to be trained, disciplined, and socialized into such things. The acquisition of concepts comes from being trained into a form of life; this was, in Hegel's mind, not simply an empirical observation about social life but a thesis about the nature of "mindedness," *Geist*, itself. As he put it to the parents and students in 1810, "As with the will, so also must thought begin with obedience."[56]

But Hegel also made it quite clear that he understood the overarching goal of such training and discipline to be *not* the production of obedient souls but rather the instilling in the students of those dispositions that enabled them to realize "the self-activity of taking hold of things."[57] Hegel stressed that the "discipline" of which he spoke could not consist in rote memorization, indeed, so he said, restricting learning to "mere reception" would have the same effect as "writing sentences on water."[58] However, such original training and socialization cannot be a matter (or cannot exclusively be a matter) for the schools; it is fundamentally a matter for the family. In the family, one acquires the basic training and discipline in the *Sitte* (ethics and mores) of a form of a life, and "the institutions of learning presuppose ethical discipline." After all, Hegel said (playing with some German terms), "institutions of study are in part institutes of instruction, not immediately those of upbringing (*Erziehung*)" but in such institutes of study, "formation (*Bildung*) in ethics (*Sitte*) stands in an immediate connection with its main business, instruction, in part as an indirect cause, in part, however, as a direct result."[59] In modern times, we no longer need to separate "head and heart or thought and feeling" as "older times" had done.[60] The new idea of *Bildung* incorporates all the aspects of our social life together; indeed, full self-direction in fact requires *Bildung*, a socialization in which we can be at home. In short, "a generally cultivated (*gebildeter*) person can also be an ethical person."[61] What the neo-humanists called "utilitarian" education, however, cannot claim this; technical knowledge has no essential connection to moral knowledge.

Hegel closed his 1810 remarks to the students, parents, and notables with a matter that was close to his heart, the idea of careers being open to talent. He called on his relatively well-heeled audience to keep in mind "the support for those students of our institution who lack external means of support for their studies. . . . how many born to parents of no means have achieved the possibility [by such support] to raise themselves above their estate or to sustain themselves in it and develop those talents which poverty would have put to sleep or have sent in a wicked direction."[62] For Hegel, coming from Württemberg, this was one of the easy parts of the set of revolutionary ideas to embrace; because of the power of the Protestant Church in Württemberg, it had long been accepted that careers in the clergy should be open to talent, so that the son of a poor minister (who was nonetheless well-educated) would have as good a chance at attending the Seminary at Tübingen as anyone else; and, indeed, the Württemberg *Landesexam* managed to make that norm into more of a reality than it would have been otherwise. Thus, although Hegel came from a fairly well-off background himself, as a Württemberger, he could easily assimilate the general idea that "careers should be open to talent" into his own life experience. (Also in keeping with his theme of recognizing the deserving, he closed out his address by congratulating all the teachers for having been raised by governmental decree to the status of civil servants.)

Religious Authority, Educational Politics

By the end of 1810, Hegel was doing well in the community and his efforts at establishing and carrying out reforms in the *Gymnasium* were clearly meeting with both success and approval. However, despite all of this, Hegel was still less than pleased with the course of things. At one point, religious control over some of the lower schools was in part reasserted, and Hegel had to report that the professors at those institutions were "extremely displeased at having to go to church for religious instruction. What is essentially at stake is the former subordination of the teaching estate to the clergy and the clerical estate," something Hegel found particularly odious.[63] He also simply did not enjoy the administrative work and resented its taking time away from his own philosophical work on the second part of his "system." He even sent out feelers to Niethammer in August of 1810 wondering if it might be possible to "be freed of the rectorship and merely to retain the professorship so as to draw closer to what I am accustomed to consider my true vocation."[64] Moreover, he and Paulus were experiencing strained relations; Paulus was a bit irascible, and his position as the school commissioner for Hegel's district put the two at odds more than once, leading Hegel to make some less than kind comments about him to Niethammer after he had learned that Paulus had Jewish origins.[65]

However, in the autumn of 1810, Hegel found himself in the middle of a short-lived crisis, which served to confirm some of his views and helped to harden his views in other ways. At that time the Bavarian government decided as a cost-cutting measure simply to close the *Gymnasium* in Nuremberg and allow the *Realinstitut* (the more technical school) to remain. Needless to say, this upset Hegel in no small way. He was, as always, dumbfounded and perplexed by what he saw as the thorough idiocy of the Bavarian government reflected in the way it decided to close the *Gymnasium* and the sloppy reasoning it used to justify itself. Hegel certainly had a right to be outraged, since the whole affair was scandalous from start to finish. Early on, the Montgelas administration had seized all the private endowments from the formerly church-run schools and administered them itself, using them instead for its state-run schools. The alleged reason for closing the Nuremberg *Gymnasium* was a purported legal irregularity in the way in which endowment money had been allotted to the *Gymnasium*; relying on this specious legal irregularity, the officials in Munich declared the school's claim on the endowment to be void; they then concluded that that since the Nuremberg institution did not have an endowment, it was useless and too costly. Besides, the officials said, it was no great loss, since the students in Nuremberg could attend the nearby *Gymnasium* in Ansbach.

The movement to close the school was led by a Catholic adviser in Nuremberg to the government in Munich, who also arranged to have the order for the closing carried out when Niethammer was absent from Munich. Hegel led the protests, although it was Paulus who saved the day, discovering at the last minute some old documents that proved the legality of the endowment for the *Gymnasium*.[66] The citizens of Nuremberg were nonetheless quite upset with the decision, and, as a sign that Hegel's status in the tradition-bound city of Nuremberg had definitely risen, the citizens gathered a petition demanding the continuance of "the venerable and now wonderfully renewed institution of our *Gymnasium*."[67] It was clear who got the credit for having accomplished that renewal, and it was clear that Hegel's success in that regard had made his star rise in the city. The *Gymnasium* was allowed to remain, and part of the funds for its maintenance for a short period were actually to come from the citizens themselves. Hegel was quite pleased with the public response, however outraged he was by the government in Munich; during the crisis, he noted that "all social classes, ages, sexes, and persons both official and private share the same sensation of the harshness of this measure against Nuremberg. The *Gymnasium* was the only establishment for which the entire population was grateful to the government."[68]

The depth of the public response strengthened for Hegel his belief in the truth of his theory about the relation between religion and modern life as laid out in the *Phenomenology*. In a telling aside to Niethammer, he spoke of "how highly Protestants esteem their institutions of *Bildung*, how these institutions are as dear to them as the churches. They are certainly worth as much as these churches. Protestantism does not so much consist in any particular creed (*Konfession*) as in the spirit of reflection (*Nachdenken*) and higher, more rational *Bildung*, not in the training for this or that type of usefulness. One could not have attacked them at a more sensitive spot than their institutions of study."[69]

That the opposition to the reformed *Gymnasium* was being led by a Catholic only hardened Hegel's views toward Catholicism. Although he had grown up in Württemberg absorbing anti-Catholic sentiments as a youngster, he had become more open to Catholicism with his brief flirtation with Nanette Endel and his growing curiosity about the religion as a young man. In his *Phenomenology*, he had fairly well skirted the whole issue of Catholicism, arguing that Christianity was the paradigmatic modern religion – although he surely meant the Protestant version, quite strikingly, he did not spell it out as such. But the experiences of his post-Jena years – his polemical encounters with Catholic philosophers such as Weiller and Salat while in Jena prior to writing the *Phenomenology*, his observation of what had happened to Schelling at the hands of the Catholic bishops in Würzburg, his experiences living in Bavaria and having to observe and personally do battle with the Catholic "old Bavarians," and the brief experience of the Austrian seizure of Nuremberg under a declaration of war drafted by the Catholic convert Schlegel – had consolidated what his Württemberg upbringing had already prepared him for, namely, the belief that Catholicism was an outmoded, paradigmatically unmodern form of Christianity, and that Catholicism was therefore a threat to the general view for which he had argued in the *Phenomenology*.

Already in 1808, in his first term as rector in Nuremberg, he had propounded to the (overwhelmingly Protestant) students in his class that the great difference between Catholicism and Protestantism had to do with issues of authority and modernity: Catholics divided the religious community between "laymen and priests," with only the priests being "invested with the full powers" of the church, and thus the "reconciliation with God" was therefore accomplished only "externally" for Catholics. For Protestants, however, "the priests are only teachers. All in the religious community are equal before God as the present spirit of the community."[70] In Nuremberg, Hegel was seeing firsthand what he took to be the practical consequences of Catholicism when it wielded social authority, and it stiffened his dislike for it. (How Hegel must have broadly smiled to himself when he read a postscript to a letter van Ghert wrote to him in February 1811, in which van Ghert asked: "Is it really true, as people say here, that Fr. Schlegel in Vienna has become so bigoted a Catholic that he does nothing other than pray?")[71]

After his stay in Nuremberg and his experience of the ongoing disputes in Bavarian life, Hegel never wavered again in his assessment of Protestantism and of the way in which it, and not Catholicism, embodied the tendencies and the secular-religious ideals of modern life. In July 1816, after the Congress of Vienna and the restoration, he was reiterating to Niethammer that the difference between Protestantism and Catholicism was that "Protestantism is not entrusted to the hierarchical organization of a church but lies solely in general insight and *Bildung*," adding, "our universities and schools are our church. It is not the clergy and religious worship that counts as in the Catholic church."[72] He reiterated this point to Niethammer a few months later in October 1816: "Our safeguard is thus not the aggregate of council pronouncements, nor a clergy empowered to preserve such pronouncements, but is rather only the common *Bildung* of the [religious] community. Our more immediate safeguard is thus the universities and general institutions of instruction. All Protestants look upon these institutions as their Rome and council of bishops . . . The sole authority [for Protestants] is the intellectual and moral *Bildung* of all, and the guarantors of such *Bildung* are these institutions . . . *general* intellectual and moral *Bildung* is what is holy to Protestants. To Catholics, however, it is something optional, since what is sacred is in the church, which is separated off in a clergy."[73]

It is, of course, obvious that Hegel was not describing Protestantism as it actually was in Germany – many and surely most Protestants did not think of the universities as their "church" – but more in terms of what he thought were the internal, logical dynamics of the Protestant commitments. His belief in the internal logic of Protestantism was strong enough to lead him to blur in his own mind the distinction between the Protestant churches that actually surrounded him and what he thought were their logical outcomes. But after Nuremberg, Hegel never again wavered in his opinion that the project of modern life required the eventual triumph of Protestantism over Catholicism, at least as Protestantism was conceptually articulated in his philosophy, and that in turn served only to strengthen his desire to pursue a career in a *university*, that "Rome and council of bishops" for modern life in general.

Marriage into the Nuremberg Patriciate

Perhaps Hegel had not understood just what success he was having in reforming the *Gymnasium* and what a high profile he had created for himself, but he was gratified that his accomplishments had been noted. When Hegel came to Nuremberg, he clearly wanted to make a name for himself – if for no other reason than to clear the way for a university appointment. It was also clear that after establishing himself as a successful rector at an important institution, Hegel had other things on his mind. Niethammer had already told him, when he first came to Nuremberg, that he should get married, and in his letters to Niethammer, Hegel also spoke of his own desire to get married. The problem, he noted – echoing the sentiments of so many single people since then – was *meeting* somebody, or, as he exclaimed to Niethammer, "I would also like to take up and successfully conclude another business, namely, to take a wife, or rather to find one!" When he announced that he was coming to Nuremberg, even Paulus had jokingly told him that his wife would inquire about a "faithful, slow Nuremberg woman" for him.[74] (Interestingly enough, Paulus apparently suggested his own daughter to Hegel, but Hegel was not interested – did Paulus think of his daughter as "slow"?)[75]

Because of his success, Hegel was soon moving in the highest circles in the city. In October 1810, a private club was founded called The Museum. The club consisted of some of the highest levels of Nuremberg society (all male, of course), and Hegel was one of the people listed in the original membership list of 318 people. It was founded for the purpose of providing a meeting point for members of the "cultivated (*gebildeten*) estates" who would be able within the confines of the club to conduct gentlemanly and learned debates about modern literature. Despite its name, the club was not in fact a museum of any type; it took its name (probably) from an earlier, extremely similar society founded in Frankfurt in 1808 (or perhaps even from another similar club in Munich that had taken *its* name from the Frankfurt club), and a good part of its membership came from a yet earlier club of the same type in Nuremberg called the Harmony. Two of the founding members were listed as "von Tucher, council director" and "von Tucher, Senator." (Also among the other members was G. A. Gabler, Hegel's former student at Jena and his eventual successor in Berlin, who at that time was a *Hofmeister* in Nuremberg.)[76]

By early October 1810, Hegel was therefore clearly consorting with the likes of the von Tuchers, who were among the most visible and notable of the Nuremberg patrician families, having been wealthy traders in the city for many centuries. His interest in the family went beyond the usual considerations: A note from the papers of Jobst Wilhelm Karl von Tucher (the "Senator" in the membership list) noted:

"At the beginning of April (1811), rector Hegel let his wishes be known
. . . to marry my daughter and to request an opportunity to speak with
the latter. On April 8 he inaugurated his request with me . . . He requested merely the permission to be allowed to pay a friendly visit to
my daughter."[77] The daughter was Marie Helena Susanna von Tucher
(his eldest daughter), who would in fact marry Hegel on September 15,
1811; she was also more than twenty years younger than he, having
been born in 1791. But the von Tucher family clearly did not assent to
this all at once, even though Marie's father said he would completely
abide by her wishes in the matter. There was clearly some negotiating
to be done if an outsider and a non-patrician such as Hegel was going
to be allowed to enter the von Tucher family. In May 1810, Hegel had
coyly written Niethammer about his being at a "turning point: if only I
am not turned down I will accede to eternal bliss. . . . It is not a subject
that permits of being much written about," adding that in any event,
the matter was "not in his own hands" but "in the good hands of City
Administrator Merkel" (with Hegel adding in the margin that Merkel's
"good hands" were "still very general and distant").[78] Whatever Merkel
did, it seemed to have worked. Hegel revealed his engagement to Marie
von Tucher in a letter to Niethammer of April, 1811, about a year after
he had hinted to Niethammer that something like negotiations were
under way.[79]

There is unfortunately no record of Hegel's and Marie von Tucher's
courtship – not of how Hegel and Marie von Tucher met, nor of how
long they might have known each other before Hegel took the step of
asking her to marry him. Hegel wrote a love poem to Marie von Tucher
on April 13, 1811, shortly before the engagement. (According to Hegel,
the offer of marriage was accepted on April 16.)[80] The poem – "verse"
would actually be a more apt description of it – is not exactly the basis
of Hegel's reputation in the history of thought; it is a more or less
humdrum, semi-Romantic poem, lacking any attempt to imitate Hölderlin's poetry as Hegel had done when he wrote "Eleusis" to Hölderlin
himself in 1796. (It may well also be true that by this time Hegel no
longer found Hölderlin's style attractive; or it may be that he did not
feel the intended recipient of the poem would appreciate Hölderlin's
style as much as she would appreciate something done in a more conventional vein.) In the verse, Hegel brought into play the standard
panoply of Romantic imagery –going to the mountaintop, nature's maj-

esty, the redness of the sunrise, and so on – but the dominant metaphor draws on an earlier idea of "life" that he had used in Frankfurt while under Hölderlin's influence. He uses the image of the phoenix to symbolize the way in which love is the union of two people, creating a bond between them that results in a common personality, a mutual emotional commitment, and not merely a set of isolated although mutual satisfactions; the phoenix symbolizes the way in which what divides two lovers falls away as genuine love takes over and re-institutes itself over and over again, creating itself, as it were, out of its own ashes – a theme certainly in keeping with Hegel's philosophical views.[81]

In any event, the verse and whatever else Hegel was doing to woo Marie von Tucher worked, and the offer of marriage was accepted. This prompted a second piece of verse, dated April 17, 1811, in which the themes are, quite naturally, the joy that comes from knowing one's love is reciprocated, the inability of words to express what one feels, the envy of the singing of the sweet and melancholy nightingale (a perennial in European poetry), how a kiss says more than words could, and, in a manner vaguely reminiscent of the seventeenth century "metaphysical poets" of England, a closing image of souls touching and flowing into one another.[82]

All was not sweetness and light. Other, more troubled parts of their courtship emerge from two letters that Hegel wrote to Marie von Tucher in the summer of 1811, a short time after the engagement had been set. The first letter responds to the way in which Marie von Tucher's feelings obviously had been hurt by a kind of squabble between them; indeed, her feelings may have been injured enough to put the whole plan for marriage in jeopardy. One must of course read a bit between the lines to get at what the dispute was about, but it is not terribly difficult to get some inkling of what was going on. Marie von Tucher was, as a child of her time, a bit of a sentimentalist. When Hegel added a postscript to a letter Marie had written to his sister noting there that he fully expected to be very happy in his and Marie's relationship "insofar as happiness belongs to my life's destiny," he obviously hurt Marie's feeling's, since it seemed to suggest to her that Hegel was saying that he really did not expect to be completely happy in the marriage, something that clearly violated Marie von Tucher's sense of what marriage was supposed to be.[83] In his response, Hegel tried to explain away his unintended gaffe. Had they not agreed the night before, Hegel reminded her, that in all "non-superficial natures every sensation of happiness is connected with sensation of melancholy," and had they not agreed that not happiness (*Glück*) but "being contented" (*Zufriedenheit*) was the true component of genuine, deep marital love?[84] (One senses that the "night before" Hegel had been lecturing Marie von Tucher on the necessity for making certain key philosophical distinctions, and that Marie von Tucher was not exactly comfortable being the object of an instructional lecture by her future husband.) Making several other argumentative, more or less philosophical distinctions about the unity found in love, about "reflection" intruding on and dividing such unity, Hegel suddenly catches himself and in a moment of self-revelation says: "Oh, how much more I could still write – about my perhaps hypochondriacal pedantry, which led me to insist so greatly on the distinction between 'being satisfied' and happiness, a distinction which is once again so useless" and about how "I have long doubted whether I should write to you . . . since I feared explanation, which once embarked upon is so dangerous."[85] Hegel's very typical self-distancing behavior, his greater comfort with dealing with personal matters from a more abstract, much more intellectual distance – something he had long before noted to Nanette Endel – appears again. He then calls on Marie von Tucher to be his "healer," to "reconcile" his "inner self" with the actual world – a conception of the relation between men and women that was later to find full expression in his mature writings on love and the family.

This was not their last tiff before the marriage. A more serious dispute took place a short time later. Marie von Tucher, the sentimentalist, someone who thought that one's deepest and truest feelings were sufficient to give one guidance in moral matters, had apparently made some kind of remark to Hegel to the effect that moral duty comes from the heart. For that, she apparently got a stern, censorious lecture from Hegel about how this was a false and maybe dangerous view of morality. Her feelings were again deeply hurt, and, once again, Hegel tried to explain things away. In his letter to her, he basically tells her that he knows that this conflation of the heart's deepest feelings with moral duty cannot *really* be her own view, but just some kind of theory (he calls it her "reflection") she has picked up along the way, and that a fine and noble nature such as hers could not *really* hold such abominable views; indeed, she only uses such wrong-headed views to excuse others (a fine sentiment and a noble gesture, revelatory of her basically good and generous nature), but she should keep in mind nonetheless that excusing is not justifying. Once again, Hegel revealingly speaks of himself when he says that for him, all such human matters appear much too much as ideas having "logical consequences, extended results, and applications."[86] Hegel's view of the difference between the sexes also appears again in his apology for his own behavior: People like Marie von Tucher (in other words, women in general) do not proceed, he says, by rules and maxims but rather by "character," and women are always willing to forego or bend the maxims when they clash with their characters, whereas men are not. Thus, men and women have problems of communication. Rest assured, he says, that it was all just a misunderstanding, and he assures Marie von Tucher that he is definitely not one of those men "who torture their wives merely so that their . . . patience and love may be constantly tested."[87]

Marie von Tucher obviously got over these slights, but it is clear that she also did not simply accept Hegel's mastery over her. She displayed, for example, some sense of independence from Hegel in her own marginal comments added to Hegel's letter to Caroline Paulus, the wife of Heinrich Paulus (both of whom had moved to Heidelberg when Heinrich assumed a post as a professor at the university there). Hegel, as usual, inquired about the possibility of his landing a position at Heidelberg, and Marie enthusiastically endorsed the idea of leaving Nuremberg, even foregoing Erlangen, for a residence in Heidelberg. With deep irony, she refers to Hegel as her "Master (*Herr*)," adding that "I have already raised my little voice earlier in conversation with my master" about the possibility of moving to Heidelberg. When Hegel speaks of the possibility of moving to Heidelberg, she writes in the margin, "Yes! Yes!" ("*Jawohl! Jawohl!*"), and also adds, "We often talk together about it."[88] It is clear that for Hegel and Marie von Tucher, their imaginative future together has become centered around the vision of the couple as university professor and wife.

There were some other bumps along the road to the marriage, but none of them was serious. In his letter to Niethammer announcing his engagement, Hegel said that Marie's father had made their engagement contingent on Hegel's landing an appointment as a professor at a university. Hegel seems to have been stretching the truth a bit here, since in fact he did not land any such appointment, and Marie von Tucher's father obviously did not prevent the wedding (nor is there any evidence that he showed the slightest consternation or hesitation about proceeding with it). Since Hegel, a nonaristocrat with no fortune of his own, was marrying into a patrician family, he knew that this claim would at least be plausible to Niethammer. Although the aristocracy had lost much of its traditional status after the Napoleonic reorganization of central Europe, it still managed to retain much of its power and to maintain a certain mystique among the populace; as an English historian remarked in 1833, "The Germans can be roughly divided into two classes, the von's and the non-von's."[89]

Hegel seemed to be trying to call Niethammer's hand with this ploy and thereby to cajole Niethammer into making some such appointment for him, but Niethammer did not play along. Instead, he wrote back to Hegel, reproaching him for his attitude, and reminding him that in Napoleonic, modern life, such titles do not mean what they formerly meant. Niethammer reminded Hegel that he was, after all, a professor at a famous *Gymnasium*, indeed the rector of it, and that that was sufficient unto itself to establish his credentials for entry into such an exalted family as the von Tuchers. Not ancestry but "personal desert and self-acquired rank," Niethammer reminded Hegel, were the criteria of achievement in modern life. To worry about his social status vis-à-vis the von Tucher family, Niethammer further admonished Hegel, simply evidenced a certain "vanity on your part, which so ill befits a philosopher."[90] Scolded in this way, Hegel had to admit in his reply to Niethammer that Niethammer was right, noting that Marie's father in fact did not take his remaining as a *Gymnasium* professor to be an impediment to the wedding, adding perhaps apologetically, and wishing to explain away his brief flirtation with social climbing, that "the wish for better employment has never been attested in me as a wish for higher employment."[91]

The chaotic state of Bavarian finances also continued to be a problem, and as the date of the wedding approached, Hegel had to complain in clamorous tones about the way his salary was five months in arrears, how other promised reimbursements for expenses had not been received and so on. Finally, Hegel borrowed money from Mr. Merkel (like the true friend he was, Niethammer had also offered to lend him some money). That hurdle too was thus cleared.

The final hurdle was the rather embarrassing fact of the existence of

Georg Ludwig Friedrich Fischer (Hegel's illegitimate son by Johanna Burkhardt). It does seem rather likely that Marie von Tucher learned of the existence of Ludwig Fischer and his relation to her prospective husband before the wedding, although it is not at all clear whether it was Hegel who told her or whether she had to learn about the matter through (what would have been the unquestionably discomfiting) arrival on the scene of Johanna Burkhardt herself. According to one story, Johanna Burkhardt in fact appeared in Nuremberg once she learned of Hegel's upcoming wedding and demanded satisfaction from him. In a letter to Mrs. Frommann of May, 1811, Hegel announced his plans to marry, adding "I ask you still to keep this circumstance a secret, since otherwise it might incite even more the impudence of that Burkhardt woman, should she find out about it before everything is completely settled with her," noting also that it would be good to speak to the Jena lawyer Ludwig C. F. Asverus (who had been Hegel's legal advisor regarding the publication of the *Phenomenology*) about the matter.[92] The tone of Hegel's earlier references to Ms. Burkhardt – about his wanting to "extricate [Ms. Burkhardt] from her present situation" and about how she "thus has a right to call upon me to perform obligations of all sorts"[93] – had obviously dropped by the wayside by 1811. Hegel's reference to her finding out about things before everything was "completely settled with her" also indicates that he most likely was trying to arrange some kind of legally binding agreement with her that would cancel any legal claims she might have had for breach of promise, and that he was also trying to make these arrangements without her learning that he was at the time actually planning to marry somebody else. What exactly happened and what negotiations there were (or even if there were any at all) cannot, however, be known on the basis of the surviving records.[94] In any event, Marie von Tucher, whatever else she really felt about the matter, did not think it serious enough to call off the engagement.

The obstacles were all cleared, and on September 15, 1811, Hegel and Marie von Tucher were wed. Hegel was now quite satisfied; in a burst of untypical enthusiasm, he announced to Niethammer, "I have now reached my earthly goal. For what more does one want in this world than an official post and a dear wife? . . . What is left over no longer makes up chapters in themselves but perhaps only paragraphs or remarks."[95] In that same letter, Hegel also quite characteristically distanced himself from any more romantic or sentimentalist notions about marriage (and his own in particular), noting that "having entered upon the honeymoon with calmer views and having gone through the period since the wedding with fewer illusions, I am of the opinion that a not far removed degree of satisfaction and especially the same inwardness of confidence can be maintained."[96] Hegel's view that marriage required more than passion, that it required a level of dutiful commitment – that, in his own words to Marie before they married, "love requires for its completion a still higher moment than that in which it consists merely in and for itself. What is perfect satisfaction, what is called being entirely happy, can only be completed by religion and a feeling of duty"[97] – also fit well into the contours of his own personality.

Hegel's uncharacteristic mood of satisfaction and repose, however, was to be only temporary. In the first two years of their marriage, Hegel and Marie von Tucher had to navigate some fairly rough weather. The continuing financial chaos of the Bavarian administration meant that every time Hegel's salary was finally paid in full, the authorities immediately let it again fall into arrears, and Hegel was thus constantly having to borrow money to stay afloat while he waited for his salary to be paid. He was also forced to continue to cajole his friend and patron Nietham-mer to look into all kinds of things, all of which prompted Hegel to begin again incessantly writing to Niethammer and to anyone else he thought could help him about securing a university post for himself. Moreover, during this period a whole series of tragedies struck the Hegel family. On June 27, 1812, the Hegels had a daughter, Susanna Maria Louisa Wilhelmine; Hegel was overjoyed. However, on August 8, 1812, their daughter suddenly died, and Marie was particularly stricken with grief. One year later, the Hegels had a healthy son, Karl Friedrich Wilhelm, born June 7, 1813; but a few months prior to his birth, Hegel's wife's father had fallen fatally ill, and about a week after Karl Hegel's birth – who was named after Marie's father – Jobst Wil-helm Karl von Tucher, who was himself not much older than Hegel, died. (Hegel was forty-three at the time; Karl von Tucher was forty-nine.) In 1812, Hegel and Marie each had a brother die in Napoleon's Russian campaign, and Napoleon's own fall from power threw into question much of what Hegel had staked his life on until that point. An enthusiastic supporter of the new modern order, Hegel suddenly found himself surrounded by those who wished to turn back the clock not merely to pre-Napoleonic days but to pre-1789 days. Hegel, a publicly recognized enthusiast for Napoleon who was newly married and starting a family, had good reason to fear for his position in such a world.

Domesticity and Turbulence

Hegel's New Family and His Work

Hegel quickly and happily settled into married life and into Nuremberg respectability, and he and Marie bore up fairly well under the tragedies, stresses, and strains that they had to endure during their first years of marriage. Hegel clearly had excellent relations with his in-laws; his status as rector of the *Gymnasium* and his connection with one of the oldest families of the city made him a full-fledged Nuremberger. After the death of his father-in-law, Hegel's mother-in-law – Susanna Maria von Tucher, born Haller von Hallerstein – who was in fact less than one year older than Hegel, seemed to turn to him as the de facto official man (and therefore titular head) of the family and displayed great admiration, pride, and affection for her daughter's husband.

Hegel acquired a taste for Nuremberg knockwurst and bratwurst, and even before his marriage had become a passionate devotee of authentic Nuremberger *Lebkuchen* (a kind of gingerbread and chocolate cookie usually made around Christmastime).[98] He would, for example, send *Lebkuchen* to Niethammer as gifts, praising them and extolling their virtues. Indeed, after he and Marie moved to Berlin, Hegel's mother-in-law made sure that he received large packets of *Lebkuchen* each year at Christmas, and much of the correspondence between Marie and her mother from October to December each year would concern itself with the progress and status of the upcoming deliverance of *Lebkuchen* for her beloved son-in-law. In keeping with the customs of the time, she always addressed Hegel with the formal "Sie" and not the familiar "Du," although she referred to her other son-in-law – "Guido" von Meyer – by his first name, noting even in one letter to Marie that "for you, dear Marie, such a Guido would have been nothing, absolutely nothing," a not terribly flattering comparison between Guido and Hegel (at least from Guido's point of view). (Hegel also addressed his mother-in-law with the more formal "Sie.") Moreover, in her letters to Marie, Hegel's mother-in-law almost always referred to Hegel as "the dear,

good Hegel" or just as "Hegel," and only very rarely as "your husband.")[99]

In 1812, Niethammer even managed to get Hegel a position as *Schulreferent* (school inspector) for Nuremberg (Paulus's old post), thus increasing his salary by 300 Guilders, whose "starlike rays," as Hegel put
it, "dazzled my wife."[100] Things were going well for him.

All the while Hegel was settling into Nuremberg respectability, he
was hard at work on his *Logic*, using whatever free time he had from
his official duties to work on the book. He certainly complained in
letters (for example, to van Ghert) that he could only "intermittently"
work on the book; despite the fact that he almost surely had a longer
manuscript on the subject that he had brought from Jena and that he
had already written a large, clean copy of a "Logic" in 1804–05 that he
then decided not to publish after all, he had nonetheless already told
Niethammer in 1808 that the "Logic" on which he was working in
Bamberg was something for which he "had hardly laid the foundation"
in Jena, indicating that he was fundamentally rethinking his own conception of what was to become his *Science of Logic* in light of his
experience in writing the *Phenomenology*.[101] He did indeed manage to
publish the first part of the *Science of Logic* in 1812, remarking at the
time to Niethammer that "it is no small matter in the first half year of
one's marriage to write a book of thirty proofsheets of the most abstruse
contents."[102]

The Pedagogy of Freedom: The 1811 Address

Hegel's address at the ceremonies marking the end of the school year in
1811 reveal both his confidence in the success of the *Gymnasium* that he
had played such a large role in restoring and the current directions of
own thought. The address was given a little less than two weeks before
his marriage, and in it, he concentrated on the theme of ethics in
education. Proudly referring to what he only half-modestly described as
the "second founding, as it were," of the school under his leadership,
Hegel outlined for his audience of students, parents, and notables –
among which were surely included his soon-to-be in-laws – what he
took to be the *moral* purpose of the school. Hegel's commitment to
modern ways of doing things and his belief in *Bildung* as the unifying
goal of modern life again made a clear and unmistakable appearance:

The purpose of education in the sense of upbringing (*Erziehung*) is, Hegel says, an "upbringing toward independence (*Selbstständigkeit*)," and this "upbringing toward independence" is indeed an essential component of the overall cultivation, *Bildung*, that is carried out in the schools.[103] Hegel found his work in the schools to have given him a particularly clear instance of the notion of mediating institutions that had played such a large role in his Jena manuscripts. The school, Hegel says, "*stands between the family and the actual world* and constitutes the linking middle member of the transition from the former into the latter."[104] As one of the key institutions of modern life, the school is essential for making the transition from childhood to adulthood in the way necessary for modern life, namely, by taking the child out of relations of familial dependence and training him so as to make him self-directing – the goal, in Hegel's mind, of all genuinely modern *Bildung*.

Hegel's own philosophical emphasis on freedom thus appeared clearly in his pedagogy: The school is the social preparation for modern self-direction and self-respect, but it likewise presupposes that parents bring up their children in a specifically modern ethical way. The students must come to the schools already possessing a certain discipline and self-respect if they are to be in the position to perform the tasks assigned to them in the school and to acquire the goods which a modern school has to offer them. It is clear that Hegel's characteristic philosophical junction of discipline, training, and freedom thus also played a central role in his pedagogical practice and took more determinate shape as he gained experience in this area. It is particularly noteworthy that Hegel did not argue that discipline should triumph over freedom, nor did he even hint that he might accept the fully specious point that discipline and obedience are really (in some obscure sense) freedom. To drive this point home, Hegel contrasted in his address what he described as modern life's "correct viewpoint" with an older conception of upbringing and cultivation: Since modern upbringing (*Erziehung*) is, he noted, "essentially more a matter of support for than suppression of the awakening feeling of the self, it must be a *Bildung* to independence," which stands of course in complete opposition to the older, outmoded manner of "giving to the young the feeling of submissiveness and unfreedom . . . of demanding empty obedience for obedience's sake."[105] That the schools accomplish their task of "refining the person" (*Bildung*) for

independence by cultivating certain habits of mind and character
through the imposition of certain types of discipline on the students
does not imply, Hegel makes abundantly clear, the older (and, as he
hopes, discredited) authoritarian concept of education.

If the school is to be a place where ethical principles are taught, he
noted, it must be kept in mind that these "principles and ways of acting
are not so much brought to mind in conscious reflection as they are a
substantial element in which the human being lives and according to
which he directs and accommodates his spiritual organization to the
extent that the principles attach themselves to him as mores (*Sitte*) and
become habits."[106] The schools play their specific role in guiding and
training the students to practice a kind of *moral* reflection on these
customary (*sittliche*) principles, so that the principles in terms of which
we "give accounts to ourselves and to others about our actions, the
orienting points which guide us through the multiplicity of appearance
and the precarious play of feelings" can be more fully grasped, understood, and made efficacious in everyday life.[107] This grasping and understanding of moral principles, moreover, is not something in which
there can be a strict, rule-guided method of instruction. The real task
for the moral agent is to learn to *perceive* what is salient about situations,
to learn how to specify his principles more concretely as needed and to
apply in varied and very different cases what can otherwise only be very
general, abstract ethical principles; or, as Hegel put it, "our whole life
consists in nothing further than learning to understand ever more
deeply [the principles'] meaning and scope, to see them resonating in
newer and ever more new examples and cases, and thus to recognize
the multiple facets in their meanings and that which is determinate in
their application."[108]

The right kind of education in the schools helps to socialize the
young so that they can come to distance themselves from their more
immediate desires, inclinations, and thoughts and thus place themselves
in a position to carry out such judgmental deliberations about the right
thing to do in particular circumstances. The school is to accomplish this
task by constituting itself as an institution that is neither the natural,
loving world of the family (in which the child is valued simply for who
he is) nor the competitive world of the marketplace (in which the
individual is valued only for what he does). It is instead the "middle
sphere" between them, in which the young student "is instructed in a

community with many others," in which "he learns to direct himself to others, to acquire trust in others who are at first alien people to him, and to acquire trust in himself in relation to them and therein make a start on *Bildung* and the practice of social virtues."[109] The school, moreover, cannot even pretend to exhaust the young student's life. Between his family and his school life, the student must be given wide latitude to pursue his own interests, to associate with others, and in general to learn to trust and train his own judgment.

The school, however, should not be a place where students are merely trained for the acquisition of neutral "skills" in preparation for a career. To be sure, Hegel notes, the school must prepare people for the real world beyond its doors. The real world, Hegel reminds the students and parents, "does not care about their particular goals, opinions, and dispositions."[110] The school prepares the student for that world by giving them *Bildung*: In Hegel's words, "the work of the schools does not have its complete end within itself but only lays the foundations for the possibility of something else, which is the essential work" – which is the whole life of the individual. The individual "can never even perfect this preliminary work, this self-cultivation (*Bildung*), he can only reach a certain level."[111] The schools prepare one for *life*, not *jobs*, even though the skills that one acquires in the schools prepare one for the kinds of careers that modern life promises.

Hegel's address thus laid out his and Niethammer's neo-humanism as the pedagogy for freedom, for putting people in the position to be able to direct their own lives by being able to engage in moral reflection on the customs and mores that make up their deep sense of who they are and by acquiring the wide-ranging skills of thought and reflection that equip them to step into the new careers opening up for the talented in the post-Revolutionary, Napoleonic world around them.

Napoleon's Fall

As Hegel gave that address, neither he nor anyone else could have predicted the upheaval that would shortly follow. In a stunning display of overconfidence and hubris, Napoleon decided in 1812 to bring Russia to the bargaining table by declaring war on it and brought his formidable Franco-German army of more than 600,000 men to bear on that end. The campaign began near the end of June, 1812, but the Russian army, refusing to act according to the plan Napoleon had laid out for it, retreated first from Poland and then deep into Russia itself. Napoleon, now an emperor himself and married to a member of the Austrian royal family, refused to use one of the most successful tactics of his youth, namely, promising to free the serfs and establish a French style republic of liberty and equality; consequently, he was not able to break the link between the czar and the Russian people, and he continually had problems in supplying his troops. By the time Napoleon arrived in Moscow in September 1812, much of the city had been evacuated, much had been burned, his own army had been badly damaged, and there was nobody there with which to deal. He had nothing to do except to wait in Moscow to see if anyone would show up to negotiate with him. Nobody did. When by October 1812 this had become obvious, he decided to return home. However, since the more attractive southern route home was blocked by the Russian army, he had to retrace his steps along his original route; his earlier campaign's pillaging and marauding had, however, left the area devastated, unable to supply his army's needs; continual Cossack attacks and an early winter (in which the temperature fell to twenty degrees below zero) proceeded to decimate Napoleon's remaining army. In a crushing blow to his chances, one of his major allies, General von Yorck, defected to the Russians (with von Clausewitz mediating for them), taking his 14,000 Prussian troops with him. When Napoleon finally arrived back in Paris in December 1812, the original army of more than 600,000 men numbered fewer than 40,000. The formidable French army had been virtually wiped out. Of the Württemberg regiments, of which Hegel's brother was a member, fewer than 1,500 of the original 16,000 troops were still alive.[112]

Napoleon's foes, sensing their opportunity, now tried to launch an unfettered war against him. A German contingent at the Russian court, including von Clausewitz and Freiherr von Stein, had begun calling for a "patriotic war" of "national liberation" against the French. (Stein had earlier been the reforming minister of the Prussian government after the debacle with the French at Jena but had lost his position in 1808; in an angry moment that he may well have later regretted, Napoleon branded Stein a criminal and ordered his arrest, thereby forcing Stein to flee first to Austria and then to Russia, where he was to become one of the major leaders of the allied opposition to Napoleon.) The rhetoric of a "war of national liberation" took hold among certain influential personages (if not among the people at large), and the Prussian king reluctantly embraced the idea. The wars against Napoleon, which commenced in 1813, thus went down in German nationalist mythology as the "wars of national liberation" and became known as the war in which "the king called and all came." (In fact, the actual participation of the people was much smaller than the German propagandists later made it out to be; the *Volk* remained relatively apathetic vis-à-vis all the appeals to defend their "Fatherland.")

The Prussian-Russian alliance and the nationalist call for the defense of the fatherland and Europe made the other German allies of Napoleon quite nervous. Napoleon refused to accept any compromises, such as the Austrian proposal to return to the borders of the Lunéville treaty of 1801; he demanded the borders of 1812. But as it gradually became clear that Napoleon's hold on power was becoming increasingly tenuous, his German allies began to cancel their treaties with him and either declare neutrality or switch sides. On April 25, 1813, the Bavarian government announced its neutrality, but when Napoleon secured some victories against the Prussian-Russian forces in May, 1813, the Bavarians abruptly canceled their negotiations with Austria. In October, 1813, Napoleon met the combined allied armies outside of Leipzig, and what became known in the propaganda of the time as the "Battle of Nations" took place (so named for all the nationalities that fought there). The French were badly outnumbered, roughly 160,000 French and allies against roughly 320,000 opponents; the result was, despite some cunning moves by Napoleon, a disaster for the French, and the list of casualties was enormous for both sides (more than 54,000 killed or wounded for the Prussian-Russian led coalition, and more than 38,000 lost for the French).[113] By March, 1814, Napoleon's reign was over; the anti-Napoleonic allies entered Paris, and Napoleon abdicated his throne and surrendered to the British on April 6, 1814.

Hegel observed all this with stunned disbelief. At first he discounted stories of allied victories, reminding people that in the past such stories had been fabricated and that the truth had always been that Napoleon had triumphed. But as the shape of things became more clear, he too began to see that Napoleon's days were numbered. Hegel could only hope that the reforms made within Napoleonic Germany could not be effectively erased and that indeed the dynamic of modern life and reform had already gone too far to be stopped. The initial events of 1813 temporarily helped to reassure people such as Hegel that things had indeed already gone too far for any reversal of the reform process to take place. In October of 1813, the Bavarians signed a treaty with the Austrians, pledging 36,000 troops to the allied cause in exchange for recognition of their sovereignty, and in the months that followed, Metternich of Austria managed to get most of the other large states of the Confederation of the Rhine to do the same thing. Those treaties with the newly formed and enlarged states of Napoleonic Germany meant that those who hoped to reconstitute the old Holy Roman Empire were bound to be disappointed, for it clearly implied that the shape of Napoleonic Germany, along with its reforming institutions, would remain intact after Napoleon's fall.

But Hegel was understandably nervous and anxious about all this and continued to seek reassurance that things were going to turn out well. This was not easy for him. He was by nature an anxious fellow – and given all that he had been through, he had good reason to be anxious – and he was certainly cynical enough about all the claims for "liberation" that were emanating from Prussian, Russian, and, increasingly, Austrian propaganda to discount the more triumphant claims on the part of the propagandists. He was always mocking the idea of "liberation" in his letters to Niethammer and was particularly scornful of the idea that the Russians could be counted as liberators at all. (Hegel's anti-Russian feelings and prejudices – that Russians were not really to be counted as Europeans – had also been evident in his Bamberg days.) But the actual fall of Napoleon obviously rattled him. In a famous letter to Niethammer in April 1814, Hegel began to come to terms with this by understanding Napoleon as a tragic figure akin to Greek tragic figures: "It is a frightening spectacle to see a great genius destroy himself," Hegel said. "That is the τραγικτατον [most tragic thing] that there is. The entire mass of mediocrity . . . presses on like lead . . . until it has succeeded in bringing down what is high to the same level as itself or even below. The turning point of the whole, the reason why this mass has power and . . . remains on top, is that the great individual must himself give that mass the right to do what it does, thus precipitating his own fall."[114]

Hegel thus skirted the issue of whether it was Napoleon's overconfidence, his refusal to play the revolutionary game anymore, or just an old-fashioned run of bad luck that had conspired to bring him down. For Hegel, Napoleon's tragedy was to be attributed to those features of his character that had originally led to his successes and which eventually necessitated his downfall. Napoleon, in Hegel's view, *had* to bring himself down by virtue of the very features that had propelled him to the top in the first place. In other words, Hegel made Napoleon fit into Hegel's model of the tragic figure as he had worked it out in the *Phenomenology*. In a letter to Niethammer, Hegel even went so far as to congratulate himself for having seen in advance that this was how things would probably end: "I may pride myself, moreover, on having predicted the entire upheaval," he said, referring Niethammer to the chapter in the *Phenomenology of Spirit* at the end of the section on "Absolute Freedom and Terror" (on the Revolution and its Napoleonic aftermath) in which he claimed that the practical project of the Revolution had to be completed in the theories of German idealist Kantian-Fichtean-Hegelian philosophy.[115] In that letter, Hegel credited himself with the prediction of Napoleon's downfall because of his belief (which he still held) that the "novel of the revolution" would *not* be finished in France but rather in Germany. For him, the downfall of Napoleon was not the downfall of the ideals of the Revolution; it was only the personal tragedy of a great man.

Nonetheless, Hegel, who was by temperament by this time much more of a European than a nationalist of any sort, was dismayed and appalled by the nationalist appeals of the "liberation" and the subsequent celebration of the "Germanic" in opposition to what was labeled the "French." As the calls for restoration of the old order grew louder and the drumbeat for returning to so-called true "German" values grew more insistent, Hegel found himself not only more and more out of step with the emotional temper of the times but also with a firm conviction that he had no obligation at all to join the trend. In a scathing pun in a letter of October 1814 to Paulus, Hegel characterized those who wish to celebrate *Deutschtum* as the *Deutschdumm* (or, roughly, those who celebrate participating in authentic "Germandom" as the "German-dumb").[116] Phony "Germanism" seemed to him both silly and dangerous, both an unhealthy desire to return to the Holy Roman Empire and a fatuous cultivation of "Germanic" particularisms to supplant the more universalist elements of modern European culture. Having argued during his Jena years against the "particularisms" of people like Hamann

and Jacobi – both of whom had wanted to keep Enlightenment universalism at bay in favor of the radically particularistic "hometown" structure of the old order – Hegel now found himself arguing against all
those who wished to reassert such particularisms in the name of "Germanness" in general. In his 1811 address at the end of the school year,
Hegel had argued before the assembled parents, students, and notables
that the Enlightenment, whatever its rationalistic failures – "how it all
too often substituted for good old mores (*Sitte*) and deep principles
(because it did not understand such things) superficial, value-less, indeed ruinous maxims"[117] – had nonetheless taught important lessons for
modern life about the necessity to incorporate right and universal ethical
dispositions and feelings into the young through social practice and not
through mindless memorization.

The Congress of Vienna

The Congress of Vienna only heightened Hegel's fears. The congress
became necessary after the conquering powers (Russia, Prussia, Austria,
and England) failed in the summer of 1814 to come to any agreement
on the division of the French empire among themselves or on how to
deal with the demands of the lesser powers (such as Sweden and
Holland) who had participated in the wars against the French. The
congress itself started slowly as delegates began arriving in September
1814 in Vienna, and it quickly became ensnared in the intricacies of
diplomacy necessarily attending such high-stakes negotiations. Before
the congress convened, the "big four" (Russia, Prussia, Austria, and
England) had pretty well decided among themselves that they alone
would make all the decisions, but, given their very different interests,
that was about all on which they could at first agree. The congress thus
became a spectacle of a rather grandiose sort as the leading statesmen of
the day debated the weighty questions of Europe's future and Germany's reorganization amid an array of balls, staged hunts, musical
events – Beethoven himself was in attendance for a festive performance
of his Seventh Symphony – and other grand social occasions. The
congress thus combined the high political drama of statecraft with lavish
frivolity of the kind that always accompanies such gatherings of the
powerful and the wealthy in a great city. The elaborately staged social
affairs, though, had a deeper purpose in the sense that they served to

entertain and distract the representatives from the smaller states while they were being excluded from the sessions where the real decisions were being made. Sometimes the powerful personalities involved in the serious statecraft inserted themselves into the frivolity of the scene, as when Metternich from Austria arranged a vote by the participants of the congress to have Viennese *Sachertorte* officially proclaimed the King of Cakes, only to have Talleyrand of France retaliate by arranging another vote that officially proclaimed brie the King of Cheeses.[118]

However, because the issues involved were indeed so weighty and because the allies had very different interests in the outcome, the congress dragged on. Napoleon's escape from exile in Elba in February 1815 followed by his triumphant return to Paris and the flight of the restored Bourbon monarchy, however, sent a shiver through the entire congress. The specter of an again-triumphant Bonaparte helped to galvanize the congress, and by May 1815 the basic elements of an agreement had been hammered out, with the agreement being ratified on June 9, 1815. The confrontation at Waterloo of June 16–18, 1815, between Napoleon's reconstituted army and the forces of Wellington of England and General Blücher of Prussia, finally ended any fears of a Napoleonic restoration for the delegates; in the new peace treaty with France signed on November 20, 1815, the treaty of the Congress of Vienna was, despite some initial opposition, upheld.

Hegel was at first both cynical and fearful of the congress and thoroughly dubious as to whether any of the high-minded talk about Germanic freedoms would translate into anything substantive (perhaps especially since the congress was being held under the auspices of the Austrians). In his October 1814 letter to Paulus (in which he spoke about *Deutschdumm*), Hegel expressed his fear that the forces of reaction in Austria – that is, the Catholics – would, in collusion with "a few tame house cats, such as the Inquisition, the Jesuit Order, and then all the armies with their sundry commissioned, betitled, and ennobled Marshalls and generals," seek to turn the clock back and trample on the newly acquired rights of the German people. However, as the congress concluded, he came to think that his diagnosis of the dynamics of modern life had been right after all, and that the so-called restoration envisioned by the congress only amounted to a kind of finery draped over the ongoing movement of modern life to make it look more respectable to its opponents. The congress, he concluded, had essentially changed nothing about modern life; instead, it had only augmented the size and power of certain states such as Prussia, leaving modern social practice and the institutional and social reforms essentially intact. Indeed, as Niethammer began complaining to Hegel about how the restoration has set loose all the old forces in Bavaria that he had been successfully battling during the reform years, Hegel began trying to soothe Niethammer, telling him that the forces of reaction could in fact do nothing to turn things completely around.

Hegel's Estrangement from Christiane Hegel

During this period, Hegel had to balance his intense interest in things political and artistic with his growing duties to his family and his professional responsibilities as professor, rector, and (since 1812) the school inspector for Nuremberg. During all this, however, he managed to arrange a visit to Niethammer in Munich in the late summer of 1815, during which he managed to take in some of the Munich art collections – he explicitly remarked on how wonderful they were, saying that because of them Munich is one of the "most excellent points in all Germany"; while in Munich, he also visited Schelling, although he did not report anything of substance about their visit.[119]

After his return from Munich, on September 25, 1814, he and Marie had a second son, Thomas Immanuel Christian Hegel (named after his three godparents, Immanuel Niethammer, Thomas Seebeck, and Hegel's sister, Christiane). In December of 1815, however, Marie Hegel suffered a traumatic miscarriage and for a short time things apparently looked somewhat bleak for her. She recovered but was bedridden for some time.

This period also led to an estrangement, at least on Hegel's side, between himself and his sister, Christiane Luise Hegel. Christiane Hegel was three years younger than Hegel and had never married despite having had some serious suitors.[120] Hegel's relation to Christiane was strained by several factors, not the least of which was Hegel's post-Enlightenment attitudes about women. Hegel accepted the view that had emerged in the eighteenth century that women were not simply "deficient men," as a long tradition of thought since Aristotle had asserted, but were radically *other* than men. Men were rational, calculating, and at one remove from nature; women, by virtue of their biology, were closer to nature and were therefore more naturally at harmony with themselves and less rational. Women's duties followed from their biology; as more naturally harmonious and intuitive, they were best suited to "heal" men – as Hegel had put it to Marie before their marriage – from the rigors imposed by the less natural, more alienated and rational constitution of masculinity. For Hegel, women had their proper sphere in the home, nurturing the children and tending to their husbands, whereas men had their proper spheres in the world of society, with its rough-and-tumble competition for status and success, and in the refined world of statecraft, the arts, and the sciences (in which women, by virtue of their more intuitive, emotional approach to things could not hope, Hegel thought, to participate with any success).[121] This attitude also extended to Christiane.

After their mother's death in 1781, Christiane came to be the "woman of the house" and devoted herself to taking care of their father. She remained at home until his death in 1799 (when she was about twenty-six). There is no evidence that Hegel saw anything amiss in this, apparently accepting it as normal. Christiane was also a middle child, having a younger brother (who died in Napoleon's 1812 campaign) and an older brother, Hegel himself.[122] Her own godparents were members of the Stuttgart non-noble notables, the *Ehrbarkeit*, and like her broth ers, she must have received some kind of education, since she was later able to make a living teaching French, and we know that she was an avid reader.[123] (It must be remembered that Hegel's mother was also apparently a highly educated woman for her time.) Christiane also apparently shared some of her older brother's interest in making excerpts from the books she was reading and in enthusiastically following the proceedings of the Württemberg political scene. She also wrote poetry, although none of it survives (apparently in the style of Schiller, a taste she shared with her brother).[124] In fact, Christiane took very much after her older brother and was obviously attached to him; staying behind to take care of their father, in becoming the "woman of the house," Christiane also stepped into the role that Hegel's mother had played. (Both Hegel and his sister revered the memory of their mother, and both intensely identified with her sense of "learnedness" as central to their own identities.) Hegel's often-repeated comments about the sanctity and closeness of the relation of brother and sister (brought out dramatically in his interpretation of *Antigone* in the *Phenomenology*) doubtless were based in part on his own relation to his sister. Hegel's relationship with his sister was heavily colored by his reverential attitude toward his mother; Christiane's attitude to her older brother was equally colored by her attitudes toward her mother (and her father). In some respects, she lived vicariously through Hegel, and he maintained the memory of his mother through her.

After their father's death, Christiane came into a small amount of money. In deference to her not having had a chance to pursue any further education, Hegel and his brother gave her the larger share: Hegel took a bit more than 3,154 Guilders, his brother took a bit more than 3,354 Guilders, and Christiane received a bit more than 4,000 Guilders. (To keep in mind what that meant, remember that Hegel was receiving the equivalent of around 1,500 Guilders for his rectorship and his school inspectorship in Nuremberg.) But those 4,000 Guilders were capable of supporting her at best for only a few years, and thus she had to face up to the fate most greatly feared at the time by unmarried middle-class women such as herself: She had to go to work as a governess, that is, essentially to become a servant in a well-to-do household. By 1814, she apparently was having some trouble with the household that employed her – she had been the governess for the family of Count von Berlichingen in Jaxthausen in Württemberg – and was dismissed in 1814, although on fairly friendly terms, with the mistress of the household promising her a small pension of 50 to 100 Guilders, depending on how the Congress of Vienna treated the von Berlichingen family's property.[125] Around the same time, Christiane had begun suffering from what was described at that time as "mental (*Geistige*) problems" and "nerve problems," and since the letter releasing her from her position cites her health as the reason, something like that might have been the grounds for dismissal. It certainly seems as if some of the "mental problems" were real. One account of Christiane, at a later period in her life, described her as frantically worrying that she was a small packet that people wanted to ship in the mail and, when she met strangers, shivering out of fear that they were going to wrap her up and ship her away.[126] After her dismissal from Count von Berlichingen's household, she went to stay with a cousin in Stuttgart, Karl Wilhelm Göriz, and then another cousin, a church deacon, Ludwig Göriz, in Aalen.

Although it is unclear if she was present at Thomas Immanuel Christian Hegel's baptism on October 16, 1814, Hegel clearly invited her to

come stay with him and Marie in a letter of April 1814. The pretext
was usual for a middle-class family of that time: One asks one's unmarried sister if she would like to live with one's family and perhaps
help out around the house with the children, and in that way, the
unmarried woman can de facto become a governess without having to
become a recognized servant, since she is one of the family. Indeed, a
sibling was more or less expected to make such an offer to an unmarried
older sister once he or she was comfortably situated in his or her own
family life. Hegel's letter to Christiane follows the pattern, noting that
if Christiane is "no longer up to these responsibilities [of her job in
Jaxthausen], we invite you to move in with us permanently, to live with
us and receive the care you need. . . . My wife will be delivering this
fall, and if you could lend her a hand your presence would be doubly
advantageous."[127] He made this offer on April 9, 1814, and repeated it
in September 1814 after Christiane had been dismissed from her position, noting again that Marie would be delivering and that "it would
be a great favor and relief for us if you were to be here with during
this period and look after the household."[128] The visit in fact came off,
and during the summer and the fall of 1815, Christiane lived with
Hegel and Marie. The visit was, however, for reasons that have never
surfaced, apparently a disaster, and there was no offer ever made for
her to return. While going through her husband's papers after his death,
Marie Hegel noted much later that when Christiane left them in Nuremberg, she was "mentally ill."[129]

One can only speculate as to why Marie Hegel thought this and why
the visit was such a disaster, but it seems very likely that there was a
deep personal conflict between Marie and Christiane (possibly over who,
the sister or the wife, was more authoritative regarding the proper care
of the "man of the house"). Ludwig Friedrich Göriz, to whose house
Christiane returned after the visit, described her at the time as being
"beside herself all the day, wailing and crying on the sofa" and venting
a "deep hatred" of Marie Hegel and a "thorough dissatisfaction with
her brother."[130] Christiane Hegel was also, whatever her other problems,
a strong-willed, intelligent woman – for example, she was at one point
in her life smuggling in correspondence to a political prisoner in one of
Württemberg's jails.[131] (Interestingly enough, she looks much like the
strong-willed woman exemplified in the figure of Antigone, a figure of
femininity that Hegel both celebrated and feared and whom he tried to

explain as motivated by pure love of her brother.) That she and Marie Hegel might have had strong personal conflicts is thus not at all out of the question. Indeed, during part of Christiane's visit, Hegel was away in Munich visiting Niethammer, and Christiane and Marie were alone together at home; some kind of friction between them could have surfaced at that time, when Hegel was not there to mediate any disputes, that was out of control by the time he returned.

It was nevertheless after this visit that Christiane had her complete psychic collapse followed by some unspecified physical ailments. Hegel's letters to her after that period become more distant and paternalistic, less and less frequent, and he began to intervene with other people to have her committed to an institution (for which he contributed the money). But he continued to send her some money, and Marie would always write short, friendly notes to her in the margins of Hegel's letters to her. She was finally committed in 1820 to a sanitarium in Zwiefalten, a pleasant town in the hills not far from Tübingen. When she was declared fully cured and released in the middle of 1821, she returned to Stuttgart, where she taught French and had a lively circle of established friends. She wrote Hegel an angry letter (long since lost) at that time accusing him of something terrible (most likely of betraying her) and accusing others of mistreating her. Hegel refused to respond to the charges – "I shall thus have as little as possible cause to want to justify others or myself here and there against you, and to stir up in you and bring before you again what you are rather to consider as over and done with"[132] – and went on to give her stern advice on how best to lead her life. He advised her to see her troubles as past and done with, to see that it was best not to think about them too much and to concentrate instead on getting on with her life on a sound footing. During this period, she also managed to alienate Göriz, who complained to her about her "arrogance," her claims to "learnedness" (which he clearly felt were out of place), her "putting on airs" and acting as if she was too good to work for others, even her "mistrust of God," and her lack of gratitude for all he and his family had done for her; but it seems likely that in this case Göriz was just as apprehensive of Christiane's independence and free-thinking nature as her brother was.[133]

The relations between the Hegel family and Christiane certainly did not become completely cold. Hegel's mother-in-law visited Christiane in Aalen in 1818, had some tea with her, and found her cheerful, although she too later came to see her as mentally unbalanced. Marie Hegel seems to have felt some sympathy with Christiane precisely because she was so troubled, and was even prepared for a while immediately after Hegel's death to turn over to Christiane her own (Marie's) widow's pension coming from Hegel's rectorship in Nuremberg in order to help out Christiane and console her for the death of her brother; those considerations, however, were abandoned when Christiane committed suicide by drowning herself about a month after her brother's death.[134] It seems most likely that Hegel himself (and probably also Marie) were made extremely uneasy by Christiane's mental problems, a not uncommon reaction for their time (and certainly also not for our own); they handled the matter by dealing with it only from a distance and by not having anything to do with Christiane on a face-to-face basis after the disastrous visit. Hegel's close friend Hölderlin suffered from madness; now the same thing seemed to be happening to his sister. Hegel reacted to both cases by distancing himself from the trouble – a move that fit his self-distancing personality, even if it did amount to dodging the more immediate and pressing aspects of the issue. The break with Christiane also meant that Hegel was from that point onward, for all practical purposes, without a family outside of the new one he had started; his emotional isolation from his own family was now complete.

Sadly, almost all of Christiane's letters to Hegel have been lost, and on the whole only his letters to her remain. It is also well established that Hegel's sons – in particular, Immanuel Hegel – destroyed large numbers of Hegel's papers many years after his death. Immanuel remarked in a letter to his brother Karl in 1889 that he had delivered a selection of his father's writings to the royal library and "the rest of the lot, in order to prevent further misuse, was delivered to a paper mill in the vicinity."[135] It can only be a matter of conjecture, but it does seem likely that Christiane's more accusatory letters to her brother – along with Frommann's letters to Hegel about his illegitimate son, Ludwig, and perhaps even Hegel's letters to his father while he was in Tübingen – were among those that Immanuel Hegel deemed unfit to preserve out of fear of "further misuse."

A Philosopher in the Post-Napoleonic Order

Hegel's Administrative Successes

Although Hegel clearly wanted to be doing something other than teaching *Gymnasium*, he nonetheless did the best he could under the circumstances. After becoming the inspector of schools, he set out to rectify the appalling situation concerning schooling for the poor that had come to exist in Nuremberg. In 1807, when the reforms first began in Nuremberg after it had been incorporated into the kingdom of Bavaria, out of the 3,516 children of school age in Nuremberg, fully 275 did not attend school for financial reasons and another 187 were for the same reasons forced to abandon their schooling early. In order to meet their needs, more teachers were needed, and therefore it was decided that a teachers training college (*Schullehrerseminar*) be erected in Nuremberg. As always, however, the good ideas behind the reform were not backed up by any funds, and the project was put to one side. As *Schulreferent*, Hegel energetically and actively stepped into the struggle to improve the school situation in Nuremberg and to see to it that the teachers training college was in fact opened. Hegel's good connections with Niethammer paid off, and on January 17, 1814, came the official decree declaring that the teachers training college was to be built. Hegel wasted no time and drew up very detailed plans for it, continuing to lobby for the requisite funds even long after they had been promised. (By this time Hegel had too much experience with the Bavarian government to believe that the mere promise of funds implied that he would actually receive them.) He succeeded, and on April 19, 1814, the requisite funds were transferred from the central accounts to those in Nuremberg so that Hegel could authorize the construction to begin; and on June 27, 1814, the teachers training college opened. (One of the first students to be accepted was a Miss Louise Götz, who was however forced to withdraw under social pressure from those who considered it completely out of the ordinary that a young woman would attempt to become a teacher.) Hegel even functioned as one of the examiners for the first batch of candidates in August 1815. Not content with his initial success, Hegel undertook some further initiatives, and the school was expanded in 1815 and 1816. In his yearly reports, Hegel proudly pointed out that he had both managed to erect and establish the "poor schools" and staff them with trained personnel who taught the children with the best and most up-to-date methods.[136]

Hegel was also incensed with the clumsy way in which a girls school had been established, mismanaged, and then forced to close for lack of funds in March 1814. Outraged, Hegel commented to Niethammer about a "botched job of Stephani's – a local secondary school for girls – collapsed the other day; and the money unjustly and improperly used, God knows how, for the school has been as good as thrown out the window."[137] Women should also acquire *Bildung*, Hegel thought, even if he also thought that they could not hope to enter the sciences or achieve anything great in the arts – only a cultured and educated woman, after all, could adequately serve as the proper companion to a cultured and educated man. (Hegel obviously saw his own wife in that light.) When three of the teachers from the terminated girls school – including a Ms. Eisen – appealed to Hegel for permission to reopen the school on a private basis, he wrote a letter of reference approving of the venture, and they were allowed to go forward with their plans. (The school they opened lasted until 1831, the year of Hegel's death, when it was absorbed into the public school for girls; Ms. Eisen was the director of the school for the entire period.)[138]

Hegel's commitment to the ideal of *Bildung* went deep, and it helps to explain his personal commitment to the duties of his job, despite his continual complaints in all of his letters about how he hoped not to have to perform such tasks forever, how he hoped he would not be a school inspector for long, and so forth. Like Wilhelm von Humboldt's, Hegel's ideals of *Bildung* were not fully egalitarian; he did not hold out any hope that *Bildung* was suitable for everyone, but he (and von Humboldt) believed it was indeed required for those who wished to pursue careers in the more powerful and prestigious professions for which university training was required. In his 1810 report on the status of the *Realschul* (the "polytechnic") vis-à-vis other lines of study, he stressed that he thought that although "mathematics, physics, chemistry, natural history" were greatly valuable, and that a student who studies only those subjects can certainly acquire "technical knowledge and skills" that are "useful," they are nevertheless not "sciences that demand real thought and, what is more important, no particular depth of mind, as the classical studies" do.[139]

Report on the Teaching of Philosophy in the Gymnasium

Niethammer also commissioned Hegel to write a report on the teaching of philosophy in the *Gymnasia* in Bavaria, since his "General Normative" of 1807 had required such teaching. Hegel responded in 1812. (He did not deliver an address at the end of the school year in 1812; it was decided that it was the turn of the director of the *Realschul* to do that.) By that time, he had become very pessimistic about the future of philosophy in the *Gymnasium*. He complained to Niethammer in 1811 that he quite honestly thought that there was simply too much philosophy already in the *Gymnasium*, that it was taking time away from other things perhaps better suited to students of that age, and that furthermore the very idea that (as had been decreed by the authorities, Niethammer included) there were supposed to be "practical exercises" in the use of "speculative thought" seemed, if not silly, then at least baffling to him.[140] By March 1812 he was repeating this to Niethammer, arguing that philosophy should be eliminated at least from the lower levels of the *Gymnasium*, and that in any event "the aim should not be to teach youth at this age the absolute standpoint of philosophy."[141] Thus, when Hegel finally made his commissioned report on the teaching of philosophy in the *Gymnasia* to Niethammer, he declared with admirable honesty in an accompanying letter that "my more immediate interest would be for professors of philosophical sciences to be declared to be superfluous in the *Gymnasia* and either given another task or sent elsewhere," adding with a tone of not quite mock despair, "Yet how am I, professor of philosophical preparatory sciences, to fight against my own discipline and post, undermining the basis of my own livelihood?"[142] (It must have been obvious to Niethammer that Hegel indeed wanted to be "sent elsewhere," namely to a university, something that, true to form, Hegel also explicitly brought up elsewhere in the letter.)

In the report, Hegel described to Niethammer his experiences in trying to adhere to Niethammer's "General Normative," which had required the teaching of "speculative" post-Kantian philosophy.[143] Hegel had run into stubborn practical difficulties in trying to carry this out. On the one hand, although he believed that the philosophical discipline ought to be divided into logic, philosophy of nature, and philosophy of spirit (in that order), he found that in fact it was pedagogically better to begin with the moral parts of the philosophy of spirit, since the students found them so much easier to grasp.[144] The students were also, he noted, not particularly smitten with the philosophy of nature, partly because (at least so he hypothesized) it was too abstract for such young students and partly because they did not have the background for such studies, since such philosophy of nature "as speculative physics presupposes an acquaintance with nature's appearances – with empirical physics – an acquaintance which at this point is not yet present."[145]

Hegel mentioned using his *Phenomenology* to introduce the students to the first part of philosophical psychology, although he added that he only did the first three stages of it, omitting what was probably the case, namely, that he had tried to do more of the *Phenomenology* but had abandoned that project in part because it had proved to be too taxing for the students.[146] (He also passed over the issue that he had decided to use the *Phenomenology* as an introduction to "philosophical psychology" instead of an introduction to the "system" itself. Hegel felt compelled at first, for more or less pedagogical reasons, to change the role of the *Phenomenology* as an introduction to the "system" – to "Logic" – but because of this he was ultimately led to rethink entirely the place of the *Phenomenology* in his system as a whole, such that by the time he got to Heidelberg, the role of the *Phenomenology* in his thought had become extremely problematic for him; his later Heidelberg and Berlin conception of the role of the *Phenomenology* in his system first found expression in his classroom instruction in Nuremberg.)[147] Metaphysics itself, which the "General Normative" had declared to be a required part of instruction, was, said Hegel, really only part of "Logic," adding in a note that made it clear what line of thought he took himself to be pursuing, "Here I can cite Kant as my precedent and authority . . . Logic can thus in the Kantian sense be understood so that, beyond the usual content of the so-called general logic, what he calls transcendental logic is bound up with it and set out prior to it."[148] Nonetheless, what was truly "speculative," the way in which human thought and human history had to be shown to be self-grounding, self-legitimating, "can only scantily appear in a *Gymnasial* lesson. It will generally be grasped only by the few, and to some extent one cannot even really know whether it is grasped by them."[149]

The idea that philosophy was only for the very few was an idea that Hegel had already brought with him to Nuremberg; he had said some-

thing to that effect in a letter to van Ghert in 1809.[150] Philosophy was
necessary for modern life, since it was the way in which modern social
practice came to a full understanding of itself, the way in which modern
life comes to understand how what is authoritative for itself is necessary
and rational, not something that is contingent and fortuitous. But it was
not something immediately accessible for everyone; its true place was in
the universities, as the "queen of the faculties," the core discipline for
the university training of a new, cultured, and cultivated elite.

That result must have been discouraging for Hegel, but Niethammer
found it even more depressing, since his ally in his fight had in effect
declared one of the main goals of the "General Normative" to be
virtually unattainable and not even worth the effort to salvage it. Ruefully, Hegel had concluded that philosophy was not best taught in the
Gymnasium at all, a conclusion that surely served to underscore for him
his distance from what he took to be the true centers of his vocation.
Hegel had to reassure Niethammer that it was not the "General Normative" he was attacking, but only one small part of it (the idea that
speculative philosophy should be a key element of Bavarian education),
and that even that criticism was aimed not at Niethammer but "against
myself, for on account of my audience I do not know how to get by
with what is speculative, while on account of myself I do not know how
to get by without it."[151] Sadly, Hegel concluded that the ideal for the
Gymnasium would be "Ciceronian philosophizing . . . but it is against
my nature."[152]

Modern Life and School Life

However discouraged Hegel was about philosophy in the *Gymnasium* in
1812, by 1816 he had become not nearly so discouraged by the course
of events in the world. His beliefs about the way in which the Napoleonic reforms were the social expression of certain key changes in how
people had come to think of themselves, the course of their lives, and
what they were committed to, seemed to be confirmed for him in the
outcome of the Congress of Vienna and events since. In a metaphor
that captured his sense of the direction of events, Hegel said to Niethammer in July 1816 that he held fast to the idea that "the world spirit
has given the times the command to advance, and the command is being
obeyed."[153] The forces of the reaction have merely taken up the reforms

and declared them to be matters they themselves have carried out, but "the sum and substance remains the same."[154] In order to genuinely turn back the clock, the forces of reaction would have to get people fully to alter their self-identities and to commit themselves to modes of self-understanding that had already proved to be insufficient.

Hegel's last graduation address in 1815 gave him a forum for asserting this more upbeat view to the assembled parents, students, and notables. In a somewhat muted rhetorical broadside against the hopes of the more conservative elements of the German population for a restoration of the pre-revolutionary social order, Hegel argued before the assemblage that it is an understandable mistake that "*change* so often presents itself as having the same meaning as *loss*," since when people continually find that the "fruits of their sacrifices are so often consigned into the future," they will tend to fasten the "object of their yearnings to the past."[155] But rather than mourn for what has been, they should instead understand that "the world has given birth to a great epoch,"[156] and that a genuine "insight into our times" "reveals in part the dawn" of a "day of essential improvement" in all things.[157] Social life had, to be sure, become more complex, and the kinds of tradition-bound private activities that had previously been the warp and woof of social life had therefore to make way for the emerging and more rational (even if more complex) social order. In particular, he reminded them, the missions of school instruction must be reformed in light of certain social goals – in particular, that of freedom – and made independent of the private, arbitrary wishes of the parents, whose own wishes for their children's personal development might be at odds with the aspirations of freedom in modern life.[158]

All practices and institutions had to be integrated into the emerging life of the modern social order and made to fit into modern life's overall goal of freedom, which itself made the reform of the schools necessary and the practical problems of pedagogy especially difficult. Sounding some older notes, Hegel noted that freedom's being the goal of modern life does not imply that the schools should dispense with discipline, even though, as Hegel noted, "it is difficult to find the middle way between too great a freedom permitted for the children and too great a restriction of them."[159] But it is necessary in light of the goals of the "new times" to find a way to impose discipline in the schools not in the name of tradition but for the sake of educating the children so that as adults they would be able to direct their own lives and be at home in the emerging, modern world in which they would live. Hegel also made it clear that he did not endorse any of the newfangled ideas about giving children complete and undisciplined freedom in the schools; that simply falsified the way in which humans become socialized and in fact undermined the goals of making them into free adults.

Hegel also assured the parents that he did not mean to argue for the complete subordination of the individual to the state, only for an integration of social life into a more rational form: "Much as on the one hand a limit must prevail as holy, within which the government of the state may not touch the private life of the citizens, so must the private lives of the citizens more closely assimilate those things connected with the purposes of the state and subordinate them to a methodical oversight."[160] Over this entire period, he had been likewise telling the students in his classroom that in the well-ordered, modern state, "the essential disposition of the citizens (*Bürger*) vis-à-vis the state and its government is [not] to consist in the blind obedience of its commands . . . but rather trust in and insightful obedience to the state's commands."[161]

University Posts

Hegel also continued his efforts to secure a position for himself in a university. Having done a commendable job of reorganizing the *Gymnasium* and Nuremberg's school system, he nevertheless began to feel more and more isolated from what for him was the center of things; he was a professor of the preparatory philosophical sciences in an institution that he had come to think should not even be teaching philosophical sciences, and the great reform movements – especially after the fall of Napoleon – seemed to be ready to take off without him. A visitor and later friend, Sulpiz Boisserée (an art collector), noted that Hegel felt so isolated from major intellectual centers that he told Boisserée that if he did not already have a wife, he would certainly leave Nuremberg and (as he had done at Jena) take his chances with an unpaid lectureship at one university or another.[162] He wrote to his old friend Friedrich Frommann in April 1816 inquiring about the possibility of a new professorship in Jena. Having heard that Schelling had been offered the position but had turned it down (since

Schelling had a nonteaching, well-paid position in Munich at the Academy of the Plastic Arts), he of course wondered if he might be considered for the slot.

He also made a revealing comment to Frommann: "My first efforts there as a lecturer, from what I hear, left behind a prejudice against me. To be sure, I was a beginner, had not yet worked my way through to clarity, and was bound to the letter of my notebook in oral presentation. I have since acquired complete freedom through almost eight years' practice at the *Gymnasium*, where one is constantly interacting in conversation with one's listeners and where being understood and expressing oneself clearly by itself is of the utmost necessity."[163] Among his teenage students in Nuremberg, however, Hegel seems to have lost the anxiety (or at least a bit of it) that led to his infamously bad public speaking, and he (unfortunately falsely) believed that his difficulties in lecturing to university students had been only a temporary problem for which he had found the solution.

When Fries accepted the position in Jena that Hegel had earlier sought and thus vacated his position at Heidelberg (which Hegel had also earlier sought), Hegel inquired to Paulus in May 1816 about the possibility of his acquiring Fries's newly unoccupied position, and he made the same point about his having overcome his old lecturing style, using almost identical words to describe the matter. (He also quite uncharacteristically says something nice about Fries in the letter, the one place in which he does so; but it was almost certainly not heartfelt and was most likely a feigned gesture of magnanimity in order not to come across to Paulus as a cranky, resentful fellow.)

Unfortunately, his anxiety about speaking authoritatively before groups – about being the "professor" addressing an audience from the lectern, a position he clearly and desperately wanted – was in fact never to leave him. Although his lecturing style irritated no small number of people, it also, curiously enough, helped to underwrite a kind of Romantic appropriation of Hegel. His followers, from Jena to Berlin, were inclined to take his monotonic delivery – punctuated by gasps, coughs, and stutters – to be a sign of his great "interiority," of the depths of his genius struggling to bring those dark, difficult thoughts to the light of day, rather than being the expressions of an anxious man doing something that he loved but which also burdened him with no small amount of agitation and anxiety.

The Misfired Offer from Berlin

Unknown to Hegel at this time, there was great maneuvering going on at Berlin University to fill the chair left empty by Fichte's death in January 1814. Hegel had already inquired in 1814 to Paulus about the possibility of his taking Fichte's position, but nothing had come of it. Paulus had reported back that he had no contacts of any importance in Berlin. Besides, as Paulus's wife and Hegel's friend sarcastically asked him, "Why would you want to be in sandy Berlin, where people drink wine out of thimbles?"[164] Two years later, after intense political maneuvering (during which Wilhelm Martin Leberecht de Wette, a theology professor who had previously been at both Jena and Heidelberg during Hegel's time, lobbied heavily for an appointment for his close friend Fries), the faculty decided to make Hegel an offer and voted decisively against Fries. However, de Wette continued his academic politics by going to the official responsible for overseeing the university, the minister of the interior, Kaspar Friedrich von Schuckmann, a self-styled "Kantian" who detested Schelling's *Naturphilosophie* – indeed, who was deeply suspicious of all philosophers and whom Wilhelm von Humboldt once dismissively characterized as somebody filled with the utilitarian projects of the Enlightenment.[165] De Wette told von Schuckmann that Hegel was only another Schellingian, that his lectures were obscure, that his *Logic* was a confused mess, and that, besides, Fries was a good Kantian. To make his point, he also gave Schuckmann a copy of a novel by Fries, which (unfortunately for Fries's and de Wette's plans) had an effect exactly the opposite of that which was intended: Von Schuckmann's immediate dislike of the novel sank Fries's already foundering candidacy once and for all.

But von Schuckmann's suspicions about Hegel had thus been aroused, and he undertook to see if Hegel's lecture style was really as bad as it was reputed to be and if his philosophy really was just another form of the Schellingian system he so disdained. Professor Friedrich von Raumer, a professor of history at Berlin university, who was going on a visit to Nuremberg for other reasons, was thus informally commissioned by Schuckmann to visit Hegel and report back on what he found. The visit took place in the summer of 1816; von Raumer found that Hegel "received him in a very friendly way, and I spent several interesting evenings with him in diverse conversations with him. . . . His conversation was fluid and reasonable, so that I cannot believe that his professorial lectures would lack these properties."[166] Von Raumer asked Hegel to sketch out a report on what he took to be goals of teaching philosophy at a university. Hegel wasted no time in responding, and wrote back to von Raumer on August 2, 1816. Hegel's reply outlines his understanding of the state of post-Kantian idealism. Metaphysics, he tells von Raumer, has vanished just like the constitutional law of the Holy Roman Empire has vanished.[167] Both of them have, as it were, collapsed under the weight of their own shortcomings. Consequently, philosophy can be of value in the universities now, so Hegel argues, only if it takes a "methodical course." This means, as Hegel outlined his position to von Raumer, that it must reject the idea that "thinking for oneself" (which Kant had identified with Enlightenment itself) is falsely opposed to learning the ways of philosophizing. As Hegel put it in his letter, philosophy is thus the basic science, even though the nature of its being basic is not such that it can be learned and understood apart from the other human endeavors on which it reflects: "Philosophy's content," he said, is "what is universal in spiritual and natural relation-ships [and] immediately *leads for itself to the positive sciences* . . . to such an extent that conversely their study proves necessary to a thorough insight into philosophy."[168] In Hegel's eyes, post-Kantian idealism had shown that the old ways of ordering the curriculum of philosophy needed to be changed; the new philosophical curriculum, Hegel claimed, should be ordered into the three spheres into which he had ordered his own system, namely, logic, philosophy of nature, and phi-losophy of spirit (which itself includes philosophical psychology, philo-sophical anthropology, morals, ethics, aesthetics and the philosophy of religion), along with the history of philosophy itself.

That was not the end of the matter. Although von Raumer found himself very satisfied with the report (which he passed on sotto voce to Minister von Schuckmann), von Schuckmann himself decided that he needed to know more, and he therefore wrote Hegel a letter telling him that it had come to his attention that Hegel might be interested in a position at his university, but that, since Hegel had been out of univer-sity teaching for some time, "doubt has been raised" about his ability to return to university lecturing, and indeed, that doubt has been raised about whether Hegel had the "skills" necessary to give "lively presen-tations" before the youthful students of Berlin.[169] The letter reached

Hegel near the end of August 1816. The tone was certainly deprecatory, but Hegel did not have to take offense. Although Hegel had already learned of Berlin's interest in him some time before he received that letter, by the time the letter finally arrived another offer had come forth: His reputation and contacts had finally landed him an offer of a position at Heidelberg, and he had, after some negotiation about salary, happily accepted.

Heidelberg had been looking for a person to fill a professorship in philosophy for some time, and Hegel had not been at the top of their list. One of the others on the list, Hegel's old nemesis and a Jacobi confidante, Köppen, had been ruled out when it was pointed out that a book he had written on natural law consisted in some parts of line-for-line copies of parts of Fries's book on the same subject.[170] The same suspicions about Hegel's lecture style, as being "not particularly good and obscure," surfaced in arguments against Hegel, but others, especially Daub, testified that these rumors were false; praise for Hegel's success in teaching at Nuremberg was offered as proof of this, along with the reports of an unnamed "competent judge, who had spent many weeks in Nuremberg and often in Hegel's company," who had also praised Hegel's teaching abilities at the *Gymnasium*. Hegel was also said to have been "recognized by some of the most competent judges in this area of human knowledge, by the late Fichte, by Fr. H. Jacobi, by Schelling, and by many others."[171]

Heidelberg originally offered him a salary of 1,300 florins, and Hegel had to point out that he already made 1,560 florins in Nuremberg when one combined his salary with the other remunerations he received as rector, school councilor and the like, and, as he reminded the authorities, he and his wife had no private "fortune."[172] Heidelberg finally agreed to pay him 1,500 florins, and, on Hegel's insistence, also to pay part of his salary "in kind," specifically, as "10 malters of grain and 20 of spelt" – Hegel's idea was to lock in his outlay on foodstuffs at the going rate, since the inflation of the time could easily cause the price of such basics to rise to such a degree that they might become virtually unaffordable. Demanding payment in kind was thus in effect a way of securing a "cost of living" increase in salary. (Hegel noted in his arguments to the officials that this was also customary in Württemberg.)[173] The increase in salary and the agreement to payment in kind sealed the deal, and Karl Daub, a distinguished theologian at Heidelberg, made him the formal offer in a letter of July 30, 1816, adding the very flattering comment that "Heidelberg, for the first time since the founding of the university, will have a philosopher – Spinoza received a call from Heidelberg, but in vain, as you undoubtedly know."[174]

The newly reformed and reconstituted university at Heidelberg was to be the place where Hegel was to make his reentry into the post-Jena world. Now, finally, everything seemed to be going his way.

8

From the *Phenomenology* to the "System": Hegel's *Logic*

Hegel's Changing Conceptions of the *Phenomenology* in Nuremberg

A S HEGEL ARRIVED IN NUREMBERG, the educational affairs of the city were in disarray, and although he was officially set to begin his teaching duties on December 12, 1808, he only learned in a letter from Paulus dated November 28, 1808 just exactly *what* it was that he was supposed to be teaching. Paulus instructed him that according to Niethammer's "General Normative," he would be teaching "Introduction to Philosophy alongside Logical Drills" for one class, and "Introduction to the Knowledge of the Universal Coherence of the Sciences" along with "Religion, Right, and Duties" for another class.[1] With virtually no time at all to prepare, Hegel did what he could by taking his recently published *Phenomenology of Spirit*, along with his compilations of notes having to do with his "system" and with the "Logic" on which he was so hard at work, and using them as the bases for his class dictations. However, this had an unintended result: Bringing his recently completed *Phenomenology of Spirit* into play as an introduction to philosophy in the context of a reformed *Gymnasium* led Hegel to rethink again what he had just spent so much time working out in the first place, namely, the place of the *Phenomenology* in his proposed system of philosophy and the shape that system was supposed to take.

As he tried to use the *Phenomenology* to introduce students to philosophy, Hegel found himself having to change his mind about how far the *Phenomenology* could take them, and no doubt some of the fortuitous circumstances surrounding his assumption of his duties had something to do with this.[2] Because of all the confusion having to do with the reorganization, the school year had begun a couple of months late, and

Hegel thus had much less time than normally to do both the required "Introduction to Philosophy" and the "Logical Drills." It is thus quite probable that Hegel simply felt he did not have enough time to do the whole *Phenomenology of Spirit* in his classes. Perhaps he also found that the students were not following his presentation as well as he had hoped and came to the conclusion that changing things in midstream would be the pedagogically prudent route. It must also be remembered that he was not using the book itself (the 1807 *Phenomenology of Spirit*) in his classroom; the course instead consisted in his giving the students dictations of one paragraph and then using that dictation as a basis for further discussion. Hegel thus had to boil down the complex content of the *Phenomenology of Spirit* into a set of distinct, clear paragraphs to serve as a basis for elaboration of details in class discussion. As things turned out, Hegel found this procedure to fit his mature personal style much better, and after the publication of his *Logic*, he composed the rest of his major works as a series of numbered paragraphs that could serve as the basis for his more detailed exposition in lectures.

In any event, it seems clear that although Hegel at first intended to use the whole *Phenomenology of Spirit* as the basis for his introductory course, he changed his mind in 1808, and after introducing the concept of "reason" in his class (corresponding to the beginning of the long chapter on "Reason" in the 1807 *Phenomenology of Spirit*), he suddenly jumped to "Logic" rather than to the corresponding passages in the *Phenomenology*. The next year, 1809, he followed more or less the same plan, except that he jumped over not into "Logic" but into "Psychology," which he then described in his dictation as the "authentic doctrine of spirit."[3] After 1809, he stayed with that line of instruction for his entire time in Nuremberg.

That Hegel was rethinking the role of the *Phenomenology of Spirit* was already clear in the 1808 course. In that course he did not even refer to his introduction to philosophy as a "phenomenology" at all but instead as only a "doctrine of consciousness" – later writing in a copy of his dictations the word "Pneumatologie" (as another way of saying "doctrine of spirit") to describe what he was doing. His marginal notes on the dictation show that he was hastily trying to give some kind of order to the whole thing, at one point characterizing it as a study of "modes of consciousness, knowing (*Wissens*) and cognizing (*Erkennens*)," but then, changing his mind, writing elsewhere on the manuscript

"Doctrine of consciousness and doctrine of the soul" (by the latter, Hegel clearly meant something like a philosophical psychology).[4] The divisions that he made for the course – "A. Consciousness of abstract objects. B. Consciousness of the world of finite spirit. C. Consciousness of absolute spirit." – seem to correspond at least roughly to the divisions of the 1807 *Phenomenology of Spirit*. Even so, Hegel was also changing his terminology a bit: Instead of the chapters on "consciousness" and "self-consciousness," he had a section called "consciousness of abstract objects"; instead of the chapters on "reason" and "spirit," he included a section on "consciousness of the world of finite spirit," and, finally, instead of the chapter on "religion," he had a section called "consciousness of absolute spirit."

The central questions for Hegel throughout his deliberations about how to use his massive work seemed to involve two issues: (1) Was the *Phenomenology* the "authentic doctrine of spirit" or was that reserved for what was to have been the last part of the "system," the doctrine of "real" spirit in its social and political forms? (2) Was the "introduction" to philosophy itself a "science" (a *Wissenschaft*), as he had clearly claimed in the 1807 *Phenomenology*, or was it merely a "nonscientific" way to introduce people to "science" proper?

As of 1808–09, he still held to the notion that the *Phenomenology* was an independent "science" itself, in fact telling the students in the dictations for the class as much.[5] But, even as Hegel was saying that, it was becoming increasingly unclear to him if the *introduction* to the system actually required the whole historical apparatus of the Jena *Phenomenology*, or if only the introductory chapters were sufficient for that purpose.

This dilemma was brought to a head for him during his teaching duties in Nuremberg. Since exigencies of time and the demands to satisfy the terms of Niethammer's "General Normative" forced him to cut short the "Introduction to Philosophy" and to move on quickly to the "Logical Drills." He was also forced to cut short his dictation based on the *Phenomenology*, rapidly concluding with a section called "Universal Self-Consciousness" and a one-paragraph dictation that in his marginal notes he titled "Reason." That notion made sense within his line of thought: The dialectics of "consciousness" and "self-consciousness" (faithfully rendered in the dictations) lead to the concept of what Hegel had called in the corresponding pages of the 1807 *Phe-*

nomenology of Spirit, "the *I* that is *We*, and the *We* that is *I*" – that is, a notion of "universal self-consciousness," a term Kant himself had used to characterize the transcendental unity of apperception and which for both Kant and Hegel expressed the idea that in making judgments, in "getting it right" in general, agents are guided by the principles that would count for all other agents as "getting it right" in this case or "applying" the norms correctly.[6] Finding the elements of a more social conception of "universal self-consciousness" in Kant's *Critique of Judgment*, Hegel had developed his own view of the nature of "universal self-consciousness" as consisting in *social* norms, and a view of rationality as having to do with those standards of evaluation that develop of the practices not only of making assertions but of coming to develop higher-order principles by which we could criticize those assertions and which, in a reflexive move, come to function as standards for *self*-criticism, and, even more self-reflexively, of the criticism of the principles of criticism themselves. The putative independence and autonomy of reason, the great legacy of the Enlightenment, was thus no more than the autonomy of *Geist* itself, of the notion that nature imposes no authoritative normative structure on our "minded" activities, that no norms could count for us unless we collectively imposed them on ourselves.

The issue then naturally suggested itself to Hegel that what was at stake in "*Wissenschaft*" as he now understood it had to do with whether any of these formations or gestalts of *Geist* could sustain our normative allegiance, could be the kinds of things in which agents could both self-consciously situate themselves and sustain that kind of self-situating in light of the inherent "negativity" of such self-situating, its tendency to dissolve under the glare of self-reflection. However, raising that question in turn threw into question the status of the *we* itself. If the status of "reason" itself was what was at issue – or, rather, if the status of which among many competing conceptions of rationality was at stake – then it might seem more straightforward to investigate rationality itself, to see if any of those principles that made up the sociality of the agents would be able to sustain a normative allegiance to itself and would not generate paradoxes and skeptical doubts about itself within its own terms. This in turn seemed to call for an investigation of whether certain particular conceptions of rationality were inherently self-undermining and others were not, and as Hegel had come to understand the term in his Jena period, this itself would be the task of a *logic*. "Logic" in this sense would investigate the structure of this kind of social thought wholly within its own terms, abstracting away from its social embodiment; "logic" would investigate the structure of thought purely in terms of its own inferential goodness, its avoidance (or lack thereof) of paradox and self-contradiction. But if "logic" in this sense could itself be a self-contained "science," then it was no longer clear, as it gradually became apparent to Hegel in Nuremberg, whether we in fact needed the long historical introduction to the "speculative standpoint" that the 1807 *Phenomenology* had offered – or at least whether we needed a separate "science" that would play that role. It thus also began to seem to Hegel in Nuremberg that at most one would need only the first part of the *Phenomenology* to introduce the "we," after which it could be discarded in favor of a more purely "logical" investigation. It would be a ladder that one kicked away once one had arrived at the proper heights. His experiences in the classroom there only confirmed that notion for him.

Going directly to "logic" after a "phenomenology" was nonetheless not completely foreign to him; indeed, he had done much the same thing in his last lecture series at Jena in 1806.[7] But the demands forced on Hegel by his teaching duties also forced on him a certain awareness of how his own work, so recently completed, was perhaps not quite in harmony with his original intentions. In his second repeat of the *Phenomenology* the following year, he stressed in his introductory dictation the theme of the objective and subjective points of view and how those two points of view needed to be combined into a conception of *Geist*. As he dictated to the students, each point of view – the subjective and objective – considered on its own without the incorporation of the other point of view was only "one-sided": The objective point of view leads one to a philosophy of *realism*, in which the objects are seen as having a determinateness on their own, which can only be "given" to consciousness; and the subjective point of view leads one to a philosophy of (subjective) *idealism*, in which consciousness is seen as positing the determinateness of the world itself.[8] The truth of the matter is, of course, the social point of view of *Geist* itself, the unity within which the competing strands of "realism" and "subjective idealism" are united.

But in this 1809 repeat of the *Phenomenology* as an introduction to philosophy, Hegel made no effort to go through the whole system, stopping this time quite self-consciously at "reason" and proceeding *not* to "logic" but instead to "psychology." By 1809, he had thus decided that, in his words, the "authentic doctrine of spirit" clearly lay in philosophical psychology, and the "introduction to philosophy" thus required for its successor a course in "psychology," by which he meant a consideration of the ways in which we necessarily individually and collectively organize our conscious and self-conscious lives in terms of certain basic norms through the processes of representing, imagining, feeling, and so on. That conception stayed with him, and in 1816, in the third volume of the *Science of Logic*, he referred to his *Phenomenology of Spirit* as having its "higher truth" in his philosophical psychology, which he there explicitly called, as he had done with his students in 1809, the "authentic doctrine of spirit."[9]

This move away from "phenomenology" to "logic" and "psychology" fit nicely with another matter that had been forced on Hegel. According to Niethammer's "General Normative," he was required to teach a course with the formidable title "Introduction to Knowledge of the Universal Coherence of the Sciences." Hegel interpreted that to mean that he was to give an overview of how the various philosophical sciences fit together and how they in turn were related to the more specific empirical sciences. Lacking any text on which he could rely, Hegel was forced to come up with a short compendium of his own system, which he called an "encyclopedia." By that he meant a rigorous theoretical (*wissenschaftlich*) arrangement and derivation of the three philosophical sciences as he saw them, which, at least by the time of his required report to Niethammer in 1812 (roughly the time at which the first volume of the *Logic* appeared), he had clearly demarcated as "*logic*, philosophy of *nature*, and philosophy of *spirit*."[10] But what place was the *Phenomenology* supposed to occupy in such an "encyclopedia"? At this time, Hegel was still holding on, however tenuously, to the thought that it was still to serve as the introduction to the whole encyclopedic system, but as he thought about it more, it increasingly seemed to him that any such "phenomenology" – especially as limited to the first two sections of the original 1807 *Phenomenology* ("consciousness" and "self-consciousness") and ending in "universal self-consciousness" and "reason" – could only be a *part* of the structure of the "doctrine" of spirit.

The exigencies of Hegel's teaching situation thus forced him to come to terms with issues on which he had been working for years, and the contingent circumstances of his arrangements quite fortuitously fit into the ways in which he was coming to think of the structure of his own still-developing system. But it also increased his ambivalence about the 1807 *Phenomenology*, an ambivalence that was to last his entire life. The Nuremberg "Phenomenology" itself became only a small part of the later *Encyclopedia of Philosophical Sciences*, his magisterial presentation of the whole "system" for use in his lectures – "phenomenology" came to be a small portion of what he called in the *Encyclopedia* "subjective spirit," which itself appeared for a few pages only after much longer sections on "anthropology" and before a longer section called "psychology." Late in his career in Berlin, he was finally to admit in print that he had in fact ceased to regard the 1807 *Phenomenology of Spirit* as the proper "introduction" to his system. Thus, the seemingly fortuitous jump to psychology necessitated by Hegel's teaching duties eventually became a hard-and-fast feature of his mature system of philosophy.

However, the problem of the status of the "we" remained with him and remained one of the most problematic aspects of his overall system of thought. Hegel's critics generally wanted to do one of three things with that "we," each of which he rejected. Many wanted to turn Hegel's conception of *Geist* into something more akin to Schelling's conception of the "world soul." Some wished to dissolve the study of the "we" into an empirical, introspective study of the processes of the social or psychological constitution of our experience of the world. Others wished to jettison the "we" entirely and study only the pure forms of thought. Hegel wanted none of these, and he often found it difficult to convince his critics that his was indeed a viable fourth option. However, the difficulty of sustaining Hegel's conception of *Geist*, coupled with the metaphorical descriptions he himself gave of it, allowed many of those who would otherwise have been critics to think that they were in fact explicating Hegel himself as they propounded doctrines of empirical history, psychology, logic, or metaphysics. This continued to make Hegel into someone around whom many different people could rally, all of them continuing to see themselves mirrored in his thought.

The Development of Hegel's *Science of Logic* in Nuremberg

Hegel's Nuremberg dictations on "logic" show more clearly than his final completed work just how much he was indebted to Kant and just how much he had in fact returned to Kant in working out his own system. Hegel's own intellectual relationship to Kant was something that he was always ready to admit and equally ready to conceal; he quite obviously possessed a bit of anxiety of influence vis-à-vis Kant, and, in fact, quite revealingly, in the draft of an 1822 letter to a friend who had first become interested in Hegel's views after reading Kant, confessed that "I cut my teeth on Kant's works," but, apparently thinking better of admitting such a thing in writing, eliminated it from the final form of the letter he actually sent.[11]

In working out his *Logic*, Hegel was particularly concerned with Kant's theory of the "Ideas" – a concern that had animated much of his thought in Jena but which had mysteriously vanished from virtually all of the *Phenomenology* except for the Preface. Kant had argued that reason, as a faculty of inference and of linking various parts of the complex web of knowledge with each other, is always pushed by its own internal dynamic to look for "first causes," "beginnings in time," "atoms by which everything is constituted," "first premises" – in other words, for the conditions that would complete what would otherwise add up to an infinite series of conditions; Kant called the representations of such completeness the "Ideas" of reason. As Kant eloquently put it in the opening statement of the *Critique of Pure Reason*, "human reason has this peculiar fate that . . . it is burdened by questions which, as prescribed by the very nature of reason itself, it is not able to ignore, but which, as transcending all its powers, it is also not able to answer."[12] Reason cannot succeed because in looking for such "wholes" it goes beyond the boundaries of possible experience and finds itself making claims that it cannot redeem. Worse, it finds itself asserting equally well grounded contradictory claims, which Kant labeled the "antinomies" of reason.

However, while still in Frankfurt, Hegel had come to believe that Kant's *own* line of reasoning in his later works had undermined Kant's rigid dualisms of "concept and intuition" and "spontaneity and receptivity," and, like almost all the post-Kantians, he entirely rejected Kant's central notion of an unbridgeable gulf between the world of appearance and the world of things-in-themselves. The notion of a realm of unknowable things-in-themselves was rejected as an empty notion, a "mere" thought, and Hegel had special reason to reject Kant's claim that the "wholes" toward which reason was pushed could be (as

Kant called them) "transcendental illusions." Indeed, Hegel had come to think (at least after the *Phenomenology* if not before) that the "wholes" toward which reason was necessarily pushed were those in terms of which the individual judgments made by agents made sense in the first place; they were the inferential structure of a distinctive way in which *Geist* had structured itself in a particular historical period, and the "whole of these wholes" was human history itself.

This line of thought suggested to him a new way of developing the "logic" that he had unsuccessfully attempted to write during his Jena years. As Hegel came to see it, at least by the time he began his career in Nuremberg, if logic was still conceived as the "self-articulation of the absolute," then it would have to be conceived as the self-articulation of the inferential structure of *Geist*, of "mindedness" itself. Hegel's project for his "logic" thus began to take shape as a kind of completion and reworking of the structures both implicitly and explicitly at work in Kant's three *Critiques* once one had jettisoned the Kantian dualisms of "concept and intuition" and "things-in-themselves and appearances." His earliest versions of an attempt at this, in his 1808–09 class on "logic," are far more tied down to Kantian notions than the *Logic* that finally emerged from it. Hegel organized his first dictations on logic by laying out his versions of the Kantian antinomies from the *Critique of Pure Reason*, ordering each of them into three of his own classifications, each of which in turn was labeled the "dialectic" of its particular region. Thus, in Hegel's provisional view of his logic in 1808–09, the divisions consisted in the "dialectic of being," the "dialectic of essence" and the "dialectic of unconditioned relationships," all of which were far more closely tied into the Kantian antinomies than his final *Logic* turned out to be. In the same year, Hegel also taught what he called "subjective logic" that consisted in the traditional logic of concepts, judgments, and syllogistic inference; and in the published program for the *Gymnasium* that year, Hegel even referred to this part as "authentic logic," a term he later used in his dictations of the 1810–11 version of the course to characterize the same thing.[13]

By 1808–09, the overall structure of the "logic" that was to emerge gradually in three volumes in 1812, 1813, and 1816 had become clear to Hegel, even if it were true, as he told Niethammer in 1808, that he "had hardly laid the foundation" for such a work in Jena (an indication, if nothing else, of how unsatisfied he had become with his very substantial earlier attempts at such a "logic" there).[14] Nonetheless, since he had to teach logic for the next few years in the *Gymnasium*, he had more time to work out his ideas on the subject, and he apparently used virtually all of his free time to work on what would become the publishable form of his *Science of Logic*. His list of classes on "Logic" and the student dictations from that period show that he was immersed in working through the material and was developing his own views on the matter quite rapidly. After the very Kantian course in "Logic" in 1808–09, he again taught two logic classes in 1809–10: a lower division class (the *Unterklasse*, restricted to fourteen- to fifteen-year-olds) in which he taught a very simplified form of his own reconstruction of traditional syllogistic logic, mentioning only in passing his own understanding of what was at stake in his grander plan for a "Logic"; and a more advanced section for the highest class in the *Gymnasium* (the *Oberklasse*), which he described in the *Gymnasium*'s program that year as a class in which "logic in its full extension would be treated, with however the exclusion of the objective or transcendental logic."[15]

By 1810–11, Hegel's conception of his "logic" as central to his overall conception of the role of philosophy in modern life finally had emerged quite clearly in his dictation to his class, in which he contrasted the "heteronomous" conception of a "given" with the way in which (modern, "logical") thought has for its object only "itself in an autonomous manner."[16] The analogy Hegel was drawing is obvious: The terms "heteronomy" and "autonomy" had been used by Kant to designate manners of action; and only autonomous action, so Kant had argued, was fully moral. Hegel thus conceived his "logic" as fulfilling an ethical mission for modern people; it taught them to think without "given" foundations, to accept only that which they could come to validate for themselves. By 1810 (if not earlier) Hegel had clearly come to believe that the discipline of logic in modern life had to be a self-founding enterprise (a view which contradicted his 1804–05 view that logic itself depended on something else that at the time he had called "metaphysics"). Indeed, as his thought matured, Hegel came to think that such a logic would be the very paradigm of modern self-founding practice, of thinking without anything except self-constructed foundations. The *Logic* and not the *Phenomenology*, therefore, would henceforth serve as the linchpin of his system of philosophy.

By the middle of his sojourn in Nuremberg, Hegel's "logic" had thus taken its shape as the key element of his own emerging philosophical system with which he wanted to provide the overall structure and legitimation of post-Napoleonic European life. If the university was to be the driving agent of reformed modern life, and if philosophy was to be the apex of the modern university, and if logic was the basic study at work in all philosophy, then logic itself had to be rethought in a nondogmatic fashion. Self-grounding "logic" would teach us how to think as free, enlightened moderns.

The *Science of Logic*

Hegel began his *Science of Logic* with his characteristic bravado: Our modern era, he said, had a profound need for a philosophy to comprehend it, and his *Logic*, he said, was to be just that. Because, as he put it, "the complete transformation which philosophical thought among us has undergone in the last twenty five years and the higher standpoint reached by spirit in its self-consciousness have had but little influence as yet on the structure of logic," he had been required "to begin once again at the beginning"[17] – strong stuff from a relatively unknown writer who was at the time still only a *Gymnasium* professor with unfulfilled aspirations for university employment.

The *Science of Logic* was in a fundamental way Hegel's elaboration once more of Hölderlin's central insight. Rejecting Fichte's "subjective idealism," which held that since nothing can count for the "I," the "subject" of knowledge, unless it actively takes it up, Hölderlin had argued that such judgmental activity on the part of the knowing agent already presupposes a unity of thought and being, a way of orienting ourselves that forms a "horizon" of all our conscious life without itself being an object of conscious life itself. To make judgments, we must distinguish "subject" from "object," but we should not take that division itself as primary, as being somehow bedrock. To do that is to fall onto the mistaken path that leads to the eternal see-sawing between "realism" and "subjective idealism" in modern philosophy. Indeed, on Hölderlin's view, that kind of fundamental orientation in terms of this primordial unity is prior to the divisions inherent in "consciousness" itself.

What seems to have been part of Hegel's development of Hölderlin's account had to do with his drawing the conclusion from Hölderlin's

thoughts that for Hölderlin *truth* itself had to be a totally primitive
conception, not something that could itself be defined in any other
terms and nonetheless was not the "object" of any sort of an "intellectual intuition." Whereas Hölderlin, however, had seen all judgment as
a rupture of that fundamental unity, Hegel drew a quite different
conclusion. In his view, the conception of truth as a "primitive" concept
was in part correct, but already in the *Phenomenology* and in some of his
earlier manuscripts, he had developed Hölderlin's insight into a conviction that the prior unity of thought and being of which Hölderlin spoke
in fact should be conceived as an *intersubjective* unity of mutually recognizing agents. We do not begin reflection as isolated individual agents,
each of which would be encapsulated in his own experiences and would
only apply conceptual form to his experiences or infer on the basis of
them whether there is a world at all corresponding to them. Instead, we
begin within a way of life, as "one among many," and the self-
consciousness of each consists not only in his locating himself in that
"social space" of shared norms, entitlements, and commitments, but in
each also being self-conscious of the others' self-conscious status. That
necessity for understanding each other as *different* points of view within
one social space necessarily introduced a kind of skepticism and rupture
into that original, primordial sense of "truth."

Hegel's major insight in his own *Logic* had to do with the way in
which he transformed Hölderlin's conception of a "unity" that preceded
all acts of judgment into his own idiom, while remaining consistent with
his views as they were articulated in the *Phenomenology*. Although understanding the nature of judgment as central, Hegel nonetheless began
his *Logic* not with the notion of a *judgment* at all but with the more
abstract conception, as he put it, of "pure knowing" itself. The *Logic*
thus began not so much with a judgment as with a general "thought"
about the world, which showed by virtue of its own internal inadequacies the necessity for making discursive judgments at all (and, ultimately, the necessity for making certain kinds of discursive judgments).
Thus, famously, Hegel began his book with the category of "*being, pure
being* – without any further determination," a "thought" that already
included within itself Hölderlin's conception of the primordial unity of
thought and being and of a "truth" that was prior to any particular
articulation of some other set of truths.[18]

Hegel's argument was that the simple and primary act of thinking involved in trying to articulate that sense of the unity of thought and being – of "being, pure being" – immediately generated various paradoxes and tensions from within itself as we attempted to articulate it. Hölderlin had thought that the rupture in that unity was somehow brought about by us; Hegel, on the other hand, argued that it was implicit in the very nature of the unity itself that our effort to think about it exposed those internal tensions in the thought itself. The rupture, as it were, between thought and being, the way in which all our attempts at "getting it right" sometimes fail, is brought about by the act of judgment itself, which was itself required once "thought," in Hegel's idiom, understood itself to be generating such paradoxes. The air of great paradox with which Hegel began his *Logic* – the assertion that "Being" and "Nothing" were the same – was intended by Hegel to bring out just how paradoxical that primordial unity of thought and being actually is when taken on its own. What for Hölderlin had been a sense of "oneness" that is always and eternally there framing the essential discordances of our conscious lives was shown by Hegel to be not so harmonious, to be itself riddled with tensions that required us to undertake further judgmental commitments in order to make sense of the kinds of basic judgments that were required of us to be judging agents at all.

Very generally, Hegel thought that in trying to articulate that primordial unity of thought and being, the sense that we are always at some deep level "in touch" with the world and that the forces of skeptical doubt cannot forever undermine that for us, we come to comprehend that the reassurance that we necessarily seek – the reassurance that we *really are* in touch with the world, that thought and being *really are* not irrevocably divorced from each other – *can only* appear at the *end* of a logical development, that the reassurance comes in articulating the whole "space of reasons," the "Idea," within which our judgmental activity necessarily moves. What drives us to complete that "whole," to develop the "space of reasons" within the terms it sets for itself, are the paradoxes that such attempts generate prior to their inclusion and resolution within that whole. Hegel's term for that resolution was "*Aufhebung*," since in German that word carried (almost paradoxically itself) the disparate meanings of "canceling," "raising," and "preserving." His point in using the term was to highlight the way in which our commitments bring certain logical stresses and strains within themselves that are necessary when viewed from the standpoint of the totality of the "space of reasons," that are also never fully abolished but always remain with us, and which finally do not prove to be destructive of the "whole" once their places and functions within that whole are properly understood.

Beginning with "being," "pure being" generates the paradoxical, contradictory assertion that "being" and "nothing" are the same. The problem with the putatively "pure thought" of "pure, indeterminate being" is that it contains nothing within itself to distinguish that thought from the thought of "nothing." That distinction is made only when one articulates the so-called "pure thoughts" of "being" and "nothing" and realizes in doing so that one is in fact speaking of "becoming," of things coming-to-be and passing away.[19] Thus, when one tries to *express* the so-called *thought* of "pure being," of the notion that the world just "is" even if we can say nothing else about it, one thereby also licenses an inference to the conception that being and nothing are the same. The attempt at making a *judgment* about the "pure thought" ends up licensing what looks like a self-contradiction. That self-contradiction vanishes only when one makes explicit that one is in fact saying something more and something different than one originally expressed – one is asserting more than just "being," that "the world is," one is making the judgment that *something*, some *one determinate thing* or another, comes to be, remains, or passes away.

The initial and core paradox that animates the "Doctrine of Being" is that which arises when we attempt to articulate the unity of thought and being, for it would seem that this "Being" taken simply as the prereflective "whole" of which Hölderlin spoke is indistinguishable, at that level of articulation, from "nothing," yet it is also just as clearly distinguishable from it. The difficulty in stating that distinction and articulation of the other commitments one implicitly undertakes in stating it begins the procedure by which the other structures of judgment are developed.[20]

Hegel divided his *Logic* into what he called three "books": Being, Essence, and Concept. The rationale for the division was that there was a different "logic" – the normative structure of our entitlements, commitments, and the paradoxes they generate – depending on the kinds of judgmental relations of which we were speaking.

The "Doctrine of Being" concerns itself with the kinds of judgments we make about finite entities that come to be and pass away, which itself includes commitments to three general types of judgments: Those relating to the qualitative aspects of things that come to be and pass away, those relating to the quantitative aspects of such things, and those relating to the ways in which our judgments about qualitative and quantitative things are combined (as when, for example, we say that streams grow larger and become rivers), which Hegel calls judgments of "measure." In each of these types of judgment, we are orienting ourselves within a conception of a "whole," the "infinite" that legitimates and guides our judgmental activities. In the section on "quality," the infinite is specified as the world process as a whole, the way in which the coming-to-be and passing-away of the world is conceived as an infinite series of comings-to-be and passings-away. Taken as a whole, the world-process is thus self-contained; it is, in Hegel's terms, a "being-for-itself," not a being for something different from and outside of itself (such as a supernaturally conceived deity). This conception of "qualitative infinity" is also *ideal*: We never encounter the "whole" of the world-process within our own experience, but we must have a conceptual grasp of it (as "Idea," in Hegel's language) in order to be able to think about it in the first place. This constitutes, as Hegel puts it, the "ideality of being-for-itself as totality."[21] "Ideality," he says, "can be called the quality of infinity";[22] or, as he also puts it, "the proposition, that the finite is ideal, constitutes idealism."[23]

The section on "quantity" shows how the conceptual grasp of the "infinite" in the differential and integral calculus in effect answers the charges (made among others by Kant) that we can have no conceptual grasp of the infinite that is not already founded in some kind of immediate experience of the infinite.[24] The quantitative infinite is thus also *ideal*; it is not an object – not even something like an "infinitesimal," conceived as a quantity that is greater than zero and smaller than any natural number, an idea that Hegel sarcastically dismissed, alluding to D'Alembert, with the remark, "it seemed perfectly clear that such an *intermediate state*, as it was called, between being and nothing does not exist."[25] The quantitative infinite is to be represented in the formulas of the calculus that express iterative operations, not "infinitesimals." In Hegel's idealism, there is simply nothing more to the quantitative infinite than what is expressed in such formulas, and the quantitative infinite is thus *ideal*, since it is never grasped in some individual experience of things but is comprehended fully and truly only in thought, in the formulas of the integral and differential calculus.

In making such qualitative and quantitative judgments about the world as a whole and uniting them in judgments of "measure," we seem to commit ourselves to a set of judgments different in normative structure from those articulated in the "Doctrine of Being." The "Doctrine of Being" seems to commit us to a conception of a world that *seems* to be the substrate of such qualitative and quantitative features of itself without itself being either qualitative or quantitative "in itself." These kinds of judgments are articulated in the "Doctrine of Essence," which thus concerns itself with the normative structures of judgments that have to do with our distinguishing how the world appears to us from the way it really is. Indeed, the initial and the core paradox that motivates the development of the "Doctrine of Essence" is the skeptical assertion that what "seems to be" cannot be equivalent to what "really is the case," since it apparently requires us to make judgments about what is the case all the while asserting that we cannot know what is the case. Such judgments thus always presume a grasp "in thought" of two elements, the *appearance* and *that which* is appearing; and without such a grasp of the "whole" in thought (a conception of the whole of "the world in itself *as* appearing to us"), we could not even begin to make the kinds of ordinary skeptical judgments that we do make (such as when we doubt whether something really is the way it looks).

What *explains* the way things "seem" to be is called the "essence" of the "appearance," and the various paradoxes that arise in the "Doctrine of Essence" thus have to do with the problems encountered when we reflectively make the link between various appearances and that *of which* we take them to be appearances. Ultimately, so Hegel argued, such kinds of judgments presume a conception of the world as *one substance* that necessarily manifests itself to judging agents in certain typical ways, and this substance behaves according to "causal relationships" among the various "accidents" of the substance. However, Hegel went on to conclude, the Spinozistic notion of substance to which we become committed by virtue of making judgments about appearances and what appears – that to which Jacobi had always asserted that any rationalist metaphysics leads – itself generates various paradoxes about causality itself, such that the resolution of those paradoxes requires a doctrine of the "whole" as a self-sufficient system of interactive, reciprocal causation.

The "Doctrine of Being" and the "Doctrine of Essence" are concerned with the normative structure of those judgments about the coming-to-be and passing-away of things in the world, and the normative structure of the reflective judgments by which we distinguish appearance from reality in that world of coming-to-be and passing-away. What they cannot account for, however, is the judging activity itself. The norms governing our judging activities are not *themselves* established by the world that comes to be and passes away, and the distinction itself between appearance and reality is already a judgmental distinction that "we" have necessarily imported into our experience.

The normative structure of our own judgmental activities thus form the third "book" of the *Logic*, the "Doctrine of the Concept." This is the structure of the types of judgments that we make within the ways of life that Hegel calls *Geist*. The structure of "the concept" therefore is the structure of intersubjective self-consciousness itself. In particular, it concerns the normative structure of how we make judgments about particular things as having certain general features. Since there are no direct, "given" encounters with particular objects – our epistemically crudest and most basic perceptions are, as the *Phenomenology* showed, infused with judgmental norms – this structure can be worked out purely conceptually without having to rely, as Kant did, on "pure intuitions." In making judgments, we articulate, quite literally, the original unity of experience and the world; judgment is thus as Hölderlin said (making a play on the German term) a primordial division, an "*Ur-Teilung.*" The demonstration that a Spinozistic conception of substance requires a conception of a thinking subject that itself cannot understand itself as explained by such a substance constitutes, Hegel proudly asserted, the "unique and truthful refutation of Spinozism."[26] Jacobi's worries, so Hegel thought, had been finally laid to rest.

What we encounter in our experiences of a world – that the world is coming to be and passing away, and that we distinguish appearance from reality – are unified experiences of particular things embodying general features, experiences of "this-suches" as having their place in a "whole." Various judgments articulate the "this-such" entities we encounter against the complex background of the world as a whole and the kinds of things at stake in "Being" and "Essence." Individual judgments themselves, however, call for grounds for their assertion, and, if one follows that out far enough – Hegel's arguments in the text are quite complex and rest on some of the same points made in his 1804–05 "Logic" about how formal classification of judgments presup poses a prior material, content-laden classification of them – one is committed to the notion that understanding what counts as "getting it right" in individual judgments has to do with the kinds of concealed inferences at work in them. Individual judgments, that is, are the kinds of things that make sense only in a larger pattern of inferences, and, likewise, that inferential pattern itself cannot be purely formally determined; material notions about what counts as logical and "pure" are brought in from outside the formal structures themselves, and thus any doctrine of formal inferential structure has to give an account of the rational structure of what those other considerations might be.

This amounts to giving an account of what *Geist's* basic *interests* are in sorting out things in the world the way that it does, what *Geist* requires in order to reassure itself about the unity of thought and being, and, so Hegel had long since concluded, *Geist's* most basic interest lay in its securing for itself the conditions for the realization of its own autonomy. Securing that autonomy, moreover, requires first of all (and almost paradoxically) that we understand the world as having a rational structure that is independent of ourselves, which Hegel calls "objectivity," which itself is divided into the ideas of mechanical, chemical, and teleological systems – roughly, into systems in which the elements are identifiable independent of the laws governing the system (such as gravitational systems); systems in which each of the elements has an "affinity" for combining with other elements (as in chemical affinities); and systems in which the elements are what they are only in terms of their functioning as organs of a "whole" (as is the case with all living things).

That this is a rational characterization of the "objective" systems of the world presupposes that we have good grounds for making such divisions, and thus a demonstration of the rationality of this more "subjective" notion of systems of classification is also required. The idea of the "true," of our getting our judgments about the world "right," is bound up with our idea of the "good," of the basic interests guiding our formulating and testing such judgments, of what ends we are trying to achieve in making such judgments. What is ultimately, however, "good" in that scheme is that we exercise our own free judgmental powers so that we do "get it right," that we learn to discipline our judgmental activities according to principles that we alone impose on ourselves, since the world does not impose those principles on us. What is rational in all this is only what can survive this internal critique of itself.

The "true" and the "good" – the theoretical and the practical – are thus bound up with each other within a larger whole. This larger "whole" within which all judgmental activity goes on is the totality of the "space of reasons," or the "Idea," as Hegel calls it. Hegel's long and complex argument in the *Logic* was intended to establish that this is not merely a game that thought plays with itself but a way of articulating the original unity of thought and being that is present and active in *Geist*, spirit, even though that original unity must itself rupture and divide itself, producing the kind of "negativity" at work in the *Logic*. As developed in this way, the "space of reasons" offers the reassurance that outside of itself there is nothing of *normative* significance and that it has generated its own structure and content in a way that both preserves the original unity of thought and being and develops it in more determinate ways so that it finally reestablishes itself at the end of that otherwise "negative" development. More concretely, the "Idea," the "space of reasons," is the idealized normative structure of a rational form of "social space" and forms the "pure normative structure" of the manners of reciprocal recognition that make up *Geist*. As having nothing outside of itself of normative significance and as self-legitimating, the "space of reasons" is thus the *absolute* Idea. It is "absolute" as having nothing outside of itself to account for its legitimacy; and it is the reassurance after the long path of "negativity" that the unity of thought and being, so abstractly articulated by Hölderlin, the notion that we are really in touch with things as they metaphysically are, can be vouchsafed only by the kind of skeptical, "negative" development of our judgmental activities found in the *Phenomenology* and the *Logic*. Returning to his earlier Schellingian formulations, Hegel noted that "this identity has therefore been rightly determined as the *subject-object*, for it is as well the formal or subjective concept as it is the Object as such."[27]

The absolute Idea is thus the "space of reasons" giving an account of itself; it is reason submitting itself to its own self-critique and demonstrating that it need not go outside of itself to ratify itself. The *Logic* has shown, Hegel thought, that being a reason for *we* "like-minded" agents is *all* that there can be to being a reason; there is no supernatural rationality outside of our own against which we measure our own rationality.

The absolute Idea, while always *implicit* in human thought, is nonetheless the logical expression of the "we" of *modern* humanity, since only in modern thought have the claims of reason been able to become fully explicit. Prior ages, to be sure, had their own versions of the "Idea," but whereas their cultures and ways of life rested on authoritative norms that they simply had to accept dogmatically as given, as lying simply "in the nature of things" and thus having to be "revealed" to humanity, the modern age has the *absolute* Idea, since modern life has come to show that it can live without some dogmatic bedrock on which to stand, that it is capable of constructing its own scaffolding as it goes along. Moreover, any attempts to articulate the absolute Idea must be circular in the sense that they must *occur* within the web of norms that make up who "we moderns" are. Thus, Hegel thought he had fulfilled his task to create a *modern* logic.

The *Logic* had finally given Hegel a structure within which he could develop his other thoughts on the possibilities for modern life in the investigation of nature, of social life, of art, religion, philosophy, and history. Just as importantly, the publication of the *Logic* established Hegel in the minds of the philosophical public as a thinker in his own right. The *Phenomenology* had somewhat puzzled that public, since it seemed to them to be a Schellingian work that was also strikingly un-Schellingian in character. With the *Logic*, however, Hegel's position as *the* non-Schellingian successor to the post-Kantians began to be secured.[28]

Heidelberg: Coming Into Focus

Family Life and the Move to Heidelberg

Leaving Bavaria: Complications

ALTHOUGH HEGEL HAD LONG YEARNED for a university professorship and, in particular, for a place in Heidelberg – and it is
clear that the possibility and desirability of such a position had long
been discussed in the Hegel household – the final decision and the move
to Heidelberg did not come easily. Hegel had settled down quite happily
into family life and into a domestic routine in Nuremberg that seemed
to suit him well, even if he was frustrated by the duties attached to his
job as rector of the *Gymnasium*. (A brief glimpse of that routine in
Nuremberg is revealed in his remark in a letter to his sister, Christiane,
shortly before the move: "My children are fine. Every day Karl comes
up to fetch me to eat, and usually remarks in the room in which you
stayed: Auntie has left on a trip.")[1] But the move to Heidelberg was
something he had long awaited and for which he had long yearned, and
it was not something therefore that he took lightly.

Hegel privately accepted the offer from Heidelberg in the summer of
1816, but since he had not yet secured his formal release from the royal
Bavarian service, he was not able to make any public announcement to
that effect. Hegel was therefore both surprised and chagrined when the
Bavarian government, complicating matters in its bumbling way, suddenly authorized the university in Erlangen to appoint him to a position
as director of the seminar of philology and professor of classical literature (both Greek and Roman), along with a professorial chair in elo-
quence, poetry, and in classical Greek and Roman literature, and even
took the step of announcing the appointment in the official government

newspaper on September 4, 1816. Since Hegel had been assuming that he was to begin teaching in Heidelberg near the end of October of that year, the news of his new appointment and the ensuing delay in securing his release was both anxiety-inducing and discomforting. Hegel had longed for eight years for that position and he had constantly badgered Niethammer about it; now it was just an embarrassment. Hegel quickly wrote to his friend and benefactor at Heidelberg, Paulus, to let him know that the newspaper announcement was not true, that he had certainly *not* accepted a position at Erlangen, and to ask him to inform any others at Heidelberg who might hear of the matter that the report was false and "to do so in my name."[2]

The delay on the part of the Bavarian authorities to act on Hegel's otherwise pro forma request for dismissal from Bavarian service –thus making his imminent move to Heidelberg a bit more stressful – certainly did nothing further to endear the Bavarians to Hegel, who had already clearly taken to detesting them and who desperately wanted to get out from under their governance.

Niethammer's own recent experiences during the period immediately following the Congress of Vienna had only further heightened Hegel's concerns. The government in Bavaria had begun both to backtrack on its commitment to full equality for Protestants in their kingdom and to overrule and censure Niethammer for his attempts to secure educational reform; the results left Niethammer disgusted and despondent over the future; congratulating Hegel on his new appointment (on Hegel's "redemption," as he called it), Niethammer despairingly added, "The way things now seem, I am going to see everything that I have aimed at unravel before my eyes."[3] To drive the point home, Niethammer related to Hegel how constant rainstorms had marred a vacation he had taken but that at least the "Bavarianlessness (*Bayerlosigkeit*)" of the place made it nonetheless attractive.[4] In a letter to Paulus, Hegel himself railed against the "Bavariana" (*Bavarica*)" that he still had to endure before what he called his "damned discharge" from the Bavarian government could be received.[5] The final letter of discharge was dated October 7, 1816, only fourteen days before Hegel was to begin lecturing in Heidelberg.[6]

There was also the lingering issue of a possible offer from Berlin. Hegel's remarks on the matter in his letters disclose what must have been an intense discussion in the Hegel household about which offer

Hegel would accept if indeed the Berlin offer were to materialize. Hegel clearly wanted at least to keep open the matter of accepting the Berlin offer and probably even would have preferred to accept the Berlin offer, but it is clear that his wife, Marie, would simply have nothing of it. Marie Hegel was firmly opposed to any move to Berlin because it would take her too far away from her family and acquaintances in Nuremberg, and she made her feelings about this quite well known to Hegel. Hegel ruefully took it all in stride. He noted to Paulus on August 8, 1816, that for Marie "the name of Berlin has a doubly discordant ring to it," and he noted a few days later to Niethammer (on August 11, 1816) that "as little as my wife wants to hear of it, the post [in Berlin] might perhaps even be the more excellent one – which it would be foolish to place behind Heidelberg."[7] A few days later (August 28, 1816), he claimed in a letter to Frommann that he was in fact happy to have been "spared the choice" of going to Berlin, since he had accepted Heidelberg's offer before receiving the official offer from Berlin (but which by that time he had reasonable expectations of receiving), remarking to Frommann that "Berlin would of course have been very attractive for me in many respects," but adding, "though not for my wife, who, after all, likewise has a voice in the matter."[8] It is not hard to see that Hegel was a bit vexed with his wife's refusal to cater to his aspirations, but at least at that time he was willing to go along with her stated wishes.

Ludwig Fischer Hegel Joins the Family

A good bit before Hegel left for Heidelberg, he and his wife had made another difficult decision. In a letter to Frommann on July 20, 1816, Hegel informed Frommann that "my wife and I are resolved to take Ludwig into our home."[9] He was, of course, referring to his illegitimate son by Johanna Burkhardt in Jena, who until then had been living in the orphanage run by Frommann's sister-in-law. The basis of the decision was surely not financial; it was not as if only at that point could Hegel have afforded to bring Ludwig into the family, since the move to Heidelberg meant that Hegel was actually taking a slight reduction in income (especially if one calculated living expenses into the whole package). One major reason surely had to do with the status of the von Tucher family in Nuremberg and the possible embarrassment that the arrival of Ludwig might have had for them in the town. But it is not clear just exactly who it was they felt would be embarrassed. On the one hand, it seems as if the von Tucher family as a whole was content, at least as long as Hegel was in Nuremberg, to let Hegel relieve himself of his obligations to young Ludwig by sending the orphanage money; but it also seems that there was no small number of rumors in Nuremberg about Hegel's little secret.[10] It is also not clear just how much of a "secret" the whole thing was. Hegel and his wife clearly discussed Ludwig quite a bit. For example, in a letter to Frommann (December 20, 1815), Hegel mentions how Marie had intended to make something for Ludwig as a Christmas present but her miscarriage and precarious health had prevented her from doing so.[11] In many letters to Frommann there are invocations to send greetings to Ludwig from Hegel and his wife, but there is never mention of doing anything more.

That all changed when Hegel accepted the position at Heidelberg. He seems to have decided almost immediately after accepting the offer that Ludwig was to become a part of the household, and his mother-in-law, Susanna Maria von Tucher, quite enthusiastically announced that she had taken it on herself to procure Ludwig's bed in Heidelberg. (Good beds were hard to come by in those days, so this was no small gesture.)[12] Since Ludwig was later to complain bitterly that his stepmother, Marie Hegel, treated him in a second-class way in comparison to her own children – and, as he put it, "I always lived in fear but never in love of my parents"[13] – it seems quite likely that Ludwig's late arrival into the Hegel household was due to Marie Hegel's objections to including Ludwig in the family. Perhaps she found herself overruled by both her husband and her own mother after the issue of the possible embarrassment for the von Tucher family in Nuremberg became a moot point.[14]

Ludwig finally joined the Hegel household in April 1817, about six months after Hegel moved to Heidelberg. It does seem clear that Ludwig was immediately included in all the family activities; Marie would, for example, take him along on her trips to various spas, and Ludwig seems to have done well in school.[15] But Ludwig had been raised in an orphanage without ever really knowing his father and mother, both of whom had abandoned him, and it is no surprise to find that he had developed some personal difficulties that were a bit abrasive in the context of the Hegel family; reflecting in 1825 on the final break between Ludwig and the family (which clearly had been encouraged by the family itself), Johanna Frommann remarked, "To be sure, Louis has a stone instead of a heart."[16]

Ludwig's initial arrival in Heidelberg had a triumphal air to it; he had been picked up in Jena and brought to Heidelberg by no less a luminary than Heinrich Voss, the son of Johann Voss and himself a Heidelberg professor of classical philology; along the way they had visited Goethe, who wrote a charming entry in Ludwig's diary. Hegel also noted at the time how happy he and his wife were with Ludwig and how well schooled he seemed to be. It seems that shortly after his arrival, Hegel informed Ludwig about his mother's death in the intervening years, which as Hegel noted to Frommann, "seemed to have affected him more than me," adding, "my heart had long ago finished with her."[17] (Hegel had also expressed a bit of relief at this news, since, as he noted, he had feared a possibly unpleasant scene between Johanna Burkhardt and his wife if Ms. Burkhardt were ever to make contact with him.)[18] Ludwig is mentioned (approvingly) in many letters by Marie's mother to her, but in a letter to Hegel himself – in which Hegel's mother-in-law recounted at secondhand (in December 1817) Marie's sister's (Sofie Marie Friederike's) recollections of her stay with Hegel and Marie in Heidelberg – Ludwig is conspicuously *not* mentioned, although Karl and Immanuel are described affectionately, a pattern that is maintained in a variety of letters for the next few years.[19]

That there were problems in integrating Ludwig into the family is hardly surprising. The difficulties inherent in the situation are familiar: Having been abandoned by both parents at an early age, Ludwig almost certainly had his share of personal and psychological difficulties, and the Hegel family had trouble dealing with him; moreover, there were the usual problems of the time associated with the relations between stepchildren and stepmothers. Even Hegel himself seems to have taken in Ludwig more out of a sense of personal responsibility than out of any deep sentiment for the boy. The result was unfortunately none too happy for all concerned, especially for Ludwig himself. Ludwig seems to have been treated more or less as a foster child, not as one of the "real sons" in the Hegel family.

The stresses of the move to Heidelberg also served to delay Ludwig's own arrival in Heidelberg. One of the reasons for Ludwig's delayed arrival had to do with Marie Hegel's recuperation from another miscarriage. It was not clear where they were going to be living until more or less at the last instant Paulus secured an apartment for the Hegel family, a place in the suburbs of the city – although the site today is more or less squarely in the center of the city – with a good view of the mountains, a pastoral view of the landlord's "large farm," around which there were "cows, horses, and the barn" and fields of wheat.[20] Paulus also secured a couple of maids for the Hegel household, since Marie Hegel was expecting another child (which, according to her note in the margin of one of Hegel's letters to Paulus on September 16, 1816, was due in January or February of 1817).[21] Besides that, there were the usual stresses and strains accompanying any family's moving – Hegel even complained that "I have pointed out a hundred times to my wife how everything on my side has already been made ready, while she for her part has put the fly in the ointment." Matters then became even worse when Marie Hegel suffered another miscarriage (because, according to Hegel, she was "exhausted by the strain of packing").[22] Although she recovered well enough, it clearly prevented her from accompanying Hegel to Heidelberg, and thus he had to leave without her. Marie's need to remain in Nuremberg and her recovery meant that Ludwig's reception into the family had to be postponed.

Hegel arrived alone in Heidelberg on October 19, 1816, nine days before his inaugural lecture. Thrilled finally to be a professor at a university and fairly content with his surroundings, he was nonetheless quite distressed about having to be away from his family. He began writing his wife letters every day remarking on his loneliness and on how especially with the onset of winter he missed seeing her and the children. Mrs. Paulus, an old friend who always joked with Hegel, played cards with him and in general saw to it that he did not fall into complete despondency.[23] But despite his initial loneliness, Hegel was satisfied with his Heidelberg surroundings; he remarked in his letters to his wife how much he liked, for example, the lack of pretentiousness in Heidelberg social life and how family-oriented the place seemed to be.[24]

Marie's Sister and Brother in Heidelberg

Not only did Marie and the two sons (and a short time later, Ludwig) soon join Hegel in Heidelberg, Marie's sixteen-year-old sister, Sofie Marie Friederike von Tucher – whose nickname in the family was "Fritz" – joined them as well. The whole group probably arrived some

time in the first or second week of November, since Marie's mother
(who accompanied Marie, the two sons, and Fritz) from Heidelberg
herself returned to Nuremberg on November 18, 1816.[25] (Ludwig came
in April, 1817.) Fritz stayed with Hegel and Marie until October 3,
1817, at which point Marie's younger brother, Christoph Karl Gottlieb
Sigmund Freiherr von Tucher (who was nineteen at the time), came to
live with them while studying at Heidelberg, where he attended Hegel's
lectures. If Hegel at first felt lonely in Heidelberg, that feeling soon
vanished; within a very short period, his house was full of family
members.

Hegel's role as the titular head of Marie's family continued in Heidelberg. He ended up having to take his (then seventeen-year-old)
sister-in-law Fritz to several balls during the *Fasching* (carnival) season
and accompanied her to several other balls afterwards and even on a
trip to Mannheim for a ball there. (There is no record anywhere that
Hegel resented accompanying the pretty young Fritz to any of these
affairs, even if during the entire ball he had nothing other to do than to
sit in a chair on the sidelines as a chaperone. Marie's mother was
extremely grateful to him for performing this task – "it was no small
sacrifice for Hegel to sit during the entire ball on account of Fritz,"
Marie's mother told her.)[26] Moreover, after Julius Niethammer (Immanuel Niethammer's son, who was Fritz's age) made some romantic over-
tures to Fritz, Hegel was forced to intervene in the matter after some
rather agitated letters from his mother-in-law about the affair. (She was
not amused by Julius's somewhat cavalier attitude toward romance,
since he was clearly too young and unestablished in the world to be in
a position to propose marriage. This was, moreover, not the first time
that Hegel had had to intervene with Julius on account of Fritz; earlier
in Nuremberg, he had been called in to chide young Julius for his bad
behavior in not having asked Fritz to dance during a ball there; a couple
of years later he was having to chide Julius for showing too much
interest in her.)[27] Hegel also had to turn away an unnamed but persist-
ent suitor who wished to propose marriage to Fritz.

He was also entrusted with looking after Marie's brother (addressed
as "Gottlieb" in the family). Gottlieb came to stay with the Hegels
immediately on Fritz's departure. He had been a student at the *Gymnasium* in Nuremberg for which Hegel was the rector, and, having lost
his father at fifteen, looked up to his sister's husband for advice (some-

thing supported and encouraged by his mother). His mother had become particularly worried about him after his graduation from the *Gymnasium* and his initial studies in Erlangen, where she felt he had become "far too modern" for her tastes (as she put it in a letter to Marie on December 4, 1816).[28] In her view, he was also becoming far too involved with "modern" political developments in Erlangen. (She was completely correct about his involvement.) Because of this, Gottlieb's mother decided it would be better if Gottlieb were to study in Heidelberg and live with his sister and brother-in-law; Hegel's mother-in-law also made it clear that it would be appreciated if he were to instill some order and discipline into Gottlieb and if Hegel were to provide "male direction" for Gottlieb and receive him in a "fatherly" way.[29] Hegel did this, and it is clear that he and Gottlieb established a good relationship; Gottlieb even attended Hegel's lectures, and Hegel gave him a personally autographed copy of the *Phenomenology*. Hegel in fact even intervened with his mother-in-law to permit Gottlieb to attend some political meetings that she had originally wished to prevent him from attending.

Hegel and his wife took numerous boat trips up and down the Rhine, took excursions to some of the pretty towns in the region around Heidelberg (such as Schwetzingen, with its lovely castle gardens), and in general seemed fully to enjoy their surroundings and their new life. His adoring mother-in-law continued to send him his favorite Nuremberg delicacies (the local bratwurst, *Lebkuchen*, and other such treats) as gifts. It is clear that Hegel both identified with his new role as paterfamilias and found it quite satisfying indeed.[30]

The New Universities in the Post-Napoleonic Order

Heidelberg University

Although Hegel found himself quite satisfied with his surroundings in Heidelberg, he was nonetheless a bit taken aback by an initial lack of enthusiasm for his courses on the part of the students. In a letter to his wife (October 29, 1816) he complained that at one session he only had four students; he also noted that he had been led to understand that the altogether practical-minded students at Heidelberg required at least a half year to warm up to new and unknown professors. Students were required to pay lecture fees directly to the professor giving the lectures, and for many professors such fees amounted to substantial and sometimes even essential additions to their incomes. Hegel's concern for his lack of students was thus not merely a matter of vanity of his part, since a lack of students quickly translated into a lower standard of living.

Although this lack of students quickly changed – in one class on the Encyclopedia of the Philosophical Sciences he soon came to have twenty students, in another class on the History of Philosophy he had thirty students, and in his lectures on Metaphysics and Logic, he had seventy students[31] – Hegel was still at first probably a bit surprised to find Heidelberg to be not quite what he had most likely been expecting. He had been expecting or at least hoping for Heidelberg to be another Jena (with the exception, of course, that this time he would be adequately paid). In 1805, for example, in his letter to Johann Heinrich Voss seeking his help for a position at Heidelberg, Hegel claimed that the spirit of Jena, with which Hegel had so much identified, had moved to Heidelberg and taken root there and that he wished to join the migration of the spirit of Jena to Heidelberg.[32]

That Heidelberg should have had any claim to being the new Jena was almost as surprising as Jena's claim to have been the intellectual and cultural center it once was. The university at Heidelberg had been a particularly antiquated and unimportant site of orthodoxy during the eighteenth century. However, in the 1803 shakeup of Germany at the hands of Napoleon, the area in which Heidelberg was situated fell out of the hands of the Palatinate and the Bavarian Wittelsbachs and into the hands of the Badenese royal family, who proceeded to order a complete reorganization of the university in the same year. As Jena's star began to sink in the early 1800s, Heidelberg (along with the newly reorganized university in Halle) stepped in to fill the role in German intellectual life that the university in Jena had begun to play, and it quickly became known as a center for the kind of Romanticism that had been born in Jena but which had then fled it. Major events in the development of Romanticism – such as Arnim's and Brentano's collection of German folk songs, *Des Knaben Wunderhorn* – took place at the university in Heidelberg during this period. The university itself thus made a claim to being the successor to the Jena ideal of a university that was to present a unified body of modern knowledge – with philosophy as the faculty that was to integrate the other bodies of knowledge – and to train a new post-Napoleonic modern elite of young men of *Bildung* who were to run the central institutions of the modern world. Heidelberg had even gone so far as to reorganize the whole conception of the various "faculties" of the university into "sections," thus indicating its modernity in an even more striking way.[33]

From being an insignificant backwater university that had only about forty students at the turn of the century, the reorganized Heidelberg had by 1808 grown into a major center of intellectual life attended by more than four hundred students. (Three-quarters of those students were studying law or cameralistics, itself an indication of the kind of practically oriented student who tended to go to Heidelberg.)[34] But the tension between the Romantics at Heidelberg and the career-oriented, practical-minded students was to prove too much, and, just as they had done at Jena, the Romantics began to desert Heidelberg for what they hoped would be more hospitable surroundings. By the time Hegel finally arrived in Heidelberg, the spirit of Jena, which he had hoped to find there, had in fact long since departed; philosophy and the neo-humanism that had developed at Jena (and with which he and Niethammer had hoped to reform the Bavarian school system) had not yet found a secure footing in the kingdom of Baden. Indeed, by 1817, it was becoming clear to all those surveying the scene that the spirit of Jena was best represented by the university in Berlin, not by the one in Heidelberg – but Hegel's wife, Marie, had ruled out a move to Berlin. Just as had happened at Jena, Hegel arrived on the scene as the scene itself was beginning to shift.

Nonetheless, there were many features of Heidelberg that fitted Hegel's idea of what a modern university that built upon the model of Jena would look like. It was oriented around the idea of *Bildung*, of training young men for the leading roles in modern life by inculcating a sense of self-direction, culture, and education; and it was a post-Enlightenment university in its dedication to *Wissenschaft*, "science," and not just the "learnedness" (*Gelehrsamkeit*) that had characterized so many Enlightenment universities. The older model of the professor as a "learned" individual who had within his grasp a great body of codified (and ossified) knowledge had become an object of scorn throughout Europe by 1800, especially to the generation to which Hegel belonged. Likewise, the emphasis on publication as a mark of a professor's "learnedness" that had emerged at the end of the eighteenth century had in the neo-humanists' view only led to professors' publishing large compendia of old knowledge – collections of, as it were, everything that had been known about a particular field, with very little original research or thought going into them. This was viewed only with the greatest scorn by the new generation of reformers; not pedantic compendia and compilations of what others had already said but new knowledge, *Wissenschaft*, with its emphasis on dynamism and discovery and on the ordering and relating of these pieces of knowledge to each other in the context of lectures and seminars, became the watchword of the reformers.

For Hegel and most of his generation, Jena's dedication to *Wissenschaft*, to the construction of rigorous theory, to a more dynamic model of learning and thinking, and to a different, nondisciplinarian relation between professor and student was clearly the preferable model of university life. The older universities had only trained and drilled people into a certain type of orthodoxy by virtue of a certain type of rote learning, and consequently, the civil servants they produced had learned things almost solely by the book and without imagination; in turn, those graduates of the older university had become the model officials of the German Enlightenment's version of the "machine state" (against which the author of the "The Oldest System Program of German Idealism" had inveighed). However, after the crushing and humbling defeat of the Prussian "machine state" by Napoleon at Jena in 1806, that ideal of learning and of the university itself had fallen from favor. Faced with the daunting task of coming to terms with the post-Napoleonic restructuring, the various reorganized governments of Germany began looking for some new way to train their civil servants so that they did not find themselves out of step with the times once again. The new, Jena-inspired university seemed therefore to be the kind of thing that could supply the new kind of educated civil servant for which they were looking.

Consequently, the number of students attending universities increased rapidly (nearly doubling between 1800 and 1835), and in places like Heidelberg, grew at an even greater rate. The new ideal of *Wissenschaft*, moreover, put new demands on those students. They could no longer be the loutish brawlers famous from earlier times, protected by the traditional medieval corporate immunities; they had to become the serious, even "moral" students committed to *Bildung* and the life of the mind that Fichte had tried to establish at Jena.

The Rise of the Philosophical Faculty

Likewise, the universities themselves and the professors within them had to change their ways. The central faculties of the traditional German university were law, medicine, theology, and philosophy. (The philosophical faculty included subjects such as history and the natural sciences.) One of the key features of the newly emerging university based on *Wissenschaft* and *Bildung* was the way in which the philosophical faculty came to be central to the mission of the university as the place where all the other subjects taught at the university were to be unified and ordered. (Niethammer's "General Normative" for schools in Bavaria, for example, had attempted to build this newly emerging centrality of the philosophical faculty into the curriculum of the *Gymnasium*.) Both law and medicine – and, increasingly, theology itself – thus began to understand themselves as guided and ordered by the philosophical faculty and, as Fichte had argued at Jena and then later at Berlin, within that faculty itself, the philosophers per se were to be the leading lights.[35]

That the philosophical faculties rose to this position had in part to do with the decline of theology as a central faculty in the university. Part of that decline was surely based on the decreasing number of jobs for trained theologians; but another and equally important part of it was the attempt by the modern faculties to free themselves from the chains of theological orthodoxy. Most of the disputes between the university and the ruling orders had traditionally been about theological matters and had usually had to do with some alleged violation or undermining of accepted orthodoxy. Kant himself, for example, had run into trouble for his writings on religious issues that challenged the governing orthodoxy. The modern concern with freedom, however, which had been so intoxicatingly developed first by Kant himself and then by his idealist successors at Jena, gave the modernist reformers a firm motivation to cut the university free from its older theological bondage, and the philosophical faculty naturally emerged as the most likely candidate to supply the missing foundation for university studies that theology had partially supplied in the past. Indeed, it was in part in order to escape from such theological control of the university that the professoriate put the philosophers in charge, and even more strikingly, many of the leading theologians of the period also enthusiastically subscribed to this view. For example, the theologians Daub and Paulus were the key figures in bringing Hegel to Heidelberg (Paulus was also a good friend of Hegel's), and Schleiermacher, the great theologian of the university at Berlin, openly lamented losing Hegel to Heidelberg, remarking in a letter in 1816 to a friend (a professor at Heidelberg), "It may be that our minister von Schuckmann is responsible for your having snatched Hegel away from under our noses. God knows what is to become of our university when it so sorely lacks philosophers."[36]

The decline in the status of theology was accompanied, naturally enough, by a huge drop in enrollments during this period. But, interestingly enough, enrollments in philosophy, at least at Heidelberg, did not necessarily increase as a result of the decline in theology. The reformed civil services were, after all, to be staffed with the graduates of the new universities, most students viewed the university simply as a path to a promising career, and since cameralistics and law seemed to be the surer path to a career, most students took that path and enrolled in that faculty. What Schiller had dismissively characterized in his address in Jena as the *Brotgelehrte* (the students studying for their "bread," that is, their careers, instead of for the joy of learning itself) had in fact become the main constituents of the new university. This put the students in direct conflict with the way that the professors understood themselves and the university at which they were working and gave a tremendous impetus for the philosophical faculty further to assert its supremacy in the curriculum and in the wider life of the country.

Tensions in the New Universities

The particular tension between a faculty devoted to *Wissenschaft* and students devoted to their careers had a special edge to it at Heidelberg, which was populated with students studying for a career but who had already absorbed a certain Romantic view of the world. Many students had been drawn to Heidelberg because of the way in which the faculty and the Romantic writers associated with the university had developed a form of Romanticism in light of an emerging sense of German identity. The bucolic setting of the town and its famous ruined castle on the hill (something that particularly caught the imagination of a generation becoming fascinated by the spectacle of ruins of all sorts) did nothing to diminish its appeal as a worthy Romantic successor to Jena. However, by the time Hegel arrived, the Romantics had themselves long since departed Heidelberg, and the more professorial, rationalist faculty soon found themselves at odds with students who were attempting to lead what was already by then the emerging myth of romantic student life at "old Heidelberg."

But in making this break with the past and setting up the university on the model of *Wissenschaft*, the reformers were also setting themselves on a course that was to lead to some unexpected collisions between themselves and the ruling powers. From then on, the main areas of dispute between the universities and the ruling powers were not so much *theological* as *political* – that is, they were concerned not so much with violations of theological orthodoxy as with breaches of political observance. This was only to be expected as states gradually assumed the financing of the universities and as the traditional medieval corporate structure of self-rule and corporate immunity vanished in the wake of the revolutionary restructuring of German life.

Several other things conspired to make life particularly chaotic for the professors in the new university. Student enrollments were going up, and professorial status and pay were on the rise; but revenues were not increasing as rapidly, inflation was running high, and the reorganized, rationalized governments were now completely footing the bill for universities in a time of fiscal chaos for themselves. Since the newly reorganized universities were more or less making up the rules as they went along, there were ongoing struggles for authority as to who was to decide which issues about university life. Roughly, those struggles broke down into conflicts between attempts by the professoriate to run the university and attempts by the government to run them. This was particularly evident in the matters of appointments. The government tended to think that since they were footing the bill, they had the right to appoint all the professors, and, not unsurprisingly, the faculty resisted that view. The government was also interested in teaching the large numbers of new students for as little money as possible, which made the government especially receptive to hiring "extraordinary" professors or *Privatdozenten* ("private academics"). The "ordinary" professors (such as Hegel) drew respectable salaries; the "extraordinary" professors, on the other hand, drew either very little salary (often only 300 Thalers or less, in contrast with Hegel's 1,500 Thalers) or even none at all; and the *Privatdozenten* drew no salary at all. Both "extraordinary professors" and *Privatdozenten* therefore had to have money from independent sources (in other words, from their families) in order to support themselves; and they were encouraged to take these positions by the lure or merely the hope of one day securing "ordinary" professorships for themselves. Since part of the "ordinary" professor's income depended on student lecture fees (along with fees for reading doctoral work and for participating in doctoral examinations), the low-paid "extraordinary" professors and *Privatdozenten* came into direct competition with the "ordinary" professors for students and the money they brought with them. This of course gave the faculties powerful incentives to make the entrance requirements to the professoriate more stringent so that there would be less competition for student fees.[37]

With regard to these kinds of disputes, Hegel on the whole displayed a certain (and in some ways, uncharacteristic) humility, claiming that since he had been out of the university for so long he felt he needed to defer to his colleagues' more seasoned judgments. (He even remarked in a letter to Niethammer about how he was "only a beginning university professor.")[38] But he was also quite forceful when it came to issues of professorial authority and autonomy. He was at the same time always very open to the particular needs of the students; in cases in which worthy students lacking money were applying for their doctoral degrees, Hegel would consistently waive his fees for examining them even though it clearly meant a reduction in his own income.

A typical struggle over authority between the government and the faculty in which Hegel was involved was the case of Joseph H. Hillebrand. Hillebrand had been a Catholic priest teaching at a Catholic seminary who had lost his teaching position after he converted to Protestantism. He then applied to be an "extraordinary" professor in Heidelberg and found support in the Badenese interior ministry for this. The Badenese ministry made his permission to teach conditional on his getting the status of doctor from the philosophical faculty. (Why the Badenese ministry was interested in his case is not clear.) The faculty countered with the claim that Hillebrand could not be allowed to teach until he had submitted an appropriate *Habilitation*, the traditional work that bestows the right to teach. Some, like the dean of the faculty (Johann Heinrich Voss), however, thought that the matter was moot, since the government had appointed Hillebrand and that was that.

Others were not so sanguine, Hegel among them. Hegel complained that the request that the faculty grant Hillebrand a doctorate was superfluous if the government really was to take unto itself the authority to appoint people to academic positions without any consultation with the faculty, and he was therefore certainly not ready in this case (as he was in so many other cases) to waive his examination fees. Hegel's friend, the classicist Creuzer, joined him and called for the universities to assert their "dignity" against governments. When Hillebrand nonetheless submitted a written work to the faculty – he submitted something he had written while still teaching at the Catholic seminary – the faculty castigated it; among the charges made against him was that he "understood no Latin" and that his work was composed mostly of "windy phrases." Although firmly on the side of upholding the rights of the faculty to oversee new appointments, Hegel was nonetheless concerned to see that Hillebrand was treated fairly and did not become a mere vehicle on which the faculty could vent its displeasure with the government's interference in the university. On reading a book by Hillebrand on pedagogy (which implicitly criticized Niethammer's own work), Hegel noted that although "it cannot be taken for a scientific work," that was not "its goal," and that it moreover displayed a good "acquaintance with many philosophical thoughts"[39] The faculty was not nearly as kind as Hegel and demanded a Latin dissertation and a Latin oration from Hillebrand before the doctorate could be conferred on him. Tempers continued to heat up over the matter, but after Hillebrand finally managed to satisfy most of the faculty that he had done the necessary work for the doctorate (after having already been appointed by the government as "extraordinary professor"), many felt quite relieved that matter was over and that they had preserved their rights to examine candidates. Hegel sarcastically commented on these reassurances by noting that he agreed that "the *rights* of the faculty have been preserved, since from this particular confrontation it has become clear that the faculty has no such rights."[40]

There were many other such cases, although none that raised tempers quite as much as Hillebrand's case. As the philosophical faculty began to emerge as the central faculty of the university, disputes between it and other faculties naturally arose. When a student (Franz Anton Regenauer) who had won a prize in cameralistics offered himself as a candidate for a doctorate from the philosophical faculty, the issue arose as to whether the faculty from the cameralistic section were to be allowed to be among the examiners for the degree in philosophy. (The degree could be conferred after an examination by the faculty; the examination consisted of answering some questions posed by the faculty.) The philosophical faculty rejected the cameralistic faculty's claims to be among the examiners, claiming that the philosophical faculty and they alone were competent to decide if the philosophical doctorate was to be conferred on Mr. Regenauer. Regenauer's claim, however, that the cameralistic faculty should question him for the philosophical degree in fact rested on a government edict of 1812 that seemed to require exactly that. In the debate, Hegel tried to compromise between the factions by arguing that the 1812 edict only had to do with "dissertations" (and not examinations) that "were to have at the same time philosophical and cameralistic content" and thus that the philosophical faculty had in fact the right to examine Regenauer by themselves. (This put Hegel on the side of Johann Voss, the dean of the faculty, who himself had sided with the philosophers.) But when the faculty required a written work from Regenauer, Hegel also argued that their original timetable was unfair to Regenauer and should be extended. (Regenauer later dropped the matter, pleading that he did not have the necessary seventy-four florins for the required doctoral fees.)[41]

Not everything turned on such weighty issues. When another student (a Mr. Franz Jakob Göbel) pleaded that he needed to put the examination quickly behind him because he had been offered a position as a professor in the Netherlands (apparently as a professor of mathematics), the dean told the faculty that in his opinion, they should expedite things. But a quick examination by some of the professors discovered great gaps in Göbel's knowledge of Greek and mechanics, and Hegel noted that to his surprise Göbel showed no understanding at all of the difference between integral and differential calculus or of the fine points of mechanics, which made Hegel all the more skeptical that any university would actually make such a person a *professor* of mathematics; if the faculty were to bestow a doctorate on Göbel, Hegel sarcastically noted, "the doctoral diploma would easily appear here as an instrument to compensate for his lack of knowledge."[42] But when the faculty finally agreed that Göbel's rewritten work was of sufficient quality, Hegel went along with their judgment. When a Mr. James Bothwell applied for the doctorate but was turned down (for being in the eyes of one of the relevant faculty members "superficial, limited ... and a shameless windbag"), he then applied for the right to conduct lectures and somehow managed to enlist the vice-rector of the university in his cause; Hegel was only too happy in that case to concur with his colleagues (who had since come to judge Mr. Bothwell even more harshly as a "liar and a braggart" about his credentials) and to deny Bothwell any consideration at all.[43]

Underlying all of Hegel's participation in the struggles over authority between the government and the university and over the newly emerging standards of learning to be expected from students was a deeper view of the role of the university and the role of the professor in the new university. As a professor in the newly reorganized university, Hegel understood himself as a man of *Bildung* and a professor devoted to *Wissenschaft*, something he shared with many other colleagues. Moreover, in understanding himself in this way, he understood himself as playing a role and occupying a social position that cut across other more familiar and more traditional social divisions, such as class and estate. Indeed, the ideal of the modern university as the linchpin of modern life was not, in Hegel's eyes, a matter of social *class* at all; it was a matter of being part of a more universalistic body of people who were not bound by the particularistic strictures of hometown life. Hegel was not in his own eyes offering up a "bourgeois" philosophy; as he would have understood himself, he was not attempting, for example, to replace the power of the aristocracy with that of the newly energized bourgeoisie. In fact, Hegel (and people like him) would not have thought of themselves as particularly "bourgeois" at all. They would instead have thought of themselves as men of *Bildung*, as not tied to *any* particular social class, since an aristocrat, a bourgeois, or even the son of a ribbon maker (such as Fichte) could become a man of *Bildung*. In fact, they would be at odds with many of the more obviously "bourgeois" values around them. That one of the great disputes in the university was that between the faculty (who were devoted to making the university a center of *Wissenschaft*) and the students (who tended to look on the university as a way to advance their careers) only illustrated the way in which people like Hegel would have thought of themselves as rejecting certain so-called bourgeois values without at the same time taking on any aristocratic affectations or necessarily identifying with aristocratic values. The university was to be the place where the particularisms –

whether regional or class-based – were to be overcome in the new, post-Napoleonic modern collection of German states, and the men of *Bildung* were to be the universalistic "movers and doers" of that social order.

The structure of the modern world, which had been so hazy in 1806, now seemed to be coming into focus, to be gaining a sharper edge and determinacy before Hegel's eyes. At this point in his life, nothing in his entire life experience seemed to be at odds with the philosophy he had begun in Frankfurt and Jena and worked out in Nuremberg; if anything, life around him seemed only to be confirming it. In light of his experience, Hegel was becoming more and more convinced that his philosophy was in fact the account that the modern world had been implicitly seeking in order to understand for itself how its attempt to base itself in freedom was in fact a real possibility and not a historical illusion. Although Heidelberg was not the central attraction it had been a few years before, nonetheless Hegel had good reason to believe that his own life, his philosophy, and the modern world in general were now finally achieving a kind of clarity about themselves and beginning to assume their proper shape.

Conviviality and Settling Down

Middle Age

Hegel was reentering the university at a relatively late stage in his life. At thirty, he had decided to prepare himself for a university career, and at forty-six, he was only acquiring for the first time a university position that actually paid him an income on which he could live (and, moreover, live quite comfortably, even if he did complain about the high rate of inflation then prevalent in all of Germany). During his period in Heidelberg, short as it was, Hegel had begun to slow down his pace of work, to enjoy his middle-aged family and professional life, and to learn to be comfortable in his own skin. His frequent excursions for boat trips and visits to local scenic spots with Marie alone, with the entire family, and in the company of other Heidelberg friends were part of this. He was particularly enamored of the natural beauty of the region while at the same time apparently completely unmoved by the famous ruins of the Heidelberg castle that inspired so many contemporary Romantics (he never even mentions the ruins); he enjoyed standing at his window in the house he had rented, staring out at the wafts of mist drifting down from the neighboring hills; indeed, the students at the time did not take him to be particularly industrious at all.[44] (Like many of Hegel's admirers in the nineteenth century, his first biographer, Karl Rosenkranz, romanticized some of Hegel's habits. He took Hegel's wistful observations out his window to be periods of "Socratic reflection," periods when the great man was lost deep in thought; and he related a story that is almost surely apocryphal but which has gone down in Hegel legend, that one day as Hegel was taking a stroll, he became so lost in thought that when one of his shoes became stuck in the mud, he remained so deeply lodged in his reflections that he did not even notice his missing shoe and simply continued walking. Although the story fits the nineteenth century image of the "genius" fairly well, it is probably not true of Hegel, who was quite aware of his professional status, and who dressed in a fairly modern style. Rosenkranz himself notes that in his walks, Hegel was typically attired in his "gray trousers and gray jacket," obviously wearing what by then was the very fashionable English-inspired – and more or less modern – suit.)[45]

That Hegel was coming to be at ease for himself was not, however, as evident in his lectures. The anxieties that drove his speech impediment and that had proved so unfortunate in his lectures in Jena – where he was obviously less sure of himself and more nervous about the impact he was making – did not go away. His stuttering, and his gasping for words, nonetheless do make a bit less of a documentary appearance in Heidelberg. In both Jena and Heidelberg, people commented on Hegel's tormented lecture style, and the few comments in Heidelberg speak of a lecturer still unsure of himself before official bodies of people. In Heidelberg, Hegel remained rather wooden in his delivery, completely beholden to his lecture notes, possessed (as one hearer put it) of an "as it were tubercular" delivery, with the tendency to begin "every third part of a sentence or every third sentence with 'thus' " (which did not stop some other students, as always less in awe of their professors than the professors might have preferred, to note how many times "thus" appeared in a Hegel lecture and compare notes afterwards).[46] The accounts of Hegel as a *Gymnasium* teacher in Nuremberg make him out to be a relatively engaging and lively teacher; and while the accounts of his lecturing in Heidelberg were on the whole not quite so negative as they had been in Jena, it seems fair to conclude that Hegel's tranquil, satisfied life at Heidelberg, while lowering the level of his anxiety, did not eradicate it.

As with many people reaching middle age, Hegel was now able to reflect more on his own youth and on the changes that had overtaken him. In offering advice to Niethammer about Niethammer's son, Julius (who was then studying at Heidelberg), Hegel autobiographically noted, "I can imagine you are dissatisfied with the state in which you found him after a year and half at the university. My father was likewise said to have been incapable of being satisfied with me at that age." It is one of the few places where Hegel mentions his father; but it is clear that at the age of forty-seven, he had come to see his father's point of view in a way that he clearly could not have done earlier in life. In speaking to Niethammer about Julius, he further reminded him that although parents must maintain certain expectations for their children, it is necessary that young people experiment with different things in order to "learn by experience of its futility" – something with which he could at that point in his life identify – and noted that much in life both depends on luck. "We know what pains we had to take, and with what ultimate consequences. You and I would like to give something else to our sons – besides, they themselves are doing something quite different with themselves."[47]

Hegel clearly thought he had reached a watershed; his youth in the old regime of Württemberg was now something belonging to distant history; the youthful enthusiasm for the Revolution, the critical decision to become a professor in the new university that was only dreamed about in Jena, the tumult of the Napoleonic period, all were now historical relics; the new world, of which Hegel was now determined to be the theorist, was developing on all sides and, in 1817, seemingly in the right direction. The Revolution was now his past; the post-revolutionary modern life was the world in which he was living and was the only real world people like Julius Niethammer or his own children would ever know. Now he felt that he, like the world around him, could really settle down.

Social Life and Friendships

Hegel's social life in Heidelberg seems to have been mostly restricted to professors (unlike his life prior to Heidelberg and later in Berlin). In part this was due of course to the nature of a small town, but in part it was due to his finding among his fellow professors kindred spirits. Socializing in general in Heidelberg was infrequent – at least according to Hegel's own account – although (again according to his own account) it was nonetheless quite cordial.[48] Two of his closest acquaintances were theologians: Karl Daub, who had been instrumental in recruiting him to Heidelberg and who then converted to Hegelian philosophy; and Friedrich Heinrich Christian Schwarz, a professor of both pedagogy and theology. Hegel's other close acquaintance at Heidelberg was someone he had known (but not well) in Jena and Nuremberg: the jurist Anton Friedrich Justus Thibaut, one of the outstanding legal thinkers of the period, whose juristical ideas Hegel in large measure shared. Hegel was to participate in the many musical evenings that Thibaut staged at his house. Besides being one of the leading legal thinkers of his day, Thibaut was also a musicologist of no small repute and had a tremendous interest in what counted as "old" music at the time. It was probably at this time and partly under Thibaut's influence that Hegel began working out his ideas on music as part of his aesthetics; indeed, Hegel was intensely interested in those evenings at Thibaut's and often volunteered his own house for such gatherings. (Thibaut's musical evenings were the beginnings of the foundation of the "choral societies" that were to become the nineteenth-century replacement for the "reading societies" of the eighteenth century to which Hegel's parents belonged.)

Hegel also became well acquainted with Georg Friedrich Creuzer, the classical philologist and founder of the scientific study of mythology; Creuzer's work clearly influenced Hegel's thoughts on theology. Creuzer, one of the more respected classicists of the period, himself openly praised Hegel's understanding of the Greeks and his philological talents, and was equally open in his admiration for Hegel's immense learning.[49] (Creuzer himself had some notoriety; he had had a passionate affair with the young Romantic poet Karoline von Günderode, but had broken it off and returned to his wife after being nursed by his wife through a crucial illness; Karoline von Günderode then committed suicide in 1806. The whole affair was later brought to public attention in Bettina von Arnim's 1840 memorial tribute to her friend, *Die Günderode*; but at the time of Hegel's stay in Heidelberg, Creuzer's past was no doubt only an element of gossip among the locals.) Hegel and his wife took many of their excursions and boat trips in the company of these people and their families.

He also maintained his friendship with Sulpiz Boisserée and came to know his brother, Melchior. Sulpiz Boisserée had known Hegel in Nuremberg, and Boisserée had played a role in bringing Hegel to Heidelberg.[50] The brothers had (together with a friend, Johann Baptist Bertram) established an outstanding collection of paintings by old German and Dutch masters (both collected under the title "Old German"), which was unique for its time, and they had been exhibiting them in an older *Palais* in Heidelberg since 1810. (Goethe himself had made two trips to see the paintings.) With the awakening interest in German national matters, the collection garnered a bit of fame for itself. The collection itself was to have quite an impact on Hegel, since it stirred his thought about early Christian art and put him on the path of thinking that eventually led to his lectures on aesthetics in Heidelberg and Berlin. He was likewise to spend many evenings and outings with the Boisserée brothers (particularly Sulpiz).

The First Edition of the Encyclopedia

Although the *Phenomenology* had been Hegel's self-described "voyage of discovery," the *Logic* became more and more for him the main instrument for his rethinking and securing the rationality of modern life. Prior to Napoleon's creation of a new Germany, Hegel had been calling for a new order. Now, having seen his call answered – although not completely and certainly not in all its details – he became increasingly interested in defending and reforming that order in the face of what he took to be its enemies. That shifted his philosophical concerns even more fundamentally toward building his "system" based on the *Logic*, for although he had never relinquished his concern for how we came to be who we are, and with both how and whether that process of coming-to-be was rational, he became more and more dedicated to showing that who we have come to be is in fact something rational and sustainable in its own right, to defending and articulating the rationality of the post-Napoleonic world. In his own mind, Hegel began to think of himself less as a philosopher sketching out the birth of a new world, and more as the philosopher of *reform* for the new order that had now been born. The world around him had changed and, correspondingly, so had his idea of his system. His earliest idea of himself as "applying" philosophical thought to the needs of the time had reappeared, only in different form.

That slightly altered conception bore fruit in Heidelberg, where Hegel managed to finish and publish his *Encyclopedia of the Philosophical Sciences* in 1817. The *Encyclopedia* (subtitled "for use in his lectures") was arranged according to the way Hegel had proceeded in the *Gymnasium* in Nuremberg, that is, according to numbered paragraphs that would then serve as the basis for discussion and extrapolation in lectures. The *Encyclopedia* presented Hegel's whole system in very brief outline; it had a short introduction, a condensed version of the *Logic*, followed by a section on the philosophy of nature, which was then followed by a section on the philosophy of spirit (*Geist*). The section on the philosophy of spirit contained a small portion in it called simply "Consciousness," in which Hegel's Nuremberg condensation of the opening sections of his *Phenomenology* appeared. It also introduced a new term, "objective spirit," to describe the social and political institutionalizations of *Geist*, and a section called "absolute spirit," which repeated the *Phenomenology*'s distinctions among the religion of art (that is, Greek religion), revealed religion (that is, Christianity), and philosophy. (He had not yet separated "art" out into its own special section in the "system.")

In his public lectures on political philosophy in Heidelberg, Hegel filled out the bare bones of the section on "objective spirit" in the *Encyclopedia* into a full theory of modern political life, but he did not put those thoughts into book form until three years later in Berlin, when he published his *Philosophy of Right* in 1820.

Hegel used the Preface to the 1817 *Encyclopedia* to express his optimism about the role that his philosophy might play in the new post-Napoleonic order and how that order represented a decisive, even fateful rupture with the past. With undisguised enthusiasm, Hegel wrote, "The first of the phenomena touched upon here can in some measure be regarded as the youthful giddiness of the new epoch that has dawned in the realm of science just as it has in that of politics. If this giddiness greeted the sunrise of the rejuvenated spirit with reveling, and began enjoying the Idea at once without any hard labor, luxuriating for a while in the hopes and prospects that the sunrise offered, it also reconciles [us] more readily to its excesses because there is a kernel [of truth] at the bottom of it, and the morning mist that covers its surface is bound to clear spontaneously."[51]

Hegel's friend Sulpiz Boisserée helped to reintroduce Hegel to Goethe via Hegel's newly published *Encyclopedia*. In the *Encyclopedia*, Hegel defended Goethe's theory of colors. Goethe had argued against Newton, who asserted that clear, white light was a collection of all colors of the spectrum. Instead, Goethe had argued in favor of what for him was a more experiential theory of color, namely, that there are in fact two primal colors (white and black), and that all other color is produced simply by a combination of these two as they are blended together when passing through various clouded media. The clouded media force the two elemental and opposed colors of black and white to combine in new ways that then produce the colors of the spectrum; without passing through such clouded media, black and white produce only gray. (Goethe envisioned this as an application of his method of studying nature by attending to the *Urphänomen*, the "primordial phenomenon" as it appears to us in experience; all the various appearances of something can be interpreted as variations on the "primordial phenomenon," that which is presupposed in any encounter with particular instances of a phenomenon.) Few natural scientists took Goethe's theory seriously as a competitor to Newton's conception, whatever their feelings about Goethe's notion of the emotional effects of color. But Hegel defended Goethe's theory, and when Boisserée sent that section of the *Encyclopedia* to Goethe, Goethe was delighted to see a major thinker taking up his cause against so much opposition. This reestablished a link between Hegel and Goethe that was not afterwards to be broken. (It also did not hurt Hegel that his old nemesis, J. F. Fries, in a highly negative review of Hegel's *Logic*, also attacked Goethe's theory of color; Goethe was thus irrevocably put on Hegel's side and against Fries.)

Not everyone was enthusiastic about Hegel's idealism as he was presenting it at Heidelberg. In particular, the Heidelberg natural scientists, who were all committed empiricists, had little time for what they saw as the extravagance and obscurity of Hegel's version of German idealism, and there were discordant rumblings from them about Hegel's philosophy, which they tended to view as something that the philosopher had simply spun out of his own head and that had little if any connection to the real world. Hegel's published defense of Goethe's theory of color only served as decisive proof for them that he did not know what he was talking about, and some actually resented the leading role that philosophy (or at least Hegel's version of it) had come to play in the new structure of the university.[52] But those rumblings were distant and faint, and Hegel could choose to ignore them if he wished. On the whole, his stay at Heidelberg was proving to be the kind of success of which he had dreamed.

Jean Paul

In 1817, Hegel befriended another literary celebrity in Germany, the poet and writer Jean Paul (Johann Paul Friedrich Richter), who came for a long visit to Heidelberg during that period to see his good friend Heinrich Voss. The visit on the part of such a literary celebrity caused a small sensation in the community. The visit was sure to interest Hegel himself. Not merely was Jean Paul one of the best known and most widely read of the generation of early Romantic writers, he had also been one of the early enthusiasts of the *Phenomenology of Spirit*, privately extolling it to Jacobi. Unlike the Jena Romantics, who had taken Fichte's thought in a certain existential direction and converted Fichte's views about the revisability of all judgments into a doctrine of irony, Jean Paul had subscribed to Jacobi's "realist" criticisms of Fichte while at the same time developing his own special notion of the author's ironic distance and displaying a sense of ironic playfulness in his writings. For him, both "realism" and Fichtean/Schellingian "idealism" needed to be combined into a more stable view of the relation of the self to the world. (Realism, as he was fond of saying, is only the Sancho Panza of idealism.) His writings combined intricate, unsummarizable plot lines with frequent intrusions by the author (who identifies himself as Jean Paul but gives fictive characterizations even of himself), shifting points of view, extensive contrapositioning of scraps of information, elaborate plays on words, confused identities (Jean Paul, after all, coined the term *Doppelgänger*), and often brilliant comic asides. Moreover, Jean Paul had throughout his writings penned some wonderfully comical and sardonic spoofs of the foibles of the Jena style of idealism and the way in which one "system" rapidly replaced another during that period. A friend and admirer of Jacobi, who also got along quite well with Fichte personally, Jean Paul had satirized Fichte's notion of the "I" positing the "Not-I"; in his *Titan*, one of the characters is driven mad by thinking of himself as the absolute "I." His parodies of Schelling had even more bite: In *Titan*, one of the characters (Schoppe) worries that reading Schelling will make him like the drunkard who on urinating at night into a running fountain ends up staying the whole night at the fountain because he is convinced he has not yet finished. Given his own way of combining opposing strands within himself and the way in which so many of his own characters end up doing something that they had not been taking themselves to have been doing, Jean Paul was in a good position to appreciate the way in which Hegel in the *Phenomenology* had tried to show how the fundamental tensions at work in the various historical shapes of "spirit" inevitably lead them to undermine themselves and to turn out to have been doing quite the opposite of what they originally thought they were doing.

Hegel had, however, at first not been so enamored of Jean Paul, having taken an indirect swipe at him in 1802 in his polemical piece "Faith and Knowledge," in which he lambasted Jacobi's use of what he called Jean Paul's "sentimentalism" to criticize the Kantian philosophy. (Hegel's criticism of what he took as Jean Paul's "subjective arbitrariness" and sentimentalism was to reappear in his Berlin lectures on aesthetics.) But in the period between 1802 and 1817, Hegel had probably come to appreciate Jean Paul's ability to unite both profound religious doubt (bordering on atheism) with equally deep religious sentiment, along with his ability to combine ironic and critical detachment with a sharp, fervid, even sentimentalized attachment to family affairs. Moreover, both he and Jean Paul shared an attachment to the French Revolution, a disinclination for its Jacobin terrors, and an attachment to the ideals of freedom and cosmopolitanism that the Revolution had fostered (even if Jean Paul eventually backslid on that attachment).

Many of Hegel's contemporaries often saw Hegel only as a serious man completely absorbed in his work, but in fact Hegel (although not always easily) combined a detached, jocular temperament with a full earnestness and seriousness about his calling, and he no doubt saw a bit of that feature echoed in Jean Paul. (That Hegel wrote "Faith and Knowledge" during his period of collaboration with Schelling and that Jean Paul had particularly singled out Schelling for his satire had no doubt played some role in Hegel's initial disinclination toward Jean Paul; Hegel's break with Schelling and Jean Paul's appreciation of the *Phenomenology* no doubt played a role in his reappraisal.)

On July 11, 1817 (a Friday), Heinrich Voss held a "punch evening" for Jean Paul (a good friend of his) and some Heidelberg luminaries. (A "punch evening" was basically a drinking party for gentlemen, with an emphasis on drinking, smoking, and jovial conversation in the absence of any women – a custom at the time newly imported from England and considered very modern and very sophisticated.) Voss served up what he described as "sweet wine" in large tureens and made sure the glasses were always full. The evening was a great success – which is to say that all the men present got thoroughly plastered, told outrageous jokes and stories, and at the end could barely walk. At one point a local pastor jokingly tried to persuade Hegel to write a philosophy book for young girls that the pastor could use for instructional purposes. Hegel excused himself, saying that not only were his thoughts not really the kinds of things that young girls could grasp but that he was not proficient enough with language to write such a book. When the minister then proposed that Jean Paul could render Hegel's thoughts into acceptable and beautiful style, Jean Paul retorted by saying, "Ah, so that's how things are to be. Our old Hegel is to deliver the spirit, I'm to put a hearty body around it and a decorative garment, and then you want to take it to market!"[53] At this remark, everyone roared with laughter, making even more jokes about a possible Hegel/Jean Paul collaboration on a philosophy for schoolgirls. (Maybe one had to be there to appreciate it.) Hegel added his own jokes, being that evening, as Voss noted, "so unrestrained, glad-hearted, so popular (something that behind the podium he isn't always), that little was lacking for him to start writing that philosophy book immediately."[54] (It seems that a bit of wine always loosened up an otherwise too-serious Hegel and brought out his more jocular side.)

As the men were staggering out at the end of the evening, Hegel looked at Jean Paul and said (no doubt in slurred tones), "He has to become a doctor of philosophy." All present agreed that this was an excellent idea, and on Monday morning, the faculty (presumably now sober) met to vote on whether to award Jean Paul an honorary doctorate; one mathematician objected, arguing that Jean Paul's Christianity was somewhat doubtful and his morals even more so. In best playacting seriousness, Hegel defended the idea that Jean Paul was not only a Christian but had to be the best of all Christians and the most moral of men. Voss – a classicist – gave a long disquisition on the difference between bacchic intemperance and bacchanalian drunkenness vis-à-vis Jean Paul. In the end, all agreed on the bestowal of the honorary doctorate; the degree was inscribed on parchment, a due ceremony was held, and more parties began, followed by days and days of excursions and carriage rides to scenic spots.

Marie Hegel joined in the festivities too, although not quite in the way Hegel anticipated. An excursion to the pretty town of Weinheim was planned. Hegel could not make it on the original wagon, so Marie, along with Jean Paul, Heinrich Voss, and Heinrich Paulus's beautiful and talented daughter, Sophie Caroline Eleutheria Paulus, were to go on ahead. (In the fashion of importing sophisticated tastes from abroad, Sophie Paulus was addressed as "Mamsell Paulus," obviously a Germanization of the French form of address.) They took off at 8:00 A.M. on Sunday, with the ensemble noting that Marie seemed to be in a particularly good mood that day. There were stopovers for breakfast, hot chocolate and coffee (the women of course had to make the hot chocolate and coffee), and after a delightful lunch with even better wine (and apparently no small amount of it), they all took a stroll, then boarded their carriage again, at which point the four of them decided to play "spin the bottle" and began trading kisses. Marie was allowed to give Jean Paul eight kisses and Voss four; "Mamsell" Paulus had no such restrictions placed on her.[55] Marie was surely also unaware that Jean Paul had in the meantime developed a great passion for Sofie Paulus, which was requited on her side, and which assuredly had something to do with the erotic overtones of the carriage ride, even if it was limited to four adults playing "spin the bottle." Nothing was to come of it, although it did lead Jean Paul for a while to mull over divorcing his wife so he could establish a union with Ms. Paulus; in late September 1817, however, the twenty-eight-year-old Sofie Paulus married August Schlegel, almost fifty-one years old at the time, only to have the marriage fall apart within weeks. (That marriage was, curiously enough, the second time that Hegel was present to witness a rapidly failed marriage on August Schlegel's part.) Hegel later showed up with the children in tow, and Heinrich Voss vowed to keep the ensemble's mildly erotic secrets from Marie's husband and Jean Paul's wife. Hegel himself drank far too much and ended up with a bad hangover. (Perhaps the reason for Hegel's ardor for Jean Paul notably cooling during his Berlin period had to do with some disclosure by Marie; but perhaps not.)

As the parties and excursions with Jean Paul continued, a pattern became established. Whatever was said, Jean Paul would take issue and wittily defend some thesis that he knew would outrage or distress those present. Hegel would counter with some abstract, rigorous argument, which rolled off Jean Paul like the proverbial water off a duck's back.[56] For example, Hegel at one point gave his version of the myth of the fall as having to do with the symbolic presentation of the idea that by eating from the tree of knowledge and not of life, men had become like God, that self-consciousness was the impetus for their being driven out of paradise; Jean Paul then wittily retorted that such a view shows that God was therefore only jealous of mankind; Hegel would reply in all seriousness, and so on.[57] Great personal differences still existed between the two men; despite his combining of seriousness with ironic distance, Jean Paul always inclined toward sentimentalist solutions, whereas Hegel took that same opposition within himself in a different direction, always inclined to a more sharply critical, even rationalist view of things. Hegel saw religion as grounded in reason, whereas Jean Paul saw it more in the way that Jacobi envisioned it, as a leap, a matter of emotional and intellectual faith. One thus gets the impression that Jean Paul's wit might have been beginning to wear a bit thin on Hegel by the end of the visit. But by all accounts, Jean Paul found himself amused if not charmed by Hegel's continual insistence on pushing their conversations in a methodical, "scientific" direction.

Victor Cousin

Hegel also received a visit from a young Frenchman, Victor Cousin, who was later to play a crucial role in introducing Hegelian philosophy to France (and was also to play crucial roles in redesigning the French educational system and in French politics). Cousin was at the time a young instructor at the École Normale Supérieure in Paris who had arranged a research visit to Germany to acquaint himself with the much vaunted innovations in idealist philosophy going on there. He of course went looking for whom he thought was the most famous living idealist, Schelling, but did not meet him; on his own account, he quite by accident encountered instead Hegel, of whom he had heard little more than that he was one of the leading exponents of the Schellingian school of thought (indicating that even by 1817 the picture of Hegel as an exponent of Schellingian philosophy still had a life of its own). He acquired a copy of Hegel's newly published *Encyclopedia of the Philosophical Sciences*, which he found somewhat obscure and scholastic. During Cousin's short visit to Heidelberg, Hegel must have been in a somewhat downcast mood, since Hegel seemed at the time to Cousin to be a man who was unsure of himself and who had little commerce with others (something which clearly was not true of Hegel in his Heidelberg period). To his great surprise, Hegel took an interest in him, although, as Cousin put it, he understood little German and Hegel understood an equivalent amount of French. Their conversations nonetheless made a deep impression on Cousin, who was both struck and quite taken with the depth of Hegel's knowledge and the scope of his system. Cousin read Hegel's newly published *Encyclopedia* together with one of Hegel's French-speaking students, Friedrich Wilhelm Carové, and together they would go in the evening to Hegel's house for tea, where they would pepper Hegel with questions (although Hegel's answers, Cousin admitted, often did not exactly clear matters up). Cousin did not become a Hegelian, but, as Cousin put it to a friend, Hegel was one of those fellows to which one "attached oneself, not to follow him but to study him and comprehend him."[58] The two men nonetheless became good friends, and later in Berlin Hegel was to play a crucial role in having Cousin freed from political imprisonment.

Hegel's Relation to Students

Cousin expressed surprise that Hegel took such an interest in such a young, unknown fellow as himself, but had he known Hegel better, he would not have been so astonished. In Jena, in Nuremberg, and in Heidelberg, numerous comments were made about Hegel's openness to students, the course of their studies, and his continual willingness to spend the necessary time with them – provided, of course, that they showed an interest in "science." Although no cult around Hegel developed at Heidelberg such as later developed at Berlin, numerous students nonetheless apparently found in Hegel someone they could trust and who was always willing to offer advice and help.[59] An example of Hegel's openness to students was the experience of the Estonian aristocrat Boris von Üxküll, who after serving in the Russian army during the wars against Napoleon, decided that he needed to become educated and showed up at the age of twenty-four in Heidelberg, where he encountered Hegel; von Üxküll remarked on how patient Hegel was with his fledgling efforts at studying philosophy, indeed, how Hegel was even amused at the way in which von Üxküll found Hegel's books unintelligible; Hegel gave him some private sessions, suggested additional reading, and even gave him some instruction in algebra and Latin.[60] Von Üxküll remembered that in their strolls, Hegel would remark that he thought that "our overly clever times . . . could only come to be satisfied through a method, because a method subdues our thoughts and leads them to the real things themselves."[61] The Jena, *Wissenschaft* conception of the university required the professor to be not a disciplinarian of students (as he had often been in the older model of the university) but a *model* for them, an adult who was a living example for the students of the "scientific" approach to things, who showed them by his own practice what it meant to pursue a modern life with its anchoring in one's own practices. This fit Hegel like a glove, and many students responded to it.

In looking back on his Heidelberg years, one former student remarked that Hegel showed the students "that one must first learn quite a lot before one can make the world a better place."[62] The enrollments in Hegel's courses correspondingly began to rise dramatically; during Hegel's last semester in Heidelberg, one student noted to his father that "Hegel's lectures are so densely filled" and that Hegel was not "preaching politics but, on the contrary, science."[63] In his inaugural lecture at Heidelberg (on October 28, 1816), Hegel had already spoken directly about what he hoped for in his students and perhaps wistfully compared the storms of his past life to what he saw as the tranquillity of the modern world that finally had been born. Obviously addressing the students in his audience, Hegel remarked, "We older men who have grown up amid the storms of the time may call you happy who in your youth can devote yourselves undisturbed to truth and philosophy. I have consecrated my life to philosophy . . . I hope I may succeed in deserving and gaining your confidence."[64] During his stay in Heidelberg, a number of students seemed to have warmly responded to Hegel's offer. Hegel was obviously fully at home in his role and satisfied with the way things were settling down for him.

Hegel's Review of Jacobi

That Hegel was feeling more at home with both himself and his work also manifested itself in one of the first pieces Hegel wrote for the *Heidelberger Jahrbücher*, a respected learned journal of the time. Shortly after his arrival in Heidelberg, Hegel had been made the editor of the journal at Daub's insistence, and in 1817 he published a very appreciative review of the third volume of Jacobi's collected works in the journal. The review was striking both for the overview Hegel gave of his own thought and the conciliatory tone he adopted throughout the piece. Missing from his review was any expression of the sharp, polemical edge that had characterized him in his thirties in Jena, when as a member of the new idealist movement, he had felt obligated to make his mark and strike out at what he saw as the opposing views. Part of his contentiousness during that period reflected the passion with which he cared about the issues at stake; for him at the time, they seemed to be no less than whether a philosophy that joined forces with the dynamics of modern life and the Revolution would succeed, or whether what he saw as a series of philosophies (Jacobi's included) that were set at halting the spread of modern ideas would prevail. By the time he reached Heidelberg, though, he was a man in his late forties with a family, a good marriage, a secure, well-paying position, and, most importantly, the world seemed to be going his way. He and what he cared about had, so it seemed at the time, won the day. He could afford to be generous.

Hegel's review of Jacobi's work also offered him a chance to make his own philosophical views known to the public in a manner less burdened with the jargon and dense formulations that he thought to be obligatory in his more scholarly, *wissenschaftliche* works. Full of praise for Jacobi's contributions, sharp insight, and good-heartedness, Hegel's review tried to show how Jacobi's thought could best be understood as a rational but incomplete response to the way modern philosophical thought had developed, and to do this, he argued, one had to set all of Jacobi's works into the context of his much earlier confrontation with Kantianism and Spinozism in his 1785 book, *On Spinoza's Doctrines in Letters to Herr Moses Mendelssohn*. As Hegel saw it, the problems to which Jacobi was responding in 1785 were something like the following. By 1785, French philosophy had forsaken Descartes' revolutionary turn in favor of the

English Lockean approach. Unlike the Cartesian system, which had implicitly proposed that we "know thinking as the ground of being and cognize the contours of the latter only within and through the resources of the former," the Lockean approach had proposed to derive all thoughts from the "immediate givens of the world of appearance."[65] But since the Lockean approach then needed to provide an account of how the "givens" of our experience could in any way be counted as authoritative for our judgments, the French were led to postulate "an indeterminate *nature*" as the metaphysical ground to explain why those "givens" of experience took the shape they did. On the other side of the Rhine, the German Enlightenment had done much the same thing with regard to received religious tradition. Finding that all received religious teaching about the "divine world" could not be found within "self-consciousness," it had effectively dissolved that tradition, leaving behind only the "*death's head* of an abstract empty essence that *cannot be cognized*" and finding within its own self-consciousness "only finite ends and utility as the relation of all things to such ends."[66] Others in the German Enlightenment had reacted against that and insisted on the priority of their religious feelings, setting out to correct what they saw as the philosophical errors of the more rationalistic Enlightenment thinkers. (Hegel might have had in mind his old mentor, J. F. Abel, who had done just that.)

It was Jacobi's good sense, Hegel argued, not to be satisfied with either the French or the German Enlightenment approaches. Instead, Jacobi's acute insight led him correctly to see that "every consistent philosophy must lead to Spinozism"; he failed, however, to see that "true philosophy" must also go beyond Spinozism.[67] As Jacobi had understood, Spinozism has no real place in it for our self-consciousness; Jacobi had grasped, if only implicitly, that the Spinozistic conception of substance cannot account for how it is that itself, this substance, can come to *be aware of* itself and *give an account* of itself, and how this insufficiency in Spinozism requires a move not back to pre-Spinozistic metaphysics but forward to idealist doctrines of self-consciousness. Jacobi, that is, did not understand that our self-consciousness essentially involved "negativity," the way in which self-conscious reflection necessarily introduces a gap between our rationality and the deliverances of our senses; the capacity for self-consciousness, for reflection itself allows us to throw into question whether we can come to regard any of the

deliverances of the senses as *reasons* for belief or action. The senses
merely give us, as Hegel says, the "being" of things, *that* they are, not
what our *norms* (our "oughts") are to be. Although he took the first
step, Jacobi thus ultimately failed to draw out the logical consequence
of this line of thought: Since the senses themselves cannot sort out
which deliverances count as reasons and which ones do not, reason, as
Kant saw, must determine for itself and itself alone what does and does
not count as rational. Thus, although Jacobi intuitively understood that
the "absolute" must be something like "spirit" (*Geist*), that "God is
spirit, the absolute is free and personal," he ended up confounding this
with a subjectivistic approach to knowledge and action.[68]

The reason why Jacobi failed to make the idealist move was that his
whole approach was, so Hegel explained, that of the "reflecting consciousness, which, disassociated from reason's intuition distances itself
from the mediating movement of the cognizing of this intuition."[69]
(Hegel also made clear that by "reason's intuition" he meant "intellectual intuition.")[70] For Hegel, "reflection" has to do with the way in
which in making certain judgments about the structure of appearance,
we commit ourselves to norms about what accounts for the structure of
appearance; for example, the way in which judging that something *seems*
to be the case commits us implicitly to general norms about something's
really being the case – such as judgments that things subjectively seem
to be such-and-such commit us to general norms about the way things
objectively are. But such "reflective" structures, as Hegel believed he
had shown in his *Logic*, presuppose the structure of the "absolute Idea,"
the unity of subjective and objective points of view, although they
cannot make those structures of the "absolute Idea" explicit within their
own structures.

By arguing that Jacobi's thought only embodied "reflection," Hegel
thus put him in the same camp as Kant (a classification that Hegel had
already made in his 1802 essay "Faith and Knowledge"). But even
though Kant's thought, like Jacobi's, was a philosophy of "reflection,"
Kant had nonetheless explicitly recognized, unlike Jacobi, that reason
had to be self-determining. Hegel put it strongly: "It is more important,
however, not to overlook in this treatment of the Kantian critique of
reason . . . that it had also cognized *spirit's freedom* in its *theoretical*
aspect as the principle. This principle, in an abstract form, of course,
lies in the idea of an original-synthetic unity of apperception of self-

consciousness, which seeks in cognition also to be essentially *self-determining*."[71] Nonetheless, although Jacobi did not explicitly grasp this Kantian point, he was, Hegel argued, on the right track and in the same spirit; in this Jacobi was not to be confused with, as Hegel mischievously notes, some of his "friends" – he clearly meant in this context his old nemesis, J. F. Fries – who, not having understood at all what was important in Jacobi's criticism of Kant, thought that they could thereby improve on Kant by transforming the critical philosophy into an "anthropology . . . into a simple narration of facts that are lighted upon in consciousness," an enterprise in which "the cognition of them then consists in nothing further than a dissection of that which is lighted upon."[72] Jacobi, with his firm "intuition" of spirit as concrete, also rightfully rejected Fichte's system, which is only Kant's system "raised to a higher abstraction and carried through more consistently."[73]

But although Jacobi thus had a concrete, intuitive feel for how both Kant and Fichte required something like a conception of spirit, *Geist*, to make good on the promises of their idealism, Jacobi's intuitive feel for the concrete nevertheless led him mistakenly to suppose that the principles making up this notion of spirit, *Geist*, therefore had to come from the "heart." In this way, Jacobi repeated an Aristotelian error, which is to misconceive what is "universal" in "impulses and mores (*Sitte*)."[74] Jacobi thus failed to learn Aristotle's other lesson, namely, the recognition that "for the higher, cultivated cast of mind and its morality, a still more general cognition is required, namely that of what *ought to be*, not only its being present to itself as the *being* of a people, but rather *knowing* it as the being which appears as *nature*, *world*, and *history*."[75]

More perplexingly, in Hegel's eyes, Jacobi – whose criticism of the Enlightenment was that it inevitably led to a devaluing of humanity and a rejection of the inherent dignity of man – had failed to see that humanity's dignity lies precisely in the human capacity to assess our beliefs and impulses in terms of their rationality and to make that assessment effective – in other words, that the dignity of humanity consists in its autonomy. Jacobi's distrust of "reason" therefore was misplaced, indeed counter to what Hegel argued was the real and legitimate core of his antagonism to the prevailing Enlightenment philosophies against which he had rebelled. In opposition to Jacobi's assertion that only the "heart" could be the basis of, in Jacobi's words, the "majesty" and "dignity" of humanity, Hegel argued that "this grandeur and majesty can only be achieved through this infinite power of *abstraction from the determinate* and independence and freedom exist only through this power, as the inwardly concrete knows itself as that which is absolutely undetermined, the *universal*, the *good in itself*, and makes itself into that which is absolutely undetermined but at the same time exactly determines itself *from its own resources* and is concrete action."[76] Jacobi's appeal to the "heart" was implicitly an appeal to this kind of rationality; his appeal implicitly committed him to saying that there is something in our capacities for self-conscious reflection that implies that no mere "impulse" can count for us as a ground for action unless the "heart" endorses it. However, the "heart," which sounds so much more concrete than "reason," can offer no consistent guidance as to which impulses should be endorsed and which should not. To do that, one requires a grasp on some admirable way of life, a detailed conception of the "well-ordered state," as the ancients had long ago recognized.[77] Even worse, the appeal merely to the "heart," like Kant's appeal merely to reason, threatens to be powerless in the face of "romantic" understandings of ethics, and in light of key elements of human nature, such as the fact that often "people would rather be magnanimous than principled (*rechtlich*)," for example.[78]

On Hegel's view, both Jacobi and Kant had therefore demonstrated the insufficiencies of the "previous metaphysics" and thereby paved the way for an "altered view of the *logical*."[79] Whereas Hegel had in 1802 portrayed Jacobi's thought as essentially a misunderstanding of what was at work in modern philosophy, by 1817, after having befriended Jacobi, Hegel had taken to portraying him as an important thinker of the first order who had helped clear the ground for *Hegelian* idealism. The difference in polemical tone was hard to miss. Jacobi was no longer seen as an opponent; he was now seen as a precursor. Hegel no longer spoke as an outsider trying to get his voice heard; he now spoke as an insider putting the list of thinkers in his own time into what he saw as their proper order.

Political Engagement

While at Heidelberg, Hegel was to become engaged in three related controversies. One was the issue of constitutions for the new German states; the other was the debate surrounding the possible codification of

German law; the third was the role of the student fraternity movement (the *Burschenschaft*) in the development of German nationalism and the call for constitutional change. Hegel's more public involvement was with the issue of constitutionalism, but the results of his involvement in all three were to have an effect on his life and thought for many years to come.

Post-Napoleonic Germany and German Nationalism

After the defeat of Napoleon, many things were obviously up for grabs in Germany. Those elements in society that had lost out during the Napoleonic reorganization of Germany hoped to reacquire the privileges they had lost; those elements that had gained or prospered in the reorganization hoped to maintain what they had acquired; and those who had hoped for more radical change but had been disappointed by the French lack of enthusiasm for fomenting revolution in Germany now hoped that the time was ripe for such change. These elements contended with each other at the Congress of Vienna, each hoping to see its particular vision of Germany's future fulfilled.

Those who wished to turn the clock back, to reacquire the rights and privileges they had lost, came face to face with the fact that to do that they had to confront the powers that had emerged in the reorganization of Germany; and those powers were simply not willing to be set aside. Württemberg, Baden, and Bavaria, for example, had vastly extended their holdings, and the rulers of those lands had no real wish to return ecclesiastical properties or cede privileges back to people who would only oppose their further institutionalizing and securing of power. There were also those who pressed for a unification of all of Germany, but the band of people making such demands was small, ineffectual, and no match for the rulers of, for example, Prussia, Baden, Bavaria, and Württemberg, who did not have the slightest intention of ceding power in order to merge with some other political body. Smaller states also feared that they might be gobbled up by the larger states and that any unification of Germany would come only at their expense.

The compromise that was reached with all these groups was the *Bundesakte* (the articles of confederation among the various German states), presented by Metternich to the delegates at the Congress of Vienna on May 23, 1815, and enacted into law in late June 1815. As its

name indicates, it constituted only a confederation of states and actually
had only one institution attached to it, the *Bundesversammlung*, the Diet,
a bureaucratically restricted body that proved to be wholly ineffectual.
Article Thirteen of the *Bundesakte* also stipulated that every state in the
confederation was to have a constitution for the land reflecting its own
particularist concatenation of estates. (Each was to have what was called
a *landständische Verfassung*.)

But the very idea of a federal Diet inspired the small minority who
hoped for a unified Germany to press their case. Some eighteenth-
century ideas that had been floated in Germany about so-called German
identity began to be revived, expanded, and in the wake of the new
breed of Romantics, transformed. In particular, Fichte in his 1808
Addresses to the German Nation managed to give a much sharper formulation to a certain Romantic view of German identity in his argument
that the Germans were unique in being an "original" people still living
in their native land, speaking their original language, and maintaining
their original customs. The French and British, on the other hand, had
lost their original languages and did not live in the lands of their
ancestors and hence could not claim to be "original peoples." (This
assertion about the Germans was false on almost all counts and rested
on what has proved to be an even more dubious if not simply outright
false assumption that the "Teutons" described by Tacitus were in fact
the ancestors, both genealogically and culturally, of the "Germans" of
Fichte's own time; but at the time, the falsity of this view was not
widely known, if it was known at all.)

Hegel was as usual completely unmoved by what he saw (correctly)
as the phony Germanness of the whole movement; while in Nuremberg,
Hegel had already characterized such celebrations of ancient "Germandom" as "German-dumb" (*Deutschdumm*), and he had not changed his
mind in the meantime.[80] The interest in glorifying supposedly ancient
German customs and literature struck him as particularly silly. His
disdain for things like the *Nibelungenlied* had already been evident in
Nuremberg; in 1810, Clemens Brentano, the poet, wrote to his friend
Josef von Görres (the Romantic arch-nationalist) that in Nuremberg he
had recently encountered Hegel, who, he said, could only appreciate the
Nibelungenlied by "translating it into Greek."[81] In speaking of the *Ni-
belungenlied* in his lectures on aesthetics a few years later in Berlin,
Hegel caustically dismissed it, arguing that "the Burgundians, Chriem-

hild's revenge, Siegfried's deeds, the whole circumstances of life, the fate and downfall of an entire race, the Nordic character, King Etzel, etc., all this has no longer any living connection whatever with our domestic, civil, legal life, and with our institutions and constitutions. The story of Christ, Jerusalem, Bethlehem, Roman law, even the Trojan war have far more presence for us than the affairs of the Nibelungs which for our national consciousness are simply a past history, swept clean away with a broom. To propose to make things of that sort into something national for us or even into the Book of the German people has been the most trivial and shallow notion."[82] (Hegel could not have even conceived that some years later the *Nibelungenlied* would be made the basis of an immensely successful series of operas; at this period, Richard Wagner was only a child whose father had been killed at the battle of Leipzig.)

The Codification Controversy

An equally important controversy taking shape in Germany at this time had to do with the issue of the possible codification of German law, a debate also prompted by the changes forced on Germany by the Revolution and the Napoleonic adventures. It had become clear to many that traditional German law was in for a full overhaul.

The fragmentation of Germany and the hometown structure of much of its life had meant that legal systems varied not just from principality to principality but from town to town, and resting on top of the tangled, messy, incoherent patchwork of German law was an overlay of Imperial law from the Holy Roman Empire. In German law, local custom mingled piecemeal with Roman law and ecclesiastical canon law in all the various domains of the legal system. Added to all this mixture were the claims of "natural law," which by the seventeenth and eighteenth centuries had come to mean any study of the normative supports of the legal system that did not rely on any "positive" statute or ruling by judges. As a result, throughout the eighteenth century, there had been a rising demand for university-trained lawyers to help run the various principalities of Germany, and there had consequently been a dramatic upsurge in enrollments in the law faculties at universities. Even Hegel himself had tried (unsuccessfully, since it was against his father's wishes) to transfer out of theological into jurisprudential studies at

Tübingen, and Goethe, the Olympian figure of the period, had studied jurisprudence, worked as an intern at the Imperial Chamber of Justice at Wetzlar, practiced law for two years in Frankfurt, and even written a best-seller – *The Sorrows of Young Werther* – whose protagonist was a lawyer.

During the upheaval of the revolutionary, Napoleonic, and post-Napoleonic reform periods, the tangled complexity of German law came under particularly close scrutiny, and its possible reform became a topic of intense public interest. Much of the debate was focused on whether the great eighteenth-century codification of law begun in Prussia under Frederick the Great in 1746 and finally enacted in 1794 under Friedrich Wilhelm II should become the model for all German law. The "Prussian general code" had, after all, neatly codified great swaths of the formerly tangled and unruly Prussian legal practice into a series of neat paragraphs in nice, clear German (some of them only one sentence long). Some regarded the Prussian code as equal in cultural importance to Luther's translation of the Bible.[83] Especially after the collapse of the Holy Roman Empire in 1806 and the consolidation of various German states, the new and old principalities were pressed to decide whether to modify their archaic legal practices in light of the Prussian code of 1794 or the new "civil code" enacted under Napoleon in France in 1804. The debate was both intense and widely followed in all the German states, as it coincided and crossed paths with the debate over whether and in what form new constitutional structures for the reformed German states should be established.

The proponents of codification tended to be on the side of the new world opened up by the Revolution, and the opponents against. Those favoring the more traditional values of tradition and aristocratic privilege – and even the relative merits of Latin over vernacular German – were set against those favoring the new ideals of reason and modernity. In the great swirl of debate animating so much of German life during that period, the codification controversy gradually settled down into a match between two of the leading lights of German intellectual life in legal matters: Hegel's good friend Anton Friedrich Justus Thibaut, a professor of law at Heidelberg, and Friedrich Karl von Savigny, the great jurist at the Berlin university and later one of Hegel's fiercest opponents.

Thibaut had sparked the controversy with his highly respected pamphlet of 1814, "On the Necessity of a Universal Civil Code for Germany."[84] In that piece, Thibaut replied to the arch-conservative royal councilor in the court of Hannover, August Rehberg, who had published a piece essentially arguing that for Germany to be "Germany," it had to reject rationalistic, egalitarian "French" models of law and reinstate its own traditional system of particularistic, hometown laws. Thibaut had countered by arguing that it would be just as "German" and indeed was far more necessary to enact a rational system of law common to all the German states. The old system of law, after all, could not possibly be characterized as "German": Large parts of it were "Roman," and many of its Roman aspects in fact derived from the very period of the Roman empire when it was in its most steep decline. A truly "German" system of law would therefore take into account the particularities of Germany and its legal traditions but would render them into a unified, rational form. Although the creation of such a rational system of law would neither imply nor bring about the unification of Germany into one state, it would serve to obviate the cultural, even if not the political, fragmentation besetting Germany. Moreover, because it was to be written in the vernacular, it would be accessible to all German citizens and lessen the dependence of citizens and even judges on the opinions of a few trained jurists fluent in Latin; and it would embody the new ideals of reason, since it would be crafted by the new generation of reform-minded law professors at work in the various newly founded universities. As such, the codification of law would embody what is best and most rational in the German spirit.

Thibaut was the descendent of French Huguenots, firmly Protestant in his faith, progressive in his views, and middle-class in his outlook. (He and Hegel shared a certain common generational outlook on life, Thibaut being only two years younger than Hegel.) Thibaut, however, found his match in Karl Friedrich von Savigny (born in 1779), who was Thibaut's mirror opposite in many ways: Savigny was aristocratic, conservative, wealthy, Catholic (and, moreover, had married into a famous and staunchly Catholic family, the Brentanos), and one of the key intellectuals of German Romanticism. Like Schelling, Savigny had become a famous scholar at an early age, having published in 1803 a landmark book, *The Right of Property*, a study of Roman law.[85] (Curiously, like Thibaut, Savigny was also descended from Huguenots.)

Savigny had been working on the follow-up to his first book, which would deal with the law of the Middle Ages, but when Thibaut's pamphlet appeared, Savigny gathered up some of his extant manuscripts and promptly answered Thibaut with his own pamphlet in 1814, "On the Vocation of Our Time for Legislation and Jurisprudence."[86] In it, he repeated and extended some of the claims made famous in his first book. Law, he claimed, grows organically within the life of a people, and it is forever in the process of development. To understand law, one therefore needs a sense of history, so that both the very uniqueness of a people – a *Volk* – and a sense of how things fit into their organic context can be grasped together. Law is founded, in Savigny's terms, in the "shared consciousness of a people"; it is an expression of a specific way of life, of what he called the "spirit of a people," their *Volksgeist*. Indeed, what counts as "law" are simply the basic normative commitments shared by such a "people" that make that way of life what it is. Law therefore can neither be justified in terms of its serving any independently identifiable social function outside of itself nor as a component of achieving some "rational" end external to itself (as Savigny thought people like Thibaut mistakenly believed). Law is an essential component of the identity of a people, and that identity cannot be broken down into paragraphs or neatly codified parts. Law therefore needs no more justification than does the identity of a people itself; a "people" simply is what it is, and the goal of legal studies should be to articulate the basic commitments of that sense of identity, not to prescribe external goals to such a people. Any attempt to codify the identity of a people would be an attempt to render what is properly only understood as an organic whole into a dead set of abstract principles.

Savigny famously concluded that what "our time" lacked was precisely that understanding of the organic connectedness of law and the *Volksgeist*, which in turn made it entirely bereft of any real "vocation" for "legislation," although the new university at Berlin perhaps gave it the basis for a new form of "jurisprudence" (more accurately, a "science of law," *Rechtswissenschaft*, a term Savigny coined).[87]

Savigny and Thibaut agreed that a unified system of law was appropriate for the post-Napoleonic German states, they agreed that a unified system of law was necessary to overcome the fragmentation of German life, and they agreed that this neither required nor recommended unification into one German state. But they disagreed sharply on what that unity meant. For Thibaut, it meant a rational recasting of German law in light of the best post-Enlightenment thought coming out of the newly reformed universities; for Savigny, it meant getting clear on the true origins of the identity of the German "people" as a whole. Thibaut was in effect recommending a form of rationalism in the appropriation of the German tradition, while Savigny was recommending a more metaphysical, and certainly more Romantic, approach. Underlying Savigny's arguments was his belief that attempting to codify German law in the way in which Napoleon had authorized the codification of French law would in effect undermine German identity and would de facto be an attempt to transform the Germans into the French. Savigny managed to stake out this claim without at the same time endorsing Rehberg's entrenched reactionary position, which held that Germans simply needed to reassert their patchwork system of hometown laws.

The Burschenschaften

The Romantic view (expressed so brilliantly by Savigny) helped to inspire among many people an ideal of "authentic" Germanness as a basis for national consciousness. This "Teutonic" element gained strength with the establishment of new student fraternities (the *Burschenschaften*) at Jena in June 1815 (in which Hegel's old antagonist J. F. Fries played a part). Even Hegel's brother-in-law, Gottlieb von Tucher, had become engaged in the movement while still at Erlangen. Some members of the *Burschenschaft* at Jena even took to wearing what they thought were authentic Teutonic costumes, and the colors of the Lützow volunteer regiment of the Napoleonic wars – black, red, and gold – became the colors of the flag of the *Burschenschaft* movement.[88] The *Burschenschaften* were intended by their founders to replace the older form of student fraternities, the *Landsmannschaften* (the "fraternity of fellow countrymen"); the latter were the characteristic beer-soaked, dueling, bawdy associations of German students that had been famous at places like Jena. The *Landsmannschaften* were "particularist" in their orientation, binding together students from a particular area or principality in the celebration of their own traditions and customs; the *Burschenschaften*, on the other hand, conceived of themselves more universalistically as "German" rather than as, for example, "Saxon" or "Hessian." The *Landsmannschaften* concentrated on rowdiness and beer drinking; the *Burschenschaften* had more explicitly political themes in mind. The older forms of *Landsmannschaften* were therefore seen by the conservative powers of the restoration as essentially harmless and as posing no threat to the established order; the *Burschenschaften*, on the other hand, quite obviously posed an implicit threat to the order that had been established at the Congress of Vienna. Hegel had at first some sympathy with the high moral tone and the commitment to constitutionalist governments for the various German states on the part of some members of the movement, and he thus tended at first to support the movement.

On October 18–19, 1817, a *Burschenschaft* celebration was held at the Wartburg (the castle in Eisenach at which Luther had translated the Bible into German while under the protection of the prince there) in commemoration of the three-hundredth anniversary of the Reformation and the victory over Napoleon at Leipzig. The whole affair was somewhat ill-conceived – how, for example, were Catholic German members of the *Burschenschaft* supposed to identify with a meeting celebrating the separation from the Catholic church? There were patriotic speeches, and as things got out of hand, a book burning of nonpatriotic works took place (a sad and vicious portent of even more vicious things to come much later in Germany's history); among the books burned were the Code Napoleon and the works of German authors considered to be "un-German." Much anti-Semitic rumbling was also heard at the festival as speakers denounced the Jews as "un-German." One of the professorial leaders of the movement who spoke at the Wartburg festival was J. F. Fries, who had already published in 1816 a pamphlet attacking "Jewishness." (The pamphlet had been written while Fries was still in Heidelberg but was only published after he had gone to Jena.) In that pamphlet, Fries argued that since Jews wanted to keep themselves apart from the "German national community," they form a "state" within the German "state" and can never be *citizens* of a German state. Jewishness itself, moreover, was only the culture of "conniving second-hand street peddlers and tradesmen," a "frightful and demoralizing power," which "should be extirpated root and branch, since of all societies and states, secret or public, it is plainly the most dangerous to the state."[89]

Although this landed Fries in quite a bit of trouble and prompted a police interrogation of him, he remained unrepentant about the matter and even found support among some of his acquaintances. His friend Jacobi wrote a letter to him, assuring him that "Roth and Niethammer

F. W. J. Schelling
(Archiv für Kunst
und Geschichte)

Friedrich Hölderlin
(Schiller Nationalmu-
seum, Marbach am
Neckar)

Immanuel Kant (Dres-
dener Kunsthandel)

F. H. Jacobi (Archiv für
Kunst und Geschichte)

H. E. G. Paulus
(Archiv für Kunst
und Geschichte)

Immanuel Niethammer
(Stadtarchiv Stuttgart)

K. L. Reinhold
(Archiv für Kunst
und Geschichte)

J. G. Fichte
(Archiv für Kunst
und Geschichte)

K. S. von Stein zum
Altenstein (Bildarchiv
Preußischer Kulturbesitz)

K. A. Varnhagen von
Ense (Bildarchiv
Preußischer Kulturbesitz)

DR EDUARD GANS

Professor der Rechte an der Universität zu Berlin.

geb. d. 22. März 1797
gest. d. 5. Mai 1839

Eduard Gans
(Bildarchiv
Preußischer Kul-
turbesitz)

K. F. Zelter (Ullstein
Bilderdienst)

Hegel: portrait by
Bollinger after Chris-
tian Xeller (Hegel-
Archiv der Ruhr-
Universität Bochum)

Hegel: lithograph by L.
Sebbers (Hegel-Archiv
der Ruhr-Universität
Bochum)

Marie Hegel (private collection)

are fully in agreement with you. I have doubts and misgivings about this and that, but that is all mitigated for me by a different and greater hate of Jewish crap."[90] For his part, Fries claimed not to understand why people thought he hated the Jews; he only wanted, in his words, to "reform Jewishness (*Judentum*)," claiming that he had not spoken of hatred for the Jews themselves, nor of depriving Jews of their rights, but had spoken out only "against Jewishness as a degenerate social formation in the life of the German people."[91] But people like Hegel and his friends were not taken in by Fries's distinction between only hating Jewishness but not hating Jews, and this was finally the last straw for Hegel with Fries. It was bad enough that Fries both continued to attack anything that Hegel would have identified as a "scientific" – *wissenschaftlich* – approach to matters of religion and morality and continued to be a competitor for influence in German philosophical circles; as far as Hegel was concerned, Fries had now come to stand for the worst elements of the new German movement, and he thought that Fries's views on nationalism and the Jews were connected to his emotionalist, psychologistic versions of post-Kantian philosophy. This assessment of Fries was shared by some of Hegel's friends; Boisserée had already written to Goethe about Fries on October 9, 1817, that "since things have gone badly for him in philosophy, he has thrown himself into astronomy for ladies, after that into a makeshift physics, and now finally into teutonism and hatred of the Jews, all of this just to earn his keep."[92]

Hegel himself was also aware of Niethammer's implicit affinity for that kind of phony Germanism, although he seemed to be more willing to forgive him on this matter. When the French philosopher Victor Cousin inquired of Hegel about a possible visit on his part to see Schelling, Jacobi, and Niethammer in Munich, Hegel (writing in French) praised his old acquaintance Niethammer and extolled Jacobi's virtues (whom he had befriended only after moving to Nuremberg), but warned Cousin about both Niethammer's and Jacobi's tendency "toward this Teutonic, anti-French patriotism."[93] Revealingly, Hegel told Cousin not to worry about these things with Schelling, since "you will no doubt receive a warm welcome from him, and find a manner of political thought free from anti-French prejudices."[94] He also warned him not to bring up Jacobi's or Schelling's name in the other's presence, since the two did not seem to get along. Hegel rightly saw that Schelling, at least at that point in his life, was not being seduced by the phony Germanisms being circulated. (In fact, the issue of the rationality of the new order emerging in Germany was to put great strains on Hegel's and Niethammer's relationship.)

Several of Hegel's students attended the Wartburg festival, and the son of his friend Friedrich Frommann and the two sons of the Wessel-höft family (the family that had taken in Ludwig Fischer and raised him until Hegel took him into his family in Heidelberg) were also present, as was Gottlieb von Tucher. (Hegel's mother-in-law was firmly and resolutely opposed to Gottlieb's attending the festival, finding his attraction to all that "teutonism" to be silly and distasteful, but Hegel talked her into allowing him to attend.)

One of Hegel's favorite students at Heidelberg, Friedrich Wilhelm Carové, attended the festival as one of the leaders of the *Burschenschaft* movement, and he spoke out strongly against the anti-Semitic tenden- cies of some of those present. Carové, who heard Hegel's lectures in 1817 on "Natural Law and Political Science," even published a series of drafts of ordinances for the *Burschenschaft* movement in which he argued that only by remaking itself along the lines of the kinds of "universal principles as realized in determinate ways" (that Hegel had been expounding in his lectures) could the *Burschenschaft* hope to realize their goal of cultural renewal in Germany. Fries's idea that national consciousness like religious consciousness was a matter of feeling was ridiculed by Carové, who dismissed it as "superficial monkey love," a confusion of what was universal with the particularities and vagaries of personal temperament. In particular, in his draft of the regulations to govern the various fraternities, Carové stressed that the basis for mem- bership should only be rational agency, not religious confession, not national origin, and not social class; to drive that point home, Carové made it quite explicit that by that he meant that Jews and foreigners should be *fully* included as members in the *Burschenschaften*. (This was to lead to Carové's defeat in the movement a year later and to his virtual expulsion from the movement.)[95]

But in 1817, it no doubt seemed to Hegel not only that Fries had disgraced himself by his comments on Jewishness, but also that the *Burschenschaft* movement itself would likely be led by Hegelians. Not only would he triumph over Fries (already a sweet enough victory personally for him), his dreams of having his philosophy accepted as the *truly* modern account of the principles in play in modern life were perhaps close to being realized – and all this only one year after having secured his first real professorship! To the extent that the dynamic of modern life seemed to be moving toward making explicit those principles to which he thought modern life had implicitly committed itself, he could expect that the *Burschenschaft* movement, whatever its momentary travails and misguided youthful exuberance (such as the affectations of old Teutonic dress), would eventually have to transform itself in the direction that his philosophy had outlined.

Württemberg, Constitutionalism, and the Estates

There were, of course, powerful countervailing tendencies at work of which Hegel was aware, even if he perhaps underestimated their strength. In Austria, Metternich opposed constitutionalism, German unification, indeed, virtually all aspects of modern post-Napoleonic Germany, because he saw them as inimical to Austria's interests in maintaining its influence in Europe. But whatever his own views about the likely success of his attempts to stop some of those developments, Metternich was determined to quash the *Burschenschaft* movement and to prevent all forms of constitutionalism from taking root in Germany. He was, of course, in large measure to succeed, although that outcome could not have been clearly foreseen in 1817.

The heated dispute over constitutionalism in the German *Länder* – over whether each German *Land* should have a constitution at all, what form they should take, whether they should centralize power or reaffirm the old state of estates – replayed the ongoing dispute between the more universalistic modernizers and the more particularistic hometowners (into which a new Romantic, nationalist element had been injected). The hometowners wanted to block reform because they had now seen up close just how traditional privileges and ways of life were being threatened and undermined by those reforms; the reformers, on the other hand, had just seen up close that the hometowners both wished to prevent the state from taxing them for developmental projects (which would hinder necessary economic development) and to prevent the state from taking away their right to exclude those whom they wished to exclude from their communities – itinerants, people of low morals, Jews – which in turn would undermine the whole idea of the "career open to talent" and therefore the ability of the state to train and recruit capable, modern ministers and leaders.[96] The debate was muddied, however, by the fact that the reformers were joined by another party, the rulers of the newly formed German states, who wanted power to be lodged solely in the state, that is, in themselves, and who did not want that power to be checked by competing authorities. Some reformers saw such sovereignty as the only way to push through modern reforms and thus came to be curiously allied with those princes and their allies who wanted to aggrandize their power, whereas in another corner, some reformers joined with the old estates because they feared a centralizing grab for power on the part of some of the more ambitious princes.

In this context, the king of Württemberg, Friedrich II, sought to use the establishment of a constitution to secure his sovereignty over the *Land* and to put to rest the elements of the "good old law," with its accouterment of rights and privileges for the Württemberg estates, that had frustrated his ancestors for centuries in their attempts to pursue their own ambitions. Moreover, like many of his predecessors, he felt it was his prerogative to *give* Württemberg a constitution and that he would never *accept* a constitution from anybody else.[97] But he was faced by opposition from the most reactionary elements of the Romantic nationalists, who called for an immediate restoration of the old Württemberg constitution, arguing that Germany itself would not be completely liberated from French interference until that had been accomplished. The king, however, set to work, and without any consultation with the other reigning powers in Württemberg, came up with a relatively liberal constitution that promised equality among his subjects, gave Jews rights of participation, lifted restrictions against Catholics, but kept the power of the government and the purse strings firmly in his own hands.[98]

His first opponents thus came from the mediatized nobility and the Protestant Church, who saw (correctly) that their old privileges would vanish forever if the king's proposal become reality. The mediatized nobility had something in particular to fear; they had once been immediate to the Holy Roman Emperor and thus had not participated in Württemberg politics at all, being immune from the duke's (and later the king's) taxes and such. Now, with the Holy Roman Empire gone, their privileges were particularly in doubt, and the king's constitution spoke of "equality" among his subjects, something that clearly would have spelled the end of their special status. They found allies in Metternich and in Baron von Stein in Prussia, and fairly soon thereafter a massive protest against the king's proposed constitution was under way, and calls for the restoration of the "old" constitution grew in intensity.

As the debate gathered force, the Württembergers calling for the reestablishment of the old constitution and the "good old law" of Württemberg asserted that they had not fought against Napoleon only to lose their rights to a Württemberg dictator (the memory of Karl Eugen and his predecessors was obviously still running strong). Many of the Württemberg pastors began offering public prayers in their services for the reestablishment of the "good old law."[99] (The Tübingen philosopher Adolph Karl August Eschenmayer, an associate and follower of Schelling's *Naturphilosophie*, published a book in which he argued for the metaphysical necessity of the threefold division of the social classes of society in Württemberg according to the three faculties of the mind – ideas, imagination, and desire; the book had a wide circulation and seemed to many to bring the intellectual force of German idealism into the argument in favor of those wishing to restore the ancient constitution of Württemberg; Eschenmayer, however, went further and argued that all the particular states of Germany ought to be subordinate to the German state as a whole. The king and his advisors were apparently baffled at the incoherence and popularity of Eschenmayer's book.)

At this point, the king began to back off from his original plans and announced that he would form a new constitution, at which point the publisher Johann Cotta weighed into the debate, arguing that the new constitution should "serve as the model for Germany."[100] Since the kingdom of Württemberg as a *state* was different and included more territories than the old *Land* of Württemberg, the king argued that the old constitution could not cover the new territories, and thus that a new constitution was needed, which, the king said, could nonetheless incorporate some key parts of the old constitution. At this point, the debate swung back in the king's favor, winning him praise from various sides that until then had opposed him, all of which aroused Metternich's suspicions and made him mistrustful of the king's motivations and control over the situation. Metternich must, however, have been satisfied with the way that affairs in Württemberg quickly settled back down into mutual mistrust and suspicion between the estates and the king, with finally virtually everything coming to a standstill. However, when a draft of the constitution finally began making its rounds, and the progressive forces realized that there were no provisions for freedom of the press or for the accountability of the ministers, the anger and suspicion against both the king and the estates once again appeared with renewed force.

The old king died, however, on October 30, 1816. The new king, Wilhelm I, was of a completely different temperament than his father; he was imbued with the ideals of state sovereignty and of the new "German" (and not just Württembergian) consciousness. All eyes, including those of the reformers in Prussia, then turned to Württemberg to see if it would indeed produce the "model constitution" for Germany; Baron von Stein expected it to be the "normal constitution" for Germany.[101] On March 3, 1817, King Wilhelm I of Württemberg called the Diet together to approve his new "German" constitution for Württemberg, with its provisions for a bicameral legislature and popular representation. A more liberalized press law with more freedom for the press was promulgated on January 30, 1817, and this led publishers such as Cotta to fall in firmly behind the king's proposal. But the estates fought back bitterly, winning to their side in the battle of words both the theologian Paulus and the poet Ludwig Uhland (who perhaps not coincidentally came from the *Ehrbarkeit*). The estates wished to maintain the old dualistic *Ständesstaat*, the "state of estates" with its dual centers of power and authority (with much of the debate centering around issues of power and money having to do with whether the council of estates and the estate treasury would continue to exist as bodies separate from the king's government).

A famine in the land during 1817 did not help matters, as it tended to turn people's sympathies away from the existing royal government. On June 2, 1817, the Diet rejected the king's new constitution (by a margin of sixty-seven to forty-two votes); the coalition defeating the vote was a curious amalgam of old imperial knights, the *Ehrbarkeit*, and some prelates who wanted their old ecclesiastical rights restored. The wide support that the constitution had garnered from reformist circles outside of Württemberg counted, if anything, against it, and the rejection of the constitution thus appalled those outside of Württemberg (for example, Baron von Stein). The rejection, however, only stiffened the king's determination to put his constitution into force, hardened his belief that no compromise with the estates was possible; he therefore concluded that it no longer made any sense to attempt to incorporate any of the "good old law" into the new constitution. The estates had rejected the more universalistic appeals to a "German" sense of freedom in favor of an all-or-nothing approach to the "good old law"; they had endorsed hometown particularism against what the reformers in Germany saw as the necessary, modern "universalism" of state sovereignty and constitutional government.

Hegel's Entry into the Württemberg Debate

Hegel simply could not resist entering such a debate on Württemberg. Not only did it concern his old homeland and birthplace, it concerned the very issues of modernism that were the centerpieces of his thought. Moreover, since all eyes were on Württemberg to see how its constitutional debate took shape, Hegel no doubt felt he had a chance to play some role in the constitutional debates going on elsewhere in Germany. The additional fact that a self-proclaimed idealist and quasi-Schellingian obscurantist such as Eschenmayer in Tübingen had also inserted German idealism into the debate only made Hegel's entry into the fray all the more likely, since it raised the stakes for someone like himself, who ten years after the publication of the *Phenomenology* was still trying to convince' much of the literary public that his philosophy was an advance on Schelling's and not just another version of it.

Hegel's essay "Proceedings of the Estates Assembly in the Kingdom of Württemberg 1815–1816" was published in the *Heidelberger Jahrbücher* in the winter of 1817 and 1818 and was clearly intended to play a role in the debate as to whether the constitution should be accepted. He was partially successful in this aim; the essay was reprinted in 1818 as an inexpensive pamphlet, subsidized and distributed by the Württemberg government, who saw to it that it was widely circulated. It provoked some people to publish attacks on it, which only served to draw even more attention to it. (In 1819, the king, exasperated, simply imposed his constitution on Württemberg and ended the debate by force; but in 1817, Hegel could have foreseen that as he was writing his piece.)

In the essay, Hegel deployed the key ideas of his own philosophy to illustrate what he took to be at stake in the whole debate. In some ways, the essay functioned as another way for Hegel to clarify for himself and for the public certain core ideas found in the *Phenomenology of Spirit* and the *Science of Logic* as they related to the way in which his own conceptions of the social and political structure of modern life were rapidly coming into focus for him in his lectures at Heidelberg. Like many of Hegel's more popular writings, it is clear and lucid, and largely free of the tortuous use of technical, abstruse language that Hegel opted for in the expositions of his philosophical works.

The article is nominally concerned with the published "Proceedings of the Württemberg Estates Assembly," but, as Hegel makes clear in the opening paragraphs, we cannot hope to get an understanding of what is at stake in the debate by approaching the documents from a "psychological view of history." No investigation of the "so-called secret motives and intentions of single individuals," whether of the king or of his opponents, can be of any help in understanding what the debate was about and what was at stake in it. The state of mind of the actors in the drama is not significant; we must, as he puts it, understand "men of action from what they *do*." From the standpoint of the *Phenomenology* and *Logic*, to make a judgment is to undertake a commitment, not to be in this or that mental state or to subjectively entertain certain thoughts, and those commitments are not a function of what we subjectively happen to be thinking about at the time. Thus, no amount of research into what actually went on "amongst the populace outside the proceedings" nor the "inner history of the labors of the Cabinet and the Ministry" could help us truly understand the debate. To do this, Hegel argued, we must understand how and why the debate *mattered* to the people involved in it. What was at stake in the debate thus had to do with what kind of commitments would have to be presupposed for the people involved in the debates to care so deeply about what they were doing.

For Hegel, the "Proceedings" therefore could be understood only in light of the specific kind of practical project in which the actors were collectively engaged; what is important, therefore, is to present the "nature and course of the substantial matter itself," that is, the common practical project and the norms that make it the specific kind of project that it is.[102] Moreover, since it a *particular* practical project that is being investigated, we cannot hope to derive those norms from any perspective outside of them; since we must understand why it matters *to these people*, we cannot, as Hegel puts it, "cull from any more remote age, especially not from the civilized age of Greece and Rome" the basic commitments by which we are to understand the issues, for those commitments "are unique to our own day."[103]

The issue had to do with the conflict between modern life and those wishing to hold onto the past, but it was not an issue, as Hegel saw it, simply of whether the Württemberg king wanted to aggrandize his own power or of whether particular members of the estates believed themselves to be defending their traditional privileges. What was at stake had to do with the differences between the commitments underlying modern life and those which had structured the preceding way of life. What compromises, if any, were possible in the debate depended on what kinds of tensions, oppositions, and compatibilities there were between those commitments, and, as Hegel argued, the pre-revolutionary and post-revolutionary forms of life had to be understood as *competing* practical projects, with the commitments of one ruling out the commitments of the other. Moreover, as Hegel reconstructed them, the modern project not merely competed with that of the *ancien regime* but emerged as that which is rational and required for us because of the failures and insufficiencies of the older project.

The older project itself had to be understood as a response to the failures of its own historical predecessors. The breakup of the powers of governments in the Middle Ages led to the emergence of free-standing individuals, who then for reasons of self-interest and self-protection had to regroup themselves into various social units of "knights, freemen, monasteries, nobility, merchants, and tradesmen."[104] These groups did not manage to reconstitute themselves as a social whole, since they shared no common interests; at best, they were able to establish only a way of cooperating and getting along without any explicitly shared commitment to principle, a kind of "tolerable existence of standing alongside each other" – in short, a modus vivendi, not something with which each member took himself (or even could have taken himself) to be identified.[105] The kind of social balance that was maintained was therefore unstable and incapable of producing what Hegel calls a "sense for the state."[106] When no such "sense for the state" exists, that is, no real identification of one's own personal ends with the ends of public life, there can be no identification with public life, no shared conception of public authority. The state then appears to individuals merely as a "government," a faction, something that can be justified only as a means of serving private interest, and the deputies to such political bodies would therefore necessarily approach their work "with the will to give and do as little as possible for the universal."[107] Within that kind of normative background, the state would have to be construed as a social *contract* between, for example, princes and estates, and *political* obligation would become mingled (and, to Hegel's mind, confused) with ties of personal dependence – exactly as Hegel thought had been the case in feudal Europe. The terms of a social contract, however, can sustain allegiance only so long as the relevant interests at stake in the contract remain satisfied; as new interests emerge, or old interests that were excluded from the original contract make their voices heard, the contractual state of affairs between prince and estates, or between government and the people, becomes eroded and the stability of the social order is weakened.

The inadequacies of the old order were, Hegel thought, almost too obvious to need spelling out. Moreover, the conflicts between the estates and the prince, between the demands of modernization (with its ways of raising revenue, forming its elite out of the universities, and so on) and the interests found in the ways of life bound up with the old order could not be reconciled. The older view, with its explicit commitment to status as adhering to individuals through ties of personal dependence, turned out to be committed to a view of social life as contractual, as a constant negotiation among parties representing independent interests; the other, modernizing view, with its commitment to a conception of political authority such as having to do with more explicitly shared reasons among all participants, was committed to a view of equality before the law, principles of universal justice, confessional freedom, and the like. The old view had collapsed under its own weight, and the new view could be shown (so Hegel thought) to have not merely reason per se on its side but the kinds of reasons with which modern individuals could subjectively identify.

As Hegel pointed out, the arguments given by the estates in Württemberg amounted to saying that since they have had these rights in the past, they should have them in the future; they made this point apparently without even noticing that the whole way of life in which those rights made sense had collapsed precisely because of its own internal insufficiencies and contradictions. The rights that the estates asserted could not be *actual* rights in the modern world; the modern rules of property, the principles of law, and the social practices of modern life make it impossible to sustain any allegiance to those principles bound up with ties of personal dependency as a basis of political life. They therefore cannot serve as the norms that can underlie any collective project in modern life. Commitments sustaining the collective projects of modern life must be those that when brought to light and articulated can also be justified so they can serve as a rational basis for self-identity in social life, and the dialectic of such reasons led (as the *Phenomenology* had shown) to a conception that reasons must be universal, must be the kind of reasons that can be good for and shared by all others; but the commitment to reasons that are good for others commits us to the idea that there must be a shared conception of authoritativeness for social life, a shared conception of how authority in social life is to be parceled out, and that in turn *commits* us to a conception of justice (with its concomitant rights to such things as freedom of religious confession) as the only commitments capable of sustaining themselves in the face of claims for universal justification. That is, a commitment to key norms implicit in the practices of modern life commits one to the existence of modern constitutional states and rules out as irrational the idea of dualistic centers of authority such as existed in the old *Ständesstaat*.

To Hegel, the Württemberg estates simply had no other argument for their assertions than that the old constitution was the way things used to be and therefore should remain the way things ought to be. But appeals to tradition per se are a dead letter in modern life; as Hegel put it, "age has nothing to do with . . . whether [such rights] are good or bad. Even the abolition of human sacrifice, slavery, feudal despotism and countless infamies was in every case the cancellation of something that was an old right."[108] What the Württemberg estates presented as a golden age of integrity and honor, Hegel argued, was in fact an age of corruption and looting of the public coffers, of the same old family names appearing over and over again with their hands in the public treasury, the whole show festering in a moral quagmire and leading to the inner collapse of the ethical life of Württemberg. In answer to those who argued that Hegel, like all the reformers, was making the specious, relativistic argument that "a century cannot make wrong into right," Hegel retorted, "but we should add: Even if this century-old wrong has been called right all the time."[109] In his most stinging indictment of the

arguments on the part of the defenders of the "good old law," Hegel
compared them to the French aristocrats who returned to France from
their exile in Germany after the downfall of Napoleon and the reestablishment of the Bourbon monarchy, for *they have forgotten nothing
and learnt nothing*. [The Württemberg estates] seem to have *slept*
through the last twenty-five years, possibly the richest that world history has had, and for us the most instructive, because it is to them that
our world and our ideas belong."[110]

Hegel – as the son of a Tübingen-educated lawyer who had not been
a member of the *Ehrbarkeit* and therefore not part of that select group
that took access to public funds as part of its birthright – was no doubt
speaking from personal experience and probably deriving no small
amount of personal satisfaction in bringing this out; the young man who
had embraced the cause of moral and spiritual renewal, who as a teenager had understood the Revolution as a new Reformation, was finally
able to get back at those in his homeland whom he had seen as morally
corrupt. Nor could Hegel conceal his distaste for what he regarded as
the retrogressive elements in German life. He noted that the whole
debate about the "good old law," with its hypocritical pretense of
invoking a past time of honor and integrity, manifests the "typical
disease of the Germans," namely, "their clinging to formalisms of this
kind and their preoccupation with them."[111] The history of the way in
which France, England, and Poland developed out of feudal ties of
personal dependence into modern states, he notes, lacks that "nauseating side of Germany, namely, the complete legal and documentary
paper-bound formalism of the German states (*Länder*)."[112]

The Reaction to Hegel's Political Essay

Hegel's decision to publish the piece had, however, one consequence
that he himself certainly could not have foreseen: It precipitated a final
and irrevocable break with his old acquaintance and fellow Württemberger, Heinrich Paulus. Paulus himself had sent a long piece to the
journal on the same topic, only to have it unanimously rejected by the
editors as too long and unsuitable. When Hegel shortly thereafter published his own piece on the subject in the journal – in which he argued
for very different conclusions than those Paulus had drawn – Paulus
took this as a personal act of betrayal on Hegel's part. Relations between

Hegel and Paulus had already been strained before this discord arose between them. Before Hegel had come to Heidelberg, Paulus had asked him for an evaluation of Hegel's friend Thomas Seebeck, in light of a possible appointment for Seebeck at Heidelberg. Hegel and Seebeck had been on good terms; Seebeck had even been one of the godfathers of Hegel's son Immanuel. But in his confidential note to Paulus, Hegel noted that Seebeck was indeed a fine fellow but not a first-rate thinker. Apparently, Paulus then indiscreetly revealed to Seebeck Hegel's less-than-enthusiastic evaluation of his intellectual credentials, and this had caused a permanent rupture between Hegel and Seebeck.[113]

After Hegel had to tell Paulus that the journal had rejected his piece, he tried to smooth things over with Paulus, reminding him that not just he himself but the entire editorial board of the journal had ruled against Paulus's piece, but Paulus would hear nothing of it and immediately broke off forever all social contact with Hegel. (Paulus's irascibility led him to publish the piece on his own; he strongly attacked the king of Württemberg in it and, displaying a complete lack of prudence, even sent the king a copy. The king was not amused. When Paulus later tried to visit his dying son in Württemberg in 1819, the king immediately had him arrested and deported.)

The reaction to Hegel's pamphlet was swift, and even his friends parted company with him on the issues. Not merely was Paulus enraged about it, Niethammer was also deeply displeased with what Hegel had done. In light of his discouraging experiences in Bavaria and the way in which the gains of the last few years (and his work) were rapidly being set aside there, Niethammer thought that Hegel's pamphlet was simply too idealistic in its treatment of what the debate was really about and that Hegel had been much too naive about the real state of affairs. "I would bet," he told Hegel, "that you would not have written your review if, like me, you had been in the position of having to see these ruling rationalities face to face." To Niethammer, the king and his ministers had behaved not as good-faith members of the German confederation established by the *Bundesakte* but instead "as if they were the Emperor and Empire themselves," whereas the estates at least (in Niethammer's view) had comported themselves as members of a federal system. The estates were not simply acting, as Hegel had insisted, as reactionary bodies wishing to turn back the clock. To be sure, Niethammer conceded, the two sides had been a bit petulant in their demands

on each other, but the estates had asked for nothing more than a voice
in deciding what was going to become of themselves and were refusing
to be simply dictated to by the king. Nonetheless, the resulting impasse
probably meant, as Niethammer sadly concluded, that the whole thing
would have to be settled by force. Ruefully, Niethammer told Hegel
that "the least that I can find to say about it is that you have ingeniously
pleaded a bad cause." (Closing on a cheerier note, Niethammer noted
that Schelling sent his greetings; although Hegel and Schelling had long
since ceased to correspond with each other, they continued to hold each
other in relatively warm regard.)[114]

To others, Hegel seemed to have simply and unjustifiably sided with
the king against the people, and that there was no talk of "democracy"
in his pamphlet (except to disparage it) strengthened that view. Hegel
had in fact argued against democracy in the piece, although he had
clearly argued for political participation. In Hegel's view, democracy –
on the French model, where individual voters select representatives to
a national assembly on the principle of majority rule – places each
individual voter in the position of having his personal interest represented by a single act, which itself only occurs every few years, and
which has only the smallest effect on the general outcome; any rational
voter is thus tempted to see his vote as not worth even the small amount
of effort it takes to exercise it. Moreover, as a doctrine of majority rule,
democracy fails to take into account the interests of the minority, and
the example of England shows that it is open to abuses and absurdities
of every sort. Thus, some other way must be found to ensure that
people's interests are represented in the political debates of the day,
which, Hegel argued, would involve some type of representation that
would incorporate already formed and articulated groups who could
then choose representatives among themselves from a variety of suitably
educated people. The "fitness of electors and elected" would be found
in there being an appropriate body of people on whom the kind of *trust*
that is necessary between elector and elected could be bestowed and
sustained and who could be expected to give the electors "an opportunity to assess and test the attitudes and competence of the elected."[115]
That could be done only by means of mediating institutions that would
gather together people of common interests and common lives and
engage them in their own common projects. Within, for example, the
guild, the members would then participate in the political life of the

state by choosing the men who would represent them at the national level. Political participation would be thus mediated by participation in more local organizations, and all interests would be represented because the national government would necessarily include all the relevant groups. (If anything, Hegel thought that the proposed Württemberg constitution was too "liberal" in the sense that it paid too little attention to these mediating groups.)

On Hegel's view, which was a version of the program he had already worked out in Jena in 1805–06, participation in the political life of the state cannot be direct but must be mediated, "organic," that is, must occur within a set of mediating institutions that weave the individual's personal projects into more general common projects, which in turn are then woven into the common project of the state (as a political community as a whole). It was, moreover, quite clear whom Hegel thought were to be the elite who would be the leaders of these groupings. Like many other reformers at that time, Hegel appealed to the (largely mythical) idea of the French having been defeated by units staffed with patriotically inspired students; in fact, the French were defeated by well-trained armies, and the size of the "volunteer" corps and its actual effect on the outcome was greatly overstated by the proponents of reform. (Educated youth never made up more than twelve percent of the army, and even in the Lützow volunteer regiment, famous for its "student composition," the educated youth only composed one-third.)[116] But Hegel, latching onto the current sentiment for his own purposes, claimed that the "great events of recent history, the fight for Germany's independence, have imbued the youth in our universities with a higher interest than mere concentration on future bread-winning and making an income. Some of them have shed their blood together that the German provinces might acquire free constitutions. They have brought back from the field of battle the hope of working some day or other toward that end and of participating in the political life of the state. Their scientific education has equipped them for this purpose and destined them in the main for public service."[117] The student elite had supposedly fought for the various states of "Germany" and thereby gained entitlement to lead those states for which they had fought. But what Hegel was of course also saying was: The various German states would be led by people trained in the universities by people like Hegel.

Berlin's Offer

But as Hegel was, all in all, comfortably settling into his Heidelberg professorial life, other matters were afoot. After Hegel had turned down the offer from Berlin, the faculty there decided that they did not wish to make an offer at that time to any other philosopher; the faculty therefore simply deferred making any such offer until a man of "decisive reputation," as they put it, could be found to fill the position.[118] Fichte's old chair thus remained vacant, and many among the faculty blamed the minister in charge of the university's affairs, K. F. von Schuckmann, for the difficulties in securing a philosopher for the empty position. Von Schuckmann was by temperament ill-disposed to philosophers in general, suspicious – as Friedrich von Raumer put it – that "with their conjurer's abracadabra they intended to be the masters of the world."[119] But in the climate of reform in the Prussian government, the faculty's displeasure with von Schuckmann led to a shake-up in the ministries, and the cultural ministry was separated from von Schuckmann's ministry of the interior.

On November 3, 1817, the position of minister of culture (although at first the position was not called that) was assumed by Karl Sigmund Franz Freiherr vom Stein zum Altenstein. Altenstein, like Hegel, had been born in 1770; he and Hegel shared not only the same generational experience of the Revolution, the Napoleonic incursions into Germany, and the so-called "wars of national liberation," but also a similar outlook with regard to the shape and pace of reforms and the crucial role of *Bildung* and of the universities in the new and still emerging social order. Moreover, Altenstein was not only acquainted with Hegel's published works, he and Hegel had some common friends, such as Sulpiz Boisserée, who pushed Hegel's cause with Altenstein. (Thomas Seebeck, Immanuel Hegel's godfather, was also a friend of Altenstein's, although Hegel's break with Seebeck did not really help matters there.) Altenstein's ascension to the leadership of the culture ministry therefore put the matter of Hegel's appointment immediately back into play.

Altenstein set to work at once to get Hegel to come to Berlin. He personally wrote a letter to Hegel on December 26, 1817 (rather than have a scribe copy it for him), inviting him to assume Fichte's chair. (Altenstein apparently went through three drafts of the letter until he felt he had gotten it just right.) The letter itself was extremely flattering to Hegel, praising him and noting how much Altenstein wished to have him in Berlin: "I am not misjudging the obligations which could detain you in Heidelberg, but you have yet greater obligations to science for which a wider and more important circle of influence is open to you here. You know what Berlin can offer you in this regard."[120] Altenstein promised to use his position to assist Hegel and offered him a salary of 2,000 Prussian Courants (Thalers) and a promise to provide something extra to cover the cost of moving. This was a sizable raise; Hegel had been getting 1,500 florins at Heidelberg; the salary being offered to him in Prussia was equivalent by Hegel's own calculations to about 3,500 florins.[121]

Hegel was delighted with the offer, which to his mind had come at just the right time. Hegel had become quite worried about Baden's future (and therefore Heidelberg's future) after the death of the grand duke of Baden; there were rumors afloat that the Wittelsbach dynasty (that is, the Bavarians) were going to do their best to reclaim the Palatinate, having never quite gotten over being constrained to cede it to Baden in the first place, and the very last thing Hegel wanted was to fall back under Bavarian rule. He therefore replied on January 24, 1818, that he would love to accept the position for all the reasons that Altenstein had mentioned, but, playing his cards carefully, noted that due to his own lack of "personal fortune" and his duties as head of a household, he could not accept the offer without some other matters being cleared up. As he told Altenstein, the cost of living and housing was much greater in Berlin than in Heidelberg, and it would quickly consume the sizable raise he was getting; moreover, he had just gone through the trouble of furnishing and preparing a house in Heidelberg, and he simply did not have the money to do that again so soon; and, finally, the payments he had already made into the widows and orphans fund (the pension fund) at Heidelberg would be completely lost were he to move to Berlin. (That Hegel was twenty-one years older than his wife made this last consideration extremely important to him.) He suggested to Altenstein that if the government were to provide him with a free apartment, that would perhaps expedite things, and he also informed him that he would request 200 Friedrichs d'or (1,000 Thalers) as compensation for moving expenses.[122]

After that, things moved relatively quickly. The Prussian cultural ministry responded to Hegel on March 26, 1818, basically granting him almost all his wishes – in other words, 2,000 Thalers salary, 1,000 Thalers as compensation for moving costs, and the promise of exemption from duties when he shipped his articles from Baden to Prussia (Prussian customs duties were especially onerous at the time) – but balking at providing him with a free apartment (it just was not possible, they said). He was also reassured about the financial stability of the widows and orphans fund at Berlin.[123] Altenstein himself responded personally on March 18, 1818, with a promise to do what he could to help Hegel financially and to get him admitted to the Prussian Academy of the Sciences, which carried a small but not insignificant stipend with it.[124] (As things turned out, Altenstein was unable to keep that latter promise, much to Hegel's subsequent disappointment.)

With his requests granted, Hegel sent his letter of acceptance to the Prussian culture ministry on March 31, 1818. Marie Hegel was not exactly enthusiastic about the prospect of moving to Berlin and even put up some resistance to the move after Hegel had already accepted the offer. Indeed, Marie's own mother had to weigh in on the issue, pointing out to Marie in a letter of April 4, 1818, that she only had "to take the map and place the little spot of land next to the large one where her children and her children's children will find enough room to build their homes. . . . You and Hegel, as you are, will both soon feel at home there."[125] But that was still not enough, and Hegel had some convincing to do with Marie: In a letter to his wife later that summer, Hegel remarked that "the Berlin sand . . . would be a more receptive sphere for philosophy than Heidelberg's romantic surroundings," showing that he apparently felt he still needed to convince her that the move to Berlin was for the best.[126]

The Prussians wanted Hegel to come to Prussia immediately for the summer semester, which was to start around May, but Hegel pointed out that it would be impossible for him to move on such short notice, and, moreover, that he had obligations in Heidelberg vis-à-vis the lectures he had already announced and which had been printed in the university's list of offerings. There followed a series of exchanges between Hegel and the Prussians, who at first said that it would be fine if Hegel were to show up for the winter semester of 1818 (which would begin in October), followed by a series of letters from the ministry first asking, then more or less insisting, that Hegel send them a list of the topics of his upcoming lectures (which he finally did).

Altenstein was quite pleased with his accomplishment and wrote to Hegel offering that his sister help Marie with regard to the move. Soon thereafter, Altenstein's sister managed to rent an apartment for the Hegel family from the widow Grabow on the Leipziger Strasse at the corner of Friedrichstrasse for 300 Thalers per year. (The apartment was centrally located and only a few blocks from the university; the Hegel family stayed there only about a year, moving to more commodious quarters at Kupfergraben no. 4, next to the river, even closer to the university and the ceremonial core of the city, and just a few blocks off the grand boulevard, Unter den Linden, on which the university stood.)[127] The news of Hegel's appointment to Berlin apparently spread quickly and was greeted with immense interest. Hegel's mother-in-law (who also had reason to exaggerate her beloved son-in-law's accomplishments) claimed that it was even being discussed among the cognoscenti in Nuremberg. Schleiermacher himself wrote to a friend, "It has been decided that we will get Hegel, and there are strong rumors that [the same is true] of A. W. Schlegel. I am curious to see how both of them will get along."[128] One of Hegel's future colleagues, Karl Wilhelm Ferdinand Solger, an aesthetician and translator of Sophocles, wrote Hegel a very warm letter informing him how eager he was to meet him, how much he valued Hegel's writings, and how he sincerely hoped that some form of friendship could develop between the two.[129] Even Goethe wryly noted to Sulpiz Boisserée that with Hegel's appointment to Berlin, "Minister Altenstein seems to want to create for himself a scientific bodyguard."[130]

Hegel had therefore every reason to be hopeful about his new appointment. Schiller had quite famously called Jena a "focal point" (*Mittelpunkt*) in the 1790s, describing it as the place where the contours of modern life were suddenly concentrated and becoming clear.[131] In a letter informing his sister, Christiane, about his upcoming move, Hegel now himself characterized Berlin as a "great focal point," and he later repeated the characterization in his inaugural lecture there.[132] His use of Schiller's old characterization of Jena was not accidental; as Hegel saw how things were shaking out in post-Napoleonic Germany, Prussia, which he had once detested, seemed to be riding the crest of modernity. It was dynamic, rapidly reforming, and seemingly dedicated to putting *Wissenschaft* at the head of its social movements. It was in Prussia – at least so it seemed in 1817 and 1818 – that he saw the shape of modern

life becoming more explicit and therefore more developed and institutionalized. In other words, it seemed to be the place at which the kinds
of things he had defended in his philosophy were starting to come
clearly into focus. Heidelberg was looking as if it might collapse into
Bavarian rule and go the way of Jena; Berlin, on the other hand, was
located in what seemed to be a vigorous state clearly and irreversibly
committed to modern reforms.

Probably suspecting that it would be his last chance, Hegel made a
quick trip to Stuttgart in the spring of 1818 for a few days to visit
friends and relatives. In fact, it was the last time he was to see his
hometown. (He apparently spent some time speaking to officials in
Württemberg about his being appointed to the post of chancellor of the
Tübingen University, but, even as those talks proceeded, the die had
already been decisively cast for Berlin.) He returned to Heidelberg,
finished his summer semester lectures, and set himself to getting the
family all ready to go. Once everything else had been taken care of,
Hegel packed himself and his family into a coach for the trip to Berlin
on September 18, 1818. They traveled from Heidelberg to Frankfurt
and from Frankfurt to Jena, where they stayed several days with his old
friends the Frommann family (who had an especially large house in
Jena); Immanuel Hegel celebrated his fourth birthday there, and Ludwig Fischer Hegel located an old friend for a happy reunion. On
September 23, Hegel took Marie to Weimar for a short visit with
Goethe; this must have pleased Marie quite a bit, since Goethe was a
great (if not the greatest) literary celebrity in Germany at the time; that
her husband was on such good and personal terms with the great man
himself would have only confirmed for Marie her sense of her husband's
importance. The meeting was scheduled for 3:00 P.M. and was apparently very short; Goethe noted he had "the pleasure of speaking with
the Hegels for a moment; how much I would have wished for a longer
conversation."[133] Another observer noted on the visit how Marie Hegel
did not appear "entirely healthy."[134] In fact, Marie Hegel had suffered
yet another miscarriage at the end of 1817; the winter had not helped
matters, and on July 28, 1818, she had gone to the fashionable spa town
of Bad Schwalbach to take the waters there and recuperate, no doubt in
part to rest up for the trip.[135] But her health was still quite fragile at the
time of the move to Berlin.

After leaving Jena, the Hegel family spent four days on what Hegel described as excellent roads, staying overnight at Weißenfels, Wittenberg (the town where by legend Luther nailed his theses to the church door), and arriving in Berlin on October 5, 1818, to take up residence in their new apartment. Marie was exhausted, but the children had held up well, and Hegel was more than pleased to be in his new environment, although he was taken aback at first by what seemed to him Berlin's oversized, chaotic urban nature.

Hegel, who always praised Aristotle and particularly his politics, had in the decade earlier been characterized as the modern Aristotle (in contrast to Schelling, who was called the modern Plato). The characterization seemed to have stuck, since others continued to use it at Heidelberg.[136] For Hegel at this point, the comparison might have seemed even more apt. Aristotle had been a Greek foreigner in Athenian life who had come to see Athens's importance for understanding ethics and politics in nonprovincial and more generally human terms; Hegel no doubt thought that his being in Berlin would be an analogous situation. His own life had come into focus in Heidelberg; now he would be at the central point where modern life itself was coming into focus. For once, he would arrive somewhere before its glory period had passed, and he would be the Swabian foreigner in place to theorize about what was living and what was dead in Berlin life in its moment of transition to the new, more rational order.

Events, however, took an unexpected turn for him. Within a year of his arrival, the reaction in Prussia began to gather force, and Hegel was once again forced to rethink what his philosophy had to say about a world that was suddenly and very disturbingly not taking the shape he thought it should have.

Berlin: Reform and Repression at the Focal Point (1818–1821)

Hegel's Prussia and the Berlin University

IN RELOCATING TO PRUSSIA, Hegel was moving to a *Land* that he had previously scorned and that lay both geographically and culturally far away from his native Württemberg. But the Prussia to which Hegel was resettling himself was no longer the Prussia of his youth; in 1818 it had come to be the focal point of the post-Napoleonic reform movement. Hegel thus had every reason to believe that he was moving to the *Land* in which the shape of modern life about which he had long reflected was emerging.

Prussia had come into this status, however, in a roundabout way. Reform had been pushed onto it rather than being developed out of it. Although in the periods preceding the nineteenth century, Prussia had been one of the European "great powers," near the beginning of the century it had come perilously close to being relegated to minor status if not vanishing altogether. It had already been put on the defensive by French military successes in the 1790s, and then after its catastrophe at Jena, it had been occupied by the French. Napoleon, moreover, insisted that Prussia bear the costs of the occupation, which amounted to the staggering sum of 216 million francs.[1] At the Treaty of Tilsit in 1807, Napoleon also reduced Prussia's size by half, depriving it of all its territories west of the Elbe River. The catastrophes at Jena and Auerstädt had left Prussia's vaunted military in tatters, and, after the court in Berlin had fled from the advancing French army, the French occupiers took over the administration of many of the provinces, thus further undermining the authority of the Prussian government. In the wake of crumbling political authority at the center, the provincial organizations of estates, encouraged by Napoleon, took over even more economic and political authority. But the widespread destruction of farmland and requisitioning of food, cattle, and horses during the war devastated the countryside; to make matters worse, Napoleon's forcible inclusion of Prussia into his continental system cut them off from the English market, and without England as an export market, grain prices, absolutely crucial to the health of Prussia's economy, collapsed. In the wake of such economic and political disintegration, disease and hunger mounted; in Berlin alone between 1807 and 1808, of the 5,846 children born, 4,300 died, and the number of suicides rose sharply.[2] Prussia's old government and army had been thoroughly discredited; and by 1810, the state debt had grown from 53 million Thalers in 1806 to over 100 million Thalers, which in turn by 1815 had increased to more than 200 million Thalers.[3] It was clear that Prussia was hemorrhaging financially and unravelling politically.

The debacle had created an opening for those who wished to introduce modern, even French-style social and political reforms into Prussia, and Hegel was one of those who sympathized deeply with this aspiration. The reformers saw that the Prussian crisis had discredited the old elites and the old way of doing things; when the crunch came, they simply had not passed the test, and it was now time for something new and different, something more along the lines that the French were pushing onto Europe. As long as Napoleon was around and was supreme, the Prussian king had little choice: He had to go along with the reforms or, so it seems, run the risk of vanishing, along with his state, altogether.

Stein's Reform Government

A reform government was installed in 1807 under the leadership of Baron von Stein as chief minister. Stein, while wanting to reshape Prussian life around his vision of a mixture of English free-market economic theory, aristocratic liberalism, and preservation of some of the old corporate structure of the ancien régime in Germany, also brought with him a firm, almost cameralistic belief that the key to success lay in a well-educated administrative bureaucracy that could bring off these reforms in a disciplined, rational manner. Stein also believed that if Prussia was to survive as a modern state, it also had to offer its citizens something with which they could identify; Stein thought that this could be achieved by opening up the society to certain liberal ideas and by developing a form of nondemocratic but nonetheless representative government, in which "property owners" would be allowed "participation in the administration," an idea for which he took England to be the model.[4] (In England, so Stein argued, the costs of national administration were lower because local communities assumed more of those costs themselves, and they were willing to take on such costs and responsibilities because they "identified" with their state.)[5]

On October 9, 1807, Stein's government issued an edict that put the French idea of "careers open to talent" into practice, declaring that henceforth all occupations were to be open to those who qualified (in other words, a free labor market), that there were to be no restrictions on the sale of noble estates, and that after 1810 there were to be no more feudal relations of subordination on landed estates.[6] A year later, Stein's "municipal ordinance" of November 19, 1808, tried to put into effect a somewhat English idea of self-governance in terms of which the state would be built up from below by local communities in which propertied citizens would be authorized to manage their local affairs.

Stein's ideas thus confronted head-on what Hegel had regarded as the clash between modernizing "universalism" and particularist hometown structures, the ways in which hometowns vigorously defended their own local senses of identity, their entrenched ideas of the way things were supposed to be done, and the various structures of local authority and privilege that had accumulated over the years. To be sure, the cities of Prussia did not have the hometown structure typical of southern Germany (where Hegel had grown up), but they still carried with them a dizzying array of local privileges, exemptions, and concessions that made each locality different from the others. The "municipal ordinance" of 1808 more or less abolished those particularisms. From now on, the "municipal ordinance" declared, there was to be "only one right of citizenship" instead of the patchwork of various different local stipulations about membership and privileges, only *one* "city-citizenship" recognized as an "estate" in Prussian law replacing the patchwork of "city-citizenships" depending on the locality. Those who had the right of "citizenship" in the cities were henceforth to concern themselves with the affairs of their localities; the older rule of guilds and corporations in league with an appointed magistrate was to be wiped out. Although Stein's "municipal ordinance" did not entirely abolish all the local privileges and laws of the cities (for political reasons it had to leave some intact), its general drift was clear: Town membership was henceforth to be continuous with state membership, not something confronting it or competing with it.[7]

In pushing through these ordinances, Stein also had to confront the problem that older Prussian policy had tended to make local government completely dependent on state autocracy, and locals thus had become alienated from their own local governmental institutions. Stein's reforms thus clearly came to grips with the idea of transforming these people from *subjects* into *citizens* in order to motivate them to produce new wealth and spiritual support. The free market and administrative reforms coupled with representation in the government through membership in estates would, he thought, provide the necessary dynamic to avoid this dilemma and would reconcile the particularist emphasis on historically grounded privileges with the modernizing demands for the citizens' allegiance to the state.[8] The identification that individuals had with their own local communities and estates would thus be organically extended to the larger community that was supposed to be the state itself.

Under Stein's leadership, the old autocratic system of governance, in which the king made all the real decisions and took advice only from a cabinet appointed by him, had been effectively dismantled in the early stages of reform, with its place being taken in November, 1807, by a more reform-minded system of ministers who each headed a specific department. Stein had made himself only the "leading minister" of such a group, a first among equals, and this was exactly how we wanted it; in Stein's eyes, the ministry should be a collegial body with no clear leader having more privileges than the rest. As Stein had organized things, Prussia was to be divided into local administrative districts, which in turn were to be combined into district governments that were themselves supposed to operate as collegial bodies (not, as the alternative centralizing French model would have had it, under the authority of a single *Prefect*).[9]

The Hardenberg Reforms

Stein never found out if his ideas for running things would work. Under French pressure, he was dismissed in 1808, and he had to flee to Russia

after Napoleon put a price on his head. In Stein's place, Friedrich
Ferdinand Count von Dohna and Karl Altenstein were placed in charge
of the government, but that arrangement proved to be short-lived. In
June 1810, the king appointed Karl August Prince von Hardenberg as
chancellor, a newly established position in the government. Having been
the chief negotiator of Prussia's 1795 Treaty of Basel with France,
Hardenberg was used to striking deals, and he thus seemed like the
right person to carry out the reform program.

Like Stein, Hardenberg had studied in Göttingen; like Stein, he was
a member of the nobility; and like Stein, he was firmly on the side of
the reformers. Unlike Stein, though, Hardenberg wished to be something more like an English prime minister, and his wish was fulfilled
when he was named chancellor. Stein was idealistic, pragmatic, and
blunt; Hardenberg was pragmatic and courtly. Stein was attached to
particularist, almost hometown life; Hardenberg continued to speak of
the "machine state," not of the "organic unities" that had come to
pervade political discourse. Although Hardenberg was no less committed to reform than Stein, his ideas on what reform consisted in and how
to achieve the goals of reform departed in certain key ways from Stein's.
Neither Stein nor Hardenberg was personally inclined toward democracy, and Hardenberg was far less inclined toward representative government than was Stein. Like Stein, Hardenberg was concerned with
how he could bind individuals to the state in a way that would
strengthen the state, but unlike Stein, Hardenberg did not have any
personal attachment to the ideals of the hometown or to the old corporate bodies. He was thus far more inclined to push liberal economic
reforms at the expense of particularist communities than was Stein, and
he was far more inclined than was Stein to more French models of
statist centralization.

For Hardenberg, the central issue was that of restoring the authority
and power of the state, and if the old particularist estates stood in the
way of that, then so much the worse for them – they would simply have
to go. Putting any kind of written constitution into place was also less
important for Hardenberg than were the economic and administrative
reforms that he was convinced had to precede any constitutional settlement. Although Hardenberg gave eloquent statements of the purpose of
reform, he had no intention of introducing genuine democratic reforms
in the more expansive sense of devolving responsibility widely onto a

popular electorate; the administration was to remain in full authority over the governance of the state.

Hardenberg moved quickly and at first with great resolve to put his reforms into practice, issuing various sweeping edicts in rapid succession. On October 20, 1810, he issued a trade edict that firmly institutionalized the idea of careers open to talent; on October 27, he issued a finance edict, which was intended to equalize tax burdens; and on October 28, he issued an edict that required that anybody running a business be licensed not by his local guild but by the state.[10]

This last edict was clearly a strike against the very heart of the particularist nature of German life, a move to shift authority decisively away from local, historically embedded authorities to the state (thereby carrying further the momentum already established by Stein's 1808 "municipal ordinance"). Many of the established powers had been firmly opposed to these reforms from the outset, and even the threat of conquest or further humiliation from Napoleonic France had only blunted their hostility to the reform process. Neither the nobility nor the military officers wished to see their traditional privileges removed. Moreover, Stein's "municipal ordinance" had had the paradoxical effect of encouraging or creating small pockets of particularism in Prussia in places where they had earlier been leveled out, as the newly enfranchised city-citizens quickly began asserting their rights against those of the state.[11] Some other elements of reform also backfired: The result of emancipating the peasants from feudal ties – a reform originally opposed by many elements of the nobility – was that large wealthy landowners simply swallowed peasant land and thereby in many cases rendered the peasants even worse off than they had been before, whereas the nobles themselves only became richer and thus more confident of their ability to forestall any further changes. When Hardenberg summoned an "Assembly of Notables" in 1811 as an effort to bypass the traditional estates, he found himself stymied by the fact that the collapse of central authority in 1807 and some of Stein's reforms not only had reinvigorated the estates, but also had made them into the hub of antagonism to further reforms; they had become a force that was impossible to dismantle immediately. The "Assembly of Notables" quickly turned into a forum for attacking the reforms instead of a body that would unify the country in favor of the reform package as Hardenberg had intended.

The reformers (Stein, Hardenberg, and all their allies) faced a terrible dilemma: They had no real social constituency for their reforms outside of a small educated sector of the Prussian bureaucracy. Many people in the countryside were either indifferent or indignant, and the nobles were dead set against the reforms. Both Stein and Hardenberg were appealing to a Prussianized version of English and French society which did not exist but which they were trying to bring about; and in order to bring it about, they had to strike deals with the elements of society that were opposed to any version of such a vision. Hardenberg, like most others involved in the reform movement, was also haunted by the idea that reform had to be carried out without revolution; indeed, the fearful example of the French Revolution and the desire to avoid at all costs provoking something similar in Prussia formed the backdrop to almost all the moves undertaken by the reform movement. The result was that Hardenberg had to zig and zag in his policies; by 1812 the reform movement was clearly beginning to run out of steam, and by 1815 the defeat of Napoleon and the Congress of Vienna had sapped even more momentum from of the reform process. After Napoleon's defeat, Prussia, which had once looked as if it might vanish altogether as a major state, suddenly found itself larger than ever with the lands that it gained as a result of the post-Napoleonic shakeout; it now controlled large areas of the Rhineland and was seen as one of "Germany's" defenders along the border with France. Berlin now assumed a status more like that of Vienna as one of the central points in the Germanic world. No longer fearing humiliation by Napoleon, the antireform group was emboldened.

In those changed circumstances, the constitution that the king had been promising since 1810 and which he had publicly promised on May 22, 1815 – as the allies were preparing for their final battle with Napoleon – was put on indefinite hold. Even the reformers believed that they could not put any constitution into place without large-scale reforms first being carried out in society; and with the interest in reform becoming progressively more faint, the promise of the constitution began to seem more and more distant. But the reformers continued to firmly believe that for Prussia to be a sustainable modern state, they had to break down the barriers between government and society, prince and people, and create a state with which people could identify; and for that they needed a constitution to provide what they thought was the only way in which citizens could be integrated with the state. Otherwise, the well-established German practice of attaching loyalty to one's locality or hometown and not to any such abstraction as the "state" or the "monarch" would remain in place; without this binding to a larger sense of the state, hometowners and other particularists would continue to play one prince off against another as they felt they needed to and as they felt they could get away with. The problem of representation in the government was thus accentuated as the actual experience of representative institutions among the reformers dampened their enthusiasm for them; whenever representative institutions were called into session, they typically turned into forums for various groups to call for the reestablishment of their old privileges.

Although the slowdown of reform was clear enough in 1817 and 1818, when Hegel was musing about whether he should go to Berlin, it was not clear to everyone whether it was dead or was just taking longer than the overly euphoric aspirations during the heyday of the so-called "wars of liberation" had led some to hope. Hegel clearly took the latter view. For him, opposition was to be expected, but the social forces that were propelling reform were not going to vanish just because the representatives of an outmoded form of life were upset at the loss of their place as the lead actors on history's stage. The various religious and economic stresses and strains that had already put England and France on the path to modern life were now in full play in Germany and especially in Prussia itself under the leadership first of Stein and then of Hardenberg. The modern reform for which Hegel had so long hoped was, by his lights, now going to be transpiring under his nose, and he was set to play his part in it.

The Berlin University

The founding and development of the university at Berlin played no small role in Hegel's conception of what his place was to be in Berlin. The virtual collapse of the Prussian state in 1806 had led a number of influential people in Berlin to advocate founding a new university in the city to attract the kind of intellectual leadership that they thought was necessary for reforming and rebuilding the Prussian state and regaining for Prussia some of the prestige that it had so abruptly lost. The idea of founding a university in Berlin had originated in the request by the faculty of Halle (which Napoleon had closed in 1807) that it be reesta-

blished in Berlin. In the context of T. A. H. Schmalz's (the rector of
Halle's) request for reestablishment of the university in Berlin, the
Prussian king, Friedrich Wilhelm III, was widely reported to have said,
"The state must replace by spiritual power what it has lost physically."
It may be the only even remotely philosophical utterance he ever made,
but it made an impact, especially on modernizing intellectuals such as
Hegel. The idea gained currency, and various versions of it began to be
cited by people in Prussia. In 1807, the king authorized the head of his
cabinet, Karl Friedrich Beyme, to investigate the possibility of erecting
a university in Berlin.[12] It was certainly not to be taken for granted that
such a university was needed or should be founded. But having been
thus charged, Beyme asked several leading figures, among them Fichte,
to draw up suggestions about what form such a university should take
were it to be established.[13]

   None of the proposals submitted to Beyme (particularly Fichte's)
proved to be feasible, but the debate took a new turn when in the spring
of 1808 Friedrich Schleiermacher published a short piece, *Occasional
Thoughts on Universities in a German Sense*. Schleiermacher, who had
not been asked by Beyme to comment on the matter, independently
published his own thoughts, in which he argued for a vision of the
university more or less on the Jena model. In Schleiermacher's formulation, since knowledge is a totality that no single scholar can encom-
pass, the state must therefore create the university as a modern institution in which scholars can come together and create this unity in concert
with each other. The central faculty in such a university must be the
philosophical faculty – and it must be remembered that Schleiermacher
was a theologian making this argument – since only the philosophical
faculty is fully autonomous (harking back to Kant's thesis in *The Conflict
of the Faculties*) and thus capable of both representing and achieving the
unity of knowledge on which a modern institution of learning must rest.

   The key practice in such a university, Schleiermacher argued, is the
lecture; indeed, lectures are the "sacred aspects" of the "scientific common life of the university."[14] In the lectures, the professor both publicly
enacts the way in which knowledge unfettered by orthodoxy is achieved
and assists the students (both as exemplar and as pedagogue) in doing
this for themselves, in making themselves into appropriately *modern*
people. (In Schleiermacher's formulation, the Fichtean-Jena conception
of the "professor as modern hero" as distinct from the older professorial

figure of ridicule clearly emerged again.) It also follows, as Schleiermacher also made explicit, that academic freedom must be the touch-
stone of such a modern university.

Schleiermacher's essay was widely read in the right circles and informed a large part of the background discussion of what a university
in Berlin should look like. Schleiermacher's essay took on particular
significance after the great shake-ups in the Prussian ministry after 1807
(after Napoleon forced Stein's resignation and Beyme was discharged as
minister). The new minister, Count von Dohna, named Wilhelm von
Humboldt in February 1809 as chief of the recently founded section of
the Prussian government on "religion and public education" and specifically charged him with drawing up plans for the university. Although
Von Humboldt himself had studied law and philology in Göttingen
(and had also studied law at the university at Frankfurt on the Oder),
he had lived in Jena from 1794 to 1797 and had been infused with the
Jena view of the world. In May 12, 1809, von Humboldt submitted his
proposal to the king. In it he argued for the establishment of a Jena-
style university (although Jena was not mentioned) in which the instructional goals were to be focused on promoting the *Bildung* – the self-
determining self-cultivation and inwardly motivated love of learning
and education – of the students there and preparing them thereby to be
fully modern citizens of a fully modern state. To accomplish this, the
university had to embody within itself the union of "teaching and
research" – the two great watchwords of the Humboldt university
which were to endure for virtually all modern universities down to our
own day. The university thus had to be organized around the notion
that *Wissenschaft*, the totality of the learned disciplines, was an end in
itself, that academic freedom was therefore of utmost importance, and
that the purpose of the university was to have students *taught* by
professors who were to impart to them the state of the art in current
research in which they themselves were engaged. Publication was not
the most important part of the envisioned university, which in Humboldt's vision was to be based on a dynamic, evolving view of knowledge; the professor was to communicate in his lectures the latest and
best thoughts on the subject, and the students were to integrate them
into their own lives and go on to extend the process. The process would
lead to students emerging from the university with the formation necessary to continue to progress through such *Bildung* in the rest of their

lives. Moreover, in Humboldt's vision, just as in the Jena view, the university was most emphatically *not* to be a training ground for the professions; it was an incubator for self-determining men of taste and learning, who would emerge as the proper leaders and state officials of a modern, free form of life.

Humboldt succeeded in convincing the authorities to go ahead, and on October 10, 1809, the faculty senate held its first meeting (headed by its first rector, T. A. H. Schmalz, the former head of Halle who was later to become a strong opponent of Hegel), followed by the first lectures held on October 29, 1809. The university was a success; at its opening, it had already attracted many of the leading lights of German intellectual life and had become the model of the reformed modern university. Reality, however, soon set in. Humboldt, disappointed with the various demands and quibbles from the luminaries of the faculty the university had attracted, soon resigned his position and left Berlin even before the university had formally opened. The professors found that the promised remuneration and financial support for which Humboldt had called was not forthcoming. Humboldt had proposed that professor's salaries start around 1,500 Thalers per year; instead, they were pegged closer to 800 Thalers, when the cost of living for a bourgeois family to maintain itself in the socially appropriate ways was between 600 to 1,000 Thalers a year.[15] The students themselves turned out be more interested in careers than in *Wissenschaft* for its own sake, and the professors complained about it. Moreover, another shake-up in the Prussian administration had put K. F. von Schuckmann in charge of the university, and he put into effect a decree that the university would be completely dependent on the government for its operating costs rather than being given some lands or foundation from which it could derive independent revenues (as had been the case with the early modern universities).

In July 1811 the faculty elected Fichte as rector. Fichte, although beginning with high-minded ideals close to those upon which Humboldt had founded the university, almost immediately alienated all of his colleagues, and a kind of academic civil war among the faculty began. Some of it had to do with the personalities involved. Fichte, for example, had the habit of issuing his rectoral edicts to his colleagues by saying, "It is not I as an individual who says and wills this, but the Idea, which speaks and acts through me."[16] Fichte's troubles with the faculty came to a head with one particular incident. In his inaugural address as rector, Fichte had warned that the most pressing threat to academic freedom, the lifeblood of the modern university, was that of the students being untrue to their vocation. A student's vocation was to immerse himself in the study of "science"; instead, the students were falling back into the old pattern of a raucous fraternity life of drinking and dueling that, Fichte claimed, had brought down the university at Jena.[17] Fichte became particularly infuriated when a Jewish student was attacked by other students (who hoped thereby to provoke him into a duel); Fichte wished to punish those who had attacked the Jewish student, and when he was not supported by key members of the faculty in his efforts, became even further incensed. Schleiermacher, among others, thought that he was being too harsh; and Schleiermacher was no friend of Fichte's, as he had insisted on holding his lectures at the same time as Fichte's, thus depriving Fichte of potential lecture fees from the students who thereby could not attend his own lectures.[18] Furious, Fichte resigned as rector.

The various clashes among the faculty then descended into desultory hostilities involving various personalities, and the so-called wars of liberation against Napoleon only took more steam out of the original idealism surrounding the founding of the university. During the wars, the number of students declined precipitously; by the summer of 1813, for example, only fifteen students were attending the university.[19] Fichte himself died of typhoid during the war (while serving as a chaplain, along with his wife, who was serving as a nurse), and after the war the university could not quite manage to regain its original idealism. It had already begun to segment itself into more narrowly professional disciplines, and the students themselves were tending more and more to professional concerns rather than to *Bildung* and the love of *Wissenschaft* for its own sake.

By the time Hegel was called to Berlin, however, things had begun to improve, and his arrival was therefore greeted with a mixture of optimism, skepticism, anxiety, and expectation. The philosophical faculty had had no systematic philosopher teaching there since Fichte's death, and while many lamented that fact, many others wanted it to remain that way. Thus, Hegel was stepping into a situation as full of promise as it was full of difficulty; but in his own mind he was going exactly to where he ought to be. Hegel had long subscribed to the Jena vision of the modern university as the central institution of modern life; he certainly shared very deeply something like von Humboldt's vision for the university (however much he and von Humboldt were to disagree over other things); and he was at that point the leading proponent of the post-Kantian line of thought that had emanated from Jena in the first place and thus the appropriate philosopher for a university founded on the basis of Jena-inspired philosophy.

Hegel's identification with the Jena ideal of philosophy had informed all of his writings and aspirations since his arrival in Jena in 1801. The status of philosophy in the older university had not been that of a science, a *Wissenschaft*; philosophy was taken as a propaedeutic to theology, as a discipline whose integrity was parasitic on that for which it was a preparation. This had been in fact the status of philosophy at Tübingen when Hegel had studied there; at Tübingen the first two years of exclusive study in philosophy were justified only to prepare one for the (supposedly) more rigorous training in theology to follow. Hegel's insistence on philosophy as a "learned discipline" on its own – on philosophy as *Wissenschaft*, science – had been a rejection of his Tübingen training and an expression of his Jena-inspired modernism. Assuming a chair at Berlin was thus assuming a chair at a university that had been founded on the very ideal on which Hegel had staked his life. Moreover, the Berlin university had also incorporated into its founding the ideal of *Bildung*, the other great Hegelian modernist ideal.

Hegel was quite clearly enthusiastic about the prospect. At some point, probably in preparing his inaugural lecture for Berlin, Hegel had jotted down as a marginal note to the text of his inaugural lecture in Heidelberg an echo of the epithet first (allegedly) enunciated by the Prussian king, "Prussia [is] built on higher intelligence – greater seriousness and higher need."[20] In his actual inaugural lecture in Berlin on October 22, 1818, Hegel proclaimed that in Prussia and at the Berlin university, "the cultivation (*Bildung*) and the flowering of the *sciences* is here one of the essential *moments* itself in the *life of the state*; at this university, the university of the focal point, *philosophy*, the *focal point* of all cultivation of the spirit, of all science and truth, must find its place and its principal furtherance."[21]

Hegel was not coming to Berlin merely to hold a job doing something he liked; he was coming to achieve his modernist program, which hinged on philosophy's becoming the unifying element of the modern university, which was itself a necessary institution if the post-revolutionary world was to succeed in its own aspirations. To many at Berlin, Hegel's arrival thus offered some hope that the Humboldtian ideal could be reinvigorated; to others, Hegel's arrival seemed like a threat to what by then had become the status quo. That Hegel would have provoked great controversy at Berlin was thus not something, at least in retrospect, that should have been surprising.

Hegel Adapts to Berlin

Hegel and his family quickly settled into their new quarters, and Hegel almost immediately began his courses, lecturing on the "Encyclopedia of Philosophy" and "Natural Right and Political Science" five times per week (from 4:00–5:00 P.M. and from 5:00–6:00 P.M. respectively). Things looked auspicious for Hegel upon his arrival in Berlin. Although the majority of people actively publishing works in philosophy at the time in all of Germany comprised an odd assortment of people practicing *Naturphilosophie* under Schellingian influence (with a heavy dose of obscurantism thrown into the mix), Hegel was the person most au courant in Germany. After 1809, Schelling had fallen silent in his literary endeavors, and, although Schelling still had the greatest number of adherents teaching philosophy in universities, the real choice in modern philosophy had come down to Fries or Hegel, both of them claiming to represent the next step in the Kantian revolution in philosophy.

Although he had arrived amid some intense speculation about what kind of impression he was going to make, to the surprise of a great many at Berlin, he at first made no impact at all. One of his younger colleagues in philosophy at Berlin, Karl Solger, who had keenly anticipated Hegel's arrival, noted soon thereafter that "nobody speaks of him because he is so still and industrious."[22] The theologian de Wette, a student and friend of Fries, noted in a letter to Fries that nobody seemed concerned with Hegel, but, as de Wette presciently warned, he had "no doubt" that [Hegel] would "soon entice a few into his net."[23]

That Hegel was at first silent is not surprising. He had to set up a new household and find his way around a new university and, having also committed himself to writing a new book on his political and moral philosophy, had to contend with concerns for his wife's health, which, already fragile before the trip to Berlin, did not improve much during their first whole winter there in 1818–1819. Hegel's silence was enough to provoke Niethammer to complain lightheartedly in a letter of January 19, 1819, about having not heard anything directly from Hegel in such a long time.[24] When Niethammer also inquired about Hegel's finding him a position in Berlin – things were going badly politically for Niethammer in Munich, and he was coming to the conclusion that he had wasted fourteen years of his professional life there – Hegel had to answer with no small regret that he was only on the "periphery" of things in Berlin, without any real connections to the movers and doers of Berlin life, and hence could not be of any help.[25] Given how much Hegel owed to Niethammer's having secured him positions in his own life, this admission of powerlessness on his own part must have seemed rather poignant to him.

However, Hegel was also slightly dissimulating in his description of himself to Niethammer. In fact, although he started slowly, Hegel had begun to find himself at home in the world of the Berlin intellectuals and elite. Very shortly after his arrival in Berlin, Schleiermacher took Hegel as his guest on October 31, 1818 to one of the prestigious genteel clubs in Berlin, the *Gesetzlose Gesellschaft* (the Lawless Lodge), and on November 28, 1818, Hegel became an official member of the club.[26] The new philosopher in town was clearly being taken seriously by his colleagues, even if he did not yet quite see himself as part of the influential circle of movers and doers in Berlin. Still, he was delighted with the reception he received. In a letter of October 30, 1819, to an old friend in Heidelberg, Creuzer, Hegel noted somewhat proudly that in Berlin, not only are the youth "receptive to and interested in philosophy. One even finds majors, colonels, and privy councilors attending one's lectures here."[27]

It was also quite clear that the Hegel family was enjoying its new surroundings and the increase in income that came with Hegel's new, better-compensated position. In addition to his salary of 2,000 Thalers, he managed in his first year to take in 533½ Thalers in lecture fees, examination fees, and the like (although he continued to waive his fees for those he thought could not afford them).[28] The Hegel family lived in a characteristically "Biedermeier" style, a particularly German style typical of the early nineteenth century.[29] The emphasis in "Biedermeier" was on domesticity, coziness, and simplicity of design. It was a thoroughly middle-class, upright attitude and outlook; it prized itself on its simplicity and practicality as distinct from what was seen as the ostentation and profligacy of the aristocracy. It was also modern in the way it reflected the ethos of the new kinds of middle-class families and living arrangements that had arisen as the sphere of work had separated itself from the home. The Biedermeier house was centered around socializing among the members of the family, and the elements of it remain familiar: The central room of the house was the appropriately titled "living room" (*Wohnzimmer*) that included a sofa, an oval table, pictures on the wall (preferably of relations – Hegel's mother-in-law proudly hung a picture of Hegel over her sofa after 1819[30]), a hanging wood-framed mirror, and various work tables and sewing tables for the women; there would be a study with a writing desk and plenty of bookcases (or if there was no study, the small writing desk and book-cases would be part of the living room); the furniture – itself solid, practical, and easily movable – would be arranged not in terms of any larger symbolic design but so as to encourage socializing; there would typically be pleated curtains; bird cages and plants would be arranged on a table built to support them; there would also be a piano (something the Hegel family had possessed already in Nuremberg in 1811). All of these, including an upright clock (purchased in 1819) were to be found in the Hegel household; the family also kept at one time or another a pair of mating doves and a canary, and they were the proud owners of a flowering cactus. (Hegel also had the habit of taking naps on the sofa, sometimes falling asleep there and sleeping a good part of the night on it.)[31]

Hegel was paid in quarterly installments of 500 Thalers, and he turned over all his honoraria to his wife. What extra money Marie had thus depended on how many students Hegel was attracting that semester and how many examinations he was presiding over. Marie's duties included overseeing the running of domestic affairs, including arranging for and paying the various artisans and jobbers who were needed to keep their middle-class household running; Hegel took it on himself to pay the rent, pay the maids, and, significantly, to buy the wine. The purchase of wine remained in the Hegel household a matter of some priority, with quite a bit of expenditure going out for it; Hegel had acquired a taste for good wine and not in niggling amounts; he not only bought wine by the bottle but also by the barrel; among his favorites while he lived in Berlin were Cahors and Haut-Sauterne from France. (Hegel was also a great devotee of snuff tobacco.) He continued, as he had done in Bavaria, regularly and with gusto to play the state lottery, hoping for a big win one day to put his financial worries at ease. (Hegel was not a shrewd handler of his money; although he kept meticulous books, he regularly overestimated how much money was going to be coming in, and thus, not infrequently, overspent himself.)[32]

Hegel and his wife went to the theater and the opera with some regularity and also went to various other concerts with some frequency. They purchased a new baby grand piano for the household, which Marie (and increasingly, the children) played, and they hosted many musical evenings in their house (a Berlin fashion at the time). The three boys were all required to take music lessons, and at least (but probably not only) Ludwig was required to take singing lessons. Their recreations were not restricted only to such highly cultural matters; in January of 1820, Hegel purchased a bolt of white satin in order for Marie to have a ball gown made for herself so that they could attend a gala *Faschings* ball in February (a Mardi Gras celebration); for himself, Hegel bought a large Venetian cape (a "Domino") and a mask to wear to the ball. Even at forty-nine, Hegel still retained his youthful passion for attending balls and enjoying the eating, drinking, dancing and socializing that went on there. (Apparently he also enjoyed the aspect of dressing up in costume.)[33] As always, he avidly read the morning newspapers; his sons remember him constantly commenting on the political events of the day as he perused the newspaper each morning, no doubt drinking the coffee of which he was so fond.

Whatever the initial difficulties of setting up a new household in a city like Berlin, Hegel was obviously quite satisfied with life in his new position and was enjoying himself; he had the family life he had wanted, and he had his career right on target in the right place (and, so it seemed) at the right time. Marie Hegel even noted in the margins of a letter that Hegel wrote to Niethammer on March 26, 1819 (she had a habit of writing small marginalia on Hegel's letters to mutual friends), "I see my Hegel content in his profession, cheerful with me and the children, and *recognized* – and that is what matters to an honorable, upright woman above all else."[34]

But there were also clearly other tensions at work in the household. In her marginal note to Niethammer, Marie spoke warmly of how Karl and Immanuel were doing but did not even mention Ludwig – a telling omission, as if in her eyes he was not one of the family, was invisible, or at least was unworthy of being mentioned. Interestingly, Marie's mother continued to send presents to all "three boys" for holidays at least until 1819 and continued to speak warmly of Ludwig until 1823.[35] It is also clear from Hegel's household budget ledger that the family spent little on Ludwig's birthday but quite a bit more on Karl and Immanuel's birthdays; there is also a notice to the effect that Hegel took the two (not three) children in January to see the elephant and the rhinoceros; it is a reasonable surmise that the two were Karl and Immanuel, not Ludwig and one of the other brothers.[36]

In the middle of all this gaiety, Hegel also clearly felt himself to have reached a certain juncture in his life. When Jacobi died on March 10, 1819, Hegel noted it as a final passing of his youth. He remarked to Niethammer, "We feel ever more abandoned as, one by one, these old stocks, to whom we looked up from youth on, pass away. He was one of those who formed a turning point in the spiritual culture not only of individuals but of the age, who were the fixed points of the world in which we think of our existence," and, he remarked sadly, "he had frequently asked of news of me, and will now never have received any from me in Berlin."[37] As the heroes of his youth began to pass from the scene, the idea that he was now becoming an old man began to occupy Hegel's thoughts more and more.

Hegel and the Prussian Reaction: 1819–1820

The Murder of Kotzebue and the Search for "Demagogues"

Happy at home and in his career, Hegel was hard at work on his book on political philosophy, now known as the *Philosophy of Right*: he unfortunately could not see the storm coming his way at that time. On March 23, 1819, the ultrareactionary playwright August von Kotzebue was murdered. His loss was not mourned by those in the reform movement, who had good reason to dislike Kotzebue: He was an agent of the Russian government informing it of the "Jacobin" tendencies in German universities, and he was an outspoken opponent of all the reform agendas that were making the rounds in Germany. A twenty-three-year-old student, Karl Sand, who had fallen under the sway of the most radical of the leaders of the *Burschenschaften*, Karl Follen, gained admittance to Kotzebue's room and stabbed him to death. Sand, a fanatic devoted to Follen's ideas and one of the "honor guards" at the infamous Wartburg festival, took himself to be performing an almost sacred deed. Only a few weeks later, another member of the *Burschenschaft*, Karl Loening, murdered Karl von Ibell, an official in the *Land* of Nassau (close to Frankfurt).[38] The murders, particularly that of Kotzebue, gained quite a bit of attention throughout the various German *Länder*. Some were horrified, and some were enthused; in fact, most reformers tended simply to explain the murders away, even to suggest that they had been brought about by the despotic conditions of the times, and to adopt a rather detached attitude. Certainly no reformer mourned Kotzebue's departure from the scene, and many regarded it ruefully as perhaps a necessary evil. (Sand was captured, tried, convicted, and executed; in an ironic turn of events, his executioner was a sympathetic democrat who then built a summerhouse out of the scaffolding on which Sand was executed and made it available to the *Burschenschaft* for secret meetings.)[39]

Hegel joined some other professors in an excursion to Pichelsberg in May 2, 1819, that was arranged by some students, most of whom were members of some *Burschenschaft* or another. Among the group was Schleiermacher, de Wette, and Johann Christian Hasse, a jurist at the university. There was much drinking and singing, particularly of patriotic songs about the spirit of the "liberation" from Napoleon. The students later noted how the professors seemed to become young again as they joined the festivities (and consumed their fair share of the wine and beer). One of the members, Friedrich Förster, who was later to become a good friend of Hegel's, read a poem on the topic of Kotzebue's death and ended with a toast: "We do not wish to drink a toast to Sand but rather to the downfall of evil, without so much as the dagger's thrust."[40] Other students chimed in to drink to Sand's memory.

Although many people in Germany had written off the murders as aberrations, the authorities were taking intense notice of them and treating them quite seriously. The more reactionary elements only saw their fears of Jacobin secret societies and potentially French-style revolutionary events confirmed in Kotzebue's assassination. The Prussian nobility especially felt itself under threat, and the reactionary camp in Prussia, aghast at the assassination and its imagination inflamed, set to work to discover if such groups existed and to weed them out if they were to find them. They were particularly suspicious of the *Burschenschaften* and what they saw as their nationalist, republican tendencies (which many of the reactionary identified as the aims of the French Revolution). A widespread search for the "demagogues" began in earnest. By the middle of July, 1819, a number of people were being arrested and interrogated.

Hegel's Students Arrested: The Case of Asverus

One of the first students to be arrested had been a student of Hegel's in Heidelberg, Gustav Asverus. His father had been both Schelling's and Hegel's lawyer in Jena, had helped Hegel out with the problems surrounding the publication of the *Phenomenology*, and later had handled the negotiations with Johanna Burkhardt concerning Hegel's marriage to Marie von Tucher. Moreover, the younger Asverus was good friends with both Julius Niethammer and Hegel's brother-in-law, Gottlieb von Tucher. On April 8, 1819, he was arrested by the Prussian police and held for fourteen days, even though there was no evidence that he had any connection with Karl Sand at all. But Asverus lacked a certain discretion, and on April 29, 1819, he wrote a letter to a friend in which he praised Sand, praised Hegel, and claimed that outside of de Wette, Hegel, and Hasse, all of the professors at Berlin were cowards. He then went on to write some other letters praising Hegel and lambasting Fries – who had been his original teacher in Heidelberg and who had tried to help out in the matter of his arrest[41] – and in one letter of May 11 to his parents, again praised Hegel and told them he wanted a unified "fatherland." The authorities intercepted the letters and arrested Asverus again on the night of July 14, 1819 on suspicions of being a "demagogue" (in the parlance of the time, a dangerous subversive). They held him incommunicado, refusing to let anybody talk to him while he was being interrogated.[42]

On July 27, 1819, at the instigation of Asverus' father, Hegel wrote to the Prussian police ministry speaking in favor of Asverus's character and assuring the officials that whatever Asverus's past had been, he had by now completely dissociated himself from the *Burschenschaft* movement, indeed, from all suspicious movements, and had devoted himself with some success to studying the learned disciplines at the university.[43]

It was to no avail. By August 24, 1819, Asverus had been held incommunicado for five weeks, and Hegel engaged an acquaintance, king's counsel K. L. Krause, to defend Asverus; Krause was also prevented from speaking with Asverus. It was not until Asverus's father managed to get the government of Sachse-Weimar to intervene diplomatically with the Prussian government that Asverus was set free – on March 3, 1820, almost nine months after he had first been arrested. Part of the terms of his release had to do with Hegel's purchasing a state bond for 500 Thalers (about one-quarter of his total yearly income) as bail for Asverus.[44]

The incident with Asverus no doubt set Hegel's nerves a bit on edge. The "focal point" to which he had just come had with rather alarming dispatch and efficiency, rounded up someone whom they suspected just might be a "demagogue" and, even worse, it was one of *his* students who had mentioned *his* name in the intercepted letters in contexts that might have made the somewhat overly zealous authorities suspicious of *him*. Moreover, his own brother-in-law, Gottlieb von Tucher, who was friendly with Asverus, was implicated in the whole affair and had ended one of his letters with the phrase, "When will the bloody-red morning ever dawn?"[45] Hegel dealt with the problem head-on and continued as he had been doing, deciding that the whole fracas represented at least no immediate threat to himself. In fact, his attitude at first seemed to be that of shrugging off the whole episode as the dying gasp of an antiquated class of people fearful of what was almost certain to happen in any event.

The Persecution of the "Demagogues": Fries and de Wette

Marie Hegel, still not having fully recovered from the health problems related to her miscarriage at the end of 1817, traveled to the spa town of Neustadt on August 1, 1819, in order to regain her health, taking the children with her (or at least Karl and Immanuel – Ludwig is not mentioned in Hegel's letters to her during her absence from him, and it is unclear if he stayed at home in Berlin with Hegel at this point). Hegel used the month by himself to work intensively on his *Philosophy of Right*, finally joining Marie and the children on September 1, 1819. They decided to catch a boat on the Oder River and make their way to the very fashionable island of Rügen in the Baltic Sea; there they could appropriately celebrate their wedding anniversary in their first year after the move to Berlin. The trip proved quite expensive – more than 238 Thalers – and it turned out to be one of those all-too-common family vacations that did not unfold quite as planned.[46] At the first town on the Ode (Schwedt), Karl Hegel was so badly bitten by mosquitoes that he could not even open his eyes; when they finally got to Rügen, it stormed ferociously, and their departure from the island was delayed for a few days because of the terrible weather.[47] But Hegel nonetheless retained fond memories of collecting shells with the boys on the beach. (The memories of the rainstorms on the Rügen vacation, however, lingered; when Hegel was later traveling, he would sometimes tell Marie in letters that it was raining as hard as it had done in Rügen.)[48] On September 23, Hegel returned to Berlin; Marie and the children stayed behind for a bit longer.

As Hegel soon learned on his return, the flap over Asverus had turned out to be more than the isolated incident he had at first taken it to be. Kotzebue's assassination had continued to provoke interest and fear, and one person paying particular attention to it was Metternich, who saw in it the means to transform the fear of revolution among the German nobility and ruling elites into a fear of reform itself and thus to shore up his continued attempts to turn back the clock for the European monarchies (and thereby protect Austria's interests). In fact, it was secret negotiations between Metternich and the Prussians (along with participation by other major powers) that had led to the first phase of the crackdowns against the "demagogues" that had landed Asverus in such trouble. These early crackdowns, however, were not enough for Metternich, who realized that he needed and probably could bring about a more far-reaching program of hunting down so-called "radical" elements in German society – which meant, in his mind, any person or group that threatened the established order imposed by the Congress of Vienna. Metternich himself had already argued at the first European Congress in September 1818 that "secret" forces of revolution threatening the established order were gathering steam and were already poised and ready to strike; Metternich advised the delegates that those forces needed to be met with firm resistance by the German princes; he also argued that social unrest, revolution, and constitutionalism were all part of the same package, so that to countenance one was to encourage all of them. He pressed his points further in a series of communications

to the Prussian king, arguing that military strength was incompatible
with representative government and that the introduction of representative government into Prussia would inevitably spell its demise. The
king, who had already been made wary of constitutionalism by various
reactionaries in his court and who had been greatly influenced by a
pamphlet written by T. A. H. Schmalz in 1815 equating constitutionalism with the French Revolution, was obviously a receptive audience
for Metternich's admonitions.

Kotzebue's assassination was, quite simply, a stroke of great luck for
Metternich, offering him the opening he had been seeking. Already
made nervous by Metternich's warnings of insurrection, the Prussian
king had issued a cabinet order on January 1, 1819, proclaiming that
"dispositions dangerous to the state" were not to be tolerated among
university professors.[49] While visiting the Prussian king in Teplitz in
August 1819, Metternich managed to convince him even further of the
rightness of his views and of the need for firm resistance to these
revolutionary tendencies in German society; the king promptly instructed his chancellor, Hardenberg, to issue a decree, using Kotzebue's
murder as the pretext, revoking all plans to introduce the constitution
including representative government that he had earlier promised the
Prussian people. Metternich also managed to persuade the king to
participate in a meeting with other German rulers at the spa resort of
Karlsbad from August 6 to August 31, 1819.

The result of that meeting was the Karlsbad decrees, which included
four essential provisions providing for political repression: First, any
lecturer or professor in a German university who was deemed to be
hostile to public order or to be undermining the basic principles of the
state – in other words, who was found to be a "subversive," a "demagogue" – was to be immediately dismissed, and there was to be a
government appointed supervisory commission for each university to
oversee whether any professors or students were guilty; furthermore, no
other German university was permitted to employ any professor who
had been dismissed on those grounds. Second, a press law established a
central commission that was to provide for the effective censorship of
all papers, books, and journals throughout the German confederation.
Third, an investigative commission was to be established in Mainz with
broad powers to ferret out "demagogues." Fourth and finally, there
were to be strong executive powers that the confederation could use

against unruly member states – in other words, against states that refused to participate in the repression that the decrees mandated.[50] By September, 1819, the federal Diet of the German confederation had enacted these decrees as law, and the Prussians began to enforce them with special ardor. Rifts within the reform movement in Prussia now opened wide; Wilhelm von Humboldt, for example, vigorously protested against the Karlsbad decrees as a violation of freedom and of the conditions under which *Bildung* could be pursued, but Hardenberg saw them as necessary to maintain order.[51] Humboldt's opposition to the Karlsbad decrees led to his being forced to resign from the government; others so inclined were also forced to resign, and the number of reformers holding governmental posts began inexorably to shrink.

The newspaper *Allgemeine Preußische Zeitung* had already reported in its July 13, 1819, issue that the measures by which people like Asverus were being arrested had been made necessary by the "conclusive proofs of the existence and revolutionary high-treasonous tendencies" of certain "demagogic machinations" abroad in the land.[52] Seven days later (July 20), the newspaper published an elaboration of the supposed necessity of and rationale for the crackdown. It claimed that there was proof of the existence throughout the various German principalities of "alliances of evil-minded people and misled youth" whose goal was the "overthrow" of the existing social order, to be replaced by a "republic grounded in unity, freedom, and so-called nationality," and these people had unfortunately already seduced many youth at German universities. The newspaper further claimed that these subversive groups were, according to their own documents, aiming at no less than the murder of princes and leading citizens. As if it were not clear what was meant, the paper described these as "authentic Jacobin doctrines" unfortunately being propagated by people "under the mask of [speaking of] holy things."[53] It was clear to all whom the last phrase referred to: the theologians at Berlin, particularly Schleiermacher and the friend and student of Fries, Wilhelm Martin Lebrecht de Wette, who were known to be sympathetic to the *Burschenschaft* and its goals. De Wette himself was summoned to an interrogation, which he refused, firing off an angry letter to the minister of police, the highly reactionary Count Wilhelm Ludwig Georg Wittgenstein zu Sayn-Wittgenstein-Hohenstein, on August 19, 1819, saying that he did not even want to give the appearance of being involved in the "demagogic machinations" and thus refused to cooperate with such a waste of time.[54] Schleiermacher organized the theologians into a protest against the measures.

   Although it was clear that it was primarily de Wette and Schleiermacher who bore the brunt of suspicion – the authorities even put Schleiermacher's sermons under surveillance to see if "demagogic" ideas were being promulgated from the pulpit – Hegel had reason to be nervous that such investigations might be extended to him. In September 1819, shortly after his return from the rainy vacation in Rügen, things began to heat up. The theologian de Wette, in what was surely an astonishing display of bad judgment, wrote a condolence letter to Sand's mother, in which he said that although Sand's act was wrong, his "conviction" was that he was doing the right thing, and that when each acts "according to his best conviction, he will do the best." Sand's act was therefore a "beautiful testimonial of the time."[55] The letter caused a furor; it was denounced as the leading wedge in a campaign to overthrow the existing order and to justify regicide. The king's cabinet order of January was invoked against de Wette, and without any due process or hearing, de Wette was summarily dismissed from the university on September 30, 1819.[56] The faculty senate, joined by even its most conservative members, protested sharply, and the king replied to them just as curtly that he would "do harm to his conscience" if he were to "further entrust the instruction of youth" to a man "who holds assassination to be justified under certain conditions and presuppositions."[57] De Wette wrote a defiant letter to the king and departed from Berlin for Weimar. The crackdown on the alleged demagogues continued and in November 1819 the Weimar government was forced, more or less against its will, to live up to the Karlsbad decrees and discharge Fries from his position at the Jena university.

Carové

Like all the other professors, Hegel was understandably anxious about this turn of events. He was, after all, linked to a student in the *Burschenschaft* (Asverus) who was still under arrest at the time of de Wette's dismissal, and even his brother-in-law was a member. Hegel had also brought Friedrich Wilhelm Carové with him to Berlin to act as his assistant and had hopes of eventually getting Carové a professorship in Berlin or elsewhere. Carové had been one of the leading lights in the

Burschenschaft movement, and Hegel especially admired Carové's devotion to philosophy. Carové had in fact given up a good career in law and his position as an official in the customs office in Cologne to dedicate himself to philosophy. Hegel brought Carové to Berlin to work as a *Repetent* for his lectures – essentially a teaching assistant who would go over the material from the professor's lectures with the students in a separate session, illustrating and elaborating on various points and giving the students various "exercises" to do so that they could better understand and integrate what they had heard in the lectures. Since there were no official posts for such teaching assistants at Berlin, Carové at first did this without remuneration, but Hegel had well founded hopes for remedying that very soon.

In August 1818, a couple of months before Hegel had arrived in Berlin, the faculty had gone to work to set the rules and regulations for a *Repetenteninstitut* (an organization of such teaching assistants that designated their rights and duties and their remuneration from the university), and Hegel participated in the final deliberations. Hegel fully agreed with the majority opinion of the faculty, that the provision of paid teaching assistants to professors (who should be allowed to choose them themselves) was not aimed so much at helping the professors with their workloads but at providing subsistence and support for young scholars who would one day become professors in their own right. In his official request of November 9, 1818, to have Carové named as his teaching assistant, Hegel also argued that such assistants were necessary for the pedagogical aims of a university such as Berlin; in philosophy such sessions led by teaching assistants were especially necessarily, Hegel argued, because only in such sessions could one have the "conversations" and "disputes" that were necessary to learning philosophy; only in such sessions could the students voice "their own views and doubts" about the material and learn to come to grips with the material; philosophical knowledge could not, Hegel argued, be gained by simply memorizing books or by requiring more reading; a level of personal involvement and disputation was necessary.[58]

To Hegel's disappointment, the faculty refused in December 1818 to accept Carové as a teaching assistant until he "habilitated." Carové continued to act as Hegel's teaching assistant but without pay. Hegel made another entreaty to officials and the faculty in April 1819 to grant the request that Carové be made his teaching assistant, but it was to no avail.[59] In June 1819, Carové himself, still not having heard from Minister Altenstein about his request to become a teaching assistant, wrote to him about it, and in what turned out to be act of consummate imprudence, also sent Altenstein a piece he had written on Sand's assassination of Kotzebue from a "Hegelian" perspective (in which he tried to show how the "one-sidedness" of the views of Kotzebue's assassination as *either* a crime *or* a beautiful deed were misguided). This was perhaps the worst possible time to be relying on subtlety of any sort or to be linking oneself in any way whatsoever to the assassination in any other manner than by wildly condemning it. To make matters worse, Carové's own links with the *Burschenschaft* had made him suspect from the outset, even before he sent the pamphlet. As if to cast even more suspicion on himself, Carové was also on relatively good terms with Gustav Asverus – the two had hated each other in Heidelberg but had reconciled in Berlin – and so when Asverus came under suspicion, Carové did too.[60]

This took a toll on Hegel; he began to be a bit gloomy about the prospects for the future. It seemed that everything for which he had been preparing himself since his youth was possibly about to be dashed. He had been dedicated to playing a part in fashioning a modern world in Germany since his youth; but his original aspirations to be a reforming "popular philosopher" had fallen short; his first professorial position in Jena had collapsed; he had been out of university life for most of his adult life; and now, just when he thought he was ready to settle down into a productive career and a satisfying domestic life, it looked like things were coming unglued again. He was also feeling more and more like an old man, not somebody who could afford to wait out the storm in hopes of a better time. In an October 30, 1819, letter to Creuzer, Hegel noted that "you will surely understand as well, moreover, that all this does not help brighten one's spirits. I am about to be fifty years old, and I have spent thirty of these fifty years in these eternally uneasy times of fear and hope. I had hoped that for once we might be done with it. Now I see that things are continuing forward as ever, indeed, in one's darker hours it seems they are getting ever worse."[61]

Feeling terribly upset with the way things were suddenly turning out, Hegel found a scapegoat: his old nemesis Fries (and his acolyte, de Wette). To his way of viewing things, it was the imprudent and ignorant actions and pronouncements of Fries and his followers that had brought all the trouble down on the universities. He had always detested Fries (the feeling was mutual); throughout most of their lives, they had been rivals, first for university positions and now for influence in the German philosophical world; now Fries seemed to Hegel to be responsible for the possible unraveling of Hegel's plans, maybe even of his career, and maybe even of the project of reforming the German world through the universities. If he had hated him before, he surely hated him even more now.

Things, however, were not just "seeming" to get worse, as Hegel said he sometimes felt in his "darker hours"; they *really* were getting worse, and not just for Carové. Altenstein, himself nervous about doing anything imprudent, put off answering Carové's June request, and on November 19, 1819, officially asked the minister of the interior, von Schuckmann, if Carové was being investigated or was a participant in any of the alleged "secret societies" that were supposed to be flourishing in Germany at the time. Altenstein's suspicions were further aroused when the director of the ministry of police, von Kamptz, answered a week later that Carové was not a member of any "secret society," but that he was reputed to have given a rather "curious" speech at the Wartburg festival, and was also reputed to have defended Kotzebue's murder, and that he therefore intended to interrogate Asverus about Carové.

Dispute with Schleiermacher

In the midst of this tension, at a gathering at the *Gesetzlose Gesellschaft* on the evening of November 13, 1819, the tensions surrounding all this bubbled over, and Hegel and Schleiermacher ended up in an ugly quarrel over the firing of de Wette, exchanging sharp words in public. By this time, Hegel had come to think that getting rid of de Wette was a good thing, that people like de Wette (in other words, any member of the Fries school) were bringing calamity on the university and that both the university and German society were simply better off without them. The confrontation began when Hegel offered the opinion that the university was justified in firing de Wette provided that it continue to pay his salary. Hegel and Schleiermacher were treading on dangerous emotional ground for both of them; Schleiermacher, after all, was already under suspicion and was having his sermons watched by the authorities;

his acquaintances were being removed from their positions by the authorities, and he had reason to worry that he might be next; Hegel, like Schleiermacher, also had reason to worry that he might be next, but he put the blame elsewhere. Schleiermacher took great umbrage at Hegel's defense of de Wette's dismissal, and the squabble began, with Hegel and Schleiermacher essentially trading insults. (Despite his deep-seated aversion to de Wette, Hegel held fast to his belief that the university had an obligation to continue to pay de Wette, and when the university refused de Wette his income, which de Wette countered by haughtily refusing a few months' severance pay, a group of professors, including Hegel, gathered up a secret fund to provide de Wette with some income during his absence from university life; each professor contributed yearly to the fund – Schleiermacher contributed 50 Thalers, while Hegel contributed 25 Thalers – and the whole thing had to be kept secret from the government, which would not have looked kindly on the professors supporting a "subversive.")[62]

The spat between Schleiermacher and Hegel was probably inevitable, and all the more unfortunate since both belonged firmly to the reformist movement in Prussian society even though they represented different points of view within that movement. But Schleiermacher had never been exactly enthusiastic about bringing Hegel to Berlin; it was in fact Karl Solger, not Schleiermacher, who had proposed Hegel for the chair, and Schleiermacher had ended up voting for Hegel, ironically enough, only because he thought it was the only way to block Fries from receiving the appointment. Schleiermacher's views on the kind of philosophy Hegel practiced, moreover, were well known; in 1811 he had publicly argued before the Academy of Sciences in Berlin that "speculative philosophy" (the kind practiced by Schelling and Hegel) was not even a discipline at all and therefore did not belong in the university. Hegel also held no love for Schleiermacher's theology; as far as he was concerned, it was to be lumped together with Fries's views as a philosophy of feeling instead of reason.

Although von Altenstein had virtually promised Hegel that he would be admitted to the Academy of Sciences in Berlin, the tiff with Schleiermacher almost ensured that Hegel would never be invited to join the academy (and indeed he never was). Besides losing a stipend that would have augmented his income, Hegel also experienced his exclusion from the academy as a personal affront, and it was probably no secret to

Hegel that Schleiermacher was one of the main opponents to his receiving such an appointment. (The other was the jurist Friedrich von Savigny.) Hegel had always been a bit touchy about his own standing and the role that "speculative philosophy" had to play in modern German life, and he had experienced several years of being passed over for important positions that were given to people to his mind not nearly as talented as himself. Moreover, he had always felt that a number of well-placed lesser lights were simply prejudiced against "speculative philosophy" (and thus against all post-Kantian attempts to craft a "modern" philosophy) and were determined to keep it (and therefore him) out of the university. The academy had previously refused to admit Fichte; now it was refusing to admit Hegel, and this refusal only stung all the worse.

Rumors of the row between Hegel and Schleiermacher quickly circulated around Berlin. The two quickly made up, exchanging letters and apologizing for their mutually uncivil behavior at the club. Schleiermacher tendered the address of a Bordeaux wine merchant on Alexanderplatz in Berlin, Hegel thanked him for it, and each apologized; but the damage was done. The Schleiermacher-Hegel enmity had become public and remained in place for a long time.

Carové's Troubles Increase

In the meantime, Carové's troubles continued to mount. On December 1, 1819, the police minister, Count Wittgenstein, one of the more reactionary and ignorant members of the antireform crowd – who, appointed to membership on the commission to draft a constitution after Humboldt's dismissal, had vehemently opposed the writing of a constitution at all – denounced Carové to Altenstein as clearly a subversive, whose bad character was evidenced by the people with whom he associated, who included, on Wittgenstein's account, other students of Hegel's. Despite Wittgenstein's allegation, von Kamptz more or less exonerated Carové on December 24, 1819, after the interrogations and further investigations; but the damage had been done; in an ominous note to the proceedings von Kamptz also remarked that although he had concluded that Carové had not in fact approved of Kotzebue's murder, his writings on the matter were so obscure that one might have mistakenly though he had, and that this was not Carové's fault –

Carové's writing could be mistaken for a justification of Kotzebue's assassination "on account of the wretched mysticism of recent German philosophy and in particular that of the Hegelian, to which Carové has dedicated himself."[63]

Although von Kamptz had exonerated Carové, Count Wittgenstein thundered back a few days later on December 29, 1819, rejecting Carové's exoneration, arguing that it seemed perfectly evident to him that Carové approved of the murderer (Sand), and that moreover Carové himself was a "mystic" who should under no conditions be appointed to the university. Wittgenstein got many of his ideas about all of this from a person even more ignorant and doctrinaire than himself, Christian Moritz Pauli, who, besides claiming that the *Burschenschaft* ideal of "Germanness" was really just "Jewishness" – which in Pauli's twisted worldview meant of course that it was depraved – also claimed explicitly that Carové's so-called defense of Kotzebue's assassination was "inspired by Hegel."[64] That settled matters for Altenstein; he told Carové that it would be better if he left Berlin, went to the university at Breslau, became a private lecturer (*Privatdozent*) and did his "habilitation" there. The writing was now starting to appear on the wall: Hegel's students were being arrested, his own choice for his teaching assistant was being denounced, and he himself was precariously close to being denounced along with him.

By March 1820, Carové's troubles were increasing. The commission in Mainz proposed to Hardenberg new interrogations of Carové, Asverus, and another of Hegel's students, Leopold Dorotheus von Henning. Carové was interrogated in Breslau on April 15, 1820, and the interrogator reported back to Hardenberg on April 28, 1820, that he indeed suspected Carové of "demagogic activity." The commission in Mainz received the report on May 13, 1820, and on May 25 Hardenberg sent it to Altenstein, remarking that many things were notable in the report. That sealed Carové's fate; having already grasped what was afoot, Carové left in April for a long trip to Cologne, Dresden, Prague, Munich, Switzerland, and then back to Cologne. When he did not promptly return, Altenstein took this as the pretext he needed; the Prussian government banned Carové from all academic life. Carové was in fact never to receive an academic position; when he tried to obtain the status of a mere *Privatdozent* at Heidelberg in 1821, the government was legally compelled to reject his request. Left without any possibility of academic employment, Carové was forced instead to eke out his livelihood for the rest of his life as an independent writer; but he never broke off his affectionate ties to Hegel, even dedicating his book *Kosmorama* in 1831 to him.[65]

As Carové's troubles were coming to a head, Hegel also heard from his cousin Ludwig Friedrich Göriz sometime around May 1820 that his sister, Christiane, had suffered a relapse in her bout with mental illness. This was one more woe to be added to Hegel's other worries. Hegel wrote to Göriz a couple of times that this was the most unhappy thing that could befall a man – there is no reason to doubt that is how he felt – and he wondered whether it was "hysteria" brought on by the physiological changes "natural" to her age. However, on June 17, 1820, feeling himself too far away to do anything himself and obviously being unwilling (given the past difficulties between Christiane and Marie) to bring her to Berlin for treatment, Hegel washed his hands of the matter and gave Göriz full authorization to serve as her guardian so that she could be committed to the sanitarium at Zwiefalten. He also contributed some money for her upkeep so that she could be well attended.

Hegel's Second Choice: von Henning

With Carové having been rejected by the authorities, Hegel had to make a second choice for teaching assistant. Somewhat defiantly, he chose Leopold von Henning, an aristocrat who had fought in the wars against Napoleon as a volunteer. Von Henning, a friend of Asverus and Carové, had also been arrested on July 8, 1819, mostly on the basis of comments in some letters that his stepmother sent to him that the authorities (after intercepting the letters) had found "suspicious." He was held for seven weeks with a policeman guarding the door to his prison cell.[66] During von Henning's imprisonment, Hegel did something a bit extraordinary. Henning's cell had a window facing the Spree River in Berlin, not far from the university and Hegel's apartment. Hegel joined his students on a skiff and at midnight they all rowed up to the point at which Henning's cell window faced the river and began a conversation with him in Latin so that it could not be understood by the guards if they were to overhear it; they wished to let him know that they were convinced of his innocence and that they were working hard to prove it. As the boat pulled up next to Henning's window, close enough for Hegel

and Henning to shake hands, Hegel, aware of the general absurdity of
the situation into which he had put himself, uttered in Latin in a mock
grave tone, "num me vides" (literally translated: "now you surely see
me"), which provoked no small amount of mirth among those present.
Hegel then continued with some vague generalities (in Latin), and the
group went home, the students amused (and probably a bit surprised)
by Hegel's ironic treatment of the situation, and all (including Hegel)
joking about the matter on the way back. (Hegel's first biographer, Karl
Rosenkranz, laconically noted that it would have been all too easy for
Hegel to have been shot by a zealous Prussian watchman.)[67] It took
Hegel another whole year, but by July 22, 1820, he had managed to
obtain Henning as an official teaching assistant (to be paid the sum of
400 Thalers per year), but Henning was unable to get a certificate of
not-guilty from the government and had to teach for a year without pay
(in his own apartment, not in a university building) in order to prove
his suitability to the authorities.[68]

Dresden: Drinking to the Revolution

Another person who had attached himself to Hegel after Hegel's move
to Berlin, Friedrich Förster, also fell into trouble with the police. Förster shared some of Henning's profile; he had fought as a volunteer in
the wars against Napoleon and, having been severely wounded, had
been brought to Berlin to teach at the Royal Artillery and Engineering
School there. He was interrogated simply because he published a piece
in 1818 that not only called for a constitution for Prussia (something
the king had previously promised), but also maintained that laws legitimately come only from the people; and he specifically charged and
criticized the director of the ministry of police, von Kamptz, for blocking access to the king. Von Kamptz, a man of little irony and a taste for
finding subversives everywhere, was enraged; he had Förster interrogated and then had him suspended from his position in the Royal
Artillery and Engineering School. On September 30, 1819, Hardenberg
declared Förster unfit for state service, and he was not to be rehabili-
tated until March 31, 1823.[69]

Förster had been a member of Fries's school, but he had quickly
shifted over to Hegelianism. Someone other than Hegel might have
taken that as a good reason to keep his distance from Förster; after all,

Hegel himself was too close for comfort to many of those being investigated, and becoming associated with Fries in any way might have seemed too dangerous. Instead, Hegel and Förster became and remained good friends. Förster wrote his brother, "Many loyal students of Fries have since come over to become loyal students of Hegel. I would like to know whether any have abandoned Hegel in order to go over to Fries."[70]

Hegel made a quick excursion with Förster in July 1820 for a few days to Dresden to see some of the various art treasures they had there. At the inn called the Blue Star (where Hegel thereafter always stayed when going to Dresden), various friends and compatriots from other universities gathered for dinner (Eduard Gans, another of Hegel's students and later a close friend, was apparently among them); when the usual local Meißner wine was offered to Hegel, he rejected it, ordering instead some bottles of Champagne Sillery, the most distinguished champagne of its day.[71] Having sent the expensive bottles of Sillery around the table, he then entreated his companions to empty their glasses in the memory of the day on which they were drinking. Everyone happily downed the Sillery, but when it became clear that nobody at the table knew exactly why they should be drinking to that particular day, Hegel turned in mock astonishment and with raised voice declared, "This glass is for the 14th of July, 1789 – to the storming of the Bastille."[72] Needless to say, those around Hegel were astonished; the old man had not only bought them the finest champagne available, he was drinking to the Revolution at the height of the reaction and at a time when he himself might have been in danger. (But maybe this was not so odd; in 1826, Hegel, once again in the company of young people, again drank a toast to the storming of the Bastille, telling Varnhagen von Ense at the time that he in fact always drank a toast to the storming of the Bastille on July 14.)[73]

From August 27 to September 11, 1820, Hegel, delighted with his first excursion to what was then known as Florence on the Elba, went for another, more extended trip to Dresden. He became acquainted at that time with Karl Förster, a relative of Friedrich Förster, who although at first finding Hegel a bit "closemouthed and taciturn" warmed up to him after they began discussing the art they were seeing. In addition to what he took to be Hegel's sharp-sighted insights into the art in Dresden, Förster especially liked the way in which Hegel seemed to be "unpretentious, straightforward, simple, and cheerful."[74] Karl

Förster was a translator (of Dante and Petrarch, among others) and poet. Hegel warmed to the company around him, even getting on well with a person who had previously published an article in 1801 after the publication of Hegel's "Difference" essay to the effect that Hegel was a "stout warrior" from Württemberg fetched by Schelling to announce to the world that Schelling was better than Fichte.[75] Hegel had angrily denounced this in the *Critical Journal of Philosophy* at the time, but by 1820, that controversy was long since over, and he and the gentleman got along famously. Förster also introduced Hegel to Dr. Heinrich Hase, the deputy director of the Royal Collection of Antiquities, with whom Hegel was also to strike up a friendship. When Förster and his group asked Hegel on August 27 if he would participate in some festivities on the next day to celebrate Goethe's birthday – a yearly gathering of the Dresden group, so he was told – Hegel whimsically replied, accentuating his Swabian accent, "Good idea, but today we'd be wanting to drink to Hegel's health, since he's born on the 27th!"[76] They all took him up on it, there was more drinking (of bubbly champagne), and the festivities spilled over into the next day for the celebration of Goethe's birthday. Hegel's wife, Marie, joined Hegel for the last part of his stay, stopping off at Dresden on her way home from a visit to her family in Nuremberg; she made a good impression on everyone – there were always lots of remarks about Hegel's quite elegant and much younger wife – and they both returned to Berlin on September 11. (Although Hegel probably did not know it, the Dresden police were also keeping secret records on his movements in Dresden during this trip, noting that he had visited with the suspicious Friedrich Förster and stayed at the Blue Star Inn; Hegel had not yet escaped suspicion that he was a "demagogue" or was harboring or associating with "demagogues.")[77]

Their remembrances of Hegel on his visits to Dresden in fact summed up what most people who met Hegel during this time remembered. Those who met Hegel in his adult life tended to have one of two impressions of him. Some saw him as reserved, even stuffy, a bit arrogant, very quick to stand on his dignity, and a bit wooden in temperament. Hegel also had a detached, sarcastic side to his personality; he was not so much ironic about things (he seems to have had little irony about himself), but he was quick to see the pretensions and even absurdities in human action, although typically that sarcasm was focused on others and not on whatever absurdities there might have been in his own conduct. Some found his acerbity and sarcasm appealing, but others just found it odious. Some confused it with cynicism, some found it tiresome; Hegel clearly felt it belonged with his philosophical understanding that any more rational way of thinking and living always and essentially brings with it stresses and strains to which one must become reconciled. Friedrich von Savigny, the conservative jurist at Berlin and one of Hegel's most dedicated opponents, for example, complained about Hegel's "droll reconciling worldly wisdom" that would appear "when the talk concerns the unpleasant events and arrangements of recent and most recent times."[78] But just as many others saw him as honest, straightforward, down to earth, ready for a joke, affable, and quite gregarious.

In fact, he was all these things, always and at the same time. He was able to have a nasty tiff with Schleiermacher at the *Gesetzlose Gesellschaft and* to sit on a boat at midnight speaking to and joking with an imprisoned student. He defended de Wette's dismissal from the university, *and* he paid into the secret fund to support de Wette. He defended the government's dismissal of de Wette and Fries, *and* he openly drank to the storming of the Bastille. He led a cozy, Biedermeier life, *and* he went to the *Faschings* ball decked out in a Venetian cape and mask. He was cordial and polite, even if a bit caustic toward views he regarded as out of step with the times, but he had a sure sense of when a fine line had been crossed – that almost always had to do with some strongly held opinion or with what he felt was an affront to his dignity as a professor – and his anger was fearsome when he thought that line had been crossed. If Hegel liked to combine oppositions in his philosophy, he apparently enjoyed doing so in his life as well.

Aftershocks

Hegel's Standing and his Proposals for a Journal

Although Hegel's first year and a half at the university had been one of great stresses, many other things had gone fairly well for him. Hegel was certainly bitterly disappointed at not having been offered a position at the Academy of Sciences. Von Altenstein, himself disconcerted at not being able to secure a place for Hegel at the academy, managed instead to get Hegel appointed to a position with the Royal Board of Scientific Examiners for Brandenburg, with a remuneration of 200 Thalers per year, which Hegel quickly and gratefully accepted. It certainly did not carry with it the prestige of an appointment to the academy, and it involved a great deal more work, since it required reading and grading essays by all students coming to the university along with testing all applicants for teaching positions in secondary schools. It was at best a consolation prize, and Hegel knew it, but he needed the money.

This pattern was to be repeated: Von Altenstein, one of the few remaining reformers in the Prussian government, became one of Hegel's few major patrons in the government. Von Altenstein did this in part because he was committed to having philosophy as the central discipline at the university, and he was convinced that Hegel was the right person to carry out such a educational program; and he was continually dismayed by efforts by such people as Schleiermacher to undermine the role of philosophy in the Academy of Sciences. He came to see that he needed people such as Hegel to balance the pro-restoration forces at work in the university; and Hegel clearly saw that he needed von Altenstein for the success of his own projects. But such support by Altenstein unfortunately also gave rise to the suspicion – fostered by people like Schleiermacher and von Savigny – that Hegel was being supported by the government, and that Hegel repaid that support by slavishly defending government policies.[79] That suspicion became a rumor, and after Hegel's death the rumor was for quite a while simply accepted as fact. Certainly people like Schleiermacher and others who were in competition with Hegel for influence in the university were deeply suspicious that Hegel was flattering officials in exchange for support, especially since they felt themselves to be so out of favor with government officers, and the intellectual competition among them was stiff – the historian Leopold von Ranke remembered his student days in Berlin during this period as one of competition between the philosophers (that is, the Hegelians) and the loosely organized historical school of thought (Schleiermacher, von Savigny, and others).[80] But this was always only a rumor, never the truth. To be sure, Altenstein and the minister of education, Johannes Schulze (who was Hegel's next-door neighbor when the Hegel family moved to Kupfergraben Street and became and remained one of Hegel's closer friends), did their best to support Hegel's efforts; but this hardly amounted to any government favoritism for Hegel or his students – especially since they were usually able to do very little for Hegel. Despite the fact that people like Schulze long argued after Hegel's death that the facts showed that Hegel had enjoyed no special influence with the government, the idea set in, even in Hegel's own lifetime, that he had become too cozy with the reigning powers.

In the winter of 1819–20, Hegel tried another, rather ambitious ploy with his friends in the ministry responsible for cultural affairs. Returning to his longstanding interest in the intersection of *Bildung* and journalism, he proposed in a lengthy memorandum to the ministry for instruction that they establish a "Critical Journal of Literature" (with Hegel presumably as editor). "Literature" at this point still had a much wider connotation than it does nowadays, including all sorts of "scholarly" publications. Indeed, so Hegel argued, "journal-science and the reading of newspapers can be said to be the sufficient means for progress in *Bildung* and knowledge and a comfortable surrogate for study and involvement" in matters of cultural concern.[81] In founding such a journal, the ministry would bring the more specialized knowledge then being produced in the German universities by the various separate "learned disciplines" (*Wissenschaften*) into more general public view and would help to identify and publicize such genuine, university-based "scientific" knowledge and distinguish it from the various forms of charlatanism-parading-as-science surfacing in society at large. The journal would therefore be a modernizing force, separating out for the general public what is really *known* from what is based on myth or superstition.

Moreover, Hegel insisted, such a journal would be especially suitable for the capital city of Berlin, where there was already a sufficient collection of modern intellectuals that formed a potential "focal point" for modern cultural life and which could thereby bestow the requisite "authority" on such an undertaking.[82] Indeed, the German states needed such an authoritative "scientific and literary focal point" if German cultural life was ever to become fully self-determining and not remain a matter of provincial life, refusing to recognize its own scholars unless they themselves have already been recognized by the authorities in England or France. Such a journal would thus be, Hegel argued, the German equivalent of the French *Journal des Savants*, and as such, it would need to be sponsored by the government (as it was in France), for just as universities throughout Germany had become government-sponsored institutions, so too should such public literary endeavors.[83] Only as a public, governmentally sponsored journal could it lay any claim to the requisite impartiality (something a privately financed journal could never do, or so Hegel thought).[84] In making his case for such a journal, Hegel thus gave, once again, full expression to his continuing admiration for the French conception of the state bequeathed by the Revolution and Napoleon; it continued to be his paradigm of what modern life should look like, and such a journal would bring modern "scientific" life finally to Germany itself.

But nothing came of the proposal, surely to Hegel's great disappointment. His first great foray into establishing his modernizing program in Berlin simply fell dead off the press. But at the same time, Hegel also began enjoying a kind of social success that he had not previously had. When he arrived in Berlin, he was quiet, and nobody at first took much notice of him. Hegel's awkward lecture style, as always, also put some people off. He stuttered, then would stop speaking altogether as he shuffled through the reams of papers he always brought along with him, looking for some reference or some jottings, sometimes pausing to take some snuff; his lectures were punctuated by gasps and coughs; to make his points, he would wave his hands at inopportune moments in not exactly graceful movements; it was remarked that Hegel seemed to begin every sentence with "therefore." At first, the joke in Berlin was that Hegel was even more unintelligible than Fichte. But he attracted quite a few students, and soon his lectures and ideas became the talk of Berlin. His halting, obscure lecture style even became a vogue unto itself; it became *Hegel's* style. When the dry, gasping lecture would be punctuated by one of Hegel's sarcastic quips, there would often be a response of resounding laughter throughout the crowded lecture hall. The fact that this was being delivered by a man whose physical appearance was almost always described as "unassuming" bestowed on what was being said exactly the kind of disembodied weightlessness it seemed to require, and for many Hegel's lecture style itself became almost paradoxically part of the attraction. Hegel became fashionable; polite society began casually throwing around terms like the "in-itself, for-itself, and the in-and-for-itself," and Hegel became recognized as one of *the* intellectuals in a city already full of them.[85]

The Reception of the Philosophy of Right

But if anything, the publication of Hegel's *Philosophy of Right* in late 1820 only helped to solidify his reputation among certain people as a person too intimate with the repressive elements in power. Hegel had been at work on his *Philosophy of Right* from the moment of his arrival in Berlin; he had hoped to get it published in 1819 or thereabouts, but, as was usual with him, he underestimated the amount of time it would actually take him to complete the manuscript. The newly installed censorship laws from the Karlsbad decrees had also thrown a spanner in the works, since it was at first not clear just what type of censorship was going to be applied. The old Prussian general law had exempted university publications from censorship, and in the initial reports of the new censorship laws, it was not clear if this exemption was to be maintained; as it turned out, it was not. But once the uncertainty about the censorship laws was cleared up, Hegel continued with his work, most likely in his usual manner of sending parts of the manuscript to the printer while still working on other parts, a pattern he had followed in the *Phenomenology of Spirit*, the *Science of Logic*, and the *Encyclopedia of the Philosophical Sciences*.

Hegel completed the work between June 9 and June 25, 1820, although since the *Philosophy of Right* appeared only near the end of 1820, its publication date was listed as 1821, the year in which it was to appear in the publisher's catalogue, a normal procedure for the time.[86] (Because of Hegel's longstanding reputation as a defender of the Prussian orthodoxy and some ambiguous phrases in his letters, it has long been accepted in accounts of the genesis of the *Philosophy of Right* that Hegel already had a finished manuscript in his hands before the Karlsbad decrees were promulgated, and that in light of those decrees, he then went back and altered his work so as to make its ideas conform to the newly altered Prussian realities; that assumption, however, is very difficult to square with the facts concerning when Hegel knew about the decrees, his work habits, and what was actually being said in those letters, not to mention the very content of the book itself.)[87]

The content and arguments of Hegel's *Philosophy of Right* constituted in large part an extended justification for the Prussian reform movement, but what made the *Philosophy of Right* so damaging to Hegel's reputation was almost entirely contained in its Preface, in which Hegel committed two very serious faux pas. First, he used it to engage in the rather unattractive process of settling some old scores with Fries, an effort which was made all the more graceless by the fact that Fries had been summarily dismissed from his position in Jena. Hegel described Fries as a "leader of this superficial brigade of so-called philosophers," and described his philosophy as "superficial" and as undermining the substance of the state. Fries, so Hegel claimed, wanted to base all social relations on simple emotions instead of on rational thought, an idea that was detrimental to any kind of decent ethical order. And in a swipe at both Schleiermacher and de Wette, Hegel also noted that after Fries' idiocies, "the next step is for this view to assume the guise of piety as well . . . by means of godliness and the Bible, however, it has presumed to gain the supreme justification for despising the ethical order and the objectivity of the laws" – the similarity between Hegel's wording and that of the *Allgemeine Preußische Zeitung*'s thinly veiled attacks on Schleiermacher and de Wette could hardly have been overlooked by Hegel's audience – and he then drove the point home with a thinly veiled reference to de Wette's letter to Sand's mother, saying that "as a result, the concepts of truth and the laws of ethics are reduced to mere opinions and subjective convictions, and the most criminal principles – since they too are *convictions* – are accorded the same status as those laws."[88] Certainly de Wette knew who was meant and even wrote an angry letter to Schleiermacher about Hegel's words, raging at them as "libel" and noting that one now "reads and hears terrible things about Hegel."[89]

Second, as if to make matters worse, Hegel also emphasized some lines that incorporated technical terms in his philosophy, centering them on the page so they could not be missed: "What is rational is actual; / and what is actual is rational."[90] Hegel meant by this what he had always meant since at least his days in Jena: that what counts as rational is what is efficacious; he had made the same point in print in his *Science of Logic* ("what is actual is what is efficacious – *was wirklich ist, kann wirken* – its actuality announces itself through that which it brings forth").[91] In terms of his political philosophy, he meant by this the idea that nothing can serve as an actual principle of ethical life unless the agent identifies with that reason, unless that reason can motivate the agent, and that purely utopian, merely ideal principles will always fail for the reason that nobody can seriously entertain them.[92] But Hegel should have known how anybody not familiar with the particular terminology of the Hegelian system would in fact interpret it, namely, as equivalent to the statement, "What is, is right, and what is right currently exists," which would imply that everything in Prussia was just fine and dandy and that any criticism of the existing order was therefore irrational and most likely something the government had the right to suppress. That was in fact how many, many people took it, and the result was a disaster for Hegel's public image, the consequences of which extend into our own day.

The polemics against Fries and his statement about the identity of the "actual" and the "rational" apparently caused people simply to overlook Hegel's scathing references to K. L. von Haller, who was more or less the "official" philosopher of the most reactionary elements of the Prussian court. Haller, only one year older than Hegel, was a Swiss aristocrat and a member of the Bernese patriciate that Hegel had learned to detest so vehemently when he lived there; even worse, Haller was an apostate of the Enlightenment, having in his youth been a committed Enlightenment liberal, and even having drafted a constitution for the revolutionary government of Bern in 1798 that called for popular sovereignty, legal equality, and freedom of religion, thought, and the press. But Haller had come to reject those ideas in favor of a more "patriarchal" view of authority as coming from the top down, rather than from the bottom up, and he identified all modern political theories as erroneously endorsing the latter. His major work, *Restauration der Staatswissenschaft* (*The Restoration of Political Science*), in which he expounded his mature ideas, first appeared in 1816. Haller argued in that work that in the state of nature (something to which, Haller claimed, all modern theories adhered), we encounter not the freedom and equality promised by modern theories, but rather only authority, inequality, and hierarchy, particularly in the family, where the father's naturally greater strength gives him natural moral and legal authority over women and children. Because nature was created by God, such "natural authority" is also "divine." All authority emanates from this "patrimonial" authority, and what people call "the state" is thus only the result of all the various private contracts of subordination and domination that exist between the weak and the strong (who have a religious and moral duty to paternally concern themselves with the welfare of the weak). This culminates in a prince subordinate to nobody but God, and a "patrimonial state" that is simply the private property of the prince who possesses it. But, likewise, the prince's authority over his subjects is only that of private property and contract; other nobles have their own "patriarchal" authority over their own subjects (and families). There can be no rule of law other than the prince's personal commandments or the commandments of a "patrimonial" noble to those over whom he has such natural or contractual authority.

In giving the prince this kind of authority and (very importantly) in claiming similar authority for the other nobles, Haller thus provided both the Prussian king and the nobles with a framework in which they could defend their old rights.[93] The prince was not absolute; the nobility had its own rights; but all of these rights were based on natural authority and contracts struck within the context of such natural inequalities. Haller thus provided the rationale for a complete restoration of the pre-Napoleonic Prussian order between prince and nobility. (The crown prince, for example, was an enthusiast for Haller's work, as were many other reactionary elements around the court.)

Hegel was even more scathing toward Haller than he was toward Fries, but since he buried his discussion of Haller much more deeply in the book, not many people noticed. Hegel described Haller's work as "totally devoid of thought," something which "therefore cannot claim to have any substance," possessing as it did such "incredible crudity."[94] Hegel provides long citations from Haller's work to illustrate what he takes to be its idiocies, and he lambastes it with the kind of sarcastic polemic that always revealed Hegel's more aggressive side. It would have been difficult (especially in those times) to launch any more clear attack on the ruling ideology of the reactionary elements at the court, but the Preface to the *Philosophy of Right* appeared so damning to so many that they either did not read the rest of the book or came to see it simply as an apology for the powers of the restoration.

Almost all the contemporary reviews virtually ignored the content of the book (or badly misunderstood it) and focused instead on the Preface; the consensus among the reviewers came down to the notion that Hegel had turned into an apologist for Prussian royalist autocracy and had come to embrace a kind of unattractive absolutistic view about his own philosophy.[95] Hegel himself was acutely stung by all these criticisms; he seemed to think that nobody who knew him or read his book could possibly think that he had become one of the reactionary apologists for the existing order, but he made life more difficult for himself by the way he aggressively staked out his own position and by his typically combative, polemical style of writing. His old friend-turned-opponent Paulus, for example, in his review of the work fastened on Hegel's use of the word "insipidity" (*Seichtigkeit*), which, Paulus scornfully remarked, Hegel seemed to apply to "just about all German philosophers" (except, of course, himself); Paulus said the author of the *Philosophy of Right* leads one to believe that "he only knows one German word: Insipid."[96] Hegel also complicated his case by the fact that although he was clearly on the side of the reformers, he was not on the side of the "liberals" in the reformist camp, and he spent a portion of his book attacking the liberals; since he was living in Berlin in a time of restoration of the old powers, and since his preface to the *Philosophy of Right* was seen by so many as an apology for the existing order, he de facto came to be seen by many liberals, with whom he could have made common cause, as being on the side of the oppressors, not the reformers.[97] Much of that was his own fault.

Quite telling in this regard is the first *Brockhaus Encyclopedia* article on Hegel that appeared in 1824; the piece was written by a friend, Professor Wendt from Leipzig, and contained biographical material that only Hegel himself could have provided, and thus one must presume that Hegel contributed some of its content. The entry says of the idea that "the actual is the rational" that "this proposition has been misinterpreted as if [it said] everything that is present in a given moment of time, even that which is most contrary to right, would be rational; this has been particularly applied enviously and in a hostile way to Hegel's philosophy of the state." The author then says that regarding the charge that Hegel added these lines to please the ruling powers, "to the extent that Hegel's view on the state are known to us through his writings, [that phrase] was in no way employed *later on* for the benefit of the ruling classes but arose out of the foundations of his philosophy, which everywhere combats *empty* ideals and seeks to reconcile thoughts and actuality in the absolute Idea through, as it were, the Idea itself."[98]

Friendships and Social Life

Hegel also continued to denounce the nationalist sentiments of many of the demagogues; he would have nothing of the kind of nationalist "Germanomania" ("*Deutschtümeri*") being propagated around him.[99]

But even the fact that key conservative figures in the government some-times advised students *not* to attend Hegel's courses did not change the way many saw Hegel.[100] Try as he might, Hegel could not undo the damage he had done, and the suspicion remained that he had allied himself with the ruling powers; and this only made the rumors that he was receiving special favors from the government seem all the more plausible to many of his detractors in Berlin.

But Hegel managed to ride out the storm and began to feel even more at home in Berlin. As his academic celebrity grew, his circle of acquaintances also rapidly expanded, and he took to spending more time with various artists and, with Marie, attending opera and musical events. One of Hegel's Heidelberg acquaintances, Bernhard Klein, was summoned to Berlin at the same time as Hegel to become part of the Institute for Sacred Music; he and Marie attended a performance of Mozart's *Don Giovanni* directed by Klein in the autumn of 1820, at which time they also met a variety of other Berlin artists.[101] He and Marie also entertained at their apartment (Hegel noted how one party even cost him seven Thalers), and they frequented some of the better "cafés" of Berlin.[102] The only dark cloud in this was that Marie's health did not improve in the winter of 1820; if anything, her health worsened somewhat; and Hegel continued to be anxious about the ongoing re-pressive measures being taken against the demagogues.[103]

During this period, he also managed to rekindle his friendship with Goethe now that he was a man of substance and some renown himself; the two exchanged warm letters and traded witticisms; and Hegel treas-ured a painted goblet that Goethe sent him as a gift. His friendship with Johannes Schulze, the minister whom von Altenstein placed in charge of *Gymnasia* and universities, grew particularly close. Schulze felt that he needed some remedial work in the philosophical sciences, so he took to attending all of Hegel's lectures between 1819 and 1821. After many of the lectures, the two men would retire to Schulze's apartment to discuss matters further or would take long walks and talk over items Hegel had covered in the lectures.[104] This kind of intellectual friendship was most valued by Hegel, and Schulze was later to be the editor of the edition of the *Phenomenology* in Hegel's *Collected Works* published after his death.

His son Karl Hegel remembered his father as having a double life; on the one hand, there was Hegel the ever-proper professor, and on the other hand, there was Hegel in his family and social life. In his social life, Hegel quite often put himself as far away from his philosophical side as possible; he loved playing cards, especially with those who would not have any inclination to talk shop. In his early years in Berlin, he would play L'Hombre – a favorite card game of his in Jena and Bamberg – until late into the night with Karl Hartwig Gregor von Meusebach of the Rhenish High Court (also an avid collector of German literature of the sixteenth and seventeenth centuries and known as a bit of an eccentric).[105] However, after a while, Hegel's preference for L'Hombre gave way to Whist (which involves four partners), and as Karl Hegel remembered things, his partners for Whist were generally "Zelter (the Director of the Voice Training Academy), the painter, Rösel, and a maritime commercial agent, Bloch," but Hegel was "not choosy about partners for playing Whist; he was also satisfied with minds subordinate to his own: Schur, the Royal Stablemaster, the industrialist, Sparkäse, and Heinrich Beer."[106]

Hegel, a product of Württemberg, where the *Ehrbarkeit*, the "non-noble notables," had been the central figures of public life, was not particularly interested in cultivating friendships with leading court figures or moving within the circles of the Prussian aristocracy. Like the Württemberger he was, he was not hostile to the aristocracy; he was simply indifferent to it. Although it had become fashionable to address high-standing civil servants or men of distinction by the noble title of "high-wellborn" (*Hochwohlgeboren*) – something many nobles deeply resented – Hegel was always addressed simply by the more bourgeois "wellborn" (*wohlgeboren*); only his friend Creuzer at first addressed letters to Hegel as "*Hochwohlgeboren*," but even he eventually ceased doing so. If Hegel had cared about the matter, he could have insisted on being addressed more regally, but it is quite clear that he did not. Although he was quite quick to stand on his dignity or to see some insult to his social status, he was not a pretentious man, at least certainly not in matters concerning noble or non-noble status. He and Zelter in particular formed a close friendship; both men were exemplars of the "career open to talent," Zelter even more so than Hegel – Zelter came from very humble origins as the son of a mason and, like Hegel, had a rough-hewn style of speaking and appearance that charmed many and irritated some others. (Zelter was also very close friends with Goethe and was a lasting influence on Goethe's understanding of music.)

Students

Hegel was also having some influence among the students, and a former student of his in Heidelberg, Hermann Friedrich Wilhelm Hinrichs, was making good progress toward becoming the first Hegelian to assume a professorship. Hinrichs would write Hegel frequently, asking for advice, trading gossip, offering his own interpretations of Hegel's philosophy, and, of course, asking for Hegel's help in obtaining a teaching post for him. Hegel would always warmly respond. He was also to hear from Hinrichs in May, 1821 that Schelling – who after fourteen years of silence had returned to public lecturing on January 4, 1821, as a professor in Erlangen – was publicly polemicizing against Hegel's views, which made it all the more clear that Hegel's competitor for philosophical influence was no longer just Fries but perhaps once again Schelling as well.[107]

Along with these more pressing problems, there were also the occasional problems with students demanding time for examinations and not always being as accommodating as one might have wished. One of these stands out. A young philosopher, Arthur Schopenhauer, requested the right to do his habilitation in Berlin and to be allowed to give lectures there; he also requested, strangely enough, that if it were possible, his lectures should be scheduled at exactly the same time as Hegel's lectures. The dean of the faculty, August Boeckh, passed along Schopenhauer's petition to the rest of the faculty, noting with displeasure the "no small arrogance and extraordinary vanity" contained in Schopenhauer's request. The rest of the faculty also took umbrage with Schopenhauer's "arrogance," but Hegel apparently had nothing against it, and he agreed to set a date for Schopenhauer's defense (March 23, 1820). Schopenhauer read a test-lecture on the traditional notions of the four causes, and in the ensuing discussion, Hegel asked him to clarify what he meant when he said that "animal functions" account for an animal's behavior; Hegel thought that in one of the examples Schopenhauer had given, he was confusing motives (reasons for action) with causal factors such as pulse, blood circulation, and the like. There ensued a bit of a to-do between Hegel and Schopenhauer on the point, with the zoologist Martin H. K. Lichtenstein cutting in to defend Schopenhauer's use of the term "animal function"; Lichtenstein claimed that Schopenhauer's use of the term as meaning only those "conscious movements of the animal body" was entirely in keeping with the way the zoologists on the faculty spoke. Although Hegel's point was not about the use of terms but about the distinction between reasons and causes, he prudently decided not to press the point any further and gave Schopenhauer a passing grade, thus clearing the way for him to begin his teaching career (fully aware of Schopenhauer's peculiar request to schedule his classes so as to challenge him for students). As he had requested, Schopenhauer was permitted to hold his lectures at the same time as Hegel's, and when hardly anyone showed up for them, he had to leave Berlin for several years in some disgrace. (But thus was born another Hegel legend, partially fostered by Schopenhauer himself – Schopenhauer thoroughly detested Hegel – that Hegel had tried to block Schopenhauer's promotion to *Privatdozent*, and that in the discussion following the lecture, Hegel had also illustrated his total ignorance of natural science.)[108]

Disturbances about Naturphilosophie at the University

Just as things looked as if they were beginning to settle down, a new series of disturbances rumbled through the university. In October 1820, a doctor of medicine from Jena, C. W. H. Fenner, appeared in Berlin claiming to have a doctorate in philosophy and wishing to hold lectures as a *Privatdozent* on *Naturphilosophie*. The faculty asked for the requisite documents; Fenner went twice to the ministry to complain about how expensive this was for someone who already supposedly had a doctorate, but the ministry referred him back to the philosophical faculty, at which point Fenner presented the faculty with a falsified habilitation document. Hegel, who was to be the dean of the philosophical faculty for 1821, was asked to write an expert opinion on it, and in so doing, he discovered the subterfuge: Lines had been rubbed out, new ones added in, and page numbers had been rubbed out so that new page numbers could be inserted. Indeed, the entire document turned out to be a ragtag compilation of very disparate material. Hegel duly reported this to the faculty, they were duly outraged, and then Hegel made the mistake of sending Fenner a letter that said only that the faculty found his habilitation unsuitable.

Undaunted by anything less than a full dismissal, Fenner then convinced his friend I. H. Fichte (the son of the famous Fichte and a

Privatdozent at the university in philosophy) to intervene for him. This caused the affair to drag on until February 1821, when the ministry asked Hegel how the situation stood vis-à-vis Fenner; Hegel replied that Fenner himself had acknowledged that he did not have a philosophical doctorate, but the ministry found that too weak. Hegel then wrote a much stronger, unequivocal letter on March 3, 1821, about Fenner, but even that did not dissuade Fenner; he took out an advertisement in a local newspaper, the *Vossische Zeitung*, on May 11, 1821, announcing that he would be giving public lectures on Oken's *Naturphilosophie* for ladies. The Karlsbad decrees had required that governments appoint a plenipotentiary to supervise the universities, and on May 11, 1821, after the government plenipotentiary announced that he had discovered that Fenner had also falsified the papers supposedly testifying to membership in the Jena Latin Society, the government issued a "ministerial warning" to all Prussian universities about Fenner. The king, incensed by this, and displaying his usual lack of subtlety, had Altenstein simply ban all teaching of Oken's *Naturphilosophie* in Prussia; as further fallout, the government plenipotentiary (Schultz) informed Hegel on May 31, 1821, that "teachers of the philosophical sciences should not, perhaps out of misguided longing for a system, set their teachings on a course that would corrupt religion and ethics."[109] Schultz even asked Hegel to "observe" his colleagues' lectures and report "orally and confidentially to him" if such was being done.[110]

The uproar surrounding Fenner's idiocy was enough to send chills down Hegel's back. By the beginning of 1821, he thought that he had successfully ridden out a passing gale in the initial frenzy about all the alleged "demagogues." But in a letter to Creuzer in May of 1821, Hegel showed that he feared he was not yet out of the woods. Since the king had banned Oken's *Naturphilosophie* because he thought it would lead to "atheism," Hegel had been led to believe that the king could also be led to think that any "speculative philosophy" leads to atheism, and Hegel feared that all the palaver over Fenner would only bring back, as Hegel put it, "into vogue the all-but-forgotten catchword, 'atheism'," a controversy he thought had been over and done with several generations before.[111] (Fichte's fate in Jena was surely still not forgotten by people like Hegel.) After all, Hegel noted, "once one has been branded in a given place – no matter where and with no matter what label such as 'demagogy' or, ultimately, 'atheism' – one carries that brand on one's forehead everywhere in the German Empire and in the regions of the Holy Alliance."[112] A few months later (September 6, 1821), Hegel was writing to Niethammer about the same thing. Mockingly speaking of himself and others in Berlin as "we patriotic Prussians," Hegel remarked on the latest fracas and said, "You know that, on the one hand, I am an anxious man and, on the other hand, that I like tranquillity. It is not exactly a comfort to see a storm rise up every year, even if I can be persuaded that at most only a few drops of a light rain will touch me."[113]

The commotion over Fenner's attempt to teach *Naturphilosophie* had, however, only further stiffened Hegel's views about the university and Prussian politics. He remarked to Niethammer vis-à-vis the search for demagogues that "I have withstood the peril of demagogy without personal risk – but not indeed without concern . . . Or at least I was concerned until I read de Wette's letter and got to know better both a few demagogical individuals and a few who had to take action against them. I then realized the wretchedness and well-deserved fate of the demagogues. And although the action of officials in such a nebulous matter was admittedly not justifiable right at the start, I came to realize its eventual justice." But, Hegel added, "I became aware of even more than this," and he told Niethammer about von Henning's arrest and imprisonment. Hegel seemed to have drawn a bitter lesson from his experience in his first couple of years in Berlin. His dislike for Fries and his conviction that too much was at stake in the formation of the university in Berlin to see it collapse under pressure from reactionary forces had led him to conclude that it was in fact a good thing that Fries and de Wette had been dismissed; but he also feared that the kind of arbitrary state intervention at work in their dismissals could lead to others, maybe even himself, being unwittingly sucked into the maelstrom.

However, he did not conclude that therefore one was safer defending academics like Fries out of fear that one might become the next victim; instead, he seems to have concluded that it had become all the more necessary to have the right people in the university and civil service who would not be subject to such retrogressive passions. Like his friend Goethe, who had failed to lift a finger to help Fichte in the atheism controversy at Jena because he thought that Fichte had quite imprudently brought his troubles down on himself, Hegel thought that Fries

and those others dismissed as "demagogues" not only had brought the
wrath of the reactionaries down on themselves, but also had in the
process also foolishly endangered everyone else and perhaps the whole
movement of reform itself. He reassured himself, perhaps even a bit
presumptuously, that since he was in *Berlin* and not in some provincial
town, and that since he was contact with people such as Altenstein and
Schulze, he knew what *really* going on and could manage things so that
he did not get caught in the snares; or, as he put to Niethammer, "being
at a focal point also has the advantage of affording more accurate
knowledge of what is *likely*, so that one can be more assured of one's
interest and situation."[114]

Hegel did not go over to the side of the reactionaries; but he did
more and more come to think that he was simply a better man than
others to be leading the university into a more modern, free life, and
that those like Fries and de Wette who seemed to threaten the whole
enterprise with all their various ill-conceived shenanigans were better
left behind. He did not disown his past; he even chided Niethammer,
who had been complaining about the deposed reformer in Bavaria,
Montgelas, that he should indeed be thanking "Montgelas . . . God, and
Napoleon" for the new constitution in Bavaria.[115] But that supreme self-
confidence that had taken him through all his early failures and that
had, for example, produced the *Phenomenology* during a time of utter
emotional despair, that conviction that deep down he was *right*, together
with the immense stresses he had experienced during his introductory
years in Berlin, had led him to adopt a somewhat rigid outlook about
his place in the capital city.

Hegel felt that he had now left his youth permanently behind, and,
feeling that he therefore did not have much time to carry out what had
been his youthful project – providing the philosophical voice for the
moral, religious, and political reform of Germany, indeed, of the modern world in general – he began to solidify his positions in philosophy
and his attitudes toward university politics. As always, Hegel combined
various contradictory features in his personality; and many features of
it would come to be expressed more and more during his last nine years
in Berlin, not always in the most attractive ways.

Hegel's *Philosophy of Right*: Freedom, History, and the Modern European State

From Nuremberg to Berlin: The Recovery of "Ethical Life"

HEGEL'S 1820 *Elements of the Philosophy of Right* was written against the background of the ongoing, intensely fierce debates over the shape Germany was to assume in the aftermath of Napoleon's spectacular fall and the conflicts between reformers and reactionaries. In fact, the basic ideas and themes of the book had already been substantially worked out at least by the time that Hegel had landed in Heidelberg, and the very general themes of the book appear even earlier in his lectures in Jena and in his dictations to his *Gymnasium* class in Nuremberg. In the 1820 book, Hegel thus put into writing the results of his sustained reflections over a long period of time on the shape of modern European life, and sharpened his thoughts on those issues in light of the controversies surrounding what constitutions, if any, German states should have and whether (and how, on what basis) German law should be codified. Both debates had surrounded him at Heidelberg, and the changes from the Heidelberg manuscripts to the finished product of 1820 reflect Hegel's ongoing attempts to demonstrate how his own idealist approach to philosophy might provide the needed orientation for those debates.

In particular, the themes of "universalism" and "particularism" that had animated so much of his thought since his Württemberg days shaped and structured the *Philosophy of Right*. Hegel had long been convinced that the purely "universalizing" demands of his Enlightenment education in hometown Württemberg were somehow too one-sided, too arrogantly dismissive of the necessity for the more particular, individual elements of human life and thought; but like so many of the people of his generation, he had also broken with any simple identification with the hometowns. Hegel thought of himself as a German *and* a European, and he thus deeply mistrusted the purely parochial and narrow structure of hometown life, rightfully seeing in it the major obstacle to the kind of spiritual, moral, and political reform with which he had come to identify as a young man; yet he was never willing to completely write it off and remained attracted by what he saw as its virtues.

Hegel had already developed a fairly clear notion of what kind of political philosophy would fit into his systematic ideas by 1806 in Jena. Nonetheless, as he had done with his *Logic*, when he began his courses on "Doctrines of Right, Duties, and Religion" in Nuremberg in 1810, he operated almost exclusively with Kantian terminology, even telling his students, for example, that the "legal, ethical, and religious concepts" they were to study were of "objects" in the "intelligible world," that is, of the "unconditioned totalities," the "Ideas" of which Kant had spoken. His course itself was even structured along the lines of Kant's *Metaphysics of Ethics*.[1] The theory of *Sittlichkeit*, which figures so prominently in the 1820 *Philosophy of Right*, played little or no role in the Nuremberg dictations.

Much of the impetus for Hegel's development of his political philosophy surely came from the events around him. By the time Hegel arrived in Heidelberg, Napoleon had fallen, the Congress of Vienna had for all practical purposes given the Napoleonic reorganization of Germany the stamp of approval, and the struggle was beginning over constitutional and legal reform. Most likely, one of the prime movers in the sharpening of his thoughts on politics and ethics was the codification debate of 1814, although he did not directly discuss that debate in any of his dictations from the Nuremberg period. In some ways, his mature work on political philosophy (already substantially worked out in Heidelberg, although not, apparently, in any finished manuscript format) was a rethinking of those debates on constitutionalism and legal codification in light of doctrines already found in his *Phenomenology*. Hegel simply needed those years to work out his own thought so as to be true to his own insights.

In particular, Hegel had to have been struck by Savigny's entry into the debate and especially by the way in which Savigny brilliantly made out the case against the need for the codification of German law by appealing to his view that law was an expression of a people's identity, of its *Geist*; in Savigny's view, it seemed that one could not criticize the identity of a people, one could only draw out the implications and commitments of such an identity. Hegel had himself held a similar (though by no means identical) view at one point in Jena (around 1802–03), but he had substantially modified his views in light of his more historically oriented *Phenomenology* by 1806. Hegel thus had to be struck by the "positivity" of Savigny's views: Expressions of a people's identity simply have to be accepted; there was no going behind them for something deeper or more critical. By 1807, nothing could have been further from Hegel's own stance.

For Hegel, this "dogmatic" insistence on a people's identity simply failed to grasp the essential "negativity" of European history and *Geist*, the way in which European life fundamentally embodied a reflective sense of self-doubt about its basic norms and commitments and how that form of self-doubt was both destructive of ways of life and also productive of new forms of *Geist*. Moreover, since what counts as authoritative for a form of *Geist* has to do with what has come to be required for it by virtue of the internal failures of the preceding normative orders, we can understand a form of *Geist* only in terms of its collective ends and projects, of what it is collectively trying to accomplish and the "negativity" involved in those collective ends. The *Phenomenology* concluded that the collective end of European life had come to be that of achieving the conditions under which a people can be said to be free. To stop short at a "people's" self-identity (the *Volksgeist*, in Savigny's terms) would be to settle for a "dogmatic" position, to refuse to examine whether that self-identity is itself rational and sustainable.

In Jena, Hegel had tried to integrate the kind of unity he thought was to be found in Greek culture in its "ethical life" – its *Sittlichkeit* – with the reflective, self-distancing aspects of modern "morality." But in the *Phenomenology*, he had shown how Greek *Sittlichkeit* was lost forever and how the modern "moral worldview" had thus necessarily supplanted it, and he had gone further to argue that the modern moral standpoint itself required a certain modern, Christian religious practice for "we moderns" to be able to reconcile ourselves to the point in history to which "we" had collectively brought ourselves. His reflection on the modern debates about legal codification and constitutionalism, however, led him to rethink his views on *Sittlichkeit* and to conclude not only that a modern *Sittlichkeit* was possible, but also that it was actually necessary if the force of modern conceptions of legality and of morality themselves were to be sustainable.

This led Hegel to reformulate and sharpen one of his most striking claims. The only reasons that can count for an agent as "unconditional" reasons are those that are necessary components of an admirable, a "worthy" form of life. This had been true of Greek life, and at one point Hegel obviously despaired of seeing how those kinds of unconditional reasons could be found in modern circumstances. The Greek form of life had been so admirable because it was so *beautiful*, but modern life, fragmented as it necessarily was and therefore necessarily lacking that kind of beauty, did not seem as if it even *could* sustain that kind of unconditional allegiance unless it were held together by a very modern religion which itself would have to be underwritten by something like Hegel's own philosophy.

However, by the time Hegel came to formulating his mature political thought, he had put more of an edge to his views on this point. Although lacking the *beauty* of Greek life, modern life was more admirable in terms of its *rationality*. The complex, not easily discerned rationality of post-revolutionary institutions and practices could be both shown and demonstrated in speculative philosophy, and that meant that modern life could manage to recapture what supposedly had been lost with the Greeks, namely, a sense of *Sittlichkeit*, possessing its own type of partially fragmented and decisively nonclassical beauty. By the time he set to writing his first edition of the *Encyclopedia* (published in Heidelberg in 1817), the idea of a modern *Sittlichkeit* had been made explicit; and that also implicitly meant for him that he had to demonstrate that Protestant Christianity, in its reinterpretation in light of his philosophy, was indeed *the* defensible modern religion and compatible with the claims to rationality embodied in modern *Sittlichkeit*.

The problem with modern life was that its rationality was not immediately apparent to its participants; for that, one required a set of reflective practices that could display and demonstrate the rationality of modern life, namely, those involved in modern art, modern religion, and, most importantly, modern *philosophy*. Thus, Hegel saw himself as critically entering the debates on legality and constitutionalism with his explicitly modern philosophy that would show how the anti-reform elements of German life (and even the odd conservative mixture of reform and anti-reform represented by Savigny and his followers) were wrong in their assessment of what European and German *Geist* actually meant and what it required.

In his letter to Schelling from Frankfurt, Hegel had asked "what return to intervention in the life of men can be found"; now he had a good example of how he might do that right in front of him.[2]

The *Philosophy of Right*

Although Hegel's 1820 *Philosophy of Right* was unfairly criticized both during and after Hegel's lifetime as being only an "apology" for Prussian absolutism, it was in fact an attempt on Hegel's part to articulate the rational form of the kind of reformed, modern European state and society that people like Baron von Stein, and later Prince von Hardenberg, had tried to establish in Prussia; and most of his friends and students understood that.

The core idea of the book is that what counts as "right" in general is what is necessary for the realization of freedom. In that respect, Hegel both adhered to his Kantian inspiration while at the same time, in a crucial and decisive way, moving away from Kant. One crucial difference from Kant was Hegel's rejection of Kant's claim that if we were to be free, we had to be capable of exercising a kind of non-natural causality on ourselves, a "transcendental causality" that stood outside the natural, causal order of things and that could initiate chains of events without itself being the effect of any earlier causal chain. Hegel, by contrast, conceived of freedom not as the exercise of any form of causality at all but as instead having to do with the nature of the way in which we are capable of assuming a "negative" stance toward our inclinations, desires, and impulses.

Hegel shared with Kant the notion that the will is essentially a form of "practical reason," of our acting according to norms, but he disagreed with the idea that for such a will to be free, it required a special form of causality on its part. Our freedom consists instead in the *stance* we take towards our actions and, on Hegel's view, I am fully free when the reasons for which I act are those that I can count as *my* reasons, that is, the ones for which *I* am the subject, with which I identify myself. The agent's preferences, desires, and impulses have a normative status for the agent only to the extent that they fit into his overall project for his life, fit into some sense of his own identity, who he *is* as the acting subject – insofar as they express a certain self-relation. (On Hegel's view, there would indeed be some empirical story to be told about how it is that we ultimately move ourselves by virtue of our decisions, but however that empirical story turns out, it would not be necessary for the account of an action's being "my own" and "expressing" my acknowledgment of my reasons for acting. Only if reasons were taken to be "things" alongside other "things" would there be a need for a special doctrine of transcendental causality.)

Thus, in humans, the capacity to have a will is the capacity, first of all, to have one's actions express one's practical commitments – to follow from and fit into one's project for one's life – to have those actions done because of those and not some other practical commitments; second, to have the capacity to reflect on those practical commitments in terms of their relations of significance to other ends and other principles the agent entertains; and third, to be able to understand those commitments as one's own and not having been imposed on oneself from something outside the structure of one's willing. To have a "will," that is, is to be able to act in a *minded* way, to be able to act according to norms. The "will," as Hegel put it, is "a form of thought."[3] The opposite of such freedom would be to act in terms of something one cannot rationally endorse for oneself, that is, ultimately to be pushed around by considerations that are not really one's own but come from or belong to something else (for example, brute desires; or mere social conventions).

To be free, however, is not to be simply "expressing" oneself in isolation, it is rather, as the *Phenomenology* had shown, to stand in a complex, mediated relation to other self-conscious entities. In Hegel's almost paradoxical way of putting it, one can be an agent only by being *recognized* as an agent, and thus the conditions of free agency exist fully in the relations of mutual recognition among agents, on the norms to which we can mutually hold each other; what counts thereby as a sustainable "reason" for action is fully social in character and depends on some sense of what it is that these agents are collectively trying to achieve, not just on what individuals are trying privately to achieve for themselves. That is, freedom must consist in a fully reciprocal, mutual imposition of norms, not in the one-sided imposition of norms by one person or group on another.

That rather bold thesis about "sociality" in itself, however, seemed to lead to another, equally paradoxical conclusion. Although each agent's "calling" is to be free, to act in terms of principles that are "his own," it is clearly the case that none of us begins life as such a free being, nor do we come to that status fully naturally. Rather, we learn to subject ourselves to principles only by at first being subjected by others to those principles. A certain kind of "obedience" to the authority of others is necessary in order to learn to be self-determining, and the goal of such obedience must be to free the agent from such obedience, since it is also clear that such obedience is incompatible with freedom in Hegel's sense.[4] That principle to which I am subjected by others comes to be my principle only when I internalize the ends of that action, when I make those alien ends into *my* ends – that is, when I come to identify with them – and I can ultimately come to identify with those ends only if I can understand them, however implicitly, as following from what is inevitably bound up in my own rational agency itself. To the extent that we cannot understand those norms as rational, we see them not as our own but as something that is "ours" and "not ours"; we become alienated from them.

Hegel's theory of practical reasoning, painfully worked out over the duration of his stays in Frankfurt, Jena, and Heidelberg, finally enabled him to articulate these lines of thought in a form he found satisfactory. For any individual agent to be free, he must be able to reason practically about what he is to do, and such practical reasoning itself would be possible only if there were some conception within it about what it is that an individual is trying to accomplish by his actions, that is, what *good* he is trying to achieve. An explicitly formulated piece of practical reasoning would thus always begin with some statement about what is ultimately good and best, to be accompanied by other premises, themselves established by reflective deliberation, about what is necessary for *this* individual to achieve *that* kind of good. There are, however, no "goods" that are immediately obvious to "we moderns." Even what look like purely natural goods must, given our own "negativity," be incorporated into our maxims, be given a rational form; the only good, therefore, that can serve as an "ultimate good" to function as the first premise of any practical reasoning must be the good of freedom itself, that whatever else is the case I be free in directing my actions and that only through this freedom can I be "at home" with myself in my actions.

Expressed so abstractly, though, such an invocation of "freedom for freedom's sake" offers little or no guidance for deliberation. The purpose of the *Philosophy of Right* was thus to demonstrate what our commitment to "freedom" itself further committed us to, such that reflection on those commitments would thereby give us a grasp of some more concrete actualizations of freedom that could serve as efficacious, more substantial first principles of practical reason. In thinking about it in this way, Hegel brought into play his reflections on Hölderlin's original insight about judgment preceding from a prereflective sense of how things stand; practical reasoning, Hegel concluded, must itself therefore come out of some type of prereflective orientation that establishes certain goods as first premises, which in turn feature in the agent's project for his life and with which the agent can later, through reflection, come to see as rational. That prereflective orientation has to do with our socialization, with the ways in which we are formed by our education and form an implicit, even at first unclear, sense of what we are about, what our identity calls on us to do. Since ultimately our "projects" for ourselves must be consistent with the "negativity" of self-consciousness – the self-distancing stance we can always assume towards ourselves, our past, and the world around us – we can never simply immediately accept the self-identity with which we have been socialized; our own "negativity" entails that we must also be able to satisfy ourselves reflectively as to whether those "projects" into which we have been socialized can themselves be rationally sustained, can maintain our allegiance to themselves.

Following this idea out, Hegel argued that in the modern world, the realization of freedom must be articulated into three more determinate spheres, which he characterized as "abstract right," "morality," and "ethical life" ("*Sittlichkeit*"). Each of these embodies a way in which institutions and practices underwrite and sustain the ways in which our freedom is actualized in that each of them provides individuals with more concrete, specific first premises about "the good" (freedom) on the basis of which they may then rationally deliberate what they are required to do.

"Abstract right" is that sphere in which individuals are committed to the mutual recognition of certain basic rights having to do with property, exchange of property, and contracts. In a finite world of limited means, embodied agents require disposition over certain material elements for them to be able to carry out any of their commitments at all. To the extent that each of them is ultimately committed to realizing his own freedom (and not, for example, something else, such as the greater glory of God), he is required to extend such commitments to others (granted certain other very "modern" premises about reasoning and agency). It is the equal claims of others – an equality won by centuries of hard struggle – that leads to the commitment to mutual and abstract rights to property; it is "abstract" in that the first premise of reasoning for these very modern agents is taken to concern itself with their getting what they contingently happen to want, within the context of a set of mutually recognized rights.

Moreover, given the finitude and fallibility of human life, there will always be wrongs committed in the context of any such social "whole" based on such rights. Some agents will refuse to see themselves as "one among many" and therefore ignore others' rights in the pursuit of getting what they want, and to the extent that they are able to do that with impunity, the entire structure of "right" would be thereby threatened. To that end, some system of "punishment" is required, some infliction on the offending party of an equivalent harm to that which he has visited on others; the function of such punishment is to express the normative force of his actions were they to be applied to himself. That itself, though, requires that at least some people be capable of speaking with the voice of "right" itself, and that the offending party not be used to satisfy somebody else's desire (even for revenge) but be punished only for the sake of "restoring" right.

The ability to put one's one interests and inclinations aside and speak and act from the standpoint of "right" itself is not, however, itself an "abstract right" but a "moral disposition," a feature of character. "Morality," the second sphere of the realization of right-as-freedom, thus concerns itself with the general and unconditional *obligations* that people have by virtue of their overall commitment to freedom. Those are, very roughly, Kantian in form: People have an obligation to do the right thing (that is, to perform actions that are in accord with reasons that could be shared by all) and to do it out of the right motives (to do the right thing because it is right, not because it satisfies some other impulse, desire, or social convention). Hegel famously argued, though, that on its own, this moral demand is relatively empty; it functions as the first premise of a piece of practical reasoning, but it leaves us in the dark as to what exactly is required by "reasons that could be shared by all." Moreover, the sheer contingency of what can actually count as an "unconditional moral obligation" is made manifest in those conditions of extreme distress, as when a desperate, starving person steals a loaf of bread to survive or to feed his family; in admitting that this "right of distress" trumps property rights, we also thereby admit that what counts as an "unconditional moral obligation" can itself be overridden by more mundane concerns having to do with individual welfare.

Kant himself had admitted that it was absurd for us to expect individuals entirely to forsake their own happiness. Therefore, for us to make sense of the contingency of right and welfare, Hegel argued, we must, as Kant himself had seen, additionally commit ourselves to a notion of a "highest good," to bringing about in this world a union of virtue and happiness, such that these contingencies of right and welfare do not throw our whole scheme of moral obligation into question.[5] Kant's own invocation of the "highest good," Hegel seems to imply, shows that Kant implicitly acknowledges the right of the individual to his own *satisfaction*. This principle, in fact, of the "right of subjective freedom," first expressed in Christianity, is, Hegel says, the "pivotal and focal point in the difference between antiquity and the modern age . . . it has become the universal and actual principle of a new form of the world. Its more specific shapes include love, the romantic, the eternal salvation of the individual as an end."[6] Hegel thus crucially reinterpreted the specifically Kantian conception of the "highest good" – conceived as the union of virtue and *happiness* – towards what he simply calls "the" good – conceived as the union of virtue and *satisfaction*. Satisfaction, for Hegel, involves the achieving of ends that are crucial for an agent's sense of the project of his life, what he is about, what "counts" for himself; as Hegel makes the distinction, an agent may be satisfied yet still be unhappy.[7] In reinterpreting Kant in that way, Hegel was stressing what he saw as the logic at work in Kant's view: What was at stake was the union of the "universal" (the moral rule as expressed in virtuous action) and the "particular" (expressed as happiness for Kant and as satisfaction for Hegel). Thus, Hegel's long-standing interest in combining Enlightenment universalism with a sort of particularism reinterpreted in very modern terms came into play.

What the "highest good" as the union of *morality* (or virtue) and personal *satisfaction* reveals is that its rational articulation requires more than "morality." In undertaking a commitment to a conception of "the good" as the unity of the "universal and the particular" (as the integration of particular aspirations with what is required by "universal" reason), the agent finds himself committed to something like a conception of a pattern of action for which no determinate "rule" can be given. General rules are appropriate to the "universal"; but there are no rules or principles for the "particular." Hegel thus brought to bear his long-standing admiration for Aristotle in his criticism of Kant; just as Aristotle had argued that "practical wisdom" was, in Aristotle's phrase, "concerned not only with universals but with particulars, which become familiar from experience," Hegel argued that an agent acting on the basis of "the good" and for the sake of duty would be committed to a conception of moral judgment that relates a "universal" principle to a "particular" case without there being any rule for how such judgments make that relation.[8] And this, Hegel argues, is exactly what the intrinsically modern appeal to *conscience* is supposed to do. Conscience is always the conscience of a particular individual and is the way in which that agent judges whether the reasons behind his actions are indeed morally satisfactory, whether they are indeed the kind of reasons that can be shared by all agents.

Because modern "morality" necessarily commits us to a conception of the priority of conscience as a way of preventing the tensions between "right" and "welfare" from bringing down the moral enterprise altogether, it also commits itself to something more than an appeal to conscience, since the appeal to conscience generates its own tensions. On the one hand, as Hegel puts it, "true conscience is the disposition to will what is good in and for itself; it therefore has fixed principles"; but since it is the conscience of an individual, it also reflects his own *personal* valuations of things.[9] The appeal to conscience, therefore, can just as well license acts that are otherwise forbidden by the rest of our practical commitments as it can lead to individuals doing the right thing, and it can also promote the most brazen forms of self-deception and hypocrisy. Nor could one eliminate those tensions within the modern appeal to conscience by eliminating the appeal to conscience altogether. Modern agents *must* think of themselves as practically committed to making judgments based on their own conscience; eliminating the appeal to conscience simply cannot be an option for "we moderns," for "conscience," Hegel says, "is a sanctuary which it would be a sacrilege to violate."[10]

To the extent that a "moral" agent can successfully make such appeals to conscience, he must instead learn to orient himself in light of some idealized community of like-minded agents, in terms of the ways in which other "like-minded" agents would also ideally judge. But that means that the appeal to conscience is both necessary for the standpoint of "Morality" and also involves, at first apparently paradoxically, an appeal to something that cannot itself be contained within the standpoint of "Morality." The practical judgments required by "conscience" cannot consist in any straightforward *application* of general principles to particular cases; there can be no universal rule for applying the universal rule to particular cases. Such conscience-guided practical judgments instead require that we be *trained* into practices that are themselves sustained by public institutions so that in being so trained into those practices and in internalizing the way of life embodied in them, we thereby acquire a certain type of skill, a character, a *virtue*, a way of orienting ourselves in social space, a kind of practice-oriented ethical "know-how," that, as Hegel characterized it in his lectures, amounts to a kind of "ethical virtuosity."[11] This sphere of practices and institutions within which we learn to orient ourselves, in which we acquire such "ethical virtuosity," is modern *Sittlichkeit*, "ethical life," the basic category of Hegel's mature ethical and political thought. In it he thought he had found something deep and, to some extent, surprising about the modern world.

If we are to have any concrete first principles for moral reasoning that specify what is ultimately good and best for us, we must grasp them not as specifications of some "master rule" but as elements of a social practice, ways in which we prereflectively learn to orient and move ourselves around in the social world. Such prereflective self-situating gives us an implicit grasp of our sense of who we are, our "project" for our lives, without our having first chosen, explicitly or implicitly, that project; and the "ethical life," *Sittlichkeit*, within which we orient ourselves must then be capable of sustaining allegiance to itself when put under the glare of reflection on its rationality, which for "we moderns" means that it must be capable of being understood also as a realization of freedom. "Moral" individuals exercising their "abstract rights" thus require a "location" in these kinds of social practices since these "ethical" practices embody within themselves determinate conceptions of what is "ultimately best," namely, as the way in which individuals exercise their rights, manage their moral obligations, and come to be "at home" in the social world by virtue of acquiring a kind of "ethical virtuosity" in being brought up and socialized in these practices.

There are three such institutionalizations of *Sittlichkeit* in the modern world, each serving to give individuals a concrete specification of this ultimate good (the union of "morality" and satisfaction) about whose more specific realization they can then rationally deliberate. These are the modern family, civil society, and the constitutionalist state. Together they form a social "whole" in terms of which individuals orient themselves and which reconciles them to modern social life, gives them good grounds for believing that modern life really is, although imperfect and finite, nonetheless for the best.

In Hegel's view, in the modern family, founded on the mutual free choice of the husband and wife, agents discover a good – romantic love (that just *this* other person is the right one for me), and the ideal of family life as a refuge from civil society – which in turn also embodies certain obligations (such as: raising children to be free, independent adults; and mutual respect in the marriage). Rational reflection, so Hegel thought, would show that the individuals in such a modern family are able to experience these obligations not as imposed on them from outside of themselves (such as by "mere" social convention) but as embodying norms that sustain a full, mutual recognition without which freedom could not be possible. Modern families give modern *individuals* a *common* project; the family is not a contractual collection of private wills but is a unity on its own possessing a common purpose.

Nonetheless, although Hegel explicitly thought of his conception of the family as nonpatriarchal and even somewhat egalitarian in its dynamic, he also strongly believed that the biological differences between the sexes entailed complementary psychological differences that made a crucial difference in the way the family was to be run.[12] Women, Hegel thought, simply were not equipped by nature for "the higher sciences, for philosophy and certain artistic productions which require a universal element," for "their actions are not based on the demands of universality but on contingent inclination and opinion."[13] Thus, although a man has "his actual substantial life in the state, in *Wissenschaft*, etc., and otherwise in work and struggle with the external world and himself," a woman "has her substantial vocation in the family, and her ethical disposition consists in this piety."[14] Women's very "estate" was to be "housewife" and mother, and the man finds in the family a "peaceful intuition of this unity and an emotive and subjective ethical life" that he would otherwise not be able to find in the harsh male world of careers and competition.[15]

Given that he held those views, it cannot be surprising that quite a few of the women in Hegel's circle of friends complained of the way he would refuse to discuss ideas with them. Even his good friend Varnhagen von Ense noted with regard to Hegel's attitude to his wife, Rahel Varnhagen – a leader of the Berlin salon culture, a figure in Berlin's Jewish circles, and a woman of no small intellect – that "Hegel knew Rahel as a clever, thoughtful woman and treated her as such, but only with great difficulty did he recognize her authentic spiritual essence."[16] She herself had "difficulty" with the fact that Hegel would not discuss his ideas with her.

Hegel also argued that the purpose of raising children was to educate them to freedom and independence; as he put it, "The services which may be required of children should therefore contribute solely to the end of their upbringing; they must not claim to be justified in their own right, for the most unethical of all relationships is that in which children are slaves."[17] In his lectures, he complained about the extent of child labor in England and the way in which in manufacturing towns the children were effectively denied all right to education, a practice he found shocking and abhorrent.[18] The children within the family also serve, Hegel argued, to make the "subjective" love of husband and wife "objective," to give an anchor to what might have been only a chancy emotional relationship through the common commitment to the education of the children.

Families, however, dissolve and form anew with the death of one or both of the parents, or with the adult children going out to form new families. This leads them into "civil society," in which, with its modern market institutions, individuals have a social space in which the pursuit of their own private interests (as in "abstract right") is allowed full play and is counted as something legitimate on its own. Hegel does not completely identify civil society with market society, although he holds that the free market is essential to civil society's functioning. Indeed, what makes such civil society "ethical," *sittlich*, what makes it a common enterprise, has to do in the first place with the way in which the structures of the market compel individuals to take account of the particular needs and wants of others, so that the individual's pursuit of his private interests turns out to require a mediated form of mutuality in order for that pursuit to be successful.

The discipline of the market requires of each participant that he bend his will to the requirements of others, and the laws of the market produce a harmony out of this reciprocal pressure each has put on the other. (Hegel drew on his readings of Adam Smith to make that point.) Civil society's harmony thus comes about not in the seemingly effortless, "beautiful" manner of the ancient Greeks. As Hegel put it, modern civil society "affords a spectacle of extravagance and misery as well as of the physical and ethical corruption common to both."[19] However, whatever civil society lacks in classical beauty, it gains in rationality and efficiency, in its accommodating a place for the modern *individual*, and it thereby acquires a kind of modern, more fragmented beauty and *Sittlichkeit* on its own.

Hegel's defense of civil society as "ethical" firmly took its stance against that line of thought, widespread in his day, that was deeply suspicious of the mores of a market society, seeing it only as crass, commercial, disrespectful of tradition, and thus completely lacking in any kind of "beauty." Indeed, nowhere was this suspicion more deeply grounded than in Prussia itself, where the *Junker*, the landed aristocratic gentry of traditional eastern Prussia, had sternly set itself against anything that challenged their authoritarian rule over their domains. Hegel's robust defense of civil society thus set him firmly at odds with the *Junker* and their allies in Prussia.[20]

The participant in civil society is not yet a "citizen"; he is a bourgeois, a *Bürger*, in pursuit of the satisfaction of his own personal interests, bending his will to the will of others, since his own satisfaction depends on others finding something in him that satisfies *their* interests. As such, the bourgeois presents a stock and somewhat comic modern figure. He fiercely defends his right to count for as much as the next person, which thus forces him to seek a kind of "equality" with others, which in turn leads to the modern phenomenon of bourgeois conformism, in which each imitates the other not out of "tradition" but out of the need simply to make himself like others. Hegel, for example, explains the modern phenomenon of the European interest in rapid change in fashion as the need to *conform* to social opinion in a way that also gives the *appearance* of distinctiveness, of "particularity" in appearance. Hegel himself, who was never exactly a slave to fashion, made his own views most clear in his Heidelberg lectures: "Fashion is one aspect of this, and to dress according to fashion is the most rational course, whereas we can leave it to others to bother about new fashions: one should not take the lead oneself, but one should avoid idiosyncrasy . . . One asserts oneself in order to be equal to others."[21] Thus, conformism takes over and in the end, as Hegel puts it, "everything particular takes on a social character; in the manner of dress and times of meals, there are certain conventions which one must accept, for in such matters, it is not worth the trouble to seek display one's own insight, and it is wisest to act as others do."[22]

Indeed, precisely because of the pressures of the market on the members of civil society, the demands to pursue their own interests and to conform, Hegel argued forcefully, as he had been doing since his arrival in Jena, for the continued legal recognition of the estates and some of the corporate structures of the ancien régime, since, so he argued, only they could serve as mediating bodies for the structures of mutual and equal recognition in the newly emerging market societies. As he had done in Jena, he gave these structures a very modern twist by interpreting them not in purely economic or even "natural" but in "ethical" terms. The estates were to be determined not by virtue of a "natural" division in society but in terms of the kinds of goods and styles of reasoning that modern individuals assumed for themselves. Each estate gives its members a kind of project for themselves, a non-prudentially determined sense of identity, a "standing" in civil society as a whole. (The very German term for an "estate" – a "*Stand*" – nicely captures that sense.) Without the estates, individuals would have only the "moral" standpoint to guide them, only a very general sense that they satisfy their "universal" obligations; with the estates, individuals have a much more concrete sense of how to orient themselves in life. Thus, on Hegel's view, the peasant estate, because of its ties to the land, finds that what is good and best for itself has to do with tradition and trust in nature, and it reasons out its life project accordingly.[23] The "reflective" or business estate finds that what is good and best for it is

the rational, "reflective" calculation of what is most efficient for producing and exchanging goods. The "universal" estate of civil servants
has as its good the overall flourishing and proper functioning of civil
society as a whole, and it thus reasons out its life projects in terms of
the virtues involved in a career in public service. The fact that one must
determine for oneself which estate is to be one's own estate marked, for
Hegel, the crucial difference "between the political life of . . . the ancient and modern worlds" and, so he also thought, between the political
life of the "East" and the "West."[24] Even if one stays in the estate into
which one is born, one's birth and family simply cannot – in a modern
civil society – determine one's estate for oneself (with the exception of
the nobility).

A simple organization into estates, however, cannot be sufficient to
sustain the *sittlich*, the ethical order of civil society. The business estate
has particular tensions within itself that must be mediated by further
institutional conditions; in the pursuit of riches and efficiency, the
members of that estate have a tendency to fall back into a blind pursuit
of self-interest and thus to undermine the overall "ethical" bonds that
hold civil society together. Within the business estate, therefore, there
should be various "corporate" orders gathered around common interests
that are to "police" their members. However, since the "corporations"
cannot be expected to do that fully and completely successfully, civil
society also requires a whole set of regulatory and legal bodies to oversee
its infrastructure and day-to-day life so that it maintains the necessary
equilibrium within itself to function properly. Likewise, for the regulatory and legal bodies to function fairly and efficiently, there had to be a
codified set of laws subject to rational review; keeping the laws uncodi-
fied, as Savigny had insisted, would be, Hegel said, irrational and
unconscionable – "to deny a civilized nation or the legal estate within it
the ability to draw up a legal code would be among the greatest insults
one could offer to either."[25] Neither Savigny nor any of his followers
could have mistaken that jab Hegel took at them; in an equally sharp
jab at the attempts by the *Junker* to maintain their traditional patrimonial courts, Hegel argued equally forcefully for public courts; and he
even broke with many of his juristic colleagues in arguing for trial by
jury, noting, "it is possible that the administration of justice in itself
could be managed well by purely professional courts . . . but even if this
possibility could be increased to probability – or indeed to necessity –

it is of no relevance, for on the opposite side there is always the *right of self-consciousness* which retains its claims and finds that they are not satisfied."[26]

Hegel was also acutely aware of the problem that extreme poverty and extreme wealth generated by industrial society poses for civil society as a whole, since at both ends of the spectrum of wealth, individuals lose their sense of obligation to the "whole" – the poor because they have no stake in it, the rich because they tend to think that they can buy themselves out of its obligations. The issue of poverty was particularly acute in Prussia; the Napoleonic wars had devastated Prussian agriculture, and the legal emancipation of the peasantry had the unintended consequence that the nobility bought up the peasants' land and ejected the peasants, who had traditionally worked on it, so as to be able to institute more efficient modes of agricultural production; the result was the creation of a "rabble" of unemployed and unemployable peasants throughout Prussia. Hegel quite candidly admitted that his speculative philosophy contained no answer to the problem of modern poverty, and he tended to see it as *the* great unresolved issue in modern life. Expansion of markets abroad, he speculated, might prove to be the only practical way of even beginning to address the issue, although he did not think it could completely resolve it.

However, no matter how prosperous it may be and how much its structures tend to check the excesses of other structures, civil society cannot on its own establish the point of view of the "whole" that is necessary for the various legal, regulatory, and corporate structures to have the "ethical" authority they must have. The *political* point of view, which is concerned explicitly not with private interests but with the collective goal of freedom that the people of modern life are trying to achieve, is embodied in the "state." Whereas civil society is the sphere of free *individuals*, political life has for its purpose the establishment of the conditions necessary for a free *people*. For this goal to be actualized, the state must be articulated into a set of appropriately modern *governmental* institutions, whose legitimating principle is again that of freedom, not efficiency or preference satisfaction.

Hegel defended a form of constitutional monarchy for the modern state, although he restricted the monarch's duties to nothing more, as he put it, than dotting the "i's" on legislation presented to him by his ministers. (The Prussian royals, almost needless to say, were not amused when told what Professor Hegel was saying in his lectures about their proper political role.) The function of the modern monarch is only to express the ungrounded (or, rather, the self-grounding) nature of the modern state, the idea that its legitimacy rests on nothing else than the collective goal of establishing the conditions under which a "people" can be free. Moreover, the monarch is as contingent as the state of which he is the monarch; his blank assertion, "I will this," serves as the expression of that element of ungrounded sovereignty that distinguishes modern states. No further appeal to God's will or to natural law serves to legitimate it; only the "moral and ethical law" as freely and collectively established by rational individuals can count and put restrictions on its activities.

Constitutional protection of basic rights must be insured if people are to identify with the collective aim of such a political society. The modern state must incorporate the specifically modern sense of humanism, in which "a *human being counts as such because he is a human being*, not because he is a Jew, Catholic, Protestant, German, Italian, etc."[27] Quite strikingly, Hegel nowhere invokes anything strongly resembling a classical doctrine of the "common good" in his theory of the state. Although the state must embody the collective aspiration for the free life of a "people," nowhere does Hegel say that it ought to prescribe some one way of life or set of virtues that would be common to all. His insistence on the plurality of estates and his "ethical" interpretation of them was intended to make clear that a modern state must incorporate within itself a plurality of ways of life and even of virtues. As ever, the nationalists who wanted to prescribe an authentic "German" way of life for all those in the former Holy Roman Empire – the people he had in Nuremberg called the *Deutschdumm* – were anathema to Hegel.

Likewise, the modern state had to keep its distance even from religion. Even though the modern state and modern Protestant Christianity share the same general aspiration (that of realizing freedom), their interests in the conditions under which freedom is actualized diverge. The rational, legal constitutional state simply cannot base its actions on "authority and faith" as religion must do.[28] Letting religious matters into state affairs only leads to fanaticism; when religion becomes political, the result can only be "folly, outrage, and the destruction of all ethical relations," since the piety of religious conviction when confronted with the manifold claims of the modern political world too easily passes over into "a sense of grievance and hence also of self-conceit" and a sense that the truly faithful can find in their "own godliness all that is required in order to see through the nature of the laws and of political institutions, to pass judgment on them, and to lay down what their character should and must be."[29] Indeed, the plurality of modern religions is itself a condition for the modern state assuming the kind of complex unity that it has: The historic split in Christendom should therefore not be lamented, Hegel argued – it is in fact "the most fortunate thing which could have happened to the church and to thought as far as their freedom and rationality is concerned."[30]

If such rights and the recognition of pluralism are to be effectively insured, then a modern state must also have some form of representative government. Hegel rejected, though, democracy and voting by geographical district: In a democracy, a majoritarian parliament may simply ignore the minority's interests; and selecting representatives on the basis of geography means selecting people without any regard to whether they represent the basic and important interests of the "whole" society or even of the people whom they are supposed to represent. Thus, to the extent that people actually identify with their estates and corporations, a system of representation based on the estates and corporations will more likely ensure that all legitimate voices are heard at the "state" level. Hegel also opted for a bicameral legislature, with a house of "lords" and a house of "commons" as a way of ensuring that society's basic interests would be heard and society's stability be maintained.

The executive portion of government should be staffed by a cadre of trained civil servants who will emerge as men of *Bildung* by virtue of their university education. The protection against what he called the "arbitrariness of officialdom" would come, Hegel seemed to think, from the pressure that would be exerted by the monarch (although how a monarch who only dotted the "i's" was supposed to do that was never explained) and by the estates from which the various individual civil servants emerged.[31] Hegel also concluded that the executive should consist in something like Baron von Stein's sense of a set of "collegial bodies," with no one official having an authoritative office over the whole set of them. In an implicit criticism of Hardenberg – only voiced in his lectures after Hardenberg's death – Hegel argued that no just state should have the position of chancellor that Hardenberg had managed to obtain for himself. Although the position of chancellor, Hegel said, "is associated with a high degree of facility, speed, and effectiveness in measures adopted for the universal interests of the state," it tends nonetheless to "have the result that everything is again controlled from above by ministerial power," and however attractive such justifications in terms of efficiency and "centralization" might be, they miss the point that the *ethical* authority of the modern state lies in the way it secures the satisfaction of the common aspiration for freedom, to which efficiency, although not being ignored, must always be subordinated. For the goal of actualizing freedom to be achieved, Hegel argued, "civil life shall be governed in a concrete manner from below . . . [even though] the business in question shall be divided into abstract branches and dealt with by specific bodies."[32]

The Philosophy of World History

Since the modern state appeals to neither God nor natural law for its legitimacy, it must appeal to some sense of what a "people" collectively establish as rational. This drives political philosophy into a philosophy of history, since the kind of critique that reason performs on itself (as Kant had said was reason's highest goal) can, if Hegel's other arguments are correct, only be performed historically. Hegel thus concluded the *Philosophy of Right* with some short paragraphs on the philosophy of world history, which he later expanded into a series of popular and well-attended lectures. Those lectures were posthumously published in his collected works under the simple title *The Philosophy of History*. (The first edition was edited by Hegel's friend Eduard Gans, and the second edition by his son Karl Hegel.) Although not actually worked up for publication by Hegel himself, those lectures have since become probably his most widely read and widely known work, showing Hegel at his least obscure and in his most dazzling manner. In them, he laid out his ideas on the progressive nature of history and advanced some views that were, to say the least, quite controversial in his own day.

The progress of world history was, Hegel argued, best understood as progress in understanding and actualizing the commitments that follow from humanity's collective undertaking to realize freedom for itself in political life along with religion, art, and philosophy. In making that point about history, Hegel cited some lines from a poem by Friedrich Schiller ("Resignation") to the effect that world history is the "final

court of the world," the "last judgment" on those states whose development makes up world history itself.[33] As with many of Hegel's other
pronouncements, particularly in the *Philosophy of Right*, this only inflamed many of those who read it as offering a kind of carte blanche to
all kinds of historical immorality and as being perhaps even a cynical
invocation of historical relativism, of the idea that winners in historical
struggles are right simply by virtue of the fact that they have won. In
truth, it was only Hegel's restatement of his own brand of radical
modernism that he had already argued at length in the *Phenomenology
of Spirit*: If there were no truths of natural law to which our ethical
actions had to conform, then the ultimate justification of our actions
had to be elaborated internally within the development of our own
"mindedness" and "like-mindedness." If the authority of the modern
state lies not in its fulfilling some ecclesiastical or merely traditional
doctrine but in institutionalizing itself in terms of the pursuit of freedom for its own sake, then such a state could be judged only by
standards internal to what is necessary to realize the dynamic of freedom
itself. Hegel's notion that "world history is the world court" amounts
to his fundamental conception that there is no firm and fast way of
saying that any state has any authority except in terms of whether it can
rationally justify itself, and, no matter how convinced it may be of its
own righteousness, other people, arriving on the scene later in history,
have the right to pronounce it to have been irrational if it failed on
those terms, even implicitly.

There is therefore in history, as Hegel explicitly put it, no "irrational
necessity of a blind fate" directing the destinies of states.[34] For Hegel,
understanding what is now authoritative and possible for us in our
political lives necessarily involves locating ourselves within history, understanding our possibilities in terms of an interpretation of what *has*
happened and *is* happening and *why* it happened. What is at stake is
always up for grabs, and it is never settled by some historical fiat or
even by some social agreement that it has been settled. The shape that
a state must assume depends on what it takes to be rational for it in
light of that kind of historical understanding of what has happened and
of what that now rules in and rules out. We simply cannot understand
history as a set of "contingent" events, or even as a contingent play of
human passions, as if the great issues about reason and truth in history

could be settled by our or somebody else's simply declaring them to be settled or by our just waiting to see who "wins."

Since world history must be seen as embodying in part the history of reason itself (and therefore, ultimately, of the "Idea" of freedom itself), it is therefore, Hegel argued, the history of "states" (in his special sense of "state"). World history is the history of humanity itself – the "world spirit," in Hegel's parlance – because, in Hegel's terms, "the history of spirit is its own deed; for spirit is what it does, and its deed is to make itself . . . the object of its own consciousness and to comprehend itself in its interpretation of itself to itself."[35] What has happened is the result of the way "spirit" has *taken* itself to be in light of the other changes (environmental, technological, and so on) surrounding it.

World history is thus fundamentally about the development of the "Idea" of freedom, that is, of our collective and individual grasp of the normative "whole" in terms of which freedom is both intelligible to us and "actual" (in Hegel's sense) for us. For Hegel, it was crucial to show that the modern "Idea" of freedom was rationally necessitated by the internal deficiencies of earlier articulations of the "Idea" such that "we moderns" were in the position to understand that the deficiencies of past articulations of the normative "whole" were deficient precisely because they had no place for an understanding of the bindingness of freedom itself; even though "our ancestors" could not have understood themselves as trying to develop a conception of freedom in our sense, "we moderns" are in the position to see that it was in fact freedom that was at stake for them and "we moderns" can explain why their articulations in terms other than that of actualizing freedom were destined to failure.

Hegel therefore concluded that the crucial epochs of world history had to be understood in terms of how a particular "Idea" of freedom was to be understood in that period and why it had to undo itself, why it had to reach the point where the participants in that way of life could no longer find those norms binding on them or even find them to be intelligible any longer, and why that grasp of the normative whole committed us to a different understanding of that whole itself.

In that light, Hegel divided world history into four major periods, depending on the "Idea" of freedom contained in each. The first phase corresponded to the beginnings of history in "Eastern" states, all of which Hegel interpreted as essentially "stalled" versions of more developed modern European states. In the early phases of world history and the nations that embodied that principle, there could only be a vague, undifferentiated sense of the normative whole, which then came to be identified with "nature," within which no sense of individuality or reflective religious practice could develop. The second stage corresponded to the Greek discovery of *Sittlichkeit* and "beautiful individuality." The third stage had to do with Roman life, with its manner of subjugating all people to its rule, and the kind of alienation and inwardness that began to develop within the heart of Roman rule itself that led to its collapse. The final and last stage of history was concerned with the "Germanic" countries of Europe (under which Hegel also included Slavic countries along with France and Italy, but which he usually tended to identify more or less with northern European Protestant countries).

Hegel summed this up for his audience with his memorable formula, that of the developments in world history we find "firstly, that of the Orientals, who knew only that *one* is free, then that of the Greek and Roman world, which knew that *some* are free, and finally our own knowledge that *all* men as such are free, and that man is by nature free."[36]

He also summarized the movement of world history for his audience in Berlin with his startling claim: "World history travels from east to west; for Europe is the absolute end of history, just as Asia is the beginning."[37] By calling Europe the "absolute end" of history, he did not intend to suggest, however, that history was in fact over (whatever that might mean), that nothing new or important would ever happen again, that there would henceforth be no grand events in the world. His point was that the destiny at which European humanity had arrived was fated also to be the destiny of humanity in general: to understand that the "Idea" of freedom was something humanity developed for itself out of itself, and that its fate was now linked to the problems of how we were to live with that freedom and its attendant dissatisfactions. What had historically taken form in "European" life, the way in which European culture embodied a fundamental "negativity" about itself, a kind of permanent self-doubt and self-questioning that constituted its peculiar energy and driving force, was to be extended to all cultures, not in terms of European conquest but in terms of the way in which such

"skeptical," "negative" practices would gradually incorporate themselves into all ways of life. (Although many of Hegel's views on other
cultures were indeed "Eurocentric," he did not seem to hold that all
ways of life would indeed eventually become "European"; rather, it was
his view that as they modernized, they would eventually come to embody within themselves something like "European negativity.")

Stung by criticisms that he was a pawn of the ruling powers in
Prussia, Hegel used his lectures to clear up several misunderstandings
that had been left over from the publication of the *Philosophy of Right*.
He thus made it clear to his audiences that despite his argument for the
"absolute right" of the bearers of the meaning of world history at any
given time to do what they had to do, he was not defending any type of
view that authorized people to do what they wished to do with those
whom they regarded as "lesser" people. In his lecture notes, Hegel
noted that the religious feeling even of a lowly shepherd or peasant had
"infinite worth" and was "just as valuable" as the feelings of those more
educated or advanced; this "focal point" of human life, this "simple
source of the rights of subjective freedom . . . remains untouched and
[protected] from the noisy clamor of world history."[38] His point about
the "absolute right" of world historical figures was that moralistic criticism of historical figures was, from the standpoint of understanding
world history and its progress, simply beside the point; condemning
Caesar as a "bad man" did not help one any better understand freedom
or Caesar's role in the history of the development of the "Idea" of
freedom. He also made it clear to his audiences in other lectures that he
was not endorsing any claims to European racial superiority. As explicitly as he could, he rejected all doctrines of racial superiority floating
around Europe at the time, which, as he told his audience, had "hoped
to prove that human beings are by nature so differently endowed with
spiritual capacities that some can be dominated like animals. But descent
affords no ground for granting or denying freedom and dominion to
human beings. Mankind is in-itself rational; herein lies the possibility
of equal rights for all people and the nothingness of a rigid distinction
between races which have rights and those which have none."[39] (However, Hegel immediately followed those pronouncements about the
"possibility of equal rights for all people" with a rather painful and
typical characterization of the kinds of traits "typical" of the different
races.)

Moreover, he also tried to make it quite explicit that he was not putting forth a view that the progress of history was equivalent to God's path through time or that it consisted of a set of processes explicitly guided by God (and by implication that the monarch on the Prussian throne was therefore God's own choice). In unequivocal language, Hegel told his audience that "the universal spirit or world spirit is not the same thing as God. It is the rationality of spirit in its worldly existence. Its movement is that it makes itself what it is, i.e., what its concept is."[40] The history of states was the history of humanity in its social and political existence, not a providential tale written by God.

More particularly, Hegel's view of history implied that humanity now had to figure out which institutions and practices in modern life could *reconcile* us to that destiny as having been "right." Ultimately, Hegel also tried to make it clear that world history in its political sense could not in principle fully reconcile humanity to the conditions of its existence. Life in the political state and the exercise of political freedom, important as they were, were only more or less abstract parts of humanity's development of its own self-understanding. True reconciliation occurred only in art, religion, and philosophy. World history was simply the arena in which "objective" spirit cleared the ground for humanity's reflections on itself in "absolute spirit."

In part because of the sheer audacity of his ideas and in part because he softened and even partially abandoned his usual fearsome technical vocabulary in his popular public lectures, Hegel's lectures on the philosophy of history firmly cemented his celebrity in Berlin and were intended by him to underwrite his insistence on the necessity of modern reform. Hegel himself thought of his political philosophy as a synthesis of all that was rational in the existing institutions of the various modern European states. Much to his disappointment, however, little of it turned out actually to be put into practice. As the years went on, his own blueprint for what was rational in the actual institutions of European modernity tended less and less to resemble what was really starting to take shape, at least in Berlin. Part of Hegel's personal struggle was thus trying to keep faith with his deepest convictions and aspirations while observing all around him what might well have seemed to him disconfirming evidence.

Consolidation: Berlin, Brussels, Vienna (1821–1824)

Finding a Balance in Berlin

H EGEL'S FIRST COUPLE OF YEARS IN BERLIN had not been especially encouraging. He had been shut out of the Academy of Sciences, and his students were in political trouble. He was not even able to get his first choice for teaching assistant confirmed by the government or the faculty, and his second choice had also run into deep trouble. That, along with his increasingly overcommitted life, only added to his disappointments, and the pressures on him steadily mounted. The demands of his lectures and the examinations of students, his commitment to being a good citizen at the university and doing his fair share of the common work there, his own ambitions for further publication, the exhausting work he had accepted for the Royal Board of Scientific Examiners for Brandenburg, his own personal commitment to his family life, and his active participation in the artistic and social life in Berlin left him constantly busy and in bad health. It did not help to ease the stress when his sister, Christiane, wrote him an apparently scathing letter, accusing of him of all sorts of wrongdoing against her, to which he responded in August 1821 with a mixture of irritation and paternalistic advice.[1]

It also did not help that after the publication of the *Philosophy of Right*, he came under attack from two different factions: The liberals attacked him for what they took to be his servility to the ruling powers in that work; and at the same time the conservative factions at the university attacked him for what they took to be his baleful influence on the students (in other words, their belief that Hegel was teaching them too many "reform" ideas). One of the leaders of the conservatives, the jurist Friedrich von Savigny, began repeating the same refrain in letters to friends during that time that Hegel was even "worse than Fichte" and, what was especially aggravating, was also attracting lots of students.[2] To Savigny's great irritation, Hegel was especially revered among the Polish students (which included many Polish nobles), who, according to Savigny's rather haughty way of seeing things, "neither understand German nor are capable of forming a concept of anything."[3] (Prussia at this point included large areas of Poland within its territories.)

Worn out by the stresses and strains of the previous year and a half, Hegel suddenly decided in September 1821 to go the "Bohemian baths" via Dresden to recoup his health. Although he showed up in Dresden unannounced, he was happily received by Förster and his other new-found friends there, and the stay in Dresden proved to be both delightful and invigorating for him. His friend Böttiger, the curator of the gallery there, even gave him a special tour by "torchlight" of the Greek and Roman statuary in the collection (which was considered a special treat during the nineteenth century, since it was by and large accepted at that time that only by torchlight could the finely wrought details of the statuary stand out sufficiently for view). Hegel was also able to revisit his other friends, attend a gathering at which Ludwig Tieck read a play by an Italian writer of farces, Goldoni, and visit the picture galleries.

Hegel's journey refreshed him, but he found on his return that the stresses on his life simply continued to mount. If anything, the controversies and the political tensions at the university were only hardening his attitudes and responses to the events around him. Hegel put his faith where it had always been, seeing the current repression in Berlin as only a temporary disturbance in the march to a more rational form of life, as the kind of brief convulsion that accompanies a dying form of authority, and seeing his philosophy as the true guide to modern affairs.

Despite the fact that the reformers by that point had been almost completely driven from office, Hegel's model of Prussia remained the Prussia of Stein's and to some extent Hardenberg's reforms. Although he made no secret of this to his students, he was nonetheless reluctant to make this point too publicly, thus helping to support the claims of all those who continued to see him as servile. The poet Heinrich Heine – a student at Berlin between 1821 and 1823 who studied with Hegel and got to know him fairly well – was even by his own account one of those who "thought of Hegel as servile at that time," and he recalled having once expressed his displeasure to Hegel over the famous phrase in the *Philosophy of Right* about the identity of the rational and the actual. Hegel, as Heine remembered it, "smiled peculiarly and noted, 'It could also be rendered, everything that is rational must be.' " (A similar rendering was used by Hegel in his 1819 lectures on the *Philosophy of Right*.) Having said that, Heine said, Hegel "looked hastily about him," but was reassured when he saw that the only person who had overheard him was one of his less-than-intellectually-inspired whist-playing friends.[4] Hegel's attitudes toward the reform movement were more than clear to those who knew him well.

Besides the political and career stresses that Hegel was under, he was also confronted with a variety of personal difficulties. Marie Hegel suffered another miscarriage in the winter of 1822, and her life was in some danger for an extended period. (Marie had very much wanted to have a daughter, and the continued attempts to bring forth another child, despite the health risks, probably had to do with that desire.)[5] Her health remained in bad shape throughout the winter, and Hegel had to contend with caring for her, worrying about her, and having to take care of his three sons while she recuperated. (No doubt the maids and servants did the lion's share of the work, but, also no doubt, Hegel felt he was being pressed into extraordinary duties.) Besides that, Marie's problems with her health obviously presented another, unexpected drain on the family's financial resources.

In February 1822, though, a review of the *Philosophy of Right* appeared in a literary journal, the *Hallesche Allgemeine Literaturzeitung*, in which the anonymous reviewer took Hegel to task for his attacks on Fries. The reviewer accused Hegel of deliberately selecting the worst possible interpretation of Fries's words and of kicking Fries while he was down. "Such conduct," he said, "is not noble, but the reviewer will refrain from calling this by its true name and will leave this choice to the thoughtful reader."[6] Already under stress from many different sides, Hegel simply exploded over this perceived insult. He was already deeply offended at having been put in the same basket as the forces of reaction, who were themselves by no means eager to have him as an ally, and this was the breaking point for him. In his anger, he wrote to the ministry for instruction demanding government protection against this denunciation, arguing that it was unconscionable that a Prussian civil servant (professors were civil servants) should be attacked by a newspaper supported by the Prussian government, and added that his attacks were never meant to be against Fries himself but only against his basic principles. This only showed, Hegel went on angrily to claim, just where too much freedom of the press can lead.[7]

Altenstein did not accede to Hegel's wishes. He certainly did not want to bring the Prussian censorship laws down on a literary newspaper. However, he wanted to split the difference, so he warned the journal that it should censor its articles more carefully, and he told Hegel that the government would not press his claim but that if he really wanted satisfaction in the matter, he could take the affair to court (if he thought he had a case), or he could publish a public explanation of his views to clear up any misunderstandings he might think had been engendered by the review.[8] The net effect, though, of Hegel's attempt to get the government to intervene for him was only to damage Hegel's reputation all the more as people began to hear about the incident. (Although the affair obviously should have thrown cold water on the continuing rumors and murmurings about Hegel's alleged coziness with the government, it did nothing to squelch the rumors.)

The Preface to Hinrichs's Book on Philosophy of Religion

Hegel also had to fulfill two other promises he had made. The ministry had asked him to write a report on the teaching of philosophy in the Prussian *Gymnasium*; and his former student at Heidelberg, Hermann Friedrich Wilhelm Hinrichs, asked him to write a preface to his recently finished book (on the philosophy of religion from a Hegelian standpoint). Hegel, already strapped for time and feeling under much pressure, nonetheless agreed to do both. He sent his preface to Hinrichs on April 4, 1822, modestly apologizing to him for not actually talking much about Hinrichs's book in the piece, excusing himself by saying, "the dispersedness of my existence simply did not permit anything else."[9]

Hegel used the opportunity of the preface to articulate his basic position on what he saw as the key modern issues in the philosophy of religion and to take some swipes at those who he thought had taken the wrong turn in the debate. The piece sets out and argues for some fairly well-established Hegelian views. The basic issue in philosophy of religion, Hegel claimed, is that of the so-called opposition of faith and reason. This is, he said, not an artificial, academic opposition; it is absolutely basic to human life: "The human spirit cannot turn away from either of the two sides" of the opposition, Hegel argued, since the opposition itself is "rooted in the most inward self-consciousness" of mankind.[10] Since the opposition cannot be avoided, we must either show how faith and reason can be reconciled (in Hegel's sense of showing how the opposition is an essential component of some more rational way of living and thinking), or be forced to live with such an unlivable fracture (*Entzweiung*) at the heart of our self-understanding.

Much depends therefore on how we understand "faith" itself. Hegel proposed that we should understand "faith" neither as merely a subjective conviction nor as simply an ecclesiastically defined set of beliefs; faith itself already involves a unity of conviction and belief, a way in which the individual person subjectively *identifies* himself with the general claims set forth in a credo and understands the act of expressing the credo as something he takes on himself, not as something that an external ecclesiastical authority imposes on him. The issue of "faith" therefore has to do with the conditions under which such self-consciousness as self-determination is possible, with the conditions that underwrite "the certainty, which the person has of himself, of having identified with the self-consciousness of mankind."[11]

It is clear, so Hegel argued, that these crucial issues for modern religion cannot be resolved by the "understanding," since the opposition between faith and reason has to do with competing conceptions of the "unconditioned." The "understanding" can at best demonstrate what follows from particular sets of propositions – what follows if one accepts, for example, Protestant declarations of faith or Catholic declarations of faith – but it cannot show which of those declarations are themselves rational, except by deriving them from yet other declarations, which for believers on either side will never resolve the real differences between them.[12] Yet, although such reasoning by the "understanding" is doomed to fail as a matter of cultural reconciliation, it still seems to many people to be what "our times" calls for, since it was the grand project of the Enlightenment – the paradigmatically modern project – to derive the principles of "faith" from something else that was "not faith." But "we" (informed by Hegelian philosophy) can now see that this approach necessarily ended up becoming a type of "vanity," a smugness among adherents of one sect who, because they mis-understood the nature of their own claims, could not understand them-selves as merely another sect, and who ended up therefore only demonstrating how the particular tenets of faith held by another sect did not follow from the basic principles held by themselves.[13]

The strangely sectarian character of the Enlightenment's struggle with faith was, however, something that emerged out of the logic inher-ent in the way in which the Enlightenment framed the opposition of faith and reason in the first place. At best, such a logic leads either to a reduction of religious faith to a matter of simple sectarian assent (to first principles to which one simply "assents," since one cannot demonstrate their truth in any non-question-begging way) or to a reduction of religious belief to some vacuous abstraction that can supposedly com-mand assent from all sects, such as the idea of a "highest essence." But it does not give modern, self-critical people anything with which they can really *identify*.

Since neither blind assent nor vacuous abstractions actually resolve the opposition between religion and faith, it might seem as if Kant's philosophy is the only other alternative. But if one accepts Kant's claim that the attempt to apply reason to the "unconditioned" necessarily results in contradictions of the deepest sort (what Kant called "antino-mies"), then it follows that "faith" in an "unconditioned" (which can never be an object of possible experience) cannot in principle have anything to do with reason. Post-Kantians therefore have drawn the conclusion that "faith" must be only a matter of emotion. Thus, we find ourselves, Hegel argued, in the very peculiar modern situation of having theologians themselves arguing for the indemonstrable nature of their discipline.

This cannot be satisfactory, since what is encountered in emotion is also formulable in words and notions (in *Vorstellungen*, "representa-tions"), and the question of justification, of whether we are "getting it right" in our professions of faith, arises again in even sharper form, which itself only shows that emotion can be no adequate guide to whether we are "getting it right"; both evil and good actions can flow from deeply held feelings, for "there is nothing that cannot be felt."[14] In fact, the proper relation of emotion to faith consists in the require-ment that we learn to have the deepest emotions about what is right, not in the requirement that we take what is right to be determined by what we contingently happen to have the deepest emotions about.[15] To understand an emotion as having connected us with what is divine is already to have made a *judgment* about it, to have a "negative" relation to the emotion, and it would clearly be circular to justify the judgment on the basis of some immediate presence of an emotion that the judgment itself supposedly justifies. The issue of what justifies what (whether our rational beliefs are taken to justify our deeply felt emotions or vice versa) simply is the crucial issue – "everything depends on this difference of stance."[16]

Hegel made it clear that he was *not* arguing that one ought to banish emotion from religion. Quite the contrary: "Religion, like duty and right, should and will become a matter of feeling and should lodge itself within the heart, just as freedom in general trickles down into the emotions and becomes in people an emotion of freedom."[17] The greatest "need of the time," Hegel said, was for a reconciliation between religion and reason, which could thus only be accomplished by a *Wissenschaft* such as philosophy – or at least by a theology that became a *Wissenschaft* through an alliance with philosophy.[18]

Had Hegel stopped there, few would have taken umbrage at what he said. But near the end of the piece, Hegel dropped his bombshell. Unable to keep his natural tendency toward sarcasm in check, he remarked, in what was a clear and unmistakable reference to Schleiermacher's key notion of religion as the feeling of absolute dependence (on God), that "if religion grounds itself in a person only on the basis of feeling, then such a feeling would have no other determination than that of a *feeling of his dependence*, and so a dog would be the best Christian, for it carries this feeling most intensely within itself and lives principally in this feeling. A dog even has feelings of salvation when its hunger is satisfied by a bone."[19] There it was: Hegel had accused his distinguished Berlin colleague of holding completely ridiculous, even insipid ideas, and of not being able to distinguish deep religious faith from the animal feelings of a happy dog wagging its tail after having been given a treat. That particular remark became instantly and widely cited, as if that were all Hegel had said in the piece. Schleiermacher was understandably deeply offended by it, and Schleiermacher's friends never forgave Hegel for it. For many of those predisposed against Hegel, this was just the last straw.

The crack about Schleiermacher was not the only gibe Hegel made in the piece. Having belittled Schleiermacher without naming him, Hegel could not resist taking another shot at his old nemesis Friedrich Schlegel, whom he did name, accusing him of the grossest sophistry in the way he based religion on feeling, indeed, of being a prime representative of the "evils of the time" and of the worst type of vanity at work in the modern world.[20] (Probably unknown to Hegel at the time, Schlegel was doing no less to Hegel, accusing him of being only a "castrated Fichte," of encouraging atheism, and of "confusing Satan with almighty God.")[21]

Mounting Stresses in Hegel's Life

The attack on Schleiermacher and the ensuing bad blood among all the parties involved only made Hegel's life at the university worse. The great disputes among the personalities involved, the political repression at the time, and the intense feeling on all sides that the stakes in these clashes were extremely high set tempers even more on edge, and Hegel showed the stress. Those who knew him began to describe him as "prematurely aged," and Hegel's own physically unassuming presence only strengthened that impression.[22] As a youth, he had been nicknamed by his friends at Tübingen as the "old man"; now in Berlin, Hegel really was becoming the "old man" right before people's eyes. His mother-in-law even worriedly wrote to Marie about how she had heard from a friend that Hegel was coughing a lot and looking quite fatigued.[23] But, throughout this, Hegel did not break with his old habits; he continued his daily walks, bent forward, lost in thought when not accompanied by one of his students or friends. He and Marie continued their active social life and socialized with other luminaries in Berlin such as Count Gneisenau (the famous army reformer) and Karl von Clausewitz, the military strategist (who had also been present at the battle of Jena); he continued to be a lover of food and a connoisseur of wine, as well as an active patron of the theater and the opera, often seeming to really come alive only in the evening at the performances he would attend after his lectures. (The figure of Hegel finishing off the last words of his lectures and then rapidly striding across the street to the opera house or to the theater became a regular Berlin feature.) And, much to the abhorrence of the conservatives who detested him, his celebrity in Berlin only continued to increase even as his life at the university became more tense.

By the spring of 1822, Marie Hegel had started to recover from her latest miscarriage. As Hegel's anxieties about her health began to wane, he was forced to turn his thoughts to what he should do with his illegitimate son, Ludwig. Since Ludwig had turned fourteen and been confirmed in church, it was high time for Hegel to begin thinking about a possible career for him, since Hegel had decided that Ludwig was destined for a trade, not for the "higher professions," as were Karl and Immanuel. That meant he would not be attending the final years of *Gymnasium*, which were only for preparation for entering the university; instead he would be apprenticing with some tradesman. It seems that the ground for this decision was not any dissatisfaction on Hegel's part with Ludwig's intellectual capabilities or his diligence in his studies; in fact, he praised Ludwig in all those respects. The real ground seems to have been Hegel's belief that the drain on the family finances brought on by the costs of education for Ludwig, Karl, and Immanuel, along with the costs having to do with Marie Hegel's health problems, simply made it unaffordable for Ludwig to attend the *Gymnasium* any longer than necessary (or, rather, his firm belief that he could not afford to send all three boys to the *Gymnasium* and to the university; and it was clear which two boys were going to get that privilege). Ludwig, as the "foster son," did not in Hegel's mind have the same claim on the family resources. The problem was finding the right opening apprentice position for Ludwig. Hegel at first inquired of his friend Frommann if he could assist with Ludwig's attaining a position in Stuttgart, where Hegel had heard that there was going to be a good possibility. He noted in passing that he would not even be able to supply the *Lehrgeld*, the money paid to a tradesman to train a young apprentice, in Ludwig's case, and that whatever apprenticeship Ludwig obtained would have to be under those conditions; but that turned out to be a blind alley, and Hegel was still left with the agonizing decision about what trade Ludwig should learn. There is also absolutely no reason to think that Hegel was happy about this decision or even satisfied with it; if anything, it only added to the many stresses he felt himself to be under.

Things did not let up. The conservative forces continued to be haunted by the idea that there were subversives everywhere, and on

April 12, 1822, a cabinet order came down enjoining all the members of
the cabinet and the ministry for culture to discipline "demagogically
disposed teachers and professors" and to report back in three months.[24]
This was yet another ominous step. Once again, the authorities were
looking not merely for those "expressly" teaching and professing subversion; they were looking for those who were simply "disposed" to
such things. This cannot have helped Hegel's anxiety level, and his own
health again began to worsen.

"On the Teaching of Philosophy in Gymnasia*"*

In the midst of all this, Hegel also managed to fulfill his other promise
to the ministry of culture and submitted his report to them, "On the
Teaching of Philosophy in *Gymnasia*," on April 16, 1822. Hegel's analysis repeated some points he had made earlier in his commissioned
report in 1812 for Niethammer in Nuremberg. Like many of his fellow
professors, he was struck by the lack of fit between the professed ideals
of the Humboldt university in Berlin – the commitment both to *Bildung*
and *Wissenschaft* and to the unity of "teaching and research" – and with
the realities of university life. He was particularly distressed at what he
saw as the lack of basic knowledge, and, even more so, at the lack of
Bildung among the students. Using Schiller's terms for describing the
goals of the university at Jena, Hegel pointed out that the purpose of
the Berlin university was to teach the students not "merely for their
vocational studies (*Brotstudium*)" but also for sake of their *Bildung*.[25]
The current Prussian laws governing university admission, however,
offered to students who in fact knew that they had "no Latin, no Greek,
nothing of mathematics nor of history" the assurance that they could
still go to university, and those students would, of course, be interested
only in "vocational" studies, *Brotstudium*.[26]

   To remedy this, Hegel recommended more study of the ancients in
the *Gymnasium*, but he specifically argued against the teaching of ancient languages as an end in itself, an issue that lay close to his heart.
He thought that the pedagogical practices and goals of the time relating
to how and why classical languages should be taught had completely
reversed the rightful priorities in education; those practices put far too
much emphasis, Hegel thought, on learning the languages for their own
sakes rather than for the sake of reading the classics. The kind of

intensive study that is necessary in learning the ancient languages for their own sakes is best left to the specialists at the university in those fields; what *Gymnasium* students need for their *Bildung* is not a thorough knowledge of all of the fine points of, for example, Greek grammar, but a grounding in and appreciation of Greek literature, for which the study of the Greek language should only be a means, not an end in itself.

He also practiced what he preached; he sent neither Ludwig nor Karl nor Immanuel to the "classical" *Gymnasium* in Berlin because he thought the curriculum and teaching there were too formal and rigid. Instead, he sent all three to the "French *Gymnasium*" in Berlin, which had been founded by the Protestant Huguenots who had fled to Berlin in Frederick the Great's time to escape persecution in France. At the "French *Gymnasium*," the classical languages were barely taught at all, and all the classes (except for the "German" class) were taught entirely in French. (The teachers and "professors" at the French *Gymnasium* were all members of the Huguenot French colony in Berlin.) Better that his sons learn to speak fluent French and study a modern curriculum, Hegel thought, than have to endure a bunch of pedants dry as dust teaching Greek as an end in itself.[27]

In the report, Hegel also argued for teaching religious dogmas in the religion classes in the *Gymnasium* as a way to get students to think in ways not entirely natural for young people, who are by nature more inclined to focus on what can be of immediate use to them; instruction in religion would thus also serve the purpose of self-formation, self-cultivation, and the acquisition of culture, that is, the purpose of *Bildung*. Hegel also recommended that empirical psychology be taught, and that the history of philosophy definitely *not* be taught – without a philosophical approach to the history of philosophy, he argued, it can only seem a meaningless recounting of a series of failures and therefore to any rational youth a vain endeavor, something not to be seriously pursued. He also recommended teaching formal logic (along with Kant's table of categories, but without teaching the Kantian metaphysics that went along with it); Hegel's point was that students first have to learn to reason correctly before they can appreciate the "speculative" aspects of logic in their university years, and to make that point, he advised that the current courses on the "Juridical Encyclopedia" in *Gymnasia* be replaced by such formal logic courses. Other classes in philosophy (instruction in morality, proofs of the existence of God) could be introduced in the *Gymnasium* simply by abolishing one of the current courses on German literature, of which Hegel felt there were already too many.

Money Worries

But by the summer of 1822 Hegel, although having fulfilled his promises, was beginning to feel a bit desperate. The year had been a mess for him, his health was bad, and he could not afford to go to the spa for recuperation or take any extended vacation. Worried about his finances, he even wrote to Niethammer in Munich (after finding some old Bavarian lottery tickets among his things) asking him to check to see if he had won anything.[28] Finally, exasperated, he wrote a letter to Altenstein on June 6, 1822, requesting an extra stipend. He explained how his various "domestic misfortunes" of the last four and one half years had made his position "pressing." The extra income from the Royal Board of Scientific Examiners for Brandenburg of 200 Thalers had been eaten up by the unexpected expenses and health costs of the last few years. Moreover, Hegel noted that he was worried about the future of his family because of his "advancing age" and about whether he would be able to leave Marie and the children with any suitable pension. He had to pay, he reminded Altenstein, 170 Thalers per year into the two pension funds at Berlin just to insure that Marie would receive 300 Thalers per year as pension, and even that depended on his "dying as a professor at the Royal university" – a clear reference to his fear that he might be caught up in the pursuit of "demagogues" and dismissed.[29]

Altenstein intervened for Hegel and wrote to Hardenberg, arguing that since Hegel had been refused admission to the Academy of Sciences, and since Hegel did not receive as much money from lecture fees as some other professors because his students tended to be so poor, the university should do something for its famous philosopher. Altenstein was able to report back to Hegel very quickly on June 25, 1822, that his request had been granted, and that Hegel was to receive 300 Thalers for the previous year and 300 Thalers for the present year. Hegel was, quite understandably, extremely grateful for the bonus. At least a little bit of the pressure had been removed; and he also felt appreciated by the two reform-minded authorities overseeing the university.

Memories of Youth and Visions of the Future:
Brussels and Holland

By the beginning of September, Hegel felt flush enough to take an extended vacation. Instead of going to a spa, he elected to travel to Holland. Hegel had never traveled extensively and, except for his brief stay in Berne, had never been outside of Germany. He especially felt that his own *Bildung* was thereby lacking; for a person of Hegel's interests, it was only natural that he wanted to see more of the world, and he himself was particularly interested in those countries where modern life was being institutionalized and worked out. He had long had an interest in seeing that part of the world; as a *Hofmeister* in Berne, he had excerpted Georg Forster's descriptions of his travels in that part of the world in the 1790's; Forster had been of particular interest to Hegel because he had become the leader of the Mainz "Jacobins" who had reconstituted Mainz as a part of the revolutionary French Republic.[30] And now, at the same time that it was becoming increasingly fashionable to travel to Italy (as Goethe had done), Hegel wanted instead to go north, to the lands, as he saw it, of the future rather than (as he saw Italy) to the lands of the past. The goal of his travels was always "uplift," a contribution to *Bildung*; for the people of Hegel's day and class, the idea of a vacation as something to be spent at the beach, a mountain resort, or a spa was starting to become fashionable (something Hegel had done with his family on the trip to Rügen), but Hegel, old-fashioned in this regard, thought a vacation was better spent in pursuit of cultural self-improvement. Hegel thus wanted to travel to see the great cathedrals and the great works of art in the major museums of his day, and, being Hegel, to see how modern life was shaping up in the avant garde countries. Although he loved Italian painting and Italian music – and Italy, of course, had the greatest repositories of such items – Italy lacked, in his mind, modernity. Hegel was not opposed to going to Italy; in Jena in 1803, Hegel had even mentioned to Schelling some plans for going to Italy, but the trip never materialized.[31] After that an Italian trip remained low on Hegel's list of things to do.

Not having much money, Hegel always traveled on the cheap, almost every time taking the least expensive postal coaches that he shared with other travelers (it was too expensive to take his own coach, which he maintained in Berlin) and staying at very modest inns. This made travel slow and tiresome; one took a coach that traveled over badly maintained, mostly dirt roads, at best at roughly five kilometers per hour (3.1 miles per hour), and one frequently traveled all night to reach a particular destination, sleeping (if one could) in the coach itself (and if the coach was crowded, having to sleep while sitting upright). One could only rarely schedule connections in advance; instead, one consulted a map that showed the major arteries leading in and out of cities, and one simply arrived in a town and then inquired when the next coach might be passing through. Sometimes if an appropriate postal coach was not coming through or was already booked up, one was obliged to wait until another coach had attracted enough passengers to make the trip profitable; improvisation was often called for when one learned that the next coach to one's destination would not be arriving for several days. Like all other travelers of the time, Hegel wrote extensive letters to Marie, describing in detail what he was seeing, what the landscape was like, and so on. Hegel's letters were typical of travel letters of his day: The equivalent of postcards (virtually nonexistent then), they would almost always be saved as mementos of the trip and would serve as triggers to memory when the traveler returned (so that he could recount in detail to family and friends the sights he had seen).

Hegel set out for Holland at the beginning of September 1822, making his first stop in Magdeburg on a Sunday (September 9) and finding to his dismay that there were no other coaches departing from Madgeburg in the right direction until Tuesday. Realizing that he had some time to kill, and finding that he had very quickly exhausted whatever charms Madgeburg had to offer him, Hegel looked up General Lazare Nicolas Marguerite Carnot, who seemed quite pleased to see him, and whom Hegel found to be a delightful fellow.[32] Carnot had been a major figure in the French Revolution. He invented the French "mass conscription" that proved to be so effective in forming the revolutionary armies, and was also responsible for significant innovations in strategy and tactics, and for reorganizing the way in which the soldiers were linked to their food supply. Having done that, he joined the Jacobin committee for public safety, during which time he continued his work with the army, often joining the troops in the field, and was given credit for many of the revolutionary army's most notable successes. When Robespierre fell, Carnot's military fame enabled him to escape prosecution, and in 1795 he became one of the members of the Directory. After Napoleon's coup d'etat, he prudently left the country for a few years, returning in 1799; in 1800, he became minister of war, but retired in 1801 to devote his time to writing significant treatises on the nature of fortifications and other treatises on mathematics. He returned to active life during Napoleon's troubles in 1814 and was given a command in the army; he acquitted himself brilliantly and was ennobled for his efforts; but after the defeat at Waterloo, his title was removed, and he lived more or less under house arrest in Magdeburg until his death in 1823. (France later had his remains transferred to the Pantheon.) Hegel's visit to Carnot was significant; right at the time that many of his opponents were accusing him of servility to the Prussian state, he himself was visiting with one of the genuine heroes of the Revolution. Carnot, he told his wife, was the most "treasured" of all his sights in Magdeburg.

Hegel, now feeling himself an "old man" of substance, had suddenly become interested in revisiting the memories of his stormy, revolutionary youth, and his visit with Carnot was either part of that or helped to provoke it. The trip to the lands of the future had become, curiously, also a trip to Hegel's own past. As the repression in Prussia grew, Hegel was tempted to think that the days of creation of the new world were perhaps now over. It was, of course, out of the question to return to the past, but the major task ahead, as Hegel started to see it, was, first, to consolidate the positions he had already worked out in philosophy and the place in the university he had created for himself, and, second, for Germany to consolidate the gains it had made in its Napoleonic and post-Napoleonic reorganization. A few days into his trip, still in that spirit, Hegel drafted a letter to Goethe, in which he spoke elegiacally of his youth as being inspired by his reading of Goethe's works, of how he had for the last thirty years been animated almost daily by Goethe himself; but, catching himself, he omitted those words from the final copy of the letter he actually sent to Goethe; the actual letter ended up consisting mostly of a long, admiring commentary on Goethe's theory of colors, some recommendations on how to improve it, and a plug for his student von Henning.[33] (Hegel finally wrote three years later a letter to Goethe in which he spoke of being one of Goethe's "spiritual sons" and explained just how important Goethe had been to his own intellectual development.)[34]

Inspired by his visit to Carnot, Hegel toyed with the idea of taking an early coach to Erfurt so he could follow the path of Napoleon's retreat to the Rhine, but, having seen the rickety nature of the only available coach, changed his mind. He finally managed to work his way to Braunschweig (and, of course, to see the picture gallery) and then work his way out of it, grumbling in his letters to Marie about how he wished he had more money so he could travel in better style. But his memories of his youth – which now seemed so far away – continued to crop up; the landscape around Kassel reminded him of home; he remarked to Marie that Berlin was enough like Nuremberg for her to feel at home there (with its "sandy" soil), whereas the area in which he was then traveling looked more like his native Swabia with its green, rolling hills. It was, he said, a "nature that was home to him," a "*heimatliche Natur.*" Berlin, which was where he nonetheless wanted to be, did not at that point seem to be really a "home," not yet a *Heimat* for him.[35]

Working his way from town to town in this way, he would strew his letters with observations about his traveling conditions (almost always bad), about the quality of the cathedral architecture he encountered (it varied), the quality of the picture galleries he visited (generally good), and the quality of the wine he was encountering (sometimes really very good, sometimes excellent). He even managed to work in a cruise along the Rhine – already by this point in the nineteenth century something de rigueur for any serious traveler in that area – but he was singularly unimpressed with all the fuss about Rhine cruises. If he and Marie ever went along the Rhine, he told her, they would do it differently and most certainly not by boat.[36] But he also enjoyed sitting in his hotel room, eating sweet grapes, looking out over the romantic panorama of the Rhine from Koblenz while writing his letters to Marie.[37] Hegel was not an enthusiastic traveler; as he told Marie, he did it more out of "duty and guilt" – in other words, a feeling that he really *should* be traveling because it "improved" a person – than out of any genuine love of roaming about.[38] He certainly enjoyed the art he saw; but he was in his heart a scholar, happier at home with his family, reading in his study, and attending the opera and theater in Berlin – at least much happier than he was traveling in crowded, rickety coaches and staying in not terribly comfortable, very modest inns.

Traveling by boat from Koblenz to Bonn, Hegel managed finally to meet personally the prominent Catholic mesmerist physician Karl J. H.

Windischmann, who lived in Bonn and who had favorably reviewed the *Phenomenology* many years earlier but had split with Hegel over what he rightfully saw as the great religious differences between them. The two found, though, that they got along quite well; Windischmann on his part was quite surprised to find Hegel as cordial and jovial as he was, since he had heard so many terrible things about him from Hegel's enemies.[39] Windischmann took Hegel to an excellent wine store in Cologne (always a sure way to Hegel's heart), and Hegel expressed an aesthetic sense of astonishment on first seeing the cathedral in Cologne; what impressed him about it was its sublimity, its seeming indifference to the human presence around it, the way it seemed almost like a huge, natural object that had somehow landed in the center of a city, and, most importantly, the way it embodied what a city, a group of people, could accomplish as a common project.[40] He even attended a Mass there. Hegel was also particularly interested in the cathedral because it was held up by Romantics as a paragon of German "Gothic" architecture in distinction from (non-German) classical architecture; Hegel's appreciation of it, though, was more historically tinged: He saw it as an aesthetically sublime leftover from a historical period now dead and gone.

One of the highlights of his trip was a stopover in Aachen, where during a visit to the church he was able to sit on Charlemagne's (stone) throne. The caretaker there assured Hegel that this was not anything special, that everyone got to sit on Charlemagne's throne; Hegel was nonplussed by the caretaker's rather blasé attitude to the grandeur of perching oneself on the slabs where Charlemagne had sat; the "whole satisfaction," he told Marie, "is that one has sat on it" for oneself.[41] Hegel, who traveled for "uplift," simply had no inhibitions about also being an ordinary tourist. And, when presented with the opportunity, he usually took it.

His arrival in Holland, however, was the genuine eye-opener for him. He was simply not prepared for the wealth and cosmopolitanism he encountered there, and the provinciality of German life suddenly stood out for him. Whereas only a few major boulevards in Berlin were surfaced with paving stones at that point, all the major roads in Holland in the cities and even in the countryside, he noticed, were so surfaced. In the Dutch cities and towns, the shops had a greater variety of goods, the goods were of higher quality and more tasteful, and the cities and towns themselves were cleaner than Berlin; one did not see, as one did in Germany, crumbling old houses falling down or poorly clothed peasant children running about (or so Hegel reported). The churches in Holland were more opulent, the collections of paintings were more spectacular (Rubens, van Eyck, one could just go on and on, Hegel remarked), and the towns were more orderly.[42] Holland was a thriving country dedicated to the virtues of modern life; not for Holland were there longings to return to some idealized Middle Ages; its painters, such as Rembrandt, celebrated the modern, this-worldly humanistic side of things, even in their religious paintings. If the trip had started elegiacally with Hegel returning to the themes of his youth, it suddenly took a turn back toward the future. Holland presented a picture of what modern life could be, and Hegel found his views of what he was trying to accomplish in Germany affirmed by everything he was seeing and experiencing.

On arriving in Brussels, he was able to get together with his former student from Jena, Pieter Gabriël van Ghert. Van Ghert in fact had become an important official in the Dutch government as head of the department in the council of state for the Catholic religion; he was involved in trying to modernize Catholic teaching and in trying to ameliorate the problems of confessional differences that were then seething in Holland. Van Ghert had always maintained fond memories of Hegel and had continued to value his friendship with Hegel; indeed, he saw himself as the agent for the propagation of Hegelianism in the Netherlands; he was therefore absolutely delighted to see Hegel. Away from the troubles in Berlin, Hegel was able to take in the sights of Brussels with an old friend and follower from what now seemed like his heroic youthful years in Jena. Together, they spent three to four hours visiting the site of the Battle of Waterloo, and Hegel was moved by his thoughts of what Napoleon (to his mind) had stood for and how he had undone himself there.[43] The trip thus merged into memories of his youth and an affirmation of what Hegel's project had come to mean.

Hegel had a wonderful time as a tourist in the Dutch cities, often escaping from the drudgery of the coaches by traveling by boat. Besides multiple visits to all the museums and picture galleries and visits to the theaters, he also managed to work in some tourist shopping. With advice from van Ghert and his wife, Hegel purchased a Flemish lace cap for Marie (at that time all the rage in women's fashion, with the Flemish articles being the crème de la crème of lace caps). He also bought some tourist gifts for his sons (a bird made of seashells – apparently some tourist items never change – out of remembrance of the time spent with the boys in Rügen collecting shells on the seashore).[44] Van Ghert also introduced him to other scholars and notables who showed him around some of the other cities. In Amsterdam – the "queen of the sea," as he described the city – one of van Ghert's friends escorted him around, and he managed to visit both Jewish synagogues in the city in the evening. Drinking, as he put it, excellent Dutch coffee in wonderful Dutch kitchens, he wrote to Marie that if they ever built a house, they would most certainly put a Dutch-style kitchen in it. The sheer number of connections to the other great outposts of the modern world also caught his eye. He noticed that for only twenty-five francs, one could leave Brussels and arrive in Paris in only thirty-six hours on a daily coach; and the steamship to London took only twenty-four hours. As he noted to Marie, he was sorely tempted to go.

He returned to Berlin via Hamburg – where he visited an acquaintance by correspondence, a French owner of a hat factory who had become interested in Hegel's philosophy after having read Kant – near the end of October, refreshed and now a man of the world, having gained invaluable firsthand knowledge of a variety of different paintings that he had only read about or seen in prints, confirmed in his opinion about the superiority of the institutions and practices of modern life and equally confirmed that the calls for a restoration of the past were not only short-sighted but, given the economic dynamism so apparent in the countries of the future such as Holland, ultimately doomed on their own terms. He immediately began lecturing on his political philosophy five times per week and on a new theme, the philosophy of world history, four times per week. Fortified by his trip and feeling that he was financially out of the woods thanks to Altenstein's intervention, he also, on December 26, 1822, resigned his commission in the Royal Board of Scientific Examiners for Brandenburg for the coming year, noting in his letter of resignation that it had become simply too great a burden on his time and that it was high time for him to return to dedicating himself to his scholarly activities.[45]

Vienna and the Universal Estate

Alienation and Increasing Stress

Hardenberg's death on November 26, 1822, fairly well signaled the definitive end of the reform era, even though the era itself had been dying and been declared for dead for some time earlier. Even before Hardenberg's death, members of the reform wing of the government had been driven out and replaced by reactionary elements intent on "restoration" of much of the pre-Napoleonic order. No successor to Hardenberg as chancellor was named; under the pretext of collegiality, a variety of different ministers now competed for influence, and whatever kind of direction there had been for the reform movement dissipated. Hardenberg's death and the disappearance of the office of chancellor left Prussia with a "constitutional torso" lacking a head.[46] Ministers such as Altenstein no longer could turn to Hardenberg, who had answered only to the king; they now had to guard themselves much more carefully.

Hegel retreated into his own studies and into the preparation of his lectures. There was little for him to do as far as his ambitions for governmental work were concerned, although he continued to lecture on the *Philosophy of Right* in the winter semester of 1822–23. He found himself, however, working extremely intensively on his lectures on the philosophy of world history; over and over again in his correspondence, he apologized profusely for not having had the time to write because of the unexpected amount of work involved in the preparation for the lectures. His trip to Holland and its rich museums behind him, he also began revising his old lectures on aesthetics and preparing new material for them, and by the summer semester of 1823, he was lecturing on aesthetics.

At the same time, various memoirs about Napoleon written by those who had accompanied him into his exile – Napoleon had died in exile on St. Helena on May 5, 1821 – began appearing, and Hegel was an enthusiastic consumer of them, even writing to van Ghert to procure a copy of one of them for him and borrowing some other volumes from von Henning. The memoirs presented Napoleon, now convinced that his final defeat was really final, in the new form that the vanquished Napoleon had decided to cast for himself: He was not the military conqueror of foreign lands, as his foes tried to portray him, but was *the* child of the Revolution, a kind of "Washington as emperor," and a partisan of a Europe united under the banner of the rights of man. This picture of Napoleon, its historical accuracy aside, must only have raised Hegel's estimation of him, since he had always seen him in more or less the same light; that Napoleon himself had claimed to be something like Hegel's version of him only reinforced Hegel's already high estimation of him.

In some ways, Hegel also seemed a bit embittered and hardened by the tribulations he had experienced since coming to Berlin. Alienated from the events around him, he threw himself into his work, his family, and his social life. His celebrity grew, and he more and more turned to the theater and the opera as well as his regular games of Whist as his recreations of choice; in fact, Hegel began to be a figure on the Berlin art scene, making friends with a variety of different singers, painters, and sculptors. His lectures in particular on the philosophy of history proved to be extremely popular, and he began to receive more and more letters extolling his greatness and asking for favors (could he read this, do that, give this or that advice, help so-and-so out, and so on). But, hardened in his views, he did not let up on his dispute with Schleier- macher, taking his polemics against him into the classroom, where he would sometimes make sarcastic and invidious comparisons between Schleiermacher and the "demagogues" (causing the students at one point to express their displeasure with his anti-Schleiermacher polemic by stomping their feet).[47] The rather acidic sarcasm expressed in some of Hegel's polemics only served to earn him more enemies, and even his most admiring students were beginning to notice that the corrosive spin he was giving his attacks on others did not present a very attractive side to Hegel.[48] Hegel had always been sure he was right; now, as he was more than ever certain of it, and as he felt himself overworked, disappointed with developments, and under attack himself, he took an increasingly aggressive stance toward his opponents that made reconcil- iation all the more difficult. Moreover, his continued defense of Goe- the's theory of color only served to cement the doubts of many of the natural scientists in Berlin about his views.[49]

Vacation Plans

Hegel did no traveling during the vacation period of 1823, preferring to stay home, catch up on his reading, and work on his lectures. He was also finally able in May 1823 to redeem the bond that he had put up as bail for Asverus and reinvest the money in other state bonds; that brought a kind of closure, so it seemed, to his troubles with his students having been arrested as demagogues.[50] But Hegel also complained during 1823 of headaches, and his health only continued to deteriorate into 1824.[51] It seems clear that the stresses on Hegel, temporarily relieved by his invigorating trip to Netherlands, had not gone away; if anything, they simply picked up again.

By the summer of 1824, Hegel was in a bad state of health again, something noted by several of his friends. Once again granted 300 Thalers from the government, Hegel set his sights on a trip to Vienna. While still in Jena in 1803, he had wanted to go to Vienna at a time when he had still been tentatively looking to Austria to save the Holy Roman Empire from its tribulations, but that trip had not worked out.[52] Hegel's ostensible reason for wanting to going to Vienna was that his friend Anna Pauline Milder-Hauptmann, a renowned soprano at the Berlin opera house from 1816 to 1829, had advised him that he simply must travel to Vienna. Certainly Hegel would have taken her advice seriously; his friendship with Ms. Milder-Hauptmann was often commented on in Berlin society; she was a sometime visitor to the Hegel household, and Hegel was one of her many enthusiastic admirers. Hegel's obvious admiration for Ms. Milder-Hauptmann even led some to think he was paying court to her. Milder-Hauptmann belonged to one of the first generation of the kind of independent women who had previously been thought of as somewhat lower in social status (actresses, singers) but who had recently risen to celebrity status and been deemed fit even for aristocratic company; these women, with their own successful careers and independent incomes, exercised a peculiar fascination on men (like Hegel) who otherwise thought of women as completely domestic and as best confined to the home. Quite a celebrity for her day, Ms. Milder-Hauptmann had been with the Viennese Opera since 1803 and had also performed in Paris; Haydn had praised her, as had Beethoven; Goethe was enamored of her singing; and she was said to have had an affair with Napoleon while she was singing in Paris. Her beauty was widely praised. She was especially famous for interpretations of Gluck and Mozart, and Hegel was an unrestricted admirer of both. When she strongly advised Hegel to hear the current fashion in Italian opera, which was best heard in Vienna, Hegel only too willingly complied.

But another reason for the visit – although Ms. Milder-Hauptmann's recommendation cannot be discounted – had to do with Hegel's interest in seeing Austria and particularly Vienna, the seat of the reaction and the restoration being carried out in Europe. Hegel's interest in what Holland had revealed to him about the future only whetted his appetite to see what Vienna, the great counterpart to Prussia in the German world, had to offer. He had long since come to the conclusion that modern freedom was only to be obtained in Protestant countries, and his experiences in Bavaria had definitely hardened his position vis-à-vis Catholicism in that regard. Since Prussia had aligned itself with the "Protestant" principle, to what Hegel saw as an inherent orientation to freedom, it held out the best hope for modern life in the German world; but recently, mostly Protestant Prussia had been rushing into the "restoration" as rapidly (if not more rapidly) than any Catholic country. If Holland was the future (a largely Protestant country in which, to Hegel's mind, enlightened Catholics like his friend van Ghert were leading the way toward making Catholicism more open to modernity), then Austria should be a land of the past. But was Prussia more like Holland (and, by implication, England)? Or more like Austria? It was therefore of the greatest interest to Hegel to see firsthand the great German Catholic power. In his introductory lectures in the philosophy of world history in 1822–23, Hegel had already claimed that the "main representatives of both European principles of the state" – the Catholic and the Protestant – now necessarily coexisted in the German world, but nonetheless "that of the old church is Austria, that of the new church is Prussia, toward which the prospect of freedom has directed itself and will eternally direct itself."[53] By 1824, he wanted to see if what he was saying in his lectures would correspond to what he was seeing on his trip.

Hegel purchased a guidebook – J. Pezzl's *Neuste Beschreibung von Wien* (1823, sixth edition) – to show him things to look for, and his friend and colleague Aloys Hirt, a professor of archaeology at Berlin, gave him some special tips on what art to see on the way. Around the beginning of September 1824, Hegel, loaded with advice, embarked on his journey. He stopped over in Dresden, but this time it felt more like a duty than a pleasure. "I've had enough of Dresden," he wrote to Marie a few days after leaving, and reminded her not to mention anything political in her letters once he got to Austria, because, as he advised her, "letters are read in Austrian territory" adding, "which in any case would not happen [coming from you]" – it being unclear whether Hegel added that qualification in case some official chanced to read the letter he was himself writing or was just implying that sweet little Marie would not have had the effrontery to have a political idea in the first place.[54] After crossing the border into Austria (with no incident, he remarked in a letter to Marie), Hegel elected to stay at an inn near the border only because, as he ironically said, it was called the King of Prussia. From there he continued on to Prague.

Hegel found to his disappointment that some of Hirt's advice was not to his liking. Hirt was an enthusiast of "old" German painting – mostly medieval and late medieval work – and advised Hegel to seek out such things in Prague. Hegel dutifully did so but was not much impressed or interested in what he saw: The pieces, he told Marie, "would be of little interest to you. Nor could I describe them with much expertise." As for another collection of similar things, he could only say that although they were quite nice, neither he nor Marie was "sufficiently learned enough for me to write any more about it to you." As for the last group of "old" German paintings, Hegel could only comment, "not much to see."[55] Hegel's interest in things exclusively "German" was small; and his sights were set on what he understood to be more worthy objects yet to come in Vienna. Hegel was, however, flattered when, as he was strolling around Prague, he found himself observing a regimental parade led by Marie's uncle; Hegel tipped his hat to him, the uncle recognized Hegel and, making his way over to him, embraced him warmly, and the two set an appointment for lunch for the next day. Tired from all his walking and not inspired by the paintings, Hegel decided to skip seeing the rest of Prague.

Viennese Opera

After a thirty-six-hour trip by coach – Hegel took one of the recently invented, lighter "express coaches" (*Eilwagen*), which still took quite a bit of time to travel the 140 miles from Prague over the partially hilly Austrian terrain to Vienna – Hegel arrived in Vienna on September 20 around 6:00 in the evening and managed to lodge himself in an inn by 7:00 (an inn called the Archduke Karl on the Kärtnerstraße, where he was pleasantly surprised to find that his Berlin friends Bernhard Klein and his wife were also staying). Having been instructed by Ms. Milder-Hauptmann under no circumstances to miss the Italian opera and having his baggage still held up at customs, Hegel, still covered, as he put it, "in the grime from the trip," went directly at 7:30 to the opera house.

He was bowled over by what he heard, and overnight he became a passionate devotee of Italian opera. In Berlin at the time, Italian opera was not held in high regard; Mozart and Gluck ruled the scene. Operating in tandem with them were the champions of recent German "Romantic" opera, in particular, the operas of Karl Maria von Weber; their partisans had even rechristened Mozart himself as the true creator of modern German Romantic opera and argued that only such German Romantic opera truly expressed "German" identity and was on those grounds to be defended against French and Italian opera.[56] Rossini's music was at that time also particularly maligned in Berlin as superficial and as at best a form of shallow entertainment. However, as always, Hegel was completely unmoved by any solicitations of "German identity," and, open-mindedly, Hegel even heard Weber's *Preziosa* in Teplitz on the way to Prague. He was not impressed, and in Vienna the experience of Italian opera finally settled the matter for him. He enthusiastically wrote to Marie extolling all the virtues of the Italian singers and praising them to the heavens; he could barely contain himself – the male voices, he said, had such "resonance, purity, force, perfect freedom . . ." and twice he repeated, "one must hear them." In love with all he had heard and seen, he playfully told Marie, "As long as there is enough money to pay for the Italian opera and the trip back home – I'm staying in Vienna!"[57]

Much to the dissatisfaction of people like Beethoven – whom Hegel never mentions, even though Pezzl's guidebook recommended Beethoven as among the great living composers in Vienna – Vienna at that time was overwhelmed by an enthusiasm for Italian music and in particular for Rossini's operas. To Hegel's advantage, the whole elite of the Italian opera was at that moment in Vienna (the reason why Milder-Hauptmann had recommended the trip), and, as he remarked to Marie, the Viennese critics were saying that nothing of that caliber had come to Vienna in fifty years and probably would not return for another fifty.[58] Interestingly, Hegel did not describe in his letters to Marie any of the staging or scenery of the operas; instead, he focused exclusively on the purely musical experience of Italian opera and the Italian *singers*, on the quality of their singing and the range the operas allowed their voices. In the power and force they gave to their roles, the Italian singers, Hegel claimed, were as much composers in their own right as the people who wrote the music, and they were so very much better than the singers in Berlin. In comparison with the "transparent, golden, fiery wine" of the Italian singers, the singers in Berlin were more like ordinary "beer."[59] (Hegel noted to Marie to exclude Milder-Hauptmann from this judgment.)

When a few days later he heard Rossini's *Barber of Seville*, he converted and became a defender of Rossini's music. It took him a couple of days to gather up his own experience of Rossini's music and to make sense of it. Even though he was certainly taken, even overwhelmed by it, he also noted, in reference to his friends in Vienna (the Kleins) finding Rossini a bit tedious at times, "at times Rossini's music is also boring to me."[60] But within a couple of days, he had reevaluated that judgment as well. After reflecting some more on the matter, Hegel concluded that Rossini's music was ridiculed in Berlin because the critics simply did not have the proper connoisseurship to appreciate it: "Just as satin is for grand ladies, *pâté de foie gras* for educated palettes, so *it* [Rossini's music] is only created for Italian throats (*Kehlen*). It is not for music as such but for the song on its own account for which all else [in Rossini's music] has been fashioned."[61] Whereas other music for voice – music that is meant to have worth as a piece of music qua music – can also be transferred to and played on various solo instruments, "Rossini's music only has sense as sung," and presumably only for the particular "instruments" – the Italian voices trained in their particular way – for which it was intended.[62] The Berlin critics simply were not appreciating the nature of the music and its purpose; they were judging it by criteria external to the music itself, failing to bring the "universal" and the "particular" together in their judgments. After seeing the *Barber of Seville* for a second time, Hegel was enough taken by Rossini that he even joked to Marie that "I have so corrupted my taste that Rossini's *Figaro* [the *Barber of Seville*] has satisfied me infinitely more than Mozart's *Nozze*" – knowing full well that he was contradicting all the official received opinion in Berlin even by entertaining such a heretical thought.[63] (Hegel also heard Mozart's *Figaro* while in Vienna.)

Viennese Splendor

Wearied by his work and travels when he arrived, Hegel found himself completely resuscitated by Vienna and its cultural treasures; for his whole visit, he was constantly in motion. He would spend the entire day walking around, visiting every gallery, every private picture collection, the libraries, the gardens, the sights and sounds of Vienna, and in the evening, he would attend opera, theater, ballet until late in the evening (or at least until 11:00 P.M.). He was not nearly as impressed with the theater as with the opera, except for a farce that he had already seen once in Berlin and which he enjoyed all the more the second time. (The theater at that time in Vienna would feature a play, then sometimes also a pantomime, followed by a ballet; Hegel thus had his hands full with an evening at the theater.)

Hegel marveled at Vienna's splendor. There was a diamond in the royal and imperial treasure collection valued at one million guilders, he told Marie; and the same collection has 300,000 volumes of books; and Prince Esterhazy can ride all the way to the Turkish border without leaving his own property (which begin just outside of Vienna). He saw the emperor and his family and even, to his great pleasure, saw Napoleon's son (who had been raised by his Habsburg relatives when his mother – Napoleon's second wife and a Habsburg – decided she had her hands full being the duchess of Parma). There were small matters that made Vienna seem more elegant than Berlin: Hegel noted approvingly that in Vienna there were no "damned Schnapps boutiques, Schnapps pubs, Schnapps bars" like the ones seemingly everywhere in Berlin.[64] Hegel was thus not exaggerating when he assured Marie – after he had postponed his departure for a few days (with her permission, of course) – that he had "been industrious" in taking in all the sights.[65]

He also found that his status as a Berlin professor gained him entry into certain places. The curators of the collections, he said, treated him as a colleague, showing him around and sometimes spending several hours with him. He was especially amazed at how each prince in his *Palais* seemed to have his own gallery, his own curator and, even more surprising, would open the collection to the public free of charge. In fact, at one point, he was making his third visit to the Esterhazy collection, which on that day was closed to the general public; the prince heard someone walking around, asked who it was and, on being told that it was a "Berlin professor already coming for the third time," he instructed his valet to show Hegel everything.[66] Hegel ruefully compared that to the situation in Berlin, where one had to pay for everything – as Hegel scornfully put it, one had to pay not merely to see Frederick the Great's tomb, one had to pay extra even to see the graves of "his dogs."[67] Hegel ironically noted that in Prussia, he (and then he gives his full title), a "Royal Professor Public *Ordinarius* at the Royal University in Berlin (and indeed Professor of the subject, Philosophy, that is the subject of all subjects," has to shell out money to see anything at all in Berlin, whereas in Vienna as an ordinary foreign tourist he can see everything free of charge and as a Berlin professor even be accepted as a colleague by Viennese curators. Hegel's advice: "Save all your Ducats and Thalers . . . and use them for a trip to Vienna."[68]

Vienna and Modernity

Not everything in Vienna, however, put Berlin to shame. Hegel also noted how much more "modern" and better laid out Berlin was in comparison to Vienna. (Vienna at that time had not yet torn down its medieval walls and built its now-famous "Ringstraße.") Although Vienna may have had greater imperial splendor and many more fine palaces, Berlin was the city of the future. Hegel also found in Vienna a certain type of cosmopolitanism among those from whom he would have expected it. A local professor invited him to lunch with another visiting professor from Padua. "We scholars," Hegel told Marie, "are immediately at home with one another in a manner quite otherwise than with bankers, for example."[69] This was exactly as Hegel would have expected; the scholars of the modern world formed a large part of the "universal estate," the movers and doers whose allegiance was not purely local and particular but general, an allegiance to the rational structures of modern life as they were concretely institutionalized in their own particular lands.

That Hegel would have found himself at home with an Italian and an Austrian professor in Vienna was, it seemed to him, only fitting. He even noted that the Berlin weather forecaster, Siegmund Dittmar, was esteemed in Vienna even though he was neither Viennese nor even Austrian, and this revealed something to Hegel about himself: He said that he came to realize that it was for "those reasons," as he told Marie, that "I also did not remain in Swabia but via Nuremberg came to Berlin" – namely, to establish himself as a member of the "universal estate," as someone whose reputation and allegiance was not purely particular and local but more cosmopolitan.[70] It was not for him to defend, for example, a form of music simply because it was "German." The rationality of modern life was spreading beyond borders and what was taking shape was a European culture that embodied the ideal of freedom, not the parochial ideals of "a culture" or of just one state. Prussia was a particular *Land*, maybe even the *Land* of the European future; but that gave it no monopoly or even peremptory claim to be right about anything.

The grandeur of Vienna gave Hegel no reason to want to return to the past. Vienna's aesthetic riches clearly outstripped Berlin's; but the modern world was not primarily about "beauty" but about freedom, and a certain diminishment of the central importance of art, of its social capacity to perform a unifying function in modern life, was the rational and inevitable accompaniment to the full realization of that freedom. Vienna, with all its cultural riches and all it had to offer, was therefore not a *home* for Hegel; his home was back in Berlin, oriented to the future, not toward merely displaying the grandeur of the past or staging the music of the present, however intoxicating that music was.

His time up, Hegel caught the express coach back to Berlin and stopped off again in Dresden. His student Heinrich Gustav Hotho (who was later to edit Hegel's lectures on aesthetics for publication and who supplied many of the supplementary notes for the posthumous editions of the *Philosophy of Right*) was in Dresden at the time and was struck by how the usually serious Hegel was so "more cheerful and communicative than I had ever seen him until then," how full he was of enthusiasm for Rossini, and how he even teased Hotho about Hotho's stolid Berlin "orthodoxy," his view that Mozart and Gluck were the be-all and end-all of opera.[71] Refreshed and reassured, Hegel thus prepared to return to Berlin, having put most of his troubles behind him, the music of Vienna still ringing in his ears. That music was soon, however, to be drowned out by other more somber tunes.

13

Assertion:
Berlin, Paris (1824–1827)

New Turmoil

Victor Cousin's Arrest, Hegel's Intervention

O N OCTOBER 14, 1824, shortly after Hegel reached Dresden from
Prague on his way home from Vienna, his old friend from France,
Victor Cousin, was arrested by the Saxon police in Dresden on suspi-
cion of being a "subversive" and was then quickly handed over to the
Prussian police. This came as a great shock; almost certainly, Hegel had
seen Cousin in Dresden and spoken with him before the arrest.[1] The
"Cousin affair" was to embroil Hegel in yet another political contro-
versy, which was once again to put him at some risk.

Word of Cousin's arrest spread throughout Europe, causing a sensation when people heard of it. However, what people did not hear at the
time was the full story behind the events: Cousin's arrest was the result
of secret machinations between the restoration French government and
the restoration Prussian government. In France, Cousin had already
been suspended on political grounds from his teaching duties during
the 1820s. (He was too liberal.) Cousin then became a tutor to the
duchess of Montebello, and when the young duke of Montebello (his
protégé) was to be married in Dresden, Cousin accompanied him. The
French director of police, Mr. Franchet-Desperey, learned of this and
alerted the representative of the Prussian government in Paris in an
official letter that Cousin was going to be in Dresden, and that "this
Professor, known for his quite dangerous opinions" had earlier traveled
to Germany to establish contacts with German professors and students
for "political" reasons – in other words, for reasons of "demagoguery"
– and Franchet-Desperey advised the Prussians that the authorities

524

should simply be "aware" of that. The note was delivered with an accompanying understanding that whatever the Prussians decided to do, neither Franchet-Desperey's name nor the involvement of the French police was to be mentioned.[2] Franchet-Desperey's involvement in this is no mystery; a fierce reactionary, he had been elevated from departmental head of the post office to being put in charge of the police by virtue of a cabal led by the Jesuits in the interests of securing the restoration in France.[3]

The French reactionaries especially suspected Cousin of being a subversive; his friendship with the Piedmont (Italian) revolutionary Count Santa Rosa had only added more sustenance to that suspicion. After the failure of the Piedmont revolution, Count Santa Rosa fled to Paris under an assumed name, where he met Cousin, and the two shared a house together in Anteuil for a while; but when the French police learned Santa Rosa's identity, they arrested him, and Cousin came to his defense. Although the police eventually released Santa Rosa, they nonetheless expelled him from all French territory. (Santa Rosa later died fighting for Greek independence; Cousin had a monument erected in Greece on the spot where his friend had died.) Cousin's involvement with and defense of Santa Rosa gave the French police a substantial interest in having Victor Cousin conveniently disappear, should that prove to be possible.

After the all-too-convenient warning from the French police, the Prussian police carried out their own investigation, and their double-agent Johann Ferdinand Witt-Döring (himself related to a reactionary official in the French government) testified not only that Cousin had met with French and German revolutionaries in Paris in the summer of 1820 for the purpose of plotting to spread the revolution to Germany, but also that Cousin was personally tied into Karl Follen, the radical leader of the *Burschenschaften*. One of the co-conspirators in the secret society was also alleged to be one of the Wesselhöft brothers, a close friend of Ludwig Fischer (who was raised by Betty Wesselhöft) and Julius Niethammer. (As became clear in his interrogation, Cousin in fact knew all of the people alleged to be part of the plot.) Since the paranoid, reactionary Prussian police were only too willing to believe in the existence of an internationally based secret society of subversives dedicated to fomenting revolution in Germany, they immediately contacted the Mainz commission, which then promptly ordered the Saxon

government in Dresden to arrest Cousin and hand him over to the
Prussian police for arrest and further interrogation. Under the terms of
the Karlsbad decrees, the Saxons had no choice but to do so. Everything
went smoothly and according to plan until some confusion in the inner
workings of the French government led a hapless French representative
in Dresden to protest the political arrest of a French citizen. The cat
was then out of the bag, and in light of the ensuing public outcry, the
French government found itself, absurdly enough, obliged to file a
formal protest with the Prussian government, even though they had
instigated the whole thing in the first place.[4]

The Prussians, on the other hand, were delighted; they clearly
thought they had caught a subversive red-handed. They demanded that
the Swiss government extradite the other co-conspirators (who were at
that time living in Switzerland), but the Swiss refused, and Follen and
Wesselhöft, seeing the writing on the wall, immediately fled to America,
while the others still in Germany immediately fled to refuge in Switzerland. The only one the Prussians could get their hands on was Victor
Cousin, whom they forthwith threw into solitary confinement and
whom they then interrogated about his subversive intentions and connections.

Schleiermacher, another of Cousin's Berlin friends, was completely
dumbfounded by Cousin's arrest and said so to his friends, noting that
he had heard from one of the other arrested people that it looked like it
was going to result in at least a fifteen-year jail sentence.[5] On November
4, 1824, Hegel courageously wrote a letter to the Prussian interior
ministry arguing on behalf of Victor Cousin. He testified to Cousin's
good character, his interest in *Wissenschaft*, and, prudently noting that
he had not been in contact with Cousin for six years, nonetheless
emphatically attested to his belief in Cousin's innocence. Hegel requested that he be allowed to visit Cousin in his confinement; the
government refused. This was no small matter; Hegel's friend Varnhagen von Ense remarked at the time (December 11, 1824) that "it
belongs to Hegel's good standing with the government not to have
become himself suspect on account of his taking such steps."[6] Word of
Hegel's note to the ministry became public and only added to the
common outcry against Cousin's imprisonment; but the Prussian government did not relent, and Cousin's interrogation continued.

The public pressure, helped along by Hegel's intervention, led to

Cousin's release from prison at the beginning of February 1825 – but only on condition that he not leave Berlin until the "investigation" of him had been completed. (He was also kept under police surveillance for this period.) Cousin spent his time during this period of "house arrest" mostly in interchanges with Hegel, Schleiermacher, and other intellectuals on the Berlin scene. (Hegel and Cousin visited Ms. Milder-Hauptmann's house together, no doubt on Hegel's instigation; Cousin was ever after always to tell Hegel to say hello to Ms. Milder for him.) The pretext for Cousin's release from prison was that since his alleged co-conspirators had fled to America, the government was left without any hard-and-fast case alleging Cousin's membership in that particular secret subversive coterie; but that did not stop the Prussians from looking for more evidence of subversion, and they proceeded to investigate whether Cousin had perhaps "conspired" during his visits between 1817 and 1818 in Germany. Schelling was even asked to testify, and he wrote that Cousin's interests in those years were purely scholarly and philosophical. On April 20, 1825, Cousin was declared officially released (although not officially cleared), and a few days later, he left for Weimar, clear in his mind about who had played the largest role in Berlin in keeping his case in the public eye and was therefore responsible for his being set free.

New Religious Troubles for Hegel

If anything, this only raised the level of Hegel's celebrity in Berlin, but it did not end his contentious relationship with Schleiermacher. Even though they had been on the same side in the Cousin affair, oddly enough, he and Schleiermacher now seemed more than ever to be rivals. As one student put it, Berlin seemed at the time to be ruled by three powers: Hegel at his lectern in the university, Schleiermacher at his pulpit in the French church, and the actor Eduard Devrient on the stage at the Berlin Theater.[7] Hegel continued to attack Schleiermacher in his lectures; indeed, his antagonistic relation to Schleiermacher seems to have become a bit of an idée fixe in Hegel's mind. But after the Cousin affair, Hegel also settled back down into his usual Berlin routines, devoting himself to games of Whist with various partners; he intensified his involvement with the theater and opera and began to solidify the school of thought that was forming around him. He also continued, as many remarked, clearly to remain a Swabian in Prussia (even though Swabians were considered to be a bit provincial by Berliners); he never lost his Swabian accent – indeed, it seems to have been fairly noticeable – and he kept his Swabian style of life. As one Swabian student jestingly remarked, he continued to look like the "genuine Tübingen Seminarian" at work in the Prussian capital.[8]

Shortly after the Cousin affair, Hegel found himself under attack again. A young philosopher, Hermann von Keyserlingk, had applied in 1816 for promotion to the status of "doctor" by the Berlin faculty. His thesis and his oral defense were so bad, however, that they only awarded him the title of "*Magister*." A few years later, in 1819, von Keyserlingk appeared again in Berlin – in the meantime, he had become a *Privatdozent* in Heidelberg – requesting permission to hold lectures in Berlin even before his *habilitation* was finished. Once again, the faculty denied the request, and von Keyserlingk then asked to be granted the status at the Berlin university of at least a *Privatdozent*. The faculty agreed to examine him, and in a lapse of judgment, Hegel approved von Keyserlingk's request for status as a *Privatdozent* even though he found his work to be substandard.

Von Keyserlingk had little success as a teacher, attracting only a handful of students, but nonetheless in December 1824 he requested that he be made an extraordinary professor, and submitted a work accusing Hegelianism of really being pantheism – which in the context of the times was equivalent to accusing Hegel of atheism, which was equivalent to calling for his dismissal from the university. The faculty refused even to respond to his request, so he resubmitted it in January 1825. The ministry and the faculty both agreed that von Keyserlingk did not have the qualifications, and his request was denied. Undaunted, von Keyserlingk passed around a circular in May 1826 announcing a public discussion he was going to host on "Hegelian pantheism." That was the last straw. The faculty was outraged, Hegel filed an official protest, and the faculty backed him up. It might have seemed like a minor matter, a tempest in a teapot, but von Keyserlingk was raising what for Hegel was a potential nightmare, namely, the problem of being publicly accused of pantheism in the already repressive atmosphere of Berlin in the 1820s.[9]

Von Keyserlingk's charges were made all the more worrisome by the fact that in March 1826 Hegel's sarcasm had gotten him into hot water again with a remark he made about Catholicism during his lectures. In his lectures on the philosophy of world history, in the discussion of the medieval period, Hegel repeated a longstanding Protestant canard about the Catholic doctrine of transubstantiation, which had to do with what would happen if a mouse were to eat the consecrated wafer (the problem being, supposedly, that the wafer actually contains the body of the Lord). On one telling of the story, Hegel is said to have repeated the old Protestant legend that Catholics would therefore be required to kneel down before the mouse and worship it as bearing the Lord's body within itself. (But, it should be noted, since that version comes from Rudolf Haym, who was notoriously unfriendly to Hegel, it may well be untrue.) According to another contemporary version (cited by Hegel's student Hotho), Hegel said that it would follow that if the mouse ate the host, then the Lord's body would be contained not only in the mouse but also in his excrement.[10] (With his penchant for inflamed sarcasm, Hegel may very well have said that.) A complaint was filed with Altenstein at the ministry that Hegel was publicly slandering the Catholic religion in his lectures (again, on one telling, by the Catholic students, who supposedly accused Hegel of blasphemy; or, on another telling, by the chaplain from the Catholic church, St. Hedwig's, who had been attending the lectures and supposedly accused Hegel of slander).[11]

Altenstein deftly passed the problem over to Schulze, who asked Hegel to respond in writing to the charges. Hegel replied on April 3, quite defiantly, that he was a Protestant teaching at a university in a Protestant *Land*, which was itself the leading Protestant state in Germany, and that the Catholics should not be surprised by that; that he had not simply taken some arbitrary opportunity to speak ill of Catholicism but had done it in the course of his lectures (noting that he had to treat Catholic doctrine in his lectures on the history of philosophy, not mentioning that the incident had occurred in his lectures on the philosophy of world history); that he was only speaking with "scientific determinateness," which required him to pronounce that Luther's doctrines were the "true ones and recognized by philosophy on its part as the true ones"; that he was only speaking in an "indeterminate, hypothetical sense" in the lectures, something indicated by his tone of voice, which was of course not replicated in the complaint. It is a matter, Hegel said, of "indifference to me, whether and which consequences the Catholic church wishes to bind to its doctrines," but, he added, some of the consequences are only too well known, and he listed among them the "presumptuousness of the Popes and the other clerics" vis-à-vis secular rulers, "presumptuousness vis-à-vis confessional freedom of Christians in general," and "presumptuousness vis-à-vis all *Wissenschaft*" that contradicts official Catholic doctrines.[12] It could be only "weak intellects" that took offense at what he said, and a professor cannot be responsible for the ridiculous conclusions drawn by such "weak intellects" from his lectures. Hegel concluded that if the Catholics did not like it, they should either blame themselves for attending or blame their Catholic superiors for not warning them, but he, a confirmed Protestant, was not about to change. That seemed to settle matters, but it was clear that life in Berlin was still not without its ups and downs for Hegel.

Eduard Gans and the "Yearbooks"

Gans and the Law Faculty

During this period, Hegel became good friends with Eduard Gans, who was to remain one of his closest friends and followers during the rest of his life in Berlin. Gans was a jurist who, although not beginning as a Hegelian, quickly and fully came to embrace Hegel's teachings. Born in 1797, Gans came from an affluent Berlin Jewish family. Gans's father, whose own background had been that of religious orthodoxy, had married into one of the prominent and wealthy Jewish families in Berlin (the Marcuse family) and had played a large role in mediating war debts for the Prussians during the wars against Napoleon, but had, at his death in 1813, left his family in great debt. Eduard Gans, ignoring his mother's family's wishes that he pursue a career in commerce so as to retire his father's debts, chose instead to go to university and study law. The Prussian "emancipation" edict of March 1812 had stated, among other things, that Jews were entitled to assume academic positions, including professorial positions, "for which they have made themselves suitable," and Gans obviously intended to take the Prussians at their word. He enrolled at the university in Berlin in 1816, during which time he became active in a circle of Jewish students who met regularly to discuss intellectual and cultural issues, especially the nature and role of Judaism in the post-Napoleonic, revolutionary time in which the Jews had supposedly been emancipated in the German confederation in general and in Prussia in particular. In 1817, Gans shifted from Berlin to Göttingen to study law, and in August 1818 he enrolled at Heidelberg, where he completed his dissertation in 1819 under Hegel's old friend Anton Friedrich Justus Thibaut.

Before coming to Heidelberg, Gans had become publicly known because of his response to an attack on his father by a reactionary nationalist Romantic at Berlin, Friedrich Rühs, who had asserted in a publication that Abraham Gans was a war profiteer and thereby typified the way in which Jews could never be fully patriotic Prussian citizens. (In 1816, Rühs had already published another pamphlet arguing against civil rights for Jews and calling for the "rooting out root and branch" of Jewry in Germany.)[13] Gans responded vehemently and analytically to Rühs's nasty invective, defending his late father's dealings as being within the letter of the law; Rühs, hateful person that he was, simply refused to respond to Gans's arguments, claiming that he would not deal with such Jewish *Burschenschaft*.

Gans had been drawn to Heidelberg undoubtedly because of Thibaut's fame both as a jurist in favor of a rational codification of law and, most importantly, as a defender of full civil rights for Jews. Thibaut, like Hegel, was a firm opponent of the Romantic nationalist sentiment bubbling up in German life.[14] Gans's dissertation was full of Thibaut's influence, and having acquired his doctorate *summa cum laude* in March 1819, Gans applied for an academic position in Berlin in December 1819. The famous and influential jurist Friedrich von Savigny – who had already in 1816 published a piece in which he had argued against civil and political equality for Jews on the grounds they were essentially "aliens" in German life – wrote a very negative review of Gans's dissertation (March 1820), and the juristic faculty voted against accepting Gans in April 1820. The letter from the faculty closed with the statement that "we would venture to point out that we do not know if Dr. Gans, who stems from a well-known Jewish family, has personally converted to the Christian faith, and whether, therefore, there may not be an obstacle to his appointment to a position of public service from this side as well."[15]

Hardenberg and Altenstein were not exactly impressed with this display of anti-Jewish sentiment among the law faculty, and Hardenberg instructed Altenstein to send Gans to Breslau and as "soon as possible" to make him an "extraordinary professor" there. Altenstein, for his part, was quite straightforward about his belief that Gans's Jewishness posed "no legal obstacle" to his assuming such an academic position.[16]

Gans, however, elected to stay in Berlin and became one of the founders and leaders of the Association for the Science and Culture of Judaism; he was first its secretary and later its president. In the summer of 1820, Gans was in Dresden and was present when Hegel purchased Sillery champagne for all and drank to the storming of the Bastille; it was most likely at this point that Gans began to become interested in Hegel as a figure around which he could orient himself.

Gans defiantly continued to apply for a position on the juristic faculty, and in 1821, Savigny wrote a long "expert's report" on behalf of the faculty to the ministry in which he argued for the impossibility of appointing Jews in general to the law faculty. Noting that the faculty had already expressed some concern over not knowing whether Gans was still Jewish, Savigny said that the matter had since become completely clear.

Savigny offered three arguments against accepting Jews into the faculty. First, they are unsuited to legal studies; it is simply unthinkable that one would appoint a Jew to the faculty of theology, and law, like theology, stands in an "immediate relation with the history and unique characteristics of our nation" and is intimately connected with the "whole way of thought" of people and "in particular, with the focal point of such thought (religious conviction)."[17] In light of this, Savigny asked the ministry to imagine what it would be like if "a significant part of the juristic professorial positions were to be held by Jews."[18] Although such teachers would almost certainly not lead their students to convert to Judaism, they would nonetheless, Savigny argued, almost certainly lead them become "non-Christian, as well as non-German and non-Prussian."[19] Second, Savigny argued, professors function as "fatherly friends and advisors" to young students, and it would be impossible for a Jewish professor, not sharing the students' religious background, to speak with the proper moral authority to a Christian student. (Savigny also noted that Christian parents would not be willing to entrust the education of their sons to Jewish professors.) Third, Jews could never possess the authority to carry out any of the "business of the university" – for example, they could never become rectors of the university – since they could never have the "dignity and esteem" necessary for such office. Thus, their presence would devalue the status of other "ordinary professors," since the ordinances of the university gave all "ordinary" professors equal entitlement to such offices.

In his report, Savigny also drew out an ambiguity in the 1812 Prussian edict of emancipation. The eighth paragraph of the edict declared that Jews are eligible for those academic positions "for which they have made themselves suitable," but the ninth paragraph stated that the eligibility of Jews for other "public services and offices of the state" was to be determined by law at some later date. But since Jews were clearly not eligible for theological positions, since they clearly could not take the oath to Christianity called for in the university regulations, and since they were not, for example, capable of giving witness in criminal cases (Savigny cited §357 of the Prussian code of criminal law to back up that statement), they were therefore wholly ineligible for university positions in the law faculty. Savigny broadened the argument to include all university positions: "general experience," he argued, shows that "suitability for a teaching position is dependent on wholly individual conditions much more so than in other offices," and Jews are therefore clearly unsuitable for all the reasons already mentioned for such academic positions.[20] In effect, Savigny argued that the Prussian emancipation edict actually did not require universities to accept Jews into professorial posts.

To Hardenberg's credit, he simply ignored Savigny's and the law faculty's anti-Semitism and instructed Altenstein to settle the case in favor of Gans. Desperate and nonetheless fully resolved against having a Jew among them, the law faculty voted again against accepting Gans and appealed to the king to decide in their favor. All this put Altenstein in a precarious position. Altenstein concurred with Hardenberg about what should be done about Gans's application; the law faculty, though, was firmly set against accepting Gans, and because of their appeal to the king, there was a threat of royal intervention; and Altenstein's own position in the government was already shaky enough. Confronted with those factors, Altenstein took the safe way out and simply prevaricated on the matter, which, however, only served further to irritate Hardenberg, who kept sending him letters instructing him again and again to settle the matter in Gans's favor. Finally, frustrated by Altenstein's inaction, he wrote Altenstein, as he put it in his letter, for the "seventh time" to order him to decide the case in Gans's favor.

The law faculty, though, knew where their king stood and where Altenstein had feared that he stood; on August 18, 1822, the king effectively abolished the emancipation edict through a cabinet order and expressly declared that Gans was not to be employed as an "extraordinary professor." Altenstein, shaken by what he had always feared was going to happen, wrote to Gans and offered him a stipend of 1,000 Thalers so that he could prepare himself for some other mode of employment.

The Jahrbücher

During this rather trying period, Gans had gradually attached himself to Hegel and perhaps by 1821 (by 1822 at the latest) had become a full-fledged Hegelian. Hegel, a good friend of his teacher, Thibaut, seemed a kind of sympathetic, fatherly figure to Gans; Hegel had a long-standing interest in students whom he thought were serious and devoted to *Wissenschaft*, and he was unsparing with his time when it came to helping them. At a time when Gans was being rejected by powerful professors such as Savigny, a supportive figure like Hegel was bound to appear all the more attractive. And was it not Hegel who, in Gans's presence, had toasted the storming of the Bastille during the height of the repression? Hegel himself was also a frequent visitor at many of the social gatherings and salons thrown by the prosperous, emancipated Berlin Jewish community (of which Gans was a member), and thus Hegel seemed to be the kind of successful academic who would be sympathetic to Gans's ambitions; and Hegel had, of course, openly declared in §270 of his *Philosophy of Right* that to be true to themselves, modern states were rationally compelled to grant full emancipation to Jews and not to make this emancipation conditional on their conversion to Christianity. Moreover, Gans's attraction to Hegel and Hegelian philosophy came at a time when he himself had begun to despair (with good reason) of ever being able to accomplish anything in Germany at all; he and some other Berlin Jews had even at one point contemplated emigrating to America and establishing a homeland for emancipated Jews like themselves on the banks of the Mississippi.[21] (His friend, the poet Heinrich Heine, a participant in the scheme, joked that the capital would be called "Ganstown.")[22]

Under Hegel's influence, friendship, and encouragement, though, Gans continued his scholarly work on his own, and in 1823 he published a historical study of the Roman law of inheritance that was expressly and openly Hegelian in its theoretical stance, and he sent Hegel a personal copy in October 1823.[23] Both Hegel and Johannes Schulze were quite impressed with Gans's work, seeing in Gans's book the best appropriation of Hegel's thought that had yet been done. In that work, Gans also took off the gloves and began attacking Savigny's jurisprudential views with a vengeance (from a more or less Hegelian perspective). Hegel even recommended the work to friends, but there was nothing, it seemed, he could do for Gans's career, since the king himself had expressly forbidden Jews from holding public offices. In the spring of 1825, Gans took his stipend from Altenstein and set out on a trip abroad, and most of his friends, including Hegel, did not expect to see him ever return to Berlin.

Gans visited Paris from May until December 1825; while in Paris, he moved in the circle of French liberal thinkers such as Benjamin Constant and liberal constitutionalists such as the philosopher-politician Pierre Paul Royer-Collard. (He also became an unabashed Francophile during this visit.) He visited with Victor Cousin, whom he had met in 1825 during the "Cousin affair" in Berlin, and he met the famous German publisher Baron von Cotta, who at that time was visiting Paris. (Von Cotta was one of the proprietors of one of the major liberal reform journals in Paris, the *Constitutionel*.) Gans and von Cotta discussed the possibility of a new literary undertaking in Germany, and on his return from Paris, Gans stopped off in Stuttgart to discuss matters with von Cotta. One of Hegel's pet projects had been the establishment of a new journal that would help to solidify the intellectual forces supporting modern life, and Gans brought up the subject with von Cotta, who was intrigued with Gans's suggestion (taken from Hegel) that German literature needed a "focal point," and that the scholars associated with the Berlin university – with its modern, nonmedieval foundation – would be ideally suited to provide such a focal point. (Gans himself was interested on his own in such a journal; in 1822, he had proposed to his friend Heinrich Heine that they edit a similar journal together.)[24]

After von Cotta expressed a firm interest in the journal (and also

agreed to publish the next volumes of Gans's work on inheritance law),
Gans straightway returned to Berlin and immediately called on Hegel
at his home on *Kupfergraben*. He found Hegel sitting at his desk,
wearing (typically) his old sleeping gown over his regular clothes while
sporting his terribly unfashionable (for the time) large black beret, all
the while sorting through a pile of disarranged papers with one hand
while taking snuff out of his tin with the other.[25] (One of the most
famous pictures of Hegel, done by the lithographer Julius Ludwig
Sebbers in 1828, portrayed him in his study wearing the same outfit –
Hegel's friend and longtime Whist partner, the musician K. F. Zelter,
described the picture to Goethe as making Hegel look some odd "Doctor Faust . . . with Aristotle at his feet" and said that if the picture had
not cost him so much, he would have been sorely tempted to draw a
big "rat's tooth" on it[26] – but despite the fame of the picture, Hegel
himself disliked it; his wife joked to Christiane Hegel that it annoyed
him because of its rather "uncomfortable likeness" to him.)[27] Hegel
greeted his friend quite jovially and with characteristic understatement:
"Eh, you're back again; we've been waiting for you for some months;
privy councilor Schulze thought you'd never come back."[28] When Gans
informed Hegel about his conversations and his agreement with von
Cotta, Hegel became quite interested, although maintaining a bit of
skepticism, but then reassured both himself and Gans with the thought
that "Cotta understands this stuff better than all of us, and when he's
started something, we might just as well hand ourselves over to his
direction."[29]

   The idea of such a journal appealed to Hegel on several levels. He
had always been interested in such undertakings. His first real academic
position had been putting out the journal that he and Schelling had
edited together, and over the years he had penned several drafts for
proposals for starting new journals, most recently in an 1819–20 report
for Altenstein. He also had a personal reason for being especially interested in the journal. The Academy of Sciences had effectively black-
balled him; Schleiermacher was one of the main obstacles to his acceptance, and Savigny was another firm opponent of Hegel's membership.
Together, they wanted to limit, if not eliminate, Hegel's influence in
Berlin and in German letters. The animosity toward Schleiermacher
was largely personal; both he and Schleiermacher belonged to the reform wings of Prussian politics. But the animosity toward Savigny was

also deeply political; Savigny stood for just about everything Hegel argued against, and the anti-Semitic attacks on Gans would only have hardened Hegel's feelings about him. The idea of setting up a "critical journal" thus offered Hegel a way in which he could set up, as it were, a counter-Academy on his own, and in fact, when the journal was finally published in January 1827, it was seen by many people as exactly that: *Hegel's* "counter-Academy," even derisively called by some the "Hegel-journal."

But Hegel's interest in the journal was based on more than settling a grudge and gaining some status for himself. Hegel's vision of the modern state gave a crucial place to the idea of trained civil servants, the *Beamte*, running things, and it was the job of the university to train such civil servants and form them, to round out and firm up their sense of *Bildung*, of self-cultivation, culture, self-direction, and good judgment. In Hegel's view of modern life, technical training for the civil servants was not enough; civil servants also had to be cultured and educated, had to be men of good judgment and character for them to be able to assume their role in the "universal estate," as the movers and doers who could assume positions of authority in any of the modern states irrespective of their own personal hometown backgrounds. Crucial therefore to a civil servant's cultural education was his acquiring a sense of philosophy – which for Hegel of course meant his own idealistic philosophy, philosophy as *Wissenschaft*, not just as a loose connection of maxims by which to live; well-educated, cultured civil servants had to have a sense of how the whole of modern life hung together, and only philosophy could give them that sense of the whole. It was not enough, though, simply to give civil servants a good education at the university and then expect that to suffice for the rest of their lives. Modern *Wissenschaft* was too dynamic, too much in process, for that to be possible. The purpose of such a journal would therefore be to give those movers and doers of post-revolutionary German life an ongoing education in progress in the "sciences" that would allow them to keep up with developments in them, not to acquaint them with new techniques or methods but to maintain their *Bildung*, their status as "learned, cultured" men.

In this respect, the Academy of Sciences was clearly not suited to the job. Besides having no real philosophy in it (thanks mostly to Schleiermacher), it had devolved into an academic clique devoted to the pursuit at best of "science" for its own sake and neglecting the public role that "science" had to play in modern life itself. Hegel thus never conceived of the new publication as a *Hegelian* journal; it was never intended to propagate Hegel's philosophy but to propagate the ideal of *Wissenschaft-connected-with-Bildung* in general. Not surprisingly, Hegel's opponents' charges that the *Jahrbücher* were only "Hegel journals" were immediately rebutted by the members of the editorial board, who quite rightly pointed out that many of the key articles were written by people who by no stretch of the imagination could be said to have anything to do with Hegel's philosophy. But given the hothouse atmosphere, the competition for status, and the sense of the stakes being high circulating in Berlin at the time, the charge of its being a "Hegel journal" proved difficult to shake.

Hegel, Gans, and Hotho continued to discuss the possibility of such a journal (with Hegel fretting over all the small details – to Gans's mild irritation – and always bringing up all the ways in which the whole enterprise could fall apart). Finally, though, the die was cast.[30] Hegel circulated a memorandum around the university to interested parties on July 16, 1826, and when Marie was away with the children, Hegel had a meeting with the interested parties at his home on July 23, 1826, at which time the *Sozietät für wissenschaftliche Kritik* (Society for Scientific Criticism) was founded pretty much along the lines Hegel had suggested, with its publication to be called the "*Jahrbücher für wissenschaftliche Kritik*" ("Yearbooks for Scientific Criticism"). The "Yearbooks" were to be a general review of progress in the sciences and of new discoveries; no scholarly compendia, no pastoral works, no schoolbooks, no editions of the classics, and no purely technical works were to be reviewed; and there was to be no anonymity among the reviewers. The general setup of the "society" was like that of the Academy of Sciences: There were three sections called "classes" – philosophical, natural scientific, and historical-philological – with secretaries for each "class" and rules and regulations binding everything. Gans was elected secretary for the whole "society" and was put in charge of all its affairs (in other words, scheduling meetings and, most importantly, taking care of all the work involved in publishing the "Yearbooks"). One obvious outcome of this (which Hegel's opponents noted) was that Hegel had finally secured a potentially powerful position for his friend and follower that skirted all the objections that the reactionary, anti-Semitic forces had mustered against Gans.

Hegel and Gans, however, differed in some crucial ways about what shape the "Yearbooks" should take. Hegel thought that the "Yearbooks" should be a state-supported institution with its impartiality and authority guaranteed; Hegel had in mind something like the independence of the judiciary and of civil servants in general, and, ever the admirer of France, he also thought that since the *Journal des Savants* in France was state-sponsored and impartial, so too should the Berlin journal be state-sponsored and impartial. Gans, on the other hand, younger and more republican-oriented, wanted it to be free of state control of all sorts (including financial control). Gans also wanted it to be modeled after *Le Globe*, a more recent, independent journal in France, and not after the *Journal des Savants* (which Gans knew to be much the stuffier of the two). *Le Globe* was edited by men of Gans's age; it was more intellectual, more romantic, less stuffy, and, curiously, more philosophical than the *Journal des Savants*. Interestingly, Victor Cousin had his feet in both camps; he was, however, much more the spiritual leader of the group putting out *Le Globe* than he was vis-à-vis the *Journal des Savants*. But Hegel was by and large to get his way on the matter, even though Gans was to inject a bit of the spirit of *Le Globe* into the life of the "Yearbooks."[31]

Thus, although the "Yearbooks" were not (as its critics charged) only "Hegel journals" dedicated to propagating Hegelianism, the society constituting it was nonetheless sharply characterized by who was *not* a member: Neither Schleiermacher nor Savigny was ever asked to join, and it was clear why. This was a bit embarrassing, since both Schleiermacher and Savigny were major intellectual figures in their time. The issue touched a nerve with Hegel. When in December 1826 (about five months after the journal's initial founding), it was proposed that Schleiermacher and Savigny be made members, Hegel exploded and flew into a rage. He leapt from his chair and angrily paced the room, muttering that bringing Schleiermacher into the "society" would be tantamount to throwing him out of it. In what members recalled as one of the "stormiest" sessions ever held (with raised voices and much contention), it was finally resolved that it was perhaps "imprudent" at that time to extend an invitation to Schleiermacher. (Even Gans thought that Hegel's opposition to Schleiermacher on this point had become purely personal.)[32] The proposal was never to be tendered again.

The "Yearbooks" were unfortunately only partially successful. They never managed to generate enough subscriptions to pay for themselves, and, to Hegel's disappointment, the government at first refused to offer any financial support for such a venture, although after Von Cotta recorded a loss of 2,700 Thalers for 1827 and 1828, Altenstein was eventually able to obtain an 800 Thaler per year subvention for the "Yearbooks," which allowed their continued publication until some years after Hegel's death.[33] Even Hegel was disappointed in the results; the articles, he thought, had turned out to be too scholarly and tedious to have the kind of general public interest he had intended. He even complained to Niethammer on August 9, 1827, that "to me [the articles] have, vis-à-vis the viewpoint taken in our original plans, turned out almost too learned. However, we German scholars – but fortunately we philosophers do not belong to the class of scholars – are only with great difficulty phased out of our learnedness, thoroughness (*Gründlichkeit*) and mere shop talk."[34] However, not everyone was disappointed with the "Yearbooks"; in a reversal, Schleiermacher himself found the first issues quite good and even found Hegel's pieces in them quite interesting; but he still found it distasteful that the "Yearbooks" were, in his opinion, only a "Hegel journal."[35]

Gans had set the ball rolling for the "Yearbooks" on his trip to Paris, which in another way had proven terribly eventful for Gans. For reasons he never publicly explained but which were obvious, Gans had himself baptized into the Christian faith in Paris on December 12, 1825. Gans's conversion was almost certainly what Heinrich Heine, Gans's close friend, described it as being: an "entry ticket" into the academic world, not a deep change of religious sentiment. Gans never expressed any particular religiosity or attachment to Christianity. Gans's official conversion, however, deeply shook the Jewish community in Berlin; it particularly distressed his friend Heine, who had already converted before Gans's change of heart for much the same reason (not a belief in Christianity but an acceptance that one had to formally acknowledge it if one was to have a career in Prussia). Gans was considered by all to be the best man to push for emancipation: Intellectually and organizationally gifted, possessing enormous energy and appeal, Gans had, after all, heroically challenged the Prussians on their own terms to live up to the edict of 1812 and had not backed down. Gans was the great hope, the hero of a multitude of people in Berlin seeking to realize the post-Napoleonic reform ideals, and his conversion was widely seen as a depressing blow to hopes for Jewish emancipation. Even those who, like Heine, had made the same decision were profoundly saddened by Gans's decision, even though its real basis was clear to all. Gans himself was reported to have said of his conversion, "If the state is so stupid as to forbid me to serve it in a capacity which suits my particular talents unless I profess something I do not believe – and something which the responsible minister knows I do not believe; all right then, it shall have its wish."[36]

His conversion did, however, serve its purpose; on March 13, 1826, Gans was appointed an "extraordinary" professor in the law faculty, and, to Savigny's horror, Hegel now had a follower on the law faculty at Berlin. Gans became a phenomenal success as a teacher, and his scholarly career continued its upward climb, but the disputes between him and Savigny became more open and bitter, and Savigny clearly felt himself under attack by the "Hegelians." ("The Hegelians passionately hang together like a sect and have become my powerful opponents," Savigny complained in 1826.)[37] On November 15, 1828, a cabinet order from the king empowered Altenstein to name Gans to a position of "ordinary" professor on the law faculty, which Altenstein promptly did on December 11 over Savigny's loud protests. Gans tried to reconcile with Savigny, but Savigny repelled Gans, refusing to have anything to do with him.[38] Savigny even enlisted the crown prince on his side in the dispute. For Savigny and his followers, Gans's conversion was irrelevant; in their eyes and in the eyes of those who sympathized with them, Gans remained a Jew on the faculty. But the deed was done: A Hegelian now held one of the most prestigious positions on the law faculty, and his charismatic personality was drawing students to his lectures not just by the hundreds but sometimes by the thousands.

Satire, Saphir, and Unexpected Troubles

Berlin Wit

The "Yearbooks" were not Hegel's only endeavor related to periodicals. During this same period, he also became good friends with one of

Berlin's leading humorists, Moritz Gottlieb Saphir. Saphir (born 1793 as Moishe Saphir) was a Hungarian Jew who came to Berlin via Vienna in 1825. He caused a scandal immediately in Berlin by publishing a poem supposedly extolling the virtues of Henriette Sontag (an extremely popular singer with the Berlin theater), who herself had also come to Berlin in 1825; Saphir revealed after the poem was published that it was an acrostic, the letters of its first lines spelling out "*ungeheure Ironie*" ("monstrous irony").[39] There was talk of a scandal, and Saphir became famous because of it. His newfound renown landed him the editorship of a recently founded newspaper, the *Berliner Schnellpost für Literatur, Theater, und Geselligkeit* (*Berlin Express for Literature, Theater and Good Fellowship*), which began publication in January 1826. (It had a postal coach on its masthead, and the additional sections of the paper were labeled "*Beiwagen*," "accompanying coaches.") Saphir and his collaborators wrote often devastating, and always very humorous, reviews of plays and operas; they commented with barbed wit on the Berlin scene, and Saphir laced it all with his own esprit, which was a combination of bon mots, word play, roguish anecdotes, and the occasional sexual innuendo. (Like all wit, it does not transfer well across time; but here is one of the favorite Saphir jokes, told all across Berlin at the time – to be expressed in the properly overdrawn, authoritative tone of voice: "Are these gentlemen brothers?" "Of the one I am sure of it; of the other one, I can't say for certain.")[40] Saphir then started another, similar paper in 1827, which was equally successful: *Der Berliner Courier, ein Morgenblatt für Theater, Mode, Eleganz, Stadtleben und Lokalität* (*The Berlin Courier, a Morning Paper for Theater, Fashion, Elegance, City Life, and Local News*) Even the king read Saphir's papers, and his pleasure in Saphir's humor gave Saphir some latitude against the censors that others did not enjoy. The *Schnellpost* was an immediate success; its circulation for the first year was 1,300, and in 1827 its circulation reached 2,500 by subscription alone. (Since Berlin at that time had a population of 220,000, one person in eighty-eight was subscribing to the *Schnellpost*, and even more – from all classes, from the king to carriage drivers – were reading it.)[41] Hegel himself began to write for the *Schnellpost*, publishing a review of a theater piece in 1826, and he encouraged his students to write for it. In 1827, Saphir also founded a society dedicated to generalized tomfoolery called the "inverted world." (Initiates were called "classics," one had to say "bad" when one meant "good," and so on.)[42] Saphir took to dressing extravagantly, if not outrageously, even sporting a curly blond wig for a while. But not everybody was equally enamored of Saphir's wit and word play; Saphir offended all kinds of official people, and the police, aware that Saphir could lose the king's protection any day, insisted on giving him only temporary residence permits instead of full Berlin citizenship. In 1829, Saphir finally went too far: He published an article calling for, of all things, freedom of the press; humor was one thing, but freedom of the press was another; the king was no longer amused, and the police immediately expelled Saphir from Prussia.

Hegel's friendship with Saphir was typical of his "dual life," as Hegel's son described it. Ever the proper bourgeois professor, Hegel also had a need to hang out with swift-tongued artists, bohemians of various stripes, and figures somewhat on the margin of things. Both Hegel and Gans were Saphir's friends and shared many evenings together with Saphir. Saphir even embroiled Hegel (or Hegel perhaps embroiled himself) in what turned out to be a legendary comical incident among that crowd in Berlin. In May 1826, Carl Schall came to Berlin; Schall was a high-living, big-spending, grandly eating (and very rotund) dilettante, a passionate devotee of the theater and of actresses in particular, who, after scoring big in the lottery, decided that Berlin would be a nice place to indulge his tastes. Like so many Berliners at the time, he was totally smitten with Henriette Sontag, the beautiful, chaste singer in the musicals staged in the main Berlin theater. (People spoke of "Sontag fever" at the time.) Saphir, always the debunker, was, on the other hand, forever making jokes at Sontag's expense in his newspaper. As Sontag announced that she was leaving Berlin for Paris, a group of admirers, including Schall, met at the Café Royal in Berlin the night before her last performance to plan an homage to her, finally deciding that they would litter the stage with poems written in her honor immediately upon conclusion of the final performance. Saphir remarked that he too would throw a poem onto the stage but in honor of one of the members of the chorus, a young woman of, as it were, tarnished reputation. Schall exploded at this perceived insult to Sontag, and, claiming to defend Sontag's honor against Saphir's insults, challenged Saphir to a duel, which Saphir accepted. The challenge itself was already absurd; Schall, whose size was round and grand, even joked that Saphir, tall and very thin, would not make as good a target as him.

The duel was set for the next day. Schall and his second showed up; Saphir showed up alone. All waited, tensely, for Saphir's second to appear. Who, after all, in Berlin would agree to be the second for that outrageous Jewish humorist? Finally, a taxi-coach pulled up bearing Saphir's second, and out stepped, of all people, Hegel! – all of which suddenly gave the whole scene, as one observer put it, an "irresistibly comical air."[43] From that moment on, it was clear that no duel was to take place; Hegel persuaded Schall – he was also one of Schall's friends – to apologize to Saphir, and everything was put back in order. Berlin wit had won the day.

The Surprise Birthday Party

For almost the entire summer of 1826, Marie and the children were away from Berlin visiting the relatives in Nuremberg. Hegel passed his time working very hard (he admitted to Marie and the boys that "I have certainly been able to work more on things since you are away"), playing Whist with his friends, and socializing with Gans.[44] In fact, by the middle of August 1826, he remarked to Marie and the children that "I'm living very quietly; I see virtually only Gans, my true friend and companion."[45] Gans quite shrewdly kept it a secret from Hegel that his friends were planning a large birthday celebration for him. On August 26 (the day before his birthday), Hegel went over to the home of his friend August Friedrich Bloch's house for (what else?) a game of Whist (with his usual partners, the painter Rösel and the music teacher Zelter). As a ruse, Hegel's partners put off beginning the game of Whist on account of a late dinner, and when midnight struck they brought out the wine and began toasting Hegel's birthday (the 27th). The next morning, well-wishers came to visit Hegel at his house, and letters with poems began arriving. (Even the powerful von Kamptz, the head of police, paid a friendly visit.)

For dinner, Hegel was invited to the opening of a new café – a *Lokal*, as the Germans call it, named after the great boulevard in Berlin, Unter den Linden – in the heart of the city for a birthday dinner, and, after the dinner, a delegation of students led by Förster and Gans suddenly arrived bringing with them a silver cup on a velvet cushion with poems inside the cup celebrating Hegel. (The poems were bound in green, and in gold lettering was inscribed, "To the 27th of August, 1827"). The silver merchant, Hegel proudly noted, had also been one of his students. Rösel presented him a small antique Egyptian statue of Isis, and he received a crystal flower vase from another student. It was then announced that his friends had commissioned the most famous student of the most famous sculptor living in Berlin (Ludwig Wilhelm Wichmann, the student of Christian Daniel Rauch) to do a bust of Hegel. (Rauch himself had pleaded that he was overcommitted and could not do it himself; Wichmann finished the bust in 1828.)

The celebration then extended late into the night amid much music and fanfare, and after midnight (the 28th), Goethe's birthday was celebrated alongside Hegel's. Gans gave a speech celebrating Goethe as having both been witness to the birth of modern German letters and having since developed that literature, and Hegel as having been witness to modern (German) philosophy that had destroyed the old metaphysics and then having also developed it. This is, Gans said, "a festival of German art and German *Wissenschaft*."[46] Zelter then read a new poem by Goethe. Hegel gave a long speech at midnight having to do with his feelings about being surrounded by such devoted friends and students. He noted how much younger he felt in the presence of those students, but also how there comes a time when one suddenly realizes that one is no longer young oneself, that one is now the elder person in relation to youth, and how that time had finally come for him (a common theme for Hegel after 1820). He also reminisced about how he himself had grown up under the influence of a great poetic spirit, Goethe, and at that he raised his glass and drank to Goethe's birthday, thereby setting off another round of celebration and drinking.

Hegel was obviously deeply moved by the occasion; the display of loyalty and affection from his friends and students was much more than he had could have expected. Exhausted, he slept until 11:00 A.M. the next day, only to rise and find yet more poems waiting for him with the post. After all his troubles, it was gratifying to see his achievements celebrated by those who clearly appreciated him as both a friend and an intellectual figure. As if to underwrite Hegel's celebrity, the local newspaper, the *Vossische Zeitung*, even reported on August 30 about the grand celebration, reprinting many of the poems and detailing the course of the evening. Hegel could not help but feel satisfied with the way things had gone.

But not everyone was as enthusiastic. The king, for one, was peeved at the coverage of Hegel's birthday. His own birthday on August 3, 1770, was close to Hegel's, and he could not help noticing that Hegel's birthday celebrations were getting perhaps a bit too much coverage in relation to the coverage of his own birthday celebrations. Being the king, however, he was not obliged to sit around and pout, since he could do something about it, and he therefore issued a cabinet order in October banning any further reporting on "private" birthday celebrations in newspapers – only truly "worthy" occasions, such as the king's own birthday or officially proclaimed festivals, could henceforth be reported in the press.

Hegel and his friends had no difficulty detecting the ominous tones in the edict and even the hint of a threat behind the king's pronouncement. Then, to make matters worse, in the same month the director of the police, von Kamptz, learned of Victor Cousin's 1826 Preface in France to his French translation of Plato's *Gorgias*, in which Cousin spoke of his arrest in Germany, his mistreatment by the Prussians, of Prussia's overly zealous police and its "odious politics," and how, in the same Preface, he had praised Hegel in lofty tones for his "noble conduct" in the whole affair, repeating how Hegel had presented himself immediately before the police to tell them that Cousin was "his friend," how Hegel had worked for Cousin's release, and how all of this displayed Hegel's "great courage" in running such a risk.[47] The king was peeved; but von Kamptz was outraged; and being on the bad side of both the king and the director of police in Berlin in those days was no trifling matter. Varnhagen von Ense noted that although philosophy was still in good standing with the ruling powers, there were those at the court who would like to pin something on it (charges of "demagoguery," for example), and it would be wise for the philosophers (in other words, Hegel) to be on their guard, since in this matter, "Hegel is no more secure than others."[48] After several years of maneuvering the treacherous waters of the reaction in Berlin while continuing to publish reform-minded pieces, Hegel needed no warning about that. For the rest of the year, he continued work on his lectures, his articles for the "Yearbooks," and resumed living "very quietly."

Ludwig's Departure

Casting a pall over all the otherwise joyous events and accentuating the more negative ones was the poignant fact of Ludwig Fischer's departure from the family (most likely earlier in 1826). It was clear that there had always been trouble with Ludwig's presence in the Hegel household. On his own account, Ludwig's life in the Hegel family had been more filled with fear than with love; more than once he had decided to run away from home, stopping only when he realized that he had no means of support by which he could make his escape. He seems to have fought often with his two brothers, who clearly were favored in the household and who rubbed that in. He wanted to study medicine and in fact was successful enough in his scholarly endeavors to qualify for such studies; instead, Hegel simply ordered him to banish that idea from his thoughts because, purely and simply, he was to be shipped off to Stuttgart to apprentice himself to a trade, and there would be no financial support from the family for any other enterprise than that.

Ludwig at first reluctantly complied with his father's wishes but quickly found the whole thing unacceptable and the man to whom he had been apprenticed more than particularly tedious. It also cannot have helped Ludwig's attitude that as more and more people flocked into the apprenticeships in post-Napoleonic Germany, the prospects for such apprentices ever becoming masters were growing fainter by the year as the economy modernized. (This was something that Hegel, for all his sharp observations of the modern economy, simply failed to see with regard to his own son.) After a sharp exchange of words one day with his employer/master, he asked for and received his discharge from his apprenticeship and managed rather quickly to acquire for himself a commission as a lower-level officer in the Dutch army for service in East India. (Legend had long had it that Hegel acquired the commission for him; that is, unfortunately, simply not the case; Ludwig got it for himself.) Ludwig felt badly treated by his father and claimed that Hegel refused to let him take any of his books and very few of his own linens with him, and that Hegel did not even communicate his farewell to him directly but only indirectly through a letter to the man to whom he had been apprenticed. (Ludwig was so incensed about this that in a letter to a friend in which he related this story, he underlined the sentence about Hegel's cold-heartedness to him; strikingly, he did not even refer to Hegel as "father" but simply as "Hegel," indicating his extreme alienation from him.)[49] He also joined the army under the name Ludwig Fisher; according to one account at the time, he had been forbidden by Hegel from using the family name after he had been caught stealing eight *Groschen* (not a large amount) from the family money-box; until then, he had gone by the name Georg Ludwig Friedrich Hegel (as noted in his matriculation papers at the French *Gymnasium*), and he took this prohibition as a severe humiliation. (It was also clear that the Hegel family took the issue of stealing money seriously; Karl Hegel related a story about how he and a brother – we presume it was Immanuel, since Karl Hegel liked to pretend that Ludwig never even existed – once stole a Thaler coin they found lying on the table and spent it; when they were caught, they were given such a burning reproach by their parents that it remained firmly implanted in his memory for the rest of his life. If the story about Ludwig and the stolen *Groschen* is true, it is merely another example of a double standard exercised in the family.)[50]

Although Ludwig perhaps justifiably felt abandoned by Hegel, it is clear that Hegel did not simply disavow Ludwig and banish him from memory. Hegel obviously knew that Ludwig had joined the Dutch army; in fact, he discussed the matter with van Ghert when he visited van Ghert during his return from Paris in 1827, and van Ghert, loyal friend that he was, wrote to Hegel wanting to know to which regiment Ludwig belonged so that he might in his official capacity be of some assistance to him.[51] But in any event, Ludwig's life in the Dutch army was tragically short; he died of a fever while serving in the Dutch army in Batavia in 1831; Hegel, who died a short while later, in fact never learned of Ludwig's death.

There can be little doubt that Hegel was deeply troubled by his relationship with Ludwig and how things had turned out, and it is also clear that he also bore a good amount of the responsibility for the fact that it went so badly. Although Hegel had always been fairly good at shaking off the messiness of private life, it is highly unlikely that he was completely able to do so vis-à-vis his failed relationship with Ludwig. For his generation, Hegel was a man quite close to his sons and clearly involved with their upbringing; his desperate failure with Ludwig must have weighed on him more than he ever admitted to anybody, maybe even to himself.

Paris: "The Capital of the Civilized World"

A Prudential Trip to Paris

At the beginning of the year (1827), Hegel and his friends were given more reason to worry about whether Hegel was in favor in the inner circles of the Prussian government. When royal awards were handed out at the beginning of the year, Prof. Ideler (one of the original members of the recently founded Society for Scientific Criticism) was awarded the Order of the Red Eagle, Third Class (which, although not bestowing the right to add a noble "von" to one's name, was nonetheless a great honor). Strikingly, Hegel was passed over, and not only that: One of the leading intellectuals in Germany, an intellectual celebrity in Berlin, had been ignored very shortly after the large and boisterous celebration of his birthday had been reported, which had angered the king.[52] His friends were appalled; Hegel himself must have been disappointed (even a bit), but he prudently kept quiet about the matter. The attacks on Hegel, however, did not let up. The Cousin affair, the Gans affair, the "counter-Academy," Hegel's own defiant, self-assured, sarcastic style – all this was simply too much for the conservatives in Berlin. Even those who did not like Hegel personally began to become worried about the passions that were boiling around him. August Boeckh, the classicist at Berlin and friend of Schleiermacher and Savigny, noted by August 1827 that Hegel "was being attacked from all sides, and indeed in a impertinent and unjust way, since he is just now starting to moderate himself . . . the people who are taking sides against him are overcome by a blind passion that knows no bounds . . . that has to do only with [Hegel's] personality."[53] And it was surely all the more vexing to Hegel's detractors that even as the atmosphere was heating up around Hegel, his own celebrity just continued to rise. Even autograph seekers were now writing to him asking for some specimen of his writing.[54]

As Hegel's birthday approached, his doctor advised him to visit a spa for his health, thus giving Hegel an excuse to be away from Berlin so that his friends could not "surprise" him again with a large celebration of his birthday. He wrote to Altenstein in June asking for money to finance a trip, and, as usual, Altenstein procured 300 Thalers to underwrite the enterprise. Hegel then wrote to Cousin, mentioning that he would like to visit Paris but that he did not think he could swing the necessary money for the trip; and Cousin replied in July asking Hegel to come visit him in Paris. This was more than just a welcome invitation; Paris was obviously a place that Hegel, with his intense interest in the Revolution and in all things French, would have loved to visit. The arrangements were finalized, and in the middle of August, Hegel set out for Paris.

The trip was in its usual way terribly uncomfortable, but Hegel made the best of it, stopping off in Halle to see his former student, F. W. Hinrichs, and stopping off to see other friends along the way, including his good friend the banker Joseph Mendelssohn, who had a large estate outside of Koblenz. Mendelssohn, born in 1770 like Hegel, was the son of the philosopher Moses Mendelssohn and the uncle of the composer Felix Mendelssohn-Bartholdy, who was later to study aesthetics with Hegel; he showed Hegel the local sights, and Hegel, ever the happy tourist and for once enjoying himself in high bourgeois surroundings, clearly enjoyed himself. From there, Hegel traveled to Trier, and managed to indulge in one of his long-standing interests, namely, drinking very good Mosel wine. But however much Hegel enjoyed being places, getting there was getting to be vexing for the fifty-seven-year-old philosopher: He told Marie, "The bodily fatigues are insignificant, but the spiritual fatigue consists in the lack of doing any work and in a lack of conversation with you that's been exchanged for conversation with meaningless company."[55]

His spirits immediately picked up after crossing the border to France and getting under way from Metz to Paris. The coach passed through important sites of the French Revolution, even going through Valmy, and Hegel could see from the coach the famous windmills where the French revolutionary army had routed the combined German forces in 1792. All of this revived, as he said, "memories of my youth, when I took the greatest interest in all this."[56] (He also, of course, stopped off to sample champagne on the way.) On September 2, Hegel arrived in Paris around 10:00 A.M. and checked into his lodgings (the Hôtel des Princes), which he discovered to be too expensive for his budget, and, after having looked up Cousin and begun his preliminary sightseeing, transferred himself to another, more suitable set of lodgings, the Hôtel Empereur Joseph II (at the corner of Rue Tournon and Rue Vaugirard, directly across from the Luxembourg Gardens).

Hegel as Parisian Tourist

Like almost all first visitors to Paris, Hegel was simply overwhelmed and enchanted. It is unclear what high expectations he had of Paris, but it is clear that the city surpassed them. The magnificence, the beauty, the wealth, and the cosmopolitan hustle and bustle fully captivated his imagination. Everything in Berlin paled before Paris; the Parisian buildings were grander, everything was in better shape, and, he noted, each faculty at the university even had its very own *palais*, which was itself as large as the single *palais* in Berlin that served for the whole university! The shops were grander, larger, and there were more of them; the café life was more vibrant – the *Café des Ambassadeurs* and the *Café de L'Aurore* were like the pub *Zelten* in Berlin "only there were ten times as many people" there and the crowds were more mixed.[57] One can, Hegel noted with great admiration, read all newspapers from everywhere in the cafés for only a pittance; the churches were grand, the libraries along with the various collections of art and of natural history were simply breathtaking, the people were industrious and honest, and the Louvre was simply incomparable. The cultural life of the city was an abundance of riches. I am, he wrote to Marie on his arrival, now in the "capital of the civilized world."[58]

Just as he had been in Holland, he was also struck by the sheer wealth of Paris as contrasted with what seemed like much more provincial Berlin. As he noted to Marie, "I especially wished you could see the *Palais Royal*, the Paris within Paris. The infinite number of boutiques, the abundance of merchandise, the most beautiful jewelry and costume jewelry shops fill one with astonishment. But every street is embellished with the same overabundance and splendor. Everything is available everywhere."[59] In Paris, everything was more spacious, more comfortable, and more elegant than in Berlin.

He also took great interest in the offerings in the various theaters in Paris. He was even able to see the great English actor Charles Kemble, and the legendary Irish actress Henrietta Smithson, perform Shakespeare at the newly opened English Theater in Paris; he followed the plays by reading along in the English editions he had procured, although it did seem to him that the actors were speaking rather fast. He was certainly not impressed with British methods of acting; they seemed too melodramatic – involving too much "growling" and "grimacing," as he put it – to be enjoyable; Hegel also remarked that it was "amazing how they [the British] botch Shakespeare," a common sentiment among the Romantic Germans and interesting for the fact that Hegel expressed it in that context; after all, only one year later he was chiding Ludwig Tieck in print for expressing very much that same view – "the English, one would think, understand their Shakespeare; they would at the least severely ridicule the petit bourgeois narrow-minded obscurity of the continent if we were . . . to elevate our studies above their esteem for their poet."[60]

He was also able to take in the French theater – he was not much impressed with much of it, but he did claim, after seeing Molière's *Tartuffe*, finally to understand why that play was a comedy and not a farce – and he went to a number of concerts and opera performances, some of which he found inferior to Vienna – but then who was he to complain amid such a surplus of cultural riches? (He was, however, puzzled why the Parisian audience would applaud even in those cases when it seemed to him clear that the cast did not deserve it.)[61] But in general the Parisian French presented a model of what civilized, modern life was supposed to be. They did not, for example, find much at stake in what Hegel described as "the idiotic German honor of having spoken with so-and-so"; it just was not done, and so much the better, he thought. The French even seemed to be able to express their emotions more calmly and with more definiteness than "we [Germans]," something he particularly recommended to Marie: "How often do I tell you that you should state the matter without such sensitivity," he wrote, adding as if to remove the potential rebuke from that remark, "yet your vivacity is often quite attractive on you."[62] When Marie observed in a letter to him that there much less fire in his tone than when he wrote from Vienna, Hegel replied by noting that he was by no means any the less enthusiastic; Paris was simply more overwhelming, there was simply too much to see and do, and one would need much more time really to take it all in.[63]

Hegel also had his ups and downs as a foreign tourist in Paris. For all its pleasures, the city seemed maybe a bit too disorderly, perhaps partaking of a little too much hustle and bustle for his more orderly, Württemberg-Berlin tastes. (He ruefully noted to Marie that the disorder of the Revolution, as far as he could see, was "still in full swing" in Paris.)[64] Hegel also had his own bit of trouble with the Parisian cuisine and the Parisian culinary mores. Hegel found it difficult to come to terms with the fact that Parisians such as Cousin liked to eat around 5:00 in the afternoon, whereas he ("like all rational Germans," he said ironically) preferred eating between 1:00 and 2:00 P.M. Moreover, his French vocabulary, so well suited to reading Montesquieu and Rousseau, completely failed him when it came to deciphering the French menus he encountered. When he and Cousin ate together (which at first was every day), Cousin took care of the ordering, but, as he complained, "if I am alone I do not know what the enormous list on the menu means."[65] (Who knows what Hegel accidentally found himself eating?) Hegel extricated himself from his culinary dilemma by finding a table d'hôte that had everything out on display so he could see what he was getting. Finally, Parisian food and libation caught up with him, and he contracted a bad case of indigestion that lasted at least a week; he squarely blamed it on the Seine water or on the Parisian way of life (by which he meant Parisian cooking). After his week-long bout with indigestion, Hegel decided to play it safe; he managed to find a table d'hôte that had German cooking and he made that his preferred haunt for the rest of his stay. Hegel, the gastronome and Francophile, loved Paris but found its Gallic cuisine to have bested him.

But there were many other things to take his mind off his gurgling stomach. He visited the libraries and met with local scholars, and although he used his Parisian stay for "uplift" (he studied the art, read books, visited libraries, and gathered impressions that he would later work into his lectures on aesthetics), he also satisfied his tourist instincts, even noting that he had to put up with the way Cousin "made fun of him" when he "saw and found noteworthy to see what the conscience of a traveler and the *Manuel des Etrangers*" told him to see.[66] He went to Versailles; he very much liked the buildings and grounds but found the gardens too "old French" to be of much interest, preferring the more English gardens of the Trianon. He went to Montmarte and admired the view. More memorably, he went to visit Rousseau's old haven at the Eremitage in Montmorency, where Rousseau had written so many of his famous works; to get there, Hegel had to ride a donkey, but, as far as Hegel was concerned, a trip on a donkey in the sun was worth it to see a Rousseau site, since such a place was, after all, a homage to his youth; he even proudly noted that he saw on the grounds a rose bush allegedly planted by Rousseau. He also attended a meeting of the French Academy of Sciences, where he met and spoke with some influential scholars, and he visited the palace of the Chambre de Députés (the old Bourbon palace transformed into the National Assembly during the Revolution). He visited with special interest the various sites associated with the Revolution, and he also visited the various modern buildings that Napoleon had erected, obviously to get some grasp on what kind of rational rebuilding the Revolution and the man who completed it had put in place. He visited the modern *abattoir* (slaughterhouse) that Napoleon had erected to rid of the city of the slaughterhouses in the middle of the city, which until then had occupied prominent places on one of the main roads (the Quai) beside the river; he visited the stock exchange that Napoleon had erected ("What a temple," Hegel exclaimed, a clear mark of his modernizing sensibility and his sense that the stock exchange was the new "sacred" site of modern society); he visited these and other modern sites that "Paris still owes Napoleon – like a hundred other great things."[67]

Hegel even got himself into an incident which would have been terribly embarrassing if he had actually realized what was going on (although, as far as we know, he never found out the details). Hegel's colleague Friedrich von Raumer (the historian) was visiting Paris at the same time as Hegel, and both von Raumer and Hegel had a reputation in Berlin as great habitués of the theater. After going to a play featuring the famous French actress Anne Françoise Mars (another favorite of Napoleon's), Hegel learned that von Raumer had in fact met Mademoiselle Mars, and when von Raumer waxed enthusiastically to Hegel about Mademoiselle Mars, Hegel, quite accustomed to being on a personal basis with such actresses as Henriette Sontag and Anna Milder-Hauptmann in Berlin, became quite excited about meeting her. Von Raumer ventured that he should ask Cousin to arrange a meeting with Mars. According to von Raumer (who made this known only after Hegel's death), Cousin, quite agitated, then came to him and explained that Hegel, with his "personality and manner of speaking," would only invite members of the French theatrical world to make fun of both of them. Von Raumer confessed to having given Hegel the idea in the first place and suggested (on his account of the affair) that Cousin explain to Hegel that he (von Raumer) was a man of notorious bad taste, that meeting Mademoiselle Mars simply was not worth it, and that there were other actresses and theatrical people who were much more interesting to meet but who were unfortunately not in town at the moment. If this was indeed the ruse that von Raumer claimed it was, it worked. Hegel wrote to his wife somewhat disdainfully of von Raumer's attentions to Mars, noting that "Raumer has an audience today at noon with Mademoiselle Mars; he just has to be with all actresses; Cousin finds it ludicrous to go to see her – he would have taken me to [François-Joseph] Talma or Mde. Pasta were they still here."[68]

Hegel and the French Liberals

His interest in the Revolution and visiting its sites also got him to read François Auguste Marie Mignet's *Histoire de la Révolution française jusqu'en 1814*, which had been published in 1824; Hegel described Mignet's history of the Revolution as "currently the best history" of the subject.[69] Around September 29, he shared a meal with Cousin, Mignet, and others (among them Adolphe Thiers, another liberal antirestoration historian, later to have a more conservative and legendary political career, and who, in 1871, after crushing the Paris Commune, became the president of the French Republic). Mignet (who was about the same age as Gans) belonged to the circle of antirestoration liberals in France who saw the Revolution through Sieyès' eyes: 1789 had been a victory for the Third Estate, and that victory could simply not be undone. The Revolution, as Mignet presented it, was a decisive watershed, a historical break which had made it impossible to "restore" the pre-revolutionary order of things; the aristocracy and nobility now had to fit themselves into the modern world created by the Third Estate of political freedom, civil equality, and careers open to talent; there was simply no going back to the age of absolute monarchy and aristocracy as the ruling powers. In Mignet's interpretation, the years of Robespierre were not to be disavowed but only to be understood as historically necessary stages of the Revolution that were nonetheless not essential to its real meaning, which was to be found in the triumph of the Third Estate in 1789 and in the end result of constitutional monarchy toward which it was progressing (and which in principle it had already reached).

To make this point, Mignet and those who shared his view turned (as had an earlier generation of French revolutionaries) to Britain as a model for how the Revolution was to proceed. In fact, Mignet's history tended to see the French Revolution as necessarily progressing through

the same stages as the earlier British upheaval: the beheading of the
king, followed by anarchy and then dictatorship, which was succeeded
and consummated by a regime of constitutional monarchy with representative government after a change of dynasties had been effected.[70]
The end result of both the English and French revolutions was emphatically not democracy (rule by the "multitude," as Mignet had put
it, and which he had seen as an unfortunate although necessary phase
of the Revolution around 1793) but constitutional monarchical rule in
which the idea of the career open to talent ruled and only those who
had the talent, the "enlightened," were to rule, for they were the ones
who were, in Mignet's words, "alone qualified to control [the force and
power of the state] because they alone had the intelligence necessary for
the control of government"; the goal of such a regime was, as Mignet
put it, to "let all share in the rights when they are capable of gaining
them."[71] The rule of the "multitude" had only been necessary in those
days when the Revolution was under attack from other countries, but it
had already run its historical course. In Mignet's analysis, what had
emerged from the "anarchy and despotism" of the Revolution was that
"the old society was destroyed during the Revolution, and the new one
established under the empire."[72]

For Mignet and other French liberals of that circle, a continental
interpretation of the English experience was crucial to figuring out how
one could institutionalize the freedom evoked and promised by the
Revolution, and Hegel, to a large extent, shared that view. Hegel's
friend Varnhagen von Ense, with whom he shared many confidences,
spoke at this same period about how Prussian officials thought they had
in Hegel a "legitimizing" and fully "Prussian" philosophy but how they
had radically failed to discern Hegel's own deep "predilection for England," his admiration of the "English life of freedom," which he
combined with his "sympathy for the French Revolution" and his full
commitment to constitutional government.[73] (Hegel's devotion to the
Revolution also appeared in some of his own personal excerpts, done
some time in 1827, from Walter Scott's *Life of Napoleon*; Scott viewed
the Revolution as a "divine punishment" for France's and Europe's
sins; Hegel scathingly remarked that his views only consisted of "arrogant phrases," and that Scott seemed to be "unacquainted with the
characteristic principles that demarcate the essence of the Revolution
and give them their almost immeasurable power over the minds of

people," concluding his remarks with (in reference to Scott) the exclamation, "insipid mind!"[74]

Varnhagen's personal analysis of Hegel's position was borne out in Hegel's appreciation of Mignet, who, coming from a much different direction, had reached conclusions very similar to Hegel's (although for very different reasons). That Hegel thought Mignet's own antirestoration history (which later generations of historians were to dismiss as more of a political broadside than real history) was the "best" currently available is extremely good evidence for what Hegel's views in 1827 about the Revolution, the restoration, and the reform movement actually were; his endorsement of Mignet is clearly evidence for his own prore-form attitudes. In Mignet's history, Hegel found his own deep commitment to a certain interpretation of the ideal of 1789 and to the reform movement affirmed; and, given the ways in which Mignet's interpretation neatly dovetailed with Hegel's own understanding of the necessary progression of modern life and the role of the Revolution in it – with the idea that "everything that is rational must be," as he had put it to Heine – it is fully intelligible that Hegel both highly valued Mignet's history and wanted to meet him while in Paris.

In 1827, in the "capital of the civilized world," Hegel happily found a circle of like-minded, well-placed reformers at work in the capital of the Revolution itself, for whom something like Hegel's own interpretation of the spirit of 1789 still ruled. It is hard to imagine what Hegel could have found more satisfying. In some sense, Hegel felt that in Paris, the city of the Revolution and the birth of modern life, of material abundance and high culture, he was finally *home*, much more, oddly enough, than when he was in German-speaking Vienna. "When I return," he teasingly wrote to Marie, "we shall speak nothing but French."[75]

Being surrounded by all these up-and-coming historians, politicians, and intellectuals – most of whom were Gans's age or younger, and many of whom knew Gans – only made Hegel sense what he took to be his old age all the more and, at the same time, it completely revivified him. In one of his letters, he noted that Immanuel wanted to know why had gotten sick, so he told Marie to tell him that "I am no longer such a spring chicken as he is, I am rather an old father, and I especially wish for an old age and health in order to see him and his brother flourish further and to do my bit to contribute to it."[76] The trip to Paris was an affirmation of so much of what he had wanted and for which he had worked; it seemed both to reanimate his faith in the progress that he himself had termed "necessary" and to mark out all the more clearly the rise of a new generation that had never experienced the ancien régime themselves, a generation for which he was to be one of the intellectual leaders. It must have struck him that Cousin, who, although born in 1792, was nonetheless older than the young intellectuals now making waves in Paris, but that even Cousin was (like Hegel himself) an embodiment of the "career open to talent" and was the intellectual leader of that circle of younger intellectuals. Hegel could easily see himself as playing Cousin's role back in Berlin.[77] In Paris, Hegel recaptured his youth; he would be an elder leader of the youthful wing of reform (represented by Gans) in Berlin.

Returning Home

Cousin, in an act expressing gratitude for Hegel's courage in Berlin, graciously offered to accompany him to Cologne, an offer that Hegel eagerly accepted. Travel was odious; it was exhausting and, most of all, boring; having Cousin along would make part of the trip at least bearable. They left Paris on October 2 and traveled to Brussels, where Hegel looked up van Ghert; the van Ghert family remarked to him how much better he looked than when he had last visited them. He and Cousin (probably at van Ghert's suggestion) visited and inspected the buildings at the Catholic university at Louvain; making reference to the troubles he had encountered in the last year with religious issues, he noted to Marie, "We have looked these universities over as a prospective resting place in case the clerics in Berlin spoil *Kupfergraben* for me. The Curia in Rome would in any event be a more honorable adversary than the misery of that miserable clerical stew in Berlin."[78] Although van Ghert, of course, would have loved to bring Hegel as a professor to any of the universities under his control – he was already at work trying to establish a Hegelian form of modernized Catholicism in the Netherlands – Hegel was probably not serious about any of this. His distaste for Catholicism had only been reawakened by the charges brought against him in 1826 by the Catholics in Berlin; his beloved trip to Paris, which at the time was governed by an old alliance of ultra-royalists and conservative Catholics, probably just reminded him of all his former troubles with the Catholics in Bavaria. If he ever had any thought of forgetting those troubles, he had recently been reminded of them when a former student, Issak Rust, wrote in March 1827 to tell him about how his (Rust's) Hegelian book on philosophy and Christianity had been described in a review in the *Bayrische Literaturzeitung für katholische Religionslehrer* (*Bavarian Literary Journal for Catholic Religion Teachers*) as an example of "Hegelian pantheism," and to inform him that he, Rust, had been labeled as an adherent of Hegel's "new, baneful philosophy."[79]

Hegel's prickly feelings about Catholicism came to the fore when he and Cousin finally reached Cologne. As Cousin remembered the scene, they approached the cathedral and noticed the usual street vendors outside the building selling sacred medals and other religious items that even Cousin himself described as "superstitious." Intensely irritated by that assemblage of peddlers of religious items, Hegel exclaimed to Cousin, "Here's your Catholic religion and the sights it offers us! Will I die before I see all this perish?"[80] Cousin took issue with him, claiming that although Christianity was simultaneously both a "religion of the masses" and the "religion of the philosophers," it ought not be viewed only from the "heights to which we have elevated Saint Augustine, Saint Anselm, Saint Thomas and Bossuet"; Hegel, although nominally agreeing with Cousin's argument, was obviously not terribly moved by it. He remained, Cousin later concluded, profoundly a man of the eighteenth century, seeing himself as working for its goals (a view that Hegel vis-à-vis his relation to Kant might not have disputed). This, however, did not in any way dampen Hegel's feelings for Cousin; he remarked to Marie that he had grown "even more fond" of Cousin, and that he immensely enjoyed their conversations amid much eating (of oysters) and drinking (of Mosel wine).[81]

After parting from Cousin, Hegel stopped in Aachen, where he once again was able to sit on Charlemagne's throne (and no doubt felt just as satisfied the second time). He then set off for Weimar (complaining along the way about how the food was no longer as good as it was in France or the Netherlands), where he visited Goethe. His friend from Berlin, Zelter, was already there, and Hegel joined Goethe, Zelter, and others for a dinner with the aging duke of Weimar at Goethe's house; the next day, he, Zelter, and other parties had lunch with Goethe. Hegel, who idolized Goethe as one of the most significant figures of his youth and who clearly treasured his friendship with the great man, talked with him at length of how things stood in Paris. (Hegel's own account of that conversation differed from that of Goethe's daughter-in-law, who was also present. Hegel noted that Goethe was very interested in what Hegel had to say about current affairs in Paris, and even virtually required Hegel to tell him; Goethe's daughter-in-law, on the other hand, seemed to think that the mysterious guest – she did not know it was Hegel – simply failed to notice that he was doing all the talking.)[82] But, in Hegel's defense, Goethe's erstwhile secretary, Eckermann, noted how much Goethe esteemed Hegel – partly, still, no doubt, for Hegel's defense of his theory of color – and even Goethe himself later noted how interesting he found Hegel's descriptions of the Parisian scene;[83] but Goethe was always more critical of and distant from Hegel than was Hegel vis-à-vis Goethe. Hegel felt he had grown up with Goethe and always related to him as the man who had been his youthful hero; Goethe, on the other hand, was never personally attracted to Hegel's philosophy and even made that clear to friends, however much he appreciated Hegel as an individual and an intellectual and valued (as Eckermann testified) Hegel's talents as a critic of modern literature.[84]

During his visit to Weimar, Hegel was also able to take in the local scenery with his good friend from Berlin, Zelter, and to walk once more along the "old, familiar paths of twenty-five years ago."[85] Probably under Zelter's prodding, he decided to spring for the extra money and rent a private coach together with Zelter for the trip back to Berlin. He rationalized this act of extravagance (at least for a Swabian like himself) to Marie by explaining that for himself and Zelter, being as they were "old men," the "comfort" of a rental coach "is agreeable and useful" and worth the extra cost.[86] The trip back, however, proved not so agreeable to Zelter; Hegel was very anxious to get home, and (probably because he was spending so much extra money) complained incessantly about the coach, the horses, the inns, and everything else along the way; he lost his hat, and he demanded that the coach, as Zelter put it, be "shut tight like an old wine cellar." When Zelter, tired of it all, finally said enough was enough, Hegel fell into a pout for the rest of the journey.[87] But both Zelter and Goethe were more amused than bothered by Hegel's uncharacteristic fall from conviviality. Goethe observed with some whimsy that Hegel, the great modern thinker, seemed to be only confirming the old prejudices about philosophers, that "these gentlemen, who take themselves to have command of God, the soul, the world (and nobody has any conception of what those are supposed to mean) are nonetheless not equipped for the ups and downs of the most ordinary days."[88]

Hegel may have been cranky on his trip from Weimar to Berlin, but, animated and affirmed by his visit to Paris, he quickly reverted to his old self. One of his students observed that "one had to have sat at Hegel's feet before and after that trip to have noticed how . . . [it] brought about a rejuvenation of the fifty-seven year old" philosopher.[89] Hegel came back from Paris seeing himself more and more as the leader of a school and as the elder statesman of a group of young intellectuals who were going to push through the reform movement in Germany – and perhaps in the Netherlands, under van Ghert, and in France, under Cousin; his trip to Paris had proved him *right*. For Hegel's personality in the last years of his life, those items stirred together were always a dangerous combination.

Thinking through Modern Life: Nature, Religion, Art, and the Absolute

The Philosophy of Nature

The Motivations for the Philosophy of Nature

HEGEL LECTURED on the "philosophy of nature" several times in his Berlin period, using his *Encyclopedia of the Philosophical Sciences* as his basis and relying on his extensive notes on the subject to give long expositions on the themes treated otherwise quite sparsely in his textbook. His own interest in the "philosophy of nature" went back to his schoolboy days in Stuttgart, where (according to his sister) physics and mathematics were among his favorite subjects. At Tübingen he attended lectures on physics, and he read extensively, wrote extensively, and lectured on topics in the "philosophy of nature" during his years in Jena. Although he never published anything on it outside of his "habilitation" thesis on the orbits of the planets and in the numbered sections of the *Encyclopedia*, the topic itself was clearly something near and dear to his heart. The extensive lecture notes and student notes compiled by his students after his death and published as "additions" to the numbered paragraphs of the *Encyclopedia* in the volume in his collected works display a wide-ranging interest and erudition regarding topics in physics, optics, chemistry, geology, biology, and the like – yet another testament to Hegel's prodigious energy and intellectual curiosity.

Although he invested a great deal of time and energy into developing his "philosophy of nature," it was also unfortunately the least successful of all his ventures. Ignored for the most part in his own time (despite his own high intellectual standing), it fell into complete disrepute immediately after his death and has rarely been looked at since by anybody other than dedicated Hegel scholars.

Hegel clearly thought, however, that the "philosophy of nature" was crucial to his whole project. If a comprehensive view of the modern world was to be constructed, there had to be an understanding of how we as free agents fit into the natural world as that world was described and explained by modern science. That particular problem was especially acute for those working in post-Kantian philosophy, since Kant's own resolution of the issue – through his distinction of the world as an appearing, causally determined unity and the world regarded as composed of unknowable things-in-themselves, and the practical necessity of regarding ourselves as free – had been accepted by virtually no post-Kantian thinker at all. Early on in his career, Hegel had become convinced that Schelling's great insight had been correct, that for the idealist project to work, one had to show that nature was such that it had room in it for the kinds of free beings that we were.

In that light, Hegel also found particularly disturbing two different conceptions at work in the milieu of his time. On the one hand, he could not abide the popular mystical conceptions of nature that relied on religious or pseudo-religious conceptions to develop a conception of nature that put it outside the realm of rational inquiry; to him, that represented both a restoration of premodern dogmatism and a possibly dangerous threat to the modern social order, since it was clear that since the old feudal social and political order could not underwrite itself by reason, the temptations to claim that the old order rested therefore on "nature" were immense, and an irrational conception of nature just might be the thing to help that reactionary cause along. On the other hand, he did not think that the post-Enlightenment mechanistic conception of nature was itself feasible as the whole story about nature; even Kant had seen that such a conception was incompatible with our necessary sense of ourselves as free, rational agents. Yet modern natural science seemed to demand such a view of nature (or so Kant had famously argued in his first *Critique*); if one was not to reject modern science therefore or make it subordinate to the quasi-mystical obscurantism of the followers of Romantic *Naturphilosophie*, one had to construct something that was neither mystical nor "Enlightenment" in its outlook.

For his mature philosophy of nature, Hegel brought the basic conceptions of his Nuremberg *Logic* into play. According to that scheme, in thinking rationally about "being" at all, we logically commit ourselves to the claim that nature contains the three following structures. First, we are committed to the view that nature must have mechanical systems in it, namely, those whose explanations come from their external interactions with each other; more determinate ideas, such as "force" and "gravitation," are only specifications of this abstract form of "externality," of explaining the determinateness of individual things in terms of their interaction with other individual things that are "external" to them; and the paradigm of such "externality" of "mechanical" systems is the planetary system. Second, it must have "chemical" systems in it, namely, a conception of some things as having a natural "affinity" for each other, of their being drawn toward each other into various combinations; more particular explanations in the science of chemistry only explain how this affinity comes about and what kinds of affinities there are. Third, it must also have some conception of "living systems," of those whose activities are to some extent self-directed, whose elements are not "external" but "organic," in the sense that the determination of what they are (hearts, livers, lungs) depends on our seeing them as fulfilling certain functions and purposes. In addition to all of these, nature must have some place in it for the self-directing, norm-governed creatures that we as humans are, for the idea of an organism that gives itself laws instead of merely following them.

Hegel's "philosophy of nature" thus built on Kant's own investigations into the a priori construction of matter and Schelling's ebullient extension of that program. We cannot gather all our knowledge of nature from experience; we are already committed to a prior idea of nature in its totality by virtue of our commitment to our view of ourselves as rational beings; we must, that is, have a view of nature as a whole to guide whatever investigations we pursue of it, and that prior idea of nature as a whole, if it is to be rational, commits us to the claim that nature can be coherently understood as a whole that includes mechanical, chemical, and living systems within itself.

There were also personal and professional reasons for Hegel vigorously to pursue the "philosophy of nature." When Hegel came to Berlin, the dominant strains in German philosophy had to do with those people influenced by his old rival Fries (who endorsed a more or less mechanistic view of nature) and an even larger group who had constructed a shadowy form of Romantic *Naturphilosophie* on the basis of Schelling's early reflections on the topic. The natural scientists of Germany quite rightfully viewed that latter form of *Naturphilosophie* with complete disdain, and it was therefore crucial for Hegel to be able to show that he was not committed to that debased form of Schellingian thought. It was also the case that the natural scientists were in the process of making a play to become the dominant faculty at the university and to arrogate to themselves the exclusive authority to interpret nature for the modern world; this was something that Hegel resisted as strongly as he could, since he thought it undermined the whole thrust of the modern university, with philosophy at its core and *Bildung* as its central ideal. He even opened his Berlin lectures on the "philosophy of nature" by reminding his audience that "philosophy must constitute the indispensable introduction and foundation for *all further* scientific education and *professional study*," even as he also bemoaned how philosophy was falling into disfavor in this regard.[1]

Hegel thus needed, so he thought, to construct a more or less a priori conception of nature that would precede any empirical investigation of it; and for that conception of nature to be properly modern, it had to eschew any religious or old-fashioned metaphysical explanation of its phenomena – it could not, for example, rely on something like the argument from God's design to have the structures that it did – and it had to be more or less consistent with what modern natural science (as it stood in the early nineteenth century) said of it. That is, it had to see what could be developed out of a conception of nature – what followed from the "Idea" of nature, as Hegel put it – that was self-contained, developing within itself (requiring, that is, no extra-natural or supernatural explanations), that was consistent with the scientific description of it, and that had a place in it for the kinds of agents who constructed those explanations of it. Hegel tried, that is, to combine the ordinary experience of nature, the poetic descriptions and evocations of nature, and the modern natural scientific explanations of nature into one overall conception of nature that would be required of modern, free, rational agents.

In all this, the relation between his "philosophy of nature" and the natural sciences was clearly the touchy point. Hegel was simply not willing to yield any pride of place to the natural sciences with regard to the authority to interpret the world, but he was also by no means willing or inclined to write off the natural sciences merely as illusions or as distortions of God's creation (as some of the Romantic followers of *Naturphilosophie* tended to do). He put it bluntly: "Not only must philosophy be in agreement with our empirical knowledge of nature, but the *origin* and *formation* of the philosophy of nature presupposes and is conditioned by empirical physics" – to which, however, he immediately added the qualification, "However, the course of a science's origin and the preliminaries of its construction are one thing, while the science itself is another. In the latter, the former can no longer appear as the foundation of the science; here, the foundation must be the necessity of the concept."[2] The empirical sciences are only, in Hegel's terminology, "finite" in that they study the ways and formulate the laws through which natural ("finite," non–self-determining) objects condition each other; they cannot claim the authority to study nature as a whole, which is to study it in terms of its "Idea," the structure of the "space of reasons" in general. We can make judgments about nature only in terms of orienting ourselves in terms of that whole, and the sciences cannot nondogmatically make any claim to formulate that whole – that would be exclusively the province of a (post-Kantian) metaphysics of nature. Or, as he put it, "it is because the method of physics does not satisfy the concept that we have to go further," which consists in part in taking "the material which physics has prepared for [philosophy] empirically, at the point to which physics has brought it, and reconstitute it so that experience is not its final warrant and base."[3] Thus, rather than explore the methods and rationality of natural science, Hegel preferred instead to look at the more basic conception of nature itself that underlies all scientific investigation in the first place; for those reasons, Hegel was much more interested in constructing a "philosophy of nature" than in anything like a "philosophy of science."

Mechanics (contra Newton)

Hegel's discussions in his "philosophy of nature" range through multifarious expositions of, for example, general issues in mechanics, optics, and biology to specific discussions of, for example, the formation of granite, disturbances in the weather, and the nature of fevers. The whole panoply must be left to one side here; only the very general structure of Hegel's thoughts on the "philosophy of nature" can be given here; and a look at how Hegel's thoughts changed as he developed his philosophy of nature must, alas, also be neglected here.

Hegel begins his "philosophy of nature" with a discussion of mechanics and, coupled with a defense of Kepler's theories, a sharp rejection of Newtonianism. Hegel's animus against Newton is directed mainly at what he sees as the purely mechanical outlook contained in Newton's works. Nature cannot, so Hegel wanted to argue, be conceived purely as a mechanical system; despite his distaste for the Romantics, Hegel shared with them the view that we had to see the universe in terms of the metaphor of an "organism" and not in terms of the metaphor of a "machine." Hegel thus entered into what ultimately amounted to a losing battle with the Newtonians about the self-sufficiency of Newtonian explanations.[4] Hegel's quarrel against the Newtonians basically had to do with his view that they claimed to be able to explain the movements of the planetary system mechanically in terms of a number of irreducible elementary (and therefore unexplained) forces; he, on the other hand, argued that the whole conception of "force" itself had to be traced back to more "logical" conceptions of attraction and repulsion (building on Kant's and Schelling's arguments to that effect). Since, so Hegel thought (following Kant), "true motion" can only be ascertained by reference to an *ideal* common center of mass, the whole construction of the elementary forces rests on the a priori conception of what this common center of mass could be, and that itself rests on an a priori understanding of the way in which these ideas can be constructed mathematically. We thus must think of such mechanical systems as "striving" to reach this ideal common center, even though this striving is not in any sense at all conscious, the parts do not "aim" at it, and even though we cannot empirically determine where, as it were, this center would be. However, once we begin thinking in those terms, Hegel argued, we find ourselves no longer simply doing Newtonian mechanics but instead involved in something like Kant's antinomies, that is, caught in the contradictions that characterize thought when it tries to apply such "finite" distinctions to the totality, the "Idea," when it leaves the realm of individual investigation and ventures into metaphysics.

In this light, Hegel tried to show that in doing mechanics, we begin with a spatial point, which as it becomes elaborated is characterized as both spatial and nonspatial; and that we dislodge that elemental contra-

diction by thinking of the point as becoming "other" than itself in
further points (as constructing a "line"). From that original unity of
points and lines, Hegel then claims to derive the unity of both spatial
and temporal divisions of such "points," which in turn have their unity
further specified in the concept of a "place," which itself then requires
a concept of "matter," whose essential feature is that of "weight," to
fill it. Matter, Hegel argued, is therefore just our abstract, ideal conception of what it means to be at a spatio-temporal "place"; and these are
all rational, a priori conceptions whose justification lies in their being
necessary components of a rational view of nature as a whole. They are
not fictions, nor are they empirically determined; rather, all empirical
investigation presupposes them. Newtonians, so Hegel thought, simply
ignore this and claim to have derived these concepts from mathematics
or from induction, something he thinks simply begs the question of
what constitutes our prior grasp of these conceptions.

Hegel also tried to show (in retrospect, without much success) that
some of the Newtonian mathematical derivations of the basic laws of
mechanics fail, and that their failure is explained precisely by both the
mechanical worldview underlying Newtonianism and by Newtonianism's commitment to there being a plurality of basic forces instead of a
commitment to understanding the necessity of deriving all those forces
from the requirements of a more general, unitary conception of nature.
That more general conception of nature, in turn, requires us to think of
the planetary system not as a purely mechanical system but as something held together by an ideal striving for a "middle point" of mass.
In that respect, Hegel simply drew out some of the conclusions he had
already reached in his *Logic*.

Physics

In the development of the philosophy of nature, Hegel moved from
"mechanics" to "physics," which he distinguished (as many still did in
the fluid situation in which physics found itself in Germany in the early
nineteenth century) in terms of its being more of an empirical science
as opposed to the strictly nonempirical, mathematical inquires of "mechanics." Hegel's arguments there have a kind of charming quaintness
to them (in the sense that virtually none of his views on any of the
subjects managed to hold their own). Light, he thinks, is the way in

which matter (which essentially possesses weight) manifests itself to an other as "weightless," as "simple being-external-to-itself," the way, that is, in which matter manifests itself to living creatures inhabiting that same world.[5] As such, light is only artificially divisible, and the idea that light is a bundle of particles or "discrete, simple rays" is, Hegel says, another one of those "barbarous categories for whose prevalence in physics Newton is chiefly responsible."[6] This conception of light, Hegel argued, is more basic and fundamental than any of the more empirical determinations of light obtained in physical investigation, and no physical investigation of things can undermine the sense that light is fundamentally the indivisible *manifestation* of matter to us as embodied beings.

The earth is the point at which light and weight come together, and it itself should be viewed as an interconnected whole constituted out of a "meteorological process" of fire, water, and air, which together create the conditions for the kind of life that can ultimately give a rational account of those conditions themselves. The line of argument is intended to provide a nonmechanical explanation of how mechanics is itself possible; the planetary system "strives" for its center, which leads the matter in it to manifest itself to itself as light. Thus, the laws of gravitation serve not merely to govern matter in motion but to lay the foundations for a living earth. If those laws were different, life would not be possible; but the nature of those laws is written in the structure of things themselves that in itself forms part of the way in which rational agents must necessarily come to think of the natural world in which they live. (In one of his typically idiosyncratic asides in his lectures, Hegel noted that in providing the conditions for life, the earth thus avoids becoming a heavenly body that is purely crystalline, such as the moon, or purely water, such as a comet; it is instead the unity of crystal and water.)

Weightless light and weighted matter come together to form "specific gravity," cohesion ("a specific mode of the connection of the material parts"), sound, and heat. Each of these individualizes "abstract matter" in a more determinate way than does the "striving" for unity found in planetary systems, such that the full panoply found on the living earth is made possible; and heat tends to dissolve the matter which has been so individualized and make possible what Hegel calls the "meteorological process" that sustains life on earth. Quaint as these view are, it should be remembered that Hegel was not claiming to offer an argument about what *causes* what, not offering, that is, any kind of alternative to the empirical causal accounts offered by "physics"; instead, he claimed to be offering an account of what kind of view of nature as a whole (as "infinite," as "Idea") we are implicitly committed to when we try to make sense of ourselves as the kind of rational creatures that do empirical physics in the first place and try to understand how the nature studied by physics is also the nature in which we are free, rational agents.

The processes of individualization in specific gravity, cohesion, sound, and heat create, according to Hegel's speculative account, a more complex dynamic system, a whole called the "meteorological process," which makes up the totality of the earth as relatively self-contained, being driven by its own nonconscious "striving" to maintain the conditions under which life is possible. Hegel argues that our conception of nature as a whole, as concretized in terms of the way we as embodied agents are committed to thinking of ourselves not merely as minds with bodies but as embodied, historical forms of *Geist* inhabiting a planet on which there is differentiated life, commits us to thinking of that dynamic process as including opposites within itself that are not related purely mechanically (not related merely by the laws governing matter in motion) but in terms of deeper affinities for other things. (Hegel's account has a more than passing resemblance to some contemporary "ecological" conceptions of life on earth.) It is part of our elemental conception of nature that not everything in it tends to combine with everything else, and thus part of the overall conception of nature is that some things have a natural "affinity" for each other such that in their independent existence, they exhibit dispositions to unite with each other. Within the "meteorological process" that makes up the earth, there are thus the individual processes of magnetism, electricity, and the chemical processes; each represents the way in which some individual elements of the process tend toward union with each other without being pushed from outside (as in a purely mechanical system). The ancient Greeks, Hegel argues, correctly understood the "meteorological process" as thereby fundamentally involving the elements of fire (as the universal agent of destruction), water (as the mutable, neutral element), and air (as "that which is active, which sublates that which is determinate").[7]

In his own elaborate way, Hegel also argued in his lectures that "finite experimental physics" misunderstood what these elements were by virtue of the way in which their experiments necessarily removed these basic elements from the context of the ideal "whole" in which they play their role, and so, he rather quirkily claimed, "finite physics" could not fully explain lightning or heat and certainly could not explain rain; some physicists even thought wrongly, he further claimed, that the sun produces its heat by consuming hydrogen; and, of course, he famously defended Goethe's theory of color against the Newtonians. To underwrite his assertions on these topics, Hegel cited published instances of anomalies in various experiments in each of these fields. His views, however engaging and sometimes charming they may be, did not exactly help to convince the community of natural scientists that Hegel's philosophy of nature was worth taking seriously.

Life on Earth: Science and Religion

But his main point was that the mechanical view of nature was thus only a *part* of the view of nature that emerges from our embodied, earthbound conception of ourselves and nature; and by virtue of being committed to those views of nature, we are also committed, so Hegel argues, to a view of earth in terms of the way its processes sustain life. Life is the penultimate stage of a conception of dynamic natural processes that begins with the mechanical conception of bodies naturally constructing themselves around an ideal center of mass, and which in turn require a conception of a more complex meteorological process that involves dynamic systems of individuals bound in affinities with each other, each seeking an ideal "middle point" in its union with its "other"; life, though, is self-directing, and the living organism has its "middle point" within itself. As a complex meteorological process sustaining life, the earth must be seen itself as an organic whole, as something akin to life itself – "springs are the lungs and secretory glands for the earth's process of evaporation, so are volcanoes the earth's liver in that they represent the earth's self-heating-within-itself"[8] – even though the earth is not actually alive ("the meteorological process is not the life-process of the earth, although the earth is vivified by it; for this vivification is the real possibility of subjectivity emerging on the earth as a living being").[9]

Hegel took over from Schelling's *Naturphilosophie* a conception of the living organism as divided into three functions: sensibility, irritability, and reproduction.[10] The basic idea, as it was worked out in Hegel's formulation, was that the *concept* of a living organism implied that it had to have some way of obtaining information about the world in which it lived (sensibility), it had to have some way of achieving its ends (irritability), and it had to have some way of maintaining itself in its environment (reproduction). All empirical biological investigations, he thought, only served to discover the "finite" factual specifications of what organs and processes fulfilled those functions in what ways.

In the other systems of nature (the mechanical system of the planets and the meteorological process), the "principle" of the system induces individuals in the system to "strive" for their center (by being forced by outside causes, as in mechanical systems, or by their natural "affinity" for each other, particularly in "chemical" systems), but that "center" remains partially outside of the identity of the individuals involved. The "end" that the system serves is "external" to that system. In organisms, so it seems, the "center" is contained within each individual organism, since each organism is its own end – Hegel describes it in Kant's language as an end unto itself, a *Selbstzweck*; and the organism, as a self-maintaining unity, has therefore an "inwardness" of feeling that is lacking in the other systems. The other systems respond only quasi-teleologically to their environments, but the organism responds to its environment by virtue of registering that environment within itself (through sensibility) and adapting itself accordingly (through irritability and reproduction) in terms of its basic ends. The organism senses that it *needs* things, and, as Hegel puts it, "only what is living feels a *lack*."[11] The organism is not merely stimulated to act by its environment; it "takes it in" and responds accordingly.

As an individual plant or animal, the organism produces the totality of which it is a part by what Hegel calls the "process of the genus," the way in which the "whole" (the genus) reproduces itself solely in the reproductive activity of the individual members of the genus. Just as the organism is driven to reproduce itself in its daily commerce with its environment, it is also driven to reproduce the genus: as Hegel bluntly puts it, "The genus is therefore present in the individual as a straining against the inadequacy of its single actuality, as the urge to obtain its self-feeling in the other of its genus, to integrate itself through union with it and through this mediation to close the genus with itself and bring it into existence – *copulation.*"[12]

In this way, so Hegel argues, we have a conception of the difference of the sexes, whatever empirical biology may tell us about the empirical makeup of that difference. Neither the planet nor the individual element of a chemical pair can "feel" the whole that directs them; the "end" that such systems serve is only an end "for us," the investigators who make judgments about those systems. Only in the division of the sexes does the individual organism in the living system come to have its own subjective feeling of the totality of nature, of the end for which it is striving. Or, as Hegel describes it, "the process consists in this, that what they are in themselves, they posit as such, namely, *one* genus, the same subjective vitality. Here, the Idea of nature is actual in the male and female couple; their identity and their being-for-self, which up till now were only for us in our reflection, are now, in the infinite reflection into self of the two sexes, felt by themselves. This feeling of universality is the highest to which the animal can attain."[13] In a way completely familiar from Hegel's attitude toward gender differences in his social philosophy, he also holds that therefore the "Idea" of nature with regard to the different sexes is that the female is passive, the male active, and that this carries over into human life.

But since the reproduction of the species is the reason for the existence of the individual organism, the organism is ready for death after it has successfully reproduced the species. In the lower animals, this occurs shortly after reproduction, but in the "higher animals," because they possess a "higher independence," death comes about by virtue of disease.[14] The organism is finite, dependent on its nonorganic environment, and its function in the species is ultimately to reproduce the species, not itself. As a finite entity, caught within the mechanical, chemical, and organic conditions of life, it cannot resist all outside causes that disrupt its functioning, and thus the necessity of disease and death is written into our very conception of organic life (so Hegel argued): The concept of disease that is prior to all empirical determination of it is that of the organism's very functioning being thrown off center, of something external to the organism causing its organs not to work in terms of the end for which they exist as organs in the first place, namely, the maintenance of the individual organism itself. The possibility of death is thus the possibility that any one of the organs can fail to play the role it is supposed to play. On its own, taken out of the context of its functioning within the organism, an individual organ cannot be said to be diseased or healthy. The whole concept of health, therefore, involves a teleological judgment about the organism as a whole, an "ideality," in Hegel's words.[15]

With the concepts of the reproduction of the species and of the health and diseases of organisms, though, the proper domain of the "philosophy of nature" is, for Hegel, closed. Although everything in nature should be interpreted from the human standpoint in terms of the relative "wholes" in which the individuals of nature relate to each other, nature itself can never rise to the level of making judgments about itself. The animal can have a "feeling" of its "universality" in the reproduction of the species, but it cannot have a "thought" about it. As natural entities, all the individuals remain subject to the laws of nature. Only in the free, rational activity of the investigators of nature, the creatures for whom these "wholes" appear, is there the possibility of the *self-determination* of principles and ends. Only in norm-governed, free activity does the Idea "break out of this circle and by shattering this inadequate form make room for itself."[16]

In his lectures on the "philosophy of nature," Hegel indulged himself in all kinds of idiosyncratic musings on various topics of the day, often taking quite a curmudgeonly attitude toward various prevailing opinions. Some of them are amusing; he offers, for example, his own explanation for the widely held belief that the legendary European wine vintage of 1811, which was the same year as the appearance of a visible, bright comet in the sky and which therefore became known as the "comet vintage" (and which commanded extraordinary prices until the end of the nineteenth century), was in fact due to the comet itself: "What makes comet wine so good is that the water-process detaches itself from the earth and thus brings about an altered state in the planet."[17] Some of them seem in retrospect a bit cranky, as when Hegel denies even the possibility of explaining the differences of species by appeal to evolution. For Hegel, to explain the origin of new species or of life in terms of some natural process – as if altering one little part somewhere could produce something new – seemed untenable; one explains a species in terms of its specific ends, not in terms of how the structure of, for example, feathers or legs was brought about.[18] Likewise, Hegel mused that water was not simply a composition of hydrogen and oxygen, despite what the chemists said on the matter.[19] On some points, he acknowledged that his views on a particular subject were not taken seriously by the natural scientists, but he claimed not to be worried about it, since he was not trying to offer an alternative to "finite" scientific explanation (even though he quite often violated that maxim in his actual lectures); with reference to his criticism of Newton, he noted, for example, that "philosophy has to start from the concept, and even if it does not assert much, we must be content with this . . . I have therefore set down here only the rudiments of a rational procedure in the comprehension of the mathematical and mechanical laws of nature as this free realm of measures. This standpoint is, I know, not reflected on by professionals in the field; but a time will come when this science will require for its satisfaction the philosophical concept."[20] In terms of his philosophy of nature, Hegel remained, as he himself would have had to admit, very much a child of his times.

The goals of Hegel's "philosophy of nature" were, whatever the failures of his own rather singular rendition of the subject, nonetheless consistent with his modernism. He wanted to construct an understanding of nature that would do service in the modern self-understanding of European culture, that would bring together the ideals of freedom driving the revolutions in European life – both political and industrial – with the ideals of the scientific investigation of nature. He was quite clear that he was not claiming to explain the processes of nature in terms of some obscure spiritual construction of the world; as he emphasized to his students, "spirit is no less before than after nature . . . spirit, just because it is the goal of nature, is *prior* to it, nature has proceeded from spirit: not empirically, however, but in such a manner that spirit is already from the very first contained in nature, which is spirit's own presupposition."[21]

Hegel also had other goals in constructing his philosophy of nature. To comprehend the "whole" as a way in which nature in all its protean multiplicity is constructed of processes that produce a planet on which rational, self-conscious life – *Geist*, spirit, mind – emerges is in fact to understand nature religiously, to know God "in this his immediate existence."[22] But in saying this, Hegel makes it clear that he does not hold the orthodox view that God created the world with certain ends in mind, nor does he think that God actually consciously guides any of the processes of nature, nor that God just *is* nature. Moreover, God can also not be understood as a "supernatural" entity *outside* of the world. Rather, God exists *only* in the world's existing and coming to have the shape it does by virtue of its own internal teleology, which can only manifest itself in terms of the emergence of spirit, of human life historically coming to reflect on itself. The view of nature as a whole required also, Hegel firmly believed, a fully modernist religious sensibility, a theme and concern that had occupied him on and off since his student days in Tübingen.

The Philosophy of Religion

The Background to the Lectures

At the same time that the natural scientists were making a play for more authority in the university, the traditional claims of the theology faculty to be central to the mission of the institution had never really completely disappeared. In part to counter his disputes with the theologians (especially Schleiermacher), Hegel, the former seminarian, found himself for the first time in his life giving lectures in Berlin on the philosophy of religion. His reasons for doing so were, however, clearly more than merely prudential, merely a way to fend off his enemies; this was a subject that had occupied him for all his life, and his attitudes toward it had probably undergone more swings and changes than had his attitudes toward anything else in his life.

Although the basic rudiments of Hegel's overall philosophy of religion had not changed since his long chapter on religion in the *Phenomenology*, much of the detail and the nature of the historical and conceptual accounts did indeed change and develop. Hegel did not simply dredge up his old account and lecture on it, nor did he simply "apply" his logical categories to religious material; he continued to develop his thoughts on religion both in terms of how it was to be given a *wissenschaftlich*, or "theoretically rigorous," account in the context of his own "system," and, most importantly, with how a fully *modern* religion could be understood.

Hegel's lectures on the topic were – like his series of lectures on the philosophy of art, the philosophy of history, and the history of philosophy – among his most successful. They were well attended and widely followed, and like the other parts of his best-attended series of lectures, they were relatively free of the dense jargon that characterized his major philosophical works. By the end of his life, Hegel was gradually moving away from the kind of opaque prose that had characterized his earlier published works and was able to formulate his views in a much more elegant and accessible manner. However, he did not publish the lectures nor make any plans for publication of them in his lifetime. Only after his death did his friends gather up his own lecture manuscripts and the various copies of student notes and render them into publishable form. In fact, his lectures on the philosophy of religion were the very first of Hegel's great posthumous works to be edited and published, and it was these works that both helped to cement the influence of "Hegelianism" after his death and that provoked the initial firestorm over his legacy. (Hegel himself, however, was not silent publicly about the issue in his lifetime; besides the long chapter in the *Phenomenology* and the cryptic paragraphs in the *Encyclopedia*, Hegel stated his views in his preface to Hinrichs's book on the philosophy of religion, and he outlined his views on Indian religion in his review of Humboldt's book on the Baghvad Gita in the *Jahrbücher für wissenschaftliche Kritik* in 1827.)

Hegel's own personal religious attitudes are more difficult to fathom. He himself does not seem in his daily life to have been particularly devout, at least in any conventional way. However, his wife, Marie, certainly was, and after his death she became more and more drawn to sentimentalist religious piety. Her own memories of Hegel were of a religious man who was drawn to the Bible; but even Marie was dismayed when, after his death, she read the published lectures and discovered the philosophy contained within them to be not quite at home with her own religious views, and she even expressed some irritation at Rosenkranz's discussions of Hegel's earlier theological studies in his biography of Hegel, which, from her point of view, contained too many things that were "vexatious for faith."[23] Marie Hegel claimed that Hegel's favorite biblical citation was Matthew 5:8 – "Blessed are the pure in heart, for they shall see God" – and Hegel certainly liked quoting that passage in his lectures; but he also gave it a much different twist than we would imagine Marie did.[24] He also once simply finessed the issue of personal immortality with Marie; when she asked him what he thought of it, he simply without speaking pointed to the Bible, which she of course interpreted in her own way.[25] It does seem to be the case, though, that Hegel had a religious sentiment of sorts; it was not something that was foreign to him, and he was not feigning religiosity when he spoke of it.

Nonetheless, it is quite clear that in Hegel's own mind, the *philosophy* of religion was crucial to his enterprise. If nothing else, how his philosophy of "freedom" and "self-determining thought" was to be squared with any account of religion in which God played an independent role was hard to see for many people; and charges of "pantheism" (and, given the current of the time, what was taken as its implication, "atheism") with regard to Hegel's attitudes toward religion were never far below the surface and in the later years of his life were being openly made against his philosophy.

Religious Reflection

Religion in Hegel's understanding is one of three basic practices within which people come to be aware of and to reflect upon humanity's highest interests – in Hegel's language, to reflect on "absolute content," "absolute essence." Art and philosophy also perform this role, but religion does it in its own particular way that cannot be reduced to aesthetic experience or conceptual reflection. In religion, one attempts to "elevate" oneself to the divine by a communal reflection on what is essentially at stake in life, and in being so elevated, one seeks to experience a "unity" with the divine. One achieves a form of reflective self-consciousness about "universal" matters that transcends one's own particular interests and viewpoint, even in principle the viewpoint of one's own culture. Religion achieves this through rite, ritual, and (symbolic) representation (*Vorstellung*).[26] In particular, religious reflection implicitly commits one to an identification with what is "absolutely" true that in its ideal form does not involve alienating one's own deepest interests and aspirations from this experience of the "absolute," of what is normatively authoritative for how one is to lead one's life and to reflect on the meaning of the full range of life – its full and deepest emotional, intellectual, and practical content.

Although philosophical reflection can also be oriented toward the "absolute" as that which is inherently authoritative for us, and indeed is better suited than religious reflection to grasp the true content of such reflection, it cannot substitute for religion. As Hegel made it pointedly clear in his 1827 lectures: "Religion is for everyone. It is not philosophy, which is not for everyone. Religion is the manner or mode by which all human beings become conscious of truth for themselves."[27] By this Hegel certainly did not mean that religion is to be regarded as a kind of lower-order social practice that has some utility in the way it sugarcoats the more pristine truths found in philosophy. Religion is the experiential "elevation" of oneself to the divine; philosophy can do this only in "thought," and cannot in principle provide the same kind of emotional, personal identification with the divine that genuine religion can.

The basic issue animating Hegel's mature philosophy of religion was how such "elevation" and "unity" with the divine could be reconciled to modern life, and his answer proved to be his most controversial. God, so Hegel argued, is spirit, *Geist*, and the "elevation" to God therefore is an "elevation" to what humans really are, namely, minded and like-minded norm-bound creatures, whose highest interests are to be found in articulating and understanding their own self-consciousness in terms of rational principles. In the language of Hegel's philosophy, humans only "become" spirit when they become norm-bound, self-conscious entities, and they can do this only in a fully social manner (in terms of structures of mutual recognition and the like); they become "spirit," that is, not just by virtue of being organisms but in becoming aware of themselves as norm-bound creatures, as self-consciously conceiving of themselves as "one of us" and as "one among many": "Spirit," Hegel says in his lectures on the philosophy of religion, "is spirit only insofar as it is for spirit. This is what constitutes the concept of spirit itself."[28] God cannot therefore be adequately conceived as a being "transcendent" to such human "minded" and "like-minded" life. As Hegel sharply phrased it in one of his many formulations of the issue: "God's spirit is [present] essentially in his community; God is spirit only insofar as God is in his community."[29]

The "Phenomenology" of Religion

Hegel's own concept of religion was thus very closely linked to his philosophy of nature and to his conception of how "spirit" emerges from nature. God is not "outside" the world; that would make Him "finite," bounded by an "other" to Himself. God is instead to be found in the "principle" of the world itself. Nature – from the organization of the solar system to the "meteorological process" that makes earth into a planet capable of sustaining life – is to be understood in terms of what is necessary for life in general, and for rational, self-conscious life in particular to be possible and actual. God is therefore not some "outside" force or entity directing nature to a certain end; God, as spirit, is already metaphorically asleep in nature, and the divine principle of "spirit" comes to fruition only as humans appear on the planet and create religions as the modes of social practice in which reflection on their relation to nature, each other, and to the divine principle itself is carried out. In the creation of the religious community, spirit, as it were, wakes up from its natural slumber and becomes conscious of itself. In holding this view, Hegel clearly did not hold (as did later French positivists) that humanity was identical to God, or that worship in church was or should be really worship of humanity. Humanity did not create the world; rather, the world was so eternally structured so that it was *necessary* that life appear on earth, that humanity come to exist, and in and through humanity's religious practices, God, the divine structure, "wakes up" and comes to be aware of Himself. Without humanity, God would be, as it were, still asleep in nature, unaware of His own existence.

In Hegel's own day, there were two obvious charges to be made against such a view. First, there was the serious charge that Hegel's doctrine was only pantheism by another name and, in the equation often made at the time, would therefore be equivalent to atheism. Second, there was the charge that whatever else it was, the view was simply not Christian; and, indeed, the view did sound suspiciously pagan and Aristotelian in the way it spoke of the unity of divinity and reason.[30] Both those charges were heating up in Hegel's day, and he needed to respond to both of them.

In one sense, Hegel simply finessed the pantheism charge by dismissing it. He asserted that taken literally, the whole idea of pantheism – that God was in everything – is simply ludicrous: As he told his audience, "It has never occurred to anyone to say that everything, all individual things collectively, in their individuality and contingency, are God – for example, that paper or this table is God."[31] What is divine in all things is their essence, and God must be understood as "subjectivity," as the divine principle of reason, not as the abstract "stuff" out of which all things are made.

For such a conception to work, Hegel realized that he needed to provide a full "phenomenology" of religion, a historical and dialectical account of the development of religious truth as that which is required by virtue of the failures of earlier religious reflections, such that (Protestant) Christianity emerges not as just one religion among many but as the paradigmatic modern religion, the only religion that is *true*, is consistent with modern social, political, and scientific life – Christianity was to be, as he described it, the "consummate religion." To show this, Hegel knew he had to show that the alternatives – including Indian and Chinese religions – were incapable of being "modern" and involved the kinds of internal strains and incoherences that conceptually required a resolution in something like modern Protestant Christianity.

From the "One That Is All" to the Greek Religion of Beauty

This required him to make a demarcation of all religions very similar to the classification made in the original *Phenomenology of Spirit*. The philosophy of religion thus begins with an account of religious reflection in its "immediacy," in what he calls "nature religion." In identifying the divine with the natural, the followers of "nature religions" undertake a set of commitments to a conception of divinity that cannot be consistently carried out and lived through; although they revere implicitly the principle of *Geist*, they can only understand it as some kind of natural force. In its most "immediate" and least articulated forms, this works itself out as "magic," as the notion that some humans can achieve a power and dominion over nature by virtue of their communion with and manipulation of its spiritual powers. Hegel identified Daoism in China and all African religions with such views.

Hegel's understanding of Eastern religions saw them as essentially stalled versions of what was later to develop in the West. They displayed a sense of the unity of the world as having to do with nature and spirit, but their development, Hegel thought, rarely got beyond anything more than a vague intuition of that unity. Interestingly, though, he also vehemently argued against simply dismissing them as "premodern," or as merely being "superstitions": With regard to Tibetan religion and its veneration of the Dalai Lama, he noted, for example, that "it is easy to say that such a religion is just senseless and irrational. What is not so easy is to recognize the necessity and truth of such religious forms, their connection with reason; and seeing that is a more difficult task than declaring something to be senseless."[32]

There was also a further point to his discussion of Eastern religion as a "stalled" version of what was to develop in the West. In his 1827 lectures on Eastern religions, Hegel returned to the themes of his youth that he had shared with Schelling and Hölderlin in Tübingen. Such Eastern religions exhibit, he says, the notion of "*Hen Kai Pan*," of the "one" that is "all," and they therefore tend to foster "tranquility, obedience, and gentleness." Indeed, Hegel argued, if one is looking for pantheism, one will find it instantiated in Eastern religions. Such religions have the idea that God is the "substance" of all that is (that the universe is so arranged so as to produce self-conscious life on earth), but they cannot have the idea that God is "subject." Eastern religions conceive Him as the unity of everything that is, but God is more correctly conceived as the principle of *Geist* itself, as that in terms of which we retrospectively understand the universe to have as its consummation. (Which is not to say that anything in the universe actually *aims* at such a conclusion; Hegel is quite clear that there are no intentional "actors" designing the universe so that it culminates in God's appearance in His religious communities; it is merely the way in which we must, so he argues, conceive of the unity of the world as structured so as to produce self-conscious life, and that this intrinsic structuring is what is "divine.") Developed into a conceptual form, such Eastern pantheism becomes Spinozism, which, because of its arid conceptual nature cannot serve as a "folk religion" or serve as the basis for a genuine "faith."[33] With those observations, Hegel thought he had fairly well answered the charges of "pantheism" swirling around him; and he had brought to closure some of his own earliest thoughts and concerns on the issue.

The Persian religion of light and the ancient Egyptian religion serve to make the transition to more developed, "subjective" religions, to break free of the stalled pantheisms of the East and set in motion the developments that would culminate in Christianity. In all forms of pantheism, the commitment to an understanding of the divine as the "one that is all" breaks apart under the difficulties of sustaining and making sense of the various incoherences and tensions that are intrinsic to such conceptions, in particular the problem of understanding how evil is possible in the world. Egyptian religion, however, with its attendant myths of Osiris dying, being restored to life, and then judging in the realm of the dead, displays a vague sense (an inner, merely "symbolic" sense, Hegel says, employing the terms of his good friend Creuzer) of the way in which the "good" has the power to enforce its authority. It is a power of *judgment* and the ability to make those judgments effective, actual, that characterize Osiris's actions. In Egyptian religion, the natural and the spiritual thus become conceptually distinguished, although still in an unclear way; Egyptian religion thus remains purely "symbolic" and embodies an enigma, a riddle (*Rätsel*), at its heart, a sense of what it is trying to assert coupled with a lack of the conceptual means to make that assertion fully explicit and "transparent."

The tensions inherent in the "enigma" of Egyptian religion thus require a move to the "religion of beauty" of ancient Greece to resolve them. Hegel thus reprieves and elaborates on the idea already developed in the *Phenomenology*, that beauty and religious truth fused in ancient Greece religious practice, that the form of reflection on mankind's highest interests in enigmatic Egyptian religion made it necessary for humanity to think of its highest interests in a more developed way that clearly distinguished the spiritual from the natural, and the Greek casting of divinity into the form of beauty allowed them to do that. The gods of Greece were thus the products of artists who projected an idealized form of humanity into them. In pantheistic religions, it is never clear to what extent the interests of the divine are congruent with humanity's interests, and often one simply has to make sacrifices or offerings to the divine to appease them or to assuage them from following out what seem to be interests contrary to human interests or even incomprehensible from a human standpoint. However, at first in Egyptian religion and then in more developed form in Greek religion, the divine's interests and humanity's interests are seen as having a kind of congruence with each other. This congruence could, however, only go so far; the Greek gods, being like humans but also being immortal, could not share humanity's concern with death; and, as he had also argued in the *Phenomenology*, the Greek conception burdened not only humanity but also the gods with being subject to yet another force, "fate," blind "necessity" – which seemed to imply that the divine itself was therefore subject to a greater power than itself and was therefore perhaps not fully "divine."

Greek conceptions of divinity thus were essentially aesthetic conceptions of the divine, and the attempts by the Greek philosophers to articulate in explicit form what was only implicit in the commitment to such religious practices had the effect of fully undermining all belief in them and thereby undermining the very structure of Greek life itself. Greek deities were, as Hegel put it, not fully "holy" in the sense that they were limited and "finite"; reflection on them only made this "finitude" and the contradictions contained in such a conception more explicit.

Judaism

Hegel's Berlin "phenomenology" of religions thus recapitulated (with much more detail and subtlety) some key themes of the earlier Jena *Phenomenology*. However, by 1827, Hegel had come to new conclusion about what followed from that. The problems of Greek religion, he now thought, required it to "elevate" itself into something more coherent, which he now for the first time identified as the Jewish religion characterized as the "religion of sublimity." The Greek gods were the embodiments of human perfection in beautiful, sensuous form; the Jewish God, however, was freed from this kind of "finite" conception of the divine and was instead conceived as "infinite," purely spiritual, without shape. The Jewish God thus is "subjectivity that relates itself to itself."[34]

In his earlier writings on Judaism, Hegel had seen it as merely a religion of legalistic servility. In the *Phenomenology*, except for a few passing comments, Judaism was simply left undiscussed, as if it did not even matter in the history of humanity's self-consciousness. However, since arriving in Berlin, Hegel had clearly been mulling over and rethinking his stance on Judaism, and the impetus for this reevaluation was almost certainly his close friendship with Eduard Gans. For his own part, Hegel remained, as far as we can tell, fully ignorant of all the nonbiblical writings of Judaism (such as the Torah), and he seems to have been more or less ignorant about the development of Judaism since Roman times.[35] Gans was himself, however, intensely interested in questions regarding Judaism and the relation of the Hegelian philosophy to them; and Hegel almost certainly began to change his mind about the status of Judaism in history in light of Gans's queries.

Judaism presented a distinct problem for Hegel's views. Given his view of history, Judaism should have vanished along with Egyptian, Greek, and Roman religions; like them, having once played its role on the stage of history, it had no longer had any reason for existing, since its own internal problems (which Hegel saw as resolved in Christianity) should have gradually undermined the ability of the Jews to sustain their religion – just as the problems with Greek religion had inevitably undermined the Greeks' ability to maintain their religious beliefs and way of life.

At first, Hegel had seemed to attribute the survival of Judaism simply to the Jews' own stubbornness in holding on to dead legalistic practices. In his first lectures on Judaism in his Berlin period in 1821, Hegel still argued that Jewish religious consciousness was essentially servile, since God was represented as an "abstract" power for whom absolute obedience was required and whose commands, because of the "abstractness" of both the Jewish conception of God and the commands themselves, could not be rationally comprehended. By the time he was again lecturing on the topic in 1824, however, things had dramatically changed; in 1824, Hegel suddenly presented the Jewish God as being more "spiritual" than were the previous religious conceptions of divinity, and "wisdom" had come to be seen as one of the defining features of the Jewish divinity. Indeed, what had seemed only servile in 1821 (the "fear of the Lord") had by 1824 – after the friendship with Gans had started – come to be seen as the "beginning of wisdom" (although Hegel had much earlier cited that same biblical passage in his section on mastery and servitude in the *Phenomenology*). By 1827, Hegel described the Jewish God as the embodiment of "goodness and wisdom," and, in an even more striking development, he ranked Jewish religion as "higher" than that of the Greeks, a complete reversal of his earlier positions.

Indeed, the Jewish religion is represented in 1827 as the point where the "divine" and the "natural" along with the "ideal" and the "real" were to be conceived as existing in a "unity." As such, the natural world in Judaism was to be conceived as a "manifestation" of the divine "subject," although this manifestation can never be adequate to that of which it is the manifestation. It is in that sense, Hegel argued, that

Judaism is the religion of "sublimity," of the unimaginable power of the divine over all else. Because of this conception, Hegel also argued, Judaism was able to conceive of nature as a "prosaic" state of affairs existing in a set of lawful connections; indeed, the whole concept of a "miracle," he argued, would not have made any sense without such a conception; and thus Judaism prepared the way for the scientific treatment of nature in terms of its lawfulness.[36] Thus, in Judaism the true "miracle" – the appearance of spirit, *Geist*, in nature – is made the explicit object of reflection, and the "true" appearance of spirit as the "spirit of humanity and the human consciousness of the world" is implicitly, although not fully, brought forth as an object of religious reflection.[37] Indeed, in Judaism, God is seen as the "creator" of the world, not as something subject to a yet higher "necessity," as were the Greek divinities. As created by God, the world is basically "good"; interpreted in that way, the Jewish religion is seen as laying the groundwork for something like Hegel's speculative philosophy of nature itself. Thus by 1824 and then decisively in 1827, Hegel had completely reversed himself, conceiving in 1827 of Judaism as the first great religion of freedom, instead of the religion of servitude, the view he had taken of Judaism for almost his entire life.

Hegel was, however, clearly not fully at ease with this analysis of Judaism, since it potentially threw into question so much of his emphasis on Christianity's claim to be the exclusively modern religion. In his final 1831 lectures on the philosophy of religion, he returned to the point about Judaism as the religion of freedom, but, much more than he had done in 1827, he stressed what he saw as its fatal internal contradictions and why it could not serve as an appropriately *modern* religion. Judaism remained one-sided, Hegel concluded, in the sense that it still represented the divine as a national deity; this was the basic contradiction, so Hegel thought, in Judaism, since it held that God was the Lord of all at the same time that it maintained that God was also the deity only of a particular, "chosen" people. Moreover, the Jewish conception of God, although sublime and deep, nonetheless was still of sufficient abstractness that "the laws do not appear as laws of reason but as prescriptions of the Lord."[38] Thus, divine and human law are not sufficiently differentiated, and a legal formalism remained intrinsic to the Jewish religion and way of life.

Roman Religion as Preparing the Ground for Christianity

Roman religion appeared consistently throughout Hegel's lectures as the proper successor to Greek and Jewish religions, although the emerging characterization of Jewish religion as the first religion of freedom made that original division difficult to maintain. The analysis of Roman religion also remained within the overall view he had first articulated in the *Phenomenology*. It was the religion of *Zweckmäßigkeit*: "expediency" or "purposiveness." As Hegel had originally thought of the matter, Roman religion was the conceptual successor to Greek religion; but as he came to think of it in Berlin, Roman religion emerged as the unsuccessful unity of the principles of the Greek and Jewish religions, in which, however, what was peculiar to both religions disappeared. The beauty of the multiple Greek divinities was relinquished in favor of a conception of multiple prosaic divinities who were little more than means for achieving secular purposes, and the unity of the Jewish God was replaced by an abstract although comprehensive and unified state purpose. For the Roman way of life, the divine was essentially thus only a manner of achieving dominion and dominance in the world for the Roman people, and the essentially practical character of the Romans expressed itself in subordinating all other peoples to their own empire and assembling their various national gods into a "pantheon," which itself could amount only to a kind of hodgepodge subordinated to the one "Jupiter Capitolinus," just as all the nations were subordinate to the will of Rome.[39] The Roman religious conception itself was virtually devoid of all meaning, having no way to conceive of the unity of the pantheon (since it was little more than an unprincipled conglomeration), but this had the effect of creating the possibility of a "world religion," which was finally to be realized in Christianity. The Romans, as Hegel puts it, believed that "God is served for the sake of . . . a human purpose. The content does not, so to speak, begin with God."[40] The alienation from the whole, the lack of a sense of any concrete common purpose, however, left individuals free to develop their own contingent projects and subjectivity. The content of Roman religion was therefore "abstract inwardness," the development of individual subjectivity as a sense of individual consciousness being the seat of normative authority, of each "self" being normatively independent of one's place in the social world of the empire.[41]

The universality of the empire and the development of "abstract inwardness," however, made it necessary for some content to be given to the idea of a divine purpose. Roman religion was virtually no religion at all, but the de facto universality of the empire and the abstractness of its religion made it therefore all the easier for one of the many "national" religions of the Roman world to elevate itself to become the official religion of Rome (and therefore of the world). The result was what Hegel had called the "unhappy consciousness" with its accompanying "anguish" in the *Phenomenology*; in his 1831 lectures he reprieved that description, describing Roman religion as the "monstrous unhappiness and anguish that were to be the birthpangs for the religion of truth."[42] That "unhappiness" created "the impulse, generated by the shattering of the particular folk-spirits and of the natural deities of the people, to know God in a universal form as spiritual."[43]

However, for such a religion to succeed, it had to be a religion within which the alienated, now "subjective" members of the empire could find themselves at home, and that in turn implied that it had to be something that reflective subjects, thinking for themselves, could rationally affirm. This came on the scene as Christianity, in which the divine fully "reveals" itself. In Hegel's understanding, that meant that what was thus "revealed" in Christian religious practice was that God was not a "beyond," not something over and against the world, not an entity existing outside of the world, but the divine "principle" itself of which human self-conscious life was the "realization." The "principle" which is implicit in nature – that the universe is so ordered so as necessarily to produce and sustain the appearance of self-conscious life on earth – is the "divine," and a human religious community in coming to understand that fully realizes in its figurative way that the divine is thereby "present" in them, that they are at one with the divine. As Hegel put it, for Christianity, "the community itself is the existing spirit, the spirit in its existence, God existing as community."[44] The implicit awareness of such a unity of the divine and the human sets the stage for a "reconciliation" between God and man; in Christianity, the divine loses its strangeness and "otherness" to mankind, and it becomes clear that humanity's highest interests and the divine itself are not at odds. In all other religions, divinity remains something strange and beyond human concerns, having, as it were, its own interests that do not necessarily coincide with those of humanity, or, when they do, coinciding with only a portion of humanity (as is the case with all "national" gods). However, since in Christianity the divine principle of the universe is that which leads to the appearance of self-conscious life on earth (the appearance, that is, of "spirit"), there can be no exclusion of anybody from the religious community. It is self-conscious human life as such, not the life of a particular nation, that embodies the divine principle. Christianity is thus the first true religion of "humanity" and not just of a particular community or tribe.

This raised all the questions that were increasingly raised against Hegel's philosophy – in particular, that it was not really a Christian philosophy at all. Hegel vehemently defended his conviction (which was surely also genuine) that this was not only a variety of Christian thought, it was itself Christianity pure and simple, Christianity "in its truth." In making that claim, Hegel was also fully aware of how his views differed from what was then being taught as orthodox Christianity. Against the criticisms, for example, that charged him with failure to match his views with scripture, Hegel simply replied that such criticisms rested on indefensible conceptions of what it means to read a text, arguing that doctrines require interpretation and that the text of the Bible is not a set of self-evident statements of Christian faith. As Hegel put it in his lectures, "It helps us not at all to say that one's thoughts are based on the Bible," since "just as soon as religion is no longer simply the reading and repetition of passages, as soon as what is called explanation or interpretation begins, as soon as an attempt is made by inference and exegesis to find out the meaning of the words in the Bible, then we embark upon the process of reasoning, reflection, thinking; and the question then becomes how we should exercise this process of thinking, and whether our thinking is correct or not." Hegel went on to note that "the interpretation of the Bible exhibits its content, however, in the form of a particular age; the form of a thousand years ago was wholly different from that of today."[45] A good portion of Hegel's lectures, therefore, had to do with his always-controversial reinterpretations of traditional Christian doctrine in light of his idealist conception of religion. This required him, of course, to see many Christian doctrines, such as that of "creation" and of God's "begetting a son," as only metaphors for the "deeper" truths about *Geist* contained within them.

Jesus and Christianity

Hegel also realized that he had to spell out what he took to be the
doctrine of Jesus as mediator and savior and to articulate what was
entailed in such a conception of God and in the Christian doctrine of
the humanity and divinity of Jesus of Nazareth. Regarded merely as a
person, Hegel argued, Jesus can only be seen as a great teacher (like
Socrates) and a martyr to the truth. As a teacher, Jesus "lives only for
the truth, only for its proclamation; his activity consists solely in completing the higher consciousness of humanity."[46] By being so focused
on the proclamation of the "truth," Jesus sets aside all his normal
interests and behaves "as a prophet," through which "God speaks";
Jesus is "God's working in a human being, so that the divine presence
is essentially identical with this human being," but "not as something
suprahuman."[47]

But that is only the doctrine of Jesus as human. It is only in his death
that the truly religious element of Jesus' life comes to its realization. In
his death, it becomes clear that he was indeed human; to his followers,
he has shown the fragility and contingency of all that is finite and
limited and thus the fragility of all that we hold most dear and valuable;
and in his attachment to the proclaimed truth, he showed that what was
at stake was not some particular teaching, not even about morality or
conscience (as important as such teaching are to Christianity), but "the
infinite relationship to God, to the present God, the certainty of the
kingdom of God."[48] This only comes about in the formation of the
Christian community giving his death a "spiritual interpretation" to
the effect that "the human, the finite, the fragile, the weak, the negative
are themselves a moment of the divine, that they are within God himself
. . . the meaning attached to death is through death the human element
is stripped away and the divine glory comes into view once more."[49]
Hegel cited John 16:13 – "He will guide you into all truth" – and
interpreted it to mean, "only that into which spirit will lead you will be
the truth."[50] Likewise, Hegel interpreted the idea that Christ died for
all as "not a single act but the eternal divine history: it is a moment in
the nature of God himself; it has taken place in God himself."[51] What
is revealed, that is, is the implicitly divine structure of rational self-
conscious life, within which individuals necessarily die and new ones
are born; and the fact that this is part of a divine "history" of the world,

not a contingent accident. Christ's death thus *reveals* the nature of God as (as Hegel put it in 1831) the "course of life that consists in being the universal that has being in and for itself, yet in so doing, being identical with itself: to be this syllogism," to be the unity of the "universal" and the "individual."[52] Jesus is divine in that his death reveals the divinity in him and, implicitly, in *all*. Jesus is thus more than merely a prophet; by virtue of his devotion to the "truth" and his prompting the community to interpret his death in a spiritual way, he embodied and "revealed" the divine structure of the world expressing itself in himself and in the interpretation given to his death by his followers.

What is revealed in Jesus' life is the everlastingness of life itself, and reconciliation is experienced when this is taken as both necessary and good. Hegel explicitly ruled out personal immortality as part of this doctrine. The "wish to live eternally," he told his audience in 1827, "is only a childlike representation. Human being as a single living thing, its singular life, its natural life, must die. . . . The fact of the matter is that humanity is immortal only through cognitive knowledge, for only in the activity of thinking is its soul pure and free rather than mortal and animallike."[53] The Christian community experiences this truth expressively as the communion of fellow worshippers who regard the divine (everlasting rational self-conscious life) as what is of absolute value and importance for them and who see themselves therefore mirrored in the structure of divinity and at one with it.

In Jesus' death, Hegel said, we encounter the "most frightful of all thoughts," that "god is dead," that everything we hold to be of value is gone or will pass away, so that a "despair as to any higher truth" sets in. That thought is, however, quickly put to rest by the "resurrection," that God rises again to life, that "God maintains Himself in death, so that this process is rather a putting to death of death, a resurrection into life."[54] *Geist*, that is, eternally renews itself, although the individual agents who make it up are born and die. It is the "representational" intuition of this in the Christian community, which institutionalizes itself in a church with a doctrine, that provides the reconciliation of the human and the divine. Christian doctrines like that of the "holy communion" mean therefore that the "conscious presence of God, of unity with God . . . the feeling of God's immediate presence within the subject" come to pass in those rites and rituals.[55] (Hegel interestingly rejects the interpretation of communion as a merely symbolic act of remembrance; in Christian communion, he thought, the believer really is in that ritual moment at one with the divine order of the world; the "body" and "blood" of Christ that is consumed is the "spirit of the religious community" itself, since Christ's physical body has been "spiritualized" in the community of faith.) But Hegel makes it clear that what is at stake is the everlastingness of life itself and the faith that life – and most importantly self-conscious rational life – is not some cosmic accident but intrinsic to the structure of the universe itself.

Christian religion thus was "universal." It was not the national religion of any one "people" or any culture but was instead the religion of humanity, the mode by which humanity could come to understand itself as it truly was; and it was also thereby the religion of realized freedom. The Christian God, interpreted as Hegel did, was not an entity outside of humanity giving it commands but was the basic principle of "subjectivity," of rational self-conscious life itself, which although already discernible in outline in nature, comes to a full awareness of its own self-determining essence in Christian religion. This was a *religious* attitude, so Hegel thought, because it expressed itself in a reverential attitude toward life and divinity in general; we could be "thankful" that we existed, we could realize that our own particular lives were only part of the divine course of life, that we were dependent on that divine course of life for our own existence and for the realization of our highest interests; we could rise above our own finite interests and elevate ourselves to a reconciling unity with the divine, understanding our own deaths as a necessary part of the divine course of life that was itself intrinsically good. What is divine is not humanity as such but the "principle" of self-determining "spirit" which humanity brings to full consciousness about itself, and the Christian religious community is thus the form by which God Himself first becomes fully conscious of His nature – that God fully *reveals* Himself by virtue of our coming to a reflectively self-conscious understanding of the divine nature of the universe. In light of this conception, Hegel concluded, there need be no cleavage between the acceptance of a Christian outlook and a fully modernist sensibility. Christianity was thus indeed the only fully *modern* religion and the only one compatible with the kind of free institutions necessary for modern life to work. Faith in God was faith in the everlastingness of life (though not of one's own individual life) and the goodness of being, in the conviction that what was absolutely good in life was written into the structure of things and that we, humanity as a whole, were collectively capable of gradual realizations of that good and of substantial realizations in our own lives.

In a remark oddly prescient in ways that Hegel could not have understood, he thus assured his readers in the *Encyclopedia* and the audiences at his lectures on the "philosophy of nature" that it was not possible, for example, for comets to strike the earth because the solar system is a *system*, and the planets in the system "protect themselves against them, i.e., that they function as necessary organic moments of the system and as such must preserve themselves."[56] Dismissing the notion that it is merely "improbable" that comets might devastatingly strike the earth because of the vastness of space, Hegel assured his audience that comets "do not come as alien visitors but are generated in the solar system, which fixes their orbits; since the other bodies in the solar system are equally necessary moments, these therefore preserve their independence in face of the comets."[57] Life itself, Hegel thought, was so important to the structure of things that it was not possible that it too was a finite, fragile thing which might pass away or be wiped out in some cataclysmic event.

The Philosophy of Art

Art as "Idea"

Hegel's lectures on aesthetics also counted as one of his most successful and best attended series, and it was clearly a subject as near and dear to him as anything else. It was also a matter about which he probably developed more new ideas during his Berlin period than about any other subject.

Art is one of the forms of "absolute spirit," the practices by which humanity collectively reflects on its "highest interests." Although art can be used to satisfy other ends, such as entertainment, amusement, and relaxation, its genuine significance has to do with the way in which it provides such reflection on our highest interests. The "universal need for art," as Hegel put it, was not just to have some relaxation at the end of a tiring day, although art also sometimes serves that need; the specific need for something that was more than entertainment was man's "rational need to lift the inner and outer world into his spiritual conscious-

ness as an object in which he cognizes again his own self."[58] Art
therefore cannot be merely a craft, the result of possessing certain skills
that can be put to use to satisfy certain pre-given ends (like the need
for diversion or amusement). In itself, it must set it own ends, and, like
the other forms of absolute spirit, fulfill its vocation, in Hegel's words,
of "bringing to our minds and expressing the *divine*, the deepest interests of mankind and the most comprehensive truths of spirit."[59]

Art did that, Hegel argued, by standing, as it were, midway between
"immediate sensuousness and ideal thought" and thereby giving us an
exhibition of the "Idea" in sensuous form.[60] The "Idea" in this sense is
the normative "whole" in terms of which we situate ourselves, and in
art (as in religion and philosophy), we get a reflection of where we stand
in relation to that normative "whole." The means by which art accomplishes this is the shaping and configuring of sensuous elements (of
stone, clay, oil on canvas, sounds and tones, words, and so on) into
forms that permit such an "Idea" to be reflectively grasped by those
who perceive the artworks and whose imaginations are thereby stimulated into thinking about that "whole." When a work of art is, moreover, fully successful in accomplishing this aim, it offers up the (virtually untranslatable) *"sinnliche Scheinen der Idee,"* the "sensuously
seeming-to-be of the Idea," and it is thereby also *beautiful.*[61] (Nature –
particularly, *living* nature – can also be beautiful but only in a derivative
way; its beauty lies in *our* perceiving the "Idea" at work in it.)

In Hegel's terminology, therefore, the *content* of art is the "Idea,"
and the *form* of a work of art is the specific way in which the sensuous
material is shaped and configured.[62] (The form of sculpture is thus, for
example, shaped stone.) In subscribing to such a conception of art,
Hegel argued, one thereby also implicitly commits oneself to a norm
having to do with what it would mean for a work of art to be totally
successful: It would present us with (what Hegel called) the "Ideal,"
namely, when the work would not only be "beautiful," but the particular "gestalt" or configuration of sensuous materials shaped by the artist
would be perfectly adequate to the conception of the normative whole
that gives it its meaning – when, that is, "form" and "content" would
fully mesh and be appropriate to each other, and the work would
present us with a full, complete, reflective understanding of the normative whole, the "Idea." Art as a social practice therefore has a teleology

inherent to it, which has to do with whether it can successfully achieve the "Ideal."

The Problem of Modern Art

As always, Hegel was especially concerned with the status of *modern* art and what role art could play in modern life. Hegel could not shake his conviction that somehow the Greeks had raised art to its highest level of achievement, to the "Ideal," and that Greek sculpture, tragedy, poetry, and comedy were superior to what the moderns could produce; but he was as equally convinced that it nonetheless would be hopeless and senseless for moderns to attempt to revivify Greek art. The question then for Hegel was what role art would play in modern life that *only* art *as art* could play.

Part of the problem was, of course, that the modern age was frag-mented in a way that the ancient world was not. In his lectures, Hegel noted that in modern life the claims residing in the everyday, mundane activities of life and those arising out of the kinds of rational, principled, reflective assertions of modern life certainly *seemed* to be in conflict with each other, such that modern culture "produces this opposition in man which makes him into an amphibious animal, because he now has to live in two worlds which contradict one another . . . and driven from one side to the other, cannot find satisfaction for himself in either the one or the other."[63] The problem is that modern life seems to embody a sense of the "whole" that cannot be fully captured in a work of art, with the result that "form" and "content" seem to drift apart from each other within modern art; modern political life modeled on constitutional law and bureaucratic practice, the practices of modern science – all seemed to be structured within a "social space" that cannot be fully captured in a work of art. Modern art seemed, that is, to be incapable in principle of achieving the "Ideal" that is at the heart of aesthetic experience.

How then could a fully *modern* art fulfill the traditional vocation of art in such a ruptured, fragmented age? To answer that question, Hegel came to believe that he also needed a "phenomenology" of the history of art in order to see what was required of art as it related to the historical development of our conceptions of the normative whole in terms of which we comprehend ourselves. In doing this, Hegel presented the audiences at his lectures over the years with both a "phenomenological" history of art from the Egyptians to the present (much as he did in the lectures on the philosophy of religion) and detailed discussions of the nature of the various arts themselves. (Hegel's very illuminating observations about the particular arts – in general, architecture, sculpture, painting, music, and literature – will unfortunately have to be left almost entirely undiscussed here.)[64]

Hegel argued that understanding art in terms of its own inherent teleology meant that we had to see art as divided into symbolic, classical, and romantic periods. These in turn were divided according to how appropriately people in those historical periods grasped the true "Idea" of things – how well and articulately people had a sense of a rational normative order. Egyptians thus formulated "symbolic" art, Greeks formulated "classical" art, and the modern period was understood to be the completion of "romantic" art.

Egyptian, Greek, and Romantic Art

Because Egyptian life was characterized by only an abstract understanding of the "Idea" that was itself not fully rational, its art, like its religion, was necessarily primarily "symbolic." The form (the way in which Egyptian architecture and sculpture in particular were shaped) could not be adequate to the content, since the content itself was already so terribly abstract and so internally flawed. Since Egyptian art was therefore necessarily unclear about what it was trying to say, it could only present its truths in a "symbolic" fashion, in a "mere search for portrayal rather than a real capacity for true presentation."[65] As such, it was "sublime," since the "Idea" expressed in it was both "measureless" and always appeared "transcendent" to the world of appearance.[66] Symbolic art thus always appears to have a deeper meaning within itself that cannot be finally fathomed, that seems to point to something beyond itself that cannot be adequately expressed.

Greek art, on the other hand, is "classical" because it alone achieves the "Ideal" in art. The Greek conception of divinity as the religion of beauty was fully capable of expressing itself in works of art that were beautiful, since there were no (putative) truths in Greek religion that were over and above their presentation in works of beauty. The gods were idealizations of humanity: free, young, and immortal. As such, they could be adequately represented in human form, particularly in sculptural form. The greater gain in realism that marked off Greek sculpture from Egyptian sculpture was therefore not merely a matter of Greek technical skill, so Hegel thought; the perfection of the skills was motivated by the nature of Greek religion itself, by a conception of what it would mean to get it right when one cast sculptures of the gods. Greater realism of the Greek variety would not, for example, have made an Egyptian statue any more representative of Egyptian divinities, and thus Egyptian sculptors had no compelling motivation to perfect their skills in that direction.

Form and content thus fused in Greek art, and the "Ideal" was achieved. In Greek art, the work of art (as a specific configuration of sensuous material) does not point to something beyond itself for its meaning; as Hegel puts it, " in external existence, as its own, it expresses and means itself alone."[67] Since the true content, that is, of the "Ideal," the "focal point" of all truly beautiful art, is, as Hegel stressed, "humanity," that implies that the particular configuration of material be such that its "meaning" be at one with that particular configuration itself.[68] Only one such configuration actually does that: the human form, since only the human bodily form expresses "knowledge and will," "the spiritual in a sensuous manner."[69] Since Greek divinity is conceived in terms of individual gods having human, bodily form, Greek divinity is ideally suited for portrayal in an "Ideal" manner; and thus Greek art successfully accomplished what is inherent in the very concept of art: As Hegel wistfully told his audiences, "Nothing can be or become more beautiful."[70] But likewise, Greek divinity is only itself ideally suited for Greek sculpture; each individual god can be represented in his or her fixed, beautiful individuality. However, the same plurality of gods in Greek religion introduces an element of contingency into the very conception of the gods, and literary and poetic representations thus inevitably bring out the more contradictory aspects of the Greek conception of the normative order and thereby undermine the "Ideal" at work in Greek art.

The romantic conception of art is necessitated by the way in which the normative order came to be conceived in terms of items that cannot be "ideally" given a specific configuration, in particular, in the ways in which Christian spirituality could not be adequately captured in sculpture or architecture. The specific configurations of such works could not fully express the "inwardness" that Christianity took as essential to human life; Christian sculpture thus tended to point beyond itself to another, "spiritual" meaning that could not be captured in a bust of, for example, a suffering Jesus or a confident apostle. In that way, Christian, "romantic" art was similar to symbolic art; but whereas in symbolic art, the meaning to which the work points is itself abstract and vague, in Christian art, the meanings can be more precisely pinned down to specific doctrines of faith and spirituality. The problem, for art, is that those meanings are not and cannot be fully specified by the art itself but by something else, theology, and, as this notion of subjectivity develops in modernity, ultimately only by philosophy itself.

The dynamic underlying the development and execution of romantic art is thus that a way of life based on the notion of this kind of inwardness must necessarily draw the conclusion that "beauty" cannot exhaust "truth," that understanding the "Idea," the normative order in its full rationality yields things that are not necessarily captured in the ideal of beauty. The "higher" beauty can only be thought about as something inward, something that is not necessarily at one with sensuous embodiment; ultimately, for such a way of life, it can only be the "beauty of deep feeling."[71]

The development of romantic art is thus the development of modernity itself out of the principle of Christian "inwardness." The "true content of romantic art," Hegel said, "is absolute inwardness," and the content of art is thereby opened up to an infinite extension of subject matter, a "multiplicity without bounds."[72] The whole range of human subjective life becomes the province of art, and, not accidentally, the primary arts of modern life become painting, music, and poetry (literature), for these are the sensuous configurations that are most capable of expressing the kind of subjectivity that comes to be the focal point and content of all modern art. It also followed, so Hegel further argued, that in modern art the whole function of the configured sensuous materiality is to point back to inwardness, to show "mind and feeling as the essential element."[73] Thus, for modern art, "any and every material" (even, Hegel notes, "flowers, trees, and the commonest household gear") can enter into the work of art; nothing in principle can be excluded, since just about anything can be employed to construct a work that reveals something about the truth of inwardness, of free, self-determining human subjective life.[74]

Romantic Art: From Religious Theme to Secular Concern

The romantic "Ideal" could not, however, begin its development at that point. Historically and conceptually, it at first had to specify itself in terms of a notion of the "reconciliation of the inner life with its reality," and thus *love* – at first in the form of Christian, religious love – became one of the defining early romantic ideals.[75] As Christianity became institutionalized and the world was reworked in light of those Christian ideals, this form of inwardness, which is "at first exclusively religious loses its negative attitude to the human as such; the spirit is spread abroad, is on the lookout for itself in its present world, and widens its actual secular heart."[76]

Once this happens, though, the themes of romantic art tend to leave the purely religious field and move toward portrayals of subjective honor, love of a more profane sort, and arrangements of chivalric fidelity. But such a move intensified the dynamic already implicit in a form of art celebrating inwardness in the first place; at first exclusively Christian and concerned to illustrate and evoke the inward spirituality of the Christian religion, art inevitably turned to secular matters, to the purely human as such.

In its initial phases, such early modern art turned at first to secular concerns with chivalry and what was involved with it, such as affronts to "honor" not in terms of any objective norm but purely in terms of whether the individual's own personal self-conception was injured (which, of course, means that just about anything could count as such an affront to honor). The notion of romantic love, however, offered a richer subject matter for such romantic art, since, like the chivalric concept of honor, it has to do with the way in which a person is recognized by another in his or her full individuality. Love is more self-contained ("infinite," as Hegel calls it) in that the parties involved (in requited love) give themselves over to each other instead of being compelled to bestow an honor or redeem some offense to honor. However, like honor, love is contingent and personal; the person loves quite contingently just this or that other person, and art naturally tends to focus on the more dramatic circumstances that collide with such love or with the attempts by lovers to come together.

Themes of loyalty and fidelity (*Treue*) completed the circuit for early modern art, since they concerned themselves with the subject's choosing for himself what obligations he would elect to impose on himself. Works that celebrated chivalrous knights defending their lords out of their own free choice embodied the idea that it is "the vassal's free choice both of the superior on whom he is to depend and also of persistence in that dependence . . . and is therefore not acknowledged as a *duty* as such, which would have to be performed even against the contingent will of the vassal."[77] Like the themes of profane love, such themes brought to the fore not a *religious* inwardness but the emerging outlines of a fully modernist, *secular* inwardness.

Modern Art and the "End" of Art's Highest Vocation

The final stage of romantic art – modern art – makes explicit what is implicit in the transformation of the Christian art of inwardness into the secular art of inwardness. The object of portrayal in art comes to be more and more the portrayal of individual characters in all their subjectivity and contingency, possessed of the specific tastes, aspirations, and projects that make them the individuals that they are. Likewise, the world surrounding the individual person becomes in all its ordinariness and contingency the object of artistic treatment. Shakespeare becomes the paradigmatic modern dramatist because his characters are wholly absorbed in their own individual aims and thus sometimes, like MacBeth, devolve into evil, or, like Hamlet, they become wholes unto themselves, a character who "feels uncanny, [that] everything is not as it ought to be . . . [and who] persists in the inactivity of a beautiful, inward soul."[78] More and more, the overt theme of the artist comes to be the portrayal of the "subjective inwardness" of an individual person, since such romantic subjective inwardness can, as Hegel points out, "display itself in *all* circumstances."[79] What is important is that subjectivity itself become displayed for reflection, and not any specific circumstances for it; art need not be religious, it need not have any particular thing at all for its content except that human, individual subjectivity itself be portrayed. The result is that "it is *subjectivity* that, with its feeling and insight, with the right and power of its wit, can rise to mastery of the whole of reality."[80]

If, however, absolutely any worldly matter can be the subject of art, if what is important in making it a work of art is that it convey some sense of the fully formed individual subjectivity at work in it, then it might seem as if fully *modern* art can no longer even get close to the "Ideal." To that skeptical worry, Hegel concluded that for modern art, "the artist's subjective conception and execution of the work of art" becomes the main thrust of achieving the "Ideal" in the work.[81] In focusing on his own skill and on what he sees at work, the artist portrays a conception of the normative order at work in modern life, namely, that we are all implicitly self-orienting, that we situate ourselves in terms no longer of a "substantially shared" social space, but of a social space that is inherently fragmented along the lines of modern individuality. And, so Hegel argued, there is no reason to deny that the results of such effort can be legitimately classified as works of art.

Such a development of the importance of the subjectivity of the artist appears in its most highlighted form, Hegel thought, in modern painting and literature. As examples of this at its best, Hegel cited Dutch genre painting. In the Dutch masters, he told his audiences, "the art of painting and of the painter is what we should be delighted and carried away by."[82] The subject matter of such paintings – still lifes, domestic scenes, outdoor scenes – is not itself of intrinsic interest; what is of interest is the very human, subjective viewpoint that is captured in them.

In more recent modern art, however, this quickly dissipates into a display of whatever the artist (and by implication, his audience) finds revelatory; the work of art in our times becomes, as Hegel put it, "a production in which the *subject* doing the producing lets us see himself alone."[83] Fully modern art thus finds that the "Idea" at work is that of modern, self-determining subjectivity. Fully *modern* art, in Hegel's words, "makes *Humanus* its new holy of holies: i.e., the depths and heights of the human heart as such, the universally human in its joys and sorrows, its strivings, deeds, and fates. Herewith the artist acquires his subject-matter in himself and is the actual self-determining human spirit and considering, meditating, and expressing the infinity of its feelings and situations."[84]

With that development, in principle romantic art reaches its full point of development as *modern* art and begins its own process of dissolution in terms of art's ability to fulfill its highest vocation. The great modern rupture in self-understanding – that there are no normative "givens," that there is no longer immediate, direct access to what tradition, nature, God, or sacred texts have to tell us – thus brings in its wake a different significance for art. In coming to understand the "Idea" as the normative order, as something that is produced by our "mindedness" and "like-mindedness" itself, humanity comes to an understanding of itself that outstrips the ability of art to fully express that modern self-understanding. Thus, by 1828, Hegel told his audience early in the series of lectures that "art, considered in its highest vocation, is and remains for us a thing of the past."[85] Nowadays, he told them, we are more "reflective," and we thus judge things in terms ultimately of principles, laws, and the like that cannot be given their clearest expression in works of art. What unity there is within the fragmentation of the modern normative order can only be grasped and understood by something fundamentally nonaesthetic, by a form of thought that Hegel identified as *philosophy*. The great issues of constitutional law or what unity there is within modern market society cannot be best captured in a poem or painting but in a series of complicated arguments; moreover, we explain nature in our "contemporary prosaic reflection . . . in accordance with universal laws and forces," and thus nature for us is also, to a certain extent, necessarily disenchanted.[86] The "Ideal" for us is thus irretrievably *lost*.

Hegel's pronouncement was quickly taken by many to be a claim about the "end of art," that there was no longer a need for art or that no new art would be created. (Even his student Felix Mendelssohn-Bartholdy misunderstood him on this point, grumbling to his sister in 1831 that "although Goethe and Thorwaldsen are still alive, and Beethoven only died a couple of years ago, Hegel asserts that German art is dead as a doornail. *Quod non.* So much the worse for him.")[87] But Hegel was not asserting any such thing; he was simply drawing the consequences from his conviction about the romantic type of art being the only suitably *modern* art. Art would still remain a basic human need, and only art could offer reflection on the "Idea" in sensuous form; however, *art* could no longer produce works whose meaning was fully contained in the work itself, and thus, although it could achieve dazzling and moving results, it could no longer achieve the "Ideal" inherent in the concept of art itself.

The superiority of classical art to romantic (modern) art is thus curiously the result of the deficiency of art itself as a mode of reflection on the "absolute." Art in general is, as are the two other modes of reflection on the "absolute" (religion and philosophy), a practice involving reflection on the normative whole, the "Idea," on the way in which our own mindedness and like-mindedness articulates its most basic normative commitments. Art does this, however, by shaping and forming sensuous elements and bringing our imagination to play in that reflection on our highest interests. No sensuous presentation, however, can comprehend the modern "Idea," the modern sense of the normative whole within which we position ourselves in order to be the self-conscious beings we are. Classical art could achieve the "Ideal" because it alone was situated within a normative whole that made it intelligible that the meaning of that "whole" could be captured in sculptural and poetic renditions of the gods, but no such thing is possible for "we moderns." The divinity that art reveals is indirect; modern art reveals *humanity's* own struggles, which are given their full religious interpretation in *religion*, nonaesthetically conceived, which is in turn made intelligible to us in principled reflection, whose institutionalized form is academic philosophy in the modern, reformed university.

Hegel's lectures on art thus summed up part of his deep sense of the breach between the modern world and what preceded it. On the one hand, it could only be experienced as a loss, and it naturally enough led to attempts at retrieval (to recapture medieval art, to write or cast a new modern epic, to reinvigorate a sense of classical sculpture). But there was nothing "there" to be regained. Humanity, even in Hegel's own lifetime, had moved on, and it could not retrieve what it now experienced as falsity, however shattering the loss was and however beautiful the results had been. Modern humanity's task was to come to terms with that modernity; and it was impossible to put all the weight on the artists to accomplish that reconciliation. Ultimately, it could only be achieved through the three forms of such "absolute reflection," and philosophy was the highest of these because only in reflective, conceptual thought was the normative whole, the "Idea," of modernity to be fully understood.

That assertion – together with Hegel's brilliant lectures on the history of philosophy, another of his best attended and most popular series of lectures – put Hegel's own views on the role of philosophy (and himself) in the modern university in full view. It also let his opponents know where they stood in Hegel's scheme of things. Art and religion remained both "absolute" and necessary; but the modern age was to be one of "thought," of science and philosophy. The modern age belonged, Hegel seemed to be saying, to Hegel, not to Hölderlin.

Home: 1827–1831

Celebrity and Strife

Reformers, Counter-reformers, Liberals, and Hegel

HAVING RETURNED FROM PARIS, renewed in his belief in the essential soundness of his own position, and convinced that the days of the Revolution and the Napoleonic adventures were definitively over, Hegel – still, as ever, true to his belief in the importance and necessity of the Revolution – was all the more convinced that for Germany, indeed for all the post-Napoleonic European states, only a gradual and inevitable process of reform by degrees was now properly on the agenda, and that the process of reform at least in Germany was essentially going to have to come from the top down, from the civil service, which meant in effect that the focal point of reform lay in the university. The bureaucrats of the civil service, trained in *Wissenschaft* and *Bildung* in the university, would gradually and rationally transform all the German principalities (the *Länder*) into modern states, and Prussia would be leading the way. Prussia was the "focal point" of German culture, Berlin was Prussia's "focal point," the university was the "focal point" of Berlin, and philosophy – *Hegel's* philosophy – was the "focal point" of the university.

The stormy days of the early reform movement in Prussia were clearly over, and the initial repression and fears of renewed revolutionary activity which had culminated in the Karlsbad decrees and the pursuit of the "demagogues" also seemed to be winding down. The 1820s were proving to be a quiet period in which the public turmoil surrounding the great political debates of the past seemed to be subsiding, and from one point of view (certainly in Hegel's view), the turbulence of the early years seemed to be transforming itself into more peaceful efforts at reforming this or that institution, putting into place this or that new piece of legislation, and, in general, into a more refined reformist period as people began to find their way about in the new, modern order of things. Quietly and without the drama and fanfare that had accompanied the reform efforts in the Napoleonic past, the civil service began once again asserting its authority over local particularism where it was necessary to achieve rational consistency or economic efficiency. Niethammer's continued complaints in letters to Hegel about how things were a mess in Bavaria only fell on deaf ears; as Hegel viewed things, everything was now going as it should: Although the great reforming minister in Bavaria, Montgelas, had indeed been dismissed, the bureaucratic structure he had put in place and most of the personnel he had picked to run it were still in power. If anything, the reactionary steps taken by various rulers (such as the Prussian king's revocation of the emancipation edict for Jews) seemed to Hegel to be temporary hiccups in what was an inevitable transition to a modern, rational state. The repression still at work in Prussian politics was, Hegel apparently thought, only a hangover from the post-Napoleonic period, something bound to vanish as time went on.

What Hegel understood to be the real issue at the time was that of how the various mediating bodies of the emerging German civil society were to be regulated and organized so as to harmonize with the aims of the modern state, instead of setting themselves in opposition to it as had been the tradition in German political life. Hegel's own political views as manifested in his *Philosophy of Right* about the necessity for "mediating institutions" such as estates and "corporations" in civil society thus neatly dovetailed with the emerging debate in German political life during the 1820s.[1] In the view of many (and almost certainly also in Hegel's view), the strong communitarian bonds of the old particularist and hometown life were not yet sufficiently weakened, and the real opposition to modernizing reform was coming not from the very vocal reactionaries in the Berlin government and the court but from the proponents of particularism and hometown life themselves. The braying of the reactionaries at the court was, Hegel no doubt thought, simply the last gasp of those fated to be swept away by modern life's innovations in science, economics, and freedom; the real issue and point of friction had to do with the strong emotional pull that German particularism still exercised on people. The hometowns still provided the average German with his or her basic sense of "belonging," and the glue that held the those communities together had to do with the communal policing of personal morality and livelihood, which put the hometown squarely in opposition to the modernizing needs such as freedom of occupation and trade and freedom of marriage.[2]

The conflict between the hometowners and reformers centered around two different senses of membership: the reformers wanted people to fuse the sense of belonging to their local communities with the sense of belonging to the larger political unity (the state); the particularists rightly saw that if membership in the state as a modern citizen was to take priority, then their right to determine who was a member of the local city or town would effectively vanish; more concretely, if people could marry whom they wanted to marry, work where they could find work, and set up businesses where they pleased, then the central institutions that protected the communal structure of particularist city and town life (such as guild laws that effectively outlawed nonmembers from setting up shop and competing with locals for business) would wither and vanish – exactly what the reformers wanted and the local particularists feared. That strong emotional pull was something Hegel himself as a Württemberger both knew and felt, so for him it was extremely important to make those hometown and particularist emotions rational, to "purify" them, as Hegel would put it, and blend them into a unity with the aims of a modern civil society and state rather than to have them blindly obstruct progress. The conflicts between particularist life and tradition and the assertions of authority by the modernizing civil servants in the various German states was becoming more and more open in the 1820s; Hegel, who followed the political events of the day closely – the reading of the morning paper was one of his unalterable rituals – was of course aware of this and quite worried about it, although his worries were to be fully expressed only after the uprisings of 1830. Indeed, the weakness and even absence of the traditional hometowns in Prussia was no doubt one of the reasons Hegel was more optimistic about the cause of modernization in Prussia than elsewhere.

But what looked like the stillness of political life in 1820s in Prussia (and in Germany in general) concealed implicit turmoil below the surface. Hegel was, of course, not the only one noticing this at the time. Metternich, as always the cynical antimodernizer when it suited his ambitions, identified the troublemakers in German society in the 1820s to the czar of Russia as "wealthy men, paid State officials, men of letters, lawyers, and the individuals charged with the public education" – in other words, modernizers and people like Hegel. The battle lines were being redrawn, even if more quietly this time.[3]

During all this, probably unwisely, Hegel continued to write and speak in opposition to the *liberal* modernizers in Prussian social life. Hegel's strong opposition to the liberal wing of reform in Prussia was based on what he saw as the consequences of the liberals' desire to transfer political power to local individuals in the name of democratic participation; in Hegel's view, this would be in effect only a recipe for restoring power to the particularists of traditional communal life. Since there simply were no such creatures as fully formed individuals outside of the social context in which they were formed, giving political power to such so-called "individuals" would only give power to what those individuals happened to value, which, under the conditions of the time, was the particularist structure in which they had grown up and whose traditions were strong enough to exercise a kind of cultural gravitational pull on people. Following the liberal path of granting political power to "individuals" would lead, Hegel was certain, to individuals exercising those powers for distinctly nonliberal ends; left to their own devices, the local particularist individuals would reassert their traditional communal structure and restrict freedom of occupation and trade, Jewish civil rights, marital freedom, and the like – in short, would institute a whole set of non-liberal ideals. The issue, so Hegel saw it, was how to have individuals formed by a *rational* community structure instead of by the older, outdated (that is, "irrational") structure of the hometowns and particularist communitarian life. And *that*, he thought, was a matter best left to the university-trained civil servants in the service of the state. It was a matter of devising structures of local government that would harmonize with rational state interests, not a matter of simply leaving matters up to what local individuals happened to want to do; prudent, rational reform had to come to terms with changing what individuals valued only very slowly and very gradually.

Hegel's visit to Paris and his heartening encounters with the liberals surrounding Victor Cousin in the city had therefore the paradoxical effect of strengthening his belief in his own views and thereby hardening his own opposition to the reforming liberals back home in Berlin.

Instead of encouraging Hegel to form an alliance with them for common cause, it led him (and consequently some of his supporters) to think that the liberals were in fact opposed in fundamental ways to Hegel's objectives. Hegel's opposition to the liberals – his belief that their philosophical error about individualism was tantamount to a political error that would undo the process of reform – thus put him, perhaps unwittingly, on the side of those who opposed the liberals, and in the eyes of his detractors, this only strengthened Hegel's image as an apologist for the restoration government.

Hegel also now clearly saw himself as an elder statesman for the younger generation, both as a man of experience who had weathered the storms of the Revolution and the Napoleonic adventures in Germany and who therefore had sage advice to give, and as someone whose philosophy could provide the needed public philosophy to guide the civil servants in their efforts to bring rational coherence to German life. Now in his late fifties, he felt that he had earned his right to be heard by Germany's youth and by his fellow academics. His Württemberg upbringing and his Stuttgart family's sense of being on the way up but still being excluded by virtue of not belonging to the "non-noble notables" had always left him a bit prickly about his status and reputation; with his new sense of having paid his dues and of being the philosopher of the reform movement, he became all the more sensitive to perceived slights against his social standing and status and all the more autocratic about the status of his philosophy. This did not go unnoticed; it was in fact becoming more and more clear to those around him that he intended not merely to expound his philosophy from the lectern at the university but to found an entire school of thought that would survive him and would provide the nucleus of reform-minded civil servants in the government.

Growing Problems: Alexander von Humboldt and Schelling

It is thus not surprising that very shortly after his return from Paris, Hegel found himself again embroiled in a controversy about some putative affront to his status. Alexander von Humboldt, having also returned from his extensive (and rather famous) travels around the world, gave a series of public lectures in Berlin on the Physical Description of the World. The lectures were an immense success; they were attended by scores of people, including members of the court and even the king himself. Although Hegel did not attend the lectures, his wife, Marie, did. In one of the lectures, Humboldt delivered a thinly veiled attack against all post-Kantian philosophy – in other words, against Hegel, among others. Humboldt began that lecture with a protest against the kind of "metaphysics" that proceeds "without a knowledge by acquaintance and experience" and that had advanced a "schematism" narrower, as he put it, than that of the scholasticism of the Middle Ages. On hearing of this, Hegel, understanding the attack on "scholasticism" to be an attack on his system, was deeply offended and made his complaints known to various people, including Varnhagen von Ense. Through Varnhagen von Ense, word got back to von Humboldt, who discreetly gave the notes for his fifth lecture to von Ense, pointing out with feigned innocence that he could not see how anybody could find any attacks on philosophy in those lectures. In putting himself forward in this way, von Humboldt knew what he was doing; his attacks on Hegel were contained not in the fifth lecture (which he gave to Varnhagen von Ense) but in the sixth lecture, and he would have known (and probably approved of the fact) that Varnhagen von Ense would show the notes to Hegel. Hegel indeed read the notes and returned them to Varnhagen von Ense two days later, his feelings mollified and himself satisfied that he had not been attacked.[4] In fact, he even wrote to Victor Cousin a few months later about the "brilliant success" of von Humboldt's Berlin lectures.[5] (As von Humboldt made clear after Hegel's death, he had indeed intended to criticize Hegel in those remarks, but the real focus of his criticism, he claimed, was Schelling and all of Schelling's followers who practiced Schelling's popular *Naturphilosophie*. That von Humboldt grouped Hegel and Schelling together was typical of many people's reactions to Hegel's thought; Hegel had always had some difficulty separating himself from Schelling in the public mind, and to many people who did not take the time to look closely at what he was actually saying, his thought seemed to be only another version of what many regarded as the overly obscurantist Schellingian line. Hegel's own less-than-perspicuous vocabulary only reinforced that view.)

Hegel also continued to hear from various friends new reports of how Schelling's own attacks on him in his lectures had been taking on an increasingly vehement and derisive tone. Schelling's denunciations of

Hegel were, as many people at the time realized, more than just philosophical disagreements. By this point, Schelling felt that Hegel had somehow stolen his ideas, bastardized them, and then somehow used that theft to unfairly displace him in the pantheon of German philosophers, and he minced no words about his feelings on the matter: He characterized Hegel as the "cuckoo" who had planted himself in the nest and complained to Victor Cousin that Hegel had appropriated his (Schelling's) ideas and claimed they were his own in the same manner that "a creeping insect can believe that by appropriating the leaf of a plant, it has wrapped itself in its own weaving."[6] (Cousin wisely stayed aloof from the quarrel, replying to Schelling that he was sorry to hear that he and Hegel were in such bad temper with each other, but that he would simply not take sides in the dispute.)[7] Schelling went so far as to tell whomever would listen that Hegel had created his "logical transposition" of his (Schelling's) system on the basis of nothing else than the fact that friends in Jena many years ago had advised Hegel that since the study of logic had been neglected at the university, he could make a nice career by offering courses on it (a little piece of history that also was almost certainly was not true). In stealing his ideas and putting them in the form of his own so-called logic and his system, Schelling said, Hegel had accomplished no more than someone "transposing a violin concerto for piano."[8] Clearly, Schelling was intensely piqued by the way in which Hegel had undeservedly (so the thought) eclipsed him in fame. As Franz von Baader observed of Schelling, he had become so famous so young and had founded his own school at such an early age that he saw his predominance in cultural and philosophical matters as something that rightfully belonged to him, as a principality belongs by right to the prince, in which light he also resented Hegel as some kind of illegitimate usurper within his rightful sovereign domains.[9]

Fueling Schelling's resentment, however, was the fact that Hegel's own celebrity in Berlin, already high, only continued to grow, and all of Hegel's otherwise irritating mannerisms had become accordingly increasingly chic. His lecture style, punctuated as always by its typical stutters, gasps, coughs, his pausing to flip through his papers, and his habit of beginning each sentence with the word "thus," only became part of the show. When Hegel walked into the lecture hall, the rumble of conversation abruptly stopped, and it became so quiet that people described it with the cliché that "one could hear a pin drop."[10] As one of his Polish hearers described him, Hegel, with his pale white face, clumsily waving his hands as he spoke – often with his eyes closed – seemed like a "phenomenon from another world."[11]

Indeed, the ideal of the Berlin lecturer found one form of its realization in Hegel: That ideal held that the professor would in his monologue actually create a dialogue – that instead of simply handing over facts to the students in the lecture hall, he would somehow embody in himself and bear witness in his lectures to the way in which one explores thinking as an ongoing process rather than as something already over and done with and whose finished results were only to be communicated. (The other form of the Berlin lecture style lay in the graceful, polished style of Schleiermacher.) Hegel had perfected this manner, turning his greatest liability – his speech impediment, his unpolished demeanor and sometimes clumsy deportment – into his greatest asset; he would formulate a sentence, pause, clear his throat, rephrase the same sentence, cough, shuffle through papers, and then finally return to yet a third formulation of the sentence that would suddenly and brilliantly distill the matter at hand. The students felt that they were witnessing the actual working out of a thought, not just being handed something that had already been decided. Hegel's improvisational style gave what might have otherwise been intolerable the air of the purely creative; his own obscure formulations and his famous one-liners would quickly circulate throughout the city, and "such speculative formulas were written on the walls of the university building in chalk or pencil" virtually everywhere.[12] Just as quickly circulated around the city were Hegel's sometimes devastatingly sarcastic remarks about colleagues and other figures in the German cultural scene. "Did you hear Hegel's remark that . . ." became part of Berlin social currency. As one observer put it, "Whether a new and famous picture emerged from the workplaces of a famous painter or whether a new, very promising invention had directed the attention of the industrialists to it, whether some thought of genius in the sciences made its way into the learned world, or Miss Sontag sang in a concert, in all cases Berlin asked: What does Hegel think about it?"[13] Hegel was deluged with people wanting to see him; he regularly received mail from people wanting him to read their work, put in a good word for them in the university, do a favor for a friend, and so on. Copies of student notes taken in his lectures became sought-after items (to Hegel's irritation and displeasure), since by this point Hegel was working out his system with regard to his positions on art, religion, the history of philosophy, and the philosophy of history only in his lectures and not in any printed form.

Attacks and Irritations

As Hegel's celebrity and reputation as the man of the hour continued to rise, his detractors only intensified their attacks on him. Professor Krug, whom Hegel had already severely criticized in his days at Jena, wrote a scathing review of the revised and greatly expanded 1827 edition of Hegel's *Encyclopedia of the Philosophical Sciences* in which he accused Hegel's entire system of being merely a large "game of ideas" that included a philosophy of religion that was no more than an attempt to "inaugurate a new mysticism of faith and knowledge" and a political philosophy in which no real difference between a citizen of a Hegelian state and the "subject of a despotic sultan" could be discerned. This was followed by another attack in another leading journal a few months later in which Hegel's *Encyclopedia* was dismissed as a book "full of empty pages," stuffed with "superstition and mysticism."[14]

Karl Ernst Schubarth, an acquaintance of Goethe's and opponent of Hegel, published a book attacking Hegel and accusing him of being anti-Prussian in his politics and revolutionary in his teachings.[15] The dispute between Hegel and Schleiermacher also hardened into a dispute between their supporters, and little middle ground seemed possible; there were those on Hegel's side, and there were those on Schleiermacher's side; Altenstein tended to side with Hegel, the faculty tended to side with Schleiermacher. As one young academic put it, it seemed that one had to choose sides when joining the faculty at Berlin.[16]

Typifying many people's reactions to all the hue and cry about Hegel was that of Wilhelm von Humboldt. Humboldt actually personally got along quite well with Hegel but was more or less dumbfounded at the success of Hegel's system. He represented a great many people who found Hegel charming as a person but who found the Hegelian system unfathomable and therefore distrusted it.[17] Hegel's very critical review of Humboldt's book on the classic Indian work the *Baghvad Gita*, in the *Jahrbuch* in 1827, also did not exactly encourage von Humboldt to change his mind about Hegel's philosophy.

The issue of Hegel's joining the Academy of Sciences also kept popping up, and the whole affair began to resemble an ongoing, badly written farce: Hegel would be proposed for membership, and then, to everyone's hard feelings, Hegel would be denied because Schleiermacher would always blackball him. Schleiermacher had in fact taken some extraordinary steps in order to keep Hegel out, including an attempt to abolish altogether the "philosophical section" of the academy; having failed at that, Schleiermacher at first simply refused to call meetings of the section and in 1826 even resigned from it and founded a new class, the "philosophical/historical section," with himself as the head. On November 12, 1827, the only two remaining members of the "philosophical class," J. P. F. Ancillon (a prominent figure in governmental circles but not a philosopher) and H. F. Link (a professor of medicine and director of the botanical garden) actually voted to accept both Hegel and Heinrich Ritter (a historian of philosophy and a Schleiermacher student) into the section, but Link (perhaps under pressure from Schleiermacher and certainly fearing bad blood between Hegel and Schleiermacher) then changed his vote. The "philosophical section" (with a new, pro-Schleiermacher member) then voted in December to merge with the "philosophical/historical section" (under Schleiermacher's leadership). That seemed to end the matter once and for all.

Hegel was surely miffed at this new rebuff, and, as if to raise his anxiety level, new matters kept popping up that could only have been disquieting. The flap over his birthday celebration in 1826 had long since blown over, and his trip to Paris the next year, which had taken him out of Berlin on his own birthday, had seemed to effectively distance him from any such recurrence. But the January 26, 1827, edition of the liberal French newspaper the *Constitutionel* included an article roundly praising Hegel for his virtuous efforts in securing Victor Cousin's release from the hands of the unscrupulous Prussian police; and when the head of the Berlin police, von Kamptz, learned of the existence of the French article, he once again became furious and told people that Hegel had in fact arranged his whole trip to Paris simply in order to arrange for the *Constitutionel* to publish the article. (Von Kamptz had been equally outraged a couple of years before on learning of Victor Cousin's praise of Hegel with regard to this affair in the Preface to his book on Plato.) Once again, Hegel found himself having to tread lightly around the police powers of the Prussian state. This had to hit Hegel particularly hard; by temperament, he was a conservative fellow, hardly one to rock the social boat, but at the same time he was a celebrator of modern life who remained firmly attached to the ideals of the Revolution. Hegel, who always combined contradictory elements in his own personality, wanted to be both a reformer and an upstanding member of the existing social order. To be accused of deliberately fomenting trouble would thus have been an offense to his sense of himself.

As if this were not enough, Marie's health also seemed to remain on the low side in 1828, which only increased Hegel's worries, especially given her past history of threatening illnesses. He dealt with this as he always did, retreating into his Whist games with Zelter and his other friends, continuing his attendance at the theater and opera, taking his daily walks, head bowed, as he strolled silently among the Berliners marveling at the pale sight moving amongst them, focusing his energy on his lectures, and churning out a series of long critical articles for the *Jahrbücher* about various literary and philosophical figures of the day (articles that, had they been collected together, would have formed a lengthy book on their own).

There were other irritations that accompanied Hegel's increasing celebrity and renown. In 1826, one of his former students, Christian Kapp, published a book, *The Concrete Universal in History*, that for all intents and purposes was plagiarized from Hegel's lectures. Hegel was, to say the least, not pleased, but he did not press the issue. Kapp later defended himself in the way that plagiarists typically do, at least at first: He claimed that the similarities were purely coincidental and that a friend on reading his first book had told him how similar his and Hegel's views were and had then communicated some Hegelian sentences to him, and, somehow, some way, those sentences became incorporated into Kapp's own system, but that, after all, he really was praising Hegel's philosophy in his book, and, besides, he had always distinguished in his lectures which were his and which were Hegel's views.[18] To make matters worse, Kapp later published another book in 1829, *Goethe, Schelling, Hegel*, which among other things made the witless claim that Schelling was the prudent Menelaos of German philosophy and Hegel the avenging Agamemnon. Hegel was again irritated at Kapp's inanities and made his feelings about them quite well known; Schelling, for his part, simply hit the roof and accused Kapp of plagiarizing both himself and Hegel, which in turn caused Kapp to reply by accusing Schelling of committing the sin of idolatry vis-à-vis himself. (Moritz Saphir remarked about the ensuing dispute among Hegel, Kapp, and Schelling that it showed that philosophers think obscurely but swear very clearly.)[19]

His experiences with Kapp made Hegel perhaps a bit too sensitive to issues of plagiarism. Copies of notes taken during his lectures were now widely in circulation, and there was nothing he could do to stop it. When he learned that his old acquaintance K. J. Windischmann had published a piece on Chinese history that seemed to him to resemble his own lectures too closely to be merely coincidence, he turned to his usual sarcasm in his lectures, making various jibes about how Windischmann had stolen his ideas. On hearing of this, Windischmann was furious and deeply insulted; he wrote to Hegel to express his displeasure, pointing out that he had been saying those things for a long time, that all his friends would attest to it, and furthermore that he had been working and publishing on that subject since 1804, hurtfully telling Hegel that as one of the very first people to have seen the importance of Hegel's work and brought it to public attention, he simply had not "deserved such a hostile allusion" on Hegel's part.[20] To others, he privately expressed his intense aggravation about the matter, claiming that he had been working on that material for much longer than Hegel had and that he could as easily say that Hegel had stolen from him rather than the other way around.[21]

The Calm before the Storm

Health Problems

Hegel's health had also taken a turn for the worse in 1829. He began complaining about chest pains, and his rather shaky financial state made him all the more nervous. Everybody who saw Hegel during this period remarked on the absolute whiteness of his face; he was quite likely suffering from some sort of anemia brought on by a chronic upper gastrointestinal disease that eventually would lead to his death. His "chest pains" were most likely not heart problems but problems associated with the kind of acid reflex that often accompanies such diseases. Hegel consulted physicians, but they could do little to help him. He also therefore had to give up drinking tea in the evenings, something he clearly much enjoyed.[22]

In May 1829, he wrote Altenstein another letter complaining of his health, how it had weakened him, how it had hampered his work, and how his physician had recommended a lengthy trip to a spa, which he could not afford. His weakness was so bad, he told Altenstein, he could offer only one set of private lectures for extra money, and that compounded the financial troubles in which he found himself. In requesting money for such an extended stay at a spa, he also pointed out that since coming to Berlin he had not had a single increase in salary, "for which I was led to hope by Your Excellency's gracious promises upon my entry into the Royal civil service, though I have not dared to inquire further about this matter."[23] (The issue of his nonappointment to the academy was clearly still on his mind, as Altenstein was only too painfully aware.) It was also clear to Hegel he could not expect automatically to receive any extra money without giving some special reasons, and he thus poignantly implored Altenstein for more money by noting that if Altenstein were to grant his request, he "might perhaps prolong the life of a man" who had taught loyally and seriously for eleven years at the university.[24] As always, Altenstein secured the money for Hegel's travels.

Adding to Hegel's stress was the fact that the building in which the Hegels lived had to be completely renovated, and Hegel and his wife had to decide whether they would move or continue to live through all the chaos that comes from construction going on in the house. They finally concluded that they liked their apartment on Kupfergraben quite a bit and that, frankly, moving the whole family would be more trouble than putting up with the construction. In the spring and summer of 1829, therefore, they shipped Karl and Immanuel off to relatives and settled into the turmoil of living in a construction zone. Despite his bad health (and being surrounded by the continuous dust accompanying construction, something about which Marie especially complained), he remained more or less in good spirits. Marie Hegel described him in a letter to his sister, Christiane, in June 1829 as being "10 years younger and 20 years more merry and high-spirited as back then in Nuremberg."[25] No doubt some of that was intended to give a cheerier picture of Hegel's health to his sister than was accurate; but no doubt part of it was also correct – Hegel was at the height of his fame and powers, and he was relishing it. In any event, whatever stresses and strains there were on the family, they did not stop the Hegels from taking in a friend's son, a Mr. von Wahl, as a sort of "foster son" while he studied at Berlin. Ludwig's place in the house was empty, and the Hegel family obviously thought that they could deal with having another young man around the house.

Zelter and Felix Mendelssohn-Bartholdy

Hegel's own interest in Berlin's musical life continued unabated, and his celebrity gave him a certain entrée into the scene. His friend Zelter, after all, was one of the dominating presences on the Berlin musical scene as the director of the *Singakademie*. Zelter, whose tastes in music were extremely conservative and who combined a kind of rough-hewn, gruff manner with an acute sensitivity, idolized Haydn and Mozart (although he rather puritanically saw Mozart as a dissolute, immoral fellow, although a genius of the first order).[26] Zelter's strong musical beliefs included his conviction that the melody of a piece should follow the words exactly, and he mightily distrusted the efforts of people like Beethoven to add color and drama to the accompaniment of a poem set to music, holding that the poetry itself had to bear the whole weight of the emotion. Zelter, whose friendship with Goethe was itself legendary, also influenced Goethe's own taste in music and probably only rein- forced Goethe's otherwise natural disinclination to the music of Schu- bert and Beethoven. Hegel shared to a large extent Zelter's taste (and that Goethe shared it would have legitimated it all the more strongly for Hegel); indeed, it may well have been Zelter's influence that kept Hegel from even mentioning, much less seriously considering Beetho- ven.

One of Zelter's protégés was Felix Mendelssohn-Bartholdy, the son of a very prominent and prosperous Berlin Jewish family and the grand- son of the famous philosopher Moses Mendelssohn. Felix had been recognized at an early age as a child prodigy in music and had been put under Zelter's wing for instruction. Zelter, proud of his charge, had even taken the twelve-year-old Felix to Weimar in 1821 to meet Goethe and show off his musical skills; when Goethe suddenly produced origi- nal scores by Mozart and Beethoven for young Felix to play on the piano, the young man acquitted himself brilliantly and then astonished the assembled group all the more with his own compositions. (Zelter of course taught Mendelssohn to ignore Schubert and Beethoven and to look instead to Mozart; however, luckily enough, another of Mendelssohn's teachers, Bernhard Klein, taught him to venerate Beethoven and Schubert, and Mendelssohn happily combined the two influences.)[27] Hegel's friendships with the Mendelssohn family, Zelter, and Klein meant that Hegel was thus acquainted with young Felix Mendelssohn-Bartholdy at an early age. During his years at the university, Felix in fact attended Hegel's lectures and assiduously took notes on Hegel's theories of aesthetics.

In 1829, young Felix Mendelssohn, who, as legend has it, had been shown the score to Bach's *Saint Matthew Passion* by Zelter, began to think about staging a performance of it; the piece had been written in 1729, the year in which his grandfather Moses Mendelssohn had been born, so Felix hit upon the idea of celebrating both occasions with some kind of public spectacle. Together with Eduard Devrient, a famous young singer in Berlin (and also another of Zelter's protégés), they conspired to practice the *Passion* secretly at his house; when the time was right, they sprang their plan on Zelter. Zelter, they knew, admired Bach but thought he was beyond the taste of the Berlin musical public and hence was disinclined to stage Bach choral pieces; but, faced with this coup from his two protégés, after much harumphing and hesitating, Zelter agreed to help them and to put the resources of the Berlin *Singakademie* behind their efforts. Ms. Milder-Hauptmann was even persuaded to be one of the soloists. On March 11, 1829, the *Passion* was staged to overwhelming public acclaim and critical success.

The production became the talk of Berlin, and the demand for another production was so high that it was restaged on March 21 (Bach's birthday); all the great Berlin notables, including Hegel, attended. Afterward, a proud Zelter held a select dinner at his house for the stars of the performance and the local luminaries. Eduard Devrient and his wife, Therese, so overwhelmed with admirers after the event that they arrived at Zelter's much later than the other guests, hurriedly took their seats at the places assigned to them. Therese was immediately told to take a seat next to Felix Mendelssohn-Bartholdy, and in her memory of things, Felix "stood up, as did the man on my left, to help me squeeze in, as things were very tight. Felix was in an effervescent mood, we chatted and laughed, so that I didn't notice the servant offering me things. The man on my left bid me to let him do it. Afterward, he continuously tried to talk me into drinking some more wine and to fill my glass, which I declined until it was proposed that we toast to the health of the artist, from which, he rather affectedly whispered, I could not exclude myself, to which he then festively clinked glasses with me. He unrelentingly gripped my furthermost lace sleeve 'in order to protect it!', as he put it when he occasionally turned to me. In short, he so annoyed me with his gallantries that I turned to Felix and asked, 'Tell me who this dumb goofball is beside me.' Felix held his handkerchief over his mouth for a moment and then whispered, 'The dumb goofball there beside you is the famous philosopher, Hegel.' "[28] Hegel, the Würt-temberger from Stuttgart, apparently liked playing the role of a "gentle-man of the old order" and apparently was oblivious to just how his affectations were being received; just as he had irritated Caroline Schle-gel Schelling at Jena with his behavior, he managed in Berlin to irritate Therese Devrient with his mannerisms vis-à-vis women.

Reunion with Schelling

The association with Mendelssohn-Bartholdy was, however, gratifying. He now had a young man billed as the "new Mozart" as one of his students, taking notes at his lectures on aesthetics, and he enjoyed chatting with young Felix, who was invited to accompany Hegel on some of his various strolls. Indeed, in the course of 1830, things began to calm down a bit for Hegel. The university celebrated the twentieth anniversary of its founding in August, and at all the gala ceremonies, people noticed how Hegel and Schleiermacher (among others) seemed to bury the hatchet and get along quite well with each other. Both Schleiermacher's and Hegel's deep commitment to the success of the new, modern Berlin university apparently brought them together, at least on this occasion.

To the surprise of some, Hegel was elected in 1830 as the rector (more or less the president) of the university, the highest administrative office for the institution. It was clear that whatever negative feelings some of the faculty had harbored about Hegel in the past, they had for the most part been put aside. He was finally being recognized by his fellow professors, something which must have moved him deeply. (But clearly some people, like the eminent theologian August Neander – who under Schleiermacher's influence had converted to Christianity from Judaism – were still ambivalent about Hegel; Neander refused to become the dean of the theological faculty because he feared there would inevitably be conflicts between himself and Hegel.)[29]

Shortly after the celebrations, Hegel – who as rector was now to be addressed as *Magnifizenz* – set off for the spas at Teplitz and Karlsbad. His mother-in-law and her sister had preceded him there, and Hegel was happy to arrive on August 26 and join them for a celebration of his birthday the next day. (Once again, he was conveniently absent from Berlin for the event.) The night he arrived, he and Marie's mother's group feasted on a *Rebhuhn* (a kind of pheasant), had a jolly time, and Hegel made a good impression on all the ladies in Marie's family.[30] (There was even a whiff of scandal in the whole stopover; Marie's Aunt Rosenhayn – her mother's sister – was traveling with a man to whom she was not married, and, as Marie's mother told Marie, she found it all, well, "shocking," but then who was she to meddle in "secrets of the heart"?)[31] Hegel stayed in Teplitz with Marie's mother and aunt for a few days, at which point they all set off for Prague, where he stayed with Marie's uncle (whom he had seen during his earlier trip to Prague).

He arrived in Karlsbad on September 3, 1829. He immediately set out on a regime of drinking the sparkling mineral water for which the spa was famous, and he was able to report back to Marie that after two or three days of hiking and drinking mineral water (and eating healthy spa food), he no longer had any chest pains at all.[32] One day during his stay at the baths, he heard that, of all people, Schelling was also at one of the spas in town. Hegel went searching and located his old friend and now adversary. He wrote his wife about it; he characterized their meeting as a very happy reunion, and described how they immediately hit it off together like "cordial friends of old."[33] Schelling, he remarked, looked very "healthy and strong," not even needing the spa's regime except as a "preservative." They took a walk together, sat in a coffee house and jointly read the newspaper accounts of the taking of Adrianapolis in the Russian-Turkish war, and then passed the evening together. The idea of the old friends effortlessly renewing their old camaraderie became Hegel's official account of his reunion with Schelling; he repeated it to others, and Marie repeated Hegel's characterization of it to all their friends – they were just like "cordial friends of old," she would say.

This reconciliation with Schelling filled an emotional hole in Hegel's life. He, Hölderlin, and Schelling had been inseparable during their youth at the university; Schelling had given him his start at Jena, and he had in fact begun his academic career as more or less a Schellingian. Thus, the bitterness and rivalry that had later emerged between them obviously did not sit well with Hegel, and he surely knew that part of the blame lay with himself. Although he had never publicly spoken badly of Schelling himself – even though he had criticized Schelling's philosophy quite a bit in his lectures – his scathing references to Schellingian thought in his *Phenomenology of Spirit*, which he had feebly tried to explain away as not directed at Schelling personally but only at the weak-minded uses to which others had put his ideas, had certainly not convinced Schelling himself, and Hegel had never even replied to Schelling's rather cold letter to him about those particular passages in the *Phenomenology* (even though Schelling had ended his letter on a somewhat conciliatory note).

As Hegel was making his own career, moreover, the tendency of many to lump him and Schelling together led him to stress their differences. The rift between them had thus grown, and Hegel seemed to have come to the conclusion that the rift had been inevitable. During his lectures in Berlin, he had once remarked on the nature of youthful friendships, and those comments seem to have been thinly disguised autobiographical reflections on his own relations with both Hölderlin and Schelling in their Tübingen days, and on his later relations with Hölderlin in Frankfurt, with Schelling in their early years in Jena together, and with Niethammer even later in Nuremberg. In each of those cases, his onetime close friendship had cooled down as Hegel had gone his own way and moved up in the world. Youth is a period, Hegel said, "in which individuals become intimate and are so closely bound into *one* disposition, will, and activity that, as a result, every undertaking of the one becomes the undertaking of the other. In the friendship of adult men this is no longer the case. A man's affairs go their own way independently and cannot be carried into effect in that firm community of mutual effort in which one man cannot achieve anything without someone else. Men find others and separate themselves from them again; their interests and occupations drift apart and unite again; friendship, the innerness of disposition, principles, and general trends of life remain, but this is not the friendship of young men. . . . It is inherent essentially in the principle of our deeper life that, on the whole, every man fends for himself, i.e., is himself proficient in his own actuality."[34]

But, however Hegel thought it necessary for each man to fend for himself, it was equally important emotionally at that point to Hegel that he and Schelling make up, and that was exactly how *he* interpreted their encounter. In fact, he even took to defending Schelling after a fashion; after Victor Cousin had published a book of "philosophical fragments," Hegel chided him (in a letter of February 1830) about the superficiality of his treatment of recent German philosophy and noted that "Schelling's philosophy, which you mention, embraces in its principles much more than you have attributed to it, and you yourself ought surely to have known that."[35]

However, Schelling's account to his wife of his meeting with Hegel diverged in important ways from Hegel's. He noted in a letter to her, "Imagine, yesterday as I was sitting in the bath, I heard a somewhat unpleasant, half-forgotten voice asking for me. Then the stranger gave his name, it was Hegel from Berlin, who had come here from Prague with some relatives and wanted to stay a couple of days here on the trip. That afternoon he came a second time, very eager and uncommonly friendly as if nothing were standing between us; however, since we haven't had any scholarly conversation up until now, which I also do not intend to let myself get induced into, and since he incidentally is a very bright person, I did spend two agreeable hours conversing with him in the evening. I haven't yet visited him again; he's a bit too far away from me in the Golden Lion."[36] There are several revealing phrases, including "as if nothing were standing between us," and his remark about refusing to engage in any "scholarly (*wissenschaftlichen*) conversation" with Hegel. Schelling had obviously felt a bit betrayed by Hegel as Hegel rose to fame, and this had tended to color Schelling's own view of Hegel as a person and as a thinker; he had known Hegel as a youth, and he was convinced that Hegel simply was not as clever as his admirers thought he was, that what was admirable in Hegel's philosophy was what he had lifted from Schelling himself, and that what was objectionable was the rationalist form he had imposed on it. Schelling was thus not ready for reconciliation with Hegel, although Hegel (perhaps because he had won the battle for public opinion) was clearly in need of reconciliation with Schelling.

The full rapprochement between the two men, however, never came about in Hegel's lifetime. A few years after Hegel's death, Hegel's son Immanuel went to Munich to study law (where he lived with his godfather, Immanuel Niethammer) and decided to hear Schelling's lectures; at first, he was incensed by what he took to be Schelling's negative views on his father's thought, but later, after having been invited to Schelling's house for several balls, having been invited for Schelling's sixtieth birthday celebration, and having met Schelling's daughters, he changed his mind. Immanuel became a frequent visitor to Schelling's house and an admirer of Schelling as a person and as a thinker, even later endorsing his appointment to his father's old chair in Berlin. Schelling himself apparently only achieved his own reconciliation with Hegel through Hegel's son, four years after Hegel's death.[37]

New Honors and New Worries

Overbearing Times

Hegel returned to Berlin feeling much better and turned his energies to his newly acquired post as rector of the university and to working on the *Jahrbücher*. Hegel's prestige with the government was such that he was allowed to hold two distinct administrative positions: In addition to his position as rector, he was also to function as the government plenipotentiary overseeing the university (a post required by the Karlsbad decrees and which until then had always been held by someone outside of the university). The latter involved being the middleman between the university and the government and overseeing the university from the government's perspective, and it was thus a great honor for Hegel and a matter of some importance to the university that for the first time since the Karlsbad decrees, the university was not being overseen by some nonuniversity government official. For his inauguration as rector, he delivered a Latin address urging the students, not surprisingly, to devote themselves to *Wissenschaft*.

But Hegel's illness did not go away, and his ill health, his anxiety about his health, and his own very typical self-assuredness about the rightness of his cause made him more and more imperious and domineering, even to his friends. In one case that illustrates many others, during a meeting of the board of the *Jahrbuch* in 1829, Hegel and Varnhagen von Ense were discussing a book dealing with the so-called "wars of liberation"; their conversation, however, quickly escalated into a heated argument about the depiction of a particular battle in the book. Hegel vehemently held that the book had gotten it all wrong; Varnhagen von Ense in fact had been an officer at the battle depicted in the book and claimed that the book's description was substantially correct, but that minor fact counted for nothing to Hegel, who simply would not be persuaded that he might be wrong about something about which, in this case, he knew little. Hegel's assistant, von Henning (who had also fought in the wars) tried to calm him down and to mediate the dispute, but Hegel's outburst, his attempt to dress down Varnhagen von Ense as if he were a some kind of schoolboy, was painfully embarrassing for all present.[38] Varnhagen von Ense, in fact, sadly recalled Hegel's comportment in his last couple of years of life as being "wholly absolutistic," how in meetings of the board of the *Jahrbücher* he was becoming "more difficult and more tyrannical" as time went on.[39] In his outbursts, he would dress down even his good friends as if they were children being scolded, something everyone concerned found both embarrassing and painful to behold.[40]

However, during the early parts of 1830, Hegel began to ease up a bit. After one of Hegel's typical explosions, Varnhagen von Ense offered his hand to Hegel to let him know that he still honored him and considered him his friend; Hegel, obviously moved by this gesture, his eyes filled with tears, instead of merely taking von Ense's hand, embraced him.[41] He even confessed to Zelter that he had allowed himself to become too caught up with his opponents.[42] He clearly was seeking some kind of reconciliation with some of the people whom he had treated so haughtily, and he was clearly, worried and stressed as he was, having a difficult time doing so.

Although Hegel's celebrity was also now so high that a tobacconist even attempted to get his endorsement for some snuff tobacco, he continued to experience rebuffs from various sides even in his newly assumed position of responsibility and honor.[43] Early in 1830, Altenstein proposed Hegel for the royal honors list (the Red Order of the Eagle, third class), but he was outright refused, while at the same time Alexander von Humboldt managed to get two of his friends on the faculty so listed.[44] And as if to continue what had long since become a farce, Wilhelm von Humboldt agreed to have Hegel accepted as a member of the Academy of Sciences in May 1830, noting that Hegel should have been accepted long ago; but, as if on cue, on December 15, 1830, the Academy once again refused to accept Hegel – refused to accept the very elected rector of the university itself!

There were also some disquieting rumblings coming from other university towns in Prussia. In Halle in January 1830, several theologians associated with the recently founded (1827), very conservative *Evangelische Kirchenzeitung* (*Journal of the Evangelical Church*) were accused of "lack of belief," the basis for the charges lying in some student notes on their lectures. After much controversy and some lawsuits, they were declared innocent. But Hegel, like all other professors, followed these events with great interest and some apprehension; if one could be denounced on the basis of student lecture notes, then clearly everybody was in danger. Worse, almost everybody, including Hegel, had thought that those kinds of inquisitions were long since over, and yet here they were, surfacing again.

Remembrances of Hölderlin

On March 6, 1830, Hegel was invited as the rector of the university to attend a luncheon with the crown prince, his wife, and other members of the court. There was some discussion among members of the court as to what they should talk about with their celebrity philosopher, and at first the conversation seemed to stall. In order to break the ice, Princess Marianne, the crown prince's wife, asked Hegel about his old friend Issak von Sinclair. The princess was Marianne of Hessen-Homburg; her father had been the *Landgraf* of Hessen-Homburg, for whom Sinclair had been the minister, and Sinclair in turn had employed Hölderlin as librarian during Hegel's stay in Frankfurt. Her older sister, Auguste, had in fact in her youth been enamored of Hölderlin. Hegel suddenly came alive; his own memories of the heady days in Frankfurt with his friend Hölderlin, now apparently living in the darkness of mental illness in Tübingen, welled up, and he began to speak with great spiritedness about the area itself, remembering the name of each small mountain that lay between Frankfurt and Homburg vor der Höhe, hills that he had often walked with Sinclair. In her diary, the princess noted

in an almost Proustian voice, "At that point, he began to speak of
Hölderlin, whom the world has forgotten – of his book, *Hyperion* – all
of which had constituted an *époque* for me on account of my sister
Auguste's relation to them – and I found by the sounding of this name
a true joy – a whole lost past went through me . . . it was a remembrance
awakened as otherwise would be done through a smell or melody or
sound."[45] The princess recalled her vivid memories of seeing the sun
coming through the window and seeing *Hyperion* bound in green lying
on the windowsill. Hegel spoke of his now-lost times with his friend
Hölderlin.

It was not the first time in Berlin that Hegel had thought of his old,
and at one time dearest, friend; in fact, Hegel had been a participant in
an effort to get Hölderlin's works published in Berlin. A fastidious
lieutenant in the Prussian army (Johann Heinrich Diest) had led the
effort, engaging Johannes Schulze (who had also been an old friend of
Sinclair's), Princess Marianne, and Hegel himself, who had offered
much advice and had spoken of the conversations that he and Hölderlin
had pursued on the topics of Hölderlin's dramas (but alas, Hegel had to
tell Diest, he personally had no manuscripts of Hölderlin's to offer for
the edition); and in 1822, a new edition of *Hyperion* was published,
followed by a new volume of Hölderlin's poetry in 1826.[46] Hegel in fact
never mentioned Hölderlin in his writings or in his lectures (even on
aesthetics); for Hegel, Hölderlin seemed to have been merely an old
friend and a failed poet; he tended, no doubt, to see Hölderlin as
someone who had not completely worked through the common revolutionary project that he, Hölderlin, and Schelling had begun as youths
in the university. But, it was clear, even though he had never spoken of
him, he had never forgotten the person who had the most influence on
him and been his dearest friend. For a moment with Princess Marianne,
Hegel was not thinking of the present but was lost in his youth again,
reliving in memory his Frankfurt days.

The Anniversary of the Augsburg Confession

The summer of 1830 marked the three hundredth anniversary of the
Augsburg Confession, and the Berlin government and university decided to make quite a show of the event. They therefore called on Hegel
as rector of the university and as the celebrity philosopher of Berlin to

deliver one of the two main Latin addresses during the official festivities on June 25. The "confession" itself had been submitted to the Holy Roman Emperor, Charles V, at the Diet of Augsburg on June 25, 1530, and, largely compiled by Melanchton and based on Luther's writings, it had set out the official doctrines of what came to be the Lutheran Church; it distinguished the Lutheran creed both from Catholicism and from other Protestant sects, it specified explicitly what the new Lutheran creed held in common with Catholic doctrine, and it laid out the bases for abolishing monastic vows, mandatory celibacy for the clergy and so on.

Hegel used the occasion to talk in a relatively accessible manner about some of the key themes in his own thought on the relation between religion and modern life, and, returning to an old theme in his thought, why the Protestant Reformation was the harbinger of the French Revolution and why it made the kind of bloodshed experienced in France unnecessary in Germany. Just how many people in the audience actually understood and followed his Latin oration is, of course, unclear. (Hegel himself prepared for his Latin duties by having Friedrich Förster help him with his Latin, though he probably needed little help, and, appropriately, by sharing several bottles of Lacrima Christi wine with him, a famous Italian wine from Vesuvius made from a variety of grapes in use since Roman times.)

Hegel began by asking what "the meaning" of that day was for us, his modern, post-revolutionary audience, and he suggested at the very beginning of his oration that it had to do with modern freedom: The "confession" showed that Christianity's evangelical teaching "had finally been purified of superstitious customs, errors, manifold deceptions, and every possible injustice and wantonness" and that the true "matter of religion" had thus been firmly taken in hand, such that what had counted earlier as the "laity had a claim to their own judgments in matters of faith" and those who authored and accepted this confession "acquired this inestimable freedom on a principled basis for all of us."[47] He even suggested with some humility to his audience that he, as a member of the laity and not a theologian (perhaps a bit of false modesty on his part) was able to speak on such matters indeed only because of the fundamental freedoms accorded by the "confession."[48] To this end, he returned to an old theme in his thought: the crucial differences between premodern, dogmatic Catholicism and the true religion of modern life, Protestantism.

Before the "confession," he said, the "Christian world was divided into two classes," one that had all the rights and privileges (the ecclesiasticals) and the other that was "reduced to servitude."[49] But since what was always implicit in Christianity was its declaration of itself as committed to the dignity of all, working out that implicit belief in Christianity came to require us to adopt the Protestant principle that each individual is ineluctably in the position such that with regard to "the relationship which he has to God and God to him, [he] himself produces it with God, and that God Himself for his part completes Himself in the human spirit."[50] This "divinity" to which we relate is a God "that is the truth, eternal reason and the consciousness of this reason, that is, is spirit. According to God's will, man is endowed with this consciousness of reason and is thereby differentiated from the animals lacking reason."[51]

This new and true understanding of the nature of the Christian religion, Hegel argued, implied a fundamental change in the very form of life for Christian peoples. With the Protestant "renewal of religion" it became necessary for "the fundamental principles of the state as well as those of civil and ethical life to change."[52] This meant that the new "confession" was not simply one set of dogmas exchanged for another set; it did not result in those accepting it only "exchanging their [old] chains" for new and different ones; it was instead the basis for a new way of life, a "community founded in this avowal" in which "culture (*Bildung*), the free arts, and the sciences were returned" to mankind, and the results of this change was there for us to observe "daily in continuous forceful progress and growth, together with freedom, which has opened access to these studies to all."[53]

Hegel also elaborated what for him was an idée fixe, that the Catholic Church had completely misunderstood this, and that modern life had both made a total break with the ancient world with its Christian emphasis on freedom while at the same time managing to appropriate the true meaning of antiquity. The old teachings of the older church – in other words, Catholic doctrine – had completely inverted, Hegel told his audience, the real meaning of Christian freedom. The "virtues, which the Greeks and the Romans bequeathed to us for admiration and imitation" – among which were "love of marital couples for each other, of parents and children for each other, from which followed integrity, fairness, and benevolence towards others, conscientiousness and honesty in the administration of property, and finally the love of king and fatherland, for whose defense we must also stake our own lives" – these were the kinds of things that the old (Catholic) church had quite incomprehensibly declared, Hegel asserted, to be vices.[54] In place of those properly Christian ideals, the Catholic Church had substituted instead another "ideal of life . . . namely, that of *holiness.*"[55] But the very notion that the ideal of "love and piety" lay in celibacy and childlessness was absurd, itself only a "corruption of ethics."[56] Equally absurdly, Hegel argued, the old (Catholic) church made "poverty into a religious virtue."[57] This meant that it did not reward industry, conscientiousness, and all the other related virtues which had made modern life so prosperous and had put the moderns in the position of *actually* being able to help others as the Christian virtues commanded them to do. Even worse, the old (Catholic) church had only put on a "show" of poverty, reserving wealth and luxury for its more highly placed clerics. Finally, the old (Catholic) church had enforced a "blind obedience" and "thrown human understanding into subjection."[58]

The German princes, in fighting for the Reformation, and those princes who accepted the Augsburg Confession, had set the scene, Hegel argued, for a genuine reconciliation between the state and religion. If one doubted the relation between religion and the modern state, Hegel said, one need only note that all the Catholic countries of the world have not yet achieved the kinds of freedoms already present in most of the Protestant countries. (One wonders whether he would have included his beloved France in this assessment.) But the Protestant reconciliation between religion and the state should not be taken to require the very modern ideal of the "separation of church and state," which, although a doctrine proposed by many "highly regarded and clever" people, was nonetheless, Hegel argued, a "weighty error," since "civil freedom and justice are solely and only the fruit of freedom attained in God."[59]

Famously, the Augsburg Confession left one thing open, stipulating that it was to be left up to each German prince to decide for himself which faith (Protestant or Catholic) he would follow, and that set the stage, as later history indeed showed, for further bloody religious wars between competing princely claims to represent the true religion. Hegel wrote off that part with a rhetorical gesture; those later religious wars were merely the price that had to be paid, he said, for the sin of having falsified Christian teaching in the first place. But, as he went on to claim near the end of the oration, those wars and that heavy price have themselves been redeemed in the modern world, in which Protestant Germans, the successors to those who fought for the Augsburg Confession, have been put in the position "to increase freedom, improve the laws, make the arrangements of the state more comfortable and more appropriate" for themselves and their posterity.[60]

Hegel's oration was received extremely well, not so much for the Hegelian philosophy of religion that was expressed in it – if the audience had reflected on that, they might not have liked it so much – but for its clear and polemical assertion of the superiority of the "Protestant principle" as the basis for a modern, efficient, prosperous state. In largely Protestant Berlin, his celebration of the superiority of the "Protestant principle" found a welcome audience.

The "July Revolution"

Hegel's time for basking in the glory of his well-received speech did not last long. Events in France upset the calm that had gradually taken root in Germany during the 1820s. The Chamber of Deputies in France (led by Royer-Collard, a philosopher and Victor Cousin's teacher and mentor) had by an overwhelming majority issued a vote of "no confidence" in the regime of the Bourbon king of France, Charles X (the successor to his restored brother, Louis XVIII), and, almost exactly one month after Hegel gave his speech, Charles X, in an attempt to shore up his weakly supported regime, issued his infamous "four ordinances" on July 25, which, among other things, at one stroke abolished freedom of the press and instituted censorship, dissolved the Chamber of Deputies, and instituted a new set of rules for the composition of a new Chamber of Deputies still to be chosen. Protests immediately broke out in Paris, and, as if in a replay of the Revolution of 1789, barricades went up in various key areas in the city, which led to battles between the populace and some highly demoralized troops who had been ordered to defend a wildly unpopular regime. After three days (July 27–29), the king withdrew his decrees on July 30, but the die had been cast: Charles X's cousin, the *Duc D'Orléans*, was ready to step in as the "bourgeois king" and assume the throne under a constitutional settlement. By August 9, it was all over, the *Duc D'Orléans* was king, and Charles X was on his way to exile in England.

Hegel's friends were overjoyed at the events in Paris. Eduard Gans, who was in Paris at the time, excitedly wrote a letter to Hegel from Paris giving him a short, quick update on the progress of events as he saw them.[61] Many liberals both in Germany and in France not only were overjoyed, but also saw in the events evidence of the historical pattern Mignet had already formulated: Just as the English "glorious revolution" had required forty years from the end of the monarchy to the limited monarchy represented by William of Orange, the French Revolution of 1789 almost forty years later seemed to be following the same, apparently predestined path; and to many liberals, the events suggested, as they had to Mignet, that some kind of progressive law of history was at work and that progress in these matters was inevitable. In Germany, many drew the implication that some form of defiance of the Prussian crown was therefore also unavoidable, as would be its foreordained constitutional aftermath. When the *Duc D'Orléans* assumed the throne, it seemed only to be a completion of what was a destined revolutionary rhythm. Hegel's younger friends and acquaintances in particular welcomed the July revolution as a harbinger of better things to come, a sign that the era of political reaction was now over, and that it would soon be their turn to participate in a new, successful revolution. The July revolution was experienced by many of these young people in the way that Hegel, Hölderlin and Schelling had experienced the Revolution of 1789, namely, as an "epochal" event, something from which there was no turning back, whose meaning for them and for their successors could not be a matter of accident but had to be a matter of destiny.

Hegel was extremely disturbed by the events in France, even though many of his friends and students themselves took the new revolution as a confirmation of his view of things. To their surprise, as things began to unfold even further, he become even more displeased at the direction events seemed to be taking. The Belgians rose against the Dutch and proclaimed their independence; in one fell swoop, van Ghert's attempts to create a "modernized" reconciliation between the Catholics and Protestants of the low countries were simply swept aside. There was unrest in Italy; in Poland, the Diet declared its independence, and by January 25, 1831, the Polish Diet had declared the czar of Russia to have "abdicated" from rule over Poland. Likewise, social unrest, partly fueled by rising prices and falling wages, began to sweep through the various German states, though the unrest took different forms in different places. In some places, such as Leipzig, there was destruction and looting of property belonging to unpopular merchants, and various small-scale "uprisings" were occurring from Hannover to Göttingen.

In Hegel's eyes, the world was in danger of falling apart right before his eyes. Karl Hegel remembered his father viewing the events starting to transpire around him with great trepidation but also with a certain equanimity: "With terror my father saw in them a catastrophe which seemed to shake the secure foundations of the rational state. But, unlike Niebuhr [a historian], he did not think that it would lead us to despotism and barbarism."[62] He even admitted to Ancillon that he thought the Prussian government could do business with the new king in France if only he would act rationally.[63]

Hegel had deeper fears, though, about the new turn of events in Europe. In Hegel's mind, the idea that there was anything like an iron law of history was just wrong; there were simply *no* laws of history at all. History was the scene of great human drama and human *meaning* but the attempt to find "laws" for history was tantamount to confusing *Geist* with nature. There was no "secret plan" of history hidden in some set of natural laws waiting to be discovered; the meaning of history lay in the way in which a kind of "mindedness" and "like-mindedness" – *Geist* – was to be understood in terms of its collective aspirations, and history was the drama of how certain forms of collective aspiration have necessarily failed and how they had been taken up by succeeding peoples. Hegel's own interpretation of that story was that humanity's collective aspiration had been "freedom," that since ancient Greece this had been more or less a self-conscious aspiration, and that the line from ancient Greece to 1830 was one of attempts to work out what was entailed by such an aspiration and was most assuredly *not* the effects of some quasi-natural law at work forcing European humanity to lurch along a preordained path from Greece to modern Europe. What was at work in world history was the "negativity" embodied in European life, a constant self-doubt and skepticism even about what mattered most to people that drove Europe to become "philosophical" and progressive.

"Who" we ended up being at the end of any historical progression, though, depended entirely on "who" we made ourselves to be. Thus, when the events of 1830 began to take shape, Hegel could not share in many of his friends' enthusiasm for the supposedly ironclad English model of revolutions.

In Hegel's mind, the Revolution had long since been over even in Germany, and what was at stake was its completion in gradual reform, not some Romantic replay of storming the Bastille. No new "epoch," in Hegel's opinion, was at hand, and on this point he split sharply with how his friends and students experienced the July revolution. True to his ideas, he also thought that the "liberal" revolution of 1830 in France and the corresponding calls for "freedom" in other parts of Europe were in fact bound to play, at least in Germany, into the hands of the hometowners. He began remarking to his friends that "everything that was formerly valid appears to have been made problematic," and that these are "anxious times in which everything that previously was taken to be solid and secure seems to totter."[64]

Hegel's friends themselves were simply dumbfounded at his negative reaction; they thought that, of all people, he would be cheering the turn of events, but instead he seemed to be sounding the same tone as Prince Metternich in Austria. He began to withdraw his interest from these affairs and began to make more and more sarcastic comments as to what he saw as the insanity and inanity of the period; it all seemed like meaningless play, like Romanticism gone amok, bringing with it the portentous threat of plunging Europe into war again. When his student Karl Ludwig Michelet tried to argue with him that the July revolution was in fact a marker of "progress" in history, Hegel simply replied sarcastically that he was talking "just like Gans." When Michelet argued that he had to admit that the new revolution was an expression of the "spirit of the people" of France, he answered curtly that one did not negotiate with the spirit of a people, one negotiated with individuals (indicating his ongoing distrust of the new regime in France).[65]

To many of his friends and students, however, Hegel seemed simply to be abandoning the ground on which he had stood; and to his detractors, who had always seen him as the "philosopher of the restoration," he only seemed to be showing his true colors, denouncing the fall of a restoration government. More and more in the eyes of his younger friends and students Hegel seemed to be becoming just a discouraged and very old man.

Hegel's Term as Rector Ends

In September 1830, both Hegel and his wife fell seriously ill with a chronic fever and some other unspecified maladies. These illnesses continued off and on (mostly on) through December; they were serious enough to provoke apprehension and anxiety among Hegel's friends such as Zelter and Varnhagen von Ense, who began to worry that something quite serious might be afoot. By the middle of December, Zelter was commenting that Hegel looked like a "shadow of himself."[66] His duties as rector were also becoming more onerous to him; in his weakened condition, he could hardly handle all the administrative, teaching, and writing projects that he had taken on, and they were simply wearing him out.

In October 1830, Hegel was finally able to relinquish his position as rector, having served his term (which was limited to one year), and he was able to return to working on the revisions of his *Science of Logic*, something about which he expressed deep satisfaction – the administrative life had not been for him – and by the end of January 1831, he had finished his revisions and expansions for the new edition.

He penned an address in October 1830 on the occasion of his handing over the office of rector to his successor (although his bad health prevented him from attending the formal occasion), in which he proudly and with some humor recounted the events in the university during the preceding year. He spoke of the necessity to fix a minimum faculty salary for "ordinary" professors and of how the university had managed to dam up the flow of *Privatdozenten* into the medical faculty and thereby to stop the lowering of living standards for the "ordinary" faculty there.[67] He proudly noted that more students – in fact, 1,909 – were attending the university than were attending any other university in Germany (at least according to the newspaper accounts, he added; but he prudently qualified that claim by noting that the real number was probably closer to 1,806, and possibly even as low as 1,744, although more likely the number actually *attending* lectures was as high as 2,200). He cited the greatest number of students – no surprise – as studying in the law faculty (633, compared with 611 for theology, 302 for medicine, and 241 for the philosophical faculty), which totaled 1,787 actually matriculated students.[68]

Hegel cited the usual problems and complaints about the dates on which semesters began and ended (absolutely nobody seemed satisfied with them). But, Hegel noted, there were many fewer disciplinary problems with the students, and no disciplinary problems at all having to do with "demagoguery." As illustration, and knowing it was bound to get a chuckle from his audience, Hegel recited the story of one student who after the July revolution went around Berlin wearing a French cockade – a little ribbon rosette that one pins onto one's hat, often worn in the *ancien régime* by nobility to show the colors of their family and during the Revolution by revolutionaries to display the red, white, and blue colors of the Revolution – but it turned out that the student actually *thought* he was wearing the colors of Brandenburg (the *Land* in which Berlin lay).[69] He was simply ignorant about his own country, hardly a revolutionary calling for the overthrow of the Prussian government.

Hegel also proudly remarked on how during his tenure, the government had finally been persuaded to build a university church for students to attend; too many students apparently did not feel welcome at one of the local congregations.[70] He closed his speech by bringing up a subject near and dear to him, the necessity to provide financial assistance for poor students who could not otherwise afford to attend university, an issue he had long championed (even though he himself had not seen fit to send Ludwig to university, apparently for financial reasons).[71]

New Hopes

Indeed, 1831 at first seemed to harbinger better things for Hegel. Hegel's son Karl graduated from *Gymnasium* in 1830 and then enrolled in the university in the autumn of that year to study history; he also began attending his father's famous lectures on the philosophy of world history. Hegel himself, although discouraged by the events of the July revolution and what had succeeded it, was beginning to take a more sanguine view of things, seeing the recent turn of events as being perhaps not quite as dreadful as he at first had understood them to be (although he still thought they were bad enough), and his celebrity and fame seemed unaffected by his sharp differences with his students and friends on the issue of the July revolution. There was the usual steady clamor of people to see him, the usual long sets of requests that he read this or that book, or that he offer his opinion on one matter or another. One person even submitted an unsolicited Latin translation of Hegel's *Encyclopedia* to him, wanting to know if perhaps Hegel just might happen to know a publisher in Berlin who just might happen to be interested in it.[72] (Hegel didn't bother.) Artists were composing and publishing pictures of him that quickly sold out, and his students had a medal struck with his likeness on one side and an allegorical scene depicting themes from his philosophy on the other. He proudly wrote his sister, "I've been engraved, sculpted, and now I'm stamped," as he sent her two copies of the medal.[73] (Indeed, in the years from 1829 to 1831, he and Marie seem to have been in closer correspondence with his sister than they had been in some time; although no new invitation for her to visit was forthcoming, Hegel was clearly trying to effect some sort of rapprochement with his sister after their long period of estrangement.) The second, expanded edition (1827) of his *Encyclopedia* had quickly sold out, and a third, even more expanded edition (1830) was doing well.

Hegel also finally became officially recognized for his achievements. In January 1831, Altenstein proudly informed Hegel that he was at last to be put on the royal honors list and to receive the Order of the Red Eagle, third class. (Schleiermacher was also to receive the same honor that year.) His mother-in-law could barely contain herself on hearing of it; in Nuremberg, news of the honor was going "from mouth to mouth," she gushed to Marie, and everyone keeps wishing to "extend their compliments to the new knight of the order."[74] Things seemed to be settling down for Hegel at home, even though his health was still not greatly improving.

Troubling Thoughts: The "July Revolution" and the English Reform Bill

The "July Revolution" and the Philosophy of History

Despite his failing health and his new officially recognized status, Hegel could still not get the recent events in France, Belgium, Poland, and

Germany out of his mind, and at the end of his lectures for the semester of 1830–1831 on the philosophy of history, Hegel turned for the first time since he had been lecturing on the subject to the historical impor- tance of contemporary events and even spoke specifically of the histori- cal meaning of the July revolution in France and the European unrest that was following on it.[75] In doing so, Hegel was clearly responding both to his critics and to his friends, and trying to think his own way through the contemporary events that troubled him so much. He viewed the establishment of the July monarchy in France as bound up with a deep mistake, since the "liberalism" on which the July monarchy was based, he argued, simply repeated one of the key errors of the 1789 Revolution (which he had criticized more than twenty years earlier in the *Phenomenology of Spirit*), namely, the inability of mere collections or aggregates of individuals to form a "universal point of view" that could carry any political or ethical authority and the consequent degeneration of "government" based on such "aggregates" into "factions." Hegel argued before the assembled students in his lecture hall that in such a "liberal" regime as that established by the July revolution, "the partic- ular arrangements of the government immediately stand in opposition to freedom, for they are particular wills and thus arbitrary," and when the opponents making the charges of arbitrariness manage themselves to form the government, they too, for the very same reasons, necessarily find "the many opposed to them. Thus, commotion and unrest are perpetuated."[76]

But Hegel made it clear to his audience that he was not praising the restoration regime that had fallen; the period since the fall of Napoleon and the restoration of the Bourbons had only been a "fifteen-year farce," as he put it.[77] And, for the first time, in his lectures on the philosophy of history, he spoke quite directly about his feelings concerning the 1789 Revolution. No doubt recalling his own experiences with Hölderlin and Schelling in Tübingen, he told the students, "The principle of the freedom of the will therefore vindicated itself against existing right . . . This was accordingly a glorious dawn. All thinking beings jointly cele- brated this epoch. Sublime emotion ruled at that time, a spiritual enthu- siasm peered into the heart of the world, as if the reconciliation between the divine and the secular were now first accomplished."[78]

The grounds for the failure of the French to establish a successful constitution, he suggested, lay to some extent in the lingering force of

Catholicism in France. Repeating some views he had long held and had
already stated in his Latin oration about the Augsburg Confession,
Hegel argued that Catholicism tends to inculcate a kind of character (a
disposition, *Gesinnung*) that is inclined towards obedience to positive
authority, and which, by denying the right of individual religious conscience, helps to shape agents who do not thereby have the personal and
ethical dispositions to become citizens of a rational, modern order. "It
must be plainly stated," he told his audience in 1831, "that with the
Catholic religion no rational constitution is possible; for the people and
the government must reciprocally have this final guarantee of 'disposition' and they can only have it in a religion that is not opposed to a
rational constitution for the state."[79] In putting it in this way, Hegel
seemed at first to be suggesting that the problems with the "liberalism"
of the July revolution were specifically French problems (or, if the
Belgian revolt was to be included, maybe problems endemic only to
"Catholic" and not to "Protestant" Europe), but not something that
was generalizable to modern life as such.

However, Hegel also suggested that he did *not* see this as merely a
passing phenomenon, as something purely "French," or, for that matter, as something for which the Hegelian philosophy had any quick and
easy solution. Something deeper was at work, a problem with a certain
dynamic of modern life that, although not challenging the overall meaning of history as having to do with a collective aspiration for freedom,
nonetheless offered up something for which there was no ready solution
at hand. Fully in keeping with his various critiques of moralism, Hegel
refused to condemn the liberal "mistake" in France as a failure of moral
will; and he did not suggest, as it were, that simply consulting the
Philosophy of Right would reveal the correct solution to the problems
raised by the events there. The July revolution and its aftermath had
revealed that the difficulty in establishing how self-determining individuals (which led to an apparently inescapable factionalism in modern life)
were institutionally and practically to be linked to a viable conception
of political authority was not merely a "French" problem or a problem
simply with "Catholicism." Instead, he told the assembled students,
"This collision, this nodal point, this problem is the point at which
history now stands and which it has to solve at some future time" –
seeming thereby to imply that the problem was coming to Germany,
even to Prussia itself, but not that he considered the problem irresolv-

able.[80] The issue of how to make the hometowns of southern Germany and the Prussian particularisms more rational had not been definitively resolved; and the "liberal" alternative seemed to him to be simply self-defeating. The overall "meaning" of history, Hegel continued to argue, had been definitively established as involving what was necessary for the realization of freedom. But history itself, so Hegel seemed to suggest in 1831, was still on the move; and Hegel himself was also on the move, starting to rethink some elements of his own position.

The Background to Hegel's Article on the Reform Bill

Hegel remained deeply disturbed by the events of the summer of 1830 and the consequent unrest, and he continued to devote a lot of his energy to trying to understand what those events might mean in terms of his own, now well-worked-out views on history, politics, and modern life. In the spring of 1831, he gave more flesh to them in a published commentary on what he saw as equally dangerous tendencies starting to emanate from England as the Parliament there was putting into motion a Reform Bill that claimed to fundamentally alter the constitutional setup of England.

Hegel published the first three parts of his highly critical four-part essay "On the English Reform Bill" in the *Allgemeine preußische Staatszeitung* (*Prussian State Gazette*) – an official and rather staid state newspaper – on April 26 and April 29, 1831. But the fourth part, which was supposed to be published on April 30 or May 2, never appeared in print in that newspaper; apparently the court thought that Hegel's rather harsh criticisms of the English government and the English king might prove too inflammatory if published in an official state organ. Nevertheless, Hegel's views had found a receptive audience, and the king apparently paid for a smaller private printing of the unpublished fourth part, which circulated around Berlin for all those who wished to read it.

Hegel had a variety of motives for writing his commentary. First, despite his great admiration for many things English, Hegel continued to be irritated at the suggestions current even among his friends that England was somehow the natural end of a line of modern development, and that the traumatic modern events of the Revolution and the reform movement were simply following out a destined path first trod by

England. He disagreed with the idea that there was any such natural line of development in history in the first place, and, despite his admiration for so many things English, he certainly did not think that England represented the ideal stopping point of modern life. Thus, he wanted to exhibit the deeper problems at work in English social and political life so as to throw cold water on both suggestions, and to show that much still needed to be thought out in modern German life that could not be resolved simply by some decision to imitate England.

Second, Hegel thought the proponents of the Reform Bill in England were irresponsibly playing with fire. They were committing the fundamental "liberal" error (as Hegel understood that) of changing the political structure of the country without first changing the social and institutional life of the country; that had been tried once before in France, and the result had been the upheaval of the Revolution and the Jacobin Terror. This was particularly bothersome to him, since his views, even a few months before, had been that the French upheaval had been in part occasioned by the influence of Catholicism, and that the Germans had been able to avoid the necessity of anything like the French explosion because of the nature of German Protestantism. But if a major Protestant power looked as if it might slip into the French pattern, something had to be fundamentally rethought in Hegel's views about the relation between religion and politics. Even in the short period between the close of his lectures in 1831 and his drafting of "On the English Reform Bill," Hegel's views were still developing.

Third, and equally important, commenting on the English Reform Bill allowed him to obliquely criticize current proposals for reform in Prussia. By pointing out the shortcomings of the English solutions, he could indirectly point to what he thought were similar shortcomings in current Prussian proposals, which, so he thought, ran the danger of repeating many of the same errors.

The English Reform Bill itself took on the whole issue of the English "constitution" and the claim that the "constitution" provided a system by which the English people were "represented" in Parliament. The background to the introduction of the bill in Parliament was itself complex. There was genuine fear among some in England about the possibility of some kind of French-style insurrection, particularly after the events of July 1830. This fear was stoked by the publications in the press of dire warnings by those influenced by James Mill and Jeremy

Bentham to the effect that revolution was inevitable if constitutional change did not come.

It had long been obvious to many in England that their system of representation did not in fact represent what had come to be crucial interests in modern English society. The parliamentary system was riddled with corruption, such as the infamous "rotten boroughs," districts where there were virtually no inhabitants and which were thus "in the pocket" of wealthy landowners, who could in effect personally appoint the representatives from those areas – one area, Old Sarum, actually had no inhabitants at all but nonetheless sent two representatives to Parliament.[81] In many areas, wealthy men could basically own the voters in a district without themselves having to live there or have anything to do with the district. Many votes (and hence offices) were simply purchased by those wealthy enough to do so.

This pattern of misrepresentation and corruption made reform seem necessary even to those who feared it. But the greater fear of instigating some wider upheaval as had happened in France had recently been used by opponents of reform to keep it off the official agenda; the example of France's calling the Estates General in 1789 and then finding itself seemingly inexorably pushed into a revolutionary vortex suggested to many that instigating even needed reforms might start a process that would end in a Jacobin eruption. These fears persisted until, under somewhat extraordinary circumstances, the Whig reformers came to power in 1831 and, although their election did not itself come about as a result of the events in France, they and their proselytizers cleverly used the events of July 1830 to stir up fear and to make the case for the necessity of reform. Under these conditions and given long pent-up demands for reform, the bill to reform Parliament and make it "more representative" of the people was introduced into Parliament by Lord John Russell (the grandfather of Bertrand Russell) and began quickly and successfully to move through the complicated legislative process. In 1831, its passage, although not guaranteed, seemed extremely likely. (In fact, it became law in 1832.)

To many in Prussia, the English Reform Bill was as important as any legislation being considered at home. Some Prussians, particularly the liberals, saw England as the very model of modernity, namely, a constitutional monarchy combined with representative government in which nonetheless only "men of substance" held the reins of power. Even those other Prussians who were not so favorably disposed to the idea of a "constitutional" monarchy nonetheless saw in England the very model for how a modern state could employ the latest technology to dominate the new modes of production and create markets for its goods. There was thus an overlapping concurrence of opinion that cemented the view of England as representing the goal of modern life.

Indeed, England's lead in modern technology had been clearly recognized by Germans; especially after 1815, Germans had begun importing English machines and English know-how and themselves even going to England to study the new techniques of manufacturing and engineering at work there.[82] The great Berlin architect Karl Friedrich Schinkel, who designed many of the glorious buildings along Berlin's imperial boulevard, Unter den Linden, was sent to England in 1826, where he made sketches of gasworks, shipyards, brick factories, and the like for use back home in Prussia. Hegel himself would also have seen much of this English technological influence firsthand. In 1816, a British firm (the Imperial Continental Gas Association of London) erected Berlin's first gaslights (and ran for the next twenty-one years a gasworks outside the Halle Gate to the old city); in 1829, gaslights of English design were made a regular feature of Berlin's environment. The firm of Humphreys and Biram were operating steamships on the Spree River in Berlin by 1816. Various other things, such as a paper mill, various engineering developments, and so on were powered by steam engines from the firm of the brothers John and Charles James Cockerill. (All told, Berlin had about thirty steam engines at work in 1830, almost all of them English by make or design.)[83]

Thus, since there were many people in Prussia who for different reasons thought that Prussia should essentially copy the English, it was important to ask what the vaunted English model really meant. Part of this had to do with a new sense of the "public" being created by England's industrial revolution and the technological gains it fostered. Improvements in printing technology in England, for example, had made newspapers there more readily available – the *Times* had gone from being printed at 250 sheets per hour in 1813 to 4,000 sheets per hour in 1829 – and hence a new force, "public opinion," was suddenly being created.[84] As a result of the widespread reading of newspapers, the corruption in the English system that had been widely practiced but largely unnoticed was rapidly becoming more and more evident to the

public. Even Hegel himself got much of his information on the Reform
Bill by reading those very same English newspapers – in particular, the
very respected *Morning Chronicle* – which, quite unbeknownst to him,
was also feeding him a good bit of radical Benthamite-Millian propaganda about the danger of revolution in England, a view which he
seemed to have wholeheartedly accepted.[85] Hegel was also intensely
interested in what this new relation of the "public" to political life
might mean, especially when seen against the background of the turbu-
lent events in Europe in 1830–31.

German "Particularism" and English Politics

It is also not accidental that Hegel began writing this article as reforms
of the Prussian "municipal ordinance" were being undertaken (they
were in fact completed in 1831). The original ordinance of 1808 in
Stein's ministry had itself been quite modernizing; but that ordinance
itself had since come under attack from a variety of quarters during its
twenty-year existence. The ordinance made city citizenship and the
subsequent right to take part in the affairs of running the city completely dependent on property qualifications instead of on the older
"corporate" qualifications; every inhabitant who owned a certain
amount of property or ran an enterprise in the city was declared to be a
"citizen"; however, all others, from ordinary laborers to ministers of
state to professors, were also thereby declared *not* to be citizens; instead,
they were all grouped together as *Schutzverwandter*, basically as "strangers" without the right to participate in urban affairs. (Consequently
some of these people were also exempted from paying city taxes.)
Hegel's colleague Friedrich von Raumer had argued in a public pamphlet in 1828 that granting city citizenship rights solely on the basis of
property qualifications could only be based on a "purely materialistic
view of public life" and should be jettisoned in favor of a more "organic" organization of citizenship rights.[86] That itself had set off a huge
debate on how the "municipal ordinance" should be reformed and how
the franchise of city citizenship should be enlarged or restricted. The
issue of the relation of state authority to local privilege was thus also
being played out on the Prussian stage; and a critique of English relations could serve as a warning to those entrusted with reforming the
Prussian municipal ordinance.

Hegel began his article by citing some of the reasons why constitutional reform in England was needed, noting how it was "difficult to point anywhere to a similar symptom of a people's political corruption," and how the usual attempts to justify that corrupt system were all themselves clearly illegitimate or moot.[87] The idea that the English could forestall reform, for example, by an appeal to "the wisdom of [their] ancestors" was clearly out of the question; modern life had broken with that idea as a sufficient source for the authority of legal arrangements.[88] Nor would an appeal to the "hidden wisdom" of the English system going to be of much help. It is not as if an invisible hand guides the patchwork English system to a more just conclusion than the more "scientifically" elaborated continental system. Instead, the various rights established by the English constitution actually form only an incoherent patchwork, each having its origins in various contracts, private arrangements, concessions wrung from the crown by force, and the like; such a hodgepodge can hardly lay claim to authority among modern subjects. As Hegel notes, "At no time more than the present has general understanding been led to distinguish between whether rights are purely positive in their material content or whether they are also in-and-for-themselves right and rational."[89] Bringing to bear his own Württemberg upbringing along with his own mature views on modern political life, Hegel tended to see in the crazy-quilt patchwork of English constitutional law essentially only another version of the German hometown life whose antiquated structures and irrational particularisms he had disparaged for a good part of his adult life.

In fact, Hegel argued, the irrational English patchwork constitution only produces irrational political policies. Taxation in England is exorbitant, the system of justice is expensive to maintain (and therefore available only to the rich), agriculture suffers under the antiquated system of taxation by tithing – Hegel even notes sarcastically that "the improvement of agriculture, in which large capital resources have been sunk in England, is burdened with a tax instead of being encouraged"[90] – the crown and the Parliament do not form a unity but are rather opposing powers, and so on. (These were not new views on Hegel's part; he had made all of these criticisms about the patchwork nature of the English constitutional system much earlier in his lectures on political philosophy in Heidelberg.)[91] Even more shocking, the status in England of church property as private property leads to ignominious moral and religious corruption, which Hegel described in only the most acerbic terms: "It is only too well known how common it is for the English clergy to occupy themselves with anything but the functions of their office, with hunting, etc. and idleness of other kinds, to dissipate the rich revenues of their places in foreign travel, and to hand over their official duties to a poor curate for a pittance that hardly saves him from dying of hunger."[92]

On the other hand, if "popular representation" is supposed to be the magic of the English constitution, and something that continental Europe is supposed to emulate, it must be asked, as Hegel rhetorically put it, what exactly it is that is supposed to be gained by shaping oneself on the much-vaunted English model. In Germany, in order to hold office, one must have gone through the university system, have studied *Wissenschaft*, and have become a cultured person, a man of *Bildung*. But in England, instead of *Wissenschaft* and university training, the "crass ignorance of fox-hunters and *Landjunker*" is prized, and the state's interests are in the hands of those whose "education [is] acquired simply through social gatherings or through newspapers."[93] As he puts it: "Nowhere more than in England is the prejudice so fixed and so naive that if birth and wealth give a man office they also give him brains."[94] (Hegel's description of the English landed gentry as "*Landjunker*" is a sly reference to Prussian conditions; the *Junker* was the reactionary, landed noble class who were most opposed to reform in Prussia.)

Hegel argued that the genuine venality of the English system is shown in the English treatment of the conquered in Ireland, where, although the majority of the population is Catholic, Catholic Church properties had been confiscated and turned over to the Anglican establishment simply because the English decided to exercise their "rights" as conquerors; Irish Catholics are still forced, he noted indignantly, to pay for their own priests, for the building and the upkeep of their churches, and, to add insult to injury, to support the Anglican clergy with their taxes. "Even the Turks," Hegel scathingly notes, "have generally left alone the churches of their subjugated Christian, Armenian, and Jewish inhabitants." The English treatment of the conquered Irish Catholic population is in fact simply "unprecedented in a civilized and Protestant nation," and the English "legal title" to Irish assets is supported only by the raw "self-interest" so much in evidence in the English system.[95]

That venality is, however, not a matter of bad character on the part of the English; it is instead a logical consequence of the modern conception of "right" at work in the English system. The treatment of the Irish peasantry by the English manorial class shows this; if judged by the standards of modern, English commercial life, it is not actually even wrong at all. The widespread practice of "enclosure" – ejecting peasants from land that their ancestors had farmed for centuries simply in order to clear the way for more efficient agricultural production, solely to the benefit of large landholders – is, Hegel notes, what the English call "right," which includes such measures as having "the huts burnt so as to make sure of getting the peasants off the ground and cut off their chance of delaying their departure or creeping in under shelter again."[96] Enclosure, of course, makes perfect economic sense, since the landlords can get far greater return from rising agricultural prices than they can get from their old leases; but it also means that "the lords of the manor have got property into their own hands so completely that they have cut themselves free from any obligation to look after the subsistence of the people who till their soil for them. . . . Those who already own nothing are deprived of their birthplace and their hereditary means of livelihood – in the name of right."[97] The darker side of modern life, expressed in purely individualist, "liberal" principles of property and right, is clearly on display here. (Hegel, whose own anti-Catholicism was fairly rigid by this time, was still obviously outraged at the treatment of Catholics in Ireland; even his view that Catholicism itself was incompatible with a modern rational constitution did not blind him to what he took to be the obvious injustice of the treatment of the Irish.)

The lesson for continental Europeans was clear: England's constitution, rather than being the guiding star of reform, should be seen as what it is – an arrangement vastly inferior to the more "scientifically" elaborated set of statutes and principles found in post-Revolutionary continental states, in which the social and political arrangements do not form a mere patchwork but instead constitute a rational whole and in which therefore justice is more likely to be obtained than in a situation like that of the English, in which various conflicting rights and privileges can be asserted from an arbitrary standpoint and in which individualist, commercial interests dominate all others at the expense of real justice.

The case for reform was thus clear. The corrupt English system, Hegel argued, has in the past refused to reform itself because sticking "to the abstract outlook of private rights is far too much to the advantage of the class with the preponderating influences in Parliament" and with those in the ministries who benefit from the corruption.[98] Clearly, something was awry in the English system, and, just as clearly, "the right way to pursue improvement is not by the moral route of using ideas, admonitions, associations of isolated individuals . . . but the alteration of institutions."[99] In that respect, at least, the proponents of reform in England were right.

It would thus seem that Hegel had set the stage for his full endorsement of the Reform Bill. Instead, having set up the case for reform, Hegel then proceeded to argue why the Reform Bill was misguided. First, since pretty much the same people would be in power after the reform, he noted, the reform cannot be expected to change much; but this was not his real objection. Since the Reform Bill aimed at changing not just this or that element of English political life but the entire constitution of England, it was crucial that any meaningful reform be based on some clear understanding of what the basic elements of a rational constitution would look like.

In one respect, the English constitution claimed to be based on a genuine constitutional idea, the notion that "the different great interests of the realm should be represented in its great deliberative assembly," which already distinguishes it from the "modern principle in accordance with which only the abstract will of individuals as such is to be represented"; this in turn requires that the real "foundations of the life of the state," these different, essential interests, have in the course of events been "consciously and expressly brought to the fore, recognized, and, when they were to be discussed or when decisions were to be taken about them, allowed to speak for themselves without this being left to chance."[100] The idea that representation of individuals amounts to representation of their crucial and basic interests, and that those interests are those that they share with others in their estate, was a linchpin of Hegel's thought on legitimate representation; what he calls the "modern principle" of representing only the "abstract wills" of individuals – so prominently displayed in the July revolution of 1830 – is both distinctly contemporary and distinctly misguided in its articulation of what freedom as self-rule means. The idea of the old English constitution, even though its actual constitutional practice had become irretrievably corrupt, at least in theory was based on correct principles.

However, the reforms being introduced in England, rather than ad-

hering to those basic precepts of a rational constitution, instead contained a fatal contradiction, for they embodied both the liberal "modern
principle," which, if carried to its logical conclusion, would ultimately
entitle each person to a vote, and, at the same time, the claims of the
old positive rights that made up the irrational, patchwork nature of the
older constitution. As Hegel put it, "In fact, the bill is a hodgepodge of
the old privileges and the general principle of the equal entitlement of
all citizens . . . carried out logically it would be a revolution rather than
a mere reform."[101] Furthermore, Hegel argued, there is no real ethical
advantage in implementing the principle of the "equal entitlement of all
citizens." Repeating some of his old arguments against democracy, he
noted that citizens in situations of universal enfranchisement come to
see that their individual vote counts for very little. Moreover, the idea
that the individual participates in the life of the state by occasionally
casting a single, numerically insignificant vote only belittles the deeper
importance of such participation and diminishes the larger importance
of having one's interests represented in the affairs of the state in the
first place. It is also the case, so Hegel thought, that individuals are
simply too rational to be fooled into thinking that their vote is sufficient
to guarantee their representation; as partial evidence for this, he claimed
that "in consequence of the feeling of the actually trivial influence of an
individual and his sovereign choice . . . experience teaches that elections
are not in general attended by many."[102] And, as Hegel notes, the whole
notion of "interests" is at stake here; he would expect, he said, that a
study of voting patterns would reveal that there is a greater turnout in
elections "where the franchise affects a much nearer interest of [the
voters], e.g., in elections for choosing the town councilors in Prussia."[103]

What in fact had saved the English system from utter collapse was
the fact that there had been and still was in Parliament a group of
"brilliant men wholly devoted to political activity and the interest of the
state," who have made "political activity the business of their life," and
who essentially carry the day against the great hoard of members "who
are incompetent and ignorant, with a veneer of current prejudices and
a culture drawn from conversation and often not even that."[104] Having
this culture of service to the state has in essence saved modern England
from what would have been the ruinous consequences of not having
such service bound up with proper, modern university training. (It must
also be remembered just how much both Oxford and Cambridge were

antiquated academic backwaters at this point.) Paradoxically, though, such men have their seats in Parliament only by virtue of the corruption endemic to the English system. The reforms unintentionally threaten to drive many of these men from the institution, and thus the reforms may quite unintentionally have the effect of bringing down the whole English system.

Since the reforms do not actually challenge the patchwork nature of the British constitution, they cannot thereby undermine the antiquated hometown nature of British political life, and at the same time, the increasing forces of technological modernization threaten to atomize British life even further and to help eliminate the communal structures of hometown life without replacing them with anything more rational. This stands in contrast to the way, so Hegel argued, that the Germans have been able to modernize so as to have "brought about the actual, peaceful, gradual, and legal transformation of the [old feudal] rights" into "the institutions of real freedom" in which the principles based on reason have become "firm principles of inner conviction and public opinion."[105] Absent the mediating structures of rational community (as contained partially in the Prussian municipal ordinance), individuals in such a state, cut loose from the socializing, mediating ties of local interests and communities, are prey to overly generalized and abstract lines of thought, and the French Revolution demonstrated what happens when such very general abstractions are made the guiding principles of action without there being any more determinate practices to mediate them.

The "knowledge, experience, and business routine" of the statesmen who have hitherto held the English system together will thus quite possibly be lost amid the clatter of such very general principles, which because "they are simple in nature, can be easily grasped by the ignorant." Their simplicity and overly general nature also lends them an illusory explanatory nature, since they are so general that they "have a claim to adequacy for everything," and they thus "suffice in a man of a certain slenderness of talent, and a certain energy of character and ambition, for the requisite all-attacking rhetoric, and they exercise a blinding effect on the reason of the populace."[106] Even worse, those men of experience and dedication to the interests of the state, those who practically and intuitively understand the complexities involved in running things, will simply be *excluded* from the Parliament, ironically enough, by a bill that claims to be "reforming" the system.

The big issue therefore at stake in the Reform Bill (and by implication, in some of the proposals for changing Prussia's municipal ordinances) was whether modern political life necessarily undermines the very authority it needs to make good on its promises. The forces of modernization, seen most starkly and clearly in England, seem themselves to atomize the populace, and because each member of that populace understands himself in the modern way as a free, self-ruling agent, each necessarily feels that his freedom can only be limited by public institutions rather than being underwritten by them. True freedom is possible only if certain collective goals can be sustained, if some common projects are articulated and developed into a set of properly mediating, concrete institutions of a modern civil society and a constitutional state. It is only in the "activity of institutions in which public order and genuine freedom consists" that the practical answer to this dilemma of modernity can be found.[107] The solution is not easy: The atomizing forces of modern life seem to "make constitutional law self-contradictory from the start. Obedience to law is granted to be necessary, but when demanded by the authorities, i.e., by individuals, it is seen to run counter to freedom. The right to command, the difference arising from this right, the general difference between commanding and obeying, is contrary to equality."[108] The *general* solution to this, of course, lies in the recognition that for the government of a free people, "more is needed . . . than principles . . . For men [only] of principles, national legislation is in essence more or less exhausted by the *droits de l'homme et du citoyen*."[109] But the events of July 1830 seem to show that people are not necessarily led to develop those mediating institutions automatically; even worse, it shows that they may not even be able to sustain such institutions at all.

The Reform Bill threatened, Hegel concluded, to reform the English constitution by creating an institutional setup that did not counteract the atomizing tendencies of modern life but instead underwrote and promoted them. It may well be, Hegel noted, that the thick hometown structure of English life and the vaunted practical sense of the English will mitigate the ill effects of such a reform and prevent a social explosion from happening; but the reformers had, he feared, taken a tiger by the tail, and, he concluded, they may find themselves faced with what he feared the French were already facing; or, as he put it in the concluding phrase of his essay, they may be faced with "an opposition which . . . might feel itself no match for the opposite party in Parliament [and] could be led to look for its strength to the people, and then introduce not reform but revolution."[110] Philosophical reflection on history, on the significance of what had happened and was now happening, Hegel hoped to have shown, still had some lessons to teach; but what those lessons were, he realized, was not as clear as perhaps he had once thought.

The Last Days

Even though Hegel was obviously very much engaged in appraising whether recent events should lead him to rethink some elements of his philosophy, he himself was simply not in good health during this period. He gave only one set of lectures during 1830–1831 because of ill health; his other announced lectures on the "Philosophy of Right" were given by his student, Michelet. To make matters worse, as the summer of 1831 approached, a new threat appeared on the horizon. In the autumn of 1830, a cholera epidemic appeared in Russia (first in Odessa, then in the Crimea, then in Moscow). After the Polish uprising in 1830 following the July revolution, the Russians dispatched troops to Poland to quash the rebellion, and the troops unwittingly brought cholera with them; soon it was breaking out in Poland. The outbreak of cholera in Russia had caused all of Europe to take note, but with its appearance in Poland, Europeans really started to pay attention. The epidemic began spreading slowly westward, and in May 1831, Danzig (a part of Poland then in Prussian territory) experienced an outbreak of the disease.[111] Cholera was seen as a dark, ominous plague coming out of the "barbarian" East to overtake the "civilized" West, and tensions began to rise in all parts of Prussia as news of the dreaded contagion spread. On orders from the Prussian king, the eastern borders of Prussia were therefore sealed, and all travelers coming from that area (and in fact all travelers in Prussia without proper papers) were to be put under quarantine.

Much learned opinion of the day held that cholera was an airborne disease carried by dirty air or "miasmas"; other learned opinion held that it was transmitted from person to person via some type of material (such that even touching the clothing of someone infected could cause a person to get the disease). There was, however, widespread agreement in learned circles that it had a tendency particularly to attack those with weakened digestive systems. Berlin was therefore divided up into medically supervised regions, and many public buildings, slaughterhouses, and even schools were closed. Even coins and mail were fumigated with smoke or sulfur. Houses with stricken members were quarantined, funerals were required to be held at night on the very day of death (the nighttime requirement was meant to minimize the contact of the infected corpse with other people), and the corpse was required to be soaked with calcium chloride. Berlin was rapidly overwhelmed with rumors, pamphlets, and books on what to do about cholera. Even in Hegel's *Jahrbücher* of 1831, there was a long review of several books dealing with the nature and history of cholera. Curiously, though, by the time it was decided that cholera had actually broken out in Berlin in August 1831, the authorities decided not, after all, to close buildings or seal the city. Sadly, Berlin did not acquire a sewerage system until 1873; until that time, sewage was carried in open gullies in the city, thereby greatly increasing the danger of cholera, although the authorities could not have known that at the time.

Those who could do so left the city intending to wait until the plague was over before returning. Hegel and his family followed suit and rented a garden house outside of the city in Kreuzberg (these days very much a part of the city of Berlin). They rented the top floor of the house, which Hegel and his wife took to calling their "little palace" (the "*Schloßchen*"). Hegel was particularly anxious about the epidemic, telling his wife over and over again that "with my weak stomach it wouldn't take much to contract cholera."[112] In fact, Hegel's health had deteriorated for the whole year of 1831. After his trip to Karlsbad in 1829, he had felt that any more travel was out of the question because it had become simply too "fatiguing" for him.[113] He had become particularly weakened after the illness which had befallen him for the autumn in 1830, and he never really recovered his strength after that. Moreover, his chronic stomach ailment made it impossible for him to eat anything more than strong soups and light meat dishes, and he began to experience more and more attacks of vomiting, after which his stomach pains would recede for a while. He withdrew from his social life; he ceased attending the opera, going to the theater, and he did not socialize very much, something which, as his wife noted, was completely out of character for him. During this period, he also experienced various sharp mood swings; he would become quite unhappy and depressed, then snap out of it and become once again his cheery self. The smallest physical activity seemed to exhaust him, and he became especially sensitive to all changes in the weather.

At the "little palace" in Kreuzberg, Hegel and his family had little contact with the city, almost entirely out of fear of the cholera epidemic spreading there. Hegel himself spent most of his time in the garden; he passed the day working on his philosophy, playing chess with his sons, entertaining some visitors, reducing his daily walk (because of fatigue) to some very short strolls, and, as always, thoroughly reading his daily newspapers (after which he would spend some time swearing about the recent events and minor rebellions taking place in various German cities in the aftermath of the rebellion in France). Some of Hegel's students visited him, and while they were there, he would regain his old cheerful air, teasing them about their prematurely taking on airs of elderly *gravitas* and ancient wisdom (all this from one dubbed by his friends "the old man" in his university days). Typical of his taste for different kinds of people, Hegel also struck up a friendship with a local fellow, an old hospital attendant, and the two men engaged in long conversations with each other about life; Hegel enjoyed teasing his student friends about his new acquaintance, telling them that the old man's simple wisdom was a match for the most abstruse consequences of his own philosophical system.[114] He also worked hard on his upcoming lectures, noting proudly that since that his son Karl was attending them, he himself was taking a particular joy in them.[115] But the anxiety of cholera hanging over the residence was palpable; Marie had been instructed to purchase various cholera preventatives at the pharmacist, and the family acquainted itself with what physicians were nearby in case worse should come to worse.

For Hegel's birthday that year, some friends came out for a visit, and it was decided to celebrate his birthday in the nearby Tivoli amusement park, where there was a suitable hall. His erstwhile Whist companions Zelter and Rösel attended, as did the painter Xeller, along with other friends who were still around. (Many of Hegel's acquaintances had left the area entirely in order to get as far away from the epidemic as possible.) The birthday celebration turned out to be a joyous event, and

Hegel clearly had a great time; it ended with the coffee and champagne being poured just as a heavy thunderstorm struck, sending most of the guests, including Hegel, rapidly packing up and returning to their respective homes.[116]

At this point, Hegel's wife wanted to get out of the Berlin area altogether and take the entire family to stay with relatives in Nuremberg, but Hegel himself did not want to go and felt quite despondent at the prospect of leaving. Berlin was now his home, it was where he wanted to be. "As a product of spirit," he would tell friends, "the most ordinary Berlin joke counts for more than the sun."[117] Hegel put his foot down, and the family stayed. At the end of October, with the new semester about to begin, it was no longer possible to stay in the "little palace," and the Hegel family therefore set itself to packing up for the return to Berlin. Hegel had been led to understand that the major wave of the epidemic was now over in Berlin. (He turned out to be wrong about that.) But even he had mixed feelings about returning; as they returned to Kupfergraben, Hegel complained bitterly about the dirty Berlin air, saying that he felt just like a fish that had been taken out of a fresh spring and thrown into a sewer.[118] (It was clear what particular fear of disease was in the back of his mind when he said that.) But he was nonetheless looking forward to the new year; he even signed a contract on October 1, 1831, for the publication of a new edition of his *Phenomenology of Spirit* and began preliminary work on it.

The return to Kupfergraben was not without its discord. Hegel was set to lecture on the "history of philosophy" and the "philosophy of right" for the winter semester of 1831–32, and the latter course was being given apparently under duress from the crown prince. Earlier in the year, Hegel had been invited to share a meal with the crown prince, and the prince had suddenly sprung on Hegel his complaint that he had heard that the lectures on the philosophy of right given by Hegel's protégé, Gans, were colored by an antimonarchical, revolutionary, republican outlook. The prince made it supremely clear that he viewed this as an outrage, and demanded to know why Hegel himself did not give the course. Hegel fumbled for words, excused himself by saying that he had not known that Gans was doing such a thing, and promised that he himself would offer the lectures the next semester and then let the matter go at that. (Gans had in fact taken on the duty of lecturing on the "philosophy of right" since 1825, which had freed Hegel to pursue his other interests in philosophy of religion, aesthetics, and philosophy of world history.)

As it turned out, that semester both Hegel and Gans had announced that they would both be lecturing on the "philosophy of right" – Gans in the law faculty, Hegel in the philosophical faculty. But at the beginning of the semester, the usual hoard of students that typically registered for Hegel's classes did not appear; those hoards had in fact registered for Gans's lectures. The implications were clear: Hegel was rapidly losing his authority with the students. In his lectures, Gans was much more lucid than Hegel was in his own, and in the heady days in the aftermath of the July revolution, it was felt among many of the students that Hegel had simply lost touch with things and that Gans was now the torchbearer of modernist idealism. Hegel was more than just a little upset with this turn of events; aggravated, he wrote a letter expressing his irritation to Gans in which he complained about the unseemliness of their both lecturing on the same topic, particularly when the topic was his own book; Gans responded sincerely enough by posting a notice that he would not be lecturing *that* semester on the "philosophy of right" but instead on legal history, and he advised the students therefore to attend Professor Hegel's lectures on the topics. But few of the students made the switch; they were clearly waiting until Gans himself lectured on the topic some other semester.

Hegel was utterly humiliated by the experience; suddenly, he, the philosophical celebrity of Berlin, was being eclipsed by his own protégé after he had been personally chastised by the crown prince, and he let his wounded feelings show. He wrote Gans a *very* angry note on November 12, 1831, letting him know that he did not take kindly to being treated as Gans's follower, and Gans, understanding quite well the tone of rejection and anger in Hegel's note, was virtually inconsolable about how he managed so deeply to offend his beloved mentor and friend. Hegel's temper at this point in his life had become well known among his friends and his illness had only exacerbated it; Gans nonetheless clearly looked forward to reconciling with his friend sometime in the next few days after Hegel had had time to cool down.

Hegel began his lectures on Thursday, November 10, 1831. To some in his audience, he did not look well; in fact, to many, he seemed quite weak: He stumbled up to the lectern, and was lacking his usual intense concentration. (Some others, though, remembered him as being in good form.) After the lectures, he remarked to Marie that he had had a particularly easy time that day. On Thursday, a newly arrived student from Württemberg (indeed, from the Protestant Seminary in Tübingen), David Friedrich Strauß, visited Hegel, and they had a jolly time exchanging news and gossip about events in Hegel's hometown and at Tübingen University; Strauß brought him up to date on what had happened to many of his old classmates at Tübingen, and Hegel made a series of humorous remarks about some of his old comrades and about Württemberg life in general. To Strauß, Hegel seemed lively, in fine form, even youthful in spirit. On Friday, after his lectures, Hegel toddled over to Zelter's house and amiably passed the time with his old friend for a while.

On Saturday, he gave some exams at the university and paid some social calls and was in good spirits. He arose on Sunday in good spirits; he and Marie had invited some old friends over for dinner that evening, and he was looking forward to it. Suddenly at 11:00 A.M. on Sunday, he began to complain of severe stomach pains. A physician was summoned, who arrived at 2:00 and, seeing nothing more than a case of irritation of the stomach, prescribed a mustard plaster for the abdomen. But shortly thereafter Hegel began vomiting "gall" (which might have been bile but might also have been stomach juices mixed with blood).[119] Dinner with their friends was postponed, and Hegel retired to bed. He had a fitful night, being in great discomfort and more or less unable to sleep. Marie, clearly worried about him, stayed up all night with him; he tried to reassure her that everything was fine, that he was just uncomfortable with his (now) usual stomach pains, and that she should get some sleep.

The next day, November 14, Hegel arose, much, much weaker than normal, and collapsed on his way to the sofa in the living room; his bed was brought into the living room, and he quickly fell asleep in it. The physician arrived again and administered another mustard plaster. (Marie had applied leeches the night before; Hegel was quite likely anemic by this time, and, although she could not have known it, this might have worsened the situation quite a bit.) As the day wore on, Hegel's condition quickly worsened; he could not urinate, and he began hiccuping wildly. At this point, the first physician summoned a second physician. Hegel, who was fully conscious during all this, must have feared the worst at this point. According to recently enacted Prussian law, if a

physician feared a patient was suffering from cholera, he was required
by law immediately to summon a second physician. Seeing those two
physicians standing beside him applying mustard plasters over his entire
body and soaking him in chamomile extract, Hegel must have known
what they thought was wrong and that his worst fears seemed to be
coming true. But he displayed complete sangfroid about the whole
thing, no doubt hoping not to give any distress to his family, said
nothing, and carried on as if he were unconcerned with the state of
affairs. At 3:00 P.M., he began to experience chest cramps and to breathe
very uneasily; he complained of lack of air and of how uncomfortable
he was and requested to be rolled onto his side; his two sons propped
his head up so he could breathe easier; he then fell asleep, and around
4:45, his pulse began rapidly to sink, his breathing became more forced,
and then it became quite weak. His face suddenly turned ice cold.

   Johannes Schulze, who lived next door, had received an anxious note
from Marie at 4:45 P.M. to come before it was too late; he had hurried
over and, coming into the room around 5:00, on finding Marie and her
two sons standing, visibly shaken, by the bedside, he went over to where
Hegel was lying and determined that he had died. He and Marie
together closed Hegel's eyes. The physicians arrived and pronounced
Hegel dead from cholera.

Epilogue

O N THE EVENING OF NOVEMBER 14, 1831, some of Hegel's students were having a merry time with a visiting American friend, Mr. A. Brisbane, at Karl Michelet's quarters. Brisbane was regaling them with stories of his adventures in Greece, when Eduard Gans, visibly shaken, burst through the door. "Hegel is dead," he announced to the stunned group. The news spread rapidly through the city; for everyone, it came as a complete shock. Hegel, one of the most celebrated and controversial intellectual celebrities on the scene, was gone.

Even more shocking, the physicians had declared the cause of death to have been cholera. But, since Hegel had none of the symptoms of cholera, they ruled that it was "intensive cholera," which supposedly attacked the body from within but did not display any of the external symptoms of typical cholera. The cause of death was, however, almost certainly not cholera; Hegel did not have the diarrhea, the swelling, or any of the other symptoms characteristic of the disease. Most likely, Hegel died of a chronic ailment from which he had suffered for some time, perhaps even since 1827 (when he had been stricken ill in Paris), and most likely this was some kind of upper gastrointestinal disease. However, because of the physicians' verdict and because cholera also carried away several other prominent intellectuals (including von Clausewitz) in Berlin, Hegel has since gone down in history as having been one of that epidemic's famous victims.[1]

Hegel's influential friends intervened with the authorities, and, although the Hegel household was fumigated and disinfected according to Prussian law, the other legal requirements (such as the immediate burial of the body at nighttime) were waived for Hegel, and, following Hegel's own wish to be buried at the Dorothea Cemetery next to Fichte and Solger, the requirement that he be buried in a special "cholera cemetery" was also waived. Altenstein also quickly intervened with the authorities to assist Marie in obtaining a more adequate pension and in securing stipends for the two sons to attend university.

The funeral on November 16 turned out to be a massive procession. The wagon carrying Hegel's body was followed by a large crowd of his students and sympathizers from all over the city. Even his opponents were shaken by the news of his sudden and unexpected death. His friend and colleague Philipp Konrad Marheineke, a theologian and the new rector of the university, was chosen to give the benediction at the Great Hall of the university; and Friedrich Förster was selected to give the speech at the grave.

It soon became apparent that Hegel had been to his loyal friends and students more than a philosophy teacher or a valuable colleague; he had come to stand for them as something much more, somebody who had provided them with a new direction in the fractious modern world, who had taught them how to navigate their way through the post-revolutionary complications of life. Hegel, his supporters felt, had formulated and expressed the sense of rupture with the past so deeply felt by the revolutionary, Napoleonic and post-Napoleonic generation; and he had formulated, as it were, the approach that humanity now needed to take in light of what so many had experienced as crucial, epochal events.

In his benediction, Marheineke drew a virtually explicit comparison between Hegel and Christ: "In a fashion similar to our savior, whose name he always honored in his thought and activity, and in whose divine teaching he recognized the deepest essence of the human spirit, and who as the son of God gave himself over to suffering and death in order to return to his community eternally as spirit, he also has now returned to his true home and through death has penetrated through to resurrection and glory."[2] Förster sounded a similar note: "Let the dead bury the dead, to us belongs the living; he who, having thrown off his earthly bonds, celebrates his transfiguration. . . . Indeed, he was for us a helper, savior, and liberator from every need and distress, for he saved us from the bonds of madness and selfish egoism."[3] It was now clear that Hegelianism, at least in the minds of its followers, had become more than just an academic doctrine. As much as anything else, this kind of reaction to Hegel as the modern thinker and guide par excellence to modern life immediately became part of his troubled legacy.

Hegel's friends immediately formed a society in his honor and dedicated themselves to raising money and performing the editorial work to put out a complete edition of his works. His good friend Johannes Schulze volunteered to edit a new edition of the *Phenomenology* incorporating the few changes Hegel had made before death had cut short his work on the project. The other students began gathering their compilations of lecture notes to spread the word that until then had been communicated only in lectures.

Hegel's death was followed about a month later by news of Christiane's suicide. Christiane, who clearly adored her brother and whose own life had been so difficult, walked down to the Nagold River and drowned herself. She had lived her life devoted to her mother and to caring for her father, and she always remained devoted to her older brother; life without him no longer seemed worthwhile.

In a very short time, the circle of "Hegelians" began to fight among themselves and even with Hegel's two sons about the meaning of Hegel's legacy. Those who understood themselves as Hegel's successors began bitterly to quarrel among themselves as to what represented the true and enduring core of Hegel's thought and about who was best entitled to interpret that thought. Quickly the Hegelians fragmented into what became known as the "right" and the "left" Hegelians (although this designation failed to do justice to the actual heterogeneity of the way Hegel's school so rapidly fragmented), and by the middle of the 1840s, the young Karl Marx had began to work out his own materialist version of "left" Hegelianism.

As his followers and his detractors competed for the authority to pronounce on his legacy, Hegel's reputation quickly plummeted. The fragmentation of modern life, a theme which had animated so much of Hegel's own thought, quickly came to seem to overwhelm Hegel's own, almost heroic efforts to overcome it in philosophy. The further rise of natural science and the birth of the "research paradigm" at the Prussian universities further eroded the standing of Hegelian thought as a piece of "philosophy" that claimed to comprehend the whole of knowledge taught at the university in an "encyclopedic" form. With the rapid collapse of what seemed like any possibility at all for anything like an "encyclopedia of the philosophical sciences" to serve as an overview and legitimation of the rapidly expanding universe of the German university, Hegel's authority simply and quietly evaporated. What had seemed unassailable had in only a few years come to seem simply one more outmoded period in the development of modern thought. Hegelianism itself quickly split into factions, into many different little, partial, fragmented forms of Hegelianism, and the possibility of Hegel's philosophy actually remaining the *Wissenschaft* that he himself took it to be seemed only illusory, something to be explained by historians of the intellectual past.

Hegel's own troubled legacy then became a matter of great contention, as the historians and the natural scientists began to compete with the philosophers for the position of authority at the German universities. Hegel quickly became a figure to combat, to refute, to refine, even to ridicule, but never to restore. He became the voice that many proponents of modern life wished to ignore or, if they could not ignore him, to dismiss him with a sneer. Emblematic of the anti-Hegelian reaction that quickly set in was an apocryphal story that quickly sprang up and was soon widely cited around all of Germany that on his deathbed Hegel had said that nobody ever understood him – except for one man, and even he didn't understand him. Stories about Hegel the humbug and Hegel the charlatan gained force and became part of intellectual currency in certain influential intellectual circles. Within a few years, his system had been debased, infamously, by crude commentators into the banal assertion that all development followed a so-called dialectical law of thesis, antithesis, and synthesis (an adulteration of his thought that continues to be taught even today).

As many of Hegel's followers, particularly those known as the "left" Hegelians, began taking Hegel's teachings in a direction that clearly frightened the Prussian authorities, the authority of Hegelianism became even further eroded; and in one of history's great ironies, in 1841 the Berlin authorities summoned Hegel's old friend Schelling, now grown quite conservative, to assume Hegel's old chair in Berlin, specifying his mission as the duty to "stamp out the dragon seed of Hegelian pantheism in Berlin." On November 15, 1841 – almost ten years to the day after Hegel's death – Schelling gave his inaugural lecture in Berlin; and, propitiously, sitting in his audience that day were Søren Kierkegaard, Michael Bakunin, and Friedrich Engels – the early exponents of what would later be called existentialism, anarchism, and Marxism. Each was disappointed with what he heard; and all three of them drifted away, deciding to come to terms with Hegel in their own ways. The liberals who were also Hegelians tried to present him as one of them; and the conservatives tried – as it turns out with more historical success – to present Hegel as a defender of the kind of nationalist state that Bismarck would eventually come to put into place – surely as ironic a development as any could be, given Hegel's own feelings about German nationalism. In 1857, Rudolf Haym, a disaffected nationalist, published his epochal study of Hegel – *Hegel und seine Zeit* (*Hegel and His Times*) – in which Haym attacked Hegel as the official philosopher of the Prussian restoration; Haym had been given access to Hegel's papers by his family, which helped to give his work an aura of authority, and Hegel's sons were particularly bitter about his misuse of them. However, through Haym, the damage had been done. Many liberals still saw in Hegel an underpinning for their own aspirations; the nationalists (represented by Haym) agreed and saw that as a reason to dismiss Hegel. Since people like Haym saw the "national question" as having been discredited by earlier Prussian absolutism, they also tended to see Hegel as an impediment to their own nationalist aspirations. Liberals themselves increasingly came to accept Haym's version of Hegel, and with the triumph of the Bismarckian state, Hegelianism's fate was sealed. Hegel, the great partisan of the Revolution, gradually came more and more to assume in the minds of posterity the shape of a narrow-minded Prussian apologist.

Both of his surviving sons had successful careers and lived until ripe old ages. Karl died in 1901, Immanuel died in 1891. In later life, Karl seemed to take more after his father, Immanuel after his mother. Much to the distress of the family, for a short while Immanuel took a job as a Prussian censor in Magdeburg before assuming his final and important position as the lay head of the Protestant Church in Prussia; Immanuel became religiously orthodox, and in his old age remarked on how his father's philosophy, heroic as it had been for its own period, was no longer fit for the times, which he thought required a restoration of something like the old religious faith. Karl decided to marry a woman much like the woman his father had married; he married a distant cousin, a von Tucher, and managed to construct a successful career as a political writer and historian of the Middle Ages (expressing his minor rebellion by focusing his historical research on the one period his father did not particularly like); he was a professor in Erlangen, just outside the traditional von Tucher home base of Nuremberg. Marie, somewhat to the distress of her two sons, became more and more religiously pious and gradually withdrew from public life but kept the flame of Hegel's reputation alive as much as she could until her own death in 1855. From time to time, she fought with the editors of her husband's posthumously collected works and was continually agitated and angry at what she saw as unfounded attacks on her late husband. Immanuel Niethammer too became more conservative and returned to a more orthodox form of Lutheran faith in his old age; he died in 1848, slightly miffed at the way Hegel seemed to have neglected him after his rise to fame. Schelling himself died in 1854.

Since Hegel's departure for Jena, his oldest and dearest friend of his youth, Hölderlin, had been living in madness in Tübingen, cared for by a carpenter and his family. He had even become by the 1820s a bit of a literary tourist attraction, and visitors would seek him out, talk with him, and often come away with a small piece of rhyming poetry as a keepsake (which Hölderlin would write for them on the spot). But at some point, most likely in the 1820s, perhaps around the same time that Hegel was having dinner with the Prussian royal family and wistfully recounting with Princess Marianne his time in Frankfurt with Hölderlin, Hölderlin himself, against the forces of his own madness, momentarily regained his powers and composed his last haunting piece of blank verse. Alone of all his poems, it is written in a woman's voice (that of his love, the long-dead Susette Gontard) addressed to him. It begins with the lines (in prose translation), "If from the distance that separated us, am I still recognizable to you, the past, O you sharer of my sufferings?", and it recounts in loving detail the enchanted days they shared in the gardens in Frankfurt, the fields in which they had met after Hölderlin's dismissal from the Gontard household – meetings that Hegel had helped to arrange for the lovers – even the flowers that populated the gardens of Homburg vor der Höhe and the Gontard house.[4] As the poem progresses, Hölderlin's sense of loss and the alienation that had settled in over him in the ensuing years of his madness and isolation from his youthful friends becomes palpable, and it concludes: "Those were beautiful days, but they were followed by a sorrowful twilight, That you are so alone in the beautiful world, you always asserted to me, darling! That, however, is something you do not know, . . ."[5]

The German literary scholar Christoph Theodor Schwab visited

Hölderlin shortly before his death on June 7, 1843. He asked him whether he had thought of Hegel. Hölderlin answered that of course he had, muttered something incomprehensible, and then noted simply, "The Absolute."[6]

Notes

Chapter One

1. Charles James Fox, "The States of Wirtemberg," *Edinburgh Review*, 29 (1818), p. 30. Cited by James Allen Vann, *The Making of a State: Württemberg 1593– 1793* (Ithaca: Cornell University Press, 1984), p. 45n.

2. The standard account of Hegel's relation to the Württemberg culture in which he was formed is Laurence Dickey, *Hegel: Religion, Economics, and the Politics of Spirit, 1770–1807* (Cambridge: Cambridge University Press, 1987). Although Dickey's account and my own overlap quite a bit – we agree on the importance of the "Old-Württemberg" culture in Hegel's development – my account none-theless differs from Dickey's in several crucial ways. First, Dickey argues that Hegel was always a "theologian manqué," whose intellectual project "was toward resolution of the religious problems of Old-Württemberg" (pp. 7–8), whereas I argue that Hegel's project must be understood more broadly in terms of his efforts to fashion a "modern" understanding of things, of which his theology is one part. Second, Dickey seems to think that Hegel's adoption of the principles of philosophical idealism was done in light of goals that were extrinsic to that idealism, namely, a set of social and religious problems that Hegel was trying to resolve; I argue that in fact it was the failure of Hegel's earlier projects and the overwhelming importance of Hölderlin's influence on Hegel that led him to shift his plans and that made the development of idealism so important for him. Third, I find the importance of the hometown structure of Württemberg (as developed by Mack Walker) and the associated problems of Enlightenment "universalism" and hometown particularism to be much more determinative of Hegel's development and to explain why he was led to his idealist position. See Mack Walker, *German Hometowns: Community, State, and General Estate 1648– 1871* (Ithaca: Cornell University Press, 1971).

3. The story the Hegel family told themselves is not completely credible. More likely, one of Hegel's ancestors went for a brief while to live in Austria, then returned to Württemberg; but the idea of their being descended from righteous Protestants who left their homeland on matters of religious principle established itself and obviously carried some emotional weight in the Hegel family memory.

4. Günther Nicolin (ed.), *Hegel in Berichten seiner Zeitgenossen* (Hamburg: Felix Meiner Verlag, 1970), #1, p. 3.

5. See Friedhelm Nicolin, " 'meine liebe Stadt Stuttgart . . . ': Hegel und die Schwäbische Metropole" in Christoph Jamme and Otto Pöggeler (eds.), *"O Fürstin der Heimath! Glükliches Stutgard": Politik, Kultur und Gesellschaft im deutschen Südwesten um 1800* (Stuttgart: Klett-Cotta Verlag, 1988), pp. 261–283.

6. *Briefe*, III, #497; *Letters*, p. 420.

7. See James Allen Vann, *The Making of a State: Württemberg 1593–1793*; see also Sheehan, *German History: 1770–1866* (Oxford: Oxford University Press, 1989), pp. 38–39.

8. See Mack Walker, *German Hometowns*.

9. Mack Walker illustrates one aspect of this with the story of how a young tinsmith in Hildesheim was not allowed by his guild to marry a certain young woman because *her* father had been born "out of wedlock and then subsequently legitimized, whether by the belated marriage of his parents or by special government decree does not appear. At any rate [her father's] legitimacy was recognized by the territorial law of the Bishopric of Hildesheim, in which the community was located, but that did not make him legitimate in the eyes of the Hildesheim guildsmen." *German Hometowns*, p. 73.

10. See John Edward Toews, *Hegelianism: The Path Toward Dialectical Humanism, 1805–1841* (Cambridge: Cambridge University Press, 1980), p. 19.

11. See G. W. F. Hegel, "Über den Unterricht in der Philosophie auf Gymnasien," *Werke*, 11, p. 38; *Letters*, p. 394: "Moreover, I also remember that when I was twelve years old, on account of my being destined (*Bestimmung*) for the theological seminary of my fatherland, I had acquired a knowledge of the Wolffian definitions of the so-called *Idea clara*."

12. The school commemorated its one hundredth anniversary in 1786, with Karl Eugen himself participating in the celebrations. (The school was actually newly founded in 1686 on the basis of the older school, which was not, however, a full *Gymnasium*.)

13. See Johannes Hoffmeister, *Dokumente zu Hegels Entwicklung* (Stuttgart-Bad Canstatt: Friedrich Frommann Verlag, 1936), p. 394.

14. See Johannes Hoffmeister, *Dokumente zu Hegels Entwicklung*, p. 394. H. S. Harris in his *Hegel's Development: Towards the Sunlight 1770–1801* (Oxford: Oxford at the Clarendon Press, 1972), notes that one of G. F. Stäudlin's sisters liked to tell the story in later life of how much she had "suffered" from Hegel's clumsy dancing at a ball. See p. 59, note 2.

15. Johannes Hoffmeister, *Dokumente zu Hegels Entwicklung*, p. 39.

16. Schopenhauer's reaction is cited in a number of places. See Franz Wiedmann, *Hegel: An Illustrated Biography* (trans. Joachim Neugroschel) (New York: Western Publishing Co., 1968), p. 13. Many of Hegel's unfriendly early biographers, such as Kuno Fischer and Rudolf Haym, immediately seized on this as proof of Hegel's bad taste. That a seventeen-year-old might be briefly attracted to all kinds of things or that the book's literary merits were not what attracted the young Hegel apparently did not occur to them.

17. Johannes Hoffmeister, *Dokumente zu Hegels Entwicklung*, p. 37.

18. Hegel's first biographer, Karl Rosenkranz, clearly had access to documents from the family that have long since vanished. In his account, he noted some excerpts from Rousseau's *Confessions*. H. S. Harris doubts this, thinking instead that Rosenkranz misread some excerpts taken during Hegel's Tübingen period and mistakenly ascribed them to Hegel's school days in Stuttgart. They agree that Hegel was already under the influence of certain Rousseauian ideas in Stuttgart. See H. S. Harris, *Hegel's Development*, p. 49, note 5.

19. Hegel's note reads: "In this time the greatly famous Moser has died, the greatest pride of our *Land*, who has written so many books that a lifetime would not suffice for reading them all, who has spent his life enduring so many blows to his destiny."

20. The difficulties with Moser's conceptions of law, namely, with how one might be able to distinguish a "true" interpretation of a social practice from a "false" understanding of that practice – to put it differently, with how one determined whether accepted practice was also rational – were themes that came to dominate Hegel's mature thought; by his late twenties, he was to vehemently reject Moser's conception of constitutional law as a compilation of what practice and tradition had come to establish and to lambaste Moser's idea that what traditional practice had produced was to be accepted as rational and in good order.

21. Frederick Beiser gives an excellent account of what he calls the "Garve affair" in his thorough study of the period, *The Fate of Reason: German Philosophy from Kant to Fichte* (Cambridge, Mass.: Harvard University Press, 1987), pp. 172–177.

22. Christiane Hegel wrote a letter to Marie Hegel, Hegel's wife, after Hegel's death, giving her account of Hegel's youth in Stuttgart. She says that "Prof Hopf u. Prälat Abel protegirten ihn schon frühe . . ."; "protegieren" is to "foster" or "sponsor" in the sense of making someone a "protégé." (I cite the letter in its original spelling.) See Johannes Hoffmeister, *Dokumente zu Hegels Entwicklung*, pp. 392–393. The letter in its original spelling is in "Errinerungen Christiane Hegels," in *Der Junge Hegel in Stuttgart: Aufsätze und Tagebuchaufzeichnungen 1785–1788*, edited by Friedhelm Nicolin (Marbach: Marbacher Schriften herausgegeben von deutschen Literaturarchiv im Schiller-Nationalmuseum, 1989), pp. 83–85.

23. See J. F. von Abel, *Versuch über die Natur der speculativen Vernunft zur Prüfung des Kantischen Systems* (Frankfurt and Leipzig: 1787; reprint Brussells: Culture et civilisation, 1968).

24. After his university years, Hegel's estimation of Abel's philosophical talents was not high. In a letter to Schelling written in 1795, he says, "The reviewer of your first work [on the form of philosophy] in the *Tübingen Scholarly Review* may in other regards be worthy of respect, but to have interpreted the writing as affirming the highest principle to be an objective one truly shows no penetration of mind. It is probably Abel!" *Briefe*, I, #14; *Letters* (trans. Clark Butler and Christiane Seiler) (Bloomington: University of Indiana Press, 1984), p. 41. Whatever Hegel thought about Abel as a philosopher, he and Abel apparently remained on good terms. The elderly Abel visited Hegel in Berlin in December

of 1825, and Hegel accepted his offer to take a gift back to Stuttgart for Hegel's sister. See *Briefe*, III, #542; *Letters*, p. 420.

Chapter Two

1. There had been an earlier attempt at constructing a more forward-looking part of the university along the lines of a *Ritterakademie* (literally, an "academy of knights"), an alternative to university education that was intended primarily for the nobility (who in general tended to avoid going to university) and that taught "useful" subjects. At Tübingen, it had been called the *Collegium Illustre* and had offered, as Walter Jens puts it, everything from criminal law to the Italian language. The non-noble faculty of Tübingen, however, sensing it as a competitor to their hidebound medieval corporate practices, successfully managed to undermine it and have it shut down. (In 1817, its delightful buildings were turned over to the Catholic faculty at Tübingen for use as a seminary. Tübingen had acquired the oddity of having two distinct faculties of theology, since it had a Catholic monarch and a mostly Protestant population.) See Walter Jens, *Eine deutsche Universität: 500 Jahre Tübingener Gelehrten Republik* (Munich: Deutscher Taschenbuch Verlag, 1981), pp. 218–221.

2. See Walter Jens, *Eine deutsche Universität*, pp. 228–234.

3. Cited in David Constantine, *Hölderlin* (Oxford: Clarendon Press, 1988), p. 20.

4. In putting things in this way, I am accepting H. S. Harris's arguments for arranging the chronology of Hegel's friendship with Hölderlin and Schelling in a way that differs from the usual accounts of the chronology. See H. S. Harris, *Hegel's Development: Towards the Sunlight 1770–1801*, pp. 60–61.

5. Friedhelm Nicolin reproduces a picture of the page in *Von Stuttgart nach Berlin: Die Lebensstationen Hegels* (Marbach am Neckar: Deutsche Schillergesellschaft, 1991), p. 20.

6. H. S. Harris gives convincing reasons to doubt the story's veracity. See H. S. Harris, *Hegel's Development*, pp. 115–116.

7. See Jacques D'Hondt, *Hegel Secret: Recherches sur les sources cachées de la pensée de Hegel* (Paris: Presses Universitaires de France, 1968), pp. 14–19. After his departure from Tübingen to go to Berne, Hegel mentions hearing about Reinhardt and his rise to prominence in a letter to Schelling in 1794. See *Briefe*, I, #6; *Letters*, p. 28. He also mentions Reinhardt in 1807 in a letter to von Knebel. See *Briefe*, I, #104; *Letters*, p. 143.

8. Karl Rosenkranz, *Georg Wilhelm Friedrich Hegels Leben* (Darmstadt: Wissenschaftliche Buchhandlung, 1969) (reprint of the 1844 edition), p. 31.

9. See *Hegel in Berichten seiner Zeitgenossen*, #19, p. 19.

10. Ibid.

11. Hegel "war gern im Umgang mit Frauenzimmer," as Christiane Hegel put it. See Friedhelm Nicolin, *Von Stuttgart nach Berlin: Die Lebensstationen Hegels*, p. 19.

12. Rosenkranz claims that Hegel's father's sympathies were "decidedly aristo-

cratic," and that the son did not hesitate to debate the matter with his father. *Georg Wilhelm Friedrich Hegels Leben*, p. 33.

13. Ibid., p. 34.

14. *Briefe*, IV, #4, p. 40.

15. See Karl Rosenkranz, *Georg Wilhelm Friedrich Hegels Leben*, p. 32. (Auguste later married a Herr Krippendorf, who became the vice-chancellor of the high court of Baden; she lived until 1840.)

16. See Dieter Henrich, *Konstellationen: Probleme und Debatten am Ursprung der idealistischen Philosophie (1789–1795)* (Stuttgart: Klett-Cotta, 1991).

17. A good account of all the background and the events comprising the "pantheism controversy" involving Jacobi, Lessing and Mendelssohn can be found in Frederick Beiser, *The Fate of Reason: German Philosophy from Kant to Fichte*, pp. 44–91.

18. See *Hegel: The Letters*, p. 32. Schelling's letter is dated February 4, 1795. ("Intimate" renders "*vertraute*.")

19. Jacobi recounted the conversation as having to do with a poem by Goethe, when Lessing (on Jacobi's unconfirmed account) volunteered that "the point of view in which the poem is cast is my own point of view. . . . The orthodox concepts of the divinity are no longer for me; I cannot stand them. *Hen kai Pan*. I know naught else . . ." When Jacobi then asked, "Then you would indeed be more or less in agreement with Spinoza," Lessing replies, "If I am to call myself by anybody's name, then I know none better." Gérard Vallée, J. B. Lawson, and C. G. Chapple (trans.), *The Spinoza Conversations between Lessing and Jacobi: Text with Excerpts from the Ensuing Controversy* (Boston: University Press of America, 1988), p. 85.

20. See Dieter Henrich, *Konstellationen*, p. 177.

21. Kant respectfully notes Storr's criticisms, and remarks about Storr, "who has examined my book with his accustomed sagacity and with an industry and fairness deserving the greatest thanks." Immanuel Kant, *Religion within the Limits of Reason Alone* (transl. Theodore M. Greene and Hoyt H. Hudson) (New York: Harper and Row, 1960), p. 12.

22. See Dieter Henrich, *Konstellationen*, p. 196.

23. Immanuel Kant, *Religion within the Limits of Reason Alone*, p. 78. Citing Matthew 7:21, Kant says, "Thus 'not they who say Lord! Lord! but they who do the will of God,' they seek to become well-pleasing to Him not by praising Him (or His envoy, as a being of divine origin) according to revealed concepts which not every man can have, but by a good course of life, regarding which everyone knows His will – these are they who offer Him the true veneration which He desires" (pp. 95–96).

24. Kant says, "An ethical commonwealth under divine moral legislation . . . is called the *church invisible* (a mere idea of the union of all the righteous under direct (*unmittelbaren*) and moral divine world-government, an idea serving all as the archetype of what is to be established by men." *Religion within the Limits of Reason Alone*, p. 92.

25. Ibid., p. 113.

26. See Karl Rosenkranz, *Georg Wilhelm Friedrich Hegels Leben*, p. 42.
27. G. W. F. Hegel, "Tübingen Essay," in Hegel, *Three Essays, 1793–1795* (edited and translated by Peter Fuss and John Dobbins) (Notre Dame: Notre Dame Press, 1984), p. 46; *Werke*, 1, p. 29.
28. Hegel, "Tübingen Essay," p. 43; *Werke*, 1, p. 25; see Aristotle, *The Nicomachean Ethics* (translated by David Ross, revised by J. L. Ackrill and J. O. Urmson (Oxford: Oxford University Press, 1992), p. 148 (1142a7–27).
29. Hegel, "Tübingen Essay," p. 44; *Werke*, 1, p. 27.
30. Hegel, "Tübingen Essay," pp. 44–45; *Werke*, 1, pp. 27–29.
31. Hegel, "Tübingen Essay," pp. 55–56; *Werke*, 1, pp. 41–42.

Chapter Three

1. See Ludwig Fertig, *Die Hofmeister: ein Beitrag zur Geschichte der Lehrerstandes und der bürgerlichen Intelligenz* (Stuttgart: Metzler, 1979), p. 53.
2. See Martin Bondeli, *Hegel in Bern* (Bonn: Bouvier Verlag, 1990), p. 59.
3. Ludwig Fertig, *Die Hofmeister*, p. 65, gives an overview of such literature.
4. See Rudolf Vierhaus, "Bildung," in Otto Brunner, Werner Conze, and Reinhart Koselleck (eds.), *Geschichtliche Grundbegriffe: Historisches Lexikon zur politisch-sozialen Sprache in Deutschland* (Stuttgart: Ernst Klett Verlag, 1972), p. 551.
5. See James Sheehan, *German History: 1770–1866*, p. 215.
6. See Rudolf Vierhaus, "Bildung," p. 525.
7. See Martin Bondeli, *Hegel in Bern*, pp. 59–60.
8. *Briefe*, I, #12; *Letters*, p. 36.
9. The letter, however, does not provide any evidence for any *especially* trustful or friendly relationship between Hegel and the von Steiger family. Such oversight and reporting duties were typical of those assigned to a trusted *Hofmeister*. See Martin Bondeli, *Hegel in Bern*, p. 59, note 9.
10. *Briefe*, I, #6; *Letters*, p. 28.
11. Cited in Martin Bondeli, *Hegel in Bern*, p. 62.
12. *Hegel in Berichten seiner Zeitgenossen*, #25, p. 24.
13. See Martin Bondeli, *Hegel in Bern*, p. 61.
14. Ibid., pp. 63–64.
15. There is plenty of circumstantial evidence to justify the presumption that Hegel read Smith during this period, not the least of which is that he had bought a 1791 Swiss edition of Smith's *Wealth of Nations* in Berne and did not have a large enough library at that time to leave books lying around unread. See H. S. Harris, *Hegel's Development: Night Thoughts (Jena 1801–1806)* (Oxford: Oxford University Press, 1983), p. 126, note 2.
16. On Hegel's encounter with English modernity and on the nature of the library at the von Steiger house, see Norbert Waszek, "Auf dem Weg zur Reformbill-Schrift: Die Ursprünge von Hegels Großbritannienrezeption," in Christoph Jamme and Elisabeth Weisser-Lohmann (eds.), *Politik und Geschichte: Zu den Intentionen von G.W.F. Hegels Reformbill-Schrift* (Bonn: Bouvier, 1995), pp.

178–190. Waszek also provides additional evidence for Hegel's having read Adam Smith during this period.

17. *Briefe*, I, #6; *Letters*, p. 28.
18. Quoted in Otto Pöggeler, *Hegels Idee einer Phänomenologie des Geistes* (Munich: Verlag Karl Alber, 1993), p. 32. The Abbé Sieyès was famous for his revolutionary work, "What Is the Third Estate?", one of the key texts of the French Revolution.
19. *Briefe*, I, #6; *Letters*, p. 29.
20. *Briefe*, I, #8; *Letters*, p. 31.
21. *Briefe*, I, #8; *Letters*, p. 32. (The term "rallying point" is a translation of "*Vereinigungspunkt.*")
22. *Briefe*, I, #11; *Letters*, p. 35.
23. *Briefe*, I, #8; *Letters*, p. 31.
24. *Briefe*, I, #11; *Letters*, p. 35.
25. *Werke*, 1, p. 258.
26. Ibid.
27. *Briefe*, I, #6; *Letters*, p. 28.
28. *Briefe*, I, #14; *Letters*, p. 43.
29. *Briefe*, I, #19; *Letters*, p. 48
30. *Briefe*, I, #21.
31. *Briefe*, I, #19; *Letters*, pp. 48–49 ("unscholarly" translates "*ungelehrten*").
32. *Briefe*, I, #14; *Letters*, p. 42.
33. *Three Essays, 1793–1795*, p. 67; *Werke*, 1, p. 57.
34. *Three Essays, 1793–1795*, pp. 64–65; *Werke*, 1, pp. 53–54.
35. *Three Essays, 1793–1795*, p. 79; *Werke*, 1, p. 71.
36. *Three Essays, 1793–1795*, p. 93; *Werke*, 1, p. 88. The phrase "motives of ethical life" is "*Triebfedern der Sittlichkeit.*"
37. *Briefe*, I, #6; *Letters*, p. 28
38. *Briefe*, I, #11; *Letters*, p. 35.
39. Ibid.
40. On the relation between the *Popularphilosophen* and the Scottish Enlightenment, see Fania Oz-Salzberger, *Translating the Enlightenment: Scottish Civic Discourse in Eighteenth-Century Germany* (Oxford: Clarendon Press, 1995); on Hegel's own reception of Scottish sources, see Norbert Waszek, *The Scottish Enlightenment and Hegel's Account of Civil Society* (Dordrecht: Kluwer Academic Publishers, 1988).
41. *Briefe*, I, #8; *Letters*, p. 30.
42. See, for example, "The Positivity of the Christian Religion," pp. 96–97, 100, 154, in Hegel, *Early Theological Writings*, (trans. T. M Knox and Richard Kroner) (Philadelphia: University of Pennsylvania Press, 1975); *Werke*, 1, pp. 135, 140, 204–205.
43. Immanuel Kant, *Groundwork of the Metaphysics of Morals* (trans. H. J. Paton) (New York: Harper and Row, 1964), p. 62 (394).
44. As Kant puts the matter in another context: "Reason has insight only into that

which it produces after a plan of its own, and that must not allow itself to be kept, as it were, in nature's leading-strings, but must itself show the way with principles of judgment based upon fixed laws, constraining nature to give answer to questions of reason's own determining." Immanuel Kant, *Critique of Pure Reason* (trans. N. K. Smith) (London: Macmillan, 1964), p. 20 (Bxiii).

45. In some ways, Kant's point is a modern radicalizing of a point that Aristotle himself makes, namely, that a person is most properly identified with what is *authoritative* in himself; the person who assigns to himself, as Aristotle puts it, what is "noble and best" therefore gratifies the most authoritative element in himself, which Aristotle takes to be his *reason*. See Aristotle, *Nicomachean Ethics* (trans. David Ross, revised by J. L Ackrill and J. O. Urmson) (Oxford: Oxford University Press, 1980), p. 236 (IX, 8).

46. "The Positivity of the Christian Religion," p. 100; *Werke*, *1*, p. 140.

47. Gibbon, of course, apparently disliked all religion, and played no real favorites between Judaism and Christianity. But consider some of what Gibbon says at the opening of the chapter: "We have already described the religious harmony of the ancient world. . . . A single people refused to join the common intercourse of mankind. The Jews . . . soon excited the curiosity and wonder of other nations. The sullen obstinacy with which they maintained their peculiar rites and unsocial manners seemed to make them out a distinct species of men, who boldly professed, or who faintly disguised, their implacable hatred to the rest of human-kind" (p. 144). Gibbon argued that Christians inherited their sectarianism from the Jews and, if anything, only made their own sectarianism worse than that of the Jews; the Christians also extended what Gibbon took to be the already incredible Jewish doctrines to new levels of incredibility.

48. "The Positivity of the Christian Religion," p. 81; *Werke*, *1*, p. 119.

49. "The Positivity of the Christian Religion," p. 82; *Werke*, *1*, p. 120.

50. "The Positivity of the Christian Religion," p. 76; *Werke*, *1*, p. 113.

51. See "The Positivity of the Christian Religion," p. 154; *Werke*, *1*, p. 205.

52. Hegel's discussions of the friendships of the early Christians is clearly a paraphrase of Aristotle's discussion of the "friendship of the good" in the *Nicomachean Ethics*. Aristotle distinguishes friendships based on virtue and the pursuit of common and good ends from friendships based on mutual utility or on mutual pleasure. He notes that "perfect friendship is the friendship of men who are good, and are alike in virtue; for these wish well alike to each other *qua* good, and they are good in themselves." See *Nicomachean Ethics*, p. 196. He also notes that such "friendships of virtue" can only exist in small societies.

53. "The Positivity of the Christian Religion," p. 152; *Werke*, *1*, p. 203.

54. Immanuel Kant, "An Answer to the Question: 'What Is Enlightenment?' " (trans. H. B. Nisbet), in Hans Reiss (ed.), *Kant: Political Writings* (Cambridge: Cambridge University Press, 1991), p. 54 (A481).

55. "The Positivity of the Christian Religion," p. 77; *Werke*, *1*, p. 114.

56. "The Positivity of the Christian Religion," p. 148; *Werke*, *1*, p. 199.

57. *Briefe*, I, #22; *Letters*, pp. 55–56.

58. *Briefe*, I, #22; *Letters*, p. 58.

59. *Briefe*, I, #25; *Letters*, p. 61.
60. See *Hegel in Berichten seiner Zeitgenossen*, p. 28: "Doch als es kam ans Ende, / Ich aufbekam die Buß, / Da streckt ich beide Hände, / Zu wehren ab den Kuß."
61. See Eric Hobsbawm, *Nations and Nationalism since 1780: Programme, Myth, Reality* (Cambridge: Cambridge University Press, 1990), p. 87. He goes on to note, "And the *patrie* to which their loyalty lay was the opposite of an existential, pre-existing unit, but a nation created by the political choice of its members who, in doing so, broke with or at least demoted their former loyalties."
62. See the discussion by Hans-Christian Lucas, " 'Sehnsucht nach einem reineren, freieren Zustande.' Hegel und der Württembergische Verfassungsstreit," in Jamme, Christoph, and Otto Pöggeler (eds.), *"Frankfurt aber ist der Narbel dieser Erde": Das Schicksal einer Generation der Goethezeit* (Stuttgart: Klett-Cotta, 1983), pp. 73–103.
63. See Karl Rosenkranz, *Georg Wilhelm Friedrich Hegels Leben*, p. 91.
64. See *Briefe*, I, #22; *Letters*, p. 57.
65. See *Briefe*, I, #23; *Letters*, p. 59.
66. *Briefe*, I, #24; *Letters*, p. 60; see also *Briefe*, I, #25; *Letters*, p. 61.
67. See *Briefe*, I, #24; *Letters*, p. 60.
68. The depth and the details of their mutual influence is brought out admirably by Christoph Jamme, "Liebe, Schicksal und Tragik: Hegels 'Geist des Christentums' und Hölderlin's 'Empedokles'," in Christoph Jamme and Otto Pöggeler (eds.), *"Frankfurt aber ist der Narbel dieser Erde,"* pp. 300–324.
69. See David Constantine, *Hölderlin*, pp. 43–46.
70. David Constantine makes this point in his *Hölderlin*, pp. 54–55.
71. See Mack Walker, *Johann Jacob Moser and the Holy Roman Empire of the German Nation* (Chapel Hill: University of North Caroline Press, 1981), pp. 172–175.
72. See David Constantine, *Hölderlin*, p. 65.
73. David Constantine makes this point in his *Hölderlin*, pp. 74–75.
74. *Hegel in Berichten seiner Zeitgenossen*, #33; Hölderlin uses the word "*Verstandesmenschen*," which means literally a "man of the intellect."
75. *Briefe*, I, #21; *Letters*, p. 50; "infernal spirits" renders *Höllengeister* and "ethereal spirits" renders *Luftgeister*.
76. There is a line of thought that attributes almost equal significance to von Sinclair and Zwilling in the course of Hegel's development. While I do not doubt that the largely "Fichtean" positions they represented were crucial in bringing Hegel to see the importance of the more theoretical idealist position in philosophy, I fail to see the influence of their ideas on Hegel's development. That influence comes much more obviously from Hölderlin. Reasons of space prevent me from arguing that point here; those looking for the counterargument will find it in Christoph Jamme and Otto Pöggeler (eds.), *Homburg vor der Höhe in der deutschen Geistesgeschichte: Studien zum Freundeskreis um Hegel und Hölderlin* (Stuttgart: Klett-Cotta, 1986); also see Dieter Henrich and Christoph

Jamme (eds.), *Jakob Zwillings Nachlaß, eine Rekonstruktion: mit Beiträgen zur Geschichte des spekulativen Denkens* (Bonn: Bouvier, 1986).

77. *Hegel in Berichten seiner Zeitgenossen*, #34.

78. See Karl Rosenkranz, *Georg Wilhelm Friedrich Hegels Leben*, pp. 86–88.

79. In his Jena "Wastebook," Hegel jotted down, "While those [thoughts (*Gedanken*)] are to be made valid *through themselves*, as concepts they ought on the contrary be made comprehensible (*begreiflich*), so the kind of writing thereby undergoes a change, [acquiring] an appearance demanding a perhaps painful effort, just as with Plato, Aristotle." "Aphorismen aus Hegels Wastebook," *Werke*, 2, p. 558; "Aphorisms from the Wastebook" (trans. Susanne Klein, David L. Roochnik, and George Eliot Tucker), *Independent Journal of Philosophy*, 3 (1979), p. 4. By the time Hegel was at work in Jena, he had fully internalized Hölderlin's idea. The kind of project he envisioned for himself clearly called for him to make his views "comprehensible," "graspable" in a manner that precluded people being able to appropriate them effortlessly. It is, interestingly, similar to the kind of strategy adopted by much later modernists such as T. S. Eliot, Ezra Pound, and James Joyce, except that Hegel certainly never intended his difficult categories to be playful, even in the slightest. For him, it was a matter of modernist *Wissenschaft* that was at stake.

80. See *Briefe*, IV/1, p. 74; Karl Rosenkranz, *Georg Wilhelm Friedrich Hegels Leben*, p. 142. It is of course virtually impossible to calculate how much this was worth in today's terms; but since a Thaler was worth 1½ Guilders (the Thaler was currency in use in northern Germany and in which he would later be paid, and the Gulden, sometimes called a florin, was in use in southern Germany), he received roughly 4,731 Thalers – one Thaler was equivalent to 288 Pfennigs, so Hegel's four Pfennigs were not much. An academic in Jena in 1800 required about 450 Thalers to have even a moderately tolerable life and probably about 800 Thalers for a comfortable life (which some academics could gain by lecture fees and by boarding students in their houses). Calculating on the basis of what he had in 1799, therefore, Hegel could look forward to enough income for several years of quite comfortable living, and, if he were frugal and inflation not too high, for even longer. But there is no doubt that the unexpected and rapid inflation set in motion by the Napoleonic wars soon depleted Hegel's capital enormously. See Hermann Aubin and Wolfgang Zorn (eds.), *Handbuch der deutschen Wirtschafts-und Sozialgeschichte* (Stuttgart: Klett-Cotta Verlag, 1976), vol. 2, pp. 936–937.

81. *Briefe*, I, #29; *Letters*, p. 64.

82. See Siegfried Schmidt (ed.), *Alma Mater Jenesis: Geschichte der Universität Jena* (Weimar: Hermann Böhlaus, 1983), p. 132.

83. See Theodore Ziolkowski, *German Romanticism and Its Institutions* (Princeton: Princeton University Press, 1990), p. 228.

84. See Theodore Ziolkowski, *German Romanticism and Its Institutions*, p. 229.

85. See the discussion by Charles E. McClelland, *State, Society, and University in Germany: 1700–1914* (Cambridge: Cambridge University Press, 1980), pp. 34–57.

86. Ibid., p. 33

87. Ibid., p. 45.
88. Siegfried Schmidt (ed.), *Alma Mater Jenesis*, p. 163.
89. See Theodore Ziolkowski, *German Romanticism and Its Institutions*, p. 241.
90. Ibid., p. 245.
91. Ibid., p. 232.
92. "A grasp of the nature of dogmatism is founded, presupposes a degree of independence and freedom of mind. . . . Hence, the dogmatist cannot be refuted by the argument we have given, however clear it may be; for it cannot be brought home to him, since he lacks the power to grasp its premise." J. G. Fichte, *Science of Knowledge* (ed. and trans. Peter Heath and John Lachs) (Cambridge: Cambridge University Press, 1982), p. 20.
93. Quoted in James Engell, *The Creative Imagination: Enlightenment to Romanticism* (Cambridge, Mass.: Harvard University Press, 1981), p. 17
94. See James Engell's discussion of the earl of Shaftesbury's role in this in *The Creative Imagination: Enlightenment to Romanticism*, pp. 23–25.
95. J. G. Fichte, *Science of Knowledge*, p. 250.
96. Quoted in Theodore Ziolkowski, *German Romanticism and Its Institutions*, p. 261
97. J. M. Raich (ed.), *Dorothea von Schlegel geb. Mendelssohn und deren Söhne Johannes und Philip Veit, Briefwechsel* (Mainz: Franz Kirchheim, 1881), vol. 1, p. 19. Quoted in Hans Eichner, *Friedrich Schlegel* (New York: Twayne Publishers, 1970), p. 91.
98. Friedrich Schlegel, "Athenäum Fragments," #216, in Kathleen M. Wheeler (ed.), *German Aesthetic and Literary Criticism: The Romantic Ironists and Goethe* (Cambridge: Cambridge University Press), p. 48
99. In his famous "fragment" also written for *Athenäum*, Friedrich Schlegel declared, "Romantic poetry (*Poesie*) is a progressive, universal poetry. Its aim is not merely to reunite all the separate species of poetry and put poetry in touch with philosophy and rhetoric. It tries to and should mix and fuse poetry and prose, inspiration and criticism, the poetry of art and the poetry of nature; and make poetry lively and sociable, and life and society poetical; poeticize wit and fill and saturate the forms of art with every kind of good, solid matter for instruction, and animate them with the pulsations of humor . . . It alone is infinite, just as it alone is free; and it recognizes as its first commandment that the free choice of the poet can tolerate no law above itself." Friedrich Schlegel, "Athenäum Fragments," #116, in Kathleen M. Wheeler (ed.), *German Aesthetic and Literary Criticism*, pp. 46–47. (Wheeler translates *Willkür* misleadingly as "will.") Schlegel's use of *Willkür* – quite often rendered as "arbitrariness" or "caprice" – to characterize the poet's freedom is significant, since in his later philosophy Hegel employs the Kantian distinction between free will (*Wille*) and *Willkür*. Hegel accused Fichte of falling into "subjective idealism," of identifying the will of the absolute "I=I" with that of an individual; that is, of mistakenly identifying the generally "groundless," nonfoundational status of our norms with the idea that each individual simply *decides for himself* what norms to adopt.
100. The uniqueness and philosophical complexities of this (and of all the Roman-

tics') positions is developed in Manfred Frank, *Unendliche Annäherung* (Frankfurt a.M.: Suhrkamp Verlag, 1997). I can, of course, here only hint broadly and obliquely at the richness contained in those texts.

101. Quoted in Hans Eichner, *Friedrich Schlegel*, p. 79.

102. Novalis, *Gedichte* (Frankfurt a.M.: Insel Verlag, 1987), p. 21. ("Was uns gesenkt in tiefe Traurigkeit, / Zieht uns mit süßer Sehnsucht nun von hinnen.")

103. Max Steinmetz (ed.), *Geschichte der Universität Jena*, (Jena: VEB Gustav Fischer Verlag, 1958), pp. 236–237.

104. Max Steinmetz (ed.), *Geschichte der Universität Jena*, quoted on p. 235.

105. The haircut was so named because it was worn by actors who played Titus in Shakespeare's play. The widespread popularity of the haircut among German men in the early nineteenth century was striking, and offers another example of the way in which theater can play over into ordinary life.

106. See Günther Nicolin (ed.), *Hegel in Berichten seiner Zeitgenossen*, #47.

107. Karl Rosenkranz claims to have had in his possession two earlier work-ups of the thesis in German, one in a "pure calculus" and another as a "very nice work on the relations between Kepler and Newton." See *Briefe*, IV/2, #63, p. 308. Both manuscripts have since been lost.

108. H. S. Harris gives a blow-by-blow account of the machinations behind Hegel's defense of his habilitation in his *Hegel's Development: Night Thoughts (Jena 1801–1806)*, pp. xxvi–xxxiii.

109. See G. W. F. Hegel, *Dissertatio Philosophica de Orbitis Planetarum: Philosophische Erörterung über die Planetenbahnen* (translation, introduction, and commentary by Wolfgang Neuser) (Weinheim: VCH Verlagsgesellschaft, 1986). The translations here are from Neuser's German translation of the Latin original, pp. 137–139. See also Neuser's discussion of the issue in his introduction, pp. 50–60.

110. Günther Nicolin, (ed.), *Hegel in Berichten seiner Zeitgenossen*, #48.

111. G. W. F. Hegel, *The Difference between Fichte's and Schelling's Systems of Philosophy* (trans. H. S. Harris and Walter Cerf) (Albany: State University of New York Press, 1977); *Werke*, 2, *Differenz des Fichteschen und Schellingschen Systems der Philosophie*, pp. 7–138.

112. See Max Steinmetz (ed.), *Geschichte der Universität Jena*, p. 252.

113. See Günther Nicolin (ed.), *Hegel in Berichten seiner Zeitgenossen*, #66, #68.

114. See H. S. Harris, *Night Thoughts*, p. xxi.

115. Max Steinmetz (ed.), *Geschichte der Universität Jena*, pp. 236–237.

116. *Briefe*, I, #40; *Letters*, p. 66.

117. See Günther Nicolin (ed.), *Hegel in Berichten seiner Zeitgenossen*, #71; see the explanation of the term on p. 577.

118. *Briefe*, I, #99; *Letters*, p. 132.

119. *Briefe*, I, #151; *Letters*, p. 205.

120. *Briefe*, I, #38; *Letters*, p. 66.

121. *Briefe*, I, #40; *Letters*, p. 66.

122. *Briefe*, I, #49; *Letters*, p. 685.

123. *Hegel in Berichten seiner Zeitgenossen*, #83a, p. 56; and #88, p. 58. Schlegel's letter is dated March 20, 1804; Frommann's letter (addressee unknown) is dated January 25, 1805.

124. *Hegel in Berichten seiner Zeitgenossen*, #92, see pp. 62–64.

125. See Hugh Johnson, *Vintage: The Story of Wine* (New York: Simon and Schuster, 1989), pp. 202–203.

Chapter Four

1. Kant began §16 of his "Transcendental Deduction of the Categories" with the claim: "It must be possible for the 'I think' to accompany all my representations (*Vorstellungen*); for otherwise something would be represented in me which could not be thought at all, and that is equivalent to saying that the representations would be impossible, or at least would be nothing to me." B131–132; *Critique of Pure Reason*, pp. 152–153. The term "representation" in this context is slightly misleading; it has become the standard English translation of Kant's use of *Vorstellung*, a term which had been used to translate Hume's use of the word "idea."

2. Kant, *Critique of Pure Reason*, B130 (§15).

3. B134n, *Critique of Pure Reason*, p. 154.

4. Hegel, *Science of Logic* (trans. A.V. Miller) (London: George Allen and Unwin, 1969), p. 584.

5. See the brief biographical description of Reinhold's career in Max Steinmetz (ed.), *Geschichte der Universität Jena*, pp. 246 247.

6. See Frederick Beiser's discussion of Reinhold's views in his *The Fate of Reason*, pp. 226–265.

7. See the discussion of Jacobi's influence on the development of German Idealism in Rolf-Peter Horstmann, *Die Grenzen der Vernunft: Eine Untersuchung zu Zielen und Motiven des deutschen Idealismus* (Frankfurt a.M.: Anton Hain, 1991).

8. On Jacobi's politics, see Frederick Beiser, *Enlightenment, Revolution, and Romanticism: The Genesis of Modern German Political Thought, 1790–1800* (Cambridge, Mass.: Harvard University Press, 1992), pp. 138–153. Beiser's account of Jacobi's progressive politics is an especially good antidote to the rather distorted view of Jacobi as the kind of dark, antirationalist "Counter-Enlightenment" figure that Isaiah Berlin made famous. (See Berlin's "Hume and the Sources of German Anti-Rationalism," in Isaiah Berlin, *Against the Current: Essays in the History of Ideas* (ed. Henry Hardy) (New York: Viking Press, 1980), pp. 162–187. See also the excellent account of Jacobi's life and thought in Fania Oz-Salzberger, *Translating the Enlightenment: Scottish Civic Discourse in Eighteenth-Century Germany*, pp. 257–279.

9. Jacobi's politics (and those of many of the other Romantics) are excellently discussed in Frederick Beiser, *Enlightenment, Revolution, and Romanticism*.

10. Cited in Frederick Neuhouser, *Fichte's Theory of Subjectivity*, p. 70; Karl

Leonhard Reinhold, *Beiträge zur Berichtigung bisheriger Mißverständnisse der Philosophie* (Jena: Mauke, 1790), p. 167.

11. See Frederick Neuhouser's short and very illuminating discussion of this issue between Reinhold and Schulze and Fichte's response to the debate in *Fichte's Theory of Subjectivity*, pp. 70–86.

12. In 1795 Schelling wrote to Hegel in the spirit of Fichte, not of Reinhold, that "Philosophy is not yet at an end. Kant has provided the results. The premises are still missing. And who can understand results without premises?" *Briefe*, #7; *Letters*, p. 29.

13. This could be seen to be the "principle" that restates Kant's own point in §16 of the "Transcendental Deduction": "In other words the *analytic* unity of apperception is possible only under the presupposition of a certain *synthetic* unity." The *synthetic* unity of apperception is the identity of the "I" that thinks X with the "I" that thinks Y. (It is "synthetic" in the sense that it does not follow logically – "analytically" – from the claims "I think X" and "I think Y" that it is the *same* "I" in both cases.) In Fichte's way of putting it, the principle of "I = I" (Kant's analytic unity of self-consciousness) requires another principle involving a "Not-I": that the "I" that thinks X (a "Not-I") is the same "I" that thinks Y (another "Not-I").

14. In offering this quick summary of Fichte's views, I am necessarily not only omitting all the subtleties, but also, although quite self-consciously for reasons of space, ignoring the way in which Fichte's philosophy itself developed during this period (roughly, 1794–1800). Fichte was forever revising his principles and starting over again. A good account of Fichte's development is given in Frederick Neuhouser, *Fichte's Theory of Subjectivity* (Cambridge: Cambridge University Press, 1990); see also Robert Pippin's discussion of Fichte in his *Hegel's Idealism* (Cambridge: Cambridge University Press, 1989), pp. 42–59.

15. See Robert Pippin's discussion of Fichte's notion of the "revisability" of all our experience in his *Hegel's Idealism*, pp. 49–51.

16. Many years later, in one of those classically odd historical quirks that turn up from time to time, Fichte's way of organizing his three principles into a scheme of thesis-antithesis-synthesis quite notoriously came to be attributed to Hegel himself, who had clearly rejected such views after 1806, if not before. On the historical roots of this confusion, see G. E. Mueller, "The Hegel Legend of 'Thesis-Antithesis-Synthesis'," *Journal of the History of Ideas*, 19 (1958), pp. 411–414.

17. Robert Pippin puts the idea of Fichte's nonrepresentational conception of self-consciousness in this way: ". . . it does not involve a commitment to some mysterious, secondary, *intentional* self-regarding, but rather defines certain cognitive abilities as conditional on other cognitive abilities; in the most obvious case, that a genuinely judgmental ability presupposes one's understanding that one is judging, making a claim subject to the rules of 'redemption' and legitimation appropriate to such claims. Or, stated in representational terms, this means that there is no internal property of a mental state's occurring in me,

and no property of that state's real relation with other states, that makes it a representation *of X*. For such a state to represent *I* must 'take it up,' unite it with other (or other possible) representations, and thereby self-consciously represent X." Pippin, *Hegel's Idealism*, p. 45.

18. See Frederick Neuhouser's good account of Fichte's conception of dogmatism in his *Fichte's Theory of Subjectivity*, pp. 55–59.

19. *Werke*, 20, p. 421.

20. F. W. J. Schelling, *Of the I as the Principle of Philosophy or On the Unconditional in Human Knowledge*, in F. W. J. Schelling, *The Unconditional in Human Knowledge: Four Early Essays (1794–1796)* (trans. Fritz Marti) (Lewisburg: Bucknell University Press, 1980), pp. 63–128, see p. 82; *Vom Ich als Prinzip der Philosophie oder über das Unbedingte im menschlichen Wissen*, in Manfred Schröter (ed.), *Schellings Werke* (C.H. Beck und Oldenburg: Munich, 1927), vol. 1, pp. 73–168, see p. 101.

21. See Manfred Frank, *Eine Einführung in Schellings Philosophie* (Frankfurt a.M.: Suhrkamp Verlag, 1985); Andrew Bowie, *Schelling and Modern European Philosophy: An Introduction* (London: Routledge, 1993). My reading of Schelling diverges somewhat from both Frank's and Bowie's in stressing the "two-track" system he pursued.

22. F. W. J. Schelling, *Of the I as the Principle of Philosophy or On the Unconditional in Human Knowledge*, pp. 103, 99 ; *Vom Ich als Prinzip der Philosophie oder über das Unbedingte im menschlichen Wissen*, pp. 130, 124.

23. The forerunner and impetus for Schelling's *Naturphilosophie* was Kant, in particular Kant's *Metaphysical Foundations of Natural Science*; that work contained Kant's attempts to show both how Newtonian physics presupposed key tenets of the Kantian transcendental philosophy and how the basic relations of matter and motion had to be constructed out of the a priori established mutual forces of attraction and repulsion. Kant's apparent success motivated Schelling to attempt to extend Kant's more narrowly focused investigations of the concepts of matter and motion into an a priori philosophy of nature in general.

24. The term "*Potenz*" was used by Fichte in a similar way at around the same time. See, for example, Fichte's statement in his attempted popular exposition of his philosophy in 1801, "We can, for example, think and conceive of ourselves as the *knowing* in that fundamental consciousness, the *living* in that fundamental life – the *second potency* of life, if I call that resting in the fundamental determinations the *first potency*. One can further conceive of oneself as the *thinker* in that thinking of the original knowledge, as the *intuiter* of one's own life in the positing of the same, which would give us the *third potency*, and so on into infinity." J. G. Fichte, "A Crystal Clear Report to the General Public Concerning the Actual Essence of the Newest Philosophy: An Attempt to Force the Reader to Understand," (trans. John Botterman and William Rasch), in Ernst Behler (ed.), *Philosophy of German Idealism* (New York: Continuum, 1987).

25. Schelling, "Einleitung zu dem Entwurf eines Systems der Naturphilosophie"

(1799), *Werke*, 1, p. 312; see also the discussion of Schelling's *Naturphilosophie* in Kenneth L. Caneva, *Robert Mayer and the Conservation of Energy* (Princeton: Princeton University Press, 1993), Chapter 7, pp. 275–319.

26. As Schelling put it, "nature cannot (as one rightly maintains against the defenders of the life force) suspend a universal law, and if chemical processes take place in an organization they must proceed according to the same laws as in dead nature." F. W. J. Schelling, "Von der Weltseele, eine Hypothese der höheren Physik zur Erklärung des allgemeinen Organismus," *Werke*, 1, p. 569; this is also quoted in Kenneth L. Caneva, *Robert Mayer and the Conservation of Energy*, pp. 299–300.

27. Edith J. Morley (ed.), *Crabb Robinson in Germany: 1800–1805: Extracts From His Correspondence* (Oxford: Oxford University Press, 1929), p. 118.

28. See the reprint in Dieter Henrich, *Der Grund im Bewußtsein: Untersuchungen zu Hölderlins Denken (1794–1795)* (Stuttgart: Klett-Cotta, 1992), pp. 854–857; also in Friedrich Hölderlin, "Sein Urteil Möglichkeit" in Friedrich Hölderlin, *Sämtliche Werke (Frankfurter Ausgabe)*, vol. 17 (ed. D. E. Sattler, Michael Franz, and Hans Gerhard Steimer) (Basel: Roter Stern, 1991), pp. 147–156.

29. Whether Hölderlin knew or could have known of Schelling's attempt cannot be definitively established, but Dieter Henrich and Manfred Frank have made a good case for claiming that he must have known. See Frank's distillation of the evidence in Manfred Frank, *Unendliche Annäherung*, pp. 692–693, note 4, and "27 *Vorlesung*," pp. 715–734, especially p. 734. Frank also makes a convincing case that Hölderlin was not completely original in this regard, that some of the ideas in the piece were clearly in the air at Jena in this period, and that Immanuel Niethammer played an absolutely crucial catalytic role in all this, especially with regard to Hölderlin.

30. See Dieter Henrich, "Hegel und Hölderlin," in Dieter Henrich, *Hegel im Kontext* (Frankfurt a.M.: Suhrkamp Verlag, 1971), pp. 9–40. My understanding of Hegel's philosophical relationship to Hölderlin is heavily indebted to Henrich's work in this area. I was originally quite skeptical of Henrich's claims in this area but have since come around to sharing them, although I continue to differ with him about the shape of Hegel's ultimate response to Hölderlin.

31. The term "horizon" is not Hölderlin's own term to characterize this aspect of conscious life. There is some evidence that Hölderlin in fact got the idea of rendering "judgment" (*Urteil*) as a "primordial splitting" (*Ur-Teilen*) from Fichte himself, specifically from some lectures Fichte gave in 1794–95 that Hölderlin attended. Manfred Frank sums up the evidence for this in his *Unendliche Annäherung*, pp. 699–700.

32. See Dieter Henrich, "Hölderlin in Jena," in Dieter Henrich, *The Course of Remembrance and Other Essays on Hölderlin* (ed. Eckart Förster) (Stanford: Stanford University Press, 1997), pp. 90–118.

33. Otto Pöggeler is the source of the most powerful line of thought that identifies Hegel as the sole author of the piece. Pöggeler argues that once one understands Hegel's development and the strong influence that Kant's thought had on him in Berne – along with, among other things, details having to do with the choice

of words and with the writing style that identify the manuscript as Hegel's – there are powerful reasons (although not conclusive ones) to cite Hegel as the author. See Otto Pöggeler, "Hegel, der Verfasser des ältesten Systemprogrammes des deutschen Idealismus," in Hans-Georg Gadamer (ed.), *Hegel-Tage Urbino* (Bouvier: Bonn, 1969), pp. 17–32. A fairly up-to-date discussion of various problems concerning the authorship and dating of the manuscript (including statistics having to do with the writing style and the watermark on the paper) can be found in the discussions in Christoph Jamme and Helmut Schneider (eds.), *Mythologie der Vernunft: Hegels >>ältestes Systemprogramm des deutschen Idealismus<<* (Frankfurt a.M.: Suhrkamp Verlag, 1984). (Pöggeler's essay is also reprinted there.) In fact, there are some good reasons to attribute the piece to Hölderlin rather than to Schelling. One of these is, of course, that during the period that the piece was written, Hegel was not in contact with Schelling, and if Hegel is not the author, then it must be either Hölderlin or one of the lesser-known figures in the circle of Hegel's and Hölderlin's friends in Frankfurt. Certainly many of the ideas in the manuscript are attributable to Hölderlin, who developed many of them on his own during his stay at Jena. To my mind, the argument for Hölderlin's authorship has been strongly established by Eckart Förster, " 'To Lend Wings to Physics Once Again': Hölderlin and the Oldest System Program of German Idealism," *European Journal of Philosophy*, 3(2) (August 1995), pp. 174–190. Moreover, at this time Hegel's self-confidence had clearly been shaken by his experience at Berne; and this was one of the last points in Hegel's life when he was willing to subordinate his own project to someone else's ideas. It is not improbable that during one of Hegel and Hölderlin's intense philosophical conversations or shortly thereafter, Hegel quickly transcribed some of Hölderlin's ideas on paper, perhaps even unconsciously parsing them into something closer to his own style, for future use by himself or, very likely, as a basis for some further common project. Indeed, it could well be that the "Oldest System Program" has a kind of dual authorship: Hegel could have very slightly reworked key ideas and phrases from Hölderlin, perhaps as an outline of some future piece that the two would write together.

34. Hegel, "Das älteste Systemprogramm des deutschen Idealismus," p. 235.
35. Ibid. It should be noted that *Poesie* is not adequately rendered simply as "poetry," since *Poesie* can also include "poetic prose." The last thesis is, of course, an interesting anticipation of Percy Shelley's later and equally Romantic dictum that poets are "the unacknowledged legislators of the world."
36. Ibid., p. 236.
37. Ibid., p. 234.
38. Ibid. The conception of the state as a machine was advanced by, for example, the philosopher Christian Wolff in a rather authoritarian way. It was also a commonplace in German jurisprudence and cameralist science: the noted eighteenth-century cameralist Johann von Justi claimed that a "properly constructed state must be exactly analogous to a machine, in which all the wheels and gears are precisely adjusted to one another; the ruler must be the . . .

mainspring, or the soul – if one must use the expression – who sets everything in motion." Cited in Dorinda Outram, *The Enlightenment* (Cambridge: Cambridge University Press, 1995), p. 96; on Justi's status and influence, see Mack Walker, *German Hometowns*, pp. 161–170.

39. See Otto Pöggeler, "Politik aus dem Abseits: Hegel und der Homburger Freundeskreis," in Christoph Jamme and Otto Pöggeler (eds.) *Homburg vor der Höhe in der deutschen Geistesgeschichte* (Stuttgart: Klett-Cotta, 1986), pp. 67–98.

40. Klaus Düsing makes a very good case that Hegel was in fact during this period briefly brought around to what he describes as Hölderlin's aesthetic Platonism. However, Düsing perhaps overestimates the extent of Hölderlin's neo-Platonism during this period, and certainly the extent of neo-Platonism on Hegel's part, which mixes very uneasily with Hegel's ongoing interest in Kantian themes and with his own emerging voice during this period. See Klaus Düsing, "Ästhetischer Platonismus bei Hölderlin und Hegel," in Christoph Jamme and Otto Pöggeler (eds.), *Homburg vor der Höhe in der deutschen Geistesgeschichte*, pp. 101–117.

41. Hegel, "The Spirit of Christianity and Its Fate," in Hegel, *Early Theological Writings*, (trans. T. M. Knox and Richard Kroner) (Philadelphia: University of Pennsylvania Press, 1975), pp. 182–301; *Werke*, 1, pp. 274–418.

42. Johann Herder's influence – particularly his ideas about the way in which what he calls a "people" (a *Volk*) should be conceived as an organic whole that develops according to its own principles in interaction with its environment – quite decisively appears in the manuscript. Nonetheless, the influence of Hölderlin's criticisms of Fichte are the most important and fully alter the shape that Herder's notions assume in Hegel's thought at this time.

43. See "The Spirit of Christianity and Its Fate," p. 191; *Werke*, 1, p. 283. (The phrase in question is *"unendliche Objekt."*)

44. See "The Spirit of Christianity and Its Fate," p. 196; *Werke*, 1, p. 288.

45. See "The Spirit of Christianity and Its Fate," pp. 199–200; *Werke*, 1, p. 292.

46. "The Spirit of Christianity and Its Fate," p. 214; *Werke*, 1, p. 326.

47. Hegel's discussion of the relation of Christianity to Judaism and his clearly negative attitude toward Judaism at this period in his development – an attitude that changed dramatically in his later life – was clearly linked to Kant's own discussions of Judaism in his religious writings. Kant argued that although Judaism and Christianity were obviously historically linked, there was nonetheless no conceptual connection, no common set of beliefs held by the two religions. Following Kant's lead, Hegel also saw Jesus as breaking free of his Jewish origins and founding an entirely new religion possessing its own distinctive "spirit." Kant says, for example, "And first of all it is evident that the Jewish faith stands in no essential connection whatever, *i.e.*, in no unity of concepts, with this ecclesiastical faith whose history we wish to consider, though the Jewish immediately preceded this (the Christian) church and provided the physical occasion for its establishment. . . . We cannot, therefore, do otherwise than begin general church history, if it is to constitute a system, with the origin of Christianity, which, completely forsaking Judaism from which it

sprang, and grounded upon a wholly new principle, effected a thoroughgoing revolution in doctrines of faith." Immanuel Kant, *Religion within the Limits of Reason Alone* (trans. Theodore M. Greene and Hoyt H. Hudson), pp. 116–118. On Hegel's own similar statement, see "The Spirit of Christianity and Its Fate," p. 206; *Werke*, 1, p. 317.

48. See "The Spirit of Christianity and Its Fate," pp. 212–213; *Werke*, 1, pp. 324–325.

49. "The Spirit of Christianity and Its Fate," p. 247; *Werke*, 1, pp. 362–363.

50. "The Spirit of Christianity and Its Fate," p. 253; *Werke*, 1, p. 370.

51. This partially preserved manuscript is known (very misleadingly) as "Fragment of a System." See Hegel, *Early Theological Writings* (trans. T. M. Knox and Richard Kroner), pp. 311–312.; *Werke*, 1, p. 421.

52. "Religion, eine Religion stiften," *Werke*, 1, p. 241. ("Imagination" renders *Einbildungskraft*.)

53. On the relation of "infinite life" and worship, see "Fragment of a System," p. 312; *Werke*, I, pp. 421–422. On the identification of beauty with truth, see "The Spirit of Christianity and Its Fate," p. 196; *Werke*, 1, p. 288: "Truth is beauty represented by the understanding; the negative character of truth is freedom."

54. "The Spirit of Christianity and Its Fate," p. 245; *Werke*, 1, p. 361.

55. "The Spirit of Christianity and Its Fate," p. 285; *Werke*, 1, p. 401.

56. "The Spirit of Christianity and Its Fate," p. 294; *Werke*, 1, p. 410–411.

57. "Religion, eine Religion stiften," *Werke*, 1, pp. 241–243.

58. Niethammer's crucial role in the "re-Kantianization" of philosophy at Jena and the way in which that charged the atmosphere at the time in Jena has been forcefully demonstrated by Manfred Frank, *Unendliche Annäherung*. See especially *Vorlesungen* 16 and 27–28.

59. G. W. F. Hegel, "The German Constitution," in *Hegel's Political Writings* (trans. T. M. Knox) (Oxford: Oxford at the Clarendon Press, 1964), p. 143; *Werke*, 1, p. 461.

60. See Hegel, "The German Constitution," p. 153; *Werke*, 1, p. 472.

61. A masterfully done version of the idea that Hegel in this essay understands the essence of the state to be its capacity for "self-assertion" ("*Selbstbehauptung*") is to be found in Otto Pöggeler, "Hegels Option für Österreich," *Hegel Studien*, 12 (1977), p. 93.

62. See Hegel, "The German Constitution," p. 167; *Werke*, 1, p. 489.

63. Quoted in James Sheehan, *German History: 1770–1866*, p. 228.

64. Hegel, "The German Constitution," p. 148; *Werke*, 1, p. 466: "Sonst – in seiner Betriebsamkeit und Tat – ließ er sich nicht vom Ganzen beschränken, sondern begrenzte sich ohne Furcht und Zweifel nur [durch] sich selbst."

65. There is obviously a good deal of similarity between this analysis of the Holy Roman Empire and his analysis in "The Spirit of Christianity" of Christianity's losing its revolutionary potential as it became an official state religion.

66. "The German Constitution," p. 203; *Werke*, 1, p. 533.

67. Ibid.

68. "The German Constitution," p. 206; *Werke*, 1, p. 537.

69. "The German Constitution," p. 180; *Werke*, 1, p. 505.

70. "But there is a higher law that the people from which the world is given a new universal impulse (*Anstoß*) perishes in the end before all the others, while its principle (*Grundsatz*), though not itself, persists." Hegel, "The German Constitution," p. 206; *Werke*, 1, p. 537.

71. Hegel, "The German Constitution," p. 220; *Werke*, 1, p. 555.

72. Hegel, "The German Constitution," p. 234; *Werke*, 1, p. 572.

73. Hegel, "The German Constitution," p. 211; *Werke*, 1, p. 543.

74. G. W. F. Hegel, "The German Constitution," p. 210; *Werke*, 1, p. 541.

75. "Freedom frenzy" renders "*Freiheitsraserei.*"

76. See Hegel, *Three Essays, 1793–1795*, p. 67; *Werke*, 1, p. 57.

77. See Hegel, "The German Constitution," pp. 220, 234; *Werke*, 1, pp. 555, 572.

78. See James Sheehan's discussion of this theme in *German History: 1770–1866*, pp. 235–238.

79. Hegel, "The German Constitution," p. 241; *Werke*, 1, p. 580.

80. This "Theseus," were he to exist, would have to have not only the political cunning to achieve this task, but also the wisdom to institute a democratic constitution of sorts for the people he otherwise would be compelling to unite and to be free. This "Theseus," that is, looks very much like the "legislator" in Rousseau's *On the Social Contract*: He would be, in Rousseau's words, "in a position to change human nature, to transform each individual . . . into part of a larger whole from which this individual receives, in a sense, his life and being." Jean-Jacques Rousseau, *On the Social Contract* (trans. Donald A. Cress) (Indianapolis: Hackett Publishing Company, 1983), p. 39. But Rousseau thought that the legislator could do this only by convincing others that he spoke with *divine* authority, since no other modern authority existed that could itself appeal to a people who were not already united by a legislator into some common project. Hegel clearly rejected that possibility.

81. Hegel said about Reinhold's position: "If thinking were a true identity and not something subjective, where should this application that is so distinct from it come from, let alone the stuff that is postulated for the sake of the application? . . . The elements that originate in the analysis are unity and a manifold opposed to it. . . . In this way thinking has become something purely limited, and its activity is an application to some independently extant material, an application which conforms to a law and is directed by a rule, but which cannot pierce through to knowledge." Hegel, *The Difference between Fichte's and Schelling's Systems of Philosophy*, p. 97; *Werke*, 2, p. 29.

82. Hegel, *The Difference between Fichte's and Schelling's Systems of Philosophy*, p. 127; *Werke*, 2, p. 62.

83. Ibid.

84. Immanuel Kant, *Critique of Pure Reason*, Bxiii (Preface to the Second Edition); Hegel, *The Difference between Fichte's and Schelling's Systems of Philosophy*, p. 87; *Werke*, 2, p. 17.

85. *Werke*, 1, p. 269.
86. Hegel, *The Difference between Fichte's and Schelling's Systems of Philosophy*, p. 91; *Werke*, 2, p. 22.
87. Hegel says, "The question that philosophy has to raise is whether the system has truly purified all finitude out of the finite appearance that it has advanced to absolute status; or whether speculation, even at its furthest distance from ordinary common sense with its typical fixation of opposites, has not still succumbed to the fate of its time, the fate of positing absolutely one form of the absolute, that is, something that is essentially an opposite." Hegel, *The Difference between Fichte's and Schelling's Systems of Philosophy*, p. 101; *Werke*, 2, pp. 33–34.
88. G. W. F. Hegel, "Notizenblattt: Bayern: Ausbruch der Volksfreude über den endlichen Untergang der Philosophie" in *Werke*, 2, p. 273. ("Pastoral duty" translates "*Seelsorge*.")
89. Hegel, *The Difference between Fichte's and Schelling's Systems of Philosophy*, p. 90; *Werke*, 2, p. 21.
90. "Aphorismen aus Hegels Wastebook," *Werke*, 2, p. 547; "Aphorisms from the Wastebook," p. 2.
91. Hegel, *The Difference between Fichte's and Schelling's Systems of Philosophy*, p. 155; *Werke*, 2, p. 94.
92. G. W. F. Hegel, *The Difference between Fichte's and Schelling's Systems of Philosophy*, p. 79; *Werke*, 2, p. 9.
93. G. W. F. Hegel, *The Difference between Fichte's and Schelling's Systems of Philosophy*, p. 88; *Werke*, 2, p. 19. Immanuel Kant, *Critique of Pure Reason*, A738–766.
94. G. W. F. Hegel, "Faith and Knowledge or the *Reflective Philosophy of Subjectivity* in the Complete Range of Its Forms as Kantian, Jacobian, and Fichtean Philosophy" (trans. Walter Cerf and H. S. Harris) (Albany: State University of New York Press, 1977); *Werke*, 2, "Glauben und Wissen oder Reflexionsphilosophie der Subjektivität in der Vollständigkeit ihrer Formen als Kantische, Jacobische und Fichtesche Philosophie," pp. 287–433. (Henceforth cited as "Faith and Knowledge."
95. Hegel, "Faith and Knowledge," p. 64; *Werke*, 2, p. 298. ("Ordinary human understanding renders "*gemeinen Menschenverstandes*"; it could also be rendered colloquially as "common sense.")
96. Rüdiger Bubner points out that shortly before Hegel wrote his own essay, Reinhold had already argued for taking the relationship between philosophy and its own age seriously, although he had done so in a very moralizing fashion; Hegel was responding to Reinhold's point and attacking its moralizing tone. See Rüdiger Bubner, "Hegel's Concept of Phenomenology," in G. K. Browning (ed.), *Hegel's Phenomenology of Spirit: A Reappraisal* (Dordrecht: Kluwer Academic Publishers, 1997), pp. 31–51
97. Hegel, "Faith and Knowledge," p. 154; *Werke*, 2, p. 394.
98. The dualisms modern philosophers find so self-evident in their own experience are really, as Hegel put it in the unmistakable Schellingian idiom, "the eternal

producing of the difference which reflected thinking is aware of always and only as a *product*. What is kept separate in appearance, the incommensurable ... is self-identical in ... the infinity, which is where the opposites vanish both together," all of which, so he claimed, Fichte made clear for "our more recent subjective culture." Hegel, "Faith and Knowledge," p. 112; *Werke*, 2, p. 351.

99. Hegel, "Faith and Knowledge," p. 126; *Werke*, 2, p. 365. ("Arbitrary" translates *"Willkürliches."*)

100. Hegel, "Faith and Knowledge," p. 75; *Werke*, 2, pp. 310–311.

101. Hegel, "Faith and Knowledge," p. 74; *Werke*, 2, p. 309. ("Project" translates *"hinauswirft."*)

102. Hegel, "Faith and Knowledge," p. 76; *Werke*, 2, p. 312.

103. Hegel, "Faith and Knowledge," p. 78; *Werke*, 2, p. 314.

104. Hegel, "Faith and Knowledge," p. 68; *Werke*, 2, p. 303.

105. Hegel, "Faith and Knowledge," p. 70; *Werke*, 2, p. 305.

106. Hegel, "Faith and Knowledge," p. 71; *Werke*, 2, p. 306.

107. Immanuel Kant, *Critique of Pure Reason*, A135–B174.

108. Kant, *Critique of Pure Reason*, A141–B180.

109. Hegel, "Faith and Knowledge," p. 73; *Werke*, 2, p. 308.

110. Hegel, "Faith and Knowledge," p. 69; *Werke*, 2, p. 304.

111. Rolf-Peter Horstmann argues that Hegel came to see the importance of the *Critique of Judgment* from Schelling's influence, not from Fichte's, and that Fichte himself came fairly late to appreciate the importance of Kant's third *Critique* for the development of idealism. See Rolf-Peter Horstmann, *Die Grenzen der Vernunft: Eine Untersuchung zu Zielen und Motiven des deutschen Idealismus*, pp. 208–219.

112. Immanuel Kant, *Critique of Judgment* (trans. Werner S. Pluhar) (Indianapolis: Hackett Publishing Company, 1987), §75, p. 280–282; *Kritik der Urteilskraft*, pp. 398–400: "But while that maxim of judgment is useful when applied to the whole of nature, it is not indispensable there, since the whole of nature is not given us as organized (in the strictest sense of *organized* as given above.) But when we deal with those products of nature that we can judge only as having intentionally been formed in just this way rather than some other, then we need that maxim of reflective judgment essentially, if we are to acquire so much as an empirical cognition of the intrinsic character of these products. For we cannot even think them as organized things without also thinking that they were produced intentionally ... The purposiveness that we must presuppose even for cognizing the inner possibility of many natural things is quite unthinkable to us and is beyond our grasp unless we think of it, and of the world as such, as a product of an intelligent cause (a God)."

113. Kant, *Critique of Judgment*, §77, p. 290; *Kritik der Urteilskraft*, p. 406.

114. Kant, *Critique of Judgment*, §77, p. 291; *Kritik der Urteilskraft*, p. 407.

115. Kant, *Critique of Judgment*, §77, p. 293; *Kritik der Urteilskraft*, p. 409.

116. Kant, *Critique of Judgment*, IX, p. 37; *Kritik der Urteilskraft*, p. 197.

117. Hegel, "Faith and Knowledge," p. 86; *Werke*, 2, p. 322.

118. Kant, *Critique of Judgment*, §22, p. 89; *Kritik der Urteilskraft*, p. 239.

119. The aspect of normativity in the *Critique of Judgment* and its relation to Hegel's project is brilliantly developed by Robert Pippin in "Avoiding German Idealism: Kant and the Reflective Judgment Problem," in his *Idealism as Modernism: Hegelian Variations* (Cambridge: Cambridge University Press, 1997). This point about the normativity of both teleological and aesthetic judgments is also argued by Hannah Ginsborg, "Purposiveness and Normativity," in Hoke Robinson (ed.), *Proceedings of the Eighth International Kant Congress* (Milwaukee: Marquette University Press, 1995), pp. 453–460. My discussion of Kant's ideas is heavily indebted to Ginsborg's and Pippin's discussions.

120. Kant, *Critique of Judgment*, First Introduction, X, p. 429; *Kritik der Urteilskraft*, p. 240: "Now if I use a stone to smash something on it, or to build [something] on it, etc., I can [regard] these effects too as purposes [and] refer them to their causes; but that does not entitle me to say that the stone was [meant] to serve for building. Only about the eye do I make the judgment that it *was* [*meant*] *to* be suitable for sight."

121. The point is made by Hannah Ginsborg, "Purposiveness and Normativity," p. 456.

122. I here follow Hannah Ginsborg's interpretation in "Purposiveness and Normativity," p. 458.

123. Kant had further grounds, however, for denying that there are rules for the making of aesthetic judgments. The aesthetic judgment could not be the application of a rule since a rule would require the application of a *concept*, and the employment of a concept would bring aesthetic judgment under "the understanding" and its set of presupposed "mechanical" laws. Hence, Kant thinks that such a use of concepts must be ruled out in aesthetic judgments. When I make such an aesthetic judgment, I experience a disinterested (not uninterested) pleasure (in the sense that I am not interested in the existence of the object), and the reflective judgment that the object is beautiful "precedes the pleasure in the object and is the basis of this pleasure, [a pleasure] in the harmony of the cognitive powers." (Kant, *Critique of Judgment*, §9, p. 62; *Kritik der Urteilskraft*, p. 218.) This harmony is said to be a matter of the "free play" of the cognitive powers, a "lawfulness without a law, and a subjective harmony of the imagination with the understanding without an objective harmony." (Kant, *Critique of Judgment*, "General Comment on the First Division of the Analytic," p. 92; *Kritik der Urteilskraft*, p. 241.) The pleasure, that is, is attendant on my understanding that my own cognitive powers are working rightfully, that they are judging the object as it ought to be judged.

124. Kant, *Critique of Judgment*, §40, p. 160; *Kritik der Urteilskraft*, pp. 293–294: "Instead, we must [here] take *sensus communis* to mean the idea of a sense *shared* [by all of us], i.e., a power to judge that in reflecting takes account (a priori), in our thought, of everyone else's way of presenting [something], in order *as it were* to compare our own judgment with human reason in general and thus escape the illusion that arises from the ease of mistaking subjective

and private conditions for objective ones . . . we compare our judgment not so much with the actual as rather with the merely possible judgments of others, and [thus] put ourselves in the position of everyone else, merely by abstracting from the limitations that [may] happen to attach to our own judging."

125. Hegel, "Faith and Knowledge," p. 87; *Werke*, 2, p. 323.

126. Among the commentators, Robert Pippin has most forcefully brought out this aspect of the theme of orientation in Hegel's appropriation of the *Critique of Judgment*. See his "Avoiding German Idealism: Kant and the Reflective Judgment Problem," in *Idealism as Modernism*.

127. The full text of Kant's footnote reads, "On the other hand, the analogy of these direct natural purposes can serve to elucidate a certain association [among people], though one found more often as an idea than in actuality: in speaking of the complete transformation of a large people into a state, which took place recently, the word *organization* was frequently and very aptly applied to the establishment of legal authorities, etc. and even to the entire body politic. For each member in such a whole should indeed be not merely a means but also an end; and while each member contributes to making the whole possible, the Idea of that whole should in turn determine the member's position and function." Kant, *Critique of Judgment*, §65, p. 254; *Kritik der Urteilskraft*, p. 375.

128. Hegel, "Faith and Knowledge," p. 70; *Werke*, 2, p. 305.

129. Hegel, "Faith and Knowledge," p. 70; *Werke*, 2, p. 305: "This relative identity and opposition is what seeing or being conscious consists in; but the identity is completely identical with the difference just as it is in the magnet."

130. Hegel, "Faith and Knowledge," p. 89; *Werke*, 2, p. 325.

131. Hegel, "Faith and Knowledge," p. 191; *Werke*, 2, p. 432.

132. G. W. F. Hegel, "Natural Law: The Scientific Ways of Treating Natural Law, Its Place in Moral Philosophy, and Its Relation to the Positive Sciences of Law" (trans. T. M. Knox) (Philadelphia: University of Pennsylvania Press, 1975); Über die wissenschaftlichen Behandlungsarten des Naturrechts, seine Stelle in der praktischen Philosophie und sein Verhältnis zu den positiven Rechtswissenschaften, *Werke*, 2, pp. 434–530. The essay's title might be misleading, since it was not concerned with what nowadays is called "natural law." By the eighteenth century, the term "natural law" was taken in general to mean a theory of the normative foundations of law in general; it was opposed to jurisprudential theories of "positive law," which merely treated the laws that were actually in force in certain communities. Despite its name, "natural law" was thus not restricted to the study of which laws were "natural" or were in keeping with the "laws of nature."

133. G. W. F. Hegel, *System of Ethical Life (1802/3) and First Philosophy of Spirit (Part III of the System of Speculative Philosophy 1803/4)* (trans. H. S. Harris and T. M.. Knox) (Albany: State University of New York Press, 1979); *System der Sittlichkeit* (Hamburg: Felix Meiner Verlag, 1967).

134. The differences between Hegel's and Schelling's use of the *Potenzen* (the "potencies") is clearly brought out by Ludwig Siep, *Praktische Philosophie im*

deutschen Idealismus (Frankfurt a.M.: Suhrkamp Verlag, 1992). See the essay "Zur praktischen Philosophie Schellings und Hegel in Jena (bis 1803)," pp. 130–141.

135. In good Schellingian fashion, he characterized spirit as "the recovery of the universe into itself, both the scattered totality of this multiplicity, which it overarches, and the absolute ideality thereof in which it annihilates this separateness," – which, in so doing, *makes itself* "higher than nature." See Hegel, "Natural Law," p. 111; *Werke*, 2, p. 503.

136. See Hegel, "Natural Law," p. 83; *Werke*, 2, pp. 469–470.

137. See Hegel, "Natural Law," p. 111; *Werke*, 2, p. 503.

138. See Hegel, *System of Ethical Life*, p. 111; *System der Sittlichkeit*, p. 18.

139. Hegel, *System of Ethical Life*, p. 116; *System der Sittlichkeit*, p. 24.

140. Hegel, *System of Ethical Life*, p. 109; *System der Sittlichkeit*, p. 16. ("Effecting this into himself" translates "*Wirken in ihn*"; "incorporation" renders "*Aufnahme*.")

141. Not all of the notes that Hegel wrote during this period have been preserved, and some of the elements of Hegel's development are difficult to glean from what is left of those writings. He did save a good bit of what he wrote on the philosophy of nature, apparently as material for use in the lectures on the topic that he gave until the end of his life. Unfortunately, whatever manuscripts he prepared for his lectures on "Logic and Metaphysics" in 1802–03 have for the most part been lost. It was, however, during the period from the last part of 1803 to 1806 that he underwent his most rapid intellectual development and finally became who he was to be. From the surviving manuscripts, it seems that Hegel began sketching out a non-Schellingian conception of a part of philosophy ("logic and metaphysics") that was to deal with the articulation and inner structure of the "absolute" abstracted out of all its manifestations in different "peoples." Schellingian "speculation" would still deal with the "intellectual intuition" of the absolute in nature and in subjective and social life; but logic and metaphysics would deal with the articulation of the absolute outside of all these ways in which it happened to appear.

142. Hegel, "First Philosophy of Spirit," p. 225; Hegel, *Jenaer Systementwürfe I: Das System der spekulativen Philosophie* (ed. Klaus Düsing and Heinz Kimmerle) (Hamburg: Felix Meiner Verlag, 1986), p. 205. ("Sensing" renders "*empfindener*.")

143. Hegel, "First Philosophy of Spirit," p. 225; *Jenaer Systementwürfe I*, p. 204. (The bracketed numbers in the text are my additions.)

144. Hegel, "First Philosophy of Spirit," p. 244; *Jenaer Systementwürfe I*, pp. 226.

145. Hegel, "First Philosophy of Spirit," p. 237; *Jenaer Systementwürfe I*, pp. 218–219.

146. Hegel, "First Philosophy of Spirit," p. 239; *Jenaer Systementwürfe I*, p. 220.

147. Hegel, "First Philosophy of Spirit," p. 239; *Jenaer Systementwürfe I*, p. 221. Hegel there speaks of a *Sklave*, a slave, not a *Knecht*, a bondsman, as he did earlier and does later in the *Phenomenology of Spirit*.

148. Hegel, "First Philosophy of Spirit," p. 239; *Jenaer Systementwürfe I*, p. 221.

149. Hegel, "First Philosophy of Spirit," p. 240; *Jenaer Systementwürfe I*, p. 221.
150. Hegel, *System of Ethical Life*, pp. 99–100; *System der Sittlichkeit*, p. 7.
151. Hegel, *System of Ethical Life*, p. 125; *System der Sittlichkeit*, p. 34. The terms for "lordship and bondage" are the same as those used in the *Phenomenology of Spirit*, "*Herrschaft und Knechtschaft*."
152. Hegel, *System of Ethical Life*, p. 128; *System der Sittlichkeit*, p. 37.
153. Hegel, "Natural Law," p. 99; *Werke*, 2, p. 488.
154. Hegel, "Natural Law," p. 112; *Werke*, 2, p. 504.
155. Hegel, "Natural Law," p. 93; *Werke*, 2, p. 481.
156. Hegel, *System of Ethical Life*, p. 144; *System der Sittlichkeit*, p. 54.
157. A "people" seems to be, at least with regard to moral and ethical life, the "subject-object" of which he had spoken in the *Difference* essay, although in these pieces he preferred to move to an even more abstract level of discussion about "unity and multiplicity." See Hegel, *System of Ethical Life*, p. 144; *System der Sittlichkeit*, p. 54. Rolf-Peter Horstmann notes this difference between the *Difference* essay and "Natural Law" in his "Jenaer Systemkonzeptionen," in Otto Pöggeler (ed.), *Hegel* (Freiburg: Karl Alber Verlag, 1977), pp. 43–58; see p. 48.
158. Hegel, "Natural Law," p. 127; *Werke*, 2, p. 522.
159. Hegel, "Natural Law," pp. 104–105; *Werke*, 2, pp. 496–497. Schelling's notion of history as the progressive revelation of God is found in his 1800 *System of Transcendental Idealism* (trans. Peter Heath) (Charlottesville: University Press of Virginia, 1978); see pp. 198–212. Hegel's view of history as a set of recurring cycles of growth, maturity, and decay, in which each form of life adopts a set of binding commitments for itself, develops its life according to those commitments, and comes to grief on the hidden pressures and strains within them, is a view of historical succession very generally shared by Johann Gottfried Herder and Johann Joachim Winckelmann (and before them, by various Enlightenment historians). For a brief account of this view among Enlightenment historians, see Peter Gay, *The Enlightenment: An Interpretation: The Science of Freedom* (New York: Norton, 1969), pp. 101–102.
160. On Hölderlin's theory of tragedy and its relation to his poetry, see Dieter Henrich, "The Course of Remembrance," in Dieter Henrich, *The Course of Remembrance and Other Essays on Hölderlin* (ed. Eckart Förster), pp. 143–247; see p. 249 in particular. A similar notion of the spirit of humanity in history was also to be found in Herder's writings (and was almost certainly an additional source for this idea in Hegel's writing at the time), but Hölderlin's own particular conception of this was surely more decisive for Hegel's development.
161. Hegel, "Natural Law," p. 116; *Werke*, 2, p. 508.
162. Hegel, *System of Ethical Life*, p. 144; *System der Sittlichkeit*, pp. 54–55.
163. Hegel, "Natural Law," p. 127; *Werke*, 2, p. 522.
164. Philip de Vitry was the secretary to Philip VI of France; he noted, "In order to escape the evils which they saw coming, the people divided themselves into three parts. One was to pray to God; for trading and ploughing the second;

and later, to guard these two parts from wrongs and injuries, knights were created." Quoted in Robert S. Lopez, *The Birth of Europe* (New York: M. Evans and Co., 1966), p. 146.

165. On the status of the estates in German law at the time, see Mack Walker, *German Hometowns*, p. 110. For Hegel's own division, see Hegel, "Natural Law," p. 100; *Werke*, 2, pp. 489–490; Hegel, *System of Ethical Life*, p. 152; *System der Sittlichkeit*, p. 63. Hegel seemed unsure in "Natural Law" about whether there are three necessary estates or two necessary estates and one extra, contingent one. In the *System of Ethical Life* he seemed quite sure that there are three. (Harris and Knox's translation of *"Stand"* – estate – as "class" is somewhat misleading on this point.)

166. This analysis of cameralism is adapted from Mack Walker's wonderful discussion of it in Chapter 5 of his *German Hometowns*, pp. 145–184.

167. Such theory was also buttressed by the philosophical doctrines (so elegantly expounded, for example, by the earl of Shaftesbury) of the reciprocal interaction of everything, of the idea that Nature was a harmonious whole and that what had "naturally" grown up over the centuries in society was therefore also in itself harmonious. See Gerhard H. Müller's discussion of the earl of Shaftesbury's influence on the ideas of reciprocity in his *"Wechselwirkung* in the Life and Other Sciences: A Word, New Claims and a Concept Around 1800 . . . and Much Later," in Stefano Poggi and Maurisio Bossi (eds.), *Romanticism in Science: Science in Europe, 1790–1840* (Dordrecht: Kluwer Academic Publishers, 1994), pp. 1–14.

168. See Mack Walker's discussion of the "Prussian solution" in *German Hometowns*, pp. 154–160.

169. See Hegel, "Natural Law," p. 100; *Werke*, 2, p. 489.

170. Ibid.

171. Hegel, "Natural Law," p. 100; *Werke*, 2, p. 489.

172. Like any "hometowner," moreover, he was concerned (as he was all his life) about what he saw as the inequities contained in there being great inequalities of wealth within a society. The classical hometown had been more or less an egalitarian community, which tolerated differences in wealth but was very suspicious of people having either "too much" or "too little" and relied on its own very particularist sense of where to draw the line. See, for example, the equation of the combination of great wealth and great poverty as the "highest barbarism" (*"höchste Rohheit"*) and the claim that it is the duty of the government to work against this in Hegel, *System of Ethical Life*, p. 171; *System der Sittlichkeit*, p. 84.

173. See Hegel, "Natural Law," p. 117; *Werke*, 2, p. 510.

174. Hegel, "Natural Law," p. 124; *Werke*, 2, p. 519.

175. *Briefe*, 1, #49; *Letters*, p. 685.

176. *Briefe*, 1, #55; *Letters*, p. 107.

177. G. W. F. Hegel, *The Jena System, 1804–1805* (trans. John W. Burbridge and George di Giovanni) (Montreal: McGill-Queen's University Press, 1986); *Jenaer Systementwürfe II: Logik, Metaphysik, Naturphilosophie* (ed. Rolf-Peter

Horstmann) (Hamburg: Felix Meiner Verlag, 1982). The former is only a partial translation of the latter, omitting all of the *Naturphilosophie*; in the citations from this text I have altered the translations quite a bit.

178. There has been some scholarly debate as to how Hegel would have begun the manuscript and how he would have divided its sections. The case for holding that he began it with "simple relation" (*einfache Beziehung*) is made by the fact that at one late stage in the manuscript Hegel actually refers to the (lost) beginning of the logic by saying, "the logic began with unity itself as that which is identical with itself." Hegel, *The Jena System, 1804–1805*, p. 134; *Jenaer Systementwürfe II*, p. 136. ("... die Logik begann mit der Einheit selbst, als dem Sichselbstgleichen.") See the discussion by Rolf-Peter Horstmann in his introduction to *Jenaer Systementwürfe II*, pp. xvi–xx.

179. As Hegel puts it, "What results is the determination (*Bestimmung*) as a determination in this inner ratio (*Verhältnis*). The moments in this ratio do not have magnitude for themselves, but rather have purely and simply a magnitude as ratio; and what is determined is not their magnitude as individuals, but only their ratio to each other." Hegel, *The Jena System, 1804–1805*, p. 22; *Jenaer Systementwürfe II*, p. 20. My use for translation's sake of "relationship" to translate "*Verhältnis*," distinguishing it thereby from relations (*Beziehungen*) is, of course, completely artificial, since the associations between the German "*Beziehungen*" and "*Verhältnisse*" are definitely not those of the English "relation" and "relationship," but there simply are no other pairs of English terms that capture the senses of "*Beziehung*" as "relation" and "*Verhältnis*" as a kind of "proportion" or "ratio."

180. "The determinate relation of the universal and the particular, their simple being-within-each-other without opposition, is the determinate concept ... what is normally understood as determinate being is rather the determinate concept." Hegel, *The Jena System, 1804–1805*, p. 80; *Jenaer Systementwürfe II*, p. 79. ("Being-within-each-other" translates "*Ineinandersein*.")

181. As Hegel prefers to put it himself, "Cognition as the in-itself – which has withdrawn from all relation to others – and its moments are themselves totalities, items which are reflected into themselves; it is no longer the object of logic, which constructs the form up to its absolute concretion, but rather of metaphysics, in which the totalities must realize themselves, just as up until now the totalities, themselves existing only as moments of the absolute totality, have proven to be." Hegel, *The Jena System, 1804–1805*, p. 130; *Jenaer Systementwürfe II*, p. 131.

182. Hegel thus says at the beginning of the section, "This different cognition (*differente Erkennen*) as relating itself to an other, itself posits this other as the other of itself, it is not any more an other for us but for itself, or it negates itself. ... The In-itself of metaphysics is this form of cognition, which is the negative for cognition. Its movement, or cognition's coming to itself out of its other, cognizing that becomes cognition, is that this indifferent other becomes different for cognition, only determining itself as the negation of cognition,

through which cognition, which is alone positive, becomes the true In-itself."
Hegel, *The Jena System, 1804–1805*, p. 132; *Jenaer Systementwürfe II*, p. 133.

183. See Rolf-Peter Horstmann, "Jenaer Systemkonzeptionen," pp. 54–55. My interpretation of Hegel's writings on nature during this period is heavily dependent on Horstmann's interpretation.

184. For example, "chemism," taken as the midpoint between "dead matter" and "life," appeared in Hegel's 1803 philosophy of nature and never left it thereafter. Indeed, this desire for a smooth transition from matter to spirit was Hegel's basic motivation for saying in the *System of Ethical Life* that the family was the "highest totality of which nature was capable," indicating thereby that he wanted to show a smooth development from the nature studied by natural science to something like "ethical nature" (specifically, the difference of the sexes and the facts of human infancy and aging), to the "ethical life" of a people, which itself has no counterpart in nature. All this was meant to be continuous, nonreductionist, and to produce at the end of the process something that was new ("spirit") that was nonetheless not some substance metaphysically distinct from nature. (See Hegel, *System of Ethical Life*, p. 128; *System der Sittlichkeit*, p. 37.) Thus he says in the *System of Ethical Life*, "In the course of nature the husband sees flesh of his flesh in the wife, but in ethical life (*Sittlichkeit*) alone does he see the spirit of his spirit in and through the ethical essence." Hegel, *System of Ethical Life*, p. 143; *System der Sittlichkeit*, p. 53.

185. Hegel's own summary of this transition is exemplary of this relative lack of clarity in his notes: "The aether as absolute pure indifference identical with itself has infinity as this determinateness, ideality external to itself in the absolute independence of the members of the opposition, of the heavenly bodies; this indifference of the aether against the existing infinity passes over in the earth into their difference over and against each other, and the heavenly bodies became elements, entities for themselves, but absolutely different over and against each other in their being-for-self; their being-for-self fell apart in the absolute numerical individuality of the earth; they became idealities, unity of universality and infinity. This unity exists (*ist*) only as something infinitely absolute to itself and moving within itself and absolutely simple in its movement, or as the absolute return of the aether into itself through the absolute concept of infinity. *Nature exists in spirit as that which it is in its essence.*" G. W. F. Hegel, *Jenaer Systementwürfe I*, p. 183.

186. Hegel, *Jenaer Systementwürfe II*, p. 192.

187. Ibid., p. 197.

188. Hegel, *Jenaer Systementwürfe II*, "Zwei Anmerkungen zum System," p. 366. ("Circular line" translates literally "*Kreislinie*," circumference.)

189. G. W. F. Hegel, *Jenaer Systementwürfe III: Naturphilosophie und Philosophie des Geistes* (ed. Rolf-Peter Horstmann) (Hamburg: Felix Meiner Verlag, 1987).

190. Hegel, *Jenaer Systementwürfe III*, p. 3.

191. The section on *Geist* has been translated: G. W. F. Hegel, *Hegel and the*

Human Spirit: A Translation of the Jena Lectures on the Philosophy of Spirit (1805–6) with Commentary (trans. Leo Rauch) (Detroit: Wayne State University Press, 1983). I have altered Rauch's translations quite a bit.

192. Hegel, *Hegel and the Human Spirit*, p. 87; *Jenaer Systementwürfe III*, p. 172.

193. See, for example, *Hegel and the Human Spirit*, p. 89; *Jenaer Systementwürfe III*, p. 175.

194. Hegel, *Hegel and the Human Spirit*, p. 105; *Jenaer Systementwürfe III*, p. 191.

195. Hegel, *Hegel and the Human Spirit*, p. 107; *Jenaer Systementwürfe III*, p. 193.

196. Hegel, *Hegel and the Human Spirit*, p. 107; *Jenaer Systementwürfe III*, p. 193.

197. Hegel, *Hegel and the Human Spirit*, p. 107; *Jenaer Systementwürfe III*, p. 193.

198. Hegel, *Hegel and the Human Spirit*, p. 105; *Jenaer Systementwürfe III*, p. 191. ("Entice" renders "*reizen*.")

199. See, for example, the passages in Hegel, *Hegel and the Human Spirit*, p. 106; *Jenaer Systementwürfe III*, p. 192.

200. Hegel, *Hegel and the Human Spirit*, p. 116; *Jenaer Systementwürfe III*, p. 202.

201. Hegel, *Hegel and the Human Spirit*, p. 116; *Jenaer Systementwürfe III*, p. 202. ("Self-knowledge" translates "*Wissen von sich*.")

202. Hegel, *Hegel and the Human Spirit*, p. 118; *Jenaer Systementwürfe III*, p. 203.

203. Hegel, *Hegel and the Human Spirit*, pp. 118–119; *Jenaer Systementwürfe III*, pp. 203–204.

204. Hegel's remarks on the economy are brief and telegraphic, obviously written as notes for lectures. They are striking only in that they show that he was grappling with the consequences of the emerging modern commercial society for the kind of modern life that he championed. He uses some words that do not occur in his more extensive discussions of the problems of poverty and the introduction of machines in his earlier manuscripts: Hegel speaks of "factory work" and "manufacturing work," and he also speaks of "industry" ("*Fabrik-, Manufacturarbeiten . . . und . . . Industrie*"), things which were of much more concern in England, and of some concern in France, but were virtually unknown in Germany at the time (at least in anything like their present forms). In Hegel's day, "*Manufactur*" was identified by the "scale of the enterprise, meaning more works in a single enterprise than guild ordinances allowed, sometimes a degree of division of labor, and a market that included customers that the producers never saw" (Mack Walker, *German Hometowns*, p. 121). It had nothing to do with production according to mechanical power. Likewise, "*Industrie*" meant only, as an economic encyclopedia of the 1780s had put it, "the active energy of free workers and of merchants, together with the so-called *savoir faire* or cleverness at extracting all possible gains from favorable opportunities" (quoted in Mack Walker, *German Hometowns*, pp. 121–122). Although Hegel was clearly using those terms in their older German senses – his example of *Manufaktur* is work in the mines – he was nonetheless drawing rather modern conclusions using them.

205. Hegel, *Hegel and the Human Spirit*, p. 140; *Jenaer Systementwürfe III*, p. 224.

206. Hegel, *Hegel and the Human Spirit*, p. 140; *Jenaer Systementwürfe III*, p. 224.

207. Abbé Sieyès, "What Is the Third Estate?", in Keith Michael Baker (ed.), *The*

Old Regime and the French Revolution (Chicago: University of Chicago Press, 1987), p. 171.

208. Hegel, *Hegel and the Human Spirit*, p. 155; *Jenaer Systementwürfe III*, p. 236.

209. Hegel, *Hegel and the Human Spirit*, pp. 161, 156n, 160; *Jenaer Systementwürfe III*, pp. 241, 236n, 240.

210. Hegel, *Hegel and the Human Spirit*, pp. 159, 160; *Jenaer Systementwürfe III*, pp. 240, 239.

211. Hegel, *Hegel and the Human Spirit*, p. 155; *Jenaer Systementwürfe III*, p. 235.

212. Hegel, *Hegel and the Human Spirit*, p. 169; *Jenaer Systementwürfe III*, p. 249.

213. Interestingly, whereas in "The German Constitution" Hegel's characterization of the "absolute estate" would have in effect excluded his father from membership, in these later lecture notes his description of the "universal state" would in effect have included him.

214. There is a long tradition of historiography on this period in Germany that tends to attribute these conservative tendencies to the growth of Pietism in Germany. While it is no doubt true that Pietism played a significant role in the development of such irrationalist strands of thought, it seems to me very overstated to attribute that trend to Pietism alone. Indeed, the appeal of Pietism itself had to do with the confrontation between hometown life and the rationalizing forces both of the modern European state and of the rationalizing movement of the Enlightenment in general. Although these were two distinct lines of development – that of course overlapped with each other at many junctures – for many Pietists and their successors the two came to be fully identified with each other. The appeal of Pietism was itself rooted in hometown reactions against the encroaching, "universalistic," centralizing forces of absolute monarchy, Enlightenment critiques of superstition, and rationalistic theology. Isaiah Berlin attributes much of the irrationalism on the part of Hamann and Jacobi to Pietism in "Hume and the Sources of German Anti-Rationalism," in Isaiah Berlin, *Against the Current: Essays in the History of Ideas*, pp. 162–187. For a representative presentation of the idea that Pietism is the core idea behind the development of German thought during this period, see Liah Greenfeld, *Nationalism: Five Roads to Modernity* (Cambridge: Harvard University Press, 1992), Chapter 4: "The Final Solution of Infinite Longing: Germany," pp. 275–395.

215. See Hegel, *Hegel and the Human Spirit*, pp. 156–157; *Jenaer Systementwürfe III*, pp. 236–237.

216. Hegel, *Hegel and the Human Spirit*, p. 157; *Jenaer Systementwürfe III*, p. 237.

217. Cited in François Furet, *Revolutionary France: 1770–1880* (trans. Antonia Nevill) (Oxford: Blackwell, 1992), p. 220.

218. Hegel, *Hegel and the Human Spirit*, p. 173; *Jenaer Systementwürfe III*, p. 253.

219. Hegel, *Hegel and the Human Spirit*, p. 175; *Jenaer Systementwürfe III*, p. 255.

220. Hegel, *Hegel and the Human Spirit*, p. 176; *Jenaer Systementwürfe III*, p. 256.

221. Ibid.

222. Hegel, *Hegel and the Human Spirit*, p. 177; *Jenaer Systementwürfe III*, p. 257.

223. Hegel, *Hegel and the Human Spirit*, p. 177; *Jenaer Systementwürfe III*, p. 257.
224. Hegel, *Hegel and the Human Spirit*, p. 181; *Jenaer Systementwürfe III*, p. 260.
225. Hegel, *Hegel and the Human Spirit*, p. 181; *Jenaer Systementwürfe III*, p. 261.
226. Hegel, *Hegel and the Human Spirit*, p. 182; *Jenaer Systementwürfe III*, p. 261.

Chapter Five

1. Günther Nicolin (ed.), *Hegel in Berichten seiner Zeitgenossen*, #107, p. 76.
2. In fact, the *Phenomenology*'s fortunes rose and fell during Hegel's own lifetime. As late as 1812 (when he was writing the first preface to his *Science of Logic*), Hegel was still speaking of a projected two-part or four-part "System of Science" consisting of a *Phenomenology of Spirit* as the first part, to be followed by "Logic and the two sciences of the 'real,' the philosophy of nature and the philosophy of spirit." See G. W. F. Hegel, *Science of Logic* (trans. A. V. Miller) (London: George Allen and Unwin, 1969), p. 29; *Werke*, 5, p. 18. That two- or four-part "system" never appeared, and soon afterwards, while not exactly disowning the work (something he never fully did), Hegel definitively downplayed it, suggesting in a footnote added in 1831 to the reprinted 1812 preface to his *Science of Logic* that the *Phenomenology* had since been superseded by his later thought and was to be replaced by the introduction to his later *Encyclopedia of the Philosophical Sciences*, the sourcebook of the "system," itself, first published in 1817 when Hegel became a professor at Heidelberg. He also downplayed the *Phenomenology* within the *Encyclopedia* itself, which included a short "Phenomenology of Spirit" that played only a small role in the development of the overall "system". See G. W. F. Hegel, *The Encyclopedia Logic: Part 1 of the Encyclopedia of the Philosophical Sciences with the Zusätze* (trans. T. F. Geraets, W. A. Suchting, H. S. Harris) (Indianapolis: Hackett Publishing Company, 1991), §25; *Enzyklopädie der philosophischen Wissenschaften*, in *Werke*, 8–10. During the first phase of Hegel's ascendancy in Berlin, as he was expounding his "system," the *Phenomenology* was thus virtually forgotten, and his students focused almost exclusively instead on the method and results found in the *Encyclopedia* "system." However, as his fame grew and time passed, his later students in Berlin reversed that trend and came more and more to treat the *Phenomenology* as the very centerpiece of their interpretation of Hegel's thought.
3. See the short discussion by the editor of the critical edition of the *Phänomenologie des Geistes*, Wolfgang Bonsiepen, in G. W. F. Hegel, *Phänomenologie des Geistes* (Hamburg: Felix Meiner Verlag, 1988), pp. 547–548; the full story is related by Friedhelm Nicolin, "Zum Titelproblem der Phänomenologie des Geistes," *Hegel-Studien*, 4 (1967), pp. 113–123.
4. Immanuel Kant, *Metaphysical Foundations of Natural Science* (trans. James W. Ellington) (Indianapolis: Hackett Publishing Company, 1985), p. 119 (AA 555).
5. Wolfgang Bonsiepen thinks that Hegel most likely took the term from an essay by K. L. Reinhold or (what he regards as much less likely) from a piece by Fichte. See Bonsiepen's introductory essay to *Phänomenologie des Geistes*, pp.

ix–xvi. Curiously, however, Bonsiepen does not even consider Kant's statement in the *Metaphysical Foundations of Natural Science* (published in 1786, a work with which Hegel was surely familiar) – despite the great similarities in wording between Kant's conception of a "phenomenology" and Hegel's description of his own "phenomenology" – as a possible reason for Hegel's decision to title his work a "phenomenology." In his piece, "Hegel's Concept of Phenomenology," Rüdiger Bubner also suggests that the name came from an 1802 piece by Reinhold, *Elemente der Phänomenologie oder Erläuterung des rationalen Realismus durch seine Anwendung auf die Erscheinungen"*; see p. 48, note 12. Michael Petry gives a good account of other uses of the term "phenomenology" among Hegel's contemporaries in G. W. F. Hegel, *The Berlin Phenomenology* (ed. and trans. Michael Petry) (Dordrecht: D. Reidel Publishing Company, 1981), pp. lxxxiii–lxxxv.

6. I have given a more developed account of the structure and philosophical importance of the *Phenomenology* in Terry Pinkard, *Hegel's Phenomenology: The Sociality of Reason* (Cambridge: Cambridge University Press, 1994).

7. See *Phenomenology of Spirit*, ¶78, p. 49; *PG*, p. 67; *PhG*, p. 61. Hegel makes a play there on the words for doubt (*Zweifel*) and despair (*Verzweiflung*).

8. *Phenomenology of Spirit* ¶78, p. 49; *PG*, p. 67; *PhG*, p. 61.

9. *Phenomenology of Spirit*, ¶481–482, pp. 292–293; *PG*, p. 345; *PhG*, pp. 318–320; see also Edward Gibbon, *The Decline and Fall of the Roman Empire* (New York: Harcourt, Brace, 1960), p. 32.

10. *Phenomenology of Spirit*, ¶591, p. 360; *PG*, p. 418; *PhG*, pp. 390–391.

11. See *Phenomenology of Spirit*, ¶595, p. 363; *PG*, p. 422; *PhG*, p. 394. In an 1814 letter to Niethammer, after Napoleon's precipitous fall from power, Hegel even congratulated himself on having predicted Napoleon's downfall in those very same passages in the *Phenomenology*, claiming to have shown that "the great individual must himself give that mass the right to do what it does, thus precipitating his own fall." *Briefe*, II, #233; *Letters*, p. 307.

12. One famous occurrence of the term "beautiful soul" occurs in Johann Wolfgang von Goethe, *Wilhelm Meister's Apprenticeship* (ed. and trans. Eric A. Blackall in cooperation with Victor Lange) (Princeton: Princeton University Press, 1995). Goethe portrays a Pietist woman in that novel, who appears in a chapter titled appropriately "Confessions of a Beautiful Soul." The character notes her "tendency to consider my body as a thing apart," and concludes her account by noting, "I cannot recall having followed any commandment that loomed before me as a law imposed from without: I was always led and guided by impulse, freely following my own persuasion, and experiencing neither restriction nor regrets" (pp. 253, 256). Hegel may have taken his inspiration from Goethe; however, in 1805 he had also read a book having to do with the "confessions of a beautiful soul" that he had borrowed from his friend Karl Ludwig von Knebel; in a letter to Knebel accompanying the return of the book, he comments on "the contrast between the time in which the story is placed and the astounding modernity (*Modernität*) of the viewpoints and the manner are expressed." There were at least three other books around at the time with that

title, and there is no univocal reference to any one of them. Hegel, *Briefe*, #690; *Letters*, p. 375. See Hoffmeister's notes, *Briefe*, p. 473. On the ubiquity of the term in European life and its development, see Robert E. Norton, *The Beautiful Soul: Aesthetic Morality in the Eighteenth Century* (Ithaca: Cornell University Press, 1995).

13. The citation on "I" and "We" occurs in *Phenomenology of Spirit*, ¶177, p. 110, *PG*, p. 140; *PhG*, p. 127. The terms themselves, "mindedness" and "like-mindedness," are taken from Jonathan Lear, "The Disappearing 'We'," in Jonathan Lear, *Open Minded: Working Out the Logic of the Soul* (Cambridge, Mass.: Harvard University Press, 1998), pp. 282–300. Lear uses the terms to discuss Wittgenstein's conception of mind, but I have adopted his terminology and some of his discussion to help to clarify Hegel's conception of *Geist*. I do not think that this does any violence to the historically situated way in which Hegel in fact understood the concept of *Geist*. Indeed, I also think that the artificial terms "mindedness" and "like-mindedness" are in fact more helpful in translating the notoriously untranslatable German term "*Geist*" than the usual cognates of either "spirit" or "mind." But, it should be noted, the use of "mindedness" and "like-mindedness" also submerges the possible religious connotations that *Geist* has in German (and which are obviously better caught by the term "spirit"). The choice of translations thus rests on an interpretive decision about how to treat the importance of religion in Hegel's system; the view I take is that Hegel's philosophically articulated views on religion (at least from Jena until the end of his life) were outgrowths of his theory of *Geist* and not vice versa (as so many Hegel interpreters have done and continue to do). In other words, I do not see Hegel as advancing his philosophical views on the basis of previously held religious views; Hegel was, as I understand him, much more radical, seeing his own personal religious views fairly completely in terms of his overall philosophical views about "mindedness" and "like-mindedness."

14. See *Phenomenology of Spirit*, ¶673, p. 410, *PG*, p. 473; *PhG*, p. 443.

15. In the *Phenomenology*, the sharp distinctions that Hegel drew between art, religion, and philosophy in his Berlin years are not made; in the *Phenomenology*, "art" is more or less subsumed under "religion."

Chapter Six

1. Jakob Friedrich Fries, *Reinhold, Fichte und Schelling* (Leipzig: A. L. Reinicke, 1803); cited in Ernst Ludwig Theodor Henke, *Jakob Friedrich Fries: Aus seinem handschriftlichen Nachlasse dargestellt* (Leipzig: F. U. Brockhaus, 1867), p. 80.
2. See Ernst Ludwig Theodor Henke, *Jakob Friedrich Fries*, p. 83.
3. See Ernst Ludwig Theodor Henke, *Jakob Friedrich Fries*, p. 94.
4. J. F. Fries, *Philosophische Rechtslehre und Kritik aller positiven Gesetzgebung* (Jena: Johann Michael Mausse, 1803).
5. *Hegel in Berichten seiner Zeitgenossen*, #93, p. 71.
6. *Briefe*, I, #55; *Letters*, pp. 106–108.
7. *Briefe*, I, #158; *Letters*, p. 561.

8. Hegel's use of the term "hypochondria" is different from its contemporary usage. He uses it to refer to a type of spiritual depression; in a letter of 1826 to his friend Karl Daub he says, "I define hypochondria as the illness that consists in the inability to come out of oneself," and he recommends "activity" as the cure. See *Briefe*, III, #519; *Letters*, p. 513. Virtually the same definition occurs in one of the *Zusätze* to his *Encyclopedia*: "In this diseased frame of mind the man will not give up his subjectivity, is unable to overcome his repugnance to the actual world, and by this very fact finds himself in a state of relative incapacity which easily becomes an actual incapacity. If therefore the man does not want to perish he . . . must accept the conditions set for him by the world and wrest from it what he wants for himself." *Enzyklopädie*, §396, *Zusatz*; *Philosophy of Mind (Part Three of the Encyclopedia of the Philosophical Sciences)* (trans. William Wallace and A. V. Miller) (Oxford: Oxford University Press, 1971), p. 62.

9. *Hegel in Berichten seiner Zeitgenossen*, #92, p. 70.

10. *Briefe*, I, #76; *Letters*, p. 116.

11. *Briefe*, I, #74; *Letters*, p. 114.

12. See *Briefe*, II, #233; *Letters*, p. 306.

13. *Hegel in Berichten seiner Zeitgenossen*, #738, p. 492.

14. See *Briefe*, II, #233; *Letters*, p. 306.

15. *Briefe*, I, #78; *Letters*, p. 117.

16. See Max Steinmetz (ed.), *Geschichte der Universität Jena*, pp. 240–241.

17. *Briefe*, I, #76; *Letters*, p. 115.

18. Max Steinmetz (ed.), *Geschichte der Universität Jena*, p. 240.

19. Cited in Max Steinmetz (ed.), *Geschichte der Universität Jena*, p. 243.

20. See Max Steinmetz (ed.), *Geschichte der Universität Jena*, p. 241.

21. *Briefe*, I, notes to #113, p. 480.

22. Cited in James Sheehan, *German History: 1770–1866*, p. 358.

23. See Nicholas Boyle, *Goethe: The Poet and the Age. Volume I: The Poetry of Desire* (Oxford: Oxford University Press, 1991), p. 175.

24. See W. H. Auden, Forward to Goethe, *The Sorrows of Young Werther and Novella* (trans. Elizabeth Meyer and Louise Bogan) (New York: Random House, 1971), p. ix.

25. *Briefe*, I, #76; *Letters*, p. 116.

26. The letter is cited in Karl Rosenkranz, *Georg Wilhelm Friedrich Hegels Leben*, pp. 230–231; it has since been lost.

27. G. W. F. Hegel, "Maximen des Journals der deutschen Literatur," *Werke*, 2, p. 568; "Guidelines for the Journal of German Literature (1807)" (trans. Christine Seiler and Clark Butler), *Clio*, vol. 13, no. 4 (1984), p. 409.

28. Hegel, "Maximen des Journals der deutschen Literatur," *Werke*, 2, pp. 569–570; "Guidelines for the Journal of German Literature (1807)," p. 410.

29. On Hegel's relation to the *Edinburgh Review*, see Norbert Waszek, "Hegels Exzerpte aus der 'Edinburgh Review' 1817–1819," *Hegel-Studien*, 20 (1985), pp. 79–111. Karl Rosenkranz notes that Hegel was reading British newspapers already in Frankfurt.

30. See John Edward Toews, *Hegelianism*, pp. 76–77.

31. Hegel "Maximen des Journals der deutschen Literatur," *Werke*, 2, p. 572; "Guidelines for the Journal of German Literature (1807)," p. 412.

32. *Briefe*, I, #90; *Letters*, pp. 75–78.

33. *Briefe*, I, #93.

34. *Briefe*, I, #87; *Letters*, p. 686.

35. *Briefe*, I, #83. Schelling continues his enthusiastic description of the diviner in his letter of March 1807, #93.

36. *Briefe*, I, #90; *Letters*, pp. 75–78.

37. *Briefe*, I, #92; *Letters*, p. 687.

38. *Briefe*, IV/1, p. 231. "Crown Prince" referred to the name of his regiment.

39. *Briefe*, I, #125; *Letters*, p. 425.

40. See Sheehan, *German History: 1770–1866*, p. 251.

41. See John Edward Toews, *Hegelianism*, pp. 75–77.

42. Wilhelm R. Beyer, *Zwischen Phänomenologie und Logik: Hegel als Redakteur der Bamberger Zeitung* (Frankfurt a.M.: G. Schulte-Bulmke Verlag, 1955), p. 19.

43. See Wilhelm R. Beyer, *Zwischen Phänomenologie und Logik: Hegel als Redakteur der Bamberger Zeitung*, p. 20.

44. *Briefe*, I, #88. Niethammer apparently found the name "Schneiderbanger" humorous, saying as an aside, "Mr. Schneidewind or Schneidewang or however the peculiarly pronounced name of the owner of the paper otherwise goes."

45. *Briefe*, I, #98; *Letters*, p. 130.

46. *Briefe*, I, #89; *Letters*, p. 126.

47. Hegel, "Aphorismen aus Hegels Wastebook," *Werke*, 2, p. 547; "Aphorisms from the Wastebook," p. 2.

48. See Wilhelm R. Beyer, *Zwischen Phänomenologie und Logik: Hegel als Redakteur der Bamberger Zeitung*, p. 31.

49. *Briefe*, I, #98; *Letters*, p. 130.

50. *Briefe*, I, #85; *Letters*, pp. 122–123.

51. *Briefe*, I, #104; *Letters*, p. 143.

52. Cited in Manfred Baum and Kurt Meist, "Politik und Philosophie in der Bamberger Zeitung: Dokumente zu Hegels Redaktionstätigkeit 1807–1808," *Hegel-Studien*, 10 (1975), p. 91. My treatment of Hegel's activity during this period is largely extracted from Baum's and Meist's account.

53. Ibid., pp. 90–91.

54. Ibid., p. 112.

55. See *Briefe*, I, notes to #101, p. 473.

56. James Sheehan, *German History: 1770–1866*, p. 260.

57. See Manfred Baum and Kurt Meist, "Politik und Philosophie in der Bamberger Zeitung," p. 99.

58. See, for example, *Briefe*, I, #117; *Letters*, p. 159.

59. See James Sheehan, *German History: 1770–1866*, p. 261.

60. Manfred Baum and Kurt Meist, "Politik und Philosophie in der Bamberger Zeitung," p. 114.

61. Manfred Baum and Kurt Meist, "Politik und Philosophie in der Bamberger

Zeitung," p. 104. Baum and Meist give a nice recounting of the articles Hegel published in the newspaper in this regard, pp. 103–107.

62. *Briefe*, I, #113.

63. Manfred Baum and Kurt Meist, "Politik und Philosophie in der Bamberger Zeitung," p. 108.

64. Baum and Meist also make this point: see ibid., p. 110.

65. Ibid., p. 95.

66. In his formerly influential and furiously anti-Hegelian book, *Hegel und seine Zeit* (Berlin, 1857), Rudolf Haym tried to explain away Hegel's editorial choices as simply a reaction to the state censors. It was Haym who promoted the idea of Hegel as the official philosopher of the Prussian state; he also wished to show that Hegel's activities in Jena proved him to be not merely duplicitous in Prussia but also unpatriotic in Bamberg. Baum and Meist show that, whatever else is the case, the charge that Hegel was only reacting to the censor cannot be supported. As they also point out, Hegel's first biographer, Karl Rosenkranz, also erred in describing Hegel's editorial activities in Jena as exhibiting "warm interest" in the fate of the Prussian throne. See ibid., pp. 95–96.

67. *Briefe*, I, #102; *Letters*, p. 135.

68. His friend from Jena Thomas Seebeck, for example, commented in January 1808 on how Frommann had mentioned that Hegel "was satisfied with his current position." See *Briefe*, I, #113. In that letter, Seebeck also asks Hegel "how things stand with the second part of your system? Have you already begun the printing?" This indicates that Hegel was known by his friends to be at work on his *Logic* and to have a substantial manuscript already in draft.

69. *Briefe*, I, #112; *Letters*, p. 156.

70. *Phenomenology of Spirit*, ¶665, p. 404; *PhG*, pp. 437–438.

71. *Briefe*, I, #112; *Letters*, p. 155. Hegel's continuing penchant for coffee after his life in Bamberg is also noted in Wilhelm R. Beyer, "Aus Hegels Familienleben: Die Briefe der Susanne von Tucher an ihre Tochter Marie Hegel," *Hegel-Jahrbuch*, 1966 (Meisenheim am Glan), pp. 52–110. The Rumford percolating-drip coffee maker was one of Count von Rumford's many inventions; Count von Rumford was actually Benjamin Thompson, an American loyal to the British cause, knighted for his service to Britain in 1784 and later made a count of the Holy Roman Empire in 1791 after having served in the Royal Bavarian Service as, among other things, minister of war – he took his title from his hometown of Rumford in New Hampshire (now Concord); at the time of the production of his coffee maker, he was living in England again, conducting important research on the nature of heat and inventing a variety of stoves and fireplaces, many of which are still in use. He also designed the famous "English Gardens" in Munich.

72. See James Sheehan, *German History: 1770–1866*, pp. 269–270.

73. See *Briefe*, I, #120a; *Letters*, p. 164.

74. *Briefe*, IV/2, #120a; *Letters*, p. 163.

75. *Briefe*, I, #108; *Letters*, p. 149. He does the same thing again, in both German and Greek, in *Briefe*, IV/2, #120a; *Letters*, p. 163.

76. *Briefe*, I, #111; *Letters*, pp. 153–54.

77. *Briefe*, I, #112; *Letters*, p. 157.

78. *Briefe*, I, #112; *Letters*, p. 157; "Daß die Magistrate von den Bürgern gewählt werden müssen," in *Werke*, 1, p. 268: "The peaceful contentedness with what is actual, the hopelessness, the patient resignation in the face of a great, all powerful fate has passed over into hope, expectation, and the courage for something else." He also speaks in the Frankfurt manuscript (p. 273) of the absolute necessity for a "common mindedness" (*Gemeingeist*) in order for such reform to be possible.

79. This information is taken from note 1 in the notes to Hegel's letter to Niethammer; *Briefe*, I, p. 479.

80. *Briefe*, I, #108; *Letters*, p. 151.

81. Ibid.

82. *Briefe*, I, #103; *Letters*, p. 141.

83. *Briefe*, I, #104; *Letters*, p. 142.

84. *Briefe*, I, #126; *Letters*, p. 166.

85. *Briefe*, I, #127; *Letters*, p. 167.

86. Ibid.

87. *Briefe*, I, #125; *Letters*, p. 425.

88. *Briefe*, I, #129; *Letters*, p. 169.

89. *Briefe*, I, #95; *Letters*, p. 80.

90. Interestingly enough, Hegel might have taken this characterization of Schelling's philosophy from Friedrich Schlegel (with whom Hegel was not on the best of terms), whom Heinrich Steffens remembered at that time in Jena as having dismissed Schelling's views with the jape, "In the darkness, all cats are gray." Wolfgang Bonsiepen, Hans-Friedrich Wessels, and Heinrich Clairmont, "Anmerkungen" to Hegel's *Phänomenologie des Geistes* (Hamburg: Felix Meiner Verlag, 1988), p. 562.

91. *Briefe*, I, #107; *Letters*, p. 80.

92. Ibid.

93. *Briefe*, I, #107; *Letters*, p. 81.

94. *Hegel in Berichten seiner Zeitgenossen*, #133, p. 89. "Rat's tails" is "*Weichselzopf.*"

95. *Briefe*, I, #211; *Letters*, p. 284.

96. See John Edward Toews, *Hegelianism*, pp. 253–254.

97. The early reviews have been excerpted and discussed by Wolfgang Bonsiepen, "Erste Zeitgenössische Rezensionen der Phänomenologie des Geistes," *Hegel-Studien*, 14 (1979), pp. 9–38.

98. Cited in Wolfgang Bonsiepen, "Erste Zeitgenössische Rezensionen der Phänomenologie des Geistes," pp. 11–13.

99. Cited in ibid., p. 14.

100. Cited in ibid., p. 16.

101. Hegel, "Notizenblattt: Bayern: Ausbruch der Volksfreude über den endlichen Untergang der Philosophie," in *Werke*, 2, pp. 275–279.

102. Cited in Wolfgang Bonsiepen, "Erste Zeitgenössische Rezensionen der Phänomenologie des Geistes," p. 17.
103. *Hegel in Berichten seiner Zeitgenossen*, #130, p. 87.
104. *Hegel in Berichten seiner Zeitgenossen*, #131, p. 87.
105. *Hegel in Berichten seiner Zeitgenossen*, #132, p. 87.
106. Cited in Wolfgang Bonsiepen, "Erste Zeitgenössische Rezensionen der Phänomenologie des Geistes," p. 24. I have rendered "philosophisches Ich" as "philosophical self."
107. Cited in ibid., p. 25.
108. Cited in ibid., p. 26.
109. Cited in ibid., p. 28.
110. Cited in ibid., p. 30.
111. K. J. H. Windischmann's review of Hegel's *Phenomenology of Spirit*; reviewed as "G. W. Fr. Hegels System der Wissenschaft. I Theil. Die Phänomenologie des Geistes" in the *Jenaische Allgemeine Literatur-Zeitung*, February 7, 1809; reprinted in Oscar Fambach, *Der Romantische Rückfall in der Kritik der Zeit* (Berlin: Akademie Verlag, 1963), p. 413. See the discussion in Wolfgang Bonsiepen, "Erste Zeitgenössische Rezensionen der Phänomenologie des Geistes," pp. 19–22.
112. *Briefe*, I, #155.
113. *Briefe*, I, #103; *Letters*, p. 140.
114. *Briefe*, I, #98; *Letters*, p. 129.
115. *Briefe*, I, #109; *Letters*, p. 145.
116. *Briefe*, #215; *Letters*, p. 591.
117. See the excepts from Bachmann's review reprinted in *Briefe*, I, notes to #155, pp. 498–498. See also Wolfgang Bonsiepen, "Erste Zeitgenössische Rezensionen der Phänomenologie des Geistes," p. 32–33. The entire review is reprinted in Oscar Fambach, *Der Romantische Rückfall in der Kritik der Zeit*, pp. 428–452. That Schelling was already being talked about as a modern Plato is supported by Henry Crabb Robinson's November 1802 letter to his brother, in which he speaks of going to hear Schelling's lectures, "hearing the modern Plato read for a whole hour his new metaphysical Theory of Aesthetick Or the Philosophy of the Arts." Edith J. Morley (ed.), *Crabb Robinson in Germany: 1800–1805: Extracts from His Correspondence)*, p. 117.
118. See the reprint in Oscar Fambach, *Der Romantische Rückfall in der Kritik der Zeit*, p. 429.
119. *Hegel in Berichten seiner Zeitgenossen*, #143, p. 95.

Chapter Seven

1. *Hegel in Berichten seiner Zeitgenossen*, # 125, p. 85.
2. *Briefe*, I, #101; *Letters*, p. 134.
3. *Briefe*, I, #108; *Letters*, p. 150.
4. *Briefe*, I, #121.

5. *Briefe*, I, #122; *Letters*, p. 173.
6. *Briefe*, I, #122; *Letters*, p. 174.
7. See *Briefe*, I, #133, for Niethammer's letter; Hegel's reply is *Briefe*, I, #135; *Letters*, p. 178.
8. *Briefe*, IV/1, #81, p. 96.
9. See Karl-Ernst Jeismann, "Zur Bedeutung der "Bildung" im 19. Jahrhundert," in Karl-Ernst Jeismann und Peter Lundgreen (eds.), *Handbuch der deutschen Bildungsgeschichte* (Munich: C.H. Beck, 1987), vol. 3, pp. 4–6.
10. See Karl-Ernst Jeismann, "Zur Bedeutung der "Bildung" im 19. Jahrhundert," p. 7.
11. *Briefe*, I, #85; *Letters*, p. 122.
12. *Briefe*, I, #135; *Letters*, p. 178.
13. See *Briefe*, I, notes to #88, p. 469.
14. See *Briefe*, I, notes to #53, p. 456.
15. See Karl-Ernst Jeismann, "Das höhere Knabenschulwesen," in *Handbuch der deutschen Bildungsgeschichte*, vol. 3, pp. 158–159.
16. There had naturally enough been great differences among all the various *Länder* in how this was implemented; there were especially great differences with regard to whether it included more modern studies. See Karl-Ernst Jeismann, "Das höhere Knabenschulwesen," p. 153.
17. Cited in Hegel, *Werke*, 4, "Anmerkung zu Redaktion zu Band 4," p. 598.
18. Cited in G. Hirschmann, "Die 'Ära Wurm' (1806–1818)," in Gerhard Pfeiffer (ed.), *Nürnberg – Geschichte einer europäischen Stadt* (Munich: C.H. Beck, 1982), p. 360.
19. Cited in G. Hirschmann, "Die 'Ära Wurm' (1806–1818)," p. 359.
20. Ibid., p. 360.
21. See Karl-Ernst Jeismann, "Zur Bedeutung der "Bildung" im 19. Jahrhundert," p. 13.
22. Baron von Lochner's report is cited in Karlheinz Goldmann, "Hegel als Referent für das Nürnberger Lehrerseminar und Volksschulwesen 1813–1816," in W. R. Beyer, K. Lanig, and K. Goldmann, *Georg Wilhelm Friedrich Hegel in Nürnberg: 1808–1816* (Nuremberg: Selbstverlag der Stadt Bibliothek Nürnberg, 1966), p. 42.
23. *Briefe*, I, #143.
24. See James Sheehan, *German History: 1770–1866*, p. 267.
25. *Briefe*, I, #143.
26. *Briefe*, I, #148; *Letters*, p. 198.
27. *Briefe*, I, #145; *Letters*, p. 191.
28. *Briefe*, I, #145; *Letters*, p. 190.
29. Ibid.
30. *Briefe*, I, #144; *Letters*, p. 188.
31. See *Hegel in Berichten seiner Zeitgenossen*, #177, p. 123; #188, p. 134.
32. *Briefe*, I, #184; *Letters*, p. 244.
33. *Hegel in Berichten seiner Zeitgenossen*, #166, p. 115.
34. Karl Lanig, "Die pädagogischen Jahre Hegels in Nürnberg," in W. R. Beyer,

K. Lanig, and K. Goldmann, *Georg Wilhelm Friedrich Hegel in Nürnberg: 1808–1816*, p. 26.

35. This at least was the memory of Friedrich Kapp, cited in Karl Lanig, "Die pädagogischen Jahre Hegels in Nürnberg," p. 20.
36. *Hegel in Berichten seiner Zeitgenossen*, #145, p. 100.
37. *Hegel in Berichten seiner Zeitgenossen*, #146, p. 103.
38. Hegel, "Rede auf den Amtsvorgänger Rektor Schenk am 10. Juli 1809," *Werke*, 4, p. 307.
39. Hegel, "Rede zum Schuljahrabschluß am 29. September, 1809," *Werke*, 4, p. 314.
40. Ibid., p. 315.
41. Ibid., p. 317.
42. Ibid., p. 321.
43. Ibid., p. 318.
44. See Robert E. Norton, *The Beautiful Soul: Aesthetic Morality in the Eighteenth Century*.
45. Hegel, "Rede zum Schuljahrabschluß am 29. September, 1809," *Werke*, 4, p. 323.
46. Ibid., p. 322.
47. Ibid., p. 325. ("Career" translates *"Laufbahn."*)
48. Cited in James Sheehan, *German History: 1770–1866*, p. 286.
49. *Briefe*, I, #147; *Letters*, p. 196.
50. See G. Hirschmann, "Die 'Ära Wurm' (1806–1818)," p. 361.
51. *Briefe*, I, #148; *Letters*, p. 200.
52. *Briefe*, I, #149.
53. See *Briefe*, I, #151; *Letters*, p. 204.
54. Hegel, "Rede zum Schuljahrabschluß am 14. September, 1810," *Werke*, 4, pp. 329–330.
55. Ibid., pp. 330–331.
56. Ibid., p. 332.
57. Ibid., p. 332. ("Self-activity" renders *"Selbsttätigkeit."*)
58. Ibid.
59. Ibid., p. 334.
60. Ibid., p. 335.
61. Ibid., p. 336.
62. Ibid., pp. 339–340.
63. *Briefe*, I, #156; *Letters*, p. 210.
64. *Briefe*, I, #161; *Letters*, p. 211.
65. *Briefe*, I, #173; *Letters*, p. 230–231.
66. See *Briefe*, I, notes to #165, pp. 501–502.
67. Cited in Karl Lanig, "Die pädagogischen Jahre Hegels in Nürnberg," p. 34.
68. *Briefe*, I, #169; *Letters*, p. 226.
69. *Briefe*, I, #169; *Letters*, p. 227.
70. Hegel, *Werke*, 4, p. 68. This citation as well as the dating of it must, however, be taken with a grain of salt. It belongs to what have come to be called Hegel's

"Philosophical Propaedeutics," a compilation of manuscripts consisting of those in Hegel's own hand and in the dictation Hegel gave to his students. They were all originally compiled by his first biographer, Karl Rosenkranz, who in fact gave them the name "Philosophical Propaedeutics." Rosenkranz's editorial methods, though, left much to be desired, and his results have been challenged by later editors. Even worse, however, for the purposes of adequately dating those manuscripts in order to construct a picture of Hegel's intellectual development during this period is the fact that many of the manuscripts that Rosenkranz had at his disposal have since vanished, and thus more modern orderings and interpretations of the surviving manuscripts must be based to some extent on conjecture. This particular citation, though, *seems* to come from 1808–09. See the discussion by the editors in Hegel, *Werke*, 4, "Anmerkung zu Redaktion zu Band 4," pp. 604–617. See also Udo Rameil's discussion of Rosenkranz's editorial mistakes in his "Der systematische Aufbau der Geisteslehre in Hegels Nürnberger Propädeutik," *Hegel-Studien*, 23 (1988), pp. 19–49, and in his "Die Phänomenologie des Geistes in Hegel's Nürnberger Propädeutik," in Lothar Eley (ed.), *Hegels Theorie des subjektiven Geistes in der "Enzyklopädie der philosophischen Wissenschaften im Grundrisse"* (Stuttgart: Bad Cannstatt: Frommann-Holzboog, 1990), pp. 84–130.

71. *Briefe*, I, #177.
72. *Briefe*, II, #272; *Letters*, p. 327.
73. *Briefe*, II, #309; *Letters*, p. 328.
74. *Briefe*, I, #143.
75. *Briefe*, I, #154; *Letters*, p. 208.
76. See *Briefe*, IV/1, notes to #84, pp. 321–322. The Frankfurt club called "Museum" is discussed by Peter Gay, *The Naked Heart: The Bourgeois Experience: Victoria to Freud, Vol. IV* (New York: Norton, 1995), p. 19.
77. *Hegel in Berichten seiner Zeitgenossen*, #150, p. 104.
78. *Briefe*, I, #156; *Letters*, pp. 209–210.
79. *Briefe*, I, #181; *Letters*, p. 239.
80. See the letter to Niethammer, *Briefe*, I, #181; *Letters*, p. 239.
81. See *Briefe*, I, #178; *Letters*, pp. 236–237. *Letters* also includes a translation of Hegel's verse to Marie.
82. See *Briefe*, I, #180; *Letters*, p. 238.
83. *Briefe*, I, #186; *Letters*, p. 243.
84. *Briefe*, I, #186; *Letters*, pp. 243–244.
85. *Briefe*, I, #186; *Letters*, p. 244. (Perhaps it goes without saying, but Hegel's linguistic use of "being satisfied" (*Zufriedenheit*) in this letter should be kept distinct from his use of "satisfaction" (*Befriedigung*) of self-consciousness in the *Phenomenology*.)
86. *Briefe*, I, #187; *Letters*, p. 245.
87. *Briefe*, I, #187; *Letters*, p. 246.
88. See *Briefe*, I, #189; *Letters*, pp. 246–248, translates some of Marie von Tucher's comments.

89. Cited in James Sheehan, *German History: 1770–1866*, p. 505. (The historian is John Lothrop Motley.)

90. *Briefe*, I, #183; *Letters*, pp. 240–241. (Niethammer closed the letter trying to soothe Hegel's worries by telling an obviously strained story about the problem of widows' pensions involved in attaining university appointments, and how he would have a better chance getting such a position *after* he was married. Hegel was, however, not fooled.)

91. *Briefe*, I, #185; *Letters*, p. 241.

92. *Briefe*, I, #184; *Letters*, p. 245.

93. *Briefe*, I, #125; *Letters*, p. 425.

94. The source of the story of Hegel's promise of marriage to Ms. Burkhardt is one of Hegel's later friends in Berlin, who was himself quite a figure in the Berlin social and political scene, Karl August Varnhagen von Ense. In 1844, thirteen years after Hegel's death, Varnhagen von Ense wrote out a notice about a conversation between himself and Heinrich Leo, in which he states that Leo told him of the promise of marriage, of Hegel's subsequent and convenient forgetting about the whole matter, and of Ms. Burkhardt's showing up before Hegel's wedding in Nuremberg demanding satisfaction. This is the only source for the account that Hegel promised marriage to Ms. Burkhardt and that she tried to disrupt Hegel's wedding. See the notes to #581 in *Briefe*, III, p. 434.

95. *Briefe*, I, #196; *Letters*, p. 255. ("Official post" translates "*Amte*.")

96. *Briefe*, I, #196; *Letters*, p. 256. The Clark-Butler translation of the letter covers over Hegel's use of the negative – "not far removed (*nicht entfernter*) degree" – in speaking of the emotional aspects of his marriage. (They translate it as "the same degree.")

97. *Briefe*, I, #186; *Letters*, p. 243.

98. See Wilhelm R. Beyer, "Aus Hegels Familienleben: Die Briefe der Susanna von Tucher an ihre Tochter Marie Hegel," *Hegel-Jahrbuch*, 1966, pp. 79–81.

99. See Wilhelm R. Beyer, "Aus Hegels Familienleben," pp. 65–66. (The letter referring to "Guido" is dated April 6, 1819, after the Hegel family had moved to Berlin.)

100. *Briefe*, I, #216; *Letters*, p. 284.

101. *Briefe*, I, #122; *Letters*, p. 175.

102. *Briefe*, I, #198; *Letters*, p. 261. ("Proofsheet" renders "*Bogen*"; a "*Bogen*" is generally a proof sheet containing sixteen pages, front and back, which can then be cut and bound into a book.)

103. Hegel, "Rede zum Schuljahrabschluß am 2. September 1811," *Werke*, 4, pp. 350–351.

104. Ibid., p. 348.

105. Ibid., p. 350.

106. Ibid., p. 346.

107. Ibid. ("Orienting points" translates "*Richtungslinien*.")

108. Ibid., p. 347.

109. Ibid., pp. 349–350.
110. Ibid., p. 352.
111. Ibid., p. 353.
112. See James Sheehan, *German History: 1770–1866*, pp. 310–315; François Furet, *Revolutionary France: 1770–1880*, pp. 263–265.
113. See James Sheehan, *German History: 1770–1866*, p. 319.
114. *Briefe*, II, #233; *Letters*, p. 307.
115. Ibid.
116. *Briefe*, II, #241; *Letters*, p. 312. The full context of the reference is not altogether a happy one: "May God only grant us not to be so stiff-necked as that dearly beloved people of His; and not to have to . . . carry around as many lice with us and even be scattered from the promised land of German-dumb into particularisms." The unflattering comparison of the German nationalists to a stereotype of the Jews does not, as it were, put Hegel in the best light. It is of course unclear how ironically Hegel might mean all this. Paulus was of Jewish origin, and Hegel knew this, so one would assume that Hegel – who desperately wanted Paulus's help in landing a position at Heidelberg and with whom he was friends – would not be trying to insult Paulus with anti-Semitic jibes. But it does point out that by 1814, Hegel was still at least entertaining the view of Jewish life that he had held in Frankfurt.
117. Hegel, "Rede zum Schuljahrabschluß am 2. September 1811," *Werke*, 4, p. 347.
118. The vote on cheeses took place at a dinner at which the guests were given fifty-two different cheeses to sample and proclaimed a Brie from the farm of Estourville at Villeroy to be the King of Cheeses. See Jenifer Harvey Lang (ed.), *Larousse Gastronomique* (New York: Crown Publishers, 1988), entry on "Brie," p. 142.
119. *Briefe*, II, #262; *Letters*, p. 431.
120. See Hans-Christian Lucas, "Die Schwester im Schatten: Bemerkungen zu Hegels Schwester Christiane," in Christoph Jamme and Otto Pöggeler (eds.), *"O Fürstin der Heimath! Glükliches Stutgard,"* pp. 284–306.
121. Hegel had good and friendly relations with Caroline Paulus, the wife of the theologian (who, like Hegel, was a Swabian and who had lived in Jena at roughly the same time as Hegel, at Nuremberg at roughly the same time as Hegel, and again at Heidelberg at roughly at the same time as Hegel). They joked with each other and seemed to be on extraordinarily good terms. But Caroline Paulus offers an interesting and revealing aside in one of her letters to Hegel. The letter is dated around the end of October, 1808 (while Hegel was still in Bamberg), and concerns the nature of things in Nuremberg (where the Paulus family was living). She says, "A custom exists here in social life that I would find very disagreeable if I had not made up mind not to respect it. Namely, on the whole, men and women keep themselves separated from each other. On account of this, I have abjured my sex (on which, as you know, I have not placed much value) and thrown myself in with the men." *Briefe*,

#134. On the one hand, Hegel insisted on a sharp difference between the sexes as far as gender roles went; on the other hand, Hegel clearly enjoyed consorting with a woman who self-consciously renounced the "female" way of doing things and thus became someone with whom Hegel could feel at home. But, to be sure, Hegel would most likely have been quite upset if his wife, Marie, had uttered similar sentiments.

122. The whole issue of Hegel's relation to his family is cloudy. It seems, for example, on Hegel's own account that nobody from his family attended his wedding. Indeed, outside of his relations with Christiane, Hegel seems to have had virtually no contact at all with his family. He almost never speaks of his father, and he never speaks of his brother. There are no extant letters between the brothers, nor is there any record of any conversations between him and Christiane about Georg Ludwig. There is no record of Hegel feeling any great loss over the death of his brother. It thus seems that one must assume that the relations between the brothers were not particularly close and may indeed have been quite strained. Moreover, the way in which Christiane elected to stay with her father and take care of him until his death (despite some apparently attractive offers of marriage for her), and the way she then transferred her interests to her older brother also suggest (to use Freud's term) a "family romance" of somewhat strained relations. That Hegel's mother died of an illness that Hegel himself survived (at the age of eleven) perhaps also affected Hegel's own emotional development, giving him an anxiety about having survived the same disease at the same time as his mother. However, given only these bare facts, the true "family romance" of the Hegel family of Stuttgart can only remain a matter for speculation, although Hegel's later speech impediment – an anxiety about speaking to large groups that led him to gasp and stutter – no doubt had some origin in the dynamics of his early family life. There is some evidence that Hegel's brother took after his father, while he and Christiane clearly took after their mother.

123. See Hans-Christian Lucas, "Die Schwester im Schatten: Bemerkungen zu Hegels Schwester Christiane," p. 293.

124. Ibid., p. 295.

125. See *Briefe*, II, notes to #238, pp. 377–378.

126. See Hans-Christian Lucas, "Die Schwester im Schatten: Bemerkungen zu Hegels Schwester Christiane," p. 297.

127. *Briefe*, II, #228; *Letters*, p. 407.

128. *Briefe*, II, #238; *Letters*, p. 410.

129. See *Briefe*, II, notes to #253, p. 383.

130. See Hans-Christian Lucas, "Die Schwester im Schatten: Bemerkungen zu Hegels Schwester Christiane," p. 297; Hegel, *Briefe*, II, notes to #395, p. 486.

131. See *Briefe*, II, notes to #395, pp. 486–487. See also Hans-Christian Lucas, "Die Schwester im Schatten: Bemerkungen zu Hegels Schwester Christiane," pp. 295–296, note 27.

132. *Briefe*, II, #395; *Letters*, p. 417.

133. See *Briefe*, II, notes to #395, p. 487.
134. See Wilhelm R. Beyer, "Aus Hegels Familienleben," *Hegel-Jahrbuch*, 1966, pp. 82–85.
135. Cited in Willi Ferdinand Becker, "Hegels Hinterlassene Schriften im Briefwechsel seines Sohnes Immanuel," *Zeitschrift für philosophische Forschung*, vol. 35, nos. 3/4 (July–December 1981), p. 613.
136. See Karlheinz Goldmann, "Hegel als Referent für das Nürnberger Lehrerseminar und Volksschulwesen 1813–1816," in W. R. Beyer, K. Lanig, and K. Goldmann, *Georg Wilhelm Friedrich Hegel in Nürnberg: 1808–1816*, pp. 39–46.
137. *Briefe*, II, #229; *Letters*, p. 304.
138. See *Briefe*, II, notes to #229, pp. 374–375. In one of the more egregious misinterpretations of some of Hegel's utterances, the English translators of Hegel's letters take him as arguing against *all* education for women as "money out the window." See *Letters*, pp. 234, 302. Hegel did not say that in the letters cited, and if he really had disapproved of education for women, he would not have gone out of his way to allow Ms. Eisen to reopen the school, much less to direct it. Hegel's belief in women's education is consistent with this belief that women cannot go as far as men in scientific matters; his beliefs on the matter are hardly commendable even if they were representative of a wider body of thought at the time.
139. Hegel, "Gutachten über die Stellung des Realinstituts zu den übrigen Studienanstalten" (1810), *Werke*, 4, p. 391.
140. See *Briefe*, I, #196; *Letters*, p. 258.
141. *Briefe*, I, #200; *Letters*, p. 264.
142. *Briefe*, I, #211; *Letters*, p. 283.
143. A short overview of the ways in which Hegel both departed from and adhered to the "General Normative" can be found in Friedhelm Nicolin, "Pädagogik – Propädeutik – Enzyklopädie," in Otto Pöggeler (ed.), *Hegel*, pp. 91–105, especially pp. 98–101.
144. See Hegel, "Über den Vortrag der Philosophie auf Gymnasien: Privatgutachten für den Königlichen Bayrischen Oberschulrat Immanuel Niethammer," *Werke*, 4, p. 404; *Letters*, p. 276.
145. Hegel, "Über den Vortrag der Philosophie auf Gymnasien: Privatgutachten für den Königlichen Bayrischen Oberschulrat Immanuel Niethammer," *Werke*, 4, pp. 408–409; *Letters*, p. 278.
146. Hegel identified those first three stages to Niethammer as "Consciousness, Self-Consciousness, and Reason," in other words, in terms of the chapters of his later *Encyclopedia* treatment of "Phenomenology."
147. See Udo Rameil, "Die Phänomenologie des Geistes in Hegel's Nürnberger Propädeutik," pp. 84–130. A shorter discussion of some of the manuscripts is also given by the editors of the *Werke*, 4, pp. 610–614. For discussion of the relation of Hegel's Nuremberg "Propaedeutics" to his later system, see Chapter 8 of this volume.
148. Hegel, "Über den Vortrag der Philosophie auf Gymnasien: Privatgutachten

für den Königlichen Bayrischen Oberschulrat Immanuel Niethammer," *Werke*, 4, p. 406; *Letters*, p. 277.

149. Hegel, "Über den Vortrag der Philosophie auf Gymnasien: Privatgutachten für den Königlichen Bayrischen Oberschulrat Immanuel Niethammer," *Werke*, 4, pp. 415–416; *Letters*, p. 282.

150. See *Briefe*, I, #152; *Letters*, p. 588.

151. *Briefe*, I, #216; *Letters*, p. 285.

152. *Briefe*, I, #216; *Letters*, p. 285.

153. *Briefe*, II, #271; *Letters*, p. 325.

154. *Briefe*, II, #271; *Letters*, p. 325.

155. Hegel, "Rede zum Schuljahrabschluß am 30. August 1815," *Werke*, 4, p. 373.

156. Ibid., p. 376.

157. Ibid., p. 373.

158. Ibid., pp. 370–371.

159. Ibid., p. 374.

160. Ibid., 4, p. 372.

161. Hegel, "Philosophische Enzyklopädie für die Oberklasse," *Werke*, 4, p. 63 (§196) (part of the "Philosophical Propaedeutics").

162. *Hegel in Berichten seiner Zeitgenossen*, #177, pp. 122–123.

163. *Briefe*, II, #262; *Letters*, p. 431.

164. *Briefe*, II, #236.

165. Von Humboldt is cited in Charles E. McClelland, *State, Society, and University in Germany: 1700–1914*, p. 121.

166. *Hegel in Berichten seiner Zeitgenossen*, #179, pp. 124–125. See also *Briefe*, II, notes to #278, pp. 397–403. ("Professorial lectures" translates "*Kathedervortrage*.") In a popular illustrated presentation of Hegel's life and thought, Lloyd Spencer takes the rest of Raumer's description of Hegel completely out of context. Raumer followed his statement about Hegel's reasonableness with a comparison of Hegel's mode of presentation to that of other popular teachers: "To be sure, there is false pathos, shouting, and roaring, little jokes, digressions, half-true comparisons, one-sided comparisons with the present, arrogant self-praise . . . and this attracts masses of students." Spencer cites this as if Raumer were describing Hegel himself. But Raumer's letter clearly says otherwise; in fact, Raumer says of such "false pathos, shouting," and so forth: "In this false sense Hegel certainly does not have a good lecture-style." Raumer also recommends to von Schuckmann that with regard to those who practice the bad style of lecturing (of "false pathos, shouting," etc.) "one ought to block it rather than promote it." For the error, see Lloyd Spencer and Andrzej Krauze, *Hegel: An Introduction* (New York: Totem Books, 1996), p. 92.

167. See *Briefe*, II, #278; *Letters*, p. 338: "For *metaphysics* has disappeared even for those who still hold on otherwise to older ways, just like German constitutional law for the law faculty."

168. *Briefe*, II, #278; *Letters*, p. 340. "Relationships" is the rendering for "*Verhältnisse*."

169. *Briefe*, II, #284.
170. See *Briefe*, II, #285, notes to p. 406.
171. See *Briefe*, II, #285, notes to p. 407.
172. Briefe, II, #286; *Letters*, p. 347.
173. See *Briefe*, II, #289, #311; *Letters*, pp. 349, 348.
174. *Briefe*, II, #277; *Letters*, p. 342. The official document naming Hegel as professor was dated August 19, 1816: See *Briefe*, II, #285, notes to p. 407.

Chapter Eight

1. *Briefe*, I, #143.
2. The details of Hegel's various changes of mind are elaborated by Udo Rameil, "Die Phänomenologie des Geistes in Hegels Nürnberger Propädeutik," in Lothar Eley (ed.), *Hegels Theorie des subjektiven Geistes in der "Enzyklopädie der philosophischen Wissenschaften im Grundrisse"* (Stuttgart: Bad Cannstatt: Frommann-Holzboog, 1990), pp. 84–130. In that piece, Rameil also discusses a more adequate dating of the manuscripts and a recently discovered student transcription of Hegel's courses that Hegel himself used as a basis for elaborating his thoughts in later years in Nuremberg. Rameil also treats this and the more general issues of the development of Hegel's philosophy of spirit during the Nuremberg period in his "Der systematische Aufbau der Geisteslehre in Hegels Nürnberger Propädeutik," *Hegel-Studien*, 23 (1988), pp. 19–49.
3. Hegel, "Bewußtseinslehre für die Mittelklasse (1809ff.)," *Werke*, 4, §5, p. 112. The phrase is "eigentliche Geisteslehre."
4. Hegel, "Bewußtseinslehre für die Mittelklasse (1808/1809)," *Werke*, 4, p. 70. See also Udo Rameil's discussion of the various marginalia in his "Die Phänomenologie des Geistes in Hegels Nürnberger Propädeutik," pp. 100–102. In a letter to Niethammer, Hegel makes explicit his identification of "doctrine of the soul" with "philosophical psychology." See *Briefe*, I, #144; *Letters*, p. 189.
5. In Hegel's own words: "An introduction to philosophy must especially examine the different make-ups and activities of spirit through which it travels in order to arrive at science. Because these spiritual compositions and activities stand in a necessary connection, this self-knowledge constitutes at the same time a science." Hegel, *Werke*, 4, p. 73 (§1). ("Compositions" translates *"Beschaffenheiten."*)
6. *Phenomenology*, ¶177, p. 110, *PG*, p. 140; *PhG*, p. 127. Kant's reference to "universal self-consciousness" in the sense in which Hegel would have been interested occurs at B132 in the 1787 (B) version of the "Transcendental Deduction": "As *my* representations (even if I am not conscious of them as such) they must conform to the condition under which alone they *can* stand together in one universal self-consciousness, because otherwise they would not all without exception belong to me."
7. See Udo Rameil, "Die Phänomenologie des Geistes in Hegels Nürnberger

Propädeutik," p. 109. Rameil summarizes the reports of Karl Rosenkranz and G. A. Gabler on this matter.

8. See Hegel, "Bewußtseinslehre für die Mittelklasse (1809 ff.) ," *Werke*, 4, pp. 111–112 (§3).

9. Hegel, *Science of Logic*, p. 702; *Wissenschaft der Logik*, II, p. 437; *Werke*, 6, p. 496.

10. See Hegel, "Über den Vortrag der Philosophie auf Gymnasien. Privatgutachten für Immanuel Niethammer," *Werke*, 4 , p. 407; *Letters*, p. 279.

11. *Briefe*, II, #422, p. 327n; the phrase "cut my teeth on Kant" is my rendering of "Ich habe mich an ihr erzogen," "an ihr" referring to Kant's works – literally, "I brought myself up on Kant's works."

12. Immanuel Kant, *Critique of Pure Reason* (A vii).

13. Hegel, "Berichte Hegels über seine Unterrichtsgegenstände: Aus dem gedruckten Gymnasialprogram," *Werke*, 4, p. 295; Hegel, "Logik für die Mittelklasse (1810/11)," *Werke*, 4, p. 164 (§6).

14. *Briefe*, I, #122; *Letters*, p. 175. It is a very minor matter, but the first book of the *Logic* probably appeared in 1811, not 1812, since in Hegel's time the "publication date" of a book was generally the year of the first book fair at which it would appear. Often a book's publication date would thus be a year later than the date of its first sale. Hegel himself refers to his *Logic* as having been published in 1811. See *Werke*, 11, p. 240n.

15. Hegel, "Berichte Hegels über seine Unterrichtsgegenstände: Aus dem gedruckten Gymnasialprogram," *Werke*, 4, p. 295.

16. Hegel, "Logik für die Mittelklasse (1810/11)," *Werke*, 4, p. 162 (§1).

17. Hegel, *Science of Logic* (trans. A. V. Miller) (Oxford: Oxford University Press, 1969), pp. 25, 27; *Wissenschaft der Logik* (Hamburg: Felix Meiner Verlag, 1971), I, pp. 3, 6; *Werke*, 5, pp. 13, 16. (The phrase "wieder einmal von vorne anzufangen" is rendered by Miller as "make a completely fresh start.")

18. Hegel, *Science of Logic*, p. 82; *Wissenschaft der Logik*, I, p. 66; *Werke*, 5, p. 82.

19. "It is the form of the simple judgment," Hegel noted, "when it is used to express speculative results, which is very often responsible for the paradoxical and bizarre light in which much of recent philosophy appears to those who are not familiar with speculative thought." Hegel, *Science of Logic*, p. 91; *Wissenschaft der Logik*, I, p. 76; *Werke*, 5, p. 93. (In saying that, unfortunately, Hegel laid himself wide open for further misunderstanding by those who wished to see his philosophy in a "paradoxical and bizarre light," namely, that he was somehow endorsing the irrationalist view that "speculative truths" could not be expressed in language at all, something that was directly at odds with what he was trying to argue but of which he has been accused ever since.)

20. Hegel notes: "Now insofar as the sentence: being and nothing are the same, expresses the identity of these determinations, but in fact equally contains them both as distinguished, the proposition itself contradicts itself and dissolves itself." Hegel, *Science of Logic*, p. 90; *Wissenschaft der Logik*, I, pp. 75–76; *Werke*, 5, p. 93.

21. Hegel, *Science of Logic*, p. 164; *Wissenschaft der Logik*, I, p. 154; *Werke*, 5, p. 183.

22. Hegel, *Science of Logic*, p. 150; *Wissenschaft der Logik*, I, p. 140; *Werke*, 5, p. 166.

23. Hegel, *Science of Logic*, p. 154; *Wissenschaft der Logik*, I, p. 145; *Werke*, 5, p. 172.

24. Michael Friedman in his *Kant and the Exact Sciences* (Cambridge, Mass.: Harvard University Press, 1992) argues that Kant's points about how space and time had to be "pure intuitions" and not "concepts" was based on Kant's understanding that traditional monadic logic could not generate a conception of an infinity of objects, whereas modern polyadic logic, with its use of quantifiers, can do so. Although modern, post-Fregean polyadic logic allows us to formulate the idea of an iterative process formally, monadic logic could not do this, and, since our idea of space is infinite, Kant concluded (rightly) that it therefore could not be a (monadic) logical concept. What Kant needed was a "new logic" to see how his argument might have gone otherwise, which was precisely Hegel's point. Hegel, though, thought that this required his own "dialectical" logic; although quite different from anything like the Fregean system, Hegel's *Logic* thus shared some of its inspiration. The most extensive comparison and critique of Hegel's *Logic* from the standpoint of Fregean and post-Fregean formal logic is to be found in Pirmin Stekeler-Weithofer, *Hegels analytische Philosophie: Die Wissenschaft der Logik als kritische Theorie der Bedeutung* (Paderborn: Ferdinand Schönigh, 1992).

25. Hegel, *Science of Logic*, p. 254; *Wissenschaft der Logik*, I, p. 255; *Werke*, 5, p. 297.

26. Hegel, *Science of Logic*, p. 581; *Wissenschaft der Logik*, II, p. 218; *Werke*, 6, p. 251.

27. Hegel, *Science of Logic*, pp. 758, 765; *Wissenschaft der Logik*, II, pp. 411, 418; *Werke*, 6, pp. 466, 475. ("Object" translates "*Objekt*," as distinct from "*Gegenstand*.")

28. Later in his lectures on the history of philosophy, Hegel distinguished his view from Schelling's by arguing that Schelling could not "demonstrate" any of his propositions, and that "[i]f one begins with intellectual intuition, that constitutes an oracle to which one is supposed to submit, because the demand is made that one intuit intellectually. . . . One aspect [of Schelling's procedure] is the conveying of nature into the subject, the other that of the I to the object (*Objekt*). The authentic execution of this [project], however, can only take place in a logical mode, for logic embodies pure thought. . . . But the consideration of the logical is what Schelling never gets to in his presentation and development." *Werke*, 20, p. 435; G. W. F. Hegel, *Lectures on the History of Philosophy* (translated by E. S. Haldane and Frances H. Simson) (New York: Humanities Press, 1974), vol. 3, p. 527; G. W. F. Hegel, *Lectures on the History of Philosophy: The Lectures of 1825–1826* (ed. Robert F. Brown) (translated by R. F. Brown and J. M. Stewart with the assistance of H. S. Harris) (Berkeley: University of California Press, 1990), p. 266.

Chapter Nine

1. *Briefe*, IV/2, # 294; *Letters*, p. 411.
2. *Briefe*, II, #296; *Letters*, p. 354.
3. *Briefe*, II, #288.
4. Ibid.
5. *Briefe*, II, #300; *Letters*, p. 355.
6. It was after receiving the notice that Hegel wrote to Niethammer on October 10, 1816, expressing his now-hardened views on the superiority of Protestantism to Catholicism and on how "the sole authority [for Protestants] is the intellectual and moral *Bildung* of all, and the guarantors of such *Bildung* are" institutions such as "universities and general institutions of instruction," not the councils of the church. *Briefe*, II, #309; *Letters*, p. 328.
7. *Briefe*, II, #281, #283; *Letters*, pp. 344, 346.
8. *Briefe*, II, #293; *Letters*, p. 433.
9. *Briefe*, II, #275; *Letters*, p. 432.
10. This is at any rate the conclusion drawn by Wilhelm R. Beyer on the basis of the letters from Marie and her mother in "Aus Hegels Familienleben," *Hegel-Jahrbuch*, 1966, p. 87.
11. *Briefe*, II, #257; *Letters*, pp. 429–430.
12. See Wilhelm R. Beyer, "Aus Hegels Familienleben," *Hegel-Jahrbuch*, 1966, p. 87.
13. *Briefe*, IV/1, p. 238: Ludwig Fischer's letter to Ebert, July 11, 1825.
14. See the excerpts cited in Wilhelm R. Beyer, "Aus Hegels Familienleben," pp. 87–88. The issue of how Ludwig was to be addressed appears in this context. For reasons of his own, Hegel had always referred to Ludwig by the French name Louis; his letter of July 20, 1816, to Frommann marked the first time he spoke of him by his given name, Ludwig. Hegel's mother-in-law was still referring to him as Louis (in letters of May 18 and May 24, 1817), although in a letter of August 21, 1817, she too finally took to referring to him as Ludwig. The Frommann family referred to him as Ludwig as he left for the Hegel household in 1817, and Elisabeth ("Betty") Wesselhöft, Frommann's sister-in-law who, together with another widowed sister (Ms. Bohn), ran the orphanage, also addressed him at that time, as did others in her family, as Ludwig; but as his troubles with the Hegel family began to reach their crescendo in the 1820s, Johanna Frommann referred to him in a letter disapprovingly as Louis, indicating that she too had returned to seeing him not as "Ludwig" (a member of the Hegel family) but as "Louis," somebody not part of the Hegel family. After the break with the family, Hegel refused to allow Ludwig to use the family name, and thus he had to go by Ludwig Fischer (his mother's maiden name), not by Ludwig Hegel. See *Briefe*, IV/1, pp. 231–237.
15. See the discussion and letters in Wilhelm R. Beyer, "Aus Hegels Familienleben," pp. 85–91. See also Hegel's comments to Frommann in *Briefe*, II, #317; *Letters*, p. 434, and Ludwig Fischer's comment that he had once been "first in

his class for a whole quarter-year in Latin and Greek," in *Briefe*, IV/1, p. 238 (Ludwig Fischer's letter to Ebert, July 11, 1825).

16. *Briefe*, IV/1, p. 237: letter from Johanna Frommann to Betty Wesselhöft (June 10, 1825).

17. *Briefe*, II, #317; *Letters*, p. 434.

18. Ibid.

19. Briefe, IV/2, #324b.

20. *Briefe*, II, #324; *Letters*, p. 412

21. See *Briefe*, II, #296, p. 127n.

22. *Briefe*, II, #310; *Letters*, p. 356.

23. See Karl Rosenkranz, *Georg Wilhelm Friedrich Hegels Leben*, pp. 299–300.

24. Ibid., p. 300; see also *Briefe*, II, #312.

25. See Wilhelm R. Beyer, "Aus Hegels Familienleben," p. 69.

26. *Hegel in Berichten seiner Zeitgenossen*, #192, p. 139.

27. See Wilhelm R. Beyer, "Aus Hegels Familienleben," pp. 99–100.

28. Ibid., p. 92.

29. Ibid., pp. 92–93 (letters of Susanna von Tucher to Marie Hegel of May 24, 1817, and September 22, 1817).

30. Although sociable and friendly and having many warm acquaintances and friendships of one sort or another, Hegel does not seem to have had many close friends. The great emotional friendships of his youth with Schelling and Hölderlin had come to an end – in one case, by the falling-out with Schelling and in the other because of Hölderlin's madness. His friendship with Niethammer, although close in one sense, never went as deep; they always addressed each other with the formal "Sie" in German. So although Hegel was friendly, he seemed to have had no close friends. His family life seems to have filled that emotional gap.

31. See Karl Rosenkranz, *Georg Wilhelm Friedrich Hegels Leben*, p. 300.

32. See *Briefe*, I, #55; *Letters*, pp. 105–106.

33. See Charles E. McClelland, *State, Society, and University in Germany: 1700–1914*, pp. 107–108.

34. Ibid., p. 108.

35. Within the terms of the contemporary American university, the older German "philosophical faculty" would be more or less equivalent to the "college of arts and sciences."

36. *Hegel in Berichten seiner Zeitgenossen*, #191, p. 139.

37. See Charles E. McClelland, *State, Society, and University in Germany: 1700–1914*, pp. 165–170.

38. *Briefe*, II, #325; *Letters*, p. 367.

39. See Friedhelm Nicolin, "Hegel als Professor in Heidelberg: Aus den Akten in der philosophischen Fakultät 1816–1818," in Friedhelm Nicolin, *Auf Hegels Spuren: Beiträge zur Hegel-Forschung* (ed. Lucia Sziborsky and Helmut Schneider) (Hamburg: Felix Meiner Verlag, 1996), pp. 149–156. Originally published in *Hegel-Studien*, 2 (1963), pp. 71–98.

40. Ibid., pp. 155–156.

41. Ibid., p. 144.
42. Ibid.
43. Ibid., pp. 147–148.
44. See Karl Rosenkranz, *Georg Wilhelm Friedrich Hegels Leben*, p. 301. This description is paraphrased from Rosenkranz's account.
45. Ibid. On the modernity of Hegel's dress, see Anne Hollander, *Sex and Suits* (New York: Alfred A. Knopf, 1996).
46. See *Hegel in Berichten seiner Zeitgenossen*, #280, p. 181.
47. *Briefe*, II, #316; *Letters*, p. 358 (April 19, 1817); Butler and Seiler translate Hegel's phrase "außerdem, daß sich von sich selbst anders macht" as "quite apart from the fact that their lives are in any case developing differently." That seems to catch the sense of what Hegel is after, but it is obviously not quite as literal.
48. See *Briefe*, II, 317; *Letters*, p. 434 (letter to Frommann, April 19, 1817).
49. *Hegel in Berichten seiner Zeitgenossen*, #275, p. 178.
50. Hegel in Berichten seiner Zeitgenossen, #177, pp. 122–123.
51. G.W.F. Hegel, *Enzyklopädie der philosophischen Wissenschaften*, Werke, 8, pp. 12–13; *The Encyclopedia Logic: Part I of the Encyclopedia of the Philosophical Sciences* (trans. T. F. Geraets, W. A. Suchting, and H. S. Harris) (Indianapolis: Hackett Publishing Co., 1991), pp. 2–3.
52. See *Hegel in Berichten seiner Zeitgenossen*, #280, pp. 182–183.
53. *Hegel in Berichten seiner Zeitgenossen*, #219, p. 150.
54. Ibid.
55. *Hegel in Berichten seiner Zeitgenossen*, #223, pp. 153–154.
56. See *Hegel in Berichten seiner Zeitgenossen*, #216, pp. 148–149 (an account given by Boisserée).
57. See *Hegel in Berichten seiner Zeitgenossen*, #221, pp. 152–153 (again taken from another account by Boisserée).
58. *Hegel in Berichten seiner Zeitgenossen*, #235, pp. 159–160.
59. See, for example, *Hegel in Berichten seiner Zeitgenossen*, #276, p. 178.
60. *Hegel in Berichten seiner Zeitgenossen*, #246, pp. 163–165.
61. *Hegel in Berichten seiner Zeitgenossen*, #246, p. 164.
62. *Hegel in Berichten seiner Zeitgenossen*, #280, p. 180.
63. *Hegel in Berichten seiner Zeitgenossen*, #243, p. 162.
64. G. W. F. Hegel, *Hegel's Introduction to the Lectures on the History of Philosophy* (trans. T. M. Knox and A. V. Miller) (Oxford: Clarendon Press, 1985), pp. 2–3; *Sämtliche Werke*, vol. 17, p. 21; *Gesammelte Werke, Vorlesungsmanuskripte II (1816–1831)* (ed. Walter Jaeschke), vol. 18, p. 6.
65. Hegel, "[Über] Friedrich Heinrich Jacobis Werke. Dritter Band," *Werke*, 4, p. 431.
66. Ibid.
67. Ibid., pp. 432–433.
68. Ibid., p. 435.
69. Ibid., p. 436.
70. Ibid., p. 433. The term in question is "*Vernunftanschauung.*"

71. Ibid., p. 442.

72. Ibid., p. 443.

73. Ibid., pp. 445–46.

74. Ibid., p. 446.

75. Ibid., p. 447. ("Cultivated" translates "*gebildete*"; "cast of mind" translates "*Gesinnung.*")

76. Ibid., p. 449. ("From its own resources" translates "*aus sich selbst.*")

77. Ibid., p. 451.

78. Ibid., p. 450.

79. Ibid., p. 455.

80. *Briefe*, II, #241; *Letters*, p. 312.

81. *Hegel in Berichten seiner Zeitgenossen*, #146, p. 103.

82. G. W. F. Hegel, *Aesthetics: Lectures on Fine Art* (trans. T. M. Knox) (Oxford: Oxford University Press), vol. II, p. 1057; *Werke*, 15, p. 347.

83. Theodore Ziolkowski, *German Romanticism and Its Institutions*, pp. 79–80.

84. Anton Thibaut, "Über die Notwendigkeit eines allgemeinen bürgerlichen Rechts für Deutschland," in Hans Hattenhauer (ed.), *Thibaut und Savigny: Ihre Programmatischen Schriften* (Munich: Franz Vahlen, 1973), pp. 61–94.

85. See Theodore Ziolkowski, *German Romanticism and Its Institutions*, pp. 82–86, for a good comparison between Savigny and Thibaut.

86. Karl Friedrich von Savigny, "Von Beruf unsrer Zeit für Gesetzgebung und Rechtswissenschaft," in Hans Hattenhauer (ed.), *Thibaut und Savigny: Ihre Programmatischen Schriften*, pp. 95–192.

87. See the discussion of Savigny's brand of historicism and his conception of *Geist* in E.-W. Böckenförde, "Die Historische Rechtsschule und das Problem der Geschichtlichkeit des Rechtes," in his *Staat, Gesellschaft, Freiheit: Studien zur Staatstheorie und zum Verfassungsrecht* (Frankfurt a.M.: Suhrkamp Verlag, 1976), pp. 9–41.

88. See James Sheehan, *German History: 1770–1866*, p. 405.

89. J. F. Fries, *Über die Gefährdung des Wohlstandes und Characters der Deutschen durch die Juden* (*The Danger Posed by the Jews to German Well-Being and Character*), cited and translated by Allen Wood in his editorial notes to G. W. F. Hegel, *Elements of the Philosophy of Right* (ed. Allen W. Wood, trans. H. B. Nisbet (Cambridge: Cambridge University Press, 1991), pp. 458–459.

90. Cited in Ernst Ludwig Theodor Henke, *Jakob Friedrich Fries*, p. 157.

91. Cited in Ernst Ludwig Theodor Henke, *Jakob Friedrich Fries*, pp. 157–158.

92. Cited in the notes to *Briefe*, #321.

93. *Briefe*, II, #344; *Letters*, p. 633.

94. *Briefe*, II, #344; *Letters*, p. 633.

95. On Carové, see John Edward Toews, *Hegelianism*, pp. 134–140.

96. See James Sheehan's similar analysis in *German History: 1770–1866*, pp. 411–425.

97. Erwin Hölzle, *Württemberg im Zeitalter Napoleons und der deutschen Erhebung: Eine deutsche Geschichte der Wendezeit im einzelstaatlichen Raum* (Stuttgart: W. Kohlhammer Verlag, 1937), p. 188.

98. Ibid., pp. 190–191.

99. Ibid., p. 202.

100. Ibid., p. 206.

101. Ibid., p. 215.

102. Hegel, "Proceedings of the Estates Assembly in the Kingdom of Württemberg 1815–1816," in *Hegel's Political Writings*, p. 247; *Werke*, 4, p. 463.

103. Ibid.

104. Hegel, "Proceedings of the Estates Assembly in the Kingdom of Württemberg 1815–1816," in *Hegel's Political Writings*, p. 263; *Werke*, 4, p. 482.

105. Ibid. The phrase in question is "*leidliches Nebeneinanderbestehen*," which Knox translates freely as "modus vivendi."

106. Hegel, "Proceedings of the Estates Assembly in the Kingdom of Württemberg 1815–1816" in *Hegel's Political Writings*, p. 257; *Werke*, 4, p. 475. In this context, Knox's translation of "*Sinn des Staates*" as "political consciousness" does not perhaps best bring out what Hegel is trying to say.

107. Ibid.

108. Hegel, "Proceedings of the Estates Assembly in the Kingdom of Württemberg 1815–1816," in *Hegel's Political Writings*, pp. 282–283; *Werke*, 4, p. 507. ("Cancellation" translates "*Aufhebung*".)

109. Hegel, "Proceedings of the Estates Assembly in the Kingdom of Württemberg 1815–1816," in *Hegel's Political Writings*, p. 283; *Werke*, 4, p. 507.

110. Hegel, "Proceedings of the Estates Assembly in the Kingdom of Württemberg 1815–1816," in *Hegel's Political Writings*, p. 282; *Werke*, 4, p. 507.

111. Hegel, "Proceedings of the Estates Assembly in the Kingdom of Württemberg 1815–1816," in *Hegel's Political Writings*, p. 283; *Werke*, 4, p. 508.

112. Hegel, "Proceedings of the Estates Assembly in the Kingdom of Württemberg 1815–1816," in *Hegel's Political Writings*, p. 277; *Werke*, 4, p. 501.

113. See *Briefe*, II, notes to #322, p. 420.

114. *Briefe*, II, #327.

115. Hegel, "Proceedings of the Estates Assembly in the Kingdom of Württemberg 1815–1816," in *Hegel's Political Writings*, p. 265; *Werke*, 4, p. 485.

116. See Thomas Nipperdey, *Germany from Napoleon to Bismarck: 1800–1866* (trans. Daniel Nolan) (Princeton: Princeton University Press, 1996), p. 68.

117. Hegel, "Proceedings of the Estates Assembly in the Kingdom of Württemberg 1815–1816," in *Hegel's Political Writings*, p. 259; *Werke*, 4, p. 478.

118. *Briefe*, II, notes to #292, p. 409.

119. *Briefe*, II, notes to #278, p. 398.

120. *Briefe*, II, #326.

121. *Briefe*, II, #347; *Letters*, p. 413; see also Hermann Kellenbenz, "Zahlungsmittel, Maße und Gewichte seit 1800," in Hermann Aubin and Wolfgang Zorn, *Handbuch der deutschen Wirtschaft-und Sozialgeschichte* (Stuttgart: Klett-Cotta, 1976), vol. 2, p. 936. On Kellenbenz's calculation, it would have worth about 3,000 florins, but Hegel probably had more specific information.

122. *Briefe*, II, #328; *Letters*, pp. 379–380; for the conversion of Friedrichs d'or to Thalers, see Hermann Kellenbenz, "Zahlungsmittel, Maße und Gewichte seit 1800," p. 936.

123. *Briefe*, II, #331.

124. *Briefe*, II, #332. The letter from the culture ministry was signed March 16 but not posted until March 26.
125. *Hegel in Berichten seiner Zeitgenossen*, #259, p. 171.
126. The letter is cited in Karl Rosenkranz, *Georg Wilhelm Friedrich Hegels Leben*, p. 319. (The letter has since been lost.)
127. *Briefe*, II, #339; notes to #343, p. 428.
128. *Briefe*, II, notes to #331, p. 424.
129. *Briefe*, II, #340.
130. *Hegel in Berichten seiner Zeitgenossen*, #264, p. 173.
131. Although "focal point" is not quite accurate as a literal translation of "*Mittel-punkt*" – "midpoint" or "central point" would be more literal – the idea of a "focal point" captures the sense of what both Hegel and Schiller mean by their use of the term.
132. *Briefe*, II, #347; *Letters*, p. 412.
133. *Hegel in Berichten seiner Zeitgenossen*, #283, p. 184.
134. *Hegel in Berichten seiner Zeitgenossen*, #286, p. 185.
135. See Wilhelm R. Beyer, "Aus Hegels Familienleben," *Hegel-Jahrbuch*, 1966, p. 72.
136. See *Hegel in Berichten seiner Zeitgenossen*, #273, p. 177.

Chapter Ten

1. See Thomas Nipperdey, *Germany from Napoleon to Bismarck: 1800–1866*, p. 11.
2. See Robert Berdahl, *The Politics of the Prussian Nobility: The Development of a Conservative Ideology, 1770–1848* (Princeton: Princeton University Press, 1988), pp. 107–109.
3. See James Sheehan, *German History: 1770–1866*, p. 424.
4. Hegel had, of course, already argued for something similar in his unpublished essay on the "German Constitution" around the turn of the century; Stein's reforming ideas thus obviously struck a chord with him.
5. Stein cited Count Ivernois's study of England in his "Nassauer Denkschrift" of June 1807. See Robert Berdahl, *The Politics of the Prussian Nobility*, pp. 110–113.
6. See James Sheehan, *German History: 1770–1866*, pp. 299–301; Thomas Nipperdey, *Germany from Napoleon to Bismarck: 1800–1866*, pp. 26–31.
7. See Reinhart Koselleck, *Preußen zwischen Reform und Revolution: Allgemeines Landrecht, Verwaltung und soziale Bewegung von 1791 bis 1848* (Stuttgart: Ernst Klett Verlag, 1975), pp. 560–564.
8. See Mack Walker, *German Hometowns*, pp. 265–267.
9. See Thomas Nipperdey, *Germany from Napoleon to Bismarck: 1800–1866*, p. 25.
10. Ibid., p. 306.
11. See Mack Walker, *German Hometowns*, pp. 265–266; also see Reinhart Koselleck, *Preußen zwischen Reform und Revolution*, pp. 560–575.

12. On the widespread notion that Prussian strength was to consist in "intelligence" and "spiritual power," see Reinhart Koselleck, *Preußen zwischen Reform und Revolution*, pp. 398–410.

13. See the discussion of the founding by Theodore Ziolkowski, *German Romanticism and Its Institutions*, pp. 286–294; Ziolkowski draws out the connections between Berlin and Jena quite explicitly.

14. Friedrich Schleiermacher, "Gelegentliche Gedanken über Universitäten in deutschem Sinn, nebst einem Anhang über eine neu zu errichtende," in Ernst Anrich (ed.), *Die Idee der deutschen Universität* (Darmstadt: Wissenschaftliche Buchgesellschaft, 1964). p. 251

15. See Charles E. McClelland, *State, Society, and University in Germany: 1700–1914*, pp. 206–211.

16. Cited in Theodore Ziolkowski, *German Romanticism and Its Institutions*, p. 306.

17. See Max Lenz, *Geschichte der königlichen Friedrich-Wilhelms-Universität zu Berlin* (Halle: Verlag der Buchhandlung des Waisenhauses, 1910), vol. 1, p. 403.

18. See Theodore Ziolkowski, *German Romanticism and Its Institutions*, p. 306.

19. Ibid.

20. Hegel, "Rede zum Antritt des philosophischen Lehramtes an der Universität Heidelberg," in G. W. F. Hegel, *Vorlesungsmanuskripte II (1816–1831)* (ed. Walter Jaeschke) in *Gesammelte Werke* (ed. Rheinisch-Westfälische Akademie der Wissenschaften, 1995), p. 4.

21. Hegel, "Rede zum Antritt des philosophischen Lehramtes an der Universität Berlin," in Hegel, *Vorlesungsmanuskripte II (1816–1831)* in *Gesammelte Werke*, p. 12–13; Hegel, *Berliner Schriften: 1818–1831* (ed. Johannes Hoffmeister), p. 4.

22. *Hegel in Berichten seiner Zeitgenossen*, #290, p. 189. In the late 1820s Solger's posthumous works were published, and in reviewing them Hegel, somewhat painfully, read Solger's rather candid comments about his arrival in Berlin. See Hegel, "Solgers nachgelassene Schriften und Briefwechsel," *Werke*, 11, p. 264.

23. *Hegel in Berichten seiner Zeitgenossen*, #291, p. 190.

24. *Briefe*, II, #354.

25. *Briefe*, II, #355; *Letters*, p. 442.

26. Andreas Arndt and Wolfgang Virmond, "Hegel und die 'Gesetzlose Gesellschaft'," *Hegel-Studien*, 20 (1985), pp. 113–116.

27. *Briefe*, II, #359; *Letters*, p. 450.

28. See *Briefe*, IV/1, p. 204 ("Haushalt 1819").

29. The term "Biedermeier" itself was originally somewhat pejorative in connotation and did not come into use until the 1850s, some twenty years after Hegel's death; on discovering some really wretched poetry written by a village schoolmaster – so bad it was unintentionally comical in its effect – two men published the poems under the pseudonym Gottlob Biedermeier in a humor magazine. The term came to characterize a style of life that people in the latter half of the nineteenth century at first viewed with irony, then later with nostalgia. See James Sheehan, *German History: 1770–1866*, p. 536.

30. See Wilhelm R. Beyer, "Aus Hegels Familienleben," *Hegel-Jahrbuch*, 1966, p. 68.
31. See *Briefe*, III, #555; *Letters*, p. 645.
32. See *Briefe*, IV/1, pp. 205–207 ("Haushalt 1819").
33. See *Briefe*, IV/1, p. 206 ("Haushalt 1819").
34. *Briefe*, II, notes to #355, p. 431.
35. See Wilhelm R. Beyer, "Aus Hegels Familienleben," *Hegel-Jahrbuch*, 1966, pp. 89–90.
36. See *Briefe*, IV/1, p. 206 ("Haushalt 1819").
37. *Briefe*, II, #355; *Letters*, p. 443.
38. See Thomas Nipperdey, *Germany from Napoleon to Bismarck: 1800–1866*, p. 246.
39. Ibid., p. 247.
40. *Hegel in Berichten seiner Zeitgenossen*, #295, p. 192.
41. See Ernst Ludwig Theodor Henke, *Jakob Friedrich Fries*, p. 207.
42. See *Briefe*, II, notes to #358, pp. 432–442; Hoffmeister gives a detailed description of the circumstances surrounding Asverus's arrest.
43. *Briefe*, II, #358; *Letters*, p. 449.
44. See *Briefe*, II, notes to #358, pp. 438–440.
45. *Briefe*, II, notes to #358, p. 437.
46. *Briefe*, IV/1, p. 207 ("Haushalt 1819").
47. *Hegel in Berichten seiner Zeitgenossen*, #307a, pp. 198–199.
48. See *Briefe*, II, #433; *Letters*, p. 582.
49. See *Briefe*, II, notes to #359, p. 445.
50. See Thomas Nipperdey, *Germany from Napoleon to Bismarck: 1800–1866*, p. 39; see also James Sheehan, *German History: 1770–1866*, pp. 408–409, 422–423.
51. See Leonard Krieger, *The German Idea of Freedom: History of a Political Tradition* (Chicago: University of Chicago Press, 1957), pp. 222–223.
52. Cited in Hans-Christian Lucas and Udo Rameil, "Furcht vor der Zensur? Zur Entstehungs-und Druckgeschichte von Hegels Grundlinien der Philosophie des Rechts," *Hegel-Studien*, 15 (1980), p. 71.
53. Ibid., pp. 71–72.
54. Ibid., pp. 72–73.
55. See *Briefe*, II, notes to #359, pp. 444–445.
56. See the account in Ernst Ludwig Theodor Henke, *Jakob Friedrich Fries*, pp. 207–208.
57. *Briefe*, II, notes to #359, p. 446.
58. G. W. F. Hegel, *Berliner Schriften: 1818–1831* (ed. Johannes Hoffmeister) (Hamburg: Felix Meiner Verlag, 1956), pp. 582–583.
59. Ibid.
60. *Briefe*, II, notes to #377, p. 460.
61. *Briefe*, II, #359; *Letters*, p. 451.
62. *Hegel in Berichten seiner Zeitgenossen*, #307b, p. 199.
63. *Briefe*, II, notes to #377, p. 460.

64. *Briefe*, II, notes to #377, p. 462.
65. See *Briefe*, II, #382, in which Hermann Friedrich Wilhelm Hinrichs reports to Hegel on Carové's rejection as a *Privatdozent*.
66. Hegel, *Berliner Schriften: 1818–1831*, p. 598. Hegel remarks in a letter to Niethammer that von Henning was held for ten weeks. *Briefe*, II, #390; *Letters*, p. 470.
67. Karl Rosenkranz, *Hegels Leben*, p. 338. The anecdote comes from Rosenkranz, who does not cite its origin; see pp. 338–339. Rosenkranz noted that "a bullet from the watchman could very easily have spared the man who turned the demagogues around any further effort" (p. 338). Rosenkranz is alluding to the idea that he helped to popularize, namely, that Hegel actually "cured" young men of their demagogic tendencies with his reconciliatory philosophy. Denis Bradley translated the Latin quotation for me.
68. Hegel, *Berliner Schriften: 1818–1831*, pp. 598–607. After Hegel's death and having become an "ordinary" professor himself, Henning abandoned Hegelianism and joined the forces of reaction.
69. See *Briefe*, notes to #377, p. 471.
70. *Hegel in Berichten seiner Zeitgenossen*, #304, p. 197.
71. On Sillery, see Hugh Johnson, *Vintage: The Story of Wine*, p. 332. The vineyards were later sold to Moët after the 1848 uprising and the resulting sacking of the château; eventually the name "Sillery" was dropped altogether.
72. *Hegel in Berichten seiner Zeitgenossen*, #323, p. 214.
73. *Hegel in Berichten seiner Zeitgenossen*, #457, p. 299.
74. See Förster's reminiscences from his diary in *Hegel in Berichten seiner Zeitgenossen*, #326, pp. 215–216.
75. See H. S. Harris, *Night Thoughts*, p. xxii
76. *Hegel in Berichten seiner Zeitgenossen*, #326, p. 216.
77. See *Briefe*, II, notes to #389, p. 482.
78. *Hegel in Berichten seiner Zeitgenossen*, #336, p. 222.
79. This characterization of Hegel has been notably disputed by Jacques D'Hondt, *Hegel in His Time: Berlin 1818–1831* (transl. John Burbridge with Nelson Roland and Judith Levasseur) (Lewiston, New York: Broadview Press, 1988).
80. Ranke's reminiscences are cited in John Edward Toews, *Hegelianism, 1805–1841*, p. 60.
81. Hegel, "Über die Einrichtung einer kritischen Zeitschrift für Literatur," *Werke*, 11, p. 10.
82. Ibid., p. 15.
83. Ibid., pp. 14–15.
84. Ibid., p. 21.
85. See *Hegel in Berichten seiner Zeitgenossen*, #314, p. 203.
86. See Hans-Christian Lucas and Udo Rameil, "Furcht vor der Zensur? Zur Entstehungs-und Druckgeschichte von Hegels Grundlinien der Philosophie des Rechts," p. 91.
87. I am here accepting what I take to be the conclusive arguments about what Hegel knew about the decrees and when he knew that are presented in Hans-

Christian Lucas and Udo Rameil, "Furcht vor der Zensur? Zur Entstehungs-
und Druckgeschichte von Hegels Grundlinien der Philosophie des Rechts."
Lucas's and Rameil's arguments also help to conclusively undermine the view
held by a number of different people that Hegel's published work is more
"reactionary" and monarchical, his lectures "liberal" and more "republican."

88. Hegel, *Elements of the Philosophy of Right*, pp. 15–19.

89. *Hegel in Berichten seiner Zeitgenossen*, #332, p. 220.

90. *Elements of the Philosophy of Right*, p. 20.

91. Hegel, *Wissenschaft der Logik*, in *Werke*, vol. 6, p. 208; *Science of Logic* (trans.
A. V. Miller), p. 546; A. V. Miller translates the relevant phrase as "what is
actual can act."

92. See Robert Pippin's discussion of this in his "Hegel's Ethical Rationalism," in
Robert Pippin, *Idealism as Modernism: Hegelian Variations*, pp. 438–440.

93. See the good discussion of Haller, especially of his unexpected modernity, in
Robert Berdahl, *The Politics of the Prussian Nobility*, pp. 232–246. A good,
very short discussion of Haller and the court is found in Jacques D'Hondt,
Hegel in His Time: Berlin 1818–1831, pp. 72–77.

94. Hegel, *Elements of the Philosophy of Right*, §258 (p. 279n).

95. See the contemporary reviews collected in Manfred Riedel (ed.), *Materialien
zu Hegels Rechtsphilosophie* (Frankfurt a.M.: Suhrkamp Verlag, 1975), pp. 53–
206.

96. H. E. G. Paulus, review of Hegel's *Philosophy of Right*, in *Heidelberger Jahrbücher für Literatur* (1821), reprinted in Manfred Riedel (ed.), *Materialien zu
Hegels Rechtsphilosophie*, see pp. 54–55.

97. A very thorough comparison of the content of Hegel's *Philosophy of Right* and
the Prussian reform program is carried out in the informative editorial notes
by Allen Wood in G. W. F. Hegel, *Elements of the Philosophy of Right*. Wood
demonstrates the clear affinity between Hegel's text and the aims of Prussian
reformers such as Stein.

98. Cited and discussed by Friedhelm Nicolin, "Der erste Lexicon-Artikel über
Hegel (1824)," in Friedhelm Nicolin, *Auf Hegels Spuren: Beiträge zur Hegel-
Forschung*, p. 212. Quite interesting is the phrase "ruling classes" ("*herrschen-
den Classe*") – interesting because it uses the word "*Classe*" and not "*Stände*"
("estates"), Hegel's own preferred term when speaking of organically developed social units in civil society. The 1827 version of the Lexicon article (with
only minor changes) is reprinted in *Hegel in Berichten seiner Zeitgenossen*, #559,
pp. 363–371.

99. This was still being remarked upon in 1820; see *Hegel in Berichten seiner
Zeitgenossen*, #324, p. 214.

100. See Karl Ludwig Michelet's remarks on how Jean Pierre Friedrich Ancillon
advised him against Hegel in *Hegel in Berichten seiner Zeitgenossen*, #325, p.
214.

101. *Hegel in Berichten seiner Zeitgenossen*, #328, p. 218.

102. See *Briefe*, IV/1, p. 205 ("Haushalt 1819").

103. See Hegel's letter to his sister, *Briefe*, II, #395; *Letters*, p. 419.

104. *Hegel in Berichten seiner Zeitgenossen*, #317, pp. 209–210.
105. *Hegel in Berichten seiner Zeitgenossen*, #708, p. 453.
106. Ibid. See also the overview of Hegel's social life in Berlin in Friedrich Hoge-
     mann, "Geselligkeit," in Otto Pöggeler (ed.), *Hegel in Berlin: Preußische Kul-
     turpolitik und idealistische Ästhetik: Zum 150. Todestags des Philosophen* (Berlin:
     Staatsbibliothek Preußischer Kulturbesitz, 1981), pp. 57–63.
107. See *Briefe*, II, #388.
108. Hegel, *Berliner Schriften: 1818–1831*, pp. 587–592.
109. Ibid., p. 597.
110. Ibid., p. 597.
111. *Briefe*, II, #390; *Letters*, p. 467.
112. Ibid.
113. *Briefe*, II, #390; *Letters*, p. 470.
114. Ibid.
115. *Briefe*, II, #390; *Letters*, p. 469.

Chapter Eleven

1. The course began with a general doctrine of "right," went on to treat the basic
   elements of "right" in terms of property and exchange, then made a transition
   from that to the "state" and the "society in the state," after which it concluded
   with a "Doctrine of Duties or Morals," which was structured in a partially Kantian way along the lines of the different duties of virtue (duties to oneself and
   duties to others, with Hegel adding separate headings for familial duties and
   civic duties) – with the whole thing being given, of course, a very Hegelian
   twist. That Hegel was so influenced by Kant's *Metaphysics of Ethics* is not surprising: He had written a long commentary on it in his Frankfurt days, the manuscript of which has since been lost. Indeed, given the immense time constraints
   and pressure he was feeling in Nuremberg, and given also the fragmentary state
   of his 1806 lecture manuscripts on this topic, Hegel may have simply felt that he
   did not have the time to work up something completely new on the topic and
   thus based his dictations in Nuremberg on that older manuscript.
2. *Briefe*, I, #29; *Letters*, p. 64.
3. Hegel, *Elements of the Philosophy of Right*, §4. Compare that with Kant's own
   statement in the *Grundlegung der Metaphysik der Sitten* that "the will is nothing
   but practical reason." See Immanuel Kant, *Grounding for the Metaphysics of
   Morals* (trans. James W. Ellington) (Indianapolis: Hackett Publishing Co.,
   1981), p. 30 (A421); p. 23 (A412); *Werke*, VII, p. 41.; "so ist der Wille nicht
   anders, als praktische Vernunft."
4. As Hegel put it in his dictations in Nuremberg, "If I act on the basis of the
   authority of others, the action is not fully my own; an alien conviction is
   acting in me." G.W.F. Hegel, "Rechts-, Pflichten-, und Religionslehre für die
   Unterklasse," in *Werke*, 4, §23, p. 229.
5. Kant himself in his *Critique of Judgment*, for example, had characterized the
   "ultimate end" of the world as "the highest good *in the world* that we can

achieve through freedom" and had gone on to say that the "highest good *in the world* consists in the combination of universal happiness, i.e., the greatest welfare of the rational beings in the world, with the supreme condition of their being good, namely, that they be moral in maximal conformity with the [moral] law." Immanuel Kant, *Critique of Judgment*, §87, p. 339 (450), and §88, p. 343 (453). (Italics are my own.) Similar formulations occur in Kant's essay "On the Common Saying: 'This May Be True in Theory, but It Does Not Apply in Practice'," in *Kant's Political Writings* (trans. H. B. Nisbet, ed. Hans Reiss) (Cambridge: Cambridge University Press, 1991), pp. 61–92. On the shift in Kant's own thought about the "highest good" from a theological conception to a more this-worldly conception, see Andrews Reath, "Two Conceptions of the Highest Good in Kant," *Journal of the History of Philosophy*, vol. 6, no. 4 (Oct. 1988), pp. 593–619.

6. Hegel, *Elements of the Philosophy of Right*, §124.

7. Hegel says, for example, in his lectures on the philosophy of world history: World historical individuals "cannot be said to have enjoyed what is commonly called happiness. They did not wish to be happy in any case, but only to attain their end, and they succeeded in doing so only by dint of arduous labors. They knew how to obtain satisfaction and to accomplish their end, which is the universal end. . . . Thus it was not happiness they chose, but exertion, conflict, and labor in the service of their end. And even when they reached their goal, peaceful enjoyment and happiness was not their lot. Their actions are their entire being, and their whole nature and character are determined by their ruling passion. G. W. F. Hegel *Lectures on the Philosophy of World History: Introduction: Reason in History* (trans. H. B. Nisbet) (Cambridge: Cambridge University Press, 1975), p. 85; *Vorlesungen über die Philosophie der Weltgeschichte: Band I: Die Vernunft in der Geschichte* (ed. Johannes Hoffmeister) (Hamburg: Felix Meiner Verlag, 1994), p. 63. In his 1827 review of Wilhelm von Humboldt in the *Jahrbücher für wissenschaftlichen Kritik* ("Über die unter den Namen Bhagavad-Ghita bekannte Episode des Mahabharata von Wilhelm von Humboldt"), he also made the following distinctions: "The actualization of an end is an achievement (*Gelingen*); that the action has success (*Erfolg*) is a *satisfaction* (*Befriedigung*), an inseparable fruit of the completed action." See *Werke*, 11, p. 152.

8. See Aristotle, *Nicomachean Ethics* (trans. W. D. Ross, revised by J. L Ackrill and J. O. Urmson) (Oxford: Oxford University Press, 1992), p. 148.

9. Hegel, *Elements of the Philosophy of Right*, §§137, 139.

10. Hegel, *Elements of the Philosophy of Right*, §137.

11. Hegel, *Elements of the Philosophy of Right*, §150 (addition).

12. In his marginal comments to his copy of the *Philosophy of Right*, Hegel scribbled in phrases for use in his lectures, such as "Respecting the woman as equal to him . . . Equality, sameness of rights and duties – the husband should not count for more than the wife," and noting how polygamy amounts to slavery for women, whereas chivalry unjustifiably elevates women to a higher plane than

men. *Werke*, 7, §167, p. 321. Hegel speaks of *"Mann"* and *"Frau"* there, which does not unambiguously translate into English, since it means both "man" and "woman" and "husband" and "wife."

13. Hegel, *Elements of the Philosophy of Right*, §166 (addition).
14. Hegel, *Elements of the Philosophy of Right*, §166.
15. Ibid. In his marginal comments to his copy of the *Philosophy of Right*, Hegel wrote, *"Stand* der Frau – ist *Hausfrau." Werke*, 7, §167, p. 320.
16. *Hegel in Berichten seiner Zeitgenossen*, #489, p. 332.
17. Hegel, *Elements of the Philosophy of Right*, §174 (addition).
18. Hegel, *Lectures on Natural Right and Political Science: The First Philosophy of Right: Heidelberg 1817–1818 with additions from the Lectures of 1818–1819*, p. 156.
19. Hegel, *Elements of the Philosophy of Right*, §185.
20. The term itself, *"Junker,"* is an ancient Prussian contraction of the old high German, *"juncherro," "jung Herr,"* that is, "young master."
21. Hegel, *Lectures on Natural Right and Political Science: The First Philosophy of Right: Heidelberg 1817–1818 with additions from the Lectures of 1818–1819* (trans. J. Michael Stewart and Peter Hodgson) (Berkeley: University of California Press, 1995), p. 169.
22. See Hegel, *Elements of the Philosophy of Right*, §192 (addition).
23. Hegel's observations on the peasantry are all the more striking in that he notes (at least in his lectures) how modern agriculture is rapidly changing from the older form he knew when he was growing up into being "run in a reflective manner, like a factory," and how that was transforming rural life so that it less and less resembled the traditional peasant "estate" and looked more and more like the business "estate" of modern times. But he nonetheless simply held onto his firm belief that the necessary dependence on nature bound up with the agricultural estate would keep that form of self-understanding in a more traditional mode, despite the evidence to the contrary of which he was, curiously enough, quite aware.
24. See Hegel, *Elements of the Philosophy of Right*, §206.
25. Hegel, *Elements of the Philosophy of Right*, §211.
26. Hegel, *Elements of the Philosophy of Right*, §228.
27. Hegel, *Elements of the Philosophy of Right*, §209.
28. Hegel, *Elements of the Philosophy of Right*, §270.
29. Ibid.
30. Ibid.
31. See Hegel, *Elements of the Philosophy of Right*, §297 (addition).
32. Hegel, *Elements of the Philosophy of Right*, §290 and addition.
33. The line from Schiller is quoted both in the lectures on the philosophy of history and in §548 of Hegel's *Encyclopedia* (§448 in the 1817 edition of the *Encyclopedia*); it is only alluded to in the *Philosophy of Right*.
34. Hegel, *Elements of the Philosophy of Right*, §342.
35. Hegel, *Elements of the Philosophy of Right*, §343.

36. Hegel, *Lectures on the Philosophy of World History: Introduction: Reason in History*, pp. 54–55; *Vorlesungen über die Philosophie der Weltgeschichte: Band I: Die Vernunft in der Geschichte*, p. 63.

37. Hegel, *Lectures on the Philosophy of World History: Introduction: Reason in History*, p. 197; *Vorlesungen über die Philosophie der Weltgeschichte: Band I: Die Vernunft in der Geschichte*, p. 243.

38. Hegel, *Lectures on the Philosophy of World History: Introduction: Reason in History*, p. 92; *Vorlesungen über die Philosophie der Weltgeschichte: Band I: Die Vernunft in der Geschichte*, p. 109.

39. G. W. F. Hegel, *Philosophy of Mind (Part Three of the Encyclopedia of the Philosophical Sciences)* (trans. William Wallace and A. V. Miller) (Oxford: Clarendon Press, 1971), p. 41; *Enzyklopädie*, §393 *Zusatz*.

40. Hegel, *Lectures on the Philosophy of World History: Introduction: Reason in History*, p. 213; *Vorlesungen über die Philosophie der Weltgeschichte: Band I: Die Vernunft in der Geschichte*, p. 262.

Chapter Twelve

1. See *Briefe*, II, #395, *Letters*, pp. 417–419; the letter is discussed in Chapter 7 of this book.

2. See *Hegel in Berichten seiner Zeitgenossen*, #336, p. 222; #357, p. 230.

3. *Hegel in Berichten seiner Zeitgenossen*, #357, p. 230.

4. *Hegel in Berichten seiner Zeitgenossen*, #363, p. 235.

5. See Wilhelm R. Beyer, "Aus Hegels Familienleben," p. 73.

6. Karl Rosenkranz, *Georg Wilhelm Friedrich Hegels Leben*, p. 336.

7. Ibid., p. 337.

8. Ibid.

9. *Briefe*, II, #409; *Letters*, p. 486.

10. Hegel, "Vorrede zu Hinrichs Religionsphilosophie," *Werke*, 11, p. 42.

11. Ibid., p. 43.

12. Ibid., pp. 45–46.

13. Ibid., pp. 48–49.

14. Ibid., p. 59.

15. Ibid., p. 57.

16. Ibid., p. 60.

17. Ibid.

18. Ibid., pp. 61–63.

19. Ibid., p. 58.

20. Ibid., p. 61.

21. *Hegel in Berichten seiner Zeitgenossen*, #349, p. 227.

22. *Hegel in Berichten seiner Zeitgenossen*, #385, p. 245.

23. *Hegel in Berichten seiner Zeitgenossen*, #378, p. 242.

24. See *Briefe*, II, notes to #421, p. 498.

25. Hegel, "Über den Unterricht in der Philosophie auf Gymnasien," *Werke*, 11, p. 32.; *Letters*, p. 391.

26. See Hegel, "Über den Unterricht in der Philosophie auf Gymnasien," *Werke*, 11, p. 33.; *Letters*, p. 391.

27. See Karl Hegel's memoirs of his family's decisions about this, cited by Nicolin in *Briefe*, IV/1, p. 334 (note to item #106).

28. See *Briefe*, II, #421; *Letters*, p. 474.

29. *Briefe*, II, #413; *Letters*, p. 576.

30. See Otto Pöggeler, "Preußische Rheinlande, Vereinigte Niederlande," in Otto Pöggeler (ed.), *Hegel in Berlin: Preußische Kulturpolitik und idealistische Ästhetik: Zum 150. Todestags des Philosophen*, p. 146.

31. See *Briefe*, I, #40; *Letters*, p. 67.

32. See *Briefe*, II, #431; *Letters*, p. 580.

33. See *Briefe*, II, #432. (The variant is missing from *Letters*.)

34. *Briefe*, III, #487; *Letters*, p. 602.

35. *Briefe*, II, #433; *Letters*, p. 581.

36. See *Briefe*, II, #436; *Letters*, p. 585.

37. See *Briefe*, II, #434; *Letters*, p. 582.

38. See *Briefe*, II, #436; *Letters*, p. 584. (The translation mentions only traveling out of "duty.")

39. See *Briefe*, II, notes to #436, p. 505.

40. See *Briefe*, II, #436; *Letters*, p. 585.

41. *Briefe*, II, #437; *Letters*, p. 595.

42. See *Briefe*, II, #438; *Letters*, pp. 596–599.

43. Ibid.

44. See *Briefe*, II, #440; *Letters*, p. 600.

45. See *Briefe*, II, #443; *Letters*, p. 580a.

46. Reinhart Koselleck, *Preußen zwischen Reform und Revolution*, p. 278.

47. See *Hegel in Berichten seiner Zeitgenossen*, #388, p. 257.

48. See Stieglitz's account in *Hegel in Berichten seiner Zeitgenossen*, #411, pp. 267–268.

49. See *Hegel in Berichten seiner Zeitgenossen*, #393, p. 259.

50. See *Briefe*, III, #451; *Letters*, p. 451.

51. See the reference by Johannes Schulze to Hegel's deteriorating health in his letter to von Kamptz asking for authorization to pay for a recuperatory trip by Hegel. Cited in Inge Blank, "Dokumente zur Hegels Reise nach Österreich," *Hegel-Studien*, vol. 16, 1981, pp. 47–48. Hegel complains to van Ghert about his frequent headaches in a letter of April 4, 1823: *Briefe*, III, #447; *Letters*, p. 603.

52. See *Briefe*, I, #40; *Letters*, p. 67.

53. Cited in Kurt Rainer Meist, "Halykonische Tage in Wien," in Otto Pöggeler (ed.), *Hegel in Berlin*, pp. 154–156.

54. *Briefe*, III, #476; *Letters*, p. 610.

55. *Briefe*, III, #478; *Letters*, pp. 612–613.

56. See Gunter Scholz, "Musikalische Erfahrungen in Oper und Singakademie," in Otto Pöggeler (ed.), *Hegel in Berlin*, pp. 86–94.

57. *Briefe*, III, #479; *Letters*, pp. 616–617.

58. *Briefe*, III, #479, #480; *Letters*, pp. 616–617, 618.
59. See *Briefe*, III, #479; *Letters*, p. 618.
60. *Briefe*, III, #480; *Letters*, p. 620.
61. *Briefe*, III, #481; *Letters*, p. 624. ("On its own account" renders "*für sich*"; "throats" renders "*Kehlen*," which might also be metaphorically rendered, as Butler and Seiler do, as "voices.")
62. *Briefe*, III, #481; *Letters*, p. 624.
63. Ibid.
64. *Briefe*, III, #483; *Letters*, p. 627.
65. *Briefe*, III, #481; *Letters*, p. 623.
66. See *Briefe*, III, #482; *Letters*, p. 626.
67. *Briefe*, III, #483; *Letters*, p. 629.
68. Ibid.
69. *Briefe*, III, #482; *Letters*, p. 626.
70. *Briefe*, III, #483; *Letters*, p. 629.
71. *Hegel in Berichten seiner Zeitgenossen*, #415, pp. 271–272.

Chapter Thirteen

1. Varnhagen von Ense remarked in his journal (November 11, 1824), "All the world is convinced of his innocence; Prof. Hegel, who spoke with him in Dresden, swears by it." *Briefe*, III, notes to # 486, p. 376.
2. Franchet-Desperey's letter is printed in Jacques D'Hondt, *Hegel in His Time: Berlin 1818–1831*, p. 134; D'Hondt's discussion of the Cousin case is very helpful; see pp. 133–162. D'Hondt bases much of his discussion on the material assembled by Hoffmeister in *Briefe*, notes to #486, pp. 374–378.
3. See Jacques D'Hondt, *Hegel in His Time: Berlin 1818–1831*, p. 136.
4. Ibid., pp. 137–140.
5. *Briefe*, notes to #486, pp. 375–376.
6. *Briefe*, notes to #486, p. 376.
7. *Hegel in Berichten seiner Zeitgenossen*, #435, p. 285.
8. *Hegel in Berichten seiner Zeitgenossen*, #435, p. 282. The phrase is "*echte Stiftler*."
9. See Hegel, *Berliner Schriften: 1818–1831*, pp. 585–587.
10. *Hegel in Berichten seiner Zeitgenossen*, #442, pp. 290–291 (from a letter from Hotho to Victor Cousin, April 1, 1826).
11. Ibid. Haym has the chaplain complaining, Hotho has the students complaining. Haym's account was published in 1857, twenty-six years after Hegel's death. Perhaps the chaplain complained after having been alerted by the students.
12. Hegel, "Über eine Anklage wegen öffentlicher Verunglimpfung der katholischen Religion," *Werke*, 11, p. 69.
13. See Hermann Klenner and Gerhard Oberkofler, "Zwei Savigny-Voten über Eduard Gans nebst Chronologie und Bibliographie," in *Weltgeschichte* (ed. Hans-Heinz Holz and Domenico Losurdo) (Bonn: Pahl-Rugenstein Verlag Nachfolger, 1993), p. 133.
14. See John Edward Toews, *Hegelianism*, p. 110. Toews provides a very good

short biography of Gans. Another short biography of Gans is given by Michael H. Hoffheimer, *Eduard Gans and the Hegelian Philosophy of Law* (Dordrecht: Kluwer Academic Publishers, 1995), pp. 1–10.

15. Cited in John Edward Toews, *Hegelianism*, p. 111.
16. See the chronology in Hermann Klenner and Gerhard Oberkofler, "Zwei Savigny-Voten über Eduard Gans nebst Chronologie und Bibliographie," in *Weltgeschichte* (ed. Hans-Heinz Holz and Domenico Losurdo) (Bonn: Pahl-Rugenstein Verlag Nachfolger, 1993), pp. 132–146.
17. Friedrich von Savigny, letter of August 7, 1821 in Hermann Klenner and Gerhard Oberkofler, "Zwei Savigny-Voten über Eduard Gans nebst Chronologie und Bibliographie," p. 125.
18. Ibid.
19. Ibid.
20. Ibid., p. 128.
21. See John Edward Toews, *Hegelianism*, p. 128.
22. Cited in S. S. Prawer, *Heine's Jewish Comedy: A Study of His Portraits of Jews and Judaism* (Oxford: Clarendon Press, 1983), p. 29. Heine and Gans shared for a while the idea of a Jewish exodus from Germany to a new homeland; Heine even fantasized about Gans leading such an expedition to Jerusalem.
23. See *Briefe*, III, #464.
24. See Friedrich Hogemann, "Die Entstehung der 'Sozietät' und der 'Jahrbücher für wissenschaftliche Kritik'," in Christoph Jamme (ed.), *Die "Jahrbücher für wissenschaftliche Kritik": Hegels Berliner Gegenakademie* (Stuttgart-Bad Cannstatt: Frommann-Holzboog, 1994), p. 60.
25. See *Briefe*, III, notes to #515, pp. 391–392.
26. *Hegel in Berichten seiner Zeitgenossen*, #577, p. 386.
27. *Hegel in Berichten seiner Zeitgenossen*, #658, p. 425. It was also the combination of gown and beret that provoked the description of Hegel as the "*echte Stiftler*," the Tübingen "Seminarian to the core." Hegel's son Immanuel found the famous (and often reproduced) Johann Jakob Schlesinger painting of Hegel to be "nice," except that "the mouth," he said, was wrong, and the "eyes" were too "sharp." See Willi Ferdinand Becker, "Hegels Hinterlassene Schriften im Briefwechsel seines Sohnes Immanuel," *Zeitschrift für philosophische Forschung*, pp. 605–606.
28. See *Briefe*, III, notes to #515, p. 392.
29. See *Briefe*, III, notes to #515, p. 393.
30. See *Briefe*, III, notes to #515, p. 394.
31. For Gans's role in the founding of the journal and his preference for *Le Globe*, see Norbert Waszek, "Eduard Gans, die 'Jahrbücher für wissenschaftliche Kritik' und die französische Publizistik der Zeit," in Christoph Jamme (ed.), *Die "Jahrbücher für wissenschaftliche Kritik"*, pp. 93–118; on the relation of the "Yearbooks" to the *Journal des Savants*, see Jacques D'Hondt, "Hegel und das 'Journal des savants'," in Christoph Jamme (ed.), *Die "Jahrbücher für wissenschaftliche Kritik"*, pp. 119–144; on the nature of *Le Globe*, see François Furet, *Revolutionary France: 1770–1880*, pp. 315–320.
32. See *Briefe*, III, notes to #515, p. 398.

33. See Sibylle Obenaus, "Berliner Allgemeine Literaturzeitung oder 'Hegelblatt'?" in Christoph Jamme (ed.), *Die "Jahrbücher für wissenschaftliche Kritik"*, pp. 15–56.

34. *Briefe*, III, #552; *Letters*, p. 529.

35. *Hegel in Berichten seiner Zeitgenossen*, #499, p. 339.

36. Cited in S. S. Prawer, *Heine's Jewish Comedy*, p. 12. Heine's portrait of Gans as drawn out by Prawer is extremely important for understanding the background of the Jewish community in Berlin with which Hegel was so familiar.

37. *Hegel in Berichten seiner Zeitgenossen*, #448, p. 294.

38. Max Lenz, *Geschichte der königlichen Friedrich-Wilhelms-Universität zu Berlin*, pp. 512–514.

39. Mary Lee Townsend, *Forbidden Laughter: Popular Humor and the Limits of Repression in Nineteenth Century Prussia* (Ann Arbor: University of Michigan Press, 1992), p. 36.

40. Cited in Mary Lee Townsend, *Forbidden Laughter*, p. 37. The joke in German: "Sind diese zwei Herrn Brüder? Von dem Einen weiß ich es gewiß, von dem Andern kann ich es nicht bestimmt sagen." (p. 37n)

41. The figures are taken from Mary Lee Townsend, *Forbidden Laughter*, p. 38.

42. See Helmut Schneider, "Komödie des Lebens – Theorie der Komödie," in Otto Pöggeler (ed.), *Hegel in Berlin*, pp. 79–85.

43. See *Hegel in Berichten seiner Zeitgenossen*, #452, p. 296; Mary Lee Townsend, *Forbidden Laughter*, pp. 15–16.

44. *Briefe*, III, #516; *Letters*, p. 184.

45. *Briefe*, III, #520, *Letters*, p. 506.

46. *Hegel in Berichten seiner Zeitgenossen*, #463, pp. 310–311.

47. *Briefe*, III, notes to #530.

48. See *Briefe*, III, notes to #524, p. 402.

49. *Briefe*, IV/1, pp. 237–240 (letter from Ludwig Fischer to Ebert, July 11, 1825).

50. See *Hegel in Berichten seiner Zeitgenossen*, #708, p. 451.

51. *Briefe*, III, #581.

52. *Hegel in Berichten seiner Zeitgenossen*, #492, p. 335.

53. *Hegel in Berichten seiner Zeitgenossen*, #513, p. 345.

54. See *Briefe*, III, #548; *Letters*, p. 402. Hegel notes that a particular request did not specify what he should write about. In light of that, he says, "I cannot make this request in writing, for this very act would render the request superfluous. So allow the superfluity of having submitted the request and thereby at once annihilating it suffice."

55. *Briefe*, III, #557; *Letters*, p. 648.

56. *Briefe*, III, #559; *Letters*, p. 649.

57. *Briefe*, III, #559; *Letters*, p. 650.

58. *Briefe*, III, #559; *Letters*, p. 649.

59. *Briefe*, III, #560; *Letters*, p. 653.

60. *Briefe*, III, #562; *Letters*, p. 657; the citation about Tieck is from Hegel's 1828 essay in the *Jahrbücher*, "Solgers nachgelassene Schriften und Briefwechsel," *Werke*, 11, 219. ("Petit bourgeois narrow-minded obscurity" translates *spießbürgerlichen Dunkel*.")

61. *Briefe*, III, #563; *Letters*, p. 658.

62. *Briefe*, III, #560; *Letters*, p. 654.

63. *Briefe*, III, #564; *Letters*, p. 660.

64. *Briefe*, III, #563; *Letters*, p. 657.

65. *Briefe*, III, #560; *Letters*, p. 654.

66. *Briefe*, III, #564; *Letters*, p. 660.

67. Ibid.

68. *Briefe*, III, #560; *Letters*, p. 654.

69. *Briefe*, III, #562; *Letters*, p. 655. See the notes to #562, p. 419.

70. See François Furet's discussion of Mignet and the liberal circles in his *Revolutionary France: 1770–1880*, pp. 306–320. This, of course, gave those liberals all the more reason to support the revolution of 1830, since it seemed to fulfill the foreordained English model.

71. Cited in Eric Hobsbawm, *Echoes of the Marseillaise: Two Centuries Look Back on the French Revolution* (New Brunswick: Rutgers University Press, 1990), p. 23.

72. Ibid., p. 14.

73. See *Hegel in Berichten seiner Zeitgenossen*, #481, pp. 322–323; and #535, p. 355.

74. Hegel, *Berliner Schriften: 1818–1831*, p. 698; *Werke*, 11, p. 566 ("*Seichter Kopf!*" for "insipid mind").

75. *Briefe*, III, #562; *Letters*, p. 656.

76. *Briefe*, III, #564; *Letters*, p. 660. (I translated Hegel's term "*kleiner Springsinfeld*" as "spring chicken.")

77. On Cousin's leadership role, see François Furet, *Revolutionary France: 1770–1880*, pp. 316–317.

78. *Briefe*, III, #566; *Letters*, p. 663.

79. *Briefe*, III, #538.

80. *Hegel in Berichten seiner Zeitgenossen*, #766, p. 528.

81. *Briefe*, III, #566; *Letters*, p. 663.

82. *Hegel in Berichten seiner Zeitgenossen*, #525, pp. 350–351.

83. See *Hegel in Berichten seiner Zeitgenossen*, #527 (Eckermann), p. 351; and #530 (Goethe to Zelter), p. 353.

84. See *Hegel in Berichten seiner Zeitgenossen*, #590, p. 392, for Eckermann's account of Goethe's appreciation of Hegel's review of Hamann's works, in which Eckermann cites Goethe as saying that "Hegel's judgments as a critic have always been good."

85. *Briefe*, III, #567; *Letters*, p. 710.

86. Ibid.

87. See *Hegel in Berichten seiner Zeitgenossen*, #528, pp. 352–353.

88. *Hegel in Berichten seiner Zeitgenossen*, #532, p. 354.

89. *Hegel in Berichten seiner Zeitgenossen*, #534, p. 355.

Chapter Fourteen

1. G. W. F. Hegel, *Hegel's Philosophy of Nature* (Oxford: Oxford at the Clarendon Press, 1970), "Introduction," p. 1; *Werke*, 9, "Einleitung," p. 9. (Italics are my own.) The original editors of Hegel's philosophy of nature apparently mixed in

citations from manuscripts of very different periods in their edition. Until the fully critical edition of the philosophy of nature appears, one must therefore continue to take the "additions" (*Zusätze*) with a grain of salt, since they contain so many additions from different years.

2. Hegel, *Hegel's Philosophy of Nature*, §246; *Werke*, 9, p. 15.
3. Hegel, *Hegel's Philosophy of Nature*, §246 (*Zusatz*); *Werke*, 9, p. 20.
4. There is an immense literature on the topic of Hegel's criticisms of Newton, some of it defending Hegel, much of it criticizing him, and some of it claiming, for example, that it is not Newton himself but Newtonians that Hegel is criticizing. A fairly comprehensive overview of the (mostly German) literature is given in Wolfgang Bonsiepen, *Die Begründung einer Naturphilosophie bei Kant, Schelling, Fries und Hegel: Mathematische versus spekulative Naturphilosophie* (Frankfurt a.M.: Vittorio Klostermann, 1997). See also Rolf-Peter Horstmann and Michael J. Petry (eds.), *Hegels Philosophie der Natur: Beziehungen zwischen empirischer und spekulativer Naturerkenntnis* (Stuttgart: Ernst Klett Verlag, 1986); Michael J. Petry (ed.), *Hegel and Newtonianism* (Kluwer Academic Publishers: Dordrecht, 1993); Michael J. Petry (ed.), *Hegel und die Naturwissenschaften* (Stuttgart-Bad Cannstatt: Frommann-Holzboog, 1987).
5. Hegel, *Hegel's Philosophy of Nature*, §276; *Werke*, 9, p. 116. ("Simple being-external-to-itself" renders "*einfaches Außersichsein.*")
6. Hegel, *Hegel's Philosophy of Nature*, §276 (remark); *Werke*, 9, p. 117.
7. Hegel, *Hegel's Philosophy of Nature*, §286 (*Zusatz*); *Werke*, 9, p. 146.
8. Hegel, *Hegel's Philosophy of Nature*, §341 (*Zusatz*); *Werke*, 9, p. 363.
9. Ibid., p. 362.
10. Schelling himself took the conceptions from C. F. Kielmeyer. On Kielmeyer's influence and ideas, see Wolfgang Bonsiepen, *Die Begründung einer Naturphilosophie bei Kant, Schelling, Fries und Hegel*, pp. 268–272.
11. Hegel, *Hegel's Philosophy of Nature*, §359 (remark); *Werke*, 9, p. 469.
12. Hegel, *Hegel's Philosophy of Nature*, §369; *Werke*, 9, p. 516. ("Copulation" is "*Begattung.*")
13. Hegel, *Hegel's Philosophy of Nature*, §369 (*Zusatz*); *Werke*, 9, p. 517.
14. Hegel, *Hegel's Philosophy of Nature*, §370 (*Zusatz*); *Werke*, 9, p. 520.
15. Hegel, *Hegel's Philosophy of Nature*, §371 (*Zusatz*); *Werke*, 9, p. 520.
16. Hegel, *Hegel's Philosophy of Nature*, §376 (*Zusatz*); *Werke*, 9, p. 538.
17. Hegel, *Hegel's Philosophy of Nature*, §279 (*Zusatz*); *Werke*, 9, p. 130.
18. See Hegel, *Hegel's Philosophy of Nature*, §249 (and *Zusatz*); *Werke*, 9, pp. 31–34.
19. Hegel, *Hegel's Philosophy of Nature*, §286 (*Zusatz*); *Werke*, 9, pp. 147–148.
20. Hegel, *Hegel's Philosophy of Nature*, §270 (*Zusatz*); *Werke*, 9, p. 106.
21. Hegel, *Hegel's Philosophy of Nature*, §376 (*Zusatz*); *Werke*, 9, pp. 538–539.
22. Hegel, *Hegel's Philosophy of Nature*, §376 (*Zusatz*); *Werke*, 9, p. 539.
23. See Marie's letters to Immanuel Hegel from 1844 in Willi Ferdinand Becker, "Hegels Hinterlassene Schriften im Briefwechsel seines Sohnes Immanuel," *Zeitschrift für philosophische Forschung*, pp. 596–597.

24. *Hegel in Berichten seiner Zeitgenossen*, #697, p. 446.
25. *Hegel in Berichten seiner Zeitgenossen*, #695, p. 445.
26. "Symbolic" is being used here in the more common sense; Hegel has his own technical sense of "symbolic," which he picked up from his Heidelberg friend Friedrich Creuzer, which is different.
27. G. W. F. Hegel, *Lectures on the Philosophy of Religion* (ed. Peter Hodgson) (trans. R. F. Brown, P. C. Hodgson, J. M. Stewart) (Berkeley: University of California Press, 1984), vol. 1, p. 180; *Vorlesungen über die Philosophie der Religion* (ed. Walter Jaeschke) (Hamburg: Felix Meiner Verlag, 1993), vol. 1, p. 88.
28. Hegel, *Lectures on the Philosophy of Religion*,, vol. 1, p. 164; *Vorlesungen über die Philosophie der Religion*, vol. 1, p. 74.
29. Hegel, *Lectures on the Philosophy of Religion*, vol. 1, p. 164; *Vorlesungen über die Philosophie der Religion*, vol. 1, p. 74.
30. See, for example, among other citations, Aristotle's claim in the *Nicomachean Ethics*: "But such a life would be too high for man; for it is not in so far as he is man that he will live so, but in so far as something divine is present in him; and by so much as this is superior to our composite nature is its activity superior to that which is the exercise of the other kind of virtue. If reason is divine, then, in comparison with man, the life according to it is divine in comparison with human life. But we must not follow those who advise us, being men, to think of human things, and, being mortal, of mortal things, but must, so far as we can, make ourselves immortal, and strain every nerve to live in accordance with the best thing in us; for even if it be small in bulk, much more does it in power and worth surpass everything. This would seem, too, to be each man himself, since it is the authoritative and better part of him." (p. 265 [X, 7])
31. Hegel, *Lectures on the Philosophy of Religion*, vol. 1, p. 375; *Vorlesungen über die Philosophie der Religion*, vol. 1, p. 273. Hegel makes a very similar point in his review of Wilhelm von Humboldt. See Hegel, "Über die unter den Namen Bhagavad-Ghita bekannte Episode des Mahabharata von Wilhelm von Humboldt," *Werke*, 11, pp. 190–191.
32. Hegel, *Lectures on the Philosophy of Religion*, vol. 2, p. 570; *Vorlesungen über die Philosophie der Religion*, vol. 2, p. 467.
33. Hegel, *Lectures on the Philosophy of Religion*, vol. 2, p. 575; *Vorlesungen über die Philosophie der Religion*, vol. 2, p. 471.
34. Hegel, *Lectures on the Philosophy of Religion*, vol. 2, p. 673; *Vorlesungen über die Philosophie der Religion*, vol. 2, p. 565.
35. For Hegel's sources, see Peter C. Hodgson, "The Metamorphosis of Judaism in Hegel's Philosophy of Religion," *Owl of Minerva*, 19 (Fall 1987), pp. 41–52. Hodgson does not speculate on Hegel's relation to Gans in this matter. See also Hodgson's discussion in his editorial introduction to Hegel, *Lectures on the Philosophy of Religion*, vol. 2, pp. 48–51.
36. Hegel, *Lectures on the Philosophy of Religion*, vol. 2, p. 673; *Vorlesungen über die Philosophie der Religion*, vol. 2, pp. 676–677.

37. Hegel, *Lectures on the Philosophy of Religion*, vol. 2, pp. 676–677; *Vorlesungen über die Philosophie der Religion*, vol. 2, pp. 568–569.

38. Hegel, *Lectures on the Philosophy of Religion*, vol. 2, p. 742; *Vorlesungen über die Philosophie der Religion*, vol. 2, p. 628.

39. Hegel, *Lectures on the Philosophy of Religion*, vol. 2, p. 696; *Vorlesungen über die Philosophie der Religion*, vol. 2, p. 588.

40. Ibid.

41. Ibid.

42. Hegel, *Lectures on the Philosophy of Religion*, vol. 2, p. 760; *Vorlesungen über die Philosophie der Religion*, vol. 2, p. 642.

43. Hegel, *Lectures on the Philosophy of Religion*, vol. 3, p. 369; *Vorlesungen über die Philosophie der Religion*, vol. 3, p. 286.

44. Hegel, *Lectures on the Philosophy of Religion*, vol. 3, p. 331; *Vorlesungen über die Philosophie der Religion*, vol. 3, p. 254.

45. Hegel, *Lectures on the Philosophy of Religion*, vol. 3, pp. 258–259; *Vorlesungen über die Philosophie der Religion*, vol. 3, pp. 185–186.

46. Hegel, *Lectures on the Philosophy of Religion*, vol. 3, p. 317; *Vorlesungen über die Philosophie der Religion*, vol. 3, p. 241.

47. Hegel, *Lectures on the Philosophy of Religion*, vol. 3, p. 320; *Vorlesungen über die Philosophie der Religion*, vol. 3, pp. 243–244.

48. Hegel, *Lectures on the Philosophy of Religion*, vol. 3, p. 322; *Vorlesungen über die Philosophie der Religion*, vol. 3, p. 245.

49. Hegel, *Lectures on the Philosophy of Religion*, vol. 3, p. 326; *Vorlesungen über die Philosophie der Religion*, vol. 3, p. 250.

50. Hegel, *Lectures on the Philosophy of Religion*, vol. 3, p. 325; *Vorlesungen über die Philosophie der Religion*, vol. 3, p. 249.

51. Hegel, *Lectures on the Philosophy of Religion*, vol. 3, p. 328; *Vorlesungen über die Philosophie der Religion*, vol. 3, p. 251.

52. Hegel, *Lectures on the Philosophy of Religion*, vol. 3, p. 369; *Vorlesungen über die Philosophie der Religion*, vol. 3, p. 285.

53. Hegel, *Lectures on the Philosophy of Religion*, vol. 3, pp. 303–304; *Vorlesungen über die Philosophie der Religion*, vol. 3, p. 228.

54. Hegel, *Lectures on the Philosophy of Religion*, vol. 3, p. 370; *Vorlesungen über die Philosophie der Religion*, vol. 3, p. 286.

55. Hegel, *Lectures on the Philosophy of Religion*, vol. 3, p. 337; *Vorlesungen über die Philosophie der Religion*, vol. 3, p. 260.

56. Hegel, *Hegel's Philosophy of Nature*, §279; *Werke*, 9, p. 127.

57. Hegel, *Hegel's Philosophy of Nature*, §279 (*Zusatz*); *Werke*, 9, p. 129.

58. G. W. F. Hegel, *Aesthetics: Lectures on Fine Art* (trans. T. M. Knox) (Oxford: Clarendon Press, 1975), vol. 1, p. 31; *Werke*, 13, p. 52.

59. Hegel, *Aesthetics*, vol. 1, p. 7; *Werke*, 13, p. 21.

60. Hegel, *Aesthetics*, vol. 1, p. 38; *Werke*, 13, p. 60.

61. Hegel, *Aesthetics*, vol. 1, p. 110; *Werke*, 13, p. 150.

62. Hegel, *Aesthetics*, vol. 1, p. 70; *Werke*, 13, p. 100.

63. Hegel, *Aesthetics*, vol. 1, p. 54; *Werke*, 13, p. 80.

64. A good and (controverersial) discussion of Hegel's aesthetics and the particular arts can be found in Stephen Bungay, *Beauty and Truth: A Study of Hegel's Aesthetics* (Oxford: Oxford University Press, 1987)

65. Hegel, *Aesthetics*, vol. 1, p. 76; *Werke*, 13, p. 106 ("*ein bloßes Suchen der Verbildlichung als ein Vermögen wahrhafter Darstellung*").

66. Hegel, *Aesthetics*, vol. 1, p. 303; *Werke*, 13, p. 394. ("Transcendent" renders "*Hinaussein.*")

67. Hegel, *Aesthetics*, vol. 1, p. 431; *Werke*, 14, p. 18.

68. Hegel, *Aesthetics*, vol. 1, p. 432; *Werke*, 14, p. 19.

69. Hegel, *Aesthetics*, vol. 1, pp. 453, 433; *Werke*, 14, pp. 21, 46.

70. Hegel, *Aesthetics*, vol. 1, p. 517; *Werke*, 14, p. 128.

71. Hegel, *Aesthetics*, vol. 1, p. 531; *Werke*, 14, p. 144. ("Deep feeling" renders "*Innigkeit.*")

72. Hegel, *Aesthetics*, vol. 1, pp. 519, 525; *Werke*, 14, pp. 129, 138.

73. Hegel, *Aesthetics*, vol. 1, p. 527; *Werke*, 14, p. 140.

74. Ibid.

75. Hegel, *Aesthetics*, vol. 1, p. 540; *Werke*, 14, p. 156.

76. Hegel, *Aesthetics*, vol. 1, p. 553; *Werke*, 14, p. 171.

77. Hegel, *Aesthetics*, vol. 1, p. 570; *Werke*, 14, p. 192.

78. Hegel, *Aesthetics*, vol. 1, pp. 583–584; *Werke*, 14, pp. 207–208.

79. Hegel, *Aesthetics*, vol. 1, p. 594; *Werke*, 14, p. 221.

80. Hegel, *Aesthetics*, vol. 1, p. 595; *Werke*, 14, p. 222.

81. Hegel, *Aesthetics*, vol. 1, p. 596; *Werke*, 14, pp. 223–224.

82. Hegel, *Aesthetics*, vol. 1, p. 598; *Werke*, 14, p. 226.

83. Hegel, *Aesthetics*, vol. 1, p. 600; *Werke*, 14, p. 229.

84. Hegel, *Aesthetics*, vol. 1, p. 607; *Werke*, 14, p. 237–238.

85. Hegel, *Aesthetics*, vol. 1, p. 11; *Werke*, 13, p. 25. The dating of the lecture as occurring in 1828 is taken from Dieter Henrich, "Art and Philosophy of Art Today: Reflections with Reference to Hegel," in R. E. Amacher and V. Lange (eds.), *New Perspectives in German Literary Criticism* (Princeton: Princeton University Press, 1979), pp. 107–133; see p. 114, note 1.

86. Hegel, *Aesthetics*, vol. 1, p. 480; *Werke*, 14, p. 79.

87. *Hegel in Berichten seiner Zeitgenossen*, #669, p. 430.

Chapter Fifteen

1. This debate is brilliantly fleshed out by Mack Walker in *German Hometowns*.

2. This characterization of hometowns is taken from Mack Walker, *German Hometowns*, especially p. 101.

3. Clemens L. W. Metternich-Winnebourg, *Memoirs* (trans. Mrs. Alexander Napier III) (London, 1881), p. 467; cited by Mack Walker, p. 305n.

4. See *Briefe*, III, notes to #572, pp. 424–426.

5. *Briefe*, III, #575; *Letters*, p. 666.
6. *Hegel in Berichten seiner Zeitgenossen*, #585, pp. 389–390; Sulpiz Boisserée made the "cuckoo" remark to Goethe, *Hegel in Berichten seiner Zeitgenossen*, #552, p. 372.
7. *Hegel in Berichten seiner Zeitgenossen*, #614, pp. 404–406.
8. *Hegel in Berichten seiner Zeitgenossen*, #630, p. 412.
9. *Hegel in Berichten seiner Zeitgenossen*, #520, p. 349.
10. See *Hegel in Berichten seiner Zeitgenossen*, #558, p. 376. (The room was described as "*mäuschen Stille*," so quiet that one could hear a pin drop.)
11. *Hegel in Berichten seiner Zeitgenossen*, #558, p. 376.
12. *Hegel in Berichten seiner Zeitgenossen*, #558, p. 379.
13. *Hegel in Berichten seiner Zeitgenossen*, #558, p. 378.
14. See *Briefe*, III, notes to #579, p. 430.
15. See *Briefe*, III, notes to #687, p. 472.
16. *Hegel in Berichten seiner Zeitgenossen*, #583, pp. 388–389.
17. *Hegel in Berichten seiner Zeitgenossen*, #558, pp. 379–380.
18. See *Briefe*, III, notes to #513, pp. 388–389.
19. See *Briefe*, III, notes to #612, pp. 447–448.
20. *Briefe*, III, #605, p. 266.
21. *Hegel in Berichten seiner Zeitgenossen*, #594, p. 394.
22. See his mother-in-law's letter to Marie noting this: *Hegel in Berichten seiner Zeitgenossen*, #603, p. 400.
23. *Briefe*, III, #599; *Letters*, p. 397.
24. *Briefe*, III, #599; *Letters*, p. 398.
25. *Hegel in Berichten seiner Zeitgenossen*, #597, p. 396.
26. See the characterization of Zelter in Heinrich Eduard Jacob, *Felix Mendelssohn and His Times* (trans. Richard and Clara Winston) (Westport, Conn.: Greenwood Press, 1973), pp. 41–47.
27. See the account of the influences of Zelter and Klein, along with the account of the meeting with Goethe and the production of the *Saint Matthew Passion*, in Heinrich Eduard Jacob, *Felix Mendelssohn and His Times*, pp. 32–41, 48–89.
28. *Hegel in Berichten seiner Zeitgenossen*, #593, pp. 393–394.
29. *Hegel in Berichten seiner Zeitgenossen*, #601, p. 399.
30. *Hegel in Berichten seiner Zeitgenossen*, #603, pp. 399–400.
31. *Hegel in Berichten seiner Zeitgenossen*, #608, pp. 402–403.
32. *Briefe*, III, #607; *Letters*, p. 398.
33. Ibid.
34. Hegel, *Aesthetics*, vol. 1, p. 569; *Werke*, 14, pp. 190–191.
35. *Briefe*, III, #630; *Letters*, p. 668.
36. *Briefe*, III, notes to #607, p. 445.
37. See Immanuel's letters to his mother from 1834–35 in Willi Ferdinand Becker, "Hegels Hinterlassene Schriften im Briefwechsel seines Sohnes Immanuel," *Zeitschrift für philosophische Forschung*, pp. 600–601.

38. *Hegel in Berichten seiner Zeitgenossen*, #622, p. 409. (These come from Rosenkranz's memoirs, not his biography of Hegel.)
39. *Hegel in Berichten seiner Zeitgenossen*, #489, pp. 332–333.
40. *Hegel in Berichten seiner Zeitgenossen*, #687, pp. 441–442.
41. *Hegel in Berichten seiner Zeitgenossen*, #489, p. 333.
42. *Hegel in Berichten seiner Zeitgenossen*, #616, p. 406.
43. *Hegel in Berichten seiner Zeitgenossen*, #615, p. 406 (on the matter of the endorsement for snuff tobacco).
44. *Hegel in Berichten seiner Zeitgenossen*, #624, p. 410.
45. Cited in Otto Pöggeler, "Einleitung," in Christoph Jamme and Otto Pöggeler (eds.), *Homburg vor der Höhe in der deutschen Geistesgeschichte*, p. 15.
46. See Christoph Jamme, "Die erste Hölderlin-Ausgabe," in Otto Pöggeler (ed.), *Hegel in Berlin*, pp. 64–71.
47. Hegel, *Berliner Schriften: 1818–1831*, "Rede bei der dritten Säkularfeier der Übergabe der Augsburgischen Konfession," pp. 31, 33 (taken from Hoffmeister's German translation of the original Latin).
48. Ibid., p. 33.
49. Ibid. (For "servitude," the word is "*Knechtschaft.*" This echoes, of course, Hegel's famous struggle between "*Herr*" and "*Knecht*" in the *Phenomenology of Spirit.*)
50. Ibid. (For "completes," the word is "vollendet," or "perfects.")
51. Ibid.
52. Ibid., p. 39.
53. Ibid., pp. 41, 43.
54. Ibid., p. 45.
55. Ibid.
56. Ibid., p. 47.
57. Ibid.
58. Ibid., p. 49.
59. Ibid., p. 51.
60. Ibid., p. 53.
61. *Briefe*, III, #644.
62. *Hegel in Berichten seiner Zeitgenossen*, #637, p. 415.
63. *Hegel in Berichten seiner Zeitgenossen*, #638, p. 6.
64. *Briefe*, III, #659, #664; *Letters*, pp. 543, 422.
65. *Hegel in Berichten seiner Zeitgenossen*, #638, p. 415.
66. *Hegel in Berichten seiner Zeitgenossen*, #652, p. 420.
67. Hegel, *Berliner Schriften: 1818–1831*, "Hegels Rede bei der Abgabe des Rektorats," p. 765.
68. Ibid., p. 767.
69. Ibid., p. 770.
70. Ibid., p. 774.
71. Ibid., pp. 777–778.
72. *Briefe*, III, #655.

73. *Briefe*, III, #664; *Letters*, p. 422.

74. *Hegel in Berichten seiner Zeitgenossen*, #659, p. 426.

75. I am following the dating of the various manuscripts on the lectures on the philosophy of history as laid out by Hans-Christian Lucas, "Die 'Tiefere Arbeit': Hegel zwischen Revolution und Reform," in Christoph Jamme and Elisabeth Weisser-Lohmann (eds.), *Politik und Geschichte: Zu den Intentionen von G.W.F. Hegels Reformbill-Schrift*, pp. 207–234.

76. Hegel, *Philosophie der Geschichte*, *Werke*, 12, pp. 534–535; *Philosophy of History* (New York: Dover Publications, 1956), p. 452. ("Arbitrary" translates *"Willkür."*)

77. Hegel, *Philosophie der Geschichte*, *Werke*, 12, p. 534; *Philosophy of History* (New York: Dover Publications, 1956), p. 451.

78. Hegel, *Philosophie der Geschichte*, *Werke*, 12, p. 529; *Philosophy of History* (New York: Dover Publications, 1956), p. 447.

79. Hegel, *Philosophie der Geschichte*, *Werke*, 12, p. 531; *Philosophy of History* (New York: Dover Publications, 1956), p. 449.

80. Hegel, *Philosophie der Geschichte*, *Werke*, 12, p. 535; *Philosophy of History* (New York: Dover Publications, 1956), p. 452.

81. See Michael Brock, *The Great Reform Act* (London: Hutchinson University Library, 1973), p. 28.

82. See James Sheehan, *German History: 1770–1866*, pp. 496–500.

83. See Anthony Read and David Fisher, *Berlin: The Biography of a City* (London: Pimlico Press, 1994), pp. 80–82.

84. See Michael Brock, *The Great Reform Act*, p. 17.

85. See Michael John Petry, "The 'Prussian State Gazette' and the 'Morning Chronicle' on Reform and Revolution," in Christoph Jamme and Elisabeth Weisser-Lohmann (eds.), *Politik und Geschichte*, pp. 61–94.

86. See Elisabeth Weisser-Lohmann, "Englische Reformbill und preußische Städteordnung: Repräsentative Staatsverfassung und vertikale Gewaltenteilung: V. Raumer, Steckfuß, Gans und Hegel," in Christoph Jamme and Elisabeth Weisser-Lohmann (eds.), *Politik und Geschichte*, p. 287.

87. Hegel, "Über die englische Reformbill," *Werke*, 11, p. 85; "The English Reform Bill," in *Hegel's Political Writings*, p. 297.

88. Hegel, "Über die englische Reformbill," *Werke*, 11, p. 87; "The English Reform Bill," in *Hegel's Political Writings*, p. 298.

89. Hegel, "Über die englische Reformbill," *Werke*, 11, p. 88; "The English Reform Bill," in *Hegel's Political Writings*, p. 299.

90. Hegel, "Über die englische Reformbill," *Werke*, 11, p. 94; "The English Reform Bill," in *Hegel's Political Writings*, p. 304.

91. See G.W.F. Hegel, *Lectures on Natural Right and Political Science: The First Philosophy of Right: Heidelberg 1817–1818 with Additions from the Lectures of 1818–1819*, pp. 276–276.

92. Hegel, "Über die englische Reformbill," *Werke*, 11, p. 95; "The English Reform Bill," in *Hegel's Political Writings*, p. 304.

93. Hegel, "Über die englische Reformbill," *Werke*, 11, p. 103; "The English Reform Bill," in *Hegel's Political Writings*, p. 310.

94. Ibid. ("Brains" is the translation of "*Verstand*" here.)

95. Hegel, "Über die englische Reformbill," *Werke*, 11, pp. 97–98; "The English Reform Bill," in *Hegel's Political Writings*, pp. 306–307.

96. Hegel, "Über die englische Reformbill," *Werke*, 11, p. 100; "The English Reform Bill," in *Hegel's Political Writings*, p. 308.

97. Hegel, "Über die englische Reformbill," *Werke*, 11, pp. 99–100; "The English Reform Bill," in *Hegel's Political Writings*, pp. 307–308.

98. Hegel, "Über die englische Reformbill," *Werke*, 11, p. 96; "The English Reform Bill," in *Hegel's Political Writings*, p. 306.

99. Hegel, "Über die englische Reformbill," *Werke*, 11, p. 86; "The English Reform Bill," in *Hegel's Political Writings*, p. 297. ("Ideas" in this context is the translation of "*Vorstellungen*.")

100. Hegel, "Über die englische Reformbill," *Werke*, 11, p. 107; "The English Reform Bill," in *Hegel's Political Writings*, p. 314.

101. Hegel, "Über die englische Reformbill," *Werke*, 11, pp. 108–109; "The English Reform Bill," in *Hegel's Political Writings*, p. 315.

102. Hegel, "Über die englische Reformbill," *Werke*, 11, p. 114; "The English Reform Bill," in *Hegel's Political Writings*, p. 319.

103. Hegel, "Über die englische Reformbill," *Werke*, 11, p. 114; "The English Reform Bill," in *Hegel's Political Writings*, p. 320.

104. Hegel, "Über die englische Reformbill," *Werke*, 11, pp. 119–120; "The English Reform Bill," in *Hegel's Political Writings*, pp. 323–324.

105. Hegel, "Über die englische Reformbill," *Werke*, 11, p. 120; "The English Reform Bill," in *Hegel's Political Writings*, p. 325.

106. Hegel, "Über die englische Reformbill," *Werke*, 11, p. 122; "The English Reform Bill," in *Hegel's Political Writings*, p. 326.

107. Hegel, "Über die englische Reformbill," *Werke*, 11, p. 127; "The English Reform Bill," in *Hegel's Political Writings*, p. 329.

108. Ibid.

109. Hegel, "Über die englische Reformbill," *Werke*, 11, p. 126; "The English Reform Bill," in *Hegel's Political Writings*, p. 329.

110. Hegel, "Über die englische Reformbill," *Werke*, 11, p. 128; "The English Reform Bill," in *Hegel's Political Writings*, p. 330.

111. Barbara Markiewicz, "Hegels Tod," in Christoph Jamme, (ed.), *Die "Jahrbücher für wissenschaftliche Kritik,"* pp. 531–556. See especially pp. 542–543, from which these dates are taken.

112. *Hegel in Berichten seiner Zeitgenossen*, #739, p. 499.

113. *Hegel in Berichten seiner Zeitgenossen*, #739, p. 497.

114. *Hegel in Berichten seiner Zeitgenossen*, #678, p. 433.

115. *Hegel in Berichten seiner Zeitgenossen*, #739, p. 498.

116. Karl Rosenkranz, *Georg Wilhelm Friedrich Hegels Leben*, pp. 419–420.

117. *Hegel in Berichten seiner Zeitgenossen*, #698, p. 446.

118. *Hegel in Berichten seiner Zeitgenossen*, #739, p. 499.

119. For the characterization of Hegel's final illness, I acknowledge my gratitude to Dr. Daniel Sulmasy, who discussed with me at length Hegel's medical symptoms and possible diagnoses of his final illness.

Epilogue

1. In fact, the true cause of cholera was discovered in 1833, only a few years after Hegel's death – in Berlin by Robert Koch, a professor at the university there.

2. *Hegel in Berichten seiner Zeitgenossen*, #723, pp. 474–475. (The translation is taken with slight alteration from that of John Edward Toews, *Hegelianism*, p. 89.)

3. *Hegel in Berichten seiner Zeitgenossen*, #724, pp. 476–477. (The translation is taken with slight alteration from that of John Edward Toews, *Hegelianism*, pp. 88–89.)

4. "Wenn aus der Ferne, da wir geschieden sind, / Ich dir noch kennbar bin, die Vergangenheit / O du Teilhaber meiner Leiden!" from *Hölderlin* (introduced and edited by Michael Hamburger) (trans. Michael Hamburger) (Baltimore: Penguin Books, 1961), p. 249.

5. "Es waren schöne Tage. Aber / Traurige Dämmerung folgte nachher / Du seiest so allen in der schönen Welt / Behauptest du mir immer, Geliebter! das / Weißt aber du nicht . . ." (*Hölderlin*, p. 251).

6. *Hegel in Berichten seiner Zeitgenossen*, #39a, p. 35.

Chronology of Hegel's Life

STUTTGART

1770 August 27: **Hegel is born in Stuttgart**
Parents: *Rentkammersekretär* Georg Ludwig Hegel and Maria Magdalena
Louisa Hegel (born Fromm)

1773 April: his sister, Christiane, is born (dies 1832). Hegel goes to the *deutsche
Schule.*

1776 Probable entrance into *Untergymnasium*
May: birth of brother Georg Ludwig (dies 1812)

1780 Hegel takes the *Landexamen* for the first time

1783 September 20: Hegel's mother dies of "*Gallenfieber*"; Hegel also is seriously
ill with it

1784 Beginning in the autumn, Hegel is a student at the *Obergymnasium*

1786 Centennial celebration of the Stuttgarter *Gymnasium*

1788 September: Hegel leaves the *Gymnasium*; he gives the *Abiturrede*

TÜBINGEN

1788 October: reception in the *Stift* at the same time as Hölderlin
Hegel begins his study with the philosophical faculty

1790 September: *Magister-Exam*
Registration in the theological faculty
He shares a room in the *Stift* with Hölderlin and Schelling

1793 June: theological disputation
Starting in July, Hegel is on leave from the Seminary and stays in Stuttgart
September 19–20: *Konsistorialexam*

BERNE

1793 October: begins his activity as house tutor with K. F. von Steiger

1795 May: trip to Geneva

1796 July: hike through the Bernese Alps
End of the year: return from Berne to Stuttgart

FRANKFURT

1797 January: Hegel begins the *Hofmeister* position that Hölderlin found for him with the wine merchant Gogel

1798 First publication: *Vertrauliche Briefe über das vormalige staatsrechtliche Verhältnis des Waatlandes zur Stadt Bern*

1799 January: death of Hegel's father in Stuttgart
March: Hegel makes the trip back to Stuttgart

1800 September: Hegel makes a trip to Mainz, which since 1798 has belonged to the French Republic

JENA

1801 January: Hegel moves to Jena
September: first philosophical book published, *The Difference Between Fichte's and Schelling's Systems of Philosophy*
August 27: habilitation submitted in Latin on the orbits of the planets; Hegel becomes a *Privatdozent* without *Besoldung* (remuneration)

1802/1803 Together with Schelling he edits the *Critical Journal of Philosophy*

1805 Named to *außerordentliche Professor*, without remuneration

1806 October: completion of the *Phenomenology of Spirit*

1807 February: birth of his illegitimate son, Ludwig Fischer (dies 1831 in Jakarta)

BAMBERG

1807 March: moves to Bamberg; editor and *Redakteur* of the *Bamberger Zeitung*
April: publication of the *Phenomenology of Spirit*

NUREMBERG

1808 November: rector of the *Gymnasium* in Nuremberg until 1815: he gives the official year-end speeches

1811 September: marries Marie von Tucher

1812 First volume of the *Science of Logic* published

1813 Named to *Lokalschulrat*
Second volume of *Science of Logic* published
Birth of son Karl (dies 1901)

1814 Birth of son Immanuel (dies 1891)

1816 Third volume of *Science of Logic* published

HEIDELBERG

1816 University Professor in Heidelberg

1817 Publication of the *Encyclopedia of the Philosophical Sciences*
Coeditor of the *Heidelberger Jahrbücher*
Hegel publishes in the *Heidelberger Jahrbücher*, "Proceedings of the Estates Assembly in the Kingdom of Württemberg 1815–1816"

BERLIN

1818 October 5: moves to Berlin
October 22: inaugural lecture
November 28: Hegel becomes a member of the *Gesetzlose Gesellschaft*

1819 June 17: Hegel turns over guardianship of his sister, Christiane, to his cousin, Ludwig Friedrich Göriz
July 27: Hegel writes to the authorities about Asversus

1820 October: publication of *Philosophy of Right*
Hegel travels in the fall to Dresden

1821 Hegel travels again in the fall to Dresden
Hegel becomes dean of the philosophical faculty for a one-year term

1822 Hegel writes the preface to Hinrichs's book on the philosophy of religion
Hallesche A. L. Zeitung publishes an attack on Hegel, and Hegel fails in his attempt to get the government to intercede for him

October: trip to the Netherlands
Hegel writes a memorandum on the teaching of philosophy and other subjects in the *Gymnasium*

1823 Hegel redeems the bond he put up for Asversus

1824 September/October: trips to Prague and Vienna
September 21–October 5: Hegel's stay in Vienna
November 4, 1824: Hegel writes the Prussian police on behalf of Victor Cousin

1825 (A quiet year for Hegel)

1826 Hegel writes "On a Complaint on Account of a Public Slander of the Catholic Religion"
Hegel writes "Über die Bekehrten" ("On the Converted") for the *Berliner Schnellpost*
July 23, 1826: Founding of the *Jahrbücher für wissenschaftliche Kritik*
Ludwig Fisher Hegel leaves the family (probable date)

1827 Publication begins of the *Jahrbücher für wissenschaftliche Kritik*
New edition of the *Encyclopedia of the Philosophical Sciences*
August–October: trip to Paris
Returning through Brussells, Hegel visits van Ghert, discusses Ludwig Fisher

1827 Hegel stops off in Weimar, visits with Goethe
Hegel publishes "On the Episode of the Mahabharata Known as the Bhagavad-Gita by Wilhelm von Humboldt" in the *Jahrbücher für wissenschaftliche Kritik*

1828 "Hamann's Writings" in the *Jahrbücher für wissenschaftliche Kritik*
Review of Solger in the *Jahrbücher für wissenschaftliche Kritik*

1829 September: trip to Prague; visit to the spa in Karlsbad where he accidentally meets Schelling; on the return trip, he visits Goethe

1829/30 Hegel is elected rector of the university
Hegel publishes his review of Goeschel's "Aphorisms on Ignorance and Absolute Knowing" in the *Jahrbücher für wissenschaftliche Kritik*
Hegel publishes his review of "On the Hegelian Doctrine or Absolute Knowing and Modern Pantheism – On Philosophy in General and Hegel's Encyclopedia of the Philosophical Sciences in Particular" in the *Jahrbücher für wissenschaftliche Kritik*

1830 Third edition of the *Encyclopedia of the Philosophical Sciences*
March 6: lunch with the royal family during which there is a remembrance of Hölderlin
June 25: Latin speech on the three hundredth anniversary of the Augsburg Confession

1831 New reworking of *Science of Logic*, Volume 1 (appears 1832)
Hegel publishes his review of "Ideal-realism" in the *Jahrbücher für wissenschaftliche Kritik*
"On the English Reform Bill"

November 14: Hegel dies in Berlin

Hegel's Works Cited

Collected Works and Collections of Articles

Werke in zwanzig Bänden (ed. Eva Moldenhauer and Karl Markus Michel) (Frankfurt a.M.: Suhrkamp Verlag, 1971) (abbreviated as *Werke* and volume number).

Sämtliche Werke (ed. Hermann Glockner) (Stuttgart: Frommans Verlag [H. Kurtz], 1928), vols. 1–20.

Gesammelte Werke (ed. Rheinisch-Westfälische Akademie der Wissenschaften) (Hamburg: Felix Meiner Verlag, 1968–   ).

Berliner Schriften: 1818–1831 (ed. Johannes Hoffmeister) (Hamburg: Felix Meiner Verlag, 1956).

Briefe von und an Hegel (ed. Johannes Hoffmeister) (Hamburg: Felix Meiner Verlag, 1969), vols. 1–4 (abbreviated as *Briefe*, volume number, and the letter number); *Hegel: The Letters* (trans. Clark Butler and Christiane Seiler) (Bloomington: University of Indiana Press, 1984) (abbreviated as *Letters* and page number).

Early Theological Writings (trans. T. M. Knox and Richard Kroner) (Philadelphia: University of Pennsylvania Press, 1975).

Hegel's Political Writings (trans. T. M. Knox) (Oxford: Oxford at the Clarendon Press, 1964).

Individual Works

"[Beurteilung der] Verhandlungen in der Versammlung der Landstände des Königreichs Württemberg im Jahr 1815 und 1816," *Werke*, 4, pp. 462–597; "Proceedings of the Estates Assembly in the Kingdom of Württemberg 1815–1816," in *Hegel's Political Writings* (trans. T. M. Knox) (Oxford: Oxford at the Clarendon Press, 1964), pp. 246–294.

"[Über] Friedrich Heinrich Jacobis *Werke*. Dritter Band," *Werke*, 4, pp. 429–461.

"Aphorismen aus Hegels Wastebook," *Werke*, 2, pp. 540–567; "Aphorisms from the Wastebook" (trans. Susanne Klein, David L. Roochnik, and George Eliot Tucker), *Independent Journal of Philosophy*, 3 (1979), pp. 1–6. (The English translation is only a selection from the whole.)

"Berichte Hegels über seine Unterrichtsgegenstände: Aus dem gedruckten Gymnasialprogram," *Werke*, 4, pp. 294–302.

"Bewußtseinslehre für die Mittelklasse (1809)," *Werke*, 4, pp. 111–123.

"Das älteste Systemprogramm des deutschen Idealismus," *Werke*, 1, pp. 234–236. (Hegel's authorship is in question.)

"Daß die Magistrate von den Bürgern gewählt werden müssen," *Werke*, 1, pp. 268–273.

"Der Geist des Christentums und sein Schicksal," *Werke*, 1, pp. 274–418; "The Spirit of Christianity and Its Fate," in Hegel, *Early Theological Writings*, pp. 182–301.

"Die Positivität der christlichen Religion," *Werke*, 1, pp. 104–229; "The Positivity of the Christian Religion," *Early Theological Writings*, pp. 67–181.

"Die Verfassung Deutschlands," *Werke*, 1, pp. 451–610; "The German Constitution," in *Hegel's Political Writings* (trans. T. M. Knox) (Oxford: Oxford at the Clarendon Press, 1964), pp. 143–242.

"Glauben und Wissen oder Reflexionsphilosophie der Subjektivität in der Vollständigkeit ihrer Formen als Kantische, Jacobische und Fichtesche Philosophie," *Werke*, 2, pp. 287–433; "Faith and Knowledge or the Reflective Philosophy of Subjectivity in the Complete Range of Its Forms as Kantian, Jacobian, and Fichtean Philosophy" (trans. Walter Cerf and H. S. Harris) (Albany: State University of New York Press, 1977).

"Gutachten über die Stellung des Realinstituts zu den übrigen Studienanstalten" (1810), *Werke*, 4, pp. 379–397.

"Hegels Rede bei der Abgabe des Rektorats," in *Berliner Schriften: 1818–1831* (ed. Johannes Hoffmeister), pp. 763–780.

"Logik für die Mittelklasse (1810/11)," *Werke*, 4, pp. 162–203.

"Maximen des Journals der deutschen Literatur," *Werke*, 2, pp. 568–574; "Guidelines for the Journal of German Literature (1807)" (trans. Christine Seiler and Clark Butler), *Clio*, 13, no. 4 (1984), pp. 409–412.

"Notizenblattt: Bayern: Ausbruch der Volksfreude über den endlichen Untergang der Philosophie," *Werke*, 2, pp. 273–279.

"Rede auf den Amtsvorgänger Rektor Schenk am 10. Juli 1809," *Werke*, 4, pp. 305–311.

"Rede bei der dritten Säkularfeier der Übergabe der Augsburgischen Konfession," in *Berliner Schriften: 1818–1831* (ed. Johannes Hoffmeister), pp. 30–55.

"Rede zum Antritt des philosophischen Lehramtes an der Universität Heidelberg" in G. W. F. Hegel, *Vorlesungsmanuskripte II (1816–1831)* (ed. Walter Jaeschke), in *Gesammelte Werke* (ed. Rheinisch-Westfälische Akademie der Wissenschaften, 1995), pp. 11–31.

"Rede zum Schuljahrabschluß am 14. September, 1810," *Werke*, 4, pp. 327–343.

"Rede zum Schuljahrabschluß am 2. September 1811," *Werke*, 4, pp. 344–359.

"Rede zum Schuljahrabschluß am 29. September, 1809," *Werke*, 4, pp. 312–326.

"Rede zum Schuljahrabschluß am 30. August 1815," *Werke*, 4, pp. 368–376.

"Über den Unterricht in der Philosophie auf Gymnasien," *Werke*, 11, pp. 31–41.

"Über den Vortrag der Philosophie auf Gymnasien: Privatgutachten für den Königlichen Bayrischen Oberschulrat Immanuel Niethammer," *Werke*, 4, pp. 4103–417; *Letters*, pp. 275–282.

"Über die Einrichtung einer kritischen Zeitschrift für Literatur," *Werke*, 11, pp. 9–30.

"Über die englische Reformbill," *Werke*, vol. 11, pp. 83–128; "The English Reform Bill," in *Hegel's Political Writings* (trans. T. M. Knox), pp. 295–330.

"Über die wissenschaftlichen Behandlungsarten des Naturrechts, seine Stelle in der praktischen Philosophie und sein Verhältnis zu den positiven Rechtswissenschaften," *Werke*, 2, pp. 434–530; "Natural Law: The Scientific Ways of Treating Natural Law, Its Place in Moral Philosophy, and Its Relation to the Positive Sciences of Law" (trans. T. M. Knox and Richard Kroner) (Philadelphia: University of Pennsylvania Press, 1975).

"Über eine Anklage wegen öffentlicher Verunglimpfung der katholischen Religion," *Werke*, 11, pp. 68–71.

"Vorrede zu Hinrichs Religionsphilosophie," *Werke*, 11, pp. 67.

Aesthetics: Lectures on Fine Art (trans. T. M. Knox) (Oxford: Clarendon Press, 1975), vols. 1–2.

Differenz des Fichteschen und Schellingschen Systems der Philosophie, Werke, 2, pp. 7–138; *The Difference Between Fichte's and Schelling's Systems of Philosophy* (trans. H. S. Harris and Walter Cerf) (Albany: State University of New York Press, 1977).

Dissertatio Philosophica de Orbitis Planetarum: Philosophische Erörterung über die Planetenbahnen (translation, introduction, and commentary by Wolfgang Neuser) (Weinheim: VCH Verlagsgesellschaft, 1986).

Elements of the Philosophy of Right (ed. Allen W. Wood, trans. H. B. Nisbet) (Cambridge: Cambridge University Press, 1991); *Werke*, 7.

Enzyklopädie der philosophischen Wissenschaften, Werke, vols. 8–10; *The Encyclopedia Logic: Part 1 of the Encyclopedia of the Philosophical Sciences* (trans. T. F. Geraets, W. A. Suchting, and H. S. Harris) (Indianapolis: Hackett Publishing Co., 1991); *Hegel's Philosophy of Nature* (trans. A. V. Miller) (Oxford: Oxford at the Clarendon Press, 1970); *Hegel's Philosophy of Mind (Part Three of the Encyclopedia of the Philosophical Sciences)* (trans. William Wallace and A. V. Miller) (Oxford: Clarendon Press, 1971).

Hegel's Introduction to the Lectures on the History of Philosophy (trans. T. M. Knox and A. V. Miller) (Oxford: Clarendon Press, 1985).

Jenaer Systementwürfe I: Das System der spekulativen Philosophie, (ed. Klaus Düsing and Heinz Kimmerle) (Hamburg: Felix Meiner Verlag, 1986).

Jenaer Systementwürfe II: Logik, Metaphysik, Naturphilosophie (ed. Rolf-Peter Horstmann) (Hamburg: Felix Meiner Verlag, 1982).

Jenaer Systementwürfe III: Naturphilosophie und Philosophie des Geistes (ed. Rolf-Peter Horstmann) (Hamburg: Felix Meiner Verlag, 1987); *Hegel and the Human Spirit: A Translation of the Jena Lectures on the Philosophy of Spirit (1805–6) with Commentary* (trans. Leo Rauch) (Detroit: Wayne State University Press, 1983).

Lectures on Natural Right and Political Science: The First Philosophy of Right: Heidelberg 1817–1818 with Additions from the Lectures of 1818–1819 (trans. J. Michael Stewart and Peter C. Hodgson) (Berkeley: University of California Press, 1995).

Phänomenologie des Geistes (ed. Hans Friedrich Wessels and Heinrich Clairmont) (Hamburg: Felix Meiner Verlag, 1988) (abbreviated as *PhG*.); *Phänomenologie des Geistes* (ed. J. Hoffmeister) (Hamburg: Felix Meiner Verlag, 1955) (abbreviated as *PG*.); *Phenomenology of Spirit* (trans. A. V. Miller) (Oxford: Oxford University Press, 1977).

Philosophie der Geschichte, Werke, vol. 12; *Philosophy of History* (trans. J. Sibree) (New York: Dover Publications, 1956).

System der Sittlichkeit (Hamburg: Felix Meiner Verlag, 1967); *System of Ethical Life (1802/3) and First Philosophy of Spirit (Part III of the System of Speculative Philosophy 1803/4)* (trans. H. S. Harris and T. M. Knox) (Albany: State University of New York Press, 1979).

Three Essays, 1793–1795 (edited and translated by Peter Fuss and John Dobbins) (Notre Dame: Notre Dame Press, 1984).

Vorlesungen über die Philosophie der Religion (ed. Walter Jaeschke) (Hamburg: Felix Meiner Verlag, 1993), vols. 1–3; *Lectures on the Philosophy of Religion* (ed. Peter Hodgson, trans. R. F. Brown, P. C. Hodgson, and J. M. Stewart) (Berkeley: University of California Press, 1984), vols. 1–3.

Vorlesungen über die Philosophie der Weltgeschichte: Band I: Die Vernunft in der Geschichte (ed. Johannes Hoffmeister) (Hamburg: Felix Meiner Verlag, 1994); *Lectures on the Philosophy of World History: Introduction: Reason in History* (trans. H. B. Nisbet) (Cambridge: Cambridge University Press, 1975).

Wissenschaft der Logik (Hamburg: Felix Meiner Verlag, 1971); *Werke*, 5–6; *Science of Logic* (trans. A. V. Miller) (Oxford: Oxford University Press, 1969).

Works Cited

J. F. von Abel, *Versuch über die Natur der speculativen Vernunft zur Prüfung des Kantischen Systems* (Frankfurt and Leipzig: 1787; reprinted Brussells: Culture et Civilisation, 1968).

Ernst Anrich (ed.), *Die Idee der deutschen Universität* (Darmstadt: Wissenschaftliche Buchgesellschaft, 1964).

Aristotle, *Nicomachean Ethics* (trans. David Ross, revised by J. L Ackrill and J. O. Urmson) (Oxford: Oxford University Press, 1992).

Andreas Arndt and Wolfgang Virmond, "Hegel und die 'Gesetzlose Gesellschaft'," *Hegel-Studien*, 20 (1985), pp. 113–116.

Hermann Aubin and Wolfgang Zorn (eds.), *Handbuch der deutschen Wirtschafts-und Sozialgeschichte* (Stuttgart: Klett-Cotta Verlag, 1976), vol. 2.

W. H. Auden, "Forward," in J. W. Goethe, *The Sorrows of Young Werther and Novella* (trans. Elizabeth Meyer and Louise Bogan) (New York: Random House, 1971).

Manfred Baum and Kurt Rainer Meist, "Politik und Philosophie in der Bamberger Zeitung: Dokumente zu Hegels Redaktionstätigkeit 1807–1808," *Hegel-Studien*, 10 (1975), pp. 87–127.

Willi Ferdinand Becker, "Hegels Hinterlassene Schriften im Briefwechsel seines Sohnes Immanuel," *Zeitschrift für philosophische Forschung*, 35, nos. 3/4 (July-December 1981), pp. 592–614.

Frederick Beiser, *Enlightenment, Revolution, and Romanticism: The Genesis of German Political Thought 1790–1800* (Cambridge, Mass.: Harvard University Press, 1992).

Frederick Beiser, *The Fate of Reason: German Philosophy from Kant to Fichte* (Cambridge, Mass.: Harvard University Press, 1987).

Robert Berdahl, *The Politics of the Prussian Nobility: The Development of a Conservative Ideology, 1770–1848* (Princeton: Princeton University Press, 1988).

Isaiah Berlin, "Hume and the Sources of German Anti-Rationalism," in Isaiah Berlin, *Against the Current: Essays in the History of Ideas* (ed. Henry Hardy) (New York: Viking Press, 1980), pp. 162–187.

W. R. Beyer, K. Lanig, and K. Goldmann, *Georg Wilhelm Friedrich Hegel in Nürnberg: 1808–1816* (Nuremberg: Selbstverlag der Stadt Bibliothek Nürnberg, 1966).

Wilhelm R. Beyer, "Aus Hegels Familienleben: Die Briefe der Susanne von Tucher an ihre Tochter Marie Hegel," *Hegel-Jahrbuch*, 1966 (Meisenheim am Glan), pp. 52–110.

Wilhelm R. Beyer, *Zwischen Phänomenologie und Logik: Hegel als Redakteur der Bamberger Zeitung* (Frankfurt a.M.: G. Schulte-Bulmke Verlag, 1955).

Inge Blank, "Dokumente zur Hegels Reise nach Österreich," *Hegel-Studien*, 16 (1981), pp. 41–55.

E.-W. Böckenförde, "Die Historische Rechtsschule und das Problem der Geschichtlichkeit des Rechtes," in his *Staat, Gesellschaft, Freiheit: Studien zur Staatstheorie und zum Verfassungsrecht* (Frankfurt a.M.: Suhrkamp Verlag, 1976), pp. 9–41.

Martin Bondeli, *Hegel in Bern* (Bonn: Bouvier Verlag, 1990).

Wolfgang Bonsiepen, *Die Begründung einer Naturphilosophie bei Kant, Schelling, Fries und Hegel: Mathematische versus spekulative Naturphilosophie* (Frankfurt a.M.: Vittorio Klostermann, 1997).

Wolfgang Bonsiepen, Hans-Friedrich Wessels, and Heinrich Clairmont, "Anmerkungen" to Hegel's *Phänomenologie des Geistes* (Hamburg: Felix Meiner Verlag, 1988).

Andrew Bowie, *Schelling and Modern European Philosophy: An Introduction* (London: Routledge, 1993).

Nicholas Boyle, *Goethe: The Poet and the Age. Volume I: The Poetry of Desire* (Oxford: Oxford University Press, 1991).

Michael Brock, *The Great Reform Act* (London: Hutchinson University Library, 1973).

Rüdiger Bubner, "Hegel's Concept of Phenomenology," in G. K. Browning (ed.), *Hegel's Phenomenology of Spirit: A Reappraisal* (Dordrecht: Kluwer Academic Publishers, 1997), pp. 31–51.

Stephen Bungay, *Beauty and Truth: A Study of Hegel's Aesthetics* (Oxford: Oxford University Press, 1987).

Kenneth L. Caneva, *Robert Mayer and the Conservation of Energy* (Princeton: Princeton University Press, 1993)

Roger Chartier, "The World Turned Upside Down," in Roger Chartier, *Cultural History* (trans. Lydia G. Cochrane) (Ithaca: Cornell University Press, 1988).

David Constantine, *Hölderlin* (Oxford: Clarendon Press, 1988).

Jacques D'Hondt, "Hegel und das 'Journal des savants'," in Christoph Jamme (ed.), *Die "Jahrbücher für wissenschaftliche Kritik": Hegels Berliner Gegenakademie*, pp. 119–144.

Jacques D'Hondt, *Hegel in His Time: Berlin 1818–1831* (trans. John Burbridge with Nelson Roland and Judith Levasseur) (Lewiston, N.Y.: Broadview Press, 1988).

Jacques D'Hondt, *Hegel Secret: Recherches sur les sources cachées de la pensée de Hegel* (Paris: Presses Universitaires de France, 1968).

Laurence Dickey, *Hegel: Religion, Economics, and the Politics of Spirit, 1770–1807* (Cambridge: Cambridge University Press, 1987).

Klaus Düsing, "Ästhetischer Platonismus bei Hölderlin und Hegel," in Christoph

Jamme and Otto Pöggeler (eds.), *Homburg vor der Höhe in der deutschen Geistesgeschichte: Studien zum Freundeskreis um Hegel und Hölderlin* (Stuttgart: Klett-Cotta, 1986), pp. 101–117.

Hans Eichner, *Friedrich Schlegel* (New York: Twayne Publishers, 1970).

James Engell, *The Creative Imagination: Enlightenment to Romanticism* (Cambridge, Mass.: Harvard University Press, 1981).

Oscar Fambach, *Der Romantische Rückfall in der Kritik der Zeit* (Berlin: Akademie Verlag, 1963), pp. 403–427.

Ludwig Fertig, *Die Hofmeister: ein Beitrag zur Geschichte der Lehrerstandes und der bürgerlichen Intelligenz* (Stuttgart: Metzler, 1979).

J. G. Fichte, "A Crystal Clear Report to the General Public Concerning the Actual Essence of the Newest Philosophy: An Attempt to Force the Reader to Understand" (trans. John Botterman and William Rasch), in Ernst Behler (ed.), *Philosophy of German Idealism* (New York: Continuum, 1987).

J. G. Fichte, *Science of Knowledge* (ed. and trans. Peter Heath and John Lachs) (Cambridge: Cambridge University Press, 1982).

Charles James Fox, "The States of Wirtemberg," *Edinburgh Review*, 29 (1818).

Eckart Förster, " 'To Lend Wings to Physics Once Again': Hölderlin and the Oldest System Program of German Idealism," *European Journal of Philosophy* 3(2) 174–190, August 1995.

Manfred Frank, *Eine Einführung in Schellings Philosophie* (Frankfurt a.M.: Suhrkamp Verlag, 1985).

Manfred Frank, *Unendliche Annäherung* (Frankfurt a.M.: Suhrkamp Verlag, 1997).

Michael Friedman, *Kant and the Exact Sciences* (Cambridge, Mass: Harvard University Press, 1992).

J. F. Fries, *Über die Gefährdung des Wohlstandes und Characters der Deutschen durch die Juden* (*The Danger Posed by the Jews to German Well-Being and Character*), partially translated by Allen Wood in his editorial notes to G. W. F. Hegel, *Elements of the Philosophy of Right* (ed. Allen W. Wood, trans. H. B. Nisbet) (Cambridge: Cambridge University Press, 1991).

François Furet, *Revolutionary France: 1770–1880* (trans. Antonia Nevill) (Oxford: Blackwell, 1992).

Peter Gay, *The Enlightenment: An Interpretation: The Science of Freedom* (New York: Norton, 1969).

Edward Gibbon, *The Decline and Fall of the Roman Empire* (New York: Harcourt, Brace, 1960).

Hannah Ginsborg, "Purposiveness and Normativity," in Hoke Robinson (ed.), *Proceedings of the Eighth International Kant Congress* (Milwaukee: Marquette University Press, 1995), pp. 453–460.

Johann Wolfgang von Goethe, *Wilhelm Meister's Apprenticeship* (ed. and trans. Eric A. Blackall in cooperation with Victor Lange) (Princeton: Princeton University Press, 1995).

Karlheinz Goldmann, "Hegel als Referent für das Nürnberger Lehrerseminar und Volksschulwesen 1813–1816," in W. R. Beyer, K. Lanig, and K. Goldmann, *Georg Wilhelm Friedrich Hegel in Nürnberg: 1808–1816.*

Liah Greenfeld, *Nationalism: Five Roads to Modernity* (Cambridge: Harvard University Press, 1992).

H. S. Harris, *Hegel's Development: Towards the Sunlight 1770–1801* (Oxford: Oxford at the Clarendon Press, 1972).

H. S. Harris, *Hegel's Development: Night Thoughts (Jena 1801–1806)* (Oxford: Oxford University Press, 1983).

Ernst Ludwig Theodor Henke, *Jakob Friedrich Fries: Aus seinem handschriftlichen Nachlasse dargestellt* (Leipzig : F.U. Brockhaus, 1867).

Dieter Henrich, "Art and Philosophy of Art Today: Reflections with Reference to Hegel," in R. E. Amacher and V. Lange (eds.), *New Perspectives in German Literary Criticism* (Princeton: Princeton University Press, 1979), pp. 107–133.

Dieter Henrich, "Hegel und Hölderlin," in Dieter Henrich, *Hegel im Kontext* (Frankfurt a.M.: Suhrkamp Verlag, 1971), pp. 9–40.

Dieter Henrich, *Der Grund im Bewußtsein: Untersuchungen zu Hölderlins Denken (1794–1795)* (Stuttgart: Klett-Cotta, 1992).

Dieter Henrich, *Konstellationen: Probleme und Debatten am Ursprung der idealistischen Philosophie (1789–1795)* (Stuttgart: Klett-Cotta, 1991).

Dieter Henrich, *The Course of Remembrance and Other Essays on Hölderlin* (ed. Eckart Förster) (Stanford: Stanford University Press, 1997).

Dieter Henrich and Christoph Jamme (eds.), *Jakob Zwillings Nachlass, eine Rekonstruktion: mit Beiträgen zur Geschichte des spekulativen Denkens* (Bonn: Bouvier, 1986).

G. Hirschmann, "Die 'Ära Wurm' (1806–1818)," in Gerhard Pfeiffer (ed.), *Nürnberg – Geschichte einer europäischen Stadt* (Munich: C. H. Beck, 1982).

Eric Hobsbawm, *Echoes of the Marseillaise: Two Centuries Look Back on the French Revolution* (New Brunswick: Rutgers University Press, 1990).

Eric Hobsbawm, *Nations and Nationalism since 1780: Programme, Myth, Reality* (Cambridge: Cambridge University Press, 1990).

Peter C. Hodgson, "The Metamorphosis of Judaism in Hegel's Philosophy of Religion," *Owl of Minerva*, 19 (Fall 1987), pp. 41–52.

Michael H. Hoffheimer, *Eduard Gans and the Hegelian Philosophy of Law* (Dordrecht: Kluwer Academic Publishers, 1995).

Johannes Hoffmeister, *Dokumente zu Hegels Entwicklung* (Stuttgart-Bad Canstatt: Friedrich Frommann Verlag, 1936).

Friedrich Hogemann, "Die Entstehung der 'Sozietät' und der 'Jahrbücher für wissenschaftliche Kritik'," in Christoph Jamme (ed.), *Die "Jahrbücher für wissenschaftliche Kritik": Hegels Berliner Gegenakademie*, pp. 57–92.

Friedrich Hogemann, "Gesellligkeit," in Otto Pöggeler (ed.), *Hegel in Berlin: Preußische Kulturpolitik und idealistische Ästhetik: Zum 150. Todestags des Philosophen*, pp. 57–63.

Friedrich Hölderlin, "Sein Urteil Möglichkeit," in Friedrich Hölderlin, *Sämtliche Werke (Frankfurter Ausgabe)*, vol. 17 (ed. D. E. Sattler, Michael Franz, and Hans Gerhard Steimer) (Basel: Roter Stern, 1991), pp. 147–156.

Friedrich Hölderlin, "Wenn aus der Ferne," in *Hölderlin* (introduced and edited by

Michael Hamburger) (trans. Michael Hamburger) (Baltimore: Penguin Books, 1961), pp. 249–251.

Anne Hollander, *Sex and Suits* (New York: Alfred A. Knopf, 1996).

Erwin Hölzle, *Württemberg im Zeitalter Napoleons und der deutschen Erhebung: Eine deutsche Geschichte der Wendezeit im einzelstaatlichen Raum* (Stuttgart: W. Kohlhammer Verlag, 1937).

Rolf-Peter Horstmann, "Jenaer Systemkonzeptionen," in Otto Pöggeler (ed.), *Hegel* (Freiburg: Karl Alber Verlag, 1977), pp. 43–58.

Rolf-Peter Horstmann and Michael J. Petry (eds.), *Hegels Philosophie der Natur: Beziehungen zwischen empirischer und spekulativer Naturerkenntnis* (Stuttgart: Ernst Klett Verlag, 1986).

Rolf-Peter Horstmann, *Die Grenzen der Vernunft: Eine Untersuchung zu Zielen und Motiven des deutschen Idealismus* (Frankfurt a.M.: Anton Hain, 1991).

David Hume, *Treatise on Human Nature* (ed. L. A. Selby-Bigge) (Oxford: Clarendon Press, 1978).

Heinrich Eduard Jacob, *Felix Mendelssohn and His Times* (trans. Richard and Clara Winston) (Westport, Conn.: Greenwood Press, 1973).

Christoph Jamme (ed.), *Die "Jahrbücher für wissenschaftliche Kritik": Hegels Berliner Gegenakademie* (Stuttgart-Bad Cannstatt: Frommann-Holzboog, 1994).

Christoph Jamme, "Die erste Hölderlin-Ausgabe," in Otto Pöggeler (ed.), *Hegel in Berlin: Preußische Kulturpolitik und idealistische Ästhetik: Zum 150. Todestags des Philosophen*, pp. 64–71.

Christoph Jamme, "Liebe, Schicksal und Tragik: Hegels 'Geist des Christentums' und Hölderlins 'Empedokles'," in Christoph Jamme and Otto Pöggeler (eds.), *"Frankfurt aber ist der Nabel dieser Erde": Das Schicksal einer Generation der Goethezeit*, pp. 300–324.

Christoph Jamme and Elisabeth Weisser-Lohmann (eds.), *Politik und Geschichte: Zu den Intentionen von G.W.F. Hegels Reformbill-Schrift* (Bonn: Bouvier, 1995).

Christoph Jamme and Helmut Schneider (eds.), *Mythologie der Vernunft: Hegels >>ältestes Systemprogramm des deutschen Idealismus<<* (Frankfurt a.M.: Suhrkamp Verlag, 1984).

Christoph Jamme and Otto Pöggeler (eds.), *"Frankfurt aber ist der Nabel dieser Erde": Das Schicksal einer Generation der Goethezeit* (Stuttgart: Klett-Cotta, 1983).

Christoph Jamme and Otto Pöggeler (eds.), *Homburg vor der Höhe in der deutschen Geistesgeschichte: Studien zum Freundeskreis um Hegel und Hölderlin* (Stuttgart: Klett-Cotta, 1986).

Karl-Ernst Jeismann and Peter Lundgreen (ed.), *Handbuch der deutschen Bildungsgeschichte* (Munich: C. H. Beck, 1987), vol. 3.

Walter Jens, *Eine deutsche Universität: 500 Jahre Tübingener Gelehrten Republik* (Munich: Deutscher Taschenbuch Verlag, 1981).

Hugh Johnson, *Vintage: The Story of Wine* (New York: Simon and Schuster, 1989).

Immanuel Kant, "An Answer to the Question: 'What Is Enlightenment?' " (trans. H. B. Nisbet), in Hans Reiss (ed.), *Kant: Political Writings* (Cambridge: Cambridge University Press, 1991).

Immanuel Kant, *Critique of Judgment* (trans. Werner S. Pluhar) (Indianapolis: Hackett Publishing Company, 1987).

Immanuel Kant, *Critique of Pure Reason* (trans. N.K. Smith) (London: Macmillan, 1964).

Immanuel Kant, *Groundwork of the Metaphysics of Morals* (trans. H. J. Paton) (New York: Harper and Row, 1964).

Immanuel Kant, *Metaphysical Foundations of Natural Science* (trans. James W. Ellington) (Indianapolis: Hackett Publishing Company, 1985).

Immanuel Kant, *Religion within the Limits of Reason Alone* (trans. Theodore M. Greene and Hoyt H. Hudson) (New York: Harper and Row, 1960).

Immanuel Kant, *The Metaphysics of Morals* (trans. Mary Gregor) (Cambridge: Cambridge University Press, 1991).

Immanuel Kant, *Werke* (ed. Wilhelm Weischedel) (Frankfurt a.M.: Suhrkamp Verlag, 1977).

Hermann Kellenbenz, "Zahlungsmittel, Maße und Gewichte seit 1800," in Hermann Aubin and Wofgang Zorn, *Handbuch der deutschen Wirtschafts-und Sozialgeschichte* (Stuttgart: Klett-Cotta, 1976), vol. 2, pp. 934–958.

Hermann Klenner and Gerhard Oberkofler, "Zwei Savigny-Voten über Eduard Gans nebst Chronologie und Bibliographie," in *Weltgeschichte* (ed. Hans-Heinz Holz and Domenico Losurdo) (Bonn: Pahl-Rugenstein Verlag Nachfolger, 1993), pp. 123–148.

Reinhart Koselleck, *Preußen zwischen Reform und Revolution: Allgemeines Landrecht, Verwaltung und soziale Bewegung von 1791 bis 1848* (Stuttgart: Ernst Klett Verlag, 1975).

Leonard Krieger, *The German Idea of Freedom: History of a Political Tradition* (Chicago: University of Chicago Press, 1957).

Jenifer Harvey Lang (ed.), *Larousse Gastronomique* (New York: Crown Publishers, 1988), entry on "Brie," pp. 142–143.

Karl Lanig, "Die pädagogischen Jahre Hegels in Nürnberg," in W. R. Beyer, K. Lanig, and K. Goldmann, *Georg Wilhelm Friedrich Hegel in Nürnberg: 1808–1816*, pp. 17–38.

Jonathan Lear, "The Disappearing 'We'," in Jonathan Lear, *Open Minded: Working Out the Logic of the Soul* (Cambridge, Mass.: Harvard University Press, 1998), pp. 282–300.

Max Lenz, *Geschichte der königlichen Friedrich-Wilhelms-Universität zu Berlin* (Halle: Verlag der Buchhandlung des Waisenhauses, 1910).

Robert S. Lopez, *The Birth of Europe* (New York: M. Evans, 1966).

Richard Lovelace, "To Lucasta, Going to the Wars," in Helen Gardner (ed.), *The Metaphysical Poets* (London: Penguin Books, 1957), pp. 231–232.

Hans-Christian Lucas, "Die 'Tiefere Arbeit': Hegel zwischen Revolution und Reform," in Christoph Jamme and Elisabeth Weisser-Lohmann (eds.), *Politik und Geschichte: Zu den Intentionen von G.W.F. Hegels Reformbill-Schrift*, pp. 207–234.

Hans-Christian Lucas, "Die Schwester im Schatten: Bemerkungen zu Hegels Schwester Christiane," in Christoph Jamme and Otto Pöggeler (eds.), *"O*

Fürstin der Heimath! Glükliches Stutgard": Politik, Kultur und Gesellschaft im deutschen Südwesten um 1800 (Stuttgart: Klett-Cotta Verlag, 1988), pp. 284–306.

Hans-Christian Lucas and Udo Rameil, "Furcht vor der Zensur? Zur Entstehungs- und Druckgeschichte von Hegels Grundlinien der Philosophie des Rechts," *Hegel-Studien*, 15 (1980), pp. 63–93.

Eric v.d. Luft, "Hegel and Judaism: A Reassessment," *Clio*, 18 (1989), pp. 361–378.

Barbara Markiewicz, "Hegels Tod," in Christoph Jamme (ed.), *Die "Jahrbücher für wissenschaftliche Kritik": Hegels Berliner Gegenakademie*, pp. 531–556.

Charles E. McClelland, *State, Society, and University in Germany: 1700–1914* (Cambridge: Cambridge University Press, 1980).

Kurt Rainer Meist, "Halykonische Tage in Wien," in Otto Pöggeler (ed.), *Hegel in Berlin: Preußische Kulturpolitik und idealistische Ästhetik: Zum 150. Todestags des Philosophen*, pp. 154–161.

Edith J. Morley (ed.), *Crabb Robinson in Germany: 1800–1805: Extracts from His Correspondence* (Oxford: Oxford University Press, 1929).

G. E. Mueller, "The Hegel Legend of 'Thesis-Antithesis-Synthesis'," *Journal of the History of Ideas*, 19 (1958), pp. 411–414.

Gerhard H. Müller, "*Wechselwirkung* in the Life and Other Sciences: A Word, New Claims and a Concept Around 1800 . . . and Much Later," in Stefano Poggi and Maurisio Bossi (eds.), *Romanticism in Science: Science in Europe, 1790–1840* (Dordrecht: Kluwer Academic Publishers, 1994), pp. 1–14.

Frederick Neuhouser, *Fichte's Theory of Subjectivity* (Cambridge: Cambridge University Press, 1990).

Frederick Neuhouser, "Freedom, Dependence, and the General Will," *The Philosophical Review*, 102 (1993), pp. 363–395.

Friedhelm Nicolin (ed.), "Errinerungen Christiane Hegels," in *Der Junge Hegel in Stuttgart: Aufsätze und Tagebuchaufzeichnungen 1785–1788* (Marbach: Marbacher Schriften herausgegeben von deutschen Literaturarchiv im Schiller-Nationalmuseum, 1989).

Friedhelm Nicolin, " 'meine liebe Stadt Stuttgart . . . ': Hegel und die Schwäbische Metropole," in Christoph Jamme and Otto Pöggeler (eds.), *"O Fürstin der Heimath! Glükliches Stutgard": Politik, Kultur und Gesellschaft im deutschen Südwesten um 1800*, pp. 261–283.

Friedhelm Nicolin, "Der erste Lexicon-Artikel über Hegel (1824)," in Friedhelm Nicolin, *Auf Hegels Spuren: Beiträge zur Hegel-Forschung*, pp. 202–213.

Friedhelm Nicolin, "Hegel als Professor in Heidelberg: Aus den Akten in der philosophischen Fakultät 1816–1818," in Friedhelm Nicolin, *Auf Hegels Spuren: Beiträge zur Hegel-Forschung*, pp. 141–173.

Friedhelm Nicolin, "Pädagogik – Propädeutik – Enzyklopädie," in Otto Pöggeler (ed.), *Hegel*, pp. 91–105.

Friedhelm Nicolin, *Auf Hegels Spuren: Beiträge zur Hegel-Forschung* (ed. by Lucia Sziborsky and Helmut Schneider) (Hamburg: Felix Meiner Verlag, 1996).

Friedhelm Nicolin, *Von Stuttgart nach Berlin: Die Lebensstationen Hegels* (Marbach am Neckar : Deutsche Schillergesellschaft, 1991).

Günther Nicolin (ed.), *Hegel in Berichten seiner Zeitgenossen* (Hamburg: Felix Meiner Verlag, 1970).

Thomas Nipperdey, *Germany From Napoleon to Bismarck: 1800–1866* (trans. Daniel Nolan) (Princeton: Princeton University Press, 1996).

Robert E. Norton, *The Beautiful Soul: Aesthetic Morality in the Eighteenth Century* (Ithaca: Cornell University Press, 1995).

Novalis, *Gedichte* (Frankfurt a.M.: Insel Verlag, 1987).

Sibylle Obenaus, "Berliner Allgemeine Literaturzeitung oder 'Hegelblatt'?" in Christoph Jamme (ed.), *Die "Jahrbücher für wissenschaftliche Kritik": Hegels Berliner Gegenakademie*, pp. 15–56.

Dorinda Outram, *The Enlightenment* (Cambridge: Cambridge University Press, 1995).

Fania Oz-Salzberger, *Translating the Enlightenment: Scottish Civic Discourse in Eighteenth-Century Germany* (Oxford: Clarendon Press, 1995)

Blaise Pascal, *Pensées* (trans. A. J. Krailsheimer) (Baltimore: Penguin Books, 1966), p. 58 (no. 110, Lafuma edition).

Michael J. Petry (ed.), *Hegel and Newtonianism* (Dordrecht: Kluwer Academic Publishers, 1993).

Michael J. Petry (ed.), *Hegel und die Naturwissenschaften* (Stuttgart-Bad Cannstatt: Frommann-Holzboog, 1987).

Terry Pinkard, *Hegel's Dialectic: The Explanation of Possibility* (Philadelphia: Temple University Press, 1987).

Terry Pinkard, *Hegel's Phenomenology: The Sociality of Reason* (Cambridge: Cambridge University Press, 1994).

Robert Pippin, "Avoiding German Idealism: Kant and the Reflective Judgment Problem," in Robert Pippin, *Idealism as Modernism: Hegelian Variations* (Cambridge: Cambridge University Press, 1997).

Robert Pippin, "Hegel's Ethical Rationalism," in Robert Pippin, *Idealism as Modernism: Hegelian Variations*, pp. 417–450.

Robert Pippin, "The Modern World of Leo Strauss," in Robert Pippin, *Idealism as Modernism: Hegelian Variations*, pp. 209–232.

Robert Pippin, *Hegel's Idealism: The Satisfactions of Self-Consciousness* (Cambridge: Cambridge University Press, 1989).

Robert Pippin, *Idealism as Modernism: Hegelian Variations* (Cambridge: Cambridge University Press, 1997).

Robert Pippin, *Kant's Theory of Form: An Essay on the Critique of Pure Reason* (New Haven: Yale University Press, 1982).

Otto Pöggeler (ed.), *Hegel* (Freiburg: Karl Alber Verlag, 1977).

Otto Pöggeler (ed.), *Hegel in Berlin: Preußische Kulturpolitik und idealistische Ästhetik: Zum 150. Todestags des Philosophen* (Berlin: Staatsbibliothek Preußischer Kulturbesitz, 1981).

Otto Pöggeler, "Hegel, der Verfasser des ältesten Systemprogrammes des deutschen Idealismus," in Hans-Georg Gadamer (ed.), *Hegel-Tage Urbino* (Bouvier: Bonn, 1969), pp. 17–32.

Otto Pöggeler, "Hegels Option für Österreich," F. Nicolin and O. Pöggeler (eds.), *Hegel Studien* (Bonn: Bouvier Verlag), vol. 12 (1977), pp. 83–128.

Otto Pöggeler, "Preußische Rheinlande, Vereinigte Niederlande," in Otto Pöggeler (ed.), *Hegel in Berlin: Preußische Kulturpolitik und idealistische Ästhetik: Zum 150. Todestags des Philosophen*, pp. 146–152.

Otto Pöggeler, *Hegels Idee einer Phänomenologie des Geistes* (Munich: Verlag Karl Alber, 1993).

S. S. Prawer, *Heine's Jewish Comedy: A Study of His Portraits of Jews and Judaism* (Oxford: Clarendon Press, 1983).

Udo Rameil, "Der systematische Aufbau der Geisteslehre in Hegels Nürnberger Propädeutik," *Hegel-Studien*, 23 (1988), pp. 19–49.

Udo Rameil, "Die Phänomenologie des Geistes in Hegel's Nürnberger Propädeutik," in Lothar Eley (ed.), *Hegels Theorie des subjektiven Geistes in der "Enzyklopädie der philosophischen Wissenschaften im Grundrisse"* (Stuttgart–Bad Cannstatt: Frommann-Holzboog, 1990), pp. 84–130.

Anthony Read and David Fisher, *Berlin: The Biography of a City* (London: Pimlico Press, 1994).

Manfred Riedel (ed.), *Materialien zu Hegels Rechtsphilosophie* (Frankfurt a.M.: Suhrkamp Verlag, 1975).

Karl Rosenkranz, *Georg Wilhelm Friedrich Hegels Leben* (Darmstadt: Wissenschaftliche Buchhandlung, 1969; reprint of the 1844 edition).

Jean-Jacques Rousseau, *On the Social Contract* (trans. Donald A. Cress) (Indianapolis: Hackett Publishing Company, 1983).

Jean-Jacques Rousseau, *The Confessions of Jean-Jacques Rousseau* (trans. J. M. Cohen) (London: Penguin Books, 1953).

Karl Friedrich von Savigny, "Von Beruf unsrer Zeit für Gesetzgebung und Rechtswissenschaft," in Hans Hattenhauer (ed.), *Thibaut und Savigny: Ihre Programmatischen Schriften* (Munich: Franz Vahlen, 1973), pp. 95–192.

F. W. J. Schelling, "Von der Weltseele, eine Hypothese der höheren Physik zur Erklärung des allgemeinen Organismus," in Manfred Schröter (ed.), *Schellings Werke*, vol. 1, pp. 413–652.

F. W. J. Schelling, *Of the I as the Principle of Philosophy or On the Unconditional in Human Knowledge*, in F. W. J. Schelling, *The Unconditional in Human Knowledge: Four Early Essays (1794–1796)* (trans. Fritz Marti) (Lewisburg: Bucknell University Press, 1980), pp. 63–128; *Vom Ich als Prinzip der Philosophie oder über das Unbedingte im menschlichen Wissen*, in F. W. J. Schelling, *Schellings Werke*, vol. 1, pp. 73–168.

F. W. J. Schelling, *Schellings Werke* (ed. Manfred Schröter) (Munich: C. H. Beck und Oldenburg, 1927).

F. W. J. Schelling, *System of Transcendental Idealism* (trans. Peter Heath) (Charlottesville: University Press of Virginia, 1978).

Schlegel, Dorothea von geb. Mendelssohn und deren Söhne Johannes und Philip Veit, Briefwechsel (ed. J.M. Raich) (Mainz: Franz Kirchheim, 1881).

Friedrich Schlegel, "Athenäum Fragments," in Kathleen M. Wheeler (ed.), *German Aesthetic and Literary Criticism: The Romantic Ironists and Goethe* (Cambridge: Cambridge University Press, 1984).

Friedrich Schleiermacher, "Gelegentliche Gedanken über Universitäten in deutschem Sinn, nebst einem Anhang über eine neu zu errichtende," in Ernst Anrich (ed.), *Die Idee der deutschen Universität*, pp. 219–307.

Siegfried Schmidt (ed.), *Alma Mater Jenesis: Geschichte der Universität Jena* (Weimar: Hermann Böhlaus, 1983).

Helmut Schneider, "Komödie des Lebens – Theorie der Komödie," in Otto Pöggeler (ed.), *Hegel in Berlin: Preußische Kulturpolitik und idealistische Ästhetik: Zum 150. Todestags des Philosophen*, pp. 79–85.

Gunter Scholz, "Musikalische Erfahrungen in Oper und Singakademie," in Otto Pöggeler (ed.), *Hegel in Berlin: Preußische Kulturpolitik und idealistische Ästhetik: Zum 150. Todestags des Philosophen*, pp. 86–94.

James Sheehan, *German History: 1770–1866* (Oxford: Oxford University Press, 1989).

Ludwig Siep, *Anerkennung als Prinzip der praktischen Philosophie: Untersuchungen zu Hegels Jenaer Philosophie des Geistes* (Munich: Alber Verlag, 1979).

Ludwig Siep, *Praktische Philosophie im deutschen Idealismus* (Frankfurt a.M.: Suhrkamp Verlag, 1992).

Abbé Sieyès (Emmanuel Joseph), "What Is the Third Estate?" in Keith Michael Baker (ed.), *The Old Regime and the French Revolution* (Chicago: University of Chicago Press, 1987), pp. 154–179.

Lloyd Spencer and Andrzej Krauze, *Hegel: An Introduction* (New York: Totem Books, 1996).

Max Steinmetz (ed.), *Geschichte der Universität Jena* (Jena: VEB Gustav Fischer Verlag, 1958).

Pirmin Stekeler-Weithofer, *Hegels analytische Philosophie: Die Wissenschaft der Logik als kritische Theorie der Bedeutung* (Paderborn: Ferdinand Schönigh, 1992).

Anton Thibaut, "Über die Notwendigkeit eines allgemeinen bürgerlichen Rechts für Deutschland," in Hans Hattenhauer (ed.), *Thibaut und Savigny: Ihre programmatischen Schriften* (Munich: Franz Vahlen, 1973), pp. 61–94.

John Edward Toews, *Hegelianism: The Path Toward Dialectical Humanism, 1805–1841* (Cambridge: Cambridge University Press, 1980).

Mary Lee Townsend, *Forbidden Laughter: Popular Humor and the Limits of Repression in Nineteenth Century Prussia* (Ann Arbor: University of Michigan Press, 1992).

James Allen Vann, *The Making of a State: Württemberg 1593–1793* (Ithaca: Cornell University Press, 1984).

Rudolf Vierhaus, "Bildung," in Otto Brunner, Werner Conze, and Reinhart Koselleck (eds.), *Geschichtliche Grundbegriffe: Historisches Lexikon zur politisch-sozialen Sprache in Deutschland* (Stuttgart: Ernst Klett Verlag, 1972).

Mack Walker, *German Hometowns: Community, State, and General Estate 1648–1871* (Ithaca: Cornell University Press, 1971).

Mack Walker, *Johann Jacob Moser and the Holy Roman Empire of the German Nation* (Chapel Hill: University of North Carolina Press, 1981).

Norbert Waszek, "Auf dem Weg zur Reformbill-Schrift: Die Ursprünge von Hegels Großbritannienrezeption," in Christoph Jamme and Elisabeth Weisser-

Lohmann (eds.), *Politik und Geschichte: Zu den Intentionen von G.W.F. Hegels Reformbill-Schrift*, pp. 178–190.

Norbert Waszek, "Eduard Gans, die 'Jahrbücher für wissenschaftliche Kritik' und die französische Publizistik der Zeit," in Christoph Jamme (ed.), *Die "Jahrbücher für wissenschaftliche Kritik": Hegels Berliner Gegenakademie*, pp. 93–118.

Norbert Waszek, *The Scottish Enlightenment and Hegel's Account of Civil Society* (Dordrecht: Kluwer Academic Publishers, 1988).

Norbert Waszek, "Hegels Exzerpte aus der 'Edinburgh Review' 1817–1819," *Hegel-Studien* 20 (1985), pp. 79–111.

Elisabeth Weisser-Lohmann, "Englische Reformbill und preußische Städteordnung: Repräsentative Staatsverfassung und vertikale Gewaltenteilung: V. Raumer, Steckfuß, Gans und Hegel," in Christoph Jamme and Elisabeth Weisser-Lohmann (eds.), *Politik und Geschichte: Zu den Intentionen von G.W.F. Hegels Reformbill-Schrift*, pp. 281–309.

Franz Wiedmann, *Hegel: An Illustrated Biography* (trans. Joachim Neugroschel) (New York: Western Publishing Co., 1968).

Ludwig Wittgenstein, *Philosophical Investigations* (trans. G. E. M. Anscombe) (New York: Macmillan, 1953).

Theodore Ziolkowski, *German Romanticism and Its Institutions* (Princeton: Princeton University Press, 1990).

Index